THE
LAST
KINGS
OF
THULE

*This book is, above all, a tribute to
the Danish explorer Knud Rasmussen,
the man "whose laughter went before him,"
the poet and ethnologist,
the founder of Thule.*

PORTRAIT BY ALBERT ENGSTRÖM, 1926

THE
LAST
KINGS
OF
THULE

With the Polar
Eskimos, As They
Face Their Destiny

JEAN
MALAURIE

TRANSLATED
FROM THE FRENCH BY
ADRIENNE FOULKE

The University of
Chicago Press

The University of Chicago Press, Chicago 60637

Library of Congress Cataloging-in-Publication Data
Malaurie, Jean.
    The last kings of Thule.

    Translation of: Les derniers rois de Thulé.
    Bibliography: p.
    Includes index.
    1. Eskimos—Greenland.   2. Malaurie, Jean.
3. Greenland—Exploring expeditions.   4. Greenland—
Description and travel.   I. Title.
[E99.E7M2313   1985]   998'.2'00497   85-8765
    ISBN 0-226-50284-8 (paper)

THIS BOOK
IS DEDICATED TO
THE POLAR ESKIMOS
OF THULE

*We cannot know a country
merely through the science of
geography . . . . I do not
believe that we can know
anything merely through
science; it is too precise, too
rigid a tool. The world has a
thousand tendernesses into
which we must lean so that
we may understand them
before we learn what the sum
of their parts represents . . . .
Only the sailor knows the
archipelago.*

—*Jean Giono*
L'eau vive

*All countries that have lost
their legends
Will be condemned to die
of cold . . . .*

—*Patrice de la Tour
du Pin*

CONTENTS

ix

PART THREE
*One Thousand Miles
of Exploring In
Inglefield Land,
Washington Land,
and on
Ellesmere Island*

PART FOUR
The Iron Age

Photo galleries follow pages
108, 124, 228, 334,
376, and 386

LIST OF MAPS

PREFACE

In the pages that follow I have tried to portray the very unusual life I have lived among the Polar Eskimos of the Thule district in northern Greenland.

When I undertook my first research in this region during the year 1950–51 (the year which serves as a framework for the present book) I was surprised to discover that its modest and proud people had never been as systematically studied as one might have expected. This was particularly curious in that this region had been the springboard for important expeditions to the North Pole and to Canada. No research in demography, social economy, or human biology had ever been devoted to them. And for the most part, a sociogeographic study of the Polar Eskimos as hunters still remained to be done. (The work of Knud Rasmussen prior to 1910 and of my friend and colleague Erik Holtved in 1936 and 1937 had provided the very foundations of the linguistic and archaeological knowledge of this people.)

Nevertheless, some people will be surprised that any research is undertaken for a handful of tribes in decline. Digs are undertaken in regions that are difficult both to reach and to remain in, in ground that thaws in summer to a depth of no more than three to six feet; the language is difficult; the population, despite its seeming graciousness, is hard and closed, and its behavior often enigmatic. Are there no more urgent tasks elsewhere? Is this search for the exotic not a mere intellectual exercise?

These studies, however, are neither narrow nor futile in their aims. Who can say that some dig or some ethnographic or geographic expedition in Eskimo territory will not one day make a decisive contribution to our knowledge of our own prehistory—which essentially took place in a cold climate—and illuminate it with fresh light? The ethnology of boreal societies, with their emphasis on the precariousness of life, on concrete reality and violence, on the most firmly asserted individuality that coexists with the most restrictive group laws, reveals too many sociological facts—for example, the frequent absence of institutions or explicit social structures—not to command the closest attention.

To know how the boreal hunter apprehends time and space can become a crucial element in our understanding of archaic thought processes. In watching the Eskimos live, in trying to grasp how they equip and organize themselves, in analyzing on the basis of little everyday scenes their real and symbolic relations with the world, the ethnologist, no matter where he is from, is at the very roots of his own civilization.

During my geomorphological and demographic research, I constantly, fanatically, observed the slightest details of the world around me. Smells, colors, words, gestures, silences, little nothings—I patiently recorded them all in my notebook. The work was difficult and lonely. Of course, sometimes the life of daily hunting was so full and absorbed me so totally that I felt like letting myself go and living as the Eskimos did rather than making the constant effort to keep a certain distance, to record, record. And then the business of spying is thankless. But by reading over now and then what I had written, I gathered fresh courage: by seeing in my notebook how additions and deletions to my descriptions of how their techniques and skill operated day after day, how a story or a personal confidence was begun and developed, it seemed to me possible to understand how a primitive society dominated by an implacable environment can persevere.

It was then that I saw things on a higher plane. Perhaps the exemplary life of these three hundred hunters who in 1818 had no driftwood, no metals; for whom a needle, a nail, or a board was a treasure, would illuminate the distant centuries that are at the very sources of human thought. Who knows? Perhaps their life could shed revolutionary light on our understanding of the development of the earliest societies. How—and with what rules—did man pass from the state of the lowest paleolithic hunter to that of the Neanderthal, hunter of the mammoth and rhinoceros, to that of the hunter of walrus and whale? How did he move on from small unorganized groups to form a communistic society?

And there is more: there are problems of understanding. It is said that a man of today could not understand his Ice Age brother. However, the Arctic in 1950 was a living Lascaux in some ways, and in this environment it was possible to attempt this understanding. After my arrival in July, a dialogue was joined. Of course, barriers still remained between us. Which? That is what I had tirelessly to explore in order to learn at the price of what theatricality and what masks we mutually distorted ourselves—they and I—as we scrutinized each other. That quest is perhaps one of the main purposes of the present book.

I owe much to these exemplary men, who obliged me to discover in depth my own identity. They reminded me that a man's life should be a constant challenge that enables him to become what he truly is. They were my second—and more important—university, and I shall be indebted to them all my life. They constituted a school of experience: they taught me all over again that the process of reasoning can be so immediate that it borders on intuition. They strengthened this capacity in me, which my French education had buried deep inside me.

Over a period of fourteen months, I learned the virtue of silence. An interior dialogue—sometimes one of physical suffering—developed between these men and me during my first "exile" among them. I learned to look on these men not as abstract ideas but as a challenge to the history of humanity; their functioning society forced me to revise my unitarian ideas about destiny and progress. Nevertheless, I do not want to start my book with a false impression. Were these hunters the last kings of Thule? Yes, they were. Their way of life, the only one possible if one wants to live entirely off the northern lands, was and is doomed. But does this mean that these people in all their individuality are doomed also?

I do not believe so, despite the difficulties ahead. The essential thing is not to regret that for the Eskimos one era is past, but to help ensure that the Eskimos' *true needs* are met.

This book is intended not only to bear witness to the past and present of the Eskimos of Greenland but also to consider their future.

I have sought to stress the vitality of the society that lives on the southwestern and eastern coasts of Greenland, and to show how exceptional it is in the Arctic regions that this ethnically mixed Eskimo community of fifty thousand Greenlanders should have come to be part of the Kingdom of Denmark. Fifty thousand: one-half of the Eskimo people deployed along the 180° longitude. One must hope that eventually successful government policies for the Polar Eskimos will crown the indisputable successes achieved by the policy on the southwestern coast.

For the isolated group of 302 Polar Eskimos, their "discovery" in 1818 by the explorer John Ross was a cardinal date in their history, not to be matched until 1951, when United States expansion into the Arctic Ocean began with the creation of the Air Force base at Thule. That was the most important—and what is more, the most critical—date in the Polar Eskimos' history. When two societies of different vocations and levels of development are brought into proximity—in this instance, Danish, not to mention American, and Eskimo—there is every risk that the weaker will suffer a decline.

With this in mind, one could have wished that the Polar Eskimos had been more stringently isolated than I observed them to be in July of 1951. Provided, of course, that such administratively protected isolation had been balanced by a policy of *radical economic expansion:* an inventory of possible new sources of income, such as the breeding of fur-bearing animals, commercial fishing, the formation and maintenance of search-and-rescue dog-team patrols for airplanes in distress; the introduction of modern methods of hunting and trapping; the extension of the hunting terrain to embrace the whole of northern Greenland; the development of broader technological training. Provided, further, that the Polar Eskimos be granted genuine power via a pricing policy that would have permanently assured them a substantial economic profit. Lastly, a vigorous birth-rate and demographic policy should have been set up for the immigration of Greenlandic families from the deprived sectors of Upernavik or, better still, of Canadian Eskimo families. It was certain already in 1951 that unless precautions were taken, the progressive insertion of this numerically small group into the much vaster population of Greenland, from which it had been separate, would lead to its decadence or to a prolonged regression of the indigenous people such as was observed earlier on the eastern Greenland coast.

I can vouch for the fact that the Thule Eskimos are aware of their situation. On a worldwide scale, their vulnerability is glaringly evident. "Don't destroy us!" they appealed to John Ross's British sailors and their interpreter, Saccheus. "We are alive, very much alive!"

The only place "primitive" man is going to find enough strength, enough "extra soul," to defend himself against the bait of our consumer civilization is in himself and within his community. There is an urgent need, then, for these people to be politically educated so that they can protect themselves from the dangers of cultural assimilation and what they have been offered in the name of technological progress.

It would be truly tragic if these northern hunters, who for thousands of years successfully met the challenge of the harsh living conditions at the Pole, went the way of so many others and were tempted to abandon their identity as free men merely for the often deceptive attraction of welfare assistance and city lights.

The Eskimo is enough of a gambler not to turn away from such a confrontation, and he owes it to himself to be man enough to take advantage of his new situation to bring about a renaissance as lively and as rich as were the first epochs of his civilization.

And this is not a Utopian point of view.

The powerful and imaginative personality of the Danish Eskimo Knud Rasmussen stands as proof of what I have been saying. He is the symbol and the hope of Greenland's future civilization.

PARIS, 1953–54

In 1950–51 the Polar Eskimos, the northernmost inhabitants of our earth, were among the rare representatives of ancient hunting times in the cold regions. They were witnesses to what the postglacial era may have been in Europe and Asia. In 1950–51, in their innermost selves and in manifest ways, they still remained at the level of this immensely important epoch in human history. The myths, ideas, sensibility, and unconscious of these hunters were, in large part, those of their remote ancestors, as was their mode of life. They had been familiar with wood since 1818–30, and with the rifle since 1880. However, in such high latitudes both mental evolution and social evolution are slow—the whole of the present book attests to this—and the rhythms of change are uneven.

The Eskimo I knew only some thirty years ago was still at a stage of cultural advancement where he felt that he was a shade of a human being who partook more of the dead than of the living, and that he could affirm himself as a man only by maintaining, via hunting, an umbilical cord with the animal.

Still unsure of what he was, he felt totally *Inuk,* totally Eskimo, only in terms of action and techniques, in doing and in the ways of doing. For his ideas he relied on the group, fearful that any error could cause a mutation that he would no longer be in control of and that might plunge him back into the earlier animal world. He built his sense of self only through the group and through being one of the group.

"The more I think as an individual, the less I feel I exist." This anguish, this ontological fear, was what drew him into contact with others and pushed him to affirm almost mechanically through group song and dance not only his reality as a man but as an Inuk. Paradoxically, at the same time, the Eskimo has always been thoroughly individualistic, and has feared the omnipresent group-refuge. To my way of thinking, one reason for the hunter's wish to deny that time has duration derived from a no less ontological concern to preserve his freedom—his marginality—by granting the group only the smallest possible hold over him. Eskimo thinking, then, did not recognize time. The hours and the days flew by according to an elusive continuance.

A human animal, a primitive? Certainly not. A *different* kind of human being. Irreducible. In the centuries-long progress of humanization, Western man has won a certain technical knowledge and has as surely lost other systems of value which the Arctic hunter used still to have at his command.

Because I lived through one historical moment in the long history of an exemplary people, I have gladly taken up *The Last Kings of Thule* again, although at the time of my writing it the book seemed to me complete.

Rereading this book after twenty years and from the perspective of intervening experience, I have felt a kind of inner need to meander and digress. For the sake of a better understanding of the facts the book records, I have integrated reflections born of my later missions among the Polar Eskimos with the events of my 1950–51 expedition. In each instance, they have been appropriately interpolated and noted. For this English-language edition, I have also added significant new material about the effect of thirty years of "modern life" upon this last tribe of independent Eskimos.

Rewriting this book has involved more than mere revision and updating. I do not refer to the length of the work—over twice as long as the first edition. There is something deeper. In rewriting, I have also relived. Perhaps I too, like the Eskimo, have sought to deny time in the narrow sense. I have in fact searched for a kind of deeper reconciliation. Amid the profusion of details of my first vision of that world, I have tried to seize the significant detail from which a larger occurrence evolves. I have had recourse not to memories relived on the frontiers of the imagined but rather to sensations that have been fugitive until now but are the more vivid as they slowly emerge in me today. And it is singular that with time one's sight does both deepen and sharpen, eliminating the superfluous in order to retain the essential that, brought into better focus, is freshly scanned and assumes its full significance. I have taken up this book again, word by word, with characteristic relish for perpetually raising the true problems and in the belief that an intensely lived passion is never all spent.

Those years continue to live within me not as a memory that blurs but as a time that draws always nearer. It is the same for the Polar Eskimos, whom I have visited often since 1951. Because these men—especially the older men —were unable to write, the past was preserved in them with a rare precision so that it might not be forgotten. They mumbled it over and over, they relived it in a half-dream; events unfolded behind their squinting eyes like a film.

When, with Inuterssuaq, Amaa, Imina, Kutsikitsoq, Bertsie, and so many others, certain scenes that we lived through together were evoked twenty years later, they were relived with infinitely greater intensity than when recalled after only a few months, as if time were needed for "the little sensation"—smell, color, emotion, astonishment—which is inscribed in the groove of memory, to protect one's recollection of the event.

It was too early for me to have written this book in 1951, but I did not know that then. Curiously enough, great travelers—Humboldt, Jack London, Père Huc—lived with their memories for years, publishing some of them only late or not at all. One lives with one's memories—in the proper sense of that phrase —in order to grasp their internal order. The weakness of big travel narratives and reportages very likely derives from the writer's haste to preserve vivacity at the expense of deeper internal experience. It is the search for time newly refound that I offer the reader.

PARIS, 1975–80

PART ONE

GREENLAND IS A GREEN LAND

"Greenland authorization officially granted."

I reread the telegram from the French ambassador in Copenhagen which a limping black man had just brought to my hut.

Thule. . . . The Polar Eskimos. . . . During earlier stays on Disko Bay, off the west coast of Greenland, I had learned from native informants that far, far to the north, near a mysterious place called Thule, there were "primitive" Eskimos among whom no Frenchman had ever lived. Everything I had ascertained about the nature of the half-Eskimo Greenlanders who lived in the southern part of that vast island had made me wish, every year more intensely, to reach back to their origins by going to more northern latitudes where, I had been told, a handful of people preserved their ethnic character to a remarkable degree.

For months I had tried repeatedly to persuade Danish officials and the scientific organizations for which I was then working how valuable it would be were a French geographical expedition to be made to the territory of this tribe before its members came into prolonged contact with whites. Now, at a desert camp in the middle of the Sahara, a favorable response to my proposal had finally arrived: a few words jotted down on a scrap of dirty paper.

The message reached me during the second of two expeditions to the Ahaggar Mountains in the winters of 1948–49 and 1949–50, the spring and summer months preceding having been spent in Greenland. A lone white man, accompanied only by two Tuareg camel drivers, I had been studying scree gradients and the erosion of desert stones in these mountains so that I might compare my findings with similar experiments in cold deserts between latitude 79° and 80° north. There, I knew, the aridity is extreme, and the annual changes in temperature are, in an inverse direction, equivalent to what rock undergoes in the Ahaggar massif region of southern Algeria—from forty to sixty degrees.

3

It is droll to reflect that I received this confirming message and worked out the details of my Arctic expedition while at a Tuareg encampment not far from Tamanrasset, the capital of the Ahaggar region in the heart of the Sahara. My mind was peopled by mirthful Eskimo faces, filled with visions of snow and ice floes. Itineraries began taking shape in my head as I paced back and forth. The camel driver Mohammed watched me, surprised and uneasy.

"Labéss, sir? Is everything all right?"

"Yes, labéss, Mohammed."

I felt that my new experience was beginning under favorable auspices.

When I arrived in Algiers, however, disastrous news was waiting for me. The director of a well-known explorers' organization on which I was counting for financial support had written, abruptly notifying me that my account with his organization was overdrawn by three thousand francs and that if I did not repay the money promptly, he would not advance me the modest sum we had long since agreed upon for the Arctic expedition. I received two letters to this effect. And so the scramble for money began, as I also plunged into the chores and rushing about that precede an imminent departure.

My departure from Copenhagen en route to Greenland had been set for July 1, 1950. In a very short time I had to get together not only several thousand francs but also my equipment, supplies, and fuel.

Thanks to the help of scientific institutions and of loyal friends, in a few days I reduced my debt to eighteen hundred francs; my sponsor considered this credit-worthy.

By June 15, my equipment was assembled, paid for, and crated; by the twenty-seventh, I was in Copenhagen.

With my passage booked, my luggage labeled, at ten o'clock on the morning of July 1, I finally boarded ship. One last farewell handshake was exchanged with some Danish friends, the ship's whistle moaned like a dumb creature, and the pier began slowly to recede. Several women passengers, their arms filled with flowers, were sniffling. "Farvelle! Farvelle!" We were off to the North Pole.

The gangplank had been pulled in and lay motionless on the deck. The wireless antenna swayed back and forth and the ship creaked as it swung about and headed northward. Everything lay before me. My "adventure," as we say, was beginning.

Its first phase, however, was to be an uneventful sea voyage. The passengers prepared to face the "angry boreal seas" in total comfort. As for me, I faced the monotony of a voyage I was making for the third time. Excited sea gulls shrieked over the garbage that spewed from the hull. Down in the messroom, a piano ground out two-four polka tunes against the steady muffled drumming of the ship's engines.

As early as 8:00 A.M., zealous stewardesses would bustle back and forth along the corridors. Twenty-odd sleep-drunk passengers would begin to stir in the belly of the ship. If it was a lovely morning, up on deck, as if risen from the deep, some tanned young Danish woman would already be stretched out in the sun; they did lend our freighter a holiday allure.

Our laconic captain habitually signaled our position by jabbing a thumb-tack on the map in the smoking room. Soon afterward, we would take our places at table. We were served true Scandinavian fare: tables were laden with platters of pink shrimp, raw fish, smoked meats, condiments, and bottles of beer and aquavit among flowers and tiny flags; smiling color photographs of the royal family presided over all.

"Skoll! Skoll!" At close range, we must have presented a strange spectacle. A gaunt, scowling pastor from Greenland brushed elbows with a civil servant's buxom wife, who was poured into her flower-printed dress. Children and workmen in open-collared, checked shirts surrounded us. Five Scottish moun-tain climbers sat among some gawky, grinning Greenlanders who tried to ape the manners of their distinguished neighbors. A few bookkeepers made sour comments.

Everyone was killing time. The daily siesta came at two o'clock. Stretched out on a banquette in the smoking room under a harsh electric light, a me-chanic snored, open-mouthed. Nearby, for lack of other excitement, a literary-minded lady smiled over her suspense novel. Weary eyes fastened on a few dirty icebergs at the far side of an expanse of dark, smooth water. To the cadence of our eight knots, they marched slowly by. One could make out far, far away, in a milky fog and beneath a red and violet sky, a sprinkling of nameless islands by an immense glacier. Not one tree. Rock, nothing but rock. Was this "the friendly Arctic"?

One morning, I changed my last kroner, a hundred pounds or so, and a few dollars into local currency. We were approaching the only large island on our planet whose inhabitants still adamantly refused to recognize banks and whose local currency could not be converted anywhere else. We had been traveling for eight days. During four of them my cabinmate, a venerable pastor from Oslo, had been lying, seasick and disgruntled, in his berth. We had some nineteen days still to go. We were aboard the S.S. *Disko*, the senior cargo ship of the Copenhagen-Disko Line, now in sight of the southeastern coast of Greenland.

The ship slowly entered the peaceful channel of Vaigat Sound. We dropped anchor off Qutligssat, a mining center on the large island of Disko.

Before us lay a cluster of checkered dollhouses, red, yellow, and blue. Colorful laundry was drying at the windows. Every householder had hoisted the handsome Dannebrog on his own flagpole, which heightened the Bastille Day atmosphere. Qutligssat belongs to modern, civilized Greenland, where nine-tenths of the island's total population lives. "They'd forgotten to remind us that this part of the country exists," the French journalist Robert Guillain once observed, rightly enough. "For you and me, the word 'Greenland' used to evoke little more than whiteness and cold. Just to live there must have called for a kind of daily heroism; in a word, to us 'Greenland' meant more or less the North Pole."[1]

A crowd of Brueghel-like people, squat, solidly built, all wearing caps, awaited us on the shore. Grown-ups, children—all ages had turned out. A nineteenth-century cannon that looked like a period stage prop boomed in our honor. The crowd cheered. It was a welcome straight out of an operetta.

Four or five at a time, we piled into a damp old tub lacking any floorboard and open to the weather. Our ferryman was a sort of elderly Mongol; the skin on his face was like parchment and wrinkles swallowed up his small, slitted eyes. "Kra! Hurry up! Let's go!" he shouted at a woman passenger who had slipped as she tried to join us. People did hurry, and the boat almost capsized. The Mongol laughed sneeringly. "Ah, these qallunaat!"*

The swell bore us to land, finally, and we fell into the arms of the welcoming throng. Lined up on the shore, plump, animal-eyed mothers in dirty, unbuttoned blouses held nursing babies at their breasts; they greeted us automatically with a friendly *go da*. A debonair native policeman moved among them, a copper badge pinned to the tunic of his symbolically black uniform.

I was whisked off to the home of O——, an old friend who had been working as an engineer in Greenland for years. His house was surprisingly comfortable: polished parquet floors, telephone, leather armchairs, a library, a record collection, a radio. Family photographs hung on the walls; green plants and flowering geranium sat on window sills. I noticed on one table a few bone figurines, examples of the first "souvenirs" produced for the Eskimo tourist industry. The floors were covered with animal skins and Moroccan rugs. "A lovely home indeed, Mr. Malaurie," a young nurse said to me, as she offered me a cognac. At dinner, the typically Danish courtesy reigned. As we were

---

Qallunaaq (pl. *qallunaat*) = white man; the literal meaning is "big eyebrows." Compare this with *Inuk* (pl. *Inuit*) = Eskimo, literally "man, human being"; and with *kalaaleq* (pl. *kalaallit*), the Eskimo name for "Greenlander," meaning a person of mixed Eskimo and Danish, Dutch, or Scottish origins. This latter term is used only on the southwest coast of Greenland.

Qallunaaq refers in general to a Dane (the Americans, the English, the French each have their own words). In the course of this book, however, when an Eskimo uses the term *qallunaaq* in referring to me or other whites, it is in an ironic or pejorative sense. After all, the Eskimo, the Inuk, is by definition a human being, whereas the white man, the qallunaaq, belongs to a species that defies definition.

The spellings used in this book follow accepted Greenlandic usage and may pose some pronunciation problems for the reader. Certain sounds in Eskimo are not easily transliterated, and have given rise to vastly different spellings over the years. Some examples: igloo, iglu, illu (the latter is the Greenlandic form); Etah, Ita, Iita; Kranaq, Qanaq, Qaanaaq. The *l* is often pronounced with more of a *dgl* sound (thus illu = idglu); *q*, except when at the end of a word, is pronounced *krr* (thus qallunaaq = krraslunaak). In most cases, words ending in *q* form their plurals by substituting a *t*. The letters *b, c, d, f,* and *x* have no equivalents in Eskimo.

leaving the table, Mr. Schultz-Lorentzen, the ranking pastor in Greenland, plucked at my sleeve.

"Why don't you go to the dance? It's something to see, believe me. I'm too old, but you . . ."

Someone lent me a pair of patent-leather pumps, and I put on a tie. On to the ball! In this instance, the ballroom was the poor people's club; from time to time, Greenlanders would get together here. Like true colonialists, the Danes who live on the island conceal their wealth. They keep to themselves, and only rarely are Greenlanders invited to their parties.

The dance must have been going full blast for an hour; from a distance, one heard a muffled din. The mail had arrived with our ship, and Qutligssat was celebrating. Near the community rain gauge, I met some ribald fellows all heading for the same place—the large frame and tar-paper shack that was the dance hall. Like a kind of advertisement, a group of girls stood by the entrance; their black hair fell below the collars of their red jackets, and they were shaking their fat behinds to the rhythm of the music. I picked one up, bought us tickets, and in we went. Immediately I was swept into a furious foxtrot. The music blared from the horn of a phonograph vintage 1900; there was indeed a modern record player, but that night it was broken. What difference did that make! At the end of each record, someone rushed over to crank the machine. Makeup began to run. A pungent, sour smell caught at one's throat. My partner, a free and easy Greenlander with cherry-red lips, pressed hard against me as we tangoed. Routine sentiment . . . I looked at her. Mascara made her eyes look even more slitted. We smiled at each other. A recollection flashed through my mind of an afternoon I spent as a schoolboy at an amusement park. My Greenlander proudly puffed out her bosom, which was covered by an openwork bodice, and drew attention to her dress, which pulled at the seams so that I could see slivers of a salmon-pink slip beneath. For an upwardly mobile woman, this was all in perfectly good taste. To own underwear was in itself a sign of wealth, was it not?

Some men were wearing white canvas anoraks. Many others, who carried their jackets slung over their arms, had donned handsome striped shirts and flowered ties for the occasion; by now, most collar buttons had popped from their owners' exertions. The men were lined up along one wall, cigarettes drooping from their mouths; facing them across the dance floor stood the women; it was as if they were at Mass—men on the right, women on the left. I sat on the bench reserved for Danes, facing the gramophone. Except for me, it was empty, as it always is, yet at such affairs a perverse custom calls for a qallunaat bench.

When the music started up again, I witnessed a tremendous rush. The men flung themselves toward the opposite wall to "get a woman." There was no possibility of cutting diagonally through that dense wave of males. Having lost ten seconds to my rivals, I was left with the choice of one elderly or one lame partner.

Before the next dance—a waltz—I stationed myself in a good spot, kept one eye on the arm of the gramophone and the other on my competitors, and used my elbows to advantage. Moments later, I was hurled against a poor girl just as a Greenlander—he seemed awfully drunk—was thrown against her from the other side. He grabbed one arm; I grabbed the other. I pulled; he pulled. Neither of us was willing to let go. "I was first, qallunaaq!" he spat at me. Then the music prevailed, and bore all three of us off. We stuck together, broke apart, and came together again. We were pushed, and we pushed back. The woman began to cry. We took turns holding her limp, clammy hand. I offered the Greenlander a cigar. He smiled at me and finally, with an understanding wink, relinquished his prey. It does not take long to acquire the colonialist mentality. . . .

Outside, men pissed against the walls. Women mopped their armpits with handkerchiefs or scarves. Some workmen joked with the girls; bottles of *immiaq* —a local beer made of imported barley—bulged in their pockets.

Greenland is a country of contrasts. When I went later to a foreman's house, I discovered an impersonal interior and a group of workers—all Danish —playing cards; now and then they would pass around pornographic pictures, while they got drunk on aquavit and whiskey.

Paradox confronted me everywhere. In Godthaab, the capital of Greenland, sheep stood on the shore munching cod while they watched icebergs float by. We passed a "native" wearing a sealskin coat, an American baseball cap, and tennis shoes. Each time we came into a different port, our travelers were astonished afresh to find that on this huge polar island nature was not untouched. Some of them were expecting to see snow igloos, savage Eskimos, and packs of ferocious dogs. Instead, we came upon colorful Scandinavian villages and Greenlanders in overalls bicycling to work.

"Travelers to Greenland saw what they wanted to see," Robert Guillain wrote. "Perhaps they dramatized it a little too much for us, made it a little too white. . . . Far be it from them to spoil the legend." In fact, as we walked through the streets of small towns on the southwest coast—Julianehaab, Frederikshaab, Holsteinsborg, Godhavn, Jakobshavn—we discovered harbor installations under construction everywhere. Trucks loaded with Mongolian-featured workers rumbled by constantly. Pneumatic drills digging into rock made a racket that would drive a lover of peace and quiet to distraction.

At noon, the overwhelmed "explorer" would lose his last illusions: the blast of a siren signaled the midday work break at the Qutligssat lignite mine. Did he wish to round out his impressions elsewhere? Well, in Godthaab he could visit the museum where the stuffed remains of a dying past were on display; also the "cod factory," the hospital, and a century-old printshop. Christianshaab offered a shrimp cannery. The larger towns had a radio station, an ultramodern "shop"—a store established by the Danish government to supply the population with European goods, called a *pisiniarfik* in Greenlandic —where you could find everything from a bar of soap to a typewriter, and lastly the vast complex of government and services that in each of Greenland's coastal cities constitutes the embryo of modern life.[2]

And what about the natives? I first met Juditha on the port road in Godthaab. It was she who struck up a conversation, with a spontaneity and openness that are still wholly Eskimo. She was gratifying two of the deepest tendencies of her race: a taste for the picturesque and a taste for the new. Juditha was comely and cheerful, and I see her still—a squat, rather stout girl, rigged out in a pair of checkered trousers that unhappily emphasized her broad, low-slung behind. For the arrival of the Danish ship that morning, she had hastily made up her face and put on nail polish.

She took me to her house.

"We get bored here," she said. "Not enough movies or dances. Luckily, we get to see some new qallunaats every spring!"

Her eyes were smiling at me.

"They're nice, you know."

Juditha's father had been a seal hunter in the south. She reminisced emotionally about her childhood, which nevertheless she considered had been miserable. She dreamed out loud: a tiny coastal village of five families tucked in the curve of a bay; facing south—facing the sun, that is—her family's igloo, a black square of peat blocks crouched at the foot of a rocky slope. "I was born there. Only one small room to live in, one window, one wooden platform for a bed. Day after day, nothing but seal to eat. With the fox skins we caught in winter we could buy sugar, coffee, and ammunition at the store. . . . The dog sledge? Well, yes! That was the one real pleasure the men had. But while they were outside all the time, we were inside—in the igloo—forever sewing and chewing skins. It was enough to wear down your teeth. . . . Once a year, the white doctor would come by. . . ."

In a few words she evoked not only the simple joys and the repetitive, monotonous work of patriarchal village life, but also the contrasting seasons —the June migration of birds, huckleberry and mushroom time, the scent of heather and the freedom of the tundra, the melting of the ice, the walrus and whale hunts in free water, the September ice field, the wind, the long winter night. Only one of the children—her younger brother—had carried on the tradition; her older brother was a baker at the Danish cryolite mine outside Ivittuut; one sister was a doctor's housekeeper.

In 1950 Godthaab was a town of twelve hundred inhabitants.

Juditha's "igloo" was like all the others in these southwestern towns: a frame cabin encased within peat walls; its two rooms were lighted by electricity and brightened by cooking pots and cheap religious pictures. (When we arrived, she had shoved a chamber pot under the bed with her foot.) A barrel of drinking water stood beside a coal stove. In the first room I entered, a wire stretched from wall to wall held drying espadrilles and basketball sneakers. Huddled together in a corner, five blue-eyed children stared at me pleasantly.

I talked with Juditha for an hour. Nothing about her suggested the primitive, except perhaps her facial features and her extreme sensitivity. While we

The attributes of civilization—among others, frame house, flag, clock, book, sailor's cap, Danish sailor, alarm clock, blackboard, ceiling light, painting, bedside photograph, chamber pot, chair—as seen by a fifteen-year-old Greenlandic girl from Godthaab, 1951.

waited for her Danish husband—a wireless operator—she served me the traditional coffee. The conversation turned to the price of sugar, the high cost of living, the minimum one needed to get by. This began to pall, so I talked to her about Paris. She told me politely how much she wanted to go there, and then took out a packet of pictures of Copenhagen and described the city's monuments for me. She did not like seals very much; they were dirty and smelled bad. With no false modesty, she described her love life as a girl. Abruptly, with the anarchic shift in conversation one grows used to in Greenland, she asked me whether I knew anything about "tourists." She had heard that plans for tourism were afoot and, like her women friends, she was looking forward to spring tourists so that she could guide these modern "polar travelers" to the souvenirmakers and to her primitive cousins.

In the coastal port where I visited Johann, one of the country's many half-Eskimos, or Greenlanders, the atmosphere was rather different. I was now in the home of an important person. A tall man with blond hair and green eyes, Johann was a cod fisherman, one of the rich urban Greenlanders; he would be the town's next mayor. His home mirrored the man: solid and middle class. The house was built entirely of wood—no peat walls here: three rooms painted in bright, high-gloss colors; a dining room boasting chocolate-brown wallpaper with gilded scrolls; floors so highly polished that you could have skated on them; on one wall, a cheap mirror; in a corner, hidden behind a jungle of plants, an enormous radio. I noted on the three shelves of his bookcase, next to the *Reader's Digest,* the Danish Yearbook; *Atuagagdliutit,* a Greenlandic newspaper founded in 1860; *Grønlandsposten,* a bilingual paper subsidized by the government; and three books—*Toi et moi* by Géraldy, *The Count of Monte Cristo,* and the Bible—all translations into Greenlandic. Beside a wood-platform bed lay a bearskin rug; trunks served as bureaus. On the central wall hung a print of *The Angelus,* by Millet, surrounded by photographs of Danish monarchs. Finally, a reproduction showing Christ at Lake Tiberius hung above the radio.

"Drink up, I'm rich!" Johann said, as he offered me a drink. A broad grin revealed his gold teeth. "The whole thing for Greenland," he went on, in a piquant pidgin of Danish, English, and Greenlandic, "is the fish business. The days of the seal and the kayak are over and done with. They were fine for the Eskimos. But what we need now is cod fishing, like in Iceland. Cod and more cod. Today we are fishing with poles and hooks, but tomorrow, if the *danskerne* keep on giving us money, it'll be with trawls. . . . And then we'll go where the big schools of fish are, like the qallunaat. Beezeness, beezeness, that's what it's all about. The past—all those peat and snow igloos, kayaks, dogs, tattoos, drums, and dancing—it's all folklore. Nobody cares about that anymore."

In Greenland, the middle class and the elite openly despise the poor people they themselves came from. They have set themselves up in a cultural exile which they flaunt, the better to assert themselves. In order to resemble that great and powerful protector the white man, my host had frozen his personality. His face had relaxed for a moment, but now it was closed again.

"Look! I eat, live, and think like the whites. I've got a bank account. You've seen my daughter; she's a secretary at the *kontor*. My youngest son, after he finishes the Godthaab Upper School, will go to the University of Copenhagen. I own a one-story house. In the port, I keep a motorboat I bought on a ten-year installment plan, again thanks to the Danes. . . . People must have pointed it out to you, because everybody knows me. I'm rich, I tell you. And I'm happy! . . . Don't tell me I'm an Eskimo, an Inuk! That's like calling me a savage. I'm a kalaaleq, a Greenlander! I went to a technical school. My wife is Danish— from Jutland—and at home we speak nothing but Danish. In fact, I'm not even a kalaaleq anymore. I'm a Dane from the North, and my children will be Danish. We're all Danes. There's no difference anymore."

We ended my visit by listening to a recording of some accordion music. Then my host reached into his vest pocket, pulled out a heavy turn-of-the-century watch on a chain, and excused himself. There was to be a speech on the radio which he wanted to hear—"On the future of the kalaaleq." . . . He put on a black felt hat, picked up his cane, and left for his neighbor's house. At important moments, Greenlanders like to be among their own kind.

"Qallunaat ajorput! The Danes aren't worth anything to us now! But welcome to you just the same!" From one igloo to the next the poor Greenlanders waved a friendly hello to the French visitor who had just got off the boat. We were in Holsteinborg. "Qaaniarit! Qaaniarit! Come in!" They wanted someone to pay them a visit. But the Greenland police officers, dressed in black with sheriff's badges and carrying big billy clubs, kept their eye on things to prevent any "familiarities" from taking place. We were not allowed to enter the houses of Greenlanders, shake hands, or talk. In 1950 the Danish government was still trying to maintain the isolation of the Greenlanders in order to protect their unique culture and history. With some ups and downs, this had been the policy since 1721.

But now there had been a war, and American bases on the southwest coast had brought with them a new traffic of men and ideas. The resentment at being treated like children had grown strong among the Greenlanders. The interjection *Qallunaat ajorput!* "The Danes aren't worth anything!" was by now a familiar greeting to me and my fellow foreigners. These fishing folk wanted us foreigners to know their thinking, wanted us to tell the world that they wanted no more of this protectionist legislation—whether or not it was conceived in their own interest. At the same time as they showed their newborn contempt for the Danes, they maintained a touching trust in the Danish king, a portrait of whom decorated every house.

Although the object of this book is not to dwell on living conditions on the southern coast of Greenland nearly thirty years ago, it will be helpful if the reader bears in mind the few stopovers I have briefly described. Beyond the trafficking in exotic goods which is typical of many other colonies as well, I discovered in each of the people I have mentioned the prototype of what the fifteen hundred to two thousand Eskimos of Angmagssalik or Thule—the last primitive people living on this large island—were likely to become within one generation. In my later isolation at Thule, the scenes of archaic life that I observed there formed a kind of counterpoint to the life I had seen in the southern coastal towns, and to the painful future of a people in the throes of gestation.

New York

C   A

Port Nelson   Churchill

Ottawa

Fort Chimo

LABRADOR

Illulik

Gander

Goose Bay

NEW-FOUNDLAND

Melville Bay

Godthaab   Skansen   Godhavn   THULE

Frederikshaab   DISKO ISLAND

Julianehaab   Holsteinsborg   Upernavik

Nanortalik   Qutligssat   Peary Land

Jakobshavn

GREENLAND   Smith Sound

Angmagssalik

ICELAND

SPITSBERGEN

Hammerfest

Murmansk

Novy P

Salekha

Leningrad

Paris   Copenhagen

EUROPE   U.

Moscow   S.

MAP 1. The Arctic: The Immense Territory Occupied by the Eskimo People

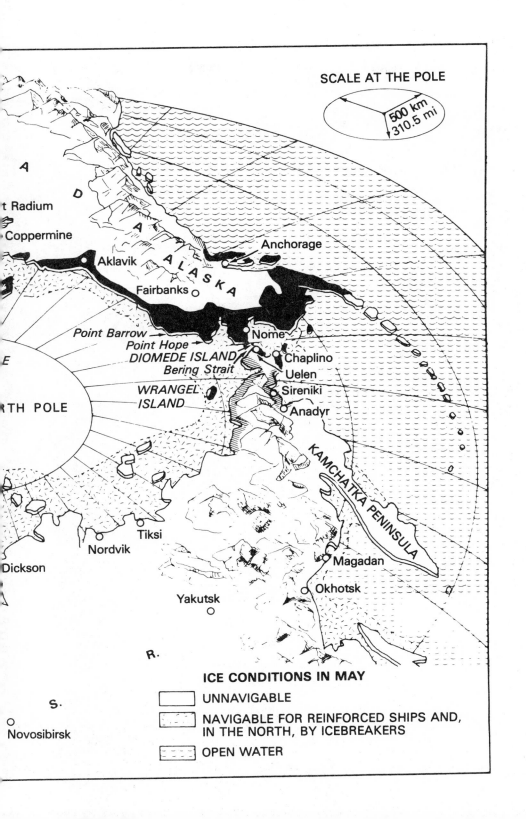

SCALE AT THE POLE

500 km
310.5 mi

t Radium

Coppermine

A

D

A L A S K A

Anchorage

Aklavik

Fairbanks

Point Barrow

Point Hope

Nome

DIOMEDE ISLAND

Chaplino

Bering Strait

Uelen

WRANGEL

Sireniki

ISLAND

Anadyr

TH POLE

E

KAMCHATKA PENINSULA

Tiksi

Nordvik

Dickson

Magadan

Yakutsk

Okhotsk

R.

ICE CONDITIONS IN MAY

S.

UNNAVIGABLE

Novosibirsk

NAVIGABLE FOR REINFORCED SHIPS AND, IN THE NORTH, BY ICEBREAKERS

OPEN WATER

PART TWO

THE
KINGS
OF THULE

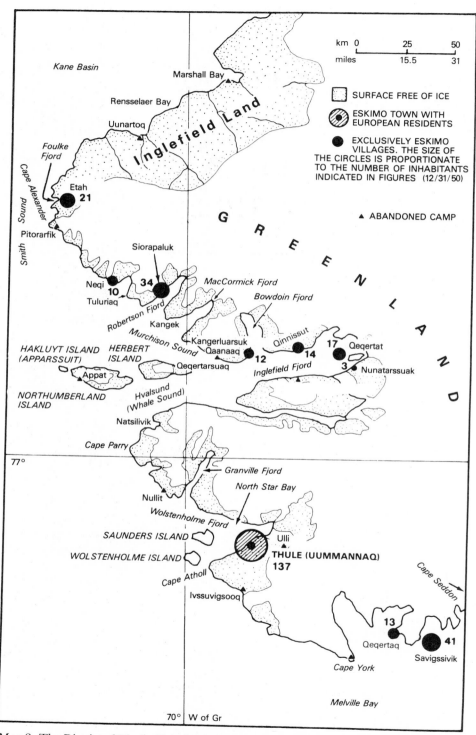

MAP 2. The District of Thule, Showing Polar Eskimo Settlements as of December 12, 1950

A return to the Stone Age, or more exactly, a return to the seal age. We were on our way to Thule.

For several hours, Cape York, a dark, towering promontory on the north-western coast of Greenland, had been in sight. Now we left Melville Bay and followed the American Polar Route, so named at the end of the nineteenth century when, after careful deliberation, Robert Peary elected to try to reach the Pole by way of Smith Sound.

Our wooden icebreaker, the *Tikerak,* which I had boarded in Jacobshavn, pushed on through fog and ice pack. Yesterday we passed the Devil's Thumb, a rock that looms high among phantom iceberg castles. Tomorrow we should reach the northernmost inhabited territory in the world. As we drew nearer our goal, some of us passengers were deeply moved. We kept pacing back and forth on the deck. We passed Cape Atholl and, in a sunless dawn, finally slipped into Uummannaq Bay. Scanning the expanse, we sighted our destination.

Uummannaq or "North Star" Bay opens onto the "free waters of the North." Its second name derives from the *North Star,* the first Scottish whaling ship to winter in these waters, in 1850–51. It is a true Arctic oasis, for it never freezes thanks to the convection of variously constituted currents. Thule, shel-tered from the Canadian winds by two islands with red sandstone cliffs, stands against the ice cap. The glacier slopes toward a nearby fjord with enormous icebergs, which attracted the large whales and, as a consequence, many hunters who lived on them. Thule—or Uummannaq—was the capital and crossroads of the district and one of the oldest Eskimo sites east of Canada.

Silently, almost as if respectfully, the ship moved forward. On July 23, we dropped anchor before the mountains of Thule, on which, it is said, mist and rock are indistinguishable. Fabled Thule had at last become a reality for all of us.

Venient Annis
Saecula seris, quibus Oceanus
Vincula rerum laxet et ingens
Pateat tellus, Tethysque novos
Detegat orbes nec sit terris
Ultima Thule.

Later, when the world has grown
In years, a moment will come
When the sea loosens the bond of things.
An immense earth will open, and Thetis
Will discover new continents.
Thule will no longer be the farthest land.

Seneca, Medea

The sun rose. This mysterious point on the globe emerged from the fog in all its bleak austerity. The landscape was severe, hostile, pitiless. A rocky, dirty beach; a small clinic; some twenty black igloos with high peat walls; a few red-and-yellow Danish houses; rags and broken crates, bones and old pots scattered along the shore. Reality gave the lie to the poets. Thule, Ultima Thule: Who had not celebrated it? Virgil, Pytheas. . . . According to Caesar, the Thule of Pytheas was a place where "night reigned for a hundred days during the winter solstice." Procopius and, after him, Dicuil honored the kings of Thule, with whom the Heruli had wanted to become allied in 512. Thule was also the myth of the magi of Germany's racist gospel: I remembered the Thule Gesellschaft, one of a number of mythic Nordic-Germanic societies that existed parallel to and helped give rise to Nazism during the Weimar Republic. Adolf Hitler belonged, in 1916, to this closed organization, as a *gast* or "visiting brother."

I thought also of the warnings Pierre Bertius, cosmographer to Louis XIII, had issued as early as 1618: "The cold there cannot be defeated . . . and . . . several people have been killed by it. The winter lasts nine months without rain. . . . The very rich protect themselves . . . with fire; others can do no more than rub their feet, while some seek warmth in caves. . . . This whole country is full of cruel bears against whom the inhabitants war continuously. Also . . . if what is said be true, there are unicorns. All maintain that there are men called pygmies. . . . The pygmies, it seems, have a human form, with hair that falls to the tips of their fingers and beards that reach to their knees, but they are brutes with neither language nor reason; they hiss like geese. . . ."

"Sainang sunai! Hello there!"

Bundled up in sweaters, we hurried to the ship's rail. The hull of the annual ship was surrounded by a dozen kayaks, their occupants staring up at us with bright albeit enigmatic smiles. They looked small, and had flat, yellow faces. Pending closer contact, they surveyed what and who made up this season's cargo.

A few minutes later, the Danish administrator himself, Torben Krogh, came aboard and cheerfully shook hands all around. A cannon boomed, rifles crackled; this tiny Danish colony of a dozen people was welcoming us as if we were lifelong friends. However, for me, Thule was simply a stopover. I had decided to spend the winter 120 miles to the north, in Siorapaluk, a settlement of natives only.*

It was a well-supervised stopover. I had to show my penis to the doctor —it is the law here—to establish the fact that I would not become the cause of any venereal infection.

Two days went by. A Danish schooner arrived. It was painted in the Danish colors, green and red. Professor Norlund, the director of the Geodesic Institute of Copenhagen, had very kindly agreed to see to it that aerial photographs of Inglefield Land, the territory north of Etah, the northernmost hamlet in the region, would be supplied to me before my expedition began (no geomorphological map of Inglefield had yet been drawn). When I passed through Copenhagen, the photos had not been ready, so they were to be sent to me in Thule via a schooner of another Greenlandic-Danish organization—the one that had just arrived. I hailed an Eskimo, who took me out to the ship in a small boat. The air was sultry. I found no one on deck. I called out. A sleepy sailor appeared. I explained my business. He said irritably that he would call the ship's captain—I recognized his name as the man I'd been told in Copenhagen would bring me the material. I waited several minutes. Suddenly I heard "Raus, Frenchman! Here Danish vessel! Get off this ship fast! You're here without authorization and Frenchmen aren't welcome!"

Raus! That cry had been heard only too often in France during the Occupation, and my blood began to boil. But the captain was shouting from his bunk and I didn't know where he was. I shouted back at him—what, have you gone crazy? I dare you to repeat that Raus face-to-face! He was careful not to come out or answer. I only heard him muttering in Danish. That cry still resounds in my memory, that Raus which was all the more out of place in Danish Greenland.

I was upset both because the Eskimo had witnessed this incident—his face has been inscrutable—and because I could not vent my anger in a man-to-man confrontation. I climbed down into the boat and returned hastily to shore. My head was in a whirl: my geomorphological mission would not be made any easier by this setback; and although the photos were delivered on my return to Copenhagen a year later, with heartfelt excuses, the delay was to upset some of my plans and increase my difficulties in making cartographic surveys. For

---

*In 1950–51, a dozen Danes—administrators, meteorologists, mechanics—lived exclusively in Thule-Uummannaq. They did not stir north or south of Thule. The seven villages and hamlets scattered over three hundred miles received only one annual regulation visit from the doctor. By settling in one of these hamlets, I could not have asked for a year of more perfect isolation.

the moment, however, I gave less thought to my difficulties and more to the Danish captain's obscene behavior. It had been like a slap in the face.

Before going off to live in my eleven-month solitude, I wanted to understand just what had happened. I went straight to the Thule doctor, who was a friend, and described the incident. "Don't get excited, Malaurie. That man's all worked up. Why?" He smiled. "Yesterday on board his ship I reminded him that he had to let me check his penis. He considered that an affront to his dignity as a man, he said. 'The law is the law,' I told him, 'and you will not go ashore unless you submit to this little formality.' I was a bit short with him. He went off in high dudgeon, and today he made you the scapegoat."

On such things hang the success or failure of scientific programs!

Several days after arriving in Thule, I got myself and my equipment aboard a freighter, the *Elin-S,* which luckily was going farther north for three days. On August 3, after a heavy squall, we sighted the Eskimo encampment.

Siorapaluk—"pretty little sandy beach" . . . I scanned it carefully: Siorapaluk had been well named. The site was extraordinarily beautiful, and my isolation would be as total as I had hoped when studying my map. To the west, high, wild slopes were surrounded by patches of bright-green grass. To the east, a romantic fjord, its walls steep, dark, and bare; two massive rivers of ice flowed down into it. Strung out along the foot of a tall, rocky talus were nine Eskimo huts. There was not a sound. The place seemed abandoned. Was everyone asleep? The launch made several trips back and forth. My equipment piled up on the fine, light sand of the beach. No other passenger was getting off here. I would be the only qallunaaq spending the winter this year north of Thule. A few natives finally came on the run, and with their help the Danes set about unloading the station's supply of provisions and coal for the winter. The season's fur catch was taken aboard. I shook hands with the pilot, Captain York, Knud Rasmussen's old companion in adventure.[1]

The launch moved off for the last time. The ship, which had to keep a schedule, headed south. For a long time I could hear the long wail of its siren, and the echoes rolling among the cliffs; the sound set the dogs at the settlement to howling. From the shore, my eyes followed "the very large boat," as the Eskimos called it. It would not return for a year. I had made a complete break. From now on I was on my own: my mission was beginning.

1

MEN
OF THE
POLE

I was still sitting on one of my bags when a woman came up to me and in sign language gave me to understand that most of the men were *avatane . . .,avatane . . .* off hunting . . . over there! Her vague gesture embraced the horizon. I set out to look for them. I followed a path that wound around a cliff, and I had been walking less than an hour when suddenly, as I came to a bend, I heard a cheeping now loud, now softer, which seemed to reach me like an echo from the cliffside. The sky darkened as thousands of tiny black birds—little auks— flew back and forth from the sea to the cliffs, chattering and noisily flapping their wings.

They dove head first into the water, to catch some fish or crustacean. After half a minute, they would surface for air, their little clown's heads glistening. Ten seconds for breathing and again they plunged their beaks into the nourishing water. At unpredictable intervals, they flew off heavily, their throats bulging with crustaceans, their legs, drawn up under their wings, slowly dripping water; in groups of five hundred to a thousand, the males came back to shore bearing food for their chicks, which had been hatched in late July and lived under the loose rocks. Flying swiftly along the face of the cliff at an altitude of some six hundred feet, they traced wide circles against the side of the talus; they flew round and round in a broad circular pattern and then, as if responding to some signal, plunged toward the ground as a group. Slowing down, they reversed the direction of their flight and climbed again to repeat their turnings. This coming and going, this round changing into an ellipse—or rather, into a kind of artificial rain—continued for a long time, interrupted by long pauses when they perched on the talus.

The noise made me almost drunk as I moved along the path. I noticed that the scree had been reddened by bird droppings. Suddenly, behind some rocks that formed a kind of screen, I glimpsed hairy heads and outstretched arms holding long-handled nets. A broad backside trousered in worn bearskin presented itself level with my eyes. I heard a hissing: "Pujulee! pujulee! Pizz . . . Pirrr . . . Pirrr." The Eskimos had stationed themselves on the scree; on tiptoe, hissing and brandishing their nets, they were trying to catch the birds as they wheeled by. In a swirl of feathers, several hundred birds spiraled directly above my head. Pizz . . . Pirrr, Pirrr! As if it were being breathed in, breathed out, the spiral expanded and contracted.

The Eskimos had large heads, long, broad torsoes, and short legs. Leaping like monkeys from rock to rock, they rapidly scaled the slope seeking an ever better vantage point from which to snare the auks.

The pace of the hunt was intense. (In eight hours, one man caught about five hundred birds.) The moment a man's net was full, he immediately dumped its own contents on a stone. From the mass of shuddering feathers he pulled out a bird, crossed its wings over its back, and pressed on its heart with his thick fingers. Then, with a slow gesture of satisfaction, he dropped the creature at his feet. His sweaty face had barely broken into a smile before he returned to the hunt.

The women moved clumsily from one man to the next; they had bags strapped around their foreheads in which they collected the dead birds by the hundreds. They called out to each other as they hurried along, "Ataa . . . qa! Hey, you up there, hand me that!" They had to work quickly. Newborn birds begin to leave in a group in late August. In mid-September, the last to go— the oldest birds, which come to reconnoiter in early May—leave to winter in southeastern Canada or the Carolinas.

Eskimo children were busy exploring the smallest holes along the slope, thrusting their little arms into the loose piles of stones. One of them called excitedly to his friends, "Assut! Assut! Come quickly!" His eyes were shining. "Appaliarssuit! Guillemots!"

He picked up a wretched little bird and, with a triumphant laugh, choked it to death.

Hunting for little auks (guillemots). (*From Kane,* Arctic Explorations)

"Eskimo meat pretty rotten, huh! What a country! Ha, ha, ha!"

As he spoke, my neighbor Sakaeunnguaq cocked his head and looked me over. I was standing near my hut, quartering a seal for my dogs; it was sticky with fat. The Eskimo eased himself down on the sand and spread his legs wide; he was laughing so loud that you would have sworn he was drunk. Then suddenly his expression became serious, and he invited me to his home. Extremely sensitive to all around him and somewhat of a marginal figure in the group, Sakaeunnguaq struck me as a little *angakkoq,* a sorcerer. In a low voice, he begged me not to think ill of him if his house was poor and dirty. I said that if he liked I would come right away, and he limped off happily to the Eskimo village.

His igloo,* standing among other identical igloos, was a hummock of peat and stones shaped like a turtle, with its head outstretched toward the shore. Sakaeunnguaq coughed to announce my arrival and lifted a plank. We bent over double and slid through an earth tunnel about twelve feet long. I pushed on the door at a second threshold which was level with my stomach. We had arrived. We hoisted ourselves up into the room. It was small, low, and pear-shaped; a black stone lamp filled with oil produced a flickering yellow light. The air was redolent of urine, fat, mold, and musk. A woman and three men were squatting along the peat walls, which were decorated for the nonce with newsprint (I recognized pages from *Politiken, Life,* and the *New York Times*). All in a heap, the children were asleep in the darkest corner of the single sleeping platform. They lay on animal skins, half naked, their genitals exposed to the air.

In the middle of the room was the Primus, the eternal, oil-burning Primus, which is used only when absolutely necessary to heat tea or coffee. The woman was sitting in front of me—squat, her face a heavy mask; she greeted me wordlessly with a vague nod. We looked each other over slowly, in silence. Not one man in the group sitting on bones and empty old containers had yet turned his head or made the slightest gesture in my direction. Sakaeunnguaq, my host, had remained by the inner door. I looked at him inquiringly. We both stood there stupidly. Having nothing else by way of a present, I offered my cigarettes. The pack was passed from hand to hand. It was examined, sniffed, assessed. My host indicated by a glance that I should sit in the place for guests, to the left of the entrance. I sat, and thus joined the circle.

"Soo, thank you," one of the men said, puffing on his cigarette. He slowly turned his head and smiled at me through the swirls of smoke. Naam-mappoq! It's good," another said. "My name is Ululik," the third said. I grinned awkwardly in reply, and, indeed, it turned out that the international language of the smile became our best interpreter. Eemmanguaq, a dark-

---

Igloo is the name of the traditional Eskimo house made of stone and peat, or of the hut enclosed by peat, and sometimes by snow. In the Thule region the *illuliaq,* or temporary snow house, was used only on long hunting expeditions.

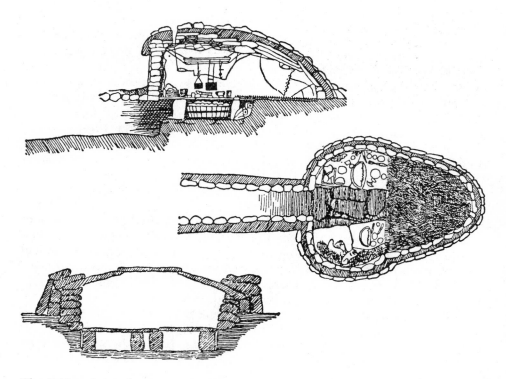

The Eskimo house in 1905 and in 1950, its structure unchanged. In the 1800s, the surface area was approximately 55 square feet; in the 1900s, approximately 132 square feet. (In 1840, it was 3 to 4 feet wide and 3 feet high.) In 1950, a rectangular igloo comprised one room measuring at most 200 to 220 square feet. It was about 5 feet high in the highest part by the entryway, 17 feet wide, and 12 feet long. In 1950, the entrance passageway, or *katak,* was about 6 to 12 feet long, 3 feet high; 2½ feet wide at the outside entrance, it gradually narrowed and usually was closed off by a skin or board some 30 inches wide and 16 inches high, which one pushed to enter the only room. During the severest winter cold, the outer end of the katak opened into a doorless stone igloo passageway that shielded the inside from snow and cold and was known as a *torssusaq.* According to Kane, in 1842 this long corridor measured 12 feet in length, 1½ feet in height, and 1 foot in width; the katak was built narrow as a defense against bears, which used to be very aggressive. (The stone igloo, being more secure, was the supreme refuge for hunters.) During the severest cold, puppies or the *iliarsuq,* the orphan, could stay in the innermost area of the katak.

In 1950, the sleeping platform was placed at the back of the room; it was 4½ feet deep, and was raised up 1 foot. A cover of roots or brush interwoven with straw was spread over the stones; over this an insulating sealskin was laid. In 1950, the oil lamps were generally 16 to 24 inches inches long and maximum 8 inches deep. Two lamps per igloo, on the average, or four at most, were surrounded by assorted objects of everyday use. The drying racks, made of strips of sealskin, hung from the ceiling. The walls were sometimes covered with sealskin (1950: five igloos out of seventy). The ventilation hole in the ceiling is called the *qingaq.* The walls, 16 inches thick, were sometimes reinforced outside by stones interfaced with peat or, more often, wood. In complexioned girl of fourteen, winked at me. The ice had been broken, and we launched into a lively, cheerful conversation. Two women neighbors entered, and I had patiently to answer a thousand and one questions: Where did I come from? Where was I going? Where was my wife? "What do the qallunaat, the white people, call you?" I tried to answer with what West Greenlandic I had learned during my previous two visits to west central Greenland. It was not much.

They appreciated the fact that when I came in I had not stridden to the middle of the room and, with never a word of greeting, stood there condescendingly inspecting the premises and the human animals within. This, I was to learn, was how qallunaat habitually behaved.

The kettle for brewing coffee was smoked and dented; someone put it on the Primus. Glazed iron bowls were brought out. With her fingers, the Eskimo woman dipped into a pail filled with a meat broth called *qajoq* and pulled out smoking chunks of seal. They were as black as soot.

"Nerniarllutit! Eat!"

She was speaking to the men. The women and the girls kept to one side, with a modest, almost apologetic air. In order to appear busy, the wife of our host remained standing, now and then poking the wick of the oil lamp. The other women clustered together, chewing on bits of skin to soften them, or mending kamiks. They would not eat until we had finished. However, some unattached women—a woman without a man is considered loose—nibbled away at the meat as we did, but off in a corner by themselves. The little boys mixed in with the men but hung back somewhat, tearing into the morsels which their elders handed them. Only the older boys dared help themselves. For a good hour, squatting or standing, the men chomped noisily on this tough, boiled meat. The more delicately mannered used their squared-off humped fingernails, which shone like black marble, to pick the meat from the bone. My attention was caught for a moment by the irregular, broken edges of those fingernails, which looked as if they had been nicked with a penknife. But most of the men held the carcass right under their noses, and with their knives chopped off chunks of seal the size of a fist, half-chewed the meat, and swallowed it in one gulp. Between servings, they licked their fingers. They spat, smoked, and drank, each in his own manner and rhythm. There was no time

---

rare cases, the walls were made entirely of peat blocks, like Sauninnguaq's igloo in Nunatarssuaq, in 1950–51.

The igloo's one window, called the *equut*, was set about 3½ feet above the floor, and was 22 inches high and 24 inches wide. It was made of seal gut, and a hole was cut in it so that one could see what was going on outside. In 1950, the seal-gut pane was preferred to the glass window available at the store because it did not frost over or crack during the severe cold.

Before the Eskimos had wood—i.e., prior to the nineteenth century—there were many double houses, which were never round, but, rather, pear-shaped. They were usually constructed against a slope that faced south, and sometimes had lateral extensions. (*Upper drawings: From Mylius-Erichsen and Moltke,* Gronland; *lower drawing: from* Steensby, Contributions)

for talk. Eyes moved back and forth, from the cut-up meat in the pot to the piece that someone else had snared and left to cool on the floor.

A dry crack: a seal rib being ground between someone's jaws.

A mound of bones—shining, clean-picked bones—grew before each man. A partridge wing was passed around with which to wipe the grease from our fingers. One of the men straightened up, happily sated, and belched. Presently, several others, replete and weary from chewing, took their leave.

"Thank you very much, Sakaeunnguaq."

"Illillo! You're welcome."*

More men came in and made themselves comfortable. Not counting the children, we had been six when I arrived. Now we were nine. It was hot. Sweat rolled down our faces; hair glistened with fat.

Some of the men opened their shirts and stretched out, bare-chested. They quenched their thirst with sips of qajoq. We chatted. The children woke up, pissed, and cried. The smell of venison and old whiting floated around us.

People patted their bellies. They were full. Inuk was content.

One of us awoke with a stomachache, unable to move. Ululik observed ironically that perhaps the meat had been rotten. The women circulated from igloo to igloo, visiting one another, joking among themselves. They would arrive in twos and threes, moving slowly and heavily, chattering and laughing. Several days after my arrival, they came to pay their first visit to me. They wanted to get their own idea of what this qallunaaq was like.

"Qaaniarit! Come in!"

The latch opened without creaking. They entered slowly, almost sidling their way in, their round faces brightened by demure smiles. They sat down on my packing cases, stretched out legs that were sheathed in long white skin boots reaching almost to their thighs, and made themselves at home. They were certainly agreeable to look at in their dark-brown and white fox furs (trousers and jacket), with their long blue-black hair secured at the nape of the neck by colored ribbons.

Pensive, attentive Nivikannguaq acted as hostess for me, and the conversation soon had us all laughing. Atangana told us the latest about poor Ululik. The night before, his bitch had attacked and killed one of Olipaluk's best dogs, and in a fury Olipaluk had shot the animal. Atangana, who had seen Ululik that morning, reported that he was resolved to beat Olipaluk up the first chance he got.

"Naagga, impossible. He's too timid," a rather forward young woman commented. "He talks bigger than he acts."

They all looked at her and smiled. Evidently she knew him well, well enough to pass such a judgment.

Nivikannguaq served the coffee. According to custom, the guests had

---

*Illillo: literally, it is I who thank you.

brought their own bowls and spoons in their pockets. While they ate and drank, the women—they all fear tuberculosis—took care to cover their mouths with their hands when they coughed. They raised the left hand rather than the right, to avoid passing on the germ when shaking hands. For the same reason, it was considered offensive to drink from a neighbor's cup. As we drank, we exchanged cigarettes; they were sticky and crushed, and had taken on the flavor of whatever pocket they had come from. Bertsie, who preferred now to use her Christian name, had come with her numerous children, who stood dutifully lined up against the partition. Sticky green mucus dribbled down onto the lips of one of them. In front of me he hesitated to blow his nose on his jacket; but no problem. He wiped his nose on the back of his hand and then licked it clean of the mucus.

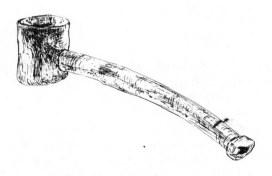

Eskimo pipe made of bone. Illulik, Canada, 1962. *(Private collection)*

"Mamaq, it's not bad," he remarked to me.

Aqatannguaq had had no qualms about bringing along her new baby. He was perched on her back, tucked in the hood of her anorak. When he began to cry, she whisked him around to the front. She raised her jacket, revealing full, light-brown breasts with a network of bluish veins, and the baby sucked voraciously at her thick, dark nipple. A few more such scenes and my hut would become a day-care center, and impossible to breathe in as well. We were enveloped by smoke, my stove having developed a case of hiccups.

No doubt as an antidote to the smells, Ann Sofia smiled and pulled a big, fat pipe from her boot: "Pujut! My pipe!" She tilted her head back and emptied the ash in the bowl into her mouth. "Mammaraai! It's good to eat, it really is." The ash made her salivate. With relish she slowly rolled the quid around with her tongue. Her face remained still, her expression fixed, inward-looking. Her dirty-yellow pupils turned blank. Time passed, a long time. Then her fingers searched in the furry top of her white boot. She pulled out a pinch of tobacco and gravely set about packing her little furnace afresh.

2

SIORAPALUK

Getting My
Winter Hut in Shape

I spent most of the first two weeks of August getting my quarters in order. I had taken possession of an unoccupied hut, and with clever help from the Eskimos, I quickly transformed it. It was rectangular and squat, with a slightly sloping double roof. There was a passageway for storing clothes and weapons, so that they would be protected from the condensation created by all the comings and goings. The interior was divided into two parts: a large room for the natives who would be working with me or simply passing by; and, separated from this room by a thin partition with a door, a small room about twelve by five feet. I had brought no furniture with me, and eventually I built tables and chairs from the lumber of my shipping cases. During the winter the ice rose a foot above ground along the partitions and had to be broken up with a knife. Heat was provided by a rusty stove that I found on arrival and that was at least thirty or forty years old. For fuel, I used the coal locally available in Greenland—imported from South Africa. And so, para-doxically, all winter long at the top of the world I burned coal from the antipodes. (During the worst cold, $-50°C/-58°F$, I also used a Coleman stove.) With Ululik's help I built, outside the wooden walls, a second wall of peat that reached roof height. When the first bad cold spells came, the house had to be completely encased by a third wall of snow blocks and the two windows equipped with double panes. The triple walls were about 2½ feet thick.

The moment I arrived from Thule, before the two feet of thawed sand could freeze again, I planted a thirteen-foot pole to which I could attach the antenna of my radio transmitter. A few yards farther away I set up a meat cache, supported on four stakes about six feet high. This protected meat and har-nesses from the dogs and the few bears who might come prowling around, though bears ventured into the outskirts of villages only rarely, particularly in autumn. The nine dogs I had bought in Thule were tethered nearby. Caporal, the puppy I had kept from the litter of one of the bitches, had firmly chosen a spot for himself next to my bed.

I made the acquaintance of the native administrator, a good-looking young South Greenlander from Julianehaab. His name was John Petrussen.[2] Through some unfortunate confusion, he had been given the multiple responsibilities of religious leader, schoolteacher, and shopkeeper. He very generously told me that whenever solitude weighed too heavily on me, his little house would be my house. As things turned out he proved true to his word, and both he and his wife, Laura, were of enormous help to me during my stay.

I had been among these men for a week. Siorapaluk seemed lulled to sleep by quiet. These were the last hours of summer. Mirages formed across the calm surface of the sound. Crystal mountains of fantastic shapes were reflected in the water as they floated toward us. On the slopes, patches of snow were melting amid tufts of green grass. Here and there you glimpsed stagnant pools; the oily surface was the color of rust, shot through with streaks of gold. Dogs lay on the ground, exhausted. An air of gaiety pervaded the encampment, nonetheless. The sun was shining, and a single ray of its warm light sufficed to make you forget the mud and vermin.

Olipaluk came to see me. He dragged his feet and his face was stiff with embarrassment, for he had come to propose that his eighteen-year-old daughter, Arnarulunguaq, become my *kiffaq*, or servant. I decided that that wouldn't work, and declined his offer.

My hut was finished; my belongings had been put in order. I became more systematic about the local language, writing down Eskimo words in my notebook and conversing as best I could in my pidgin version. I now spent hours on the beach learning to drive my dogs. I handed out presents right and left, I smiled, I talked. The Eskimos said nothing and gradually got used to my presence, but it would be going too far to say that bonds were formed. Far from it. They were reserved, mistrustful, ever on their guard.

"Qallunaaq? Sunaana? A white man here? What does that mean?"

Whenever the children saw me, from no matter how far away, they would run off whimpering.[3]

It is hard to convey how disconcerting the phases of this period of observation were, how patient I had to be, and how discouraged I felt when confronted by these fickle people, now smiling, now ironic, now kindly, now duplicitous; it was a double game calculated to exhaust the nerves of a solitary white man in an alien environment.

Only intuition can tell you when the moment has come to penetrate some area of their reserve. It is your own pleasure in living among them which will charm them into a reluctant liking for you (which will remain a tacit, loyal tenderness) and establish your own worth in their eyes.

When will the signs be given to you? Perhaps the day when the women become gentle and attentive, and openly, stubbornly insist on wasting spoon-

The Eskimo village of Siorapaluk. In the right foreground, near the stick figure, is my hut. Above, left, is Imina's hut. Meat caches are located near the shore. The village lies on the right bank of the torrent. Drawing by Sakaeunnguaq (thirty-six years old).

fuls of your best jams in their tea. It is only when the men at last begin to "talk dogs" with you that insofar as they forget you are white you will be able to get to know these people in their daily reality. But even then you must not fool yourself. Most of the time Eskimos are acting; rarely are their masks off. It is only during brief, unthinking moments, or in the friendly give-and-take of a holiday or hunting expedition, or in the face of shared danger that they will trust you as they trust one another.

As I have said, the Danish post of Thule was 120 miles to the south of Siorapaluk. Sixty miles to the north was Etah, and beyond that, the desert. One might think that my isolation was lessened by my having a radio, but making contact was difficult. For one thing, my transmitter was weak. It worked by battery, which was recharged by a hand-operated generator. In principle, I was in contact with Thule once a week (Thule was soon replaced by a small American station). Every Saturday I would confidently attach the antenna to the pole by my hut, an Eskimo would start to crank the generator, and at nine o'clock in the evening I would begin calling: "Thule . . . Thule—radio, come in. . . . Siorapaluk calling!" This might go on for five or ten minutes. The Eskimo, in his bearskin pants and sealskin anorak, would be sweating like a pig from his exertions.

"Tipi! It smells bad!" he would say to me, lifting his flushed face. "Tipi ajorpoq. It really smells bad!" he would repeat.

"Tipi . . . good heavens, it's time. . . . Turn, turn it faster! . . . That's right. . . . Thanks."

A distant Danish voice, fuzzy with static, would come through: "Change over from megacycles—I'm calling on fifty-two hundred kilocycles." Better. I was hooked in. Now the voice would be loud and clear. We would speak in English.

"Hello, hello, Malaurie, hello, hello, Malaurie. . . . How are you? Aren't you getting tired of living with those savages?"

"You can hear him, I think," the delighted native would say to me.

"And the best to you," I would say. "We lost the motor launch during a spell of bad weather last week. The administrator is furious. . . . Panippat, an Eskimo from Kangerluarsuk—only twenty years old—died in early September, right after the doctor had been here. We'd been expecting it, I don't exactly know why. We're not sure what he died of."

Thule would answer: "Hello, Malaurie. I couldn't really hear you. You'll be happy to know that everything is going well. . . . Those fellows from the south who were passing through have left us for good on the *Tikerak,* the last ship of the year. . . . Two oil tanks were put up near the beach and painted with red lead. The view's completely spoiled. The war's still going on in Korea. Strikes in England. . . . What else? Oh, I almost forgot the most important thing. The *Tikerak* left us a little present, thanks to a friendly Greenlander woman. She's not a Polar Eskimo,* she's a South Greenlander, from south of Melville Bay. You understand what I'm saying? Not an Eskimo woman from Thule. . . . The doctor's not entirely sure yet, but it's probably gonorrhea.[4] The administration will be issuing medical advice so people can protect themselves. That's all for now. Good night. Until next Saturday."

The Other Couple:
A Man and His
Dogs

Several months hence I was supposed to lead a geodynamic and geomorphological expedition to Inglefield and Washington lands. Throughout the winter, I was going to have to visit each igloo for my anthropological study. Owing to my meager funds and the workings of the French bureaucracy, which allowed me only six months' credit for a fourteen-month stay,† I could survive only by living and hunting as the nomad Eskimos did. So I spent the last weeks of

---

*The Eskimos from the Thule region are the earth's northernmost inhabitants. Since of all Eskimos they live nearest to the Pole, ethnologists usually call them Polar Eskimos. They sometimes call themselves *Aavannaamioq,* or Men of the North.

†I should explain that I was a research fellow of the CNRS (*Centre Nationale de la Recherche Scientifique*) and that the funds for my expedition were very modest. I had asked to be paid my monthly allotment in advance—to September 1951—because I would be in such an isolated area, with only one boat a year and no way to wire money. My Dean of Faculty, who had supported my request, was told that the law was the same for everyone and that the fiscal year ended on December 31, 1950. Bless all accountants!

summer training my team of dogs on the beach, learning how to handle the whip and to use the proper cries. My goal was to learn how to achieve the right tone, pace, and coordination that create the essential unit between a man and his dogs. Little by little, my basic education progressed.

The Eskimo and his dogs form a very real "couple," and their relationship is as close as a marriage. The team is like someone you marry and who marries *you*. It functions as a single person: the leader is the head, and the dogs are, literally, the torso and limbs. Without his dogs the Eskimo is not himself. He is a widower who has lost his strength, his capacity for action, his joy in life.

I first established the necessary link between the dogs and myself by feeding them regularly. Every three days in summer—every two in winter—they had to be fed about two pounds of meat per animal. The dogs were tied at some fixed point, and they strained toward the twenty or thirty chunks of meat that I had cut up with a knife or hatchet. It was absolutely essential to respect team hierarchies when throwing the meat to the dogs. They watched me intently; their brown eyes followed the slightest movement of my hand. I tossed the meat, to be caught in midair: the dog's teeth would snap as he devoured his chunk of frozen meat in one gulp, without chewing it. He would eat on all fours, then quickly resume a waiting position on his haunches. If a piece happened to fall on the ground, the pact between me and the team was broken: the meat was personalized by the giver's gesture, and by falling it lost its aura. A noisy battle would ensue as the dogs tore into one another. In the presence of a man, the strongest must establish his authority.

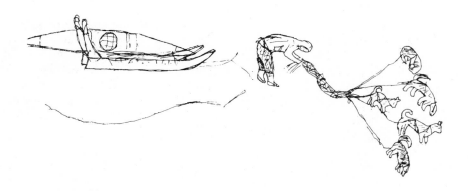

Dog team. Drawing by Appalinnguaq. Siorapaluk, December 1950. *(Private collection)*

The *naalagaq*—the leader or head dog—stood apart from the others, wait-ing. His calm, masterful eye observed the scene with seeming indifference, although now and then he would nip this dog or that if the commotion began to get out of hand. "Qanormi illit! Whenever you wish!" he seemed to be saying to me. Depending on the nature of the waiting, the size of the chunks reserved for him, and the unmistakable, sometimes ostentatious manner in which I would destine them for him, I would—or would not—receive from him a confirmation of my role.

Naalagaq is indeed the right word. I knew that my life might depend on this dog's authority. The story of X might serve as a reminder. As he was coming back from a long hunt, X's sled smashed into a big stone on the moraine of a glacier. The main strap that held each dog's trace in place broke. Suddenly free, the dogs took off on the double, following the familiar trail which led along the glacier toward their village. The man called after them, whistled to them, but to no avail. Then he fired his rifle into the air. This signals distress or promises game, and usually it brings the team back. But X's dogs, which he had mistreated, now took their revenge and ran on without a back-ward glance. They soon vanished in the fog. The hunter had to fight his way through a storm on foot. He was exhausted by his trek through the snow; presently, as he was pushing forward with his sled, he could not believe his ears: he heard muted cries that seemed to be coming from a crevasse. He ran ahead. At the foot of a cliff-slide, by a glacial cave, he found his lead dog, barking for him; the animal stood a little to one side of the other dogs, who had fallen all over one another and were entangled in their traces. A bridge of snow that concealed a crevasse had collapsed under their weight as they tried to reach the rock. Any other man would have been overjoyed. But this Eskimo was a mean fellow. He pulled the animals out of the fault, one by one, and then—impetuous man—he hauled off and killed two of them with a single blow. The next time a similar incident occurred, the remaining dogs did not let their chance for revenge slip by. A naalagaq, dog though he is, has a long memory, and he does not like gratuitous brutality.

As the weeks passed, I learned more about the dogs' habits and the methods of training them. The dogs always slept outside the igloo, no matter how severe the weather. To have done otherwise—to let them sleep in the shelter of the katak—would have weakened the team. Until a bitch throws her pups, she is part of the team. For both strength and quality of the fur, pups are best dropped in early spring. You then hold them up by the neck. By the way they arch their little backs, you can tell the strong ones from the weak. (The weak ones are thrown to the mother and the pack and are swallowed in one gulp.) At eight months, the dogs should be harnessed. Their molars are dulled with stones so that when the dogs are hungry they cannot chew through their leather traces and get free. When they are past eight years, they are killed, usually by hanging. A good team—six to ten dogs—includes only one female. (Opinions do differ on this point.) The naalagaq asserts his authority by his domination of the female. It is an authority that both physically and psychologically the other dogs constantly challenge.

In October, I had to resort to barbarous measures with Alineq—the Ugly One. He would not submit to team discipline, and he kept trying to gnaw through the harness. As is the Eskimo practice, Alineq was strung up on a meat dryer, released, and then strung up again so that he "saw" death (asuleerpa). Then, after I had tied the dog's paws together, Sakaeunnguaq helped me throw him to the pack, which proceeded to nip him just as much as necessary. The animal's fear was visible: his hair stood on end and his eyes rolled.

Eskimos are deeply attached to their dogs, and when an opportunity to cross-breed arises, they try to produce ever stronger and more high-strung teams. I knew one man who bred his dogs according to principles that I had previously heard invoked only by bull breeders: courage and audacity (very precious in hunting bear) come from the mother, and she should be chosen accordingly; strength and gait come from the father.

With such thoughts in mind, sparked by daily observation, I would set out for the great fjord with my twelve-foot sledge to which the dogs were attached by twenty-foot-long traces. I used to leave as if I were going to a training camp. On the shore of a convenient bay, where no one could see me, I drilled myself for ten weeks in the difficult skill of handling the ship. Then I tried to direct the team with speech: Assut! (Fast!) . . . Aroo! Aroo! (To the left!) . . . Assut! Assut! (To the right!) . . . Aak! Aak! (Forward!) . . . Qaa! Qaa! (Come! Come! —this is said when you are in front of the dogs) . . . Holetti! (Watch out for the harness!) . . . Aqi! Aqi! (Back!) . . . Qorfa! (A bear! Forward!) . . . Qaqortorssuaq! (Polar bear!). This last cry is infallible in getting the dogs to move, whether there is a bear or not.

During the first weeks, no matter what, the twenty-five-foot lash would wrap itself around my body, my legs, or my right sleeve. Sometimes the tip stung my face. I had to protect myself. One unlucky flick and I could lose an eye. (An Eskimo I know was blinded in one eye this way.) Little by little, my self-confidence grew. My movements became surer. Taking my dogs' traces from a hole in the ice, I would prepare to harness them. This is a moment that calls for the sharpest attention: your whip is under your arm and the traces are, so to speak, attached to nothing. Once they have been assembled, you simply put your foot on them. But if suddenly the dogs are attracted by some smell or the whim seizes them and they want to dash off, the only way you can stop them is to throw yourself on the pile of twenty-five-foot leather lines and be prepared to be dragged a few hundred yards. One morning, about a half day's journey from Etah, I met a different problem. As the Eskimos do, I had secured the dogs' traces to a rope that I passed through an ice bore and tied off above with a slip knot. Presently, wanting to free the rope from the frozen upper surface of the little tunnel and give it some play, I inserted a finger in the slip knot. The dogs thought I was about to let them

Whip (*iperaataq*). The old-style whip was made of pieces of bone and wood joined together. The lash was made of sealskin, progressively thinned to the tip. In 1950, a whip might be seven or eight yards long, and the tip alone a yard long. (*From Kane, Arctic Explorations*)

start off, and they began to pull as if they were already harnessed to the sledge. The knot closed tight around my finger. The dogs kept leaping and trying to push off, and my finger was jerked back and forth until I thought the rope would cut through to the bone. My whip lay out of reach. Was I going to have to wait for hours, would I be forced to cut off my finger? I was on the verge of doing just that. The dogs clung to the ice, yelping with impatience, eager to run across the deserted ice field. They started to pull again when Paapa, the naalagaq, finally understood his mistake and made them back up slightly . . . and saved my finger!

You must have your whip in your hand at all times. An accident that happened many years later reminds me of this. The sledges were proceeding single file at the foot of a high cliff that edges the southern coast of Herbert Island. I was behind the *napariaq,* * guiding the dogs and trying to avoid blocks of ice and the stones that came tumbling down from the ledge above. My foot had been run over by a sledge two days before and my left big toe had been broken. I hadn't wanted to slow down our group, which was in a hurry because of the weather, so I said nothing about it to the Eskimos. Each morning, I had to force myself to walk, and I was becoming more and more unsteady on my feet. As we were going through a narrow, slippery passage in drift ice, I stumbled and fell. The dogs of the team behind me were close on my heels, yelping. They were aggressive, and their fangs had not been filed. All fourteen

---

*The pair of wooden stanchions with a crossbeam at the rear of a sledge that make driving easier. The sledges of Canadian Eskimos (at least of those in northeastern Canada) do not have them.

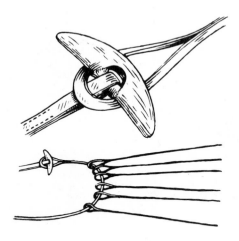

The method of harnessing dogs. The buckle *(pituutaq)*, shaped like a half-moon, and the rings *(orseq)* of each trace are made of bone.

dogs immediately threw themselves on me, the more ferocious, perhaps, because my bearskin pants and boots still smelled of bear, and these dogs, furiously tearing up everything on the ground within their reach, were starving. As I lay on the ice, covered from head to foot in my furs, I tried to fight them off. I had dropped my whip, but with luck the thick skins would protect me. Some dogs were biting my thigh while others lunged at my face. I shielded myself with my arm, shouting "Aqi! Aqi! Back!" It did no good. In the blur of hairy bodies, I could make out only fangs and blazing eyes. I rolled myself into a ball so there would be less of me for them to get at.

The savage dogs tried to tear the bearskin off me—its silky feel excited them even more—but the leather pants held. Three, four seconds passed. Time was running out. The instant blood flowed, the dogs would become drunk, like wolves. The driver of the team—Anaakkarsuaq—did not know how to help. If he used his whip, he might slice one of my eyes out. To shoot into that mass of fur would do no good. By chance—by a very lucky chance—it happened that for a moment the dogs stepped back, as they sometimes do, in order to carry out a fresh attack on this strange bear, and I was given a split-second respite. I sprang to my feet and snatched up my whip. Saved! For several weeks, my right thigh bore dark scars where the dogs had bitten my flesh.

The winter before, a child, going from one igloo to another in the dark, had fallen in similar circumstances. His little bones were found the next morning, picked clean.

A male narwhal with a long tusk—the unicorn's horn—has been harpooned off Siorapaluk: the harpoon shaft is still buried in the animal.[6] The Eskimos run from their
tents down to the shore to welcome the hunters returning by kayak or boat. A kayak
is being put into the water. Nivikannguaq has climbed up on the roof to see better. The
tents are secured by large stones. Drawing by Sarfak, Ululik's daughter, eight years old.
(*Private collection*)

End of Summer

The summer had passed amazingly fast. Some families had gone off to camp
near the lakes and fish for salmon. For almost a month, we fished the torrents
that rush down the scree slopes.[5] In the green valley of Kukkaat, the children
gathered huckleberries by the handfuls. Our tea and meat tasted of juniper and
wood smoke. The endless daylight was harsh, but the air seemed very light;
the effect was inebriating and, heedless of time, the men roamed the countryside, indulging their passion for hunting.

One day, out in the fjord, a kayak skimmed over the oily water, which was
ashimmer with huge reflections of the cliffs along the shore. It was Sakaeunnguaq. Alone and rejoicing in his freedom, he was hunting seal for his own
pleasure. His family had plenty, but what did that matter? He was hunting out
in salt water, where a wounded seal does not sink quickly—*kivivoq!*—as it does
in the fresh water near icebergs or at the mouths of the big streams.

A scent of snow in the air told us that winter was coming. We could hear the sea birds—*taatseraat, naajat, mitit* (kittiwakes, gulls, ducks)—crying. They were preparing to leave us. The moment was near when we would abandon the fragrant and transparent sealskin tents for stone-and-peat igloos, which would be dark and cold when the oil lamps burned low. Everyone felt languid and lazy; we would have liked to make time stop. The boys would stretch out on the springy tundra and watch the clouds pass by. Down on the beach, facing the sea, a dozen children and a young girl who was playing mother, with a baby on her back, gathered to enjoy these last moments of sunlight. Charmed by the peacefulness of the day, they sang old laments and made up little poems.

In the distance, above Appalersooq (a cluster of abandoned igloos west of Siorapaluk), rose, tall and straight, the smoke from a dwarf-willow fire. It was probably the women and girls of Siorapaluk lingering there to eat huckleberries.

Offshore, glacier and rock blended in the expanse of blue water. Thus time flowed by.

And then, on the morning of August 30, everything was changed. One night had sufficed to make the countryside unrecognizable. The day before, the ground had been a dirty gray, as if old beyond time. Within a few hours a new universe had been created under velvety white, crystalline snow. The light snow melted, but on September 7, it refroze. The ground was firm now, and thudded dully underfoot. Winter had come, the Arctic winter which is so long that the Eskimo uses the same word—*ukioq*—to denote both year and winter itself.*

---

*The lowest temperature registered in Thule in 1950–51 was −50°C (−58°F), in February, and the highest was +20°C (+68°F), in August. The average monthly temperature was above freezing for only ten or twelve weeks. Winds are frequent and affect thermal conditions considerably. It has been estimated that the wind-chill factor of 30-mph wind (24.28 knots) reduces a temperature of −37.2°C (−34.6°F) to −73.3°C (−99.4°F) and a temperature of −26.1°C (−14.8°F) to −56.6°C (−69.8°F). The annual rainfall in these desertlike regions is around 4 inches. Total darkness obtains from October to February, continuous daylight from April to August.

The climate grows harsher the higher the latitude. Siorapaluk and Etah have lower temperatures than Thule. And those in Inglefield Land are lower still.

3

THE
FOX
CYCLE

La Fontaine at the
North Pole

Our Western fabulists saw the world as it is—even at the North Pole. The cunning of the *terianniaq*, the fox, is as proverbial among Eskimos as among our schoolchildren.

La Fontaine's *Fables,* especially the "Roman de Renart," enchanted all of Siorapaluk. I must have told them a hundred times about the hungry wolf who gets his tail caught in the ice. They would hang on every word, and at the end they would say to me, "Suna! An Inuit story."

"Foxes do not lack good appetites, for sure. And young as he was, Reynard the Fox was still one of the sharpest. . . ." Eskimo tales and legends dwell lovingly on all such details. So it was easy for me to win real success for La Fontaine among my Inuit friends. Given that ironic, observant audience, it would have been surprising had I not.

I know that several of his fables—"The Crow and the Fox," "The Fox and the Stork," and "The Dog and the Wolf," for example—were "Eskimoized" in some fashion and incorporated in the stock of native folklore. Heaven grant that future ethnologists will know how to disentangle the true sources!

The fox is man's seasonal friend, so to speak—when the hunting season has ended. If you move quietly, he even allows you to get near him. During the mating season to come (March–April), the nearby mountain which reared above the settlement was to resound with his harsh, piercing yelps. One day I would meet a fox trotting along the crest of the mountain, his tail horizontal, his pace even and brisk. But he seemed nervous, almost possessed, and accordingly, my presence hardly mattered to him. In the hollow of a slope, he sat down on a stone, his triangular ears perked, his pointed little head alert to the slightest sound. For a long time, he called to his mate with his hoarse double or triple cry. But the tundra was empty. The wind carried no message. . . . After calling for ten minutes, the fox trotted off again on his search.

The kits are thrown in June. At that time, the fox lives with the vixen and her large litter (as many as twelve) in a den that has been built the previous September among the debris of the screes. During the periods of severest cold, the fox digs out from under balanced stones the provisions—eggs and small birds—that were collected during the summer. In one such cache on the east coast of Greenland, a naturalist found 38 little auks, 2 young guillemots, 466 snow buntings, and many auk eggs: this was one month's food supply for one fox. Active as the animal is, such reserves will not be enough to keep him going until good weather. Through the *allu*—the seal's breathing hole out on the ice field—he now and then finds scraps of seal meat left by bears, who are greedy for the fat but disdain the meat. Tracking the partridge, which he kills, and the bear, from whom he steals, the fox travels the ice floes and burrows in the snow. Man travels behind him.

During the long winter night the Eskimo's principal game is the fox, second only to subsistence hunting. This has been true since the days of Peary's expeditions in 1880 and later. The Eskimo brings himself to eat the tasteless meat only after boiling it—otherwise it causes trichinosis—and during periods of severe want. The animal is caught in a trap, which once was a small but solid stone structure, but since Peary's time has been made of steel.

The Eskimo has always hunted the fox.[7] The women use its supple and very warm fur to make their hooded jackets, or *kapataks,* which take ten skins, and their short trousers of blue fox, with a white yoke (two skins). Until the nineteenth century, men wore fox-skin jackets. Today, during severe cold, the Eskimos often wear abdominal belts, mufflers, and knee pads made of fox tails. The children of the best hunters sometimes have fox-skin anoraks.

Commercial hunting of foxes began around 1820, when whalers started to come by regularly and barter for skins. Almost a century later, in 1909–10, when the store in Thule was established, some fifty hunters accounted for 347 blue foxes and 64 whites, but that was the store's first year of operation. Stimulated by the manager, Rasmussen, commercial hunting intensified: in 1911, 514 blue foxes and 114 white were caught; in 1913–14, 628 blues and 434 whites. The price for a blue fox having been set at one hundred dollars per pelt during some of those years, one can grasp how much money the store made.

String game representing a fox on the trail, made by Pualuna. Siorapaluk, December 1950. (*Private collection*)

Population figures also increased, of course. In Thule, in 1906, the total was 209 persons; in 1918, 235 persons. In 1950–51, the population numbered 302 people, 70 of whom were hunters who accounted for 642 blue foxes and 528 whites.

The fur of this animal reaches its top quality and commands its peak price starting in early September, when the polar night begins steadily to lengthen and the weather begins to turn really cold. Ukioq—winter—is the season Eskimos choose for trapping foxes.

On September 15 the *naalaqarssuaq*, the "great leader of the white men" (actually the government in Copenhagen), gave the signal.

First
Hunting Expeditions

Each Eskimo immediately set from five to fifteen metal traps along the coast, over a distance of six to eighteen miles. He would visit them at least once a week during the winter to empty and rebait them.

Ululik and Iggianguaq invited me to go along with them on their first sortie. They intended not only to set traps in a valley where they had seen an unusually large number of tracks but also to hunt fox on foot. In a matter of minutes I was ready. I took only my rifle and a knapsack, expecting that we would be gone for a day, but in fact we did not return until much later.

We had to follow the tracks and, Iggianguaq kept telling me, the trail was good. (Ululik had stayed behind in the area of two of his traps.) Silent, intent, and imperturbable, as most of these men are when hunting, Iggianguaq went along, observing the slightest detail, sniffing the air. We caught gulls and especially hares and snow partridges for food.

Poor partridge! Her gentleness is supposed to disarm the hunter. There she stood, motionless, unsuspecting, offering herself to death. *A! . . . aaah! A! . . . aaah!* In surprise, she turned her head—absurdly small for her heavy body —and looked at us with a large, mournful eye. . . . *A! Aaah!* Suddenly uneasy, she batted her eyes and turned from side to side. She sensed danger and felt fear rising within her. *Prrrrttt, prrrttt! . . .* Her wings fluttered. She tried to hop away, to take off. Too late. A stone not even very accurately thrown felled her. Her head came off with a flick of the whip.

We did not go hungry one single day. Lichens, grasses, and especially willow roots were our fuel. On the plateau, I was strongly reminded of the Sahara. The same expanses of sand and stone; the same slow, steady plodding among rocks that have broken through the hard, crackled earth; space, and more space . . . valleys of white pebbles, desolate peaks that catch the eye, their tawny colors heightened by patches of persistent snow; here and there, in hollows and at the foot of slopes, tufts of dry, yellow grass turned always

An old-style fox trap, built of stones. Tempted into the structure by strong-smelling meat, the fox would knock down a stone which stunned or crushed him. In another type of stone trap, cleverly placed stones were dislodged when the fox took the bait, and they obstructed both exits. The fox died of hunger and cold. (*From Kane,* Arctic Explorations)

southward. . . . As we moved north, we came to the glacier. Gleaming in the sun, powerful, majestic, it made this immensity greater still. The glacier reigned over everything. We kept close to its side, tramping through sticky mud and small streams, and then crossed its promontory. Walking along the edge of the cliff that dominated the fjord of the Morris Jessup glaciers, on the south I glimpsed Smith Sound. Far to the west we could vaguely make out the snowy profile of the coast of Ellesmere Island, Canada. Water and ice surrounded us. From Etah to Savigssivik, the kingdom of Thule spreads 360 miles. But here it is a mere strip of land no more than 3 to 6 miles wide. Space was the sea. Sea and ice fields, the sources of life and of freedom. . . .

The wind came up. We had been walking, single file, for hours. The tracks on the snow were becoming more distinct. A sharp cry came from the right. Iggianguaq leaped forward, then crawled to the shelter of a mound of snow. I waited, listening. The vast emptiness was filled with countless noises—a creaking, the beating of wings, the scream of the naajat, the gulls, the crack of splitting icebergs, the muffled crunch of lake ice under too great pressure.

A dry crack: Iggianguaq had fired. At that precise moment, I saw two magnificent foxes already some distance away: their light, swift trot was of an elegance so perfect that the disappointment of the squat Eskimo in his dirty, worn-out skins could only make me smile.

We were to return to Siorapaluk without any foxes. Iggianguaq explained to me that his rifle was suffering from the evil eye. So we fell back on white hares and bagged five.

The skin on my face was burning and taut from the wind and cold. "Just a little longer," the Eskimo said to me, "and Siorapaluk will be giving us a feast. The women in their beautiful white kamiks will give us coffee, and we will go from igloo to igloo, welcomed everywhere like brothers."

After nine hours of walking, I imagined an unreal Siorapaluk, a polar oasis on a timeless summer evening. I visualized groups of animated hunters, light, a beautiful taper illuminating a snow igloo, ice walls shining in the glow of oil lamps. From all sides, Inuit came running. . . .

But this was Illulorsuit. We had come to the very place where Lauge Koch, the Danish explorer and geologist, had built his winter hut thirty years earlier, in 1922. Koch (1892–1964) produced the first map and geological analysis of the northern and eastern coasts of Greenland. The large wooden house where he had wintered in 1922 had disappeared, and the site was now deserted. Over the years, here as elsewhere, the Inuit had removed whatever was useful to them.

As Iggianguaq and I walked, each pursued his own thoughts. The massive bare blocks of the torrential deltas caught my geologist's eye. On the other hand, each bay, cape, and cliff spoke to the Eskimo. "There's Aappilattoq," Iggianguaq said to me suddenly. "That's where two children from Siorapaluk fell into a hole. It was spring. A hunter who was a little bit of a sorcerer was not far away—he was out on the ice by his allu—his seal's breathing hole. He heard the children. 'Qusuiluk-pikau!' he swore. 'May the crevasse close over those accursed children!'

"Words of ill omen. . . . Days went by and still the children did not come back. . . . People began to worry. The children were struggling to keep from freezing in the crevasse with just a small sealskin. They managed to survive only by drawing water from the bottom of the hole. The father was greatly concerned, and he went here and there for news of them. Finally he learned what had happened. Without a word, he prepared to kill the hunter-sorcerer. He drew near, harpoon in hand, but his opponent had been duly alerted by magic, and as the father approached, he fled to the west. He was an angakkoq, a sorcerer, a powerful, evil angakkoq. . . ."[8]

The hours passed like this: we swapped stories. I noticed that Iggianguaq showed polite interest in my tales about camel caravans. In general, the Eskimo is utterly indifferent to anything that does not directly concern his own people.

Finally, from atop a slope, we caught sight of Siorapaluk. The igloos looked like molehills. We stopped for a moment, and crouching on the stones of a scree shelf, we pointed out each house to one another. The dogs' baying carried all the way up to us. Iggianguaq, who had only recently married, flushed with emotion. Juditha was near. But when we arrived in the settlement, we discovered that all the hunters had left.

However, a thin column of smoke rising from Pualuna's tent bespoke some human presence there.

"Sainang sunai!" he shouted from inside his shelter, and a moment later his fine old head appeared at his wooden door.

"Taavane. Over that way, there were a lot of seals. Imina came in his kayak and told us. They took off assut, quickly, very quickly. . . . Sakaeunnguaq, Ingapaluk—even Juditha," he said, addressing my companion. "I'm all alone. Innuttaavunga. Ajorput!"

And so our return was celebrated in a humble tent of heavy white canvas spotted black by dampness, where an ailing old man and a disappointed lover sat around a stove, sharing a can of food and morose conversation.

The Pisiniarfik: Den of Magic

Twice a week, I saw my neighbors, loaded with skins, both fox and seal, pass by my window. They were on their way to the store, the pisiniarfik, to sell them and with the proceeds buy European goods.

The government made the rules; that was its right and function. It had decided that the store would be open only on *pingasunngorneq* and *arfininngorneq* (Wednesdays and Saturdays). But I never knew a day, scarcely an hour, when an Eskimo did not knock at the administrator's door to ask him to open the store. The Eskimos preferred to ignore the rule, and indeed it was doubtful whether they could ever be made to understand it. Hadn't the administrator been sent precisely to buy and sell? Didn't the Eskimos, trading with him, justify his being there? It was also beyond a native's comprehension that a white man or his representative would travel so far for any purpose other than to do some profitable business. Service for service: the white man, so reasoned the Eskimo, should hand over his merchandise upon request. (Although in small settlements such as Siorapaluk, the storekeeper—the representative of qallunaat authority—was not white but rather a Greenlander.)

It was a Tuesday. All over Greenland stores were closed. Those in high places might insist that the native must be disciplined, but that could not prevent Ululik from having a yen for some candy, Tuesday or no Tuesday.

And so, at four in the afternoon he went to the house of John Petrussen, where a few of us happened to be. John was the storekeeper. Without ado, Ululik knocked on the door and came in; he was awkward and embarrassed, for he knew he was in the wrong. We pretended to pay no attention to him. John made a show of continuing his conversation with me, but Ululik's presence weighed too heavily for that. Gripping a sorry little bag under his arm, the hunter sat down in a dark corner of the room. The comedy began.

"Niivertoq?"

We looked up; Ululik looked down. A few moments passed. He watched us furtively. The atmosphere was promising. We were obviously ready to be taken, for at that moment he took out a superb blue-fox skin and handed it around. He stood up and turned to us as if he were about to make a deal.

"Niivertoq, it's beautiful, isn't it?"

And then, in his most winning voice: "I do like candy so much."

"All right!" John said finally. "You'll have your 'store'! Qaa, let's go, come along."

He opened the door, and the two of them went out together. The Eskimo was delighted with his little act, and before making his exit, he winked at us and said: "Pissortut Inuit! Eskimos always get what they want!"*

No man would fail to show up at the store on the days it is open. For them, it's like going to a party. The pisiniarfik, just think of it! First of all, it offers an opportunity to get together, and Eskimos love to gossip. They crowd in front of the door. Once inside, some of them sit down—oh, so casually—on crates. Is the store not their house, its contents what they work for? People come and go. The wives chatter, the husbands grumble. This chamber pot, that perfume, this red cloth—"she" wants them, and "she" will have them, no matter what "he" wants. The husband is outmaneuvered, but nonetheless he will not leave the store. He doesn't want to miss the pleasure and consolation of seeing one or another of his peers even more outrageously worsted than he has been.

Every Wednesday, then, through my window I saw all of Siorapaluk trooping from its igloos to the store. Like sailors on shore leave, people rolled from house to house. They kept passing by nonchalantly, this one pushing a child's sledge, that one carrying a smooth hide bag on his back, its strap secured around his forehead or chest. Often I joined the procession.

"Sainang Imina! Hello, Imina!"

"Asukiaq. . . . Illit aamma pisiniarfimmut. Sunko! You're going to the store, too. Sunaana! So you ate up all your cans of food! What a surprise!"

I followed Imina into the hut. The room was dark, only dimly lighted by an Argand lamp. John, the shopkeeper, and an Eskimo employee, both gloved

---

*The phrase is used often and in many situations. Because the meaning changes according to the context, it is difficult to translate. Some equivalents are: "Look at us Eskimos, aren't we men!" or "Obviously, for an Eskimo, it's easy"; or "In the end, Eskimos always get what they want." The best general sense of it is, perhaps, "We are the strongest."

and bundled up in jackets, were bustling about. It was cold. To prevent fires, a Danish regulation forbids lighting any kind of fire in a pisiniarfik, and on a February day the temperature ranges from −20° to −30°C (−4° to −22°F).

In the shadowy recesses of the room I could make out Ingapaluk, Atangana, and Ussaqaq. Ululik was leaning with his elbows on the big black display table. A dozen women and children stood around him. All were wearing blue or brown canvas anoraks, their finest bearskin trousers, and their whitest boots. Pingasunngorneq, Wednesday, the big day. Some men, incongruously, sported imported sailor caps—here symbols of wealth and authority. Once inside the store, people spoke softly, showing their immense respect for this "den of magic." In this isolated spot, wasn't it marvelous to see assembled so much neqe*—so much food—and so many products all in one place: boxes of biscuits and margarine, bags of flour and nails, cans of milk by the hundreds, and cloth, matches, tobacco, coffee, and tea. . . . Hanging on the wall were axes, Primus stoves, alarm clocks, pots, and rifles. Supplies of gas and coal were kept outside the store. The abundance both stunned and intimidated people.

"Terianniaq ataaseq—one fox—number 1A. That's 42 kroner. . . . Terianniat pingasut—three foxes—number 3B. That's 105 kroner. . . . Terianniat marlluk—two foxes—2. That's 56 kroner. . . ."

In front of the Eskimo and his pile of furs, John opened a black cardboard notebook and carefully noted: "Terianniaq ataaseq number 1A, 42 kroner, Ululik, Siorapaluk. Terianniat marlluk . . ."

Intent on his notes, John scribbled on and on, but Ululik and Imina would wait as long as need be. These endless jottings flattered their vanity.

John estimated the value of a skin by its length, the glossiness and thickness of the fur, and the bushiness of the tail. From his corner, Ululik observed the procedure in silence. He would not interrupt. He was trusting.

"Sixty-five kroner for Ululik," John muttered, throwing the furs over his shoulder.

"Sixty-five kroner for Ululik," the admiring and discreet audience echoed.

The Eskimo went up to the table.

"Qaa! Take them!"

His head lowered, Ululik gathered up the big bills spread out on the table, as if with reluctance.

"Sixty-five kroner for Ululik," he grumbled under his breath.

With great care, he counted his bundle.

". . . Ieh,"† he said finally. "Naammappa, that's right, we're square."

---

*Literally, meat. By extension, neqe denotes all food.
†Ieh ("yes") is most frequently pronounced yay. (The Greenlandic spelling of this word, which has not been adopted for this book, is jii.) When agreement is self-evident, so much so as to verge on the annoying, or when the matter at hand is very serious, ieh is pronounced yeah. As a comment made during the recital of a story, the ieh is prolonged—yaaaaay—and supports the narrator when he falters. The intonation varies, permitting the speaker to express astonishment, curiosity, approbation. At least, this is how I sensed the nuances.

49

You might think that at this point he would leave. But that would be to
mistake Ululik. The money was burning his fingers. All of a sudden he became
another man. His extraordinarily mobile face changed. Always the actor, in a
flash he took on another role. He was in complete control of himself as he now
played the angry man. He became rough and peremptory; he was not about
to leave the store until he had spent all his money, down to his last öre.
Clutching the table so that he would not lose his turn, it was he who was now
in charge.

"Niivertoq! Give me that, that, and that. Massakkut! *Right away!* Tuavi!
Hurry up!" He threw his kroner on the table.

"Give you what?" was John's calm rejoinder.

"The rifle, that pot on the right, a kilo of coffee, those cartridges at the
back on the left, twenty cigarettes, that pipe over there in the corner," and then
at the very end: "Tamassa! Tamassa, everything!" He wheeled around and
laughed uproariously.

People looked at him respectfully. With his back against the counter, very
much at his ease, Ululik commented on his purchases before the assembled
Inuit.

"Kiffaq!"* he growled self-importantly, addressing John's assistant and,
by extension, John himself.

The assistant kept trotting back and forth from the back of the store to the
display table. John interpreted Ululik's confused wishes, gave them shape and
dimension. Counting and weighing were practices unknown to the Eskimos
before 1910, and to use them in trading with white men in these pisiniarfik
seemed unworthy to them.

Ululik's kroner reverted to John. Glancing over his purchases, the Eskimo
suddenly turned furiously toward John.

"Niivertoq! The rifle! Where's the rifle? I remember I asked you for a rifle.
. . . Where is it? Give me that one. That's right," he shouted to the assistant,
"the best one!"

"Be quiet," the Inuit said to him, in lowered voices. "You'll see, you'll get
into trouble. You don't understand, you've spent almost all your money.

"Look," Imina said to him gently, "there are only three kroner left."

"What do you mean, only three kroner! Thief! With all that money I don't
even have the right to a rifle? A pack of thieves! Sallutooq![9] Liar! . . . Qallunaat!" he said contemptuously. "They're all alike. . . . I'm going to tell the
governor. . . . Thief! Sixty-five kroner, and all I get is this hammer, this poor
little hammer that's worth nothing? Sixty-five kroner, and you give me this
heavy pipe that isn't even well carved? Qallunaat ajorput! White men are a
worthless lot!"

John did not answer. He was attending to a woman customer who had
given him an endless list of perfumes and chocolates.

---

*Any man who is not a hunter, who does not have his own dog team, is said to be a
kiffaq. Applied to a man, or to a grown woman, it is a pejorative term.

"There's my husband, he'll be along to pay," she kept saying turning toward the door. "Give me my chocolate."

John was a true métis. Because he identified with white authority, he believed he should keep his distance with regard to the Eskimo, and the gap between the young teacher-shopkeeper and the population—which considered itself much superior to him—seemed to grow wider as the months passed. I never had the feeling that it bothered him greatly.

"They are so different from us kalaallit, us Greenlanders," he had said to me. "The Thule Eskimos belong to another world! . . . For all their friendly smiles, they are suspicious of us, of you and me. In varying degrees, we're all foreigners to them. You'll see, you'll see. . . ."

Now, without looking at the impatient Eskimo woman, John pushed her aside.

"No husband, no store for you. . . . Next!"

By cutting into line, Ululik managed to take the woman's place. His face was angry, his hair disheveled. He leaned on the counter.

"The rifle, I want my rifle! Niivertoq! Shopkeeper! Take everything back! The pipe, the hammer—naaga, I don't want them anymore. But, if you please," he said, with a pathetic smile, "the rifle . . ."

He whimpered like a child.

John lost patience and made a gesture as if to throw him out. The Eskimo, seemingly cast down, went off to squat in a corner. In the half-darkness, he dumped the shoddy goods he no longer wanted onto the floor.

"Come on, take your rifle. Here it is. Take it. You'll pay me later," John said to him, after a silence. "But that's enough for now. What's sold is sold."

A few moments later, I ran into Ululik.

"You see," he said to me with a smile, "to me, Ululik, they gave a rifle. Seventy kroner . . . I have everything I want. It is enough"—and he spoke with slow emphasis—"that Ululik go hunting for the foxes to run to him."

This declaration visibly pleased him, and as ostentatiously as he could, he staggered off, bent under the weight of his purchases. He headed for his igloo, humming to himself.

He had not got very far when I saw him slow down, poor man, and lower his head. His real troubles were just beginning. Standing by the igloo, waiting for him, was his wife and he had forgotten her list.

4

PUALUNA

The encounter with Pualuna after my unsuccessful fox hunt turned out to be the beginning of a friendship with the old man. Pualuna was Bertsie's father, and Sakaeunnguaq's father-in-law. In bygone days, the Eskimo did not allow old people to "enjoy the freedom of the city." Times had changed, of course, but even if old people were no longer encouraged to let themselves die in 1950, they were still treated with bald indifference. They were just barely tolerated.

As recently as the 1940s, hunters in Canada still abandoned their old people on the ice field during hunting expeditions. To abandon them thus was necessary in time of extreme hardship, and was done with their elders' full consent in the course of long journeys. At winter's end, Eskimos used to flee villages where famine had struck. They would push on for forty-eight hours without food or sleep, trying to join others who would share supplies with them. It was a dreadful sight: two or three dogs, rarely more, pulling a poor sledge (less than a century ago, the Thule Eskimos were so impoverished that they could not allow themselves larger teams). The father and son would walk in front, the wife and daughter behind. Only the old man—the old woman too, but she less often because women usually died early—would sit at the rear of the sledge. Knowing only too well what must be done, the old man would finally let himself slip off. . . . No one would turn around. Nonetheless, as the sledge drew inexorably farther and farther away, he would think to himself: I have lived my life. Go on, the rest of you. Quickly, go eat the seal of neighbors, of those who will be willing to share with you. The sledge would become a speck on the horizon. Stoically, the man would wait for the end, letting himself gradually freeze to death. The father had chosen the hour of his death and of his rebirth in his son.

Traces of this custom still remained, if only "in the mind." Pualuna, who was one of the oldest men in the tribe, lived alone in his tent, in great poverty.[10]

People treated him with more or less contempt—"the old man!"—and he was therefore very grateful for my visits and kindness to him.

I wanted to get to know Pualuna and often went to see him. As I had suspected, he was one of the memory sources for the entire group.

Pualuna had set up his shelter at some distance from the Inuit, on a rocky, flat-topped embankment. It was a low tent. I remember a sheet of canvas riddled with holes, which he had mounted on two stakes, one of them an old harpoon. A few heavy stones secured it. Scraps of metal and garbage lay about; there was the smell of rancid fat. The man, crouched under his tent, waited. His stove was no longer lighted. Fuel was expensive.

On one of my early visits, I noticed his provisions for the week lying on a board to the right of the entrance: a quarter of seal, which his son-in-law Sakaeunnguaq had—quite exceptionally—given him a few days before; six cubes of sugar; two halves of a cigarette; a few matches. Pualuna vegetated; he was worn out; his days were numbered.

Wrapped in dog skins, he was lying on a platform of planks that took up two-thirds of the tent. He always kept on his pants and boots. He seldom undressed and washed. "It's warmer this way," he used to say.

The small round face that emerged from the pile of skins and fur had been sculpted by time into a hard mask. Almost lost in folds of skin, his eyes were running; now and then he wiped away the rheumy flow with a filthy rag. The face he turned toward me was melancholy, for his lips were so chapped that he could not smile. His last remaining glory was his abundant coarse hair, which was still completely black (the hair of the ethnically pure Eskimo almost never turns white). With a weary gesture that had become second nature to him, he picked up a stone to scratch his head. Then, looking at the door of the tent with a vacant expression, he pensively pulled out the few graying hairs on his chin with the dirty fingernails of his left hand. I remained standing before him, not knowing where to sit, then I stepped back tentatively. There the ground was already muddy. Pualuna sat facing me. He pushed aside his dented Primus, some tins of food, and the chamber pot he used as a spittoon. I could settle down then, and our conversation could begin.

In this way, I discovered a true personality. Pualuna had taken part in American expeditions that in the late nineteenth century went above latitude 80° north. He had gone on several of Peary's expeditions to the Pole. On March 21, 1908, by arrangement with Peary's rival, Dr. Frederick A. Cook, he had dropped off large stocks of foodstuffs at Cape Stallworthy, the northernmost point of Axel Heiberg Island, for Cook's use on his return from the Pole to the coast.

Pualuna always spoke of Cook, the controversial explorer accused by the press and by Peary of being a charlatan, with great personal esteem. "North Pole or not . . . that's the white men's business!" Pualuna's brother Uutaaq was Peary's favorite Eskimo companion and a great hunter. It was he who, on April 6, 1909, had raised the American flag as a sign of victory at the North Pole—or what was taken to be the Pole.

The brothers did not suffer from the rivalry between their "patrons." The family shared the advantages of having one brother work for Cook and the other for Peary. When one recalls the antagonism between the two Americans —which led Peary to forbid "his" Eskimos to work for or follow Cook—one can appreciate the two brothers' spirit of enterprise and complicitous cunning.

Pualuna had once been a shaman, an angakkoq; he had been married four times, and was only recently separated from his last wife, Atitak. He had six children, fifteen grandchildren, and thirteen great-grandchildren.

I quickly directed the conversation to one of my projected subjects of research: the genealogy of the eighty Eskimo families that made up the entire group at any time of my stay among them. Some twelve hundred individuals, both living and dead, were involved. Pualuna, like several others—particularly the old women—had a very reliable memory and became a precious informant.

In connection with this genealogical study, I eventually interviewed every adult man and woman in the settlement, embracing, naturally, all heads of families, all the old people. I identified and counted over four generations, twelve hundred individuals. Pualuna, like many of his contemporaries, was quick to show a keen interest in the work's being successfully carried out. "Good for the Eskimos," he often whispered to me. "A record of our past must be kept in writing. The young people today have no memory."

At the outset, our interviews went more or less like this: "Let's see, Pualuna, how old are you?"

"Fifty to seventy years old. Ittoq! Old! A good-for-nothing, an old man. I am not worth much." He answered my questions with the greatest good will. He made an effort, closing his eyes the better to remember, or counting on his fat, twisted fingers: "My, that's a long time ago!"

"Come on, Pualuna, how old are you? Or rather, how old were you when Kunúnnguaq [Knud Rasmussen] left with Kuukkok [Lauge Koch] and Inukit-supaluk for the other side of the big glacier with the second Thule expedition [April 1917]?"

"Asukiaq. That doesn't interest me and I absolutely don't remember anymore. . . . Assorsuaq puigorpakka! Taamannarsuaq. Taammaappoq! I have no idea. . . . I've forgotten, I can't find myself anymore!"

"Listen, Pualuna, surely you remember how old you were when Piulissuaq [Peary] went with your brother to the North Pole." (It was in February 1909.)

"Ieh . . . ieh . . . uvatsi. . . . Wait a minute. Yes, I know. I married the beautiful Aviaq, my third wife, in Etah when they came back. That was a summer for salmon, salmon half as long as a man's arm. There were many Inuit around our sealskin tents. All the hunters who came back with Piulissuaq had new rifles. And that was the last year we saw a big baleen whale spouting near Qaanaaq. At that time I was . . . a bit older than you are now. Yes, really. The same age Ululik or Angutilluarssuk from Savigssivik is now. Three winters later, I had my first child. Is that all? Wait. . . . Wait. . . . I was near Illulorsuit, very near, when Kuukkok set up his base there [1922]! The autumn when

Amaroq [Thorild Wulff] did not come back with Kununnguaq from Inglefield Land [1917], I was in Etah, as old as Nassapaluk is now. When Aqajak left Neqi with two qallunaat, a young one and an old one [the German geologist H. U. E. Krüger], and never came back I was in Qeqertaq [1937], much older than Imina is today, much older. When the big boat came to Etah [the American meteorological expedition led by Clifford James McGregor], I was in Etah [1937–38]. When Knudguak's son came to Neqi, I was in Neqi, too [1939]; and now for your first winter, I am here, in Siorapaluk, with you. Is this what you want to know?"

A cross-check resulted in a consensus that in 1909 Pualuna was between thirty-three and thirty-seven. Therefore, in 1950, when these interviews took place, he was around seventy-eight.

It is remarkable that if an Eskimo's memory is just jogged a little, he is able, without paper, without any written documents whatever, to provide a great deal of information about his past which is far more precise than what Pualuna recalled in our initial conversations.

My genealogical research was not without its ups and downs. The Eskimos' impulse was to mock a person who asked such questions. This, when joined to their respect for their cherished dead—as late as 1950 it was taboo to mention them by name—meant that at first they would pretend not to remember very well and would feign indifference. But as I discovered the right way to question them, they soon began to answer clearly and with considerable precision. Through my knowledge of West Greenlandic, my communications in the Polar Eskimo dialect were improving progressively.

"You know Atitak—the Inuit have surely talked to you about her. Well . . . I've had enough of her. No, but have you seen her?" Pualuna was alluding to an affair of his that had been going on for a dozen years. Against the advice of some people, when he was sixty-six he had wanted to marry a woman of almost the same age. Both people were so implacably independent that soon after their marriage—duly and properly performed by a government official—they divorced. But it was a friendly—actually only a seasonal—divorce; if for three-quarters of the year they preferred to go their separate ways from settlement to settlement, living off their relatives, in spring they did come together for a few weeks under the same roof. This was a festive interlude. You would see Pualuna and Atitak walking together along the beach. Two old people hobbling over the sand. Their neighbors used to watch them and laugh. The idyll was short-lived; within a month, they would be regretting their lost freedom.

A little boy came into Pualuna's tent. He had surely been sent by Olipaluk, who had seen me walking in that direction. By now I was on more familiar terms with Pualuna, and we were sitting side by side on his bed platform. The child sat down in the opposite corner; he seemed indifferent, and kept his head lowered. He was waiting for me to leave, and then he would clean the tent. Olipaluk would certainly have wished the child had come before I did. Eskimos do not like to see their elders, no matter how old, appear too miserable in front of a qallunaaq. Native dignity has its exigencies in this area, no doubt ever since the Eskimos learned that in the white man's world old people are respected, at least to the extent of being given pensions.

I got up to leave.

"Thank you ever so much, Pualuna."

"Illillo, not at all," he said, almost cutting me short. "It is I who thank you."

His face brightened with malice. He turned and rummaged among his vile cans of food. He half-raised himself on his bed, and held out his arm.

"This yellow-looking sugar—here, would you like it?"

Dear Pualuna, I do believe I can hear you still.

5

WALRUS HUNT

When the Inuk sleeps, do not disturb him. Sleeping is one of his greatest pleasures and his principal activity in his free time. He will hunt for sixty hours at a stretch, but he also sleeps longer than we do in our latitudes—in winter, for as long as twelve to fifteen hours at one time. Now it was the end of September, and supplies were getting low. The women grew fretful and complained; the children whimpered. Soon there would be nothing to eat. "That's all right, that's all right," Olipaluk grunted. "We'll go hunting aaveq. . . ."

The aaveq, or walrus, that heaven-sent animal which is particularly abundant around Pitorarfik-Neqi—an ancestral meeting ground—provided the tribe with enough meat to feed its dogs during the hard weeks of December and January. In October and November, the ice is still thin and soft, and the moonless days are too dark for the men readily to hunt seal by the holes in the ice field.[11] The fox is the only source of fresh meat from December to March. But its flesh is nauseating to eat, and it is not a meat that the Eskimos actively seek. Hare and partridge are to be found on the green slopes and in the grassy valleys, but hunting such game is for women and adolescents—and for times of dire need. Only the tough meat of the walrus is considered nourishing. Throughout the autumn, the walrus is pursued systematically. Any surplus quarters of meat are buried here and there along the shore, in stone caches that in January and February will be the main meat-supply centers.[12]

"Imina and Ululik will go by umiaq, by boat, the others by land," Olipaluk specified. "The kayakers are on their own."

Word spread quickly. Activity was frenzied. Hunters ran this way and that. Imina jumbled the orders he gave his wife and son. "Go fetch the Primus. No . . . see to the dogs. . . . The tobacco, where's the tobacco?"

Imina's hut was crowded with hunters. You couldn't take a step without bumping into someone. Doors slammed; people rushed in and out. Heads were awhirl, and the most conflicting ideas flew about. No sooner would someone make a proposal than it would be seconded by someone else with a low, approving "ieh" and a nod, only to be promptly contradicted by another idea.

John, the niivertoq, was roused from his bed. The storekeeper did not like hunting, and he was groggy with boredom. We provisioned ourselves abundantly with ammunition, sugar, and tea. I attended to the tent; food we would hunt for along the way. "Well, when do we leave?"

"Massakkut, right away!" Ululik shouted to me as he ran by.

I stared at him, nonplussed. He was half naked.

The Dead Gods

We would not be setting out for a good two hours. To escape the crowd, I sought refuge in old Pualuna's tent. The atmosphere there was comfortable; the mild weather had made for a relaxed mood and, when amused, people became more outgoing. The women and old men made the first overtures to me. I had coffee and tobacco. Pualuna looked at me with a noncommittal smile; he settled down with his back against a crate, propped his forearms on his knees, and bent his head. Was he about to speak? No. . . . He was not comfortable yet. He shifted position, cleared his throat, and wiped his swollen blue lips with the back of his hand. Some chunks of seal remained in his pot. He examined them and chose a morsel to suck on. Pualuna enjoyed being pressed to talk. Finally, he was ready.

"A long time ago—you weren't even born yet—the angakkoq, the shaman, was the most important person among us. He was the anga, the elder, the one who is first, who precedes. Hold on . . . pass me the spittoon—yes, that tin can with a lid. . . . What used to happen at the shaman's? . . . Always the same thing. In the evening, we would all get together in someone's igloo—not always his. The Inuit, the real hunters—no young people but the women, too, the ones who knew how—would begin to recite ritual phrases. The shaman would look at us with vague eyes. Then people—all the Inuit—would shout louder, each one according to his own nature.

"The angakkoq would not get up until there was silence again. He would hide behind a sealskin and begin to talk. He talked and talked. His voice would be low—muffled—and then, little by little, it would grow louder and louder until it filled the whole igloo. The women would begin to *aja—aja-ja-aja-ja—* you've probably heard us chant like that. At first, the rhythm is very slow. The angakkoq would begin to fidget and fret; he grimaced and grunted as if he were possessed by 'powers' that were making him suffer so that they could escape from inside him. He panted and trembled, and in a jerky voice, he would cry out in a special language that we did not always understand. Appeals, exclamations. . . . Then he would collapse in a heap. The Inuit used to say that they could hear a long whistling that came out of the ground. The *aja-ja-aja-ja* continued but became inaudible. The angakkoq would no longer be breathing."

"What? What do you mean?"

Pualuna tapped his belly.

"You are like all qallunaat. You will never understand anything—nothing, but not a thing about the Inuit. . . . So listen to me. Pissortut—obviously—the shaman only *seemed* to be dead. At that very moment, his spirit had escaped through a hole—a very little hole—in the floor of the hut. The whistling? That was his breath, which had gone away. It had left to consult with Nerrivik, the great goddess of the waters.

"Ah, there is a beautiful woman, and she has great powers. . . . A cigarette? Soo! Thank you. . . . All that time, the rest of us would sit with our eyes closed, babbling I don't know what anymore. . . . Sometimes that went on for a long time. It depended on the days.[13]

"So we would stay there, crouching in front of the angakkoq, and we would be worried and tense. Suddenly there would be a loud noise. The sealskin had fallen. The angakkoq was back. One arm would move. He would open one eye, shake one leg. He was coming back to life, trembling from head to foot. He would get to his feet, all pale, his lips shaking, and incomprehensible words[14] would come from his mouth in spurts. He would chew his lips. 'Soo!' we would say. 'Soo! You have done well.' He would raise his head. We would all move closer. Sometimes he would sing an angakkoq song. He had seen Nerrivik, he had spoken with our dead, our great ancestors. 'Nerrivik is great and powerful. This is what she wills: 'I thank you, angakkoq, for having kindly caressed and untangled my hair in the depths of the waters. . . . In your tribe there is a woman who did not respect the taboos during menstruation. Therefore, blood will continue to flow from her entrails and the sea animals will flee from the bad odor. But because it is you, once again I will move my oil lamp to your shore at Kiataq. The water there will be warm and nourishing, and you will find seals by the score, pointing their heads above the water again and again, and white whales[15] will come and go in the bay close by the shore. . . . Go!' "

"That was more or less what used to happen," Pualuna said. "If the angakkoq did not speak clearly because he was tired, very tired from his

The angakkoq's spirit visits the whale, while an Eskimo beats a drum. Ivory intaglio (Alaska). *(From Gessain,* Les Esquimaux du Groenland à l'Alaska; *Collection Joie de connaître, Bourrelier)*

journey under the sea, one of the hunters would repeat what he had said. And who was Nerrivik? Where did she come from? . . . It's a long story. Every child knows it. In the evening, the old women who know everything would tell you the story without leaving out a word or detail. Go see Amannalik, in Uuminan- naq! She talks a lot, but she doesn't lie. . . . Have you any tobacco left? . . . Thank you! . . . I could also tell you the story right now, after all. It's cozy being together like this, and you're truly interested in us. So listen to me again. . . .

"Nerrivik had married a bird, a kind of sea gull. They went off together to live on a small island. Every morning, the husband went out hunting. While his wife waited patiently for him to return, she scraped skins with her ulu which would be used for tents. Now and then her parents came to see her. The sea gull had been in the habit of wearing glasses when he came home. His eyes were indeed hideous. But one day he came back without the glasses.

" 'Have you ever seen my eyes?' he asked his wife, and he laughed. She was intrigued, and she looked at him. But when she saw how ugly his eyes were, she burst into tears and she never left off crying.

"Her parents urged her to flee in a little sealskin boat while the sea gull was out hunting.

"So, one evening, they hurriedly left the island. But when the sea gull returned and saw that his wife had left him, he became very angry. He set out after her, and soon he caught sight of the boat. He quickly reached it, and flew so close that he brushed against it. The parents were afraid, and the father decided to throw his daughter into the sea. This was done.

"No sooner was she in the water than she clung to the boat and almost made it tip over. The father then took his heavy, broad knife and chopped off a few fingers from each of her hands. When she continued to cling to the boat, he cut off all the fingers that were left. . . . But poor Nerrivik did not give in, and she held on with her bleeding palms. To make an end of it, the father cut off both her hands. Nerrivik tried hard to hold on with her stumps. But they had no grip and slowly they slipped off. This did not take long, and presently her parents were able to finish their journey in peace.

"After sinking to the bottom of the sea, Nerrivik became the goddess of the waters.

"It is certain that she answers the prayers only of the great shamans. Only they know how to talk to her, to soothe her, to arrange the bun at the back of her neck properly, and to sweep her house."

"A shaman is immortal," Pualuna added. "What I mean is, he can come back to life if need be.

"In our long history there was once a shaman who came back from death five times. There was even an angakkoq who fell from a cliff to his death and whose remains were eaten by a dog. But blessed be he! Even though this dog had eaten him, he came back to life and walked into the village with the dog, whose jaws were still dripping with blood, trotting at his side. . . .

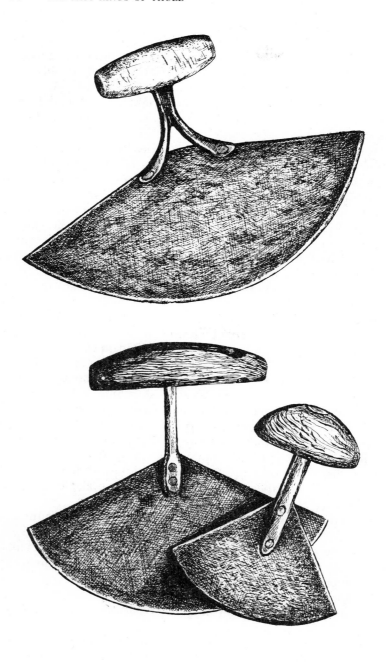

Ulus, knives with curved blades used by women throughout the Arctic. The larger two are from the Thule district, 1950–51. The third, lower right, is from Spence Bay, Boothia Peninsula, Canada. September 1961. (*Private collection*)

"The history of our ancestors, you see, has taught us how to discover the great mysteries. Nothing surprises us, and we do not stop trying to understand the meaning of everything around us. . . .

"The Inuit," Pualuna went on, "by using their poor means of observation have understood that things are connected, that they depend on each other. Nothing upsets us more, us Inuit, than to interfere with this natural order. So we make sure that we only float with it, without changing its course. Hunters are forbidden to eat malemuk eggs in June if earlier in the year they have not caught one animal from all the kinds that live on the earth and in the sea. And then there are other allernersuit.* Wait a minute, I'm going to tell you about these allernersuit. When I was young, life was very complicated. An angakkoq —myself, for example—might not use a knife or a harpoon for several days after he had seen Nerrivik. A young hunter must not touch the water he drank; he had to suck it up with a special tube made of bone. During her period, a woman could not urinate on the ice field. Oh! I forgot to tell you that the only wound that can kill a shaman, so the Inuit say, is in the throat. . . .

"Everything is spirit. This is the essential thing for you to remember. The forces are our friends, our relatives. Still, we must be able to understand them in order to make them useful to us. A woman could be an angakkoq also, but almost always they were men. Some powerful angakkoqs could foresee the great changes of cold and heat; they could foresee how long the warm spells would last, when the narwhals and seals would leave and return, and why the fjord would suddenly be blocked with ice and for how long. In those days, the angakkoq was our most dependable protector. Without him, the Inuit would all have died. Each of us and the angakkoq, too—since we are all Inuit—have guardian spirits that help us win out over the forces. We keep these familiars secret, and often they come to us in our dreams.

"How does one become an angakkoq? By inspiration. Your familiar speaks to you. Afterward . . . there are many tests in solitude. Another angakkoq teaches you the vast knowledge and the great language. We believe that the spirits go off to other worlds and that except in rare cases we do not see them again.

"On certain special occasions they change themselves into birds or seals, or they live inside one of these animals. . . . There is no limit to these transformations. Uutaaq would explain these things to you very well. You'll speak with him when you pass through Uummannaq. He also has been an angakkoq.

"But I should also say that there are evil spirits—the ilisiitsoqs—whom no one here likes to talk about. They take possession of a man and make him qivittoq. The man goes crazy, he shouts shaman words, and he writhes as if possessed, as if another being has taken him and is tearing him apart. Then he goes off to the mountains where, they say, men who are half-savage and

---

*Allerpoq = "one under taboo"; allernersuit = "one is under a very strict taboo." Allernersuit are the most stringent of taboos, the absolute prohibitions.

half-animal live in the earth and ice. Some return from the mountains. I met such people when I was a boy. I hope for your sake you never see any up there. These ilisiitsoqs—these soul-robbers, these manipulators of tupilat, of spirits —used to be killed, but people were afraid of them even after they were dead. To be completely rid of them, one had to kill them in a special way. Otherwise they would be reborn in animals. The hunter who captured one of those strange animals—they looked like seal-walruses made by a man-sorcerer— would fall very sick, and after that he would be paralyzed.

"There is this, too—and pay careful attention: an angakkoq is capable of bringing about great changes. We all know the story of Arnattartoq, the wandering spirit with which a man had impregnated a sterile woman. This spirit left the woman's belly after a while. Each time someone tried to kill him, he changed himself into a fox or a seal or a bird. . . . He would always change. They would harpoon him, they would kill him. People would think that they had killed him, but he would breathe through his little finger, and when he breathed hard through his little finger no one could catch him. Once he even became a dog. But no sooner had they put him next to a cache of meat he could feed on than he lay down and changed himself into something else.

"He was afraid of the water and when he became a walrus did not know how to dive. 'Strike the vault of the sky with your flippers and you will dive,' his brother walruses told him.

"In the end, he changed himself into a bear. The dogs smelled him, chased him, and ran him down. They seized him, one by a paw, another by the belly. This time he didn't have time to become another creature. So ended 'the Wandering Spirit' who had turned himself into a bear."

Hunting
Walrus in Kayaks

Strident shouts sounded through the settlement. I left Pualuna to his memories. Finally the Eskimos were leaving, more or less according to plan: one group by boat, one group by land, others—on their own—by kayak. The only boat in the village—an open wooden boat with no mast, no sail—was pushed into the water. A few men and I jumped in. The wind took hold, and it moved off.

"Well, which way are we going?" the men asked.

"Follow the wind," the genial Olipaluk answered.

I looked at him, stunned.

"The wind's good," he said to me. "In Innartalik there is walrus."

The men began to row. Some sang. *Nuannarpoq!* How pleasant it is! Those of us who were going on foot followed them with our eyes as we trudged along the sweeping, graceful curves of the silver-white beach. The sun was shining; the air rustled; it was warm. The men's leathery faces were sweaty. The smell of animal skins and grease filled our nostrils. The warmth of the ground, which had thawed only on the surface, rose visibly as steam to the height of six or nine feet. The birds were excited by the harshness of a never-ending day, and they kept circling back and forth between slope and shore. I blinked; the blue-black sea was smooth, without a ripple. The flat expanse of water flashed shimmering mirages from iceberg to iceberg. My glance traveled from the wet, gleaming glacier to the motionless sea. Beyond the straits, some twenty-five miles distant, the tall mauve cliffs of Northumberland Island floated as if on a cloud. Suddenly, the umiaq stopped.[16]

"Hey, Arnarulunguaq, is there any gasoline? . . . Where are my gloves, Aqatannguaq? . . . Look for some matches—mine are wet."

Questions flew back and forth between the shore and the boat. The Eskimo makes no inventory of his baggage until he is under way, and our great setting forth was nearly a false departure.

We passed Illulorsuit. The broad, flat torrent, strewn with pebbles and sea ice at its delta, was now frozen to a depth of two inches. With Appalinnguaq last month I had had trouble crossing the icy current.

As the Eskimos got farther away from the village and its psychological pressures, they began to speak to me about themselves more spontaneously —I would even say more freely. Each cliff, each valley, was recognized and named. A hunter would see the place where he had set his traps or where, the summer before, he had made love under a tent. Each man took pleasure in drawing me aside and pointing out places that held memories for him, but when they were all together, they would never confide in me. We were walking

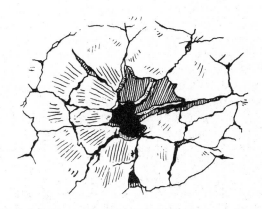

Breathing hole made by a walrus in the ice. See note 12, part 2. (*From Kane*, Arctic Explorations)

on over hard, clean ground, smoking our pipes, our rifles slung over our shoulders. They told stories from the past—tales they shared in common—of famine, deaths, women, and amorous exploits. Their recitals would be interrupted by gusts of laughter and corrections, the older men intervening to set things straight.

"Takkuut! Look! . . . Naajat!"

We threw ourselves down on the sand. We whistled piercing bird cries and waved feathers. Five large gulls approached, hesitated. . . . Too late. One volley brought them down. A black crow flying out from the mountain circled some seventy-five feet above us. Unlike the Bering Strait Eskimos, the Eskimos here look upon the crow with contempt—"Tulugaq! A crow!" Because the bird lives on offal, "he's a piece of dung." The crow is perfectly adapted to the cold, although it has no fat or down, and is one of the few birds to winter over here.

At Kuugarssuk, luck smiled on us again. A dead seal[17] was lying on the shore; its skin was good, the fur still adhering. The beach, indented by deltas and lagoons, now formed a sweeping curve. We were walking on wet sand and beneath our feet could feel the permanently frozen subsoil slowly rising.

"Do you see the rock at the foot of that tall cliff, that steep mountain—the rock to the right of the iceberg? That's it!"

Soon afterward the group halted. On all sides, bones and blackened rocks: this was Innartalik. On a long slope covered with small stones stood a dozen piles of big stones, each pile about three feet high, each stone weighing about twenty pounds; the stones were welded together by ice. Appearances to the contrary, they were not cairns or small *inussut,* but caches. (Inussut and cairns are bigger, and in silhouette look like a man. The inussut are intended to frighten reindeer and drive them where they can be killed—to a lake or a narrow passage.) These caches were well-built, and bears and foxes could not break into them to devour the stores of meat buried inside.

We pitched camp around a fire of fat. Several hunters built low stone walls, behind which they would sleep under the open sky. When the tea was ready, we clustered around some unspeakable brew, bowl in hand.

"Only one serving apiece," Ingapaluk informed me.

A yellowish liquid mixed with tea leaves was poured to the rim of each container. The craftier Eskimos held out big tin cans. My regulation army mug looked rather pathetic. No matter. Thank you, Ingapaluk! The tea warmed us. We drank standing up, stamping our feet on the ground. The sun would soon be gone. "What are we waiting for? Let's get some sleep."

The Eskimo was hungry and he wanted his walrus. He was on its track, he could already smell it, and he would wait as long as need be. . . .

A dozen walruses were running straight toward us. Three hunters ran for their kayaks and, with help from some younger men, got them into the water in a flash. The rest of us climbed into the boat and rowed hard to keep up. We stopped when we came within firing range.

Two walruses. A female and her calf were playing in the icy water, beside

Walrus cache. *(From Kane,* Arctic Explorations*)*

an iceberg. Five hundred yards away, fifteen or twenty others were tumbling about in the choppy water, and bellowing.

"Hy-yy. . . . Hy-yyy. . . ."

Ululik drew near the female in his kayak. He was trying to stay to windward and to keep the sun behind him. She was intrigued by his imitative cry, and raised her head. A male approached.

"Hy-yy. . . . Hy-yyy. . . ."

Those of us in the boat were watching intently. This type of hunting is extremely dangerous. The Eskimo must strike the animal near the head with his harpoon. If he misses, the enraged walrus will go on the offensive. He will charge straight on. With his red eye, the walrus quickly takes the measure of the battlefield, and the hunter must absolutely not let the animal drag him toward the *querencia,* the territory where the animal and the rest of the herd like to stay. A kayak is very likely to be overturned in this area and stove in by the maddened beast. This had happened recently to Kaalipaluk, Peary's Eskimo son. He described to me how the summer before, his kayak had been

Walrus hunting. *(Schneider collection, Musée de l'Homme, Paris)*

dragged toward the main herd and had been literally crushed by one of these formidable sea elephants as he was getting ready to harpoon it. He couldn't get clear of the wreckage in that icy water. Had he been alone, he would have been lost. His companions were hard put to create the necessary diversion by shouting and striking the water with their paddles.

The suddenness of such attacks is another danger. The walrus is even more aggressive and unpredictable if he is an old loner who has already been wounded by a man. Once, in an area where walrus were being hunted from the edge of the ice floe, a walrus suddenly surfaced, lifted one hunter between his tusks, and carried him off the way a mother would have picked up one of her calves and borne him between her flippers. The Eskimo was dragged down to the bottom. The walrus resurfaced to breathe; so did the hunter but, swimming beneath unbroken ice, he could not find the walrus's breathing hole. . . . The men who recounted this true story, said Rasmussen, were luckily able to follow the movements of their companion. They made a hole in the ice and saved him.

"Hy-yyy. . . . Hy-yyy. . . ."

The walrus was finally answering Ululik. The Eskimo was perfectly calm. He followed the animal's every movement with the closest attention. He must be able to anticipate its lightninglike reactions. This time he was in a good position . . . and he moved in to attack. Twenty yards . . . ten yards . . . five . . . four. . . . The hunter handled his double paddle with such consummate skill that it did not ripple the water. He had already checked his harpoon; his rope was carefully coiled.

The two walruses, isolated now, were looking in another direction. The male had moved off. In the evening light, we could see the mother playing with her calf in the satin-smooth water. It was she whom Ululik had chosen. But now she shifted position slightly. Her splashing allowed the hunter, who was already very near, to draw even closer.

Three . . . two. . . . Strike! He hurled the harpoon, then backpaddled with rapid, powerful strokes. In a great spray of water the walrus dove to escape from this sudden blow which it probably thought had come from a bear, or perhaps—though this would be unusual—from a great killer whale.[18] The buoy,* which was attached to the harpoon line, floated in a widening circle of blood.

We followed the buoy as the poor animal dragged it along. Was the walrus coming up for air? Our five rifles spat. . . . "It's a big one!" Imina shouted, turning his clown's face toward us. The walrus finally did surface; it was breathing deeply and fairly regularly, and measured about nine feet in length. We finished it off with a club and lashed its head to the boat. We inserted a tube into its stomach and took turns blowing into it, as if it were a balloon. Once inflated, the carcass could be towed to shore more easily. Two more walruses

---

*To fashion the buoy, or *avataq*, a seal is gutted, inflated by mouth with air, and attached by three yards of sealskin rope to a piece of wood.

were caught by another hunter. The men left behind on the beach had followed the hunt with passionate interest, and now they started large fat and oil fires. Fantastic shadows danced in the light of the flames; they weaved about, laughing and talking. We could hear the sound of knives being sharpened on stones. A few moments more and the shadows would be flinging themselves on the raw flesh.

We were none too many to lever and push the three enormous mountains of flesh out of the water. Aaveq, the walrus! Now that it was secured by the heavy sealskin lines, we could get a good look at the elephantine sea creature. Olipaluk approached his catch, carrying a large tapering blade. As camp leader, the honor fell to him of being the first to "stick" the animal. Blood spurted. Maneuvering skillfully to avoid soiling his bearskin trousers, a hunter collected the blood in a gasoline can. This would be our soup, or qajoq. The men began to carve up the carcass. The belly was slit down the middle, from the neck to the genitals, and then the carcass was methodically cut up. We were soon squelching around in sticky mud. Encased in thick white fat, the red nourishing meat excited the hunters. Everyone was impatient to cut off the piece due him. The flippers were eaten as the carving progressed. The hunters permitted Ingapaluk and Appalinnguaq, who were the last arrivals, to slice off their geometric shares. The Inuit half-chewed the raw meat and talked at the top of their lungs as, brandishing huge knives, they circled around what would soon be a mere pile of bones. They relished plunging their blades into the carcass to free the remaining blood. Ululik had sat down on a stone and was sipping warm blood from a tin can.

"Mammaraai! It's good!"

He invited me to drink, too. Appalinnguaq, to make himself thoroughly comfortable, blew his nose with his fingers. A blob of mucus fell onto the meat, but who would pay that any mind? Ingapaluk was carefully separating the intestines and emptying them of a yellowish mixture; he pressed the white gelatinous membrane of the big intestine to force out the light-colored contents. His example was contagious. When the hunting is good, the tripes belong to everyone. Imina emptied the stomach of its predigested brown mussels. The hunters kneeled down in the snow to help him so that none of this delectable food would be lost. With the tacit agreement of the others, one man had reserved the eyes for himself.

"Prima . . . prima," he said to me. "First-rate."

He sucked on them, then crunched them between his teeth. The Eskimos were so busy that they had forgotten the tide. The waves licked our feet; the sea was rising.

"Hey, Imina—give me a hand, will you?"

High time—the water was beginning to cover the animal, which was far from being all carved up. Each man dropped his share and ran to save what could be saved. They grasped straps made of walrus and bearded-seal skins, and hauled the two other carcasses higher up on the beach. There it was dry and the carving could go on.

Hunting an isolated walrus with a harpoon. The village boat is in the background, on the open sea (1). The handle of the harpoon breaks off when the head sinks into the animal's flesh (7). A buoy, or avataq, enables the hunters in the boat to locate the animal (8) and finish it off (11). As shown in the drawing, the walrus used to be killed with long

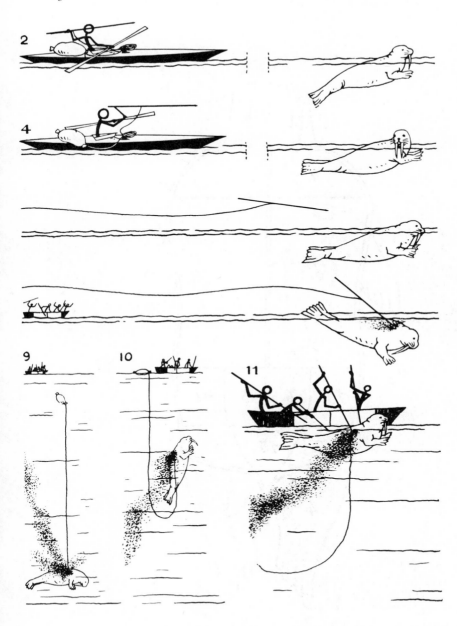

poles; today, the Eskimos hunt with rifles. A tube is inserted into the walrus's body, which, if the carcass has not been too badly damaged, is then inflated so that it will be lighter to pull ashore, where it is cut up. (*Based on Gessain,* Les Esquimaux du Groenland à l'Alaska)

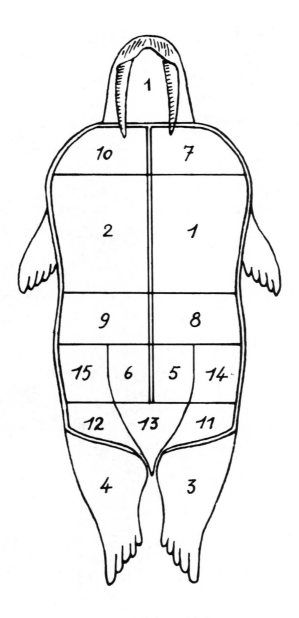

The pattern governing the division of a walrus among fifteen hunters. A slightly modified version of a drawing by Christian Vibe which shows a division among nineteen hunters. The portions are hierarchically determined.

By ten o'clock that evening, everything was finished. During the cutting up, which followed traditional rules that harked back to very old socioeconomic structures, each man had made a mark on the piece he received and carried it to his pile of belongings. Without discussion, some men were given extra shares. The walrus head, the two ivory tusks, and the heart, which weighed a good seventeen pounds, went by rights to the hunter who had harpooned the animal.

An Eskimo Dream

Hands greasy, stomachs full, we repaired to our tents. Primuses purred. Pipes were lighted. One man told us a story, picking his teeth the while. Sprawled on his sack, my neighbor belched and burped. His lips were still flecked with tiny morsels of fat.

The next day, one of the hunters who, like all Eskimos, dreamed a great deal, told me his dream[19] more or less as follows:

"Last night I saw a broad, bright, and icy hall, where tall women were coming and going with what looked like socks sticking to their skin. When I entered, they nodded slightly and smiled. I was charmed as I watched them pass before me, one by one. Just as one of them held out her hand and seemed to be inviting me to follow her, an enormous voice boomed out at me:

" 'Eskimo! Ha! ha! ha! ha! Always loafing around, aren't you! Eskimo! Ha! ha! ha! ha! . . . You surely do stink. Here we have—What? You don't know? Why, this is the big qallunaat store. . . . Very large. Nothing like that shop in Siorapaluk. Butik-kasik! A no-account little shop that is. . . . But look at what's here.'

"The women were wearing white smocks, like the nurses at the clinic in Thule, and were leaning their elbows on the clean tables. Everything was rich and shining. . . . Goods everywhere—hanging up, stacked in piles.

" 'Do you want something?' the voice asked me.

I held out my arms joyously to accept some cans of food.

" 'Thank you,' I said to one of the women. 'Thank you very much,' I said to another. 'It's very kind of you.'

"I was confused and went to the door.

" 'Hey, Eskimo?'

"I could hear giggling behind me. I turned around and suddenly the cans came tumbling down from everywhere. I was covered with them. Then the nurses pointed at me. They were in stitches of laughter! . . . I had three eyes and enormous hare's ears. Blood was flowing from a deep wound in my right hand. My legs were gone. I was a freak Eskimo, a beggar Eskimo, a crippled Eskimo. I was finished. Piniartoq tammaq—a washed-up hunter!' "

The Sun
Disappears

Week by week the days had grown shorter. Near the white heights of Cape Kangek, in a wash of theatrical colors, an orange-red disk crept over the ice pack—the last gleam of a sun that was about to disappear for long months. At five minutes past eleven this morning, it appeared at the top of the cliff, followed an almost horizontal trajectory, and sank from sight a few hours later. During the brief twilight, the emerald-green horizon, flecked with white, burned purple, violet, and orange. To the southwest, against a monochrome yellow sky, translucent clouds high above the horizon were brightened from behind, reminding me of a Georges de La Tour painting. The cliff cast strange shadows down its sloping sides, enlivening the snowy landscape for a few hours more.

As the pale daytime light haloed this wan landscape, the winter wind began to rise, and caused the rust-colored scree slopes to become streaked with narrow, shining trails. Olipaluk came to see me. He seemed to be in high spirits. We walked along together, talking about this and that. Suddenly he grasped my arm.

"You don't have sick blood, do you? Your nose is all red."

The Eskimo was making fun of my nose, which was more or less frozen and was now peeling.

"It's magnificent," he went on, "that big red qallunaaq nose of yours. Ha, ha, ha! It'll serve as a sun for us this winter. . . . Do you see Qeqertaq [Herbert Island]? Yes, behind that iceberg that looks like an ear. . . . The sun went down right there."

The Eskimo talked and talked. He was now completely at ease. He even took hold of my arm again!

"Is it possible that you, qallunaaq, know why the sun disappears? And why the stars—the Great Caribou, the Big and the Little Dipper, the Milky Way— why all these stars, these ulloriat,[20] are going to shine for four months at midday just as they do at midnight?"

I made a vague gesture.

"Stupid Inuk that I am, I will explain it to you."

He picked up a large round stone.

"This white stone"—he passed it before my eyes—"let us say it's the moon —aningaaq."

He laid it down on the ground.

"Push it. . . . Good. Wait. . . . Yes, that's it. When the sun is here, we don't see it anymore. It's cold. But when the sun comes back—oh, oh, it gets even colder."

His thick fingers quickly pushed the stones around—the sun, the stars— and the universe swayed.

"You see this star?"

He was holding a vertebra in his hand.

"You see this one, and that one?"

A chaotic cosmos spread out at our feet. On all fours, we moved about the beach like gods among the stars. The Eskimos can work such a spell that, I swear, they make you feel that they are always right. If ever I doubted it, the Eskimo would be right there, his brilliant eyes staring into mine to convince me.

The Drowning of Mitsoq

Mitsoq was dead! A sledge coming from Kangerluarsuk told us that Mitsoq, of Qeqertaq, had drowned a few days before, on November 1, 1950. The ice had broken under his sledge. He was frozen solid when they fished him out, just like the Danish doctor who had died in the same way five or six years earlier, not far from Thule.

In spite of his splendid cheerfulness, the hunter is no fool. He is aware of the dangers that surround him constantly: a fall into a glacier crevasse, the possibility of the ice field's breaking up and drifting, kayak accidents, rock showers from high cliffs, avalanches, rotten ice in the vicinity of headlands. The tribe has quite frequent cause to grieve over the tragic disappearance of one of its members. . . .

As soon as the ice had formed on the sea and thickened a little, he decided to go seal hunting in Wolstenholme Fjord, near Ulli. He set out alone from Thule. After cutting across the mountain, he ventured out on the ice field right near Ulli. His trail thereafter was lost.

That evening, some people in the camp began to worry. Uneasy neighbors kept coming to the igloo Mitsoq shared with Avoortungiaq and Maassannguar-suaq for news of him. Two sledges left to search for him. It was the middle of the night; the two hunters had difficulty in following the trail even as far as Ulli. From the shore, however, Maassannguarsuaq thought he could see the place where Mitsoq had disappeared. The moon illuminated an area of broken ice blocks where the unfortunate man had shattered the ice as he thrashed about in an agonized, desperate attempt to save himself. Later, his torn fingernails showed that he had clutched at the ice and fought to the very end.

One had to wait until the ice grew thicker. Two days later, the Eskimos returned with four sledges carrying poles, planks, harpoons, and sealskin robes. The gray-green ice field was now smooth and solid, but by examining the composition of the ice, they were able to locate the place where Mitsoq had sunk. The men probed the water with their harpoons. Suddenly Uissakassek felt something resist. They broke up the ice and pulled. It was only the dogs. One by one they fished them out; upon contact with the air, the dogs' carcasses instantly turned into rigid blocks. Traces and leashes were all chewed up. The poor animals had tried desperately to free themselves from the harness, which was immobilizing them. Laboriously, the Eskimos continued their task in silence. They dragged the sledge up out of the water. Everything was just where it should be. Ironically, the ice knife had slid within the driver's reach. If Mitsoq could have grabbed it, perhaps he would have been able to chop a handhold for himself. The men could see his rifle and oil heater. But they still could not find the man. He must have sunk to the bottom. Who could tell? It was now three days since the accident had happened, and the currents there were very strong. For more than an hour, the Eskimos probed the sea with large hooks attached to ropes. They were beginning to lose hope when one of the hooks snagged several yards from where the dogs had been fished up. Directly above the hole, the men pulled with infinite caution. At last Mitsoq's head emerged. His face was contorted and his mouth gaped horribly. The hook had caught him under the arm, and now the Eskimos could catch hold of their friend by his armpits. They carried him home, wrapped in a caribou skin.

He was not quite twenty-four years old.

6

FOUR MONTHS OF POLAR NIGHT

Tutsarfik

Tutsarfik—"one is listening"—denotes the month of November. With its arrival, some word finally reached us from Neqi. Qavianguaq and Ussaqaq pulled in to Siorapaluk on November 10. Because for six weeks we had heard nothing from this little hamlet, which was about twenty-five miles away, the Inuit had begun to be very worried. Nothing serious had gone wrong, however. The condition of the ice had not permitted the three families living there to keep in touch.

Qavianguaq, accompanied by Ussaqaq, had come to announce the birth of his second baby. *Pulaarupunga:* I am here with her to visit you. He went from igloo to igloo with his news. He accepted our congratulations with great dignity. Each of us had prepared his own compliment. I congratulated him warmly.

"Soo. Thank you."

And then he added this flowery sentence: "As you can see, I am a happy man. This baby, my first daughter, will be a light and joy for our whole igloo all through the winter."

Still dressed in his furs and looking like a young bear, he rocked back and forth for a few minutes. He was obviously satisfied with his image. When the occasion called for it, he, too, was capable of manifesting "fine feelings."

In his role as catechist, John Petrussen did his best to keep the registry-office records up to date. He questioned the new father about the baby's date of birth. All in vain. Without his wife, Qavianguaq could no longer quite remember when the event had taken place.

"It wasn't very cold that day," he kept saying over and over. "Yes, it must have been a rather nice day. . . . The sky was clear. You could see all the way to Apparssuit [Hakluyt] Island, but there was a lot of wind. It just might have been *ataasinngorneq,* Monday. . . ."[21]

Qavianguaq did his best. But without a calendar—the calendar was only then coming into common use—he could not remember by himself the day of the week when "the light and joy" had been bestowed upon him. On the other hand, he very well knew the exact number of walruses, seals, foxes, and hares caught that autumn. In Neqi, the season seemed to have been good. Since August, the two men of the remote settlement had harpooned seven walruses and thirty-two seals. Among the scree and on the low, grassy hills around Neqi, a hundred partridges and fifty hares had been caught during the same period by the two hunters, with the help of their wives and children. Some fowl—ducks and sea gulls—were mentioned for the record. Only a few foxes had been caught so far, but the season was just beginning.

We still had no news, however, from Etah. The Neqi people were as worried about this as we. Four families were spending the winter in Etah, the northernmost encampment in the district. It was the first time in many years that so large a group had settled at that latitude, on a site that had been inhabited from time immemorial. Eskimos' expansion northward during the Middle Ages had taken them as far as Inuarfissuaq, at the edge of Kane Basin, a territory rich in reindeer and bear, and even beyond it, all the way to the edge of Cape Scott. Now and then families would settle there for one or two years, but the last time had been at least twenty years ago. This year, Etah was the northernmost inhabited village. Why had Etah not been in touch with Siorapaluk? Would we have to wait for the sun to return before Imina would have news of his son and Sakaeunnguaq word from his father, the famous Nukapianguaq?

For two days our Neqi visitors, Ussaqaq and Qavianguaq, went from igloo to igloo, talking and chatting. News of everything that had happened to everyone during the summer, no matter how trivial, was exchanged. The people of Siorapaluk overwhelmed the two men with messages.

"Tell Atitak . . ."

"Ieh . . . Ieh," they would answer politely.

"Don't forget to give this . . ."

"Ieh . . . Ieh . . ."

The days were growing short. The shadows were lengthening. The wide expanse of water was like a pale desert. Night was near. Every day the temperature dropped. It was time for our friends from Neqi to set off for the north. On the afternoon of November 14, Qavianguaq and Ussaqaq said good-bye to each of us individually and went silently to pick up their whips. The short, ragged barks of the dogs, who had sniffed departure in the air, filled the camp. The two hunters walked over to their sledge; everything was in place. The two men glanced at each other, then looked back gravely at us. What actors, and what a sense of formalities!

One last wave of the hand. The whips cracked. The heavy sledge, unstuck by a kick of the heel to the front runners, moved off. We watched until the outlines of men and dogs, strung out against the horizon, disappeared to the west among icebergs and milky fog.

The Sea Freezes

After this visit, we settled back into our daily routine. It was a monotonous life. For the hunter, autumn is the dead season. He drifts from igloo to igloo, eating in one, pausing to chat in another. He is waiting for the sea to freeze over and form the bridge of ice that will enable him to make new trips.

What about the kayak?[22] It could not be used in November because sharp-edged drift ice floated over the surface of the water. Eventually it would become cold enough for the ice pack to fuse, but the battle between the free water and the frost that was trying to congeal it was far from over. For the moment, the sea was only a kind of black gelatinous paste with a film of soft, whitish ice. Gontran de Poncins put it very well: it is a long struggle between two elements, and the sea's ally—the wind—regularly destroys the thin milky belt that slowly builds up along the shore and the patterns of water lilies that flower there.

Yet it would not be long before the ice-field bridge formed and winter was upon us. At that moment, group living would take on its true meaning.[23]

Polar Hysteria

I did not realize what was causing a very noticeable moodiness in some people. The most trivial discussion grew heated over a yea or nay. For several mornings, I had been waking up with nausea and a severe migraine. I mentioned my uneasiness about all this to a neighbor. His wife had not even got up yet, and he himself, usually cheerful and forthcoming, seemed depressed.

"It will pass," he said, "but not before the sun disappears. You're not the only one. The few qallunaat I've known to spend the winter here were all uncomfortable when winter was coming on. Now it's nothing compared with how it used to be. Ah! the old days. . . . Taamanarssuaq, allanik. Listen, I'll tell you an old story. It's very ancient. It must have happened in the autumn. As now, there was still a little bit of sun left.

"A whole family had gone to spend the winter in Neqi. . . . You know Neqi, I think. . . . Everything seemed favorable—the hunting had been good that summer. In June, the sky had been so full of birds that it was black, the way it is black with big clouds when the weather is turning bad. The appaliarsuit—the sea kings—had been plentiful, and they had caught hundreds of them. A little before September, the eqaluit (salmon trout) rivers were boiling with fish. And foxes . . . well, in October there were foxes everywhere, not to mention walruses and seals. There were so many you couldn't count them. The dogs were fat and strong.

" 'We are rich,' the father said.

" 'Ieh,' the family chorused. 'We are rich.'

"But when winter came, perlerorneq [hysteria] fell upon them. For some time, now that the sun was low on the horizon, the mother had not been herself. She who used to work from morning till night, who could be heard laughing from the moment she got up, now remained in the igloo for hours, sitting idle and silent, staring blankly before her. The others were not too much worried, because the Inuit know that occasionally people are a little 'funny' at this time. Once or twice, however, the mother had said some very strange things.

"One evening when the father and one son had gone off to eat seal with some neighbors, the mother had remained behind, stretched out on the illeq—the sleeping platform. She felt tired, she said. The father and son were talking, eating and drinking tea with the neighbors. Everyone was all excited, for an Eskimo was telling how he had seen fresh bear tracks not far from the encampment. Suddenly, toward midnight, they heard the dogs howl.

" 'Let's go back,' the father said. 'This has nothing to do with bears. I can feel it here,' and he pointed to his head.

"Outside, the dogs were barking their heads off. In the meantime, the wind had risen. The son went first. They could see the light in their igloo, which seemed to be going on and off; it was as if someone was constantly walking back and forth in front of the only window. Beside the house, the dogs were straining with all their might against their leashes. When the father and son opened the door, they saw a dreadful sight. The house had been turned upside down. Torn caribou skins were scattered over the floor amid seal meat and streams of blood. The younger children stood trembling in the corner. The mother's face was dark and flushed; her clothing was disheveled, and she was running back and forth clutching her ulu, her knife.

"The sound of the door made her jump. She leaped toward it, but she had not taken three steps before the father was upon her. Not to restrain her, but to help her free herself of the evil that was oppressing her within. Her skin turned even darker all over; her body was hot. Alerted by her cries, men—neighbors—rushed to the igloo.

"The unfortunate woman, who was foaming at the mouth, broke free—her strength had increased tenfold—and in spite of the cold and although she was wearing hardly any clothes, she ran off toward the ice pack, shouting 'ajaja!' She held her knife in one hand and, never stopping, with the other she snatched up everything that looked solid to her—pebbles, pieces of wood, and so on. If she felt the men getting too close, she hurled everything at them over her shoulder. Whenever she saw dogs' droppings she sniffed them, rubbed them on her face, and then devoured them greedily. The men chased her as far as an iceberg that lay on the way to Tuluriaq. She tried to hoist herself up the side, but she wasn't wearing the right shoes and she slid back. She finally caught at a spur and managed to sit astride a ridge of ice.

From there she cursed the men gathered below. One last time she managed to break away. Running over ice that the wind had broken up, she jumped from one floe to another, turning aggressively toward her pursuers and defying them.

"It was a terrible situation. Time and again she almost fell into the water. Luckily, her strength suddenly began to fail. When the Inuit caught up with her at last, they were quite far from the encampment. The woman began to ajaja again.

"They tied her to a sledge and hauled her back to a warm igloo. Her face was pale, her pupils yellow, and her skin was now uncongested and cold. Quite soon she lost consciousness and sank into a deep peaceful sleep. When she awoke much later—normal and fit—she remembered nothing of her experience."

Cases of hysteria occurred primarily among women, the Eskimo explained. But such serious attacks were no longer seen. "And these fits of perlerorneq never killed anyone, as far as I know."

Despite these precise details, the story, which reminded me of cases of amok in Malaysia, struck me as going beyond the bounds of credibility. However, I was less surprised when I heard similar stories a few weeks later and learned what had happened, for example, to Rasmussen.

During Rasmussen's second expedition, in 1907, which took place at the beginning of winter, he nearly fell victim to perlerorneq. He was writing at his table when he heard shrill cries outside. He went at once to his window; according to custom—and this was still the case in 1950 in Neqi and Qeqertaq —the "pane" was a stretched bladder membrane in the center of which there was a small hole enabling one to see what was happening outside. As he put his eye to the hole, a knife ripped through the window. Rasmussen was slightly wounded. Wiping his face, he retreated to a corner of the room. Then from outside stones began raining in on him. Some Eskimos came on the run, but, as in the story just related, it was impossible to catch the seizure victim. On the advice of friends, Rasmussen left his house, but the possessed man still would not relinquish his prey, and he chased the explorer toward the ice field. It was a moonless night. Rasmussen could not run because he was hindered by his boots, which he had not had time to lace properly. With each step, he lost his footing. Luckily, the hysteric began to run out of breath and the Eskimos were finally able to nab him.

Eager for precise details, I went to Imina for further information.

"Sauninnguaq, a woman who lives with two men in Nunatarssuak, is still subject to perlerorneq," he told me. "You will see her one day, but now she is isolated for other reasons. All young adults are more or less susceptible to perlerorneq, women more than men. Never children or old people. You see perlerorneq in all seasons, but most often in autumn and winter." As he spoke, Imina stood watch by the door so that no one would disturb us; he did not like telling me these stories in front of any and every body.

According to Imina, perlerorneq is brought on by what he called the "weight of life." When the adolescent begins to think about life and what lies ahead of him, he explodes. "A rising of the sap, of young blood nourished by qajoq soup and the blood of walruses, seals, and whales, that's perlerorneq," he told me. "Sadness takes hold of you. Then it's enough for a visitor to attack you with an ill-chosen word or a sidelong glance, and perlerorneq begins. At first, you are agitated. You sing, you start to tear your clothes. The perlerorneq tries to get out at any price into the open, to breathe, to shout at the top of his lungs, to unburden his heart—but without being judged by the village, which is watching him, for being perlerorneq, beside himself, he cannot be judged. Perlerorneq is to be sick of life."

In Illulik, to the north of Foxe Basin, in the eastern Canadian Arctic, numerous similar cases were recounted to me. Aggiaq told me that his mother had often been subject to such attacks. "Everyone would be sitting on the illeq. My mother would begin to breathe heavily, her eyes would bulge and become incandescent," he explained. "Then she would get up, go toward the katak, and start striking out at the falling snow with her fists. She used to crouch down and breathe like the wind: *pffffffff*. . . . People watching from the illeq were terrified. She would run out onto the ice field half-naked, shouting at the top of her voice."

An hour would pass, he added, before fatigue got the best of her.

In Rankin, on Hudson Bay, a priest named Didier explained to me that the "hysterics" seemed to be suffering from tightness of the chest. He did not consider them "possessed," and would offer them a bromide, which they took with ill grace. "Why are you giving me that?" one woman asked him. "I'm not really sick. . . . There's too much energy in me. It has to get out. We Inuit know that very well. It does good to let it out. The whites don't understand anything about the Inuit, that's for sure."

Perlerorneq (Peary called it *piblockto*) can, for other reasons, also affect dogs, which then are called *pillerorput*. My dogs were not affected by piblockto, some of whose symptoms resemble rabies, during my stay. Thank God! For it is an endemic sickness that manifests itself at unpredictable times and can cause great losses among the teams. The American explorer Elisha Kent Kane, whose dogs suffered from it, has given an admirable description of this illness. Canine piblockto resembles human hysteria in only some respects. Men do not die from it; it is fatal only to animals. A dog afflicted by pillerorput barks continuously and, according to Kane, groans, yelps, and walks zigzag, as if chased by a demon or an inner affliction; his bloodshot eyes stare unseeingly ahead; he foams at the mouth, shakes his head, and presently falls prostrate, his jaw gaping. According to the American explorer and author Donald Baxter MacMillan, who knew what he was talking about, the dog needs to be petted to help him calm down a little. In April 1967, near Savigssivik, I saw foxes run around in circles until sometimes they dropped dead in their tracks from exhaustion.

Trip to
the South

The sea froze over; a rumor circulated through the village: "They're leaving."
With the first freeze in November, four sledges from Siorapaluk were preparing to go to Kangerluarsuk, thirty miles to the southeast. This three-igloo
hamlet was rich in salmon and shark's meat. Inuterssuaq, the tiny encampment's best hunter, was all the more willing to share his reserves because his
wife was Imina's sister and here in Siorapaluk food was scarce. Oil lamps were
now burning weakly. In the various semidark houses—Olipaluk's, Sakaeunnguaq's, and Aqattaq's—everyone was shivering. At my place, too! There was
no fat, no meat, and the Eskimos were beginning to be hungry. Several had
already eaten boiled fox. There was no tobacco, either. No one had any money
left. X kept coming to see me all the time, I noticed—and then, one day, he
stalled more than an hour until finally he told me what was on his mind: he
would offer me his wife in exchange for ten Gauloise cigarettes.

The ice field was still too hazardous, too thin, for hunting seals, and kayaks
were now useless in the water full of floating ice. Few partridges were to be
found on the plateau. The Eskimos had been so improvident as to put aside
only one or two *kiviaqs*—guillemots left to rot under stones—which they preferred to keep for the hard month of February. The traditional solidarity
among the villagers in sharing supplies would have to come into play—and it
did. Already, the people of Kangerluarsuk were fishing for the oily shark
beneath the ice. In December, the people of Siorapaluk would start hunting
walrus near Neqi. Constant exchanges would ensue.

One day, the activity in front of my cabin accelerated. I learned that the
plan was for a group of scouts to leave that night. I immediately resolved to
join them. Because I could not afford to pay a guide, I would simply have to
follow them. And because I did not ask for help, I knew that, according to
custom, I should expect none. November is a month of unbroken night, weakly
lighted when there is a moon. "There'll be bad weather for sure," Olipaluk
remarked as he went by. The Inuit were in a hurry, and all the more so because
they had come to a group decision: they would have to get a head start on the
storm. And since the qallunaaq was foolhardy enough to risk following them,
they intended to give him a taste of what it was really like. This is the Eskimo
style of "education."

Early that November, the ice was twelve to fifteen inches thick. Being soft
underneath, it sagged; over a broad expanse, it gave way treacherously. The
ice belt near the headlands and in the straits was even thinner and more
fissured because the waves and currents constantly nibbled at it and wore it
away. The cold was not yet sharp enough for these part-fresh, part-salt waters
to freeze deep.[24]

I looked over my nine motley dogs: their coats were, variously, black and white; brown; gray and white; and reddish. I checked their harnesses and assembled my pack. I put on my hunting clothes: deerskin *qulitsaq;* bearskin pants *(nanu),* bearskin boots (kamiks); and sealskin gloves *(aaqqatit),* with the fur on the inside. I lugged the sledge equipment outside. A sealskin was laid on the floor of the sledge, fur facing up. To the front, for me to sit on, a good, warm dogskin, and a duffel bag that I could lean my elbow on and that held the things I would need most often. Also in the front, two reindeer skins and a box to protect the Primus and shield it from the wind when in use. In the back of the sledge, I put a jerrycan of oil and a few provisions—some tea and five ribs of old frozen walrus meat. On top of this small package and within reach, a rifle.

It was nine o'clock in the evening. I mustn't delay any longer. The first sledges were already on their way. I set out in the dark behind the last straggler. It was not an easy departure, what with Olipaluk and Bertsie watching me uneasily. Siorapaluk was separated from the shore by low ruiniform walls formed by a jumble of hummocks.* Once past these, you had to cross, head on, a wide, treacherous crevasse chewed out by the tides. Beyond lay the ice field.

The fjord can be crossed in two hours. Once I had skirted Cape Kangek, the best thing for me to do next would be to enter MacCormick Fjord and follow it to the end, where I would come upon a wide snowy valley and cross a short glacial spit which linked the central ice cap with the Qaanaaq Peninsula. At the foot of a steep slope, I would come to a third fjord, at the edge of which would be Kangerluarsuk.

So, first would be Kangek, then the fjord, then a *kuuk* (torrent), the *sermek* (glacier), the glacial gorge, and finally the last fjord. That night, along the way, I went over this itinerary, which the Eskimos had hastily outlined for me. The dogs were moving at a good pace, following the double track left in the snow by the four sledges that had gone before me. I listened contentedly to the steady crunch of the steel runners. The sledge, its wood frame secured by loose-fitting leather ties, jounced and labored over bumps and holes. An easy trip; I was relaxing a bit when suddenly there was a long, piercing howl, and the sledge tipped halfway over. The dogs braced themselves, pulled ahead, and the obstacle was behind us. I had not seen a large hummock, and the sledge had run head on into it. The dogs were eager to catch up with their mates, and they stepped up the pace. Now the silence seemed muffled; was the crunch—cr-i-i-i-i—fading away? We had come upon a wind-blown snowdrift. Tails up, the dogs plunged into it, the snow reaching to their breast straps. After a five-minute struggle, we were clear of the worst. I was able to make out details better in the dim light of the quarter moon. The trail of droppings from the dogs ahead—ink-black turds and light-brown stains—

---

*Irregularly jagged accumulations of ice that seem pushed up from the ice field by pressure. Depending on the barometer and the wind direction, hummocks can form real barriers for hundreds of yards.

made the path seem familiar. Each lump, slightly irregular in shape, gleamed with flecks of gold. My dogs, whom I was handling badly, saw the droppings as so many opportunities to scatter, change places and thereby tangle the traces, sniff, and sometimes stop for a second or two to pee also. I paid scant attention to this; time passed, and I was losing considerable ground. Was it because of the freedom I felt on this first trip? I was now far behind the group. I whipped my team. I was so busy spurring on this dog and then that one with my whip that I did not notice a warm wind coming from the east. I should have been on my guard: streaks of snow on the ice were racing straight ahead, then zigzagging, and they should have warned me. But how can you learn everything in a few months? Ten minutes later, the storm broke. Snow was falling on all sides and the warm wind was bellowing like an organ. Before and behind me all tracks were obliterated, and my tactic of effortlessly following the Eskimos became useless. I could no longer see even my own team, but the dogs were still valiantly pulling ahead. The foehn drove the temperature up several degrees. Peering through wet eyelashes at the trembling wall of snow, I glimpsed a whirling horizon of mad flakes being sucked up only to be blown down again. Without guidance, the dogs' pace became hesitant.

Then the lead dog lost the trail. During a break in the snowfall, I saw him turn back toward me, looking for a signal, a direction. But to the east, north, and south there was nothing but sticky whiteness. How was I to get my bearings! At these latitudes and in such circumstances, a compass is of no help. The wind, I thought, was coming from the east—the foehn can come only from the inland ice cap—but it had no real direction. It was blowing from all sides at once, and the snow was too light to preserve any striae. My disoriented dogs came to a halt, and I no longer heard the familiar crunch of the runners. The muffled, numbing silence was broken by blasts of wind. It snowed and it snowed. The air was suffocating. My skin felt heavy, thick. I grew drowsy. Five minutes, ten minutes—I'm not sure how much time went by. Then I got hold of myself and raised my head, trying to avoid the snow that was sifting under my hood. As I peered, blinking, through the milky, flaky wall of randomly whirling snowflakes, I was trying to make out against the horizon the dark, towering cliff of Kangek—the last landmark that could spare me from getting lost far from the Greenland shore—in Canada, on Baffin Island, three hundred miles away.

The dogs had sensed my uncertainty. I might almost say that they read my thoughts. They had stopped, lain down, and curled their tails over their heads for protection. I kept my head protected too, turned my back to the wind, and as I hacked away at one of my four walrus ribs, I strove to think like an Eskimo. I thought. . . . Most important, don't run. For when I stopped the sweat would congeal and encase my body in ice. Crazy things came to mind. I recalled a conversation about the tragic story of two Danish radio operators who were caught in a storm on the east coast of Greenland, a few hundred yards from their cabin. They lay down under the slats of their sledge for fear of being eaten by their own dogs. After three days of blizzard, a fox hunter found them dead, frozen fast to each other.

Closing one eye, I looked toward the horizon. The storm was redoubling in force and the wind was turning cold. Already, all melted snow was refreezing. The swirling wind swept down in violent blasts and the ice field shook from the motion of the waves beneath it. Would it sunder? That happens. Suddenly . . . yes, over there . . . for a mere instant, far, far to the left, there was a spark! An Eskimo, as I learned later, had been lighting his pipe. Now I had my bearings. I roused the dogs and led them on by clearing a path in front of them. "Qaa! . . . Qorfa! . . ." They had seen the flash, too. They were excited and eagerly worked their way through the snow. Their sense of smell kept them heading in the right direction. Fifteen minutes later, I was shaking the hand of this heaven-sent pipe smoker. We exchanged only a few words. The Eskimos had already pushed on, after warming themselves with a meal of frozen walrus they had found in a stone cache, and he was the last of the group to set out. During the next three stops in the eighteen-hour journey—one on the ice field, one at the foot and one at the top of the glacier—it was pretty much the same story. When I arrived the four hunters did not so much as glance at me, and promptly moved on. They even quickened their pace for fear the bad weather would get worse. Nor were they displeased to break "the white man" in my person. What's more—one of them explained this to me several years later—they wanted to give me to understand unequivocally that I should expect nothing from them. (The Eskimo considers himself bound to the white man's fate only when he is hired for an expedition and is paid. Except on my long trips, such an arrangement was not possible in my case, for lack of funds.)

Here any man, whether qallunaaq or Inuk, must be able to deal with all sorts of situations: he must be able to kill, to cut up a carcass, to sew, to find his bearings at night and in fog and storms, and to struggle unremittingly against his fear and exhaustion. The worst adversity—and who here has not met with it several times in his life?—must be met with a defiant laugh or, at the very least, with a show of indifference. Tacitly, through the example of a man's being constantly forced to surpass himself, these rules, which inhere in the hearts of even the least among them, were harshly taught me every day; the men were concerned that I watch them not with my eyes but with my hands. And the pitiless chorus of the women and the young—who notice everything, repeat everything, and pass judgment on everything—sanctioned the wordless initiation that escaped no one's attention.

It was as an apprentice hunter that, like a thief, I came into this proud, closed society to attend my first classes in anthropology. Anthropology? The Eskimos used to smile.

"You want to learn about us . . . in a year. . . . We who have centuries behind us. . . . Keep trying! . . . Inuusuppoq! Presumptuous young fellow!"

My sledge was gliding along smoothly and I let my mind wander. Half-seated up front, my feet tucked under me, ready to jump down and run, I thought about the past weeks, about this man, that woman, a few friendships, and about the man I was becoming in this world where environment is sovereign. What would be left of the bantering Frenchman? But the trail demanded my attention again, and I concentrated on my dogs. What gallant creatures! They are so closely allied to the Eskimo that they share with him a distinctive characteristic found in no other group of the human race: a heavy mesial bone in the skull.

As I thought about this singular physical kinship, I observed my dogs even more carefully. They were spread out like a fan, the lead dog in the middle and slightly to the fore. Their paws arched from the effort of pulling the sledge. Their broad tongues hung, red and rough, from their jaws. In one motion, they would casually lap up fresh snow. Why do they pull so hard? Probably because the implacable Eskimo keeps them near starvation. In this way, the Eskimo reasons, they will always be fired by the illusory hope of finally being fed at the end of the day's trek and therefore they will exert themselves to cover the distance as fast as possible. . . . Each dog has his own trace, which is fastened above the spine to the *anu* or breast strap. Is it too loose, will it drag? With a flick of his whip, the driver strikes a few sensitive spots: the dog's legs, the tips of his ears, his sides, or his nose. A good driver can strike within one-sixteenth of a square inch of what he aims at; a patch of missing hair bears witness to that accuracy. The Eskimo smiles when he hears a yelp of pain: the dog has acknowledged the blow and is already pulling harder. Out of fear, some dogs will plunge ahead violently, sensing that a blow is about to fall on them. Puffing like a small steam engine, one or another dog will turn his frosted muzzle for an instant and blink his slanting, black-ringed eyes connivingly: he is watching for a sign of approval from the Eskimo. "Am I not—and have I not always been—with you?" Reassured by a word or a glance, the dog blinks again and forges happily ahead, his ears pointed forward, rubbing against the female as he passes, and, if the reins slacken at all, slyly mounting her as he runs. Satisfied, the dog lopes back to his proper place, and, as if to thank the man for his complicity, he gives a good hard pull on the harness.

When you are on the sledge behind the dogs, nothing they do escapes you: the romances, the friendships they form in the course of a day. The raised tail reveals their most intimate secrets. The female has her menstrual period; this dog has bowel trouble; another reminds you every time you start out that he is suffering from a disagreeable flatulence. And their droppings! You see nothing else! Their dung is their message. During the first half hour of a trip, the scenario is always the same. The dogs rear up on their hind legs, which get tangled in the reins of the others. One of them, whining and lifting his back legs as if he were galloping, tries to dung. But the feces are too dry and do not come out easily; just a black fiber extrudes from his anus, which spasmodically expands his pinkish-gray sphincter. A lash from the driver's sadistic whip makes his initial desire pass for the moment. But then the dog braces himself again, growling softly, afraid of being noticed. The long dry turd scrapes the membrane that is so delicate just at that place. He yelps. For an instant he slows down and moves slightly to the left. Nothing doing: the turd does not pass. He starts to limp, he leans to one side as he runs, hoping this will be of some help. Nothing works. Now he must find out how the man will react. . . . He waddles along, to make sure the man is not watching and will not notice him when the right moment comes. Very likely, in his mind he thinks that the man's mind is on other things. Taking his time now, he boldly moves apart from the team and, pushing with all his might, lets himself be dragged along, his hind legs tangled up in his own reins. He pushes and pushes. . . . The sledge is almost on top of him! No matter. The dog is concentrating entirely on his gut. The black fiber emerges slowly. Liquid excrement follows, and then a blackish diarrhetic torrent spurts forth. "Qujanaq! So much the better!" And the Eskimo, who has been watching the whole scene closely, lashes the animal's rear end, from testicles to fibrous anus. With another yelp of pain, the animal resumes his place, whining plaintively as the Eskimo jeers: "Seqajuk! Lazy good-for-nothing!" The team sides with the man. Not one of these low vassals comes to the aid of a comrade who had trouble defecating.

The hours passed. We were approaching the mouth of the fjord. The shelf was becoming a tiered bank of ice and looked like an ancient ruin. I was about to whip the team when Alineq—so appropriately named the Ugly One, the dog I had had to discipline so harshly—let his slack trace get snagged on an outcropping of ice. He pulled, but the spur held. The team, either indifferent or clumsy, ran straight on. The sledge was about to crush Alineq. There was no time for me to run to release him. But at the last moment, with a supreme effort, the dog managed to wrench free because I kicked the sledge into a skid so that it swerved into the ice spur and smashed it. Alineq was saved, and trotted happily back to his place. But I might very well have broken the tip of the sledge. I therefore intervened in Eskimo fashion. I had been shown often enough what to do. I stopped the team and clubbed the offender. Grasping the top of the harness firmly, I yanked Alineq up into the air, so that his body arched and his legs hung limp. I rained blows on his head and back until I nearly snapped the whip handle. Alineq, the individualist, the rebel, could only huddle against the naalagaq, the leader. He limped for several hours. The other dogs, who had watched with intense interest and had approved my action —because Alineq had really made trouble for them—now pulled better than ever. If coddled, Eskimo dogs do not perform well. The team is, above all, a tool that must not fail you. A man may pay with his life for forgetting this. Actually, the Eskimo treats his dogs in the same way he treats himself. The more I got to know them, the more clearly I saw that the Eskimos' way of life is very similar to their teams' way of life. One lives, one struggles, one dies. If there is nothing to eat, you lie down and wait. Emotional involvements are brief. Trouble always lies in the offing: to forget that for one moment is to accept it, to allow it to take you over. Tomorrow, of course, spells hope, but it is also the unknown. Nothing here below is ever to be counted on; everything is precarious.

We were at the upper reaches of the MacCormick Fjord. I was still very far
behind. I entered a valley of snow and followed it for several miles alone.
Moving quite quickly now, I reached the foot of the glacial spit just as the
Eskimos were about to climb it. In spite of the moonlight, one could see hardly
anything. Too many clouds. But I could still see well enough to imitate the
Eskimos. Like them, I unharnessed my dogs, unloaded the sledge, turned it
over, and with emery paper polished the runners, which had been pitted by
stones in the valley where the snow was not deep enough. The job took twenty
minutes, and it made me sweat. They took off again; I took off again. The angle
of glacial slope was steep—about twenty-seven degrees. The dogs clawed their
way up the ice. I had to push the sledge, run ahead to urge on the team, run
back to correct our direction by grasping the napariaq, and keep my companions in sight. My boots would slip, and the dogs would hesitate. The glacier
had been deeply furrowed over the last summer by torrents of melted ice. Now
snow had gathered only in these gullies. I had to follow them one after another,
climbing like an insect, glued to the wall of the glacier. I watched the terrain
closely: there were many gray-green veins of ice intersected by paths of black;
an occasional snowdrift. Almost smashing my foot against the ice to keep from
slipping, I negotiated the slope, at each step pushing on the back of the sledge
with my knee to steer it away from snow furrows where the runners would stick
and freeze. At the exact moment I pushed hardest, I whipped the dogs. They
would give a vigorous tug skillfully coordinated by a yank from the naalagaq.
Thus they paid out the friendly feelings I had aroused in them during earlier
halts by speaking to them, encouraging them, and sharing my thoughts. The
dogs are very sensitive to this, especially the lead. You can tell from the way
they wag their tails. At such moments, man and dogs are absolutely one.

The higher we climbed, the more intense the cold became. The northeast

Sledge in the night. (*From French magazine* Le tour du monde, *1878*)

wind was blowing at us from the side. I was working so hard, however, that I didn't notice. Our pace quickened. The dogs seemed to be drawn forward by the summit. Suddenly, I collided with a dark mass and found myself face-to-face with . . . a man on his way north, someone I will never in my whole life forget. It was Kutsikitsoq, the son of Uutaaq, from Qinnissut, the village beyond Kangerluarsuk. Standing beside his sledge and sixteen dogs like an ancient monarch, whip in hand, he challenged me. "Ah-ha! Here he is, the poor qallunaaq. Let me have a look at this little fellow everyone is talking about and whom I'm about to eat alive!"

We exchanged a few words, and with a flourish I took off for the south. I was alone again, now facing the task of going down the uneven half-mile slope of the crevassed glacier. My efforts now were exactly the opposite of what they had been before: I had to hold the sledge back as it headed down an increasingly steep slope toward the frozen sea. I fastened heavy seal straps under the front runners; I shifted the dogs to the rear. The middle rein now ran from front to back, floating between my feet, with the risk that if I braked abruptly the dogs might be caught by these straps coiling into knots. I had to hang on to the napariaq and brake the sledge by bending my whole body backward and letting myself slide along on the heels of my boots; the dogs, kept to the rear by the constant snapping of the whip before their eyes, also were braking the sledge just by dint of their weight. But sometimes they gave out and tumbled. I had to jump free of their traces and legs, guide the sledge by the napariaq in order to divert it from the crevasse toward which it seemed to be heading, brace myself again with my heels, and continually zigzag the sledge through a rough patch so that it would not slip sideways. Our speed increased. I had to watch out: not all the summer crevasses here were filled with snow, it seemed, and we could easily be swallowed up. Above all, I must not miss the pass that had been described to me at Siorapaluk, or I risked ending up at a sixty-foot cliff and, in the dark, crashing over it and breaking my back. All these actions had to be performed while moving at a speed of about four miles per hour over a dark sheet of ice, the features of which I could not see until I was upon them.

It was thanks more to chance than to skill that I did find the pass and the ice field. The ice field! After so many dangers, the frozen sea seemed like a royal highroad. However, although the dogs trotted contentedly over the firm, flat ice, the cold was biting into my eyebrows and nose. This always happens in the Arctic after great physical exertion: your face cooks. With their gift of invention, the Eskimos have devised sealskin mittens that allow you to curl your fingers now and then to stimulate circulation. With my warmed hand I slapped my face for a few seconds. My left big toe was becoming very sensitive to frostbite. . . .

To run behind the sledge, then to speed along with it at about three miles an hour to warm up; better, to run in front of the dogs to encourage them: sixty seconds' worth of racing, while taking care not to let your lungs freeze in the icy air. Another forty seconds behind the sledge, holding on to the napariaq;

a ten-second sprint to get ahead of the sledge and then to jump on from the side, making sure not to miss it, for the solitary traveler risks seeing his archaic vehicle vanish into the night. The dogs are famished and race on toward some unknown prey or village. There is no question of catching up with the dogs on a straightaway. At such temperatures and with such equipment, a man can't run for long.

So I jumped, shouted, whipped. . . . Finally, after four more arduous hours, I saw a single beacon light shining to the right of my route. This was how Inuterssuaq, the camp's hunter, had told me I would recognize Kangerluarsuk, with its three igloos. The four hunters from Siorapaluk had arrived a good three hours before me. The igloo I went into was dark and dirty. The men were eating kiviaq, precious, rotting kiviaq, and their mouths were covered with blood and feathers. Not one man looked up. Not one said a word about the trip. They belched, they cracked bones, they bolstered one another's spirits. "The storm? Bah! Nothing to speak of. This great meat! . . . I could go on eating it forever. . . . Ah! This was the qallunaaq's baptism! He got here after all. Who would ever have believed it! We leave tomorrow for Qeqertaq! Twenty-five miles to the east. Five igloos. Pissortut Inuit! Aren't we men!"

It was not until twenty-two years later—in 1972—that I spoke with Inuterssuaq about that blessed beacon. A hunting expedition we went on together for white whale gave me the opportunity. To have mentioned it before would have been in bad taste.

The journey from Kangerluarsuk to Qeqertaq taught me still more. To make better time, I rode on Iggianguaq's sledge. We had doubled the strength of his team by adding my dogs so that we could go faster. Everything went well until I jumped off the sledge to run behind the napariaq and warm myself up. I realized that it would take an enormous effort for me to run ahead of the sledge in order to jump on and take my seat again. No sooner had I made a move than Iggianguaq, who sensed I was behind him, whipped the dogs to make it all the more difficult for me. The stupidest thing would have been for me to get on my high horse and demand a man-to-man explanation. Better to laugh it off, to "take it" as the Eskimos do—grit my teeth and wait for a chance to get even with him for his rather tedious joke. But I was so tense and so enormously concerned not to lose face that when I stepped to the side for a moment to pee while the tired dogs were walking slowly, I was gripped by anxiety and then panic. My fingers were so numb that I couldn't close my fly (a flap that folded in the front of my bearskin trousers). With the temperature at $-20°C$ ($-4°F$), would I have to stand there abjectly and call after the hunter? The group commiseration and irony sure to ensue would ruin my reputation for good. I got hold of myself and by patiently turning the bone buttons one by one, this way and that, with my stiff fingers, I managed to fasten them. Praise be to heaven! I did it! And the Eskimo jokester did stop at a moraine and wait for me. There are days in the Eskimo world when life seems to be made up of nothing but such tiny triumphs.

The education I was receiving was unusually effective: in a very short time I was able to find my way alone at night and in fog. On the return trip from Kangerluarsuk to Siorapaluk, I was neither preceded nor accompanied by the Eskimo hunters. I was entirely alone on the ice field except for my dear companions, the dogs, and I passed the test.

Living in our latitudes, we find it hard to imagine that, at the seventy-eighth parallel, the Eskimos not only endure temperatures and storms of extreme severity but also accommodate themselves to a pattern of daylight very different from the one we are familiar with, since for them four months of unbroken Polar night are followed by eight months of unbroken Polar day.

Because I was deeply absorbed in becoming gradually integrated into Eskimo life and its techniques (feeding and driving my dogs, etc.) and in carrying out my winter project (the genealogical and socioeconomic studies of the entire group), I insensibly adapted to the Arctic climate without too much discomfort. What I did mind was not to be governed by the daily alternation of day and night. At what hour do you get up during an endless night? How do you find your way in the dark and, generally, in fog to boot? These are a few of the questions that must occur to the reader who has never been in the Arctic.

The Polar night should not be visualized as being pitch black, which it never is. Either it is lighted by the moon and stars—what we would call a clear night—or the moon and stars are hidden by clouds but still provide some kind of light. The Eskimos are obliged to hunt in all kinds of weather, and I shared that experience in that I used to follow them with my own sledge and observe them during all their activities. They are able to find their bearings, no matter how dark it is, by using the snow as a reflector. Also, after mid-January, far away to the south at the far reaches of the horizon, a pale, sometimes reddish, solar halo appears; it emerges from behind the ice field in the southern latitudes and transforms the darkness into an eerie twilight. Both good and evil spirits delight in this glow, and legends are born of it.

During a clear or total night, the ice is a bluish gray spotted with grayish white; coastal spurs loom in the distance, shadowy and hostile. Icebergs are immobilized in the frozen sea and become friendly dark masses that serve as landmarks. When men move about, they are silhouettes darker than the night itself, and they seem to sense each other's presence rather than actually to see one another. I very quickly became able to see in the dark, but, of course, my night vision will never be as good as that of an Eskimo, which is prodigious. One night early in January, on the big slope at Innartalik, I saw Iggianguaq shoot at a white hare from fifteen hundred feet and kill him outright, although I could not even make out the animal.

During the four months of the Polar night—fortunately, they are not the coldest months of the long winter—this group of nomads and individualists is brought closer together; relationships become warmer. Yet the group is turned in upon itself, as it were. Even though the ice field has formed and people exchange visits during this period, their moving around does not loosen the ties among members of the group but rather holds them, binds them together more closely. During the time I traveled about from November to March, from village to village, and even within a village, I sensed an oppression; it was as if an invisible circle, larger than family or village, a circle enclosing the entire group of people in their ten hamlets, was tightening around us. It was like one of Solzhenitsyn's circles. A reaction to this burdensome closeness is the liberating perlerorneq, the seasonal hysteria.

As I mentioned earlier, even dogs suffer from this oppression. In fact, it is especially during the winter that, unpredictably (or sometimes when strange teams arrive), they sit on their haunches, tilt their triangular heads toward the moon, half-close their eyes, and, after one dog has given an exploratory cry, they howl in chorus. It is a long, hoarse yowl that starts deep in the throat and is modulated over a long interval as the huddled dogs despairingly launch their appeal to some unknown propitiatory force. The cry lasts three or four minutes, and stops all of a sudden. Some blunderer may hazard a solitary fresh call, but instantly recognizes his mistake and falls silent.

In the course of a week, the collective cry is repeated irregularly. I noticed that dogs trained for hunting did not howl when we were camping on the ice field.

In 1950, the Eskimos of Siorapaluk owned few alarm clocks and fewer wristwatches. But by observing the movements of the moon and stars, they kept an accurate enough idea of time never to make a mistake about the only fixed schedules they were required—by the whites, of course—to observe: the days and hours when the store was open, their children's school schedule, and the time of the Sunday church services.

By contrast to the night, the Polar day brings an extraordinary liberation. One never stops discovering the limitless space, observing colors, watching the vital forces of nature explode. It is a happy, sunny time that is vitalized by the free movement of the sea, the sound of the waves, the ceaseless coming and going of birds. It is the time when for twenty-four hours a day, day after day, the repressed individualistic instinct can express itself. The prohibitions of the night are lifted. Sexual life is quickened by the light and made freer thanks to the mobility of tent camps—they are set up apart from the igloos, which are under the constant surveillance of child-spies and visitors. It is at once the season for hunting and the season for love. In his passion for the former, the Eskimo often forgets the latter, and he usually goes off to hunt bear, leaving his wife behind. I have often noticed that to hunt and kill bear gives him a gratification (sexual?) as great as that when he makes love to his wife.

The same schedule is kept winter and summer—at least this was so in 1950. I was unable to find out whether this had been the case in, say, 1900, or earlier. The only difference I noticed was that everyone got up later in winter—between one and three in the afternoon.

It should be made clear, however, that the Eskimo's notions of a "sched-

How in earlier days the Thule Eskimos got water. They used warm stones to melt snow, or else hung a sealskin sack filled with packed snow from the top of the igloo (heat rises); hour by hour, the melting snow dripped through a hole in the bottom of the sack. Stone jugs were very rare. The Thule Eskimos—unlike those of southwestern Alaska—did not develop the art of pottery, although clay is abundant in the area. On their travels, the hunters always carried with them their oil lamp, wicks, fat, and flint for lighting it. They obtained water by placing the lamp near the overhangs of icebergs exposed to the sun. When meat could be boiled—if there was enough fat for the lamp—it was put in rectangular pots cut and shaped out of soapstone, which were hung above the oil lamp. (*From Kane,* Arctic Explorations)

ule" are very hazy. Actually, there are three schedules. First, which I have just described, the one for the village's daily life. Second, there is the hunter's schedule, which depends on the wind, the temperature, and the weather in general.* Finally, there is the schedule of the white man.

Unquestionably, the annual alternation of light—the long periods of night and the day "without frontier" helps account for the unpredictability of the Eskimo and the richness of his sensations.

Eskimo Food

As a visitor, I was often offered kiviaq. It would have been improper to refuse; it is the choice dish, reserved for guests. My neighbors watched as I applied

*In May, for example, you travel when the sun is low, because the frozen snow helps the sledge to slide; from November to January, the determining factors are the moon, the clouds, the hunter's mood . . . and the game. The hunting schedule completely upsets that of the village. The most important rule, of course, is to get up when a visitor enters the igloo and not to go to sleep until news has been exchanged and you have eaten together, no matter what the hour.

myself to the job of eating. I pulled on a leg, and the carcass slipped free of the skin and feathers. The bird was well rotted indeed. Flesh, heart, coagulated blood, and fat virtually ran into my hand. I let the meat melt slowly in my mouth.

Guillemots, out of which kiviaq is made, have always been an important source of food in the Eskimo economy. During periods of extreme hardship in the seventeenth and eighteenth centuries, at the time of the Dorset culture, the group was saved by catching these birds.

In 1950, a hunter netted an average of five hundred birds a day. He did not pluck or clean them, but simply stuffed them into bags made of sealskin from which half the fat had been scraped; he stored these bags under stones, where the sun could not reach them. The fat melted slowly in the heat, and as the birds' flesh rotted it was bathed in fat. A large kiviaq (the word applies to the cache as well as to the birds it contains) contained five hundred birds, a small one two hundred and fifty. After it had had time to decompose and ferment slowly, the whole bird, feathers and all, was served up as an exquisite dish. Every house stunk with a fetid smell like that of overripe cheese.

Kiviaq has definite dietary merits. The Eskimo eats the bird's flesh and innards, leaving aside only the beak, feathers, and feet. He carefully licks all the bones, then breaks the smallest ones between his teeth and sucks them thoroughly.

In 1850, ten kiviaqs were needed to feed a family for four to five months. In 1950, at most only two or three kiviaqs per family were required because most food now came from hunting seal and walrus with rifles and from the store (coffee, tea, sugar, oatmeal). February and March continued to be hardship months, when the very poor ate nothing but kiviaq for weeks on end. In these straitened times my neighbors would eat four to six of these birds every day. Kiviaq was never traded for meat, a dog, or ammunition. Kiviaq was eaten *together*. The hunter invited you to eat *his* kiviaq with his family.

There were three methods of keeping these birds: the most common (called *kiviaq*) was, as described above, to put the birds in a sealskin bag together with the fat and place the container under stones; the second method (*krigneq*) was to put the birds directly under a stone cairn; and the third (*sioraga*) was to put them directly in sand.

Any meat that has turned is called *igunaq* by the Eskimos; igunaq has always been an essential winter food. In these regions, both Eskimos and white men feel a great need for strong-smelling, tainted meat during the coldest

Bird net. (*From* Kane, Arctic Explorations)

months. The Eskimos had an unparalleled method for controlling the decomposition. The meat would rot more or less depending on the amount of air allowed in the stone cache. (Unfermented bird flesh was considered flavorless and without "character.") The birds dried beneath the rocks were exposed to the air depending on how they were piled on top of one another, and the arrangement was carefully calculated. (I should point out that the Eskimos took very quickly to pepper and mustard, and they made great use of those condiments when they could get hold of them.)

The Eskimos' favorite food was reindeer marrow.[25] Hunters were mad for it. In the spring, they ate nothing else for several days. They cleaned the bones almost reverently, cracked them with rocks or even their teeth, and sucked them clean. One could actually see the men put on weight. This nourishment was available only rarely and for a short time, however, because reindeer lived in few and faraway areas of Inglefield Land.

The basic food was seal and walrus meat, which was always eaten with a morsel of fat. Except for the liver and the fat, freshly cut-up seal and walrus meat, ergo not frozen, was always boiled before it was eaten. In winter four or five days were allowed to go by before the meat was frozen. According to the explorer Elisha Kane, in 1853–55 the Thule Eskimos each ate nine to eleven pounds of meat per day (according to his fellow explorer Isaac Hayes, it was thirteen to fifteen pounds) plus half a gallon of soup made of blood and water. The figures for meat surprise me. I can testify to the fact that in 1950–51 they ate four to seven pounds of meat (in other words, half as much), one-quarter of which was fat. Meals were frequent—a visitor was always an excuse for a meal—and lasted for varying lengths of time: people could sit over a meal for several hours. Given ample supplies, more meat and fat was eaten in the winter; it was not boiled for eating in the fall and winter. Some seals—those caught in the spring—were held in reserve under the snow and the rocks along the shores. One precaution was taken: the belly was pierced to let any gas escape. The meat had a very strong smell. Skinned or unskinned but with the

Reindeer hunt. When the reindeer looms up over the tundra, he seems to occupy it completely. Notice the relative smallness of the hunter. Drawing by Akitseq. Illulik, Canada, May 1961. (*Private collection*)

fat always intact, the seal could be kept under stones for one year at the most, frozen by the cold rising from the ground.

Fresh blood was collected and frozen. In winter, the Eskimos drank it while they chewed raw, frozen meat. When there was no blood in reserve, they drank fresh blood, but they boiled it first. The baby seal (*qeersoq*) yielded their favorite blood. After being boiled briefly, it was allowed to freeze and was then consumed with great gusto.

Every part of the adult seal was eaten except the skin, the anus, the water surrounding the lungs, any extra fat, the bones (though their marrow was eaten), and the flippers. Favorite parts were the meat; the liver; the eyes, which were usually given to the children to munch on; the layer of fat directly in contact with the skin, which was set aside for children and old people; the contents of the stomach; and the intestines, which they cleared of dung with their fingers. The intestine muscle was boiled, filled with fat, and eaten in small pieces about three-quarters of an inch long; the taste was like margarine.

I might say, in passing, that lice used to be a much sought-after food. In 1904, Arnaluk told Harald Moltke that there was no better food than lice. Also much relished was a preparation called *oruneq*. The base of this dish was partridge droppings. They were gathered in the winter as they lay frozen on the snow, mixed with seal fat, then beaten and heated up. When ready, oruneq smelled like a hen house. A dish more common in Thule, though oruneq was not totally unknown there, was narwhal fat and water, to which walrus brain was added to give body; the mixture was stirred briskly and then combined with digested grasses from the first stomach of a reindeer.

What the Eskimos liked best about the narwhal—they did not drink its blood—was its famous *mattak* or skin, which was eaten raw; the mattak was very effective in preventing scurvy.

Lastly, for two weeks in June, the Eskimos ate birds' eggs, either raw or boiled. Sometimes the egg was not very fresh and could not be swallowed raw. A hunter told Moltke once that that did not matter: "A little bird that hasn't been born yet can't taste worse than a bird that has been born." For two months in the summer, meals were enlivened by the addition of sea birds, whortleberries, and at least nine species of plant roots (*naassut*) that I know of. From time to time, they also ate three kinds of algae, one of which (*qimerluusaat*) is taken together with seal and walrus fat, as well as the mussels (*imaneq* and *qammajoq*) they gathered along the shore in August and ate raw. (So it is not entirely accurate to say that the Eskimos were exclusively carnivorous.)

It took the Polar Eskimos nearly four generations to get used to white men's food; at first, they found it inedible. In 1853–55, Hans Hendrick, a Greenlander and companion of Kane and Hayes, described the Eskimos repugnance for "white" food: "The Tuluks offered them something to eat, bread and beef and such like, with tea, but they did not relish them, they only tried some little bits. They said 'we cannot eat it' and added that they should like to have some hare-meat."

Eskimo souvenirs: Paper knife and bear sculpted by Kigutika (thirty years old), Thule, 1951; sledge, standing hunter, and harpooner sculpted by Pualuna (seventy-six years old), Siorapaluk, 1950; fork and knife with fish handle and small black leather bag by Martha and Jacob Geisler (thirty and forty years old), Greenlanders from Skansen, or Aumarutigssat (Disko).

Gradually, the Eskimos became used to the white man's staples and adopted them, often passionately, in this order: tobacco, sugar, tea, and coffee.

How the
First Men Were Born

A door. I pulled it open toward me and crawled on hands and knees through the low, narrow peat corridor that smelled of cold mildew. I came to a second door and this time pushed inward, raising my frost-whitened head, which had brushed against the passageway walls. I entered the brightness and intimacy of the igloo and hurried to sit down on the illeq, the ceiling being too low for me.

"Sainang, qallunaaq! Greetings, white man!"

Bertsie, Sakaeunnguaq's wife, stopped her work for a moment, glanced at me sidewise, gave a smile that revealed her worn-down teeth, and then resumed her task in silence: chewing, chewing skins, her daily chore.

I crouched beside Sakaeunnguaq in front of the Primus, which in emergencies was used to implement the seal-oil lamp. In 1950, about 25 percent of Eskimo houses in the Thule region—the poorest houses—were both heated and lighted by seal-oil lamps.[26] We stretched our fingers above the flame and began to feel warmer. As we leaned our dirty bearded faces over our "hearth," I followed the movements of the thick blue flame. It ran, danced, leaped, and coiled around the black remains of a match. Pressed against each other, we watched in childish suspense as this little piece of wood twisted and flickered in the fire.

"Cigarette?"

The Eskimo had pulled a precious Lucky Strike from his pocket. We settled down comfortably on the only platform in the igloo, built of stones and boards and covered with layered skins of seals, dogs, and bears. To my right, watching over the seal-oil lamp (when it got colder there would be two of them), Bertsie was now cutting up a fox. Her husband sat to my left. Far to the right and by the wall, as if in isolation, was the old father, Pualuna, bent double. In the middle of the room a young hunter who was passing through the encampment had just awakened. He was naked from the waist up, and held his bearskin pants, his nanu,[27] in one hand; he snuffled as he washed his face in a tub of ice that was slowly melting above the oil lamp. Only rarely do men and women wash more thoroughly. Often the water is icy, and I have seen Eskimos take a mouthful to warm it, and then gradually spit it out as they washed their hands and face. A hare's pelt serves as scrubber and towel.

In the old days, they used to wash their hair in urine.

The atmosphere in the igloo was one of patience and waiting. Each of us stared straight ahead, our elbows resting on our knees. The position is so common that the bearskin pants show the wear. After six or eight months, a long furrow—flattened fur, then bare skin—personalizes the upper front of a man's nanu.

The Eskimo will putter around while his mind is somewhere else. He waits, he hopes for something to happen that will pull him out of his monotonous idleness.

That night, Pualuna was the first to provide us with such a happening.

These primitive people have a well-known love of legends, and their fables express their deepest, most secret thoughts; they summon up the beginning of time, when men and animals talked to each other. The storyteller's face assumes an inward expression; his eyes are open, as if he were watching a scene unfold. His grave tone of voice, even his hesitations as he searches for some ancient knowledge, give the listener a strange sensation of "having lived through it before."

Pualuna moved closer to me. At first, his eyes were fixed on the ground and he hugged his knees as he began to speak in a low voice:

"Once upon a time, when the world had just begun to be, in Nuliuer-qaarfik, which was near Nunatarssuaq, there lived a man and his wife and their daughter, and they mightily wished the girl to have a husband, because the man wanted a son-in-law so he would not have to go out hunting alone. But the daughter wanted no part of this under any circumstances; she wanted no husband. . . .

" 'You don't want a man,' the father said. 'All right. . . . You see this dog. Take him. He's quite good enough for you.'

"Hardly had he spoken these words when a sort of man made of dogs' droppings in a gut cocoon entered the igloo. No sooner was he inside than he wanted to leave, for he feared the effect the warmth might have on him.

"Once he was outside, he howled, for he had smelled her strong scent.

"He wanted to get back inside, and he found a passageway. . . . With a single bound he leaped on the daughter, clutched her to him, ripped off her clothes, and covered her. . . .

"And the parents could do nothing.

"Step by step, the daughter pushed the man made of dogs' droppings outside, and the father managed to tie him up. . . . But soon he howled louder than before, snapped his ropes, and again he went in and again he clove to the girl.

"And the parents could do nothing. . . .

"Finally, the father had an idea. He filled a sealskin with very heavy stones, tied the man made of dogs' droppings to this skin as tightly as he could, and then took his daughter by kayak to a small island, Qimmiuuneqarfik, and left her there.

"The man made of dogs' droppings thereupon began to howl pitifully; he jerked his neck free and rushed with his sack full of stones to the shore:

" 'Sealskin, great sealskin, do you want to float?

" 'Ha! ha! ha!'

"When he had repeated these magic words twice, the skin began to float as if it were empty, and the man made of dogs' droppings stretched out on it. He crossed the water, rejoined the daughter, who was, as one might say, his woman, and he fed her. But alas, shortly after, he died of hunger and soon after that the poor girl gave birth to babies who were half man and half dog. . . . It was their grandfather who fed them. Every time he came, they were very hungry and ate all that he brought.

"'Qaa, qaa, qaa, qaa, qaa. . . . Eat, eat,' the mother said over and over, and she blinked her black eyes. 'Leave nothing for the old scoundrel. . . .'

"The children even licked the kayak, partly out of gratitude, partly out of hunger.

"And one day their mother added: 'Qaa, qaa, qaa, now eat your old grandfather, eat the fool who gave me a man made of dogs' droppings for a husband, and while you're eating him, tell him what I have just told you!'

"But when the grandfather was eaten, the woman alone could not feed her sons. So she threw them into the water in big skin boots, and chased them, two by two, out to sea. . . .

"Facing the water, she cried majestically: 'You two,' she said to the first pair, 'go and give birth to seals, who are not very dangerous.

"'You two,' she said to the second pair, 'go and give birth to wicked wolves.

"'You two,' she said to the third pair, 'go and give birth to white men, who will be lords but who will not be very dangerous.

"'You two,' she said to the fourth and last pair, 'go and give birth to Tornit, to vile and destructive Tornit.'*

"In this way, the world was created."

Pualuna had not finished speaking when I felt a foot gently scratching my back. Behind me, the fur covers began to move, as if the skinned animals had come to life again. The children of the igloo were waking up. Immediately there were all manner of shouts and cries. This one wanted to pee; that one whined and pulled at his mother's breast. Armed with a stick, Kaali went for my black shoes.

"They're seals," he said.

And he took aim. If he hit my foot, I had to give him a shoe. All the children screamed and rushed over to harpoon me, the way their father harpooned a seal out on the ice field.

"Taama! Stop!" their father shouted.

Nonplussed, the children about-faced. The shoe fell.

I barely had time to pick it up before we grown-ups were assailed from all sides. Armed with knives, skin sacks, and rope and gesturing wildly, the chil-

---

Tornit, Tunit: an imaginary people. See the Tornit legend in chapter 7, "The Legend of the Son and the Moon."

dren ran from one corner of the igloo to another under the direction of Uummaq, the youngest.

"Sak! Sak! . . . Nanoq. . . . Qorfa! . . . Sak! Sak! Sak! Forward! Forward! . . . The bear. . . . Faster! . . . Forward!"

It was a bear hunt, and the greedy beast was everywhere. The moment for cutting up their prey came—alas. An old boot was dragged back and forth across the room: it was the bear. They recaptured my shoe: it was the seal. The laces were stripped, the tongue was ripped out. This "seal" was going to be carved up according to the rules. There was barely time to intervene. . . .

Pigtail
and Narwhal Tusk

Pualuna continued: "Long ago, a very long time ago, a woman and her two grandchildren—a boy and a girl—had left their group. The grandmother and the two children were dying of hunger. They had nothing left. The boy, the older child, had been blind from birth.

"So all alone in the igloo, they waited. A fat bear came up to the igalaaq —the window—and he planted himself in front of it, and he began to sniff.

"The grandmother said to the blind boy, 'You try to shoot. I'll bend the bow and aim.'

"She aimed and he shot. They heard a loud noise.

" 'Oh, what a shame! We missed the bear. The arrow hit the wall by the window. What a shame,' she added, 'that you were not able to kill him!'

"The blind young hunter knew that she was lying. And he was right, for the big bear had been hit in the middle of his chest.

" 'What a shame you did not shoot straight,' the grandmother said again. To the granddaughter she whispered, 'We won't give anything to your brother. He's blind and doesn't need to eat. Let's push and drag the bear away from here. We'll eat him nearby. But be sure to say nothing to your brother.'

"The meat was boiled. The grandmother and granddaughter fell to gorging themselves. But the girl had tied off the bottom of her kapatak. She hid her chin as she ate, and let little bites of meat fall down, which she held against her naked skin. This she did several times. The grandmother remarked, 'It's really extraordinary how voracious you are. You're stuffing yourself for sure.'

" 'That's because I'm very hungry, and I'm always the one to finish first.' When she went back to the igloo with her grandmother, the girl gave the pieces of meat to her brother.

"The blind boy said to his sister, 'I'm terribly thirsty. Lead me to the lake so that I can drink.'

"She took him there, crying all the way. When they arrived, the blind boy begged his sister to leave him and to go back to their grandmother, but not to forget to lay stones along the path to the igloo so that they could guide him back. And this she did, crying all the way.

"Sitting by the shore of the lake, he realized that in spite of his great thirst he was unable to drink. Suddenly he heard a terrible whistling. A bird had alighted beside him. 'Hang on to my neck,' the bird said. Which the boy did, and the bird carried him under the water. Four times they went under, and each time they stayed longer and the boy had more and more trouble breathing.

" 'How do you feel?'

" 'Better . . . I'm beginning to see!'

"After the fourth dive, he had completely recovered his sight.

" 'You are all right now,' the bird said. 'When I can, I will come back to bring you food.'

"The boy found the stones along the path and returned to the igloo. 'There's a bearskin on the path,' he said as he entered. 'A big stretched skin.'

" 'That skin was given to us as a present,' the grandmother answered, and she was lying. 'Persorssuaq's family left it for us.'

"The three of them stayed on in this encampment for the days that followed. . . .

"One day they happened to be nearby when some white whales were playing offshore. The young boy prepared to harpoon them. He tied the end of the harpoon line to his little sister's leg; in this way she would, according to tradition, become his 'whale's tail' and when he had killed the animal she would be given the portion due a hunting partner.

" 'Tie me too,' the grandmother said. This was done. A small whale was harpooned. The grandmother shouted, 'Hurry! One more!' So he harpooned another—a big one—which was swimming farther out in the water.

"The great white whale had been wounded, and it pulled on the line. The grandmother tried to hold on, to keep her balance. But she was unable to fight for long. She grabbed onto her granddaughter's boot. The whale was stronger, and the boot gave way. Little by little, the whale was dragging her off . . . into the water, far off, and down toward the bottom. Several times they both came up to the surface. The grandmother kept shouting. 'My ulu, my knife! . . . My ulu! My ulu! My ulu!' For she hoped to free herself by cutting the line.

"At the very moment her hair was being braided into a pigtail, she was once and for all dragged by the whale down to the bottom of the water. There she was transformed into a narwhal, a black male narwhal that had a long twisted tusk in its mouth."[28]

When I left to go back to my hut, Sakaeunnguaq accompanied me to the outer opening of the entrance tunnel, as is the custom. We exchanged a few words. Then there was a long silence, the kind that prefaces a true conversation and is voluntarily reserved for moments of closeness between men when they are apart from the children, women, and old people. I raised my head and looked at the sky. I wanted to speak in a voice that would be steadier than my heart, which was heavy with conflicting feelings I longed to express but could not. I wanted to remain equally close to everyone, and I felt unable to turn the empathy between Sakaeunnguaq and myself into something special. "Why only him?" And so I remained silent, except to thank my host briefly. I walked slowly over the crunchy snow toward the shore. It was dark and cold. The wind plastered my face with icy snow. I stumbled over a dog, then over a walrus bone, and fell into a hole. This confounded land of legends! . . . Before returning alone to my hut, I turned around for a last look. The nine igloos of Siorapaluk were pinpointed in the night, nine small flames that for four months would not stop burning.

Where Did the Eskimos Come From?

Where did they come from? Pualuna and his stories aside, let me give a brief account of the facts modern science has been able to determine.

As of 1979, there were some 100,000 Eskimos inhabiting the Arctic: 39,000 Eskimos in Greenland; 35,000 in Alaska; 23,000 in Canada; and 1,600 in the Chukotski region of Siberia, in the U.S.S.R. By what migration did the ancestors of these Eskimos come to the shores where the white man eventually found them? Today archaeological digs are to be found from the Chukotski coast to Greenland. For three-quarters of a century, archaeologists from Denmark, Canada, the United States, and the Soviet Union have studied and compared fragments of weapons, harpoon heads, tools, and food midden. Philologists have been noting linguistic variants, and ethnologists have observed the various techniques used by these tribes. New findings in each area are set side by side, compared, studied, and restudied. But the further we advance in our knowledge of those distant centuries, the more complex, elusive, and difficult to grasp they appear. Luckily, in recent years, the findings of paleoclimatologists (students of ancient climates), glaciologists, and geomorphologists have enabled them to establish the framework for numerous changes in this social history.

One thing is certain: in North America the Arctic past goes back very far (10,000 years) and in northeastern Siberia even further (50,000 years). This hyperborean civilization has its own prehistory. From the mesolithic culture of Denbigh (which dates back 8,000 years) to the Greenland culture of Independence, Sarqaq, pre-Dorset, Dorset, and Thule (beginning of the Christian era), to the protohistoric cultures of Inussuk (A.D. 1200–1800), to the historic cultures following the "discovery" of the Eskimos (1721 in southern Greenland, 1818 in Thule), the ethnologist is now able to make a continuous, unbroken study of evolutionary changes in this unique Eskimo culture.

It seems to have been established that the natives of Thule, in northern Greenland, who possess undeniable similarities to Asian and Indian peoples, came from races that originally inhabited another continent. It seems clear that northern Greenland was not their original home: they came from somewhere else, and have been on the north Greenland coast for at least 4,000 years.

Did they originally come from the heart of America, pushed back by the Indians or Eqqillit, their hereditary enemies who came to the North American prairies 40,000 years ago?[29] Or did they come from Asia? "It is probably somewhere to the north and east of Lake Baikal that the unexplored remains of the immediate ancestors of the Eskimos lie," H. B. Collins wrote in 1942. On the other hand, the Danish archaeologist Helge Larsen, who discovered the largest Eskimo site in the Arctic, Ipiutaq or Point Hope, Alaska—600 to 700 houses; 550 tombs—came to the conclusion in 1953 that "archaeologists might profitably turn their attention once more to Canada, the cradle of Eskimo archaeology." In other words, this civilization would have originated on the American continent, and the Caribou Eskimos of Hudson Bay would have been its last representatives. The culture of sea-oriented Eskimo societies, as is the case with Thule, would be a derivative (non-Eskimo) culture that sprang from an earlier (paleo-Eskimo) land-oriented culture. Only gradually would the natives have turned from the sea.

The Greenland society of Thule is so perfectly adapted to its surroundings and takes such full advantage of them that its name—Thule—has been given to all maritime Eskimo cultures, whether in Siberia, Alaska, Canada, or Greenland. There is the Thule *culture,* and there is the *place* Thule.

In specialized journals and at scientific congresses, opposing ideas about the origins of the Eskimo people have been competing with one another for years, until Féderica de Laguna pointed out that it was a false problem: "Eskimo culture is probably quite recent," she wrote. "It includes many currents of diverse origins, none of which was originally Eskimo." The increasing evidence that the North American Arctic civilizations date back at least 8,000 years leads one to question the validity of the notion of an Eskimo prehistory. The Eskimo is but one part, the only visible part, of that iceberg which is boreal history. In him we see the very particular expression of an upper paleolithic period that has deep roots that are still largely unknown. Today there is general agreement that pre-Eskimos who came from North China 10,000 to 15,000 years ago after the most recent Ice Age, established themselves in the regions of Baikal and Chukotski and, developing from an upper paleolithic culture, gradually adapted to the cold world and conquered the frozen seas. The unity of an "Arctic" culture came about through late and repeated migrations toward eastern North America and Greenland by Siberian-Bering peoples with a strong north Japanese and north Chinese stamp. It would appear that the Eskimos began using the sea only 2,000 years ago. But there are certain indications that in the Bering Sea—the cradle of Eskimo cultures—men were capable of hunting in the sea and of navigating by the end of the upper paleolithic period, or 10,000 years ago.

The discovery by the Danish archaeologist Eigil Knuth of the Independence culture—which dates back 4,000 years—to the northeast of the unfrozen

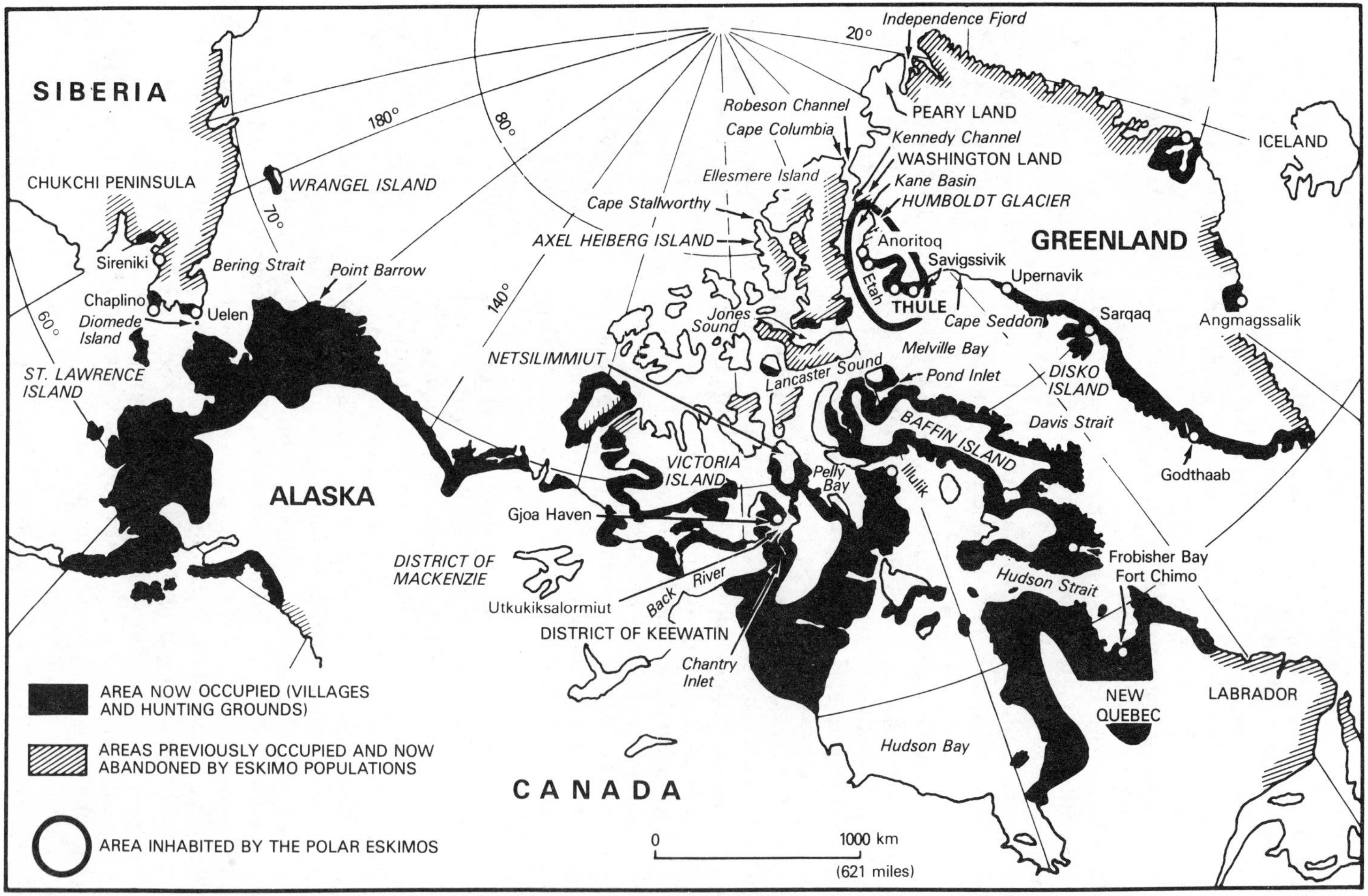

MAP 3. The Eskimo Arctic

SIBERIA

ICELAND

GREENLAND

CANADA

ALASKA

CHUKCHI PENINSULA

WRANGEL ISLAND

Point Barrow

Bering Strait

Uelen

Sireniki

Chaplino

Diomede Island

ST. LAWRENCE ISLAND

Independence Fjord

PEARY LAND

Kennedy Channel

WASHINGTON LAND

Kane Basin

HUMBOLDT GLACIER

Robeson Channel

Cape Columbia

Ellesmere Island

Cape Stallworthy

AXEL HEIBERG ISLAND

NETSILIMMIUT

Anoritoq

Savigssivik

Etah

THULE

Cape Seddon

Upernavik

Sarqaq

Angmagssalik

Godthaab

DISKO ISLAND

Davis Strait

Melville Bay

Pond Inlet

Lancaster Sound

Jones Sound

BAFFIN ISLAND

Illulik

Frobisher Bay

Fort Chimo

Hudson Strait

NEW QUEBEC

LABRADOR

Hudson Bay

Pelly Bay

Chantry Inlet

Back River

DISTRICT OF KEEWATIN

VICTORIA ISLAND

Gjoa Haven

Utkukiksalormiut

DISTRICT OF MACKENZIE

20°

80°

140°

180°

70°

60°

1000 km

(621 miles)

0

AREA NOW OCCUPIED (VILLAGES AND HUNTING GROUNDS)

AREAS PREVIOUSLY OCCUPIED AND NOW ABANDONED BY ESKIMO POPULATIONS

AREA INHABITED BY THE POLAR ESKIMOS

Peary Land and of the Sarqaq culture—which goes back 3,000 years—by the Danish archaeologist Jorgen Meldgaard in Disko Bay, western Greenland, has led to a reconsideration of how long the Thule region has been occupied. The first settlements at Thule must go back as far as those at Peary Land or Disko; Thule is a necessary point on the way from Canada to Greenland, and the country has been unfrozen for 8,000 years.

In its most recent phase, the Thule tribe came from northeast Canada— Baffin Island, near Illulik and Pond Inlet—and settled on this coast as early as the twelfth century, if not before. It was on the route of all the Eskimo migrations from Canada to the west and east coasts of Greenland, and was cut off from the west coast—specifically Upernavik—in around 1600. On August 9, 1818, John Ross discovered the tribe, which he picturesquely named "Arctic Highlanders." The American expeditions to the Pole by Kane, Hayes, and Hall (led by Bessels after Hall's death) spent winters in the Thule region in 1853– 55, 1860–61, and 1872–73.

In addition, each spring after the warming period of 1819, whalers put into Cape York. Some of them spent the winters there. Trading and interbreeding began. Though the whites took a great deal from the Eskimo in an uneven barter—a few needles and tobacco for two foxes or a narwhal tooth—they also taught him much. Without question Peary was responsible for bringing about a decisive technological development during his five stays among the tribe,

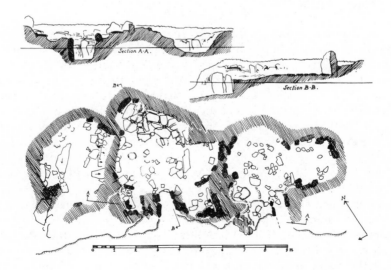

Archaeological digs carried out by the Danish ethnographer Erik Holtved in Nullit (Thule district). These remarkable digs enabled Holtved to study in particular an old type of igloo from the Middle Ages that had party walls. The drawings distinctly show the entrance passageways, which have partially disintegrated. The igloo on the right, shown in cross section, is a double igloo. (*From Holtved,* The Polar Eskimos)

from 1891 to 1909. The first European store was founded by Knud Rasmussen, after Peary's departure, at Uummannaq.

From the examination of technical and social changes over time, we have learned that the economic arrangements adopted by Eskimo cultures in order to survive in their environment of limited resources has varied relatively little over a long period. The study of strata of food midden—food debris accumulated over the centuries at the entrance to igloos—has shown that the differences in development from one level to another, from one culture to another, are very slight. Eskimo history seems closed. Because the Eskimo economy could not be improved from within, many concluded that any genuine material improvement would have required a radical change in the methods used to exploit resources, and that new resources had to be found. Raising domesticated reindeer is one example: the Laps of Scandinavia—who had formerly been hunters—brought about this radical cultural change themselves in the fourteenth century, and were one of the rare Arctic people to have independently changed their economic patterns. The Eskimo has been unable or unwilling to adopt this evolution on his own, even when encouraged to do so. How is this absence of inventive and evolutionary capacities to be accounted for? Perhaps the extreme specialization that resulted from the harshness of the climate as well as from the geographic isolation which lasted until the mid–nineteenth century, with all its attendant consequences—a lack of new ideas, technical stagnation, etc.—reduced the ability of this archaic society to adapt, as it had been able to do in the beginning?

To the Eskimos' slow cultural regression—which continued even as more advanced techniques became available to them, such as the rifle, the steel trap, etc.—must be added the considerable loss of territory they suffered. This occurred in the Canadian archipelago and on both the northwest and the northeast coasts of Greenland. It was particularly pronounced during the so-called Little Ice Age, which lasted from 1600 to 1800. Since 1800 the Eskimos of Thule have reduced their hunting terrain by a third. In the best periods it extended over 750 miles, from the southern coast of Washington Land to Cape Seddon in Melville Bay, the continuously occupied strongholds being Inuarfissuaq, Etah, Pitorarfik, Neqi, Appat, Qaanaaq, Qeqertaq, Natsilivik, Nullit, Uummannaq, Cape York, and Savigssivik.

Another consideration is that of place. As we know, there is an intimate connection between the structures of the land and the human activities that land supports. Extending from Humboldt Glacier in the north to Melville Bay in the south and winding down by frozen seas westward to the North American continent, the Thule area is a prime example of a place in which natural factors have had a dominant effect on history. Thule is a crossroads of routes and of ideas. To understand the permanence of such a northerly outpost, we have to go back in time. Since Dorset and Sarqaq (in other words, for the last 3,000 years) Thule has been the only practicable passage between the Canadian Arctic and Greenland—the last territory in the east to have been reached by

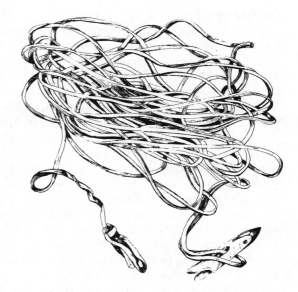

Seal leather thong attached to a harpoon (made of ivory with an iron head) for hunting walrus. Siorapaluk, October 1950. (*Private collection*)

Ancient harpoon heads made of bone, from the Kangerluarsuk digs (restored by Inuterssuaq), November 1950. (*Private collection*)

the Eskimos. There was the "Bering Bridge" in the west, the cradle of Eskimo culture, and the "Thule Bridge" from Canada to Greenland, for all hyperborean human groups. Thule represented one stage in the vast expansion that led the Eskimos in the second millennium B.C. from the extreme west (Siberia, Alaska) to the extreme east (the eastern coast of Greenland) in search of the whale and the musk ox. From the far west of Alaska to the east and southwest of Greenland, the lines of cultural ebb and flow crossed at Thule. To speak of Thule is to speak of the complexity of this society.

Consider the preeminence of the place. Thule is bordered by the "northern water," a vast polynya of free waters at the extremities of the large straits of northeastern Canada—the Lancaster and Jones straits. This polynya owes its existence to its location: at a triple confluence of Polar waters that come from the glacial Arctic Ocean, flowing along the Canadian coasts; of warm waters that are the distant reaches of the Gulf Stream and that flow along the northern coast of Greenland; and of Canadian waters that come from the Beaufort Sea through Jones and Lancaster straits. This triple encounter of waters differing in temperature, salinity, density, and depth governs the movement of ice and animal life. Their mixture gives rise to rich plankton and a dense fish population, which in turn explains the preference of pinnipeds for these waters—as well as of the bowhead or Greenland right whale, the most powerful of the cetaceans.[30] The whales mate and reproduce in specific fjords —for example Inglefield Fjord, south of Siorapaluk. There is another result: in coastal waters, plankton and small fish are so abundant that guillemots from southern Greenland and the Gulf of St. Lawrence come by the millions to nest in May or June, as we have seen. These birds—at their own expense—enable the fox to winter here. The presence of these millions of guillemots accounts for the abundance of foxes in Thule. Thanks to the plankton, seals and walruses are also very numerous. At 78° latitude, Thule is an oasis in terms of climate and fauna. In the whole of the Arctic at this latitude, there is no livelier animal or human society.

Threshold of all the large Eskimo migrations that have peopled western and eastern Greenland, a place of confluence for many waters, a biogeographic crossroads and cradle, and the territory of the northernmost tribe in the world, Thule has benefited from another unique attribute: it is very near the magnetic axis pole and at the center of the auroral zone.

Pulaarpunga:
I Pay You a Visit

Alone, the Eskimo is nothing: he needs to relate to other people; he needs human bonds. To facilitate contact, fixed meeting places are established at a distance of two or three days' travel from Eskimo camps and villages.

SUMMER INTO WINTER

Farewell to the annual boat on its return south. Siorapaluk fjord (Robertson's Bay), August 7, 1950. *(All uncredited photos in this section and throughout are by Jean Malaurie)*

Sakaeunnguaq's and Pualuna's peat house. The framework is sandstone. In the foreground are Bertsie's kamiks, drying, and katak (passageway). Siorapaluk, September 1950.

The tranquillity of Siorapaluk. August 1972.

The Saharalike slopes of the northern
Greenland plateaus. Innartalik, west of
Siorapaluk. August 1972.

(RIGHT) Sealskin tent. Ussaqaq (forty years old),
sitting beside Nivikannguaq (eighteen),
Avikinnguaq (fourteen), and Simigak (twelve).
Standing to left: Avoortungiaq (fifty-five) and
little Peter (Peary), an adopted child (eleven).
Etah, August 1950.

Illuliaq with its katak and torssusaq (igloolike passageway and snow shield). Siorapaluk, March 1951.

Dear shadows! January 1951.

Perlerorneq (Arctic hysteria) of a Polar Eskimo woman. (*The Peary expedition, Museum of Natural History, New York*)

Sakaeunnguaq (born March 31, 1914). *Ingmerneq*, or drum song, on the Thule glacier, on the expedition's return route. June 5, 1951.

Pualuna (born 1874). Siorapaluk, October
1950.

Maassannguapaluk (born 1926). Thule,
July 1951.

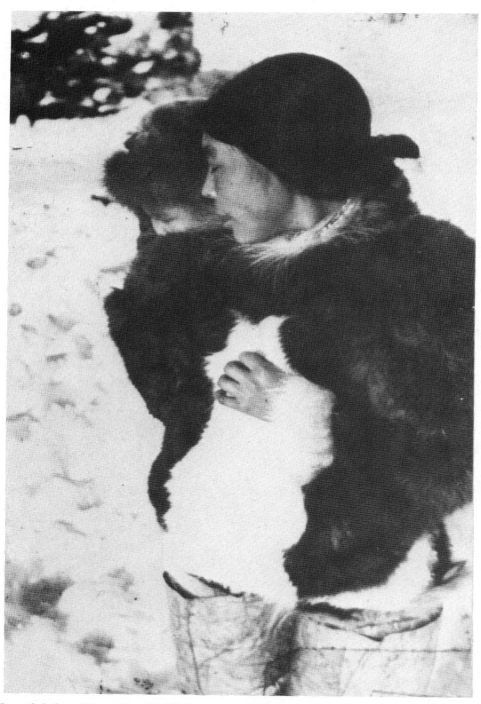

Inapaluk (born December 22, 1923), wearing her blue-fox kapatak and with her baby in the amaaq (hood). Neqi, March 1951.

For instance, every spring in the Thule region, the main families of the group gathered at Neqi-Pitorarfik for one week to hunt walrus. In April and May, little bands of two or three sledges went to Canada or Melville Bay to hunt bear. Villages joined forces to snare birds on and around the cliffs at Etah, Siorapaluk, Cape York, and Savigssivik. In August, the best hunters met at Qeqertaq on Inglefield Fjord to hunt narwhal.

In addition to these seasonal encounters, the Eskimos made two or three trips a year to Uummannaq (or Thule), the administrative center. Many went to Thule in August, when the annual provision ship was unloaded. For two or three weeks, a whole family dragged itself from igloo to igloo, pretending to while away its boredom.

There is an often dramatic contradiction between the Eskimo's basically individualistic temperament and his conscious belief that solitude is synonymous with unhappiness. He knows that an igloo which is seldom or never visited will be engulfed in the cold of the earth, wrapped in the shroud of death. Even though he may have the security of a family, if the Eskimo is abandoned by his fellowmen, he is overcome by the depression that always lies in wait for him. He needs to respond to people, to put on a smile, to win people over with his clowning, to relax. . . . Contacts with other people comfort him, warm him, reassure him. Is this race too old, perhaps? Does it perhaps know too much? Is the communal life of the group too much to bear? However that may be, in order to mislead people—and to deceive himself—the Eskimo wears a succession of masks: friendly although inscrutable with his friends; ironic and bantering with a visitor who needs his help; embarrassed and pitiful when he is in want; skilled and unerring while hunting; bold and theatrical on returning from the hunt; opaque and evasive when he has been swindled; violent or whining when he is drunk; solemn and sententious in church; closed, almost mean when he is affecting anger. The mask changes as the Eskimo's quick eye and wary sensitivity perceive the situation to change. But varied and mobile as his masks may be, there are times when he apparently feels uncomfortable, very uncomfortable in himself. So he multiplies the reasons and opportunities to escape from himself in the company of other people. The contradiction that everyone harbors in his innermost self—that solitude is soothing and company revivifying—finds expression here in the institution called the *pulaar* or visit—actually, a network of obligations that link one person to another and make a voluntary prisoner of the Eskimo.

A village comprises many communities: first of all, the network of relatives, with its mutual obligations; then the *peqatigiit,* the group of hunters. In 1950, in Siorapaluk there were two such groups, hunters who were related by blood or adoption, held their resources—dogs, motorboat—in common, and shared their time and manpower in order to hunt more effectively.

Although the men had plenty of opportunities to get together, it was not quite the same for the women. There was, of course, always the store. People continued to think up good reasons to go to the store many times in a week —for tobacco, oil, sugar, or what have you. They bought something, they contemplated buying something, or they watched other people doing the same. On such occasions, some conversation took place, but it was brief and utterly superficial. In the store's narrow passageway, everyone was observing everyone else, and since everything one said would be overheard, appraised, and passed on, people hardly spoke their innermost thoughts.

On Sundays, the church became the village square. The bell rang three times to remind everyone that it was Sunday. The crowd assembled silently around the flagpole while the flag was raised. Each person surveyed the panorama of the fjord as if he were seeing it for the first time in his life. One final peal from the bell and they ceremoniously entered the chapel. Singing hymns, the Eskimos stilled their visceral fear of the dead and of the spirits. After the service, they again gathered briefly in front of the chapel: this time they were free to be noisy.

Only the pulaar, the visit, could make up for what other institutions, which combined people without truly bringing them close to one another, lacked. *Pulaarpunga* means "I pay you a visit." The pulaar is initiated by one person and develops into a complex network of relationships, visits, and the obligation to repay visits which is superimposed on the web of family relationships. The chain cannot be broken even when it becomes suffocating. In a village of only a few igloos, like Siorapaluk, you would be visited by the same neighbor four or five times in the course of a day, and you had to return his courtesy as soon as possible. Only the length of the visit could reduce the number of visits. The scenario was invariable, and the respective roles of visitor and host never changed. There might not be a shred of desire left to see each other again; no matter: the visiting pattern had been established and visits went on most of the time.

One coughs outside to signal that one is about to enter, and one goes in, for the door is open to all. However, woe to him who has not noticed by some almost imperceptible sign outside that he should not intrude! He will be stung by the most haughty, icy, unbending stare as he arrives inside. He can do no more than beat a retreat, and a not very honorable one. He will have lost face and will be the butt of much mockery.

Around seven in the evening, Asarpanguaq, who was lame, stamped on the snow as if he were cleaning the soles of his sealskin boots—his way of making sure he would be welcome—and went into the igloo of his neighbor Qaarnaaq. This was his fourth visit of the day. There were only nine igloos in Siorapaluk, nothing had happened that particular day, not one hunter had returned to the village since morning, and so he had nothing, but not one thing, to talk about. Yet there he was. He took his "visitor's bath." He got warm again. Physically and psychologically, he had drawn close to his neighbor: contact—sensory contact—had been reestablished.

He had sat down on the crate to the left of the door. Qaarnaaq, his host, had remained seated on the illeq and had welcomed his visitor with a warm but brief greeting while he continued talking garrulously to his wife and several other women who were visiting. Qaarnaaq spoke of the weather; he said how hard it was for them not to have more reserves of meat; he talked about everything and nothing. He said that soon he would go to Inuarfissuaq to hunt reindeer: "Oh, one's well off there, there are lots of reindeer, but what snow! . . . So when do we leave? . . ." The words did not matter; they were part of a ritual. Qaarnaaq's mind was wandering; he was seeking for some distraction —an ax, the loan of a dog—and the more keenly on the track he was, the vaguer he allowed himself to seem. The way he glanced around the room with narrowed eyes—pretending to focus on something else—fooled no one. Ostensibly, his wife was sweeping the dark earthen floor of the igloo with a gull's feather. As she squatted, she looked approvingly at her husband when he spoke of his future departure. Asarpanguaq, who had not yet been offered anything to eat, was talking to himself, punctuating his monologue with noncommittal ieh, ieh's. For the nth time, Qaarnaaq's wife made a thing of showing a little boy and girl a worn photograph that she picked from a pile containing letters and odds and ends of newspapers and skins. She polished the photo with her broad thumb before handing it over. Then she passed out other photographs which had already made the rounds more than once. Everyone showed the same emotion all over again; people were so anxious to be amused that they could admire something ten or twenty times in succession with the same air of surprise. Then the woman made some string figures. Pleased to be entertained in a new way, the men watched her out of the corners of their eyes, with the weary smiles of people who have been watching age-old games for too long. Conversation lagged; silences lengthened. Boredom enveloped the greasy igloo. It was as if the tension of the hunters' group pursuit of food had so enervated them that they took rather morose delight in relaxing together like this, in a kind of playful masturbation. It was as if they had to drink the very dregs of their boredom, so that by way of reaction, the desire to get out into the open again would suddenly be rekindled.

Asarpanguaq's visit did not last ten minutes; when he left he murmured "Soo"—Thank you—as he disappeared through the door. Qaarnaaq's wife, who had been mulling over the pulaar she was going to pay Imina—her fifth for the day—immediately hurried out. Qaarnaaq left also, to visit Olipaluk. He had not been invited, but the rule is, never wait for an invitation. One honors the host by visiting him; one does not solicit that honor. And so the Eskimos exchange visits all day long, from midday until late at night. They wear themselves out with pulaars to the point of nausea.

This is why on an average of one day out of three the Eskimo did not leave his village. In the first place, he was obliged to be present for birthday pulaars, for group sharing of kiviaqs, and for the arrival of hunters from neighboring villages. Bad weather might keep him at home, or his own bad humor. But if his mood—or hunger—drove him to go hunting, he might be gone for weeks, pursuing bear or walrus far out on the ice. . . . He was just as likely to remain indoors for weeks.

And finally, the Eskimo slept a great deal. He hibernated rather, like a bear, more in winter than in summer but quite a lot, all told, when you consider that half his life is spent dozing and napping. I kept no precise records, but I would venture to say that the other half was divided thus: one-third spent in making pulaars, one-third in traveling to hunting grounds, and only one-third in actually hunting. This may come as a surprise, since as a people Eskimos are supposed to be so active. Indolence may be a sign of wisdom. It is how a society protects itself physically against an exhaustingly hard life.

The young men were the sole exception, naturally enough, to this balanced rhythm of life: seasonally, a large part of their time was taken up by their sex drive. Spring and summer, from one hamlet to the next, they pursued girls whom they had had their eye on, using all sorts of different ploys—the excuses of hunters.

Festivities in the Night

During the winter of 1950, the Eskimos of Siorapaluk became extremely uneasy. They had heard that as a result of market fluctuations in Europe, Copenhagen would increase commodity prices substantially. The summer mail had already brought word of a rise in prices, but it was still a matter of rumor. There was no question of the Eskimos' laying in reserves; even if their means would have allowed it, the idea would never have entered their minds. It was an old habit with them to rely on the white man for anything having to do with price lists and schedules. We were having our first snowfall when a hunter who had come on from Kangerluarsuk told the villagers that coffee, sugar, and cigarette prices would go up. Throughout the early autumn, I had sensed how people felt their habits were threatened. Would they be able to continue to buy wood and oil? Would they have to do without European goods that had become almost necessities for them—especially tobacco, tea, coffee, and sugar?

No sooner would two hunters get together—for example, in the house of old Inuk, the former catechist—than these problems would be brought up immediately. The men argued like shopkeepers. Their faces, usually so open, would close and become hard as soon as they spoke of foxes or kroner. I was constantly brought into the discussion.

"You'll tell the governor, right? After all, you go to Copenhagen, don't you? Wood is too expensive, but we have to have it for the thwarts on the sledges. Nobody's going to go back to building them out of bits of bone, the way our grandfathers did. We can't do it that way anymore. Tell him that! It probably wouldn't be hard for you to tell him that. . . . Oh, those skis that arrived in Thule on the last boat. . . . There's no danger that they'll go up in price! Because we can't use them! No, did you ever see an Eskimo ski?* Ha, ha, ha!"

"Here, look at this electric battery," old Inuk said. "It was all damp when I bought it. Now the light is so mikivoq—so little—that even when I put it right in front of my eyes I can't see any light. I told John about it, but do you think he wanted to take it back?

" 'What's sold is sold.' That's all he said to me."

We were to receive the first official communications about the new prices at the beginning of winter. John's receiver set, definitely 1900 vintage, did not work well. Nevertheless, he tried to get the biweekly messages. One evening at seven, his room was full of men and women. I think at that minute the scene must have been the same in all three of the huts in the district which had radios. In one corner sat the little varnished wooden case. Everyone was crowding around it. Big people pushed little people; everyone stepped on everyone else's toes. The sound was weak, and everybody wanted to get closer. A faraway voice could barely be heard, and was interrupted by static. John had his head practically in the box, trying to catch snatches of the Danish, which no one else could understand. He kept turning around to ask people not to blow their noses into their fingers, to keep the noise down. People waited three, four, five minutes. . . . John was on his knees, jotting down figures. He could not catch a repeat of the message. The only transmitter was in Thule.

"Thule said . . . Thule said," he began gravely, "that the store prices must be changed at once. Massakkut—now. A kilo of coffee will cost seven kroner . . . a hundred grams of tea ninety öre . . . one kilo of oatmeal fifty öre . . . one kilo of hardtack one kroner seventy . . . one kilo of corned beef five kroner fifty . . . one kilo of margarine three kroner fifty . . . one kilo of sugar eighty öre . . . one Stevens 16-caliber gun seventy-two kroner . . . two gun barrels two hundred four kroner . . . one 1889 model bullet fifteen öre . . . one kilo of coal ten öre . . . one kilo of oil thirty-four öre."[31]

The increase in prices was very marked, but the Eskimos showed no emotion. No one batted an eye. They sensed that the most important part was still to come.

"Well," John said, at last. "The terianniaq prices have been raised. Sixty kroner for a blue fox, forty for a prime-quality white, and four to seven kroner for a seal."

Sunaana! What's this?! The small room resounded as people commented on this news. Amid much laughter, each man tried to figure out how much he was worth. I overheard Sakaeunnguaq making the most extravagant projec-

---

*In this region the snow cover is thin, and the Eskimos do not use skis or snowshoes. Precipitation is slight: the annual rainfall in 1946–49 averaged 2½ inches. On the extremely windy north shore at Etah, the snow was about 6 inches deep. Wind and evaporation reduce the depth of snow on the plateaus by half.

tions. Meanwhile, Thule was drowning us in a flood of music. All broadcasts ended the same way, with a cultural program for the native stations. Culture . . . culture . . . yet how inappropriate the choice was for the Eskimo: the Overture to *Tannhäuser,* Mozart's Quartet in E Flat, then some waltzes and polkas.

"Why don't you listen?" I said to Olipaluk. "It's pretty."

"Bah! Qallunaat music—it's always the same. That's your kind of music. Damned qallunaat!" And he went on talking to the person beside him.

Several Eskimos were spending the evening together. The door creaked and opened halfway.

"Can I come in too?"

"Of course. Come in, little one."

She was eleven years old. Covered with snow, red-faced, she slipped timidly into our hut.

"Utoqqatserpunga. . . . Utoqqatserpunga. Excuse me. . . . Excuse me."

Tripping over people's legs, she went to sit on Iggianguaq's knee. There were six of us. Some leaned against crates; others squatted along the wall. Pipes were lighted. The room was warm. Everyone felt pleasantly at ease.

At midnight, all six were still there. Doing what? Nothing—just talking. The Eskimos were happy about the latest news, and their desire to comment on it, to discuss it out loud, was irrepressible. On important occasions, they instinctively rejoined the group. In the course of group discussion they formed their own opinions, which were then voiced by the naalagaq, the leader, who was the real midwife for the group. When the naalagaq deemed the moment right, he would express the group thought, but he added a dash of something to it, a little spice, the mark of his personality.

Typically, at the outset the group finds little to say. People talk routinely about daily tasks; they stare at the rising wreaths of smoke. They watch each other covertly, nose each other's intentions. After a half hour or so of this, someone—usually a stranger to the village—speaks amid a general silence. His head is bowed; his elbows are propped on his thighs; he speaks in a low, half-swallowed voice; his lips hardly move. He is serving as a kind of trailblazer; he is setting the tone. Usually he is a quite mediocre person and the person to respond is a marginal member of the village—one of the rare atypical individuals the community, which generally diminishes strong personalities, tolerates in its midst. His function is, by means of sarcastic remarks and critical allusions, to cause each person's deepest, innermost thoughts to surface. To keep himself in countenance, to fill the vacuum a bit, a hunter will go over to one corner of the igloo and cut himself a chunk of seal. To affect importance, another will cough or stretch his legs. More silence. Then one of the prominent men present speaks, but he is carefully noncommittal. An elder questions him. Although the man keeps insisting on his own incompetence, his insignificance, his advanced age, he is urged by everyone to be more specific. Now conversation begins to flow. Different points of view are expressed, but there is no argument; consensus is reached, rather, by a kind of wordless interchange. The decision will be the echo of each person's thought, which is communal in its origin. If the naalagaq has a strong personality and has been able to raise the tone of the discussion, for which everyone will be secretly grateful, the decision will discreetly bear his mark.

That evening, Imina, who was highly regarded, was talking about prices at the store. From now on, a skillful hunter would easily be able to make fifty to sixty-five kroner (or eight to ten dollars) a week on foxes alone. Old Inuk, like an inexhaustible chorus, once again told of how, in 1920, he was the first catechist in the district. Sakaeunnguaq, who would carry no weight here if his presence did not evoke the authority of his father, the famous Nukapianguaq, said nothing, but nonetheless he was "present." He was giving me a demonstration lesson in a string game. His hands were extraordinarily agile, and formed the oddest knots one after another, out of which he made little pictures.

"There. . . . Now don't you see?"

At least the figure was realistic: a woman and a man were represented by their respective sexual organs, one inside the other.

"You don't understand anything."

His kindly neighbor intervened: "Watch. . . ."

With several motions of his fingers, he wove us another design: the subject was the same, but the pattern was for homosexuals. Too bad! Again the effect was lost. Attention shifted elsewhere. Young Appalinnguaq, who was fourteen and not yet old enough to join the talk, captured people's notice for a few seconds by humming a Lutheran hymn.

There was a long silence. Suddenly, Ingapaluk spoke up; his speech was hoarse and rapid, as if he were afraid. He was talking from deep in his throat, his words were slurred and half-swallowed—the way hunters here talk when they are excited and feel that an event must be communicated immediately. With almost telegraphic terseness, Ingapaluk criticized the white men for not consulting the hunters, for laying down the law from far away, in the country of the qallunaat. "We should be the ones to set the prices," he said, in effect. "Piuli [Peary, in 1908–9] wanted ten foxes for one rifle, but among the qallunaat foxes were certainly worth more than that!" There was a long, heavy silence, approving yet uneasy. The Eskimos were afraid of challenging the white man this way, even from a distance. Imina assumed a conciliatory role; holding his head high, speaking slowly, enunciating each syllable clearly, he closed the discussion for now. He postponed the question until the annual meeting of the Council of Hunters: "In March, at the plenary assembly in Thule, the Inuit will have to settle the matter. Firmly!" Everyone listened to him with bowed head, uttering iehs of approval. . . . "He has perfectly expressed what everyone was thinking!" Imina's prompt decision was the more definitive because each man's thought had developed and found expression in the midst of the group and in silence.

A current of cold air: Ussaqaq had just come in the igloo. We made room

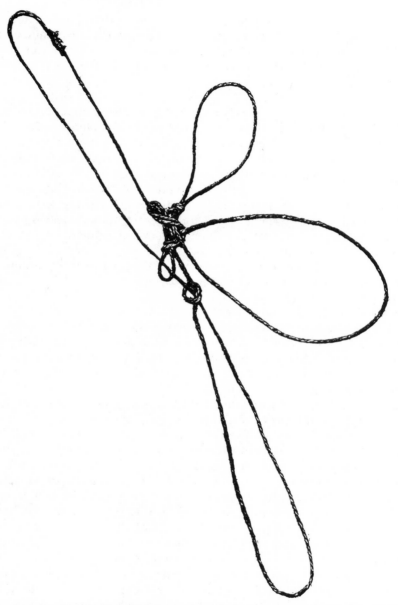

String game, or ajaraarutit, by Sakaeunnguaq. It shows a woman in a defecating position who seems to be suffering from flatulence—note the size of the loop! One can observe the fall of the feces.

A leather string or, in 1950, a thin rope about three feet long is knotted at both ends. The game consists of stretching the rope between your hands, passing from the thumb to the little finger or from ring finger to ring finger. The other fingers, particularly the index, work out the figures. Siorapaluk, December 1950. *(Private collection)* for him. The igloo was quiet. Imina let himself be prevailed upon to dance. An eighteen-year-old hunter turned a pail upside down and beat out a sort of tom-tom in three-quarter time on the metal: "Aja-a . . . aja-a . . . aja-ja. . . ." An old man looked at the youth, and he stopped.

Then, his eyes closed, his body leaning forward, his knees slightly bent, Imina accompanied himself by tapping the rim of his drum sharply with a length of seal rib.

The sound was dull, the rhythm pulsated.

The drum, or *qilaat,* is made of skin stretched over two seal or walrus ribs, or over a deer's antler. The skin is often from the throat of a walrus, although the lining of a dog's stomach is said to give a clearer sound.

That night, Imina's drum was a small one. He beat more and more loudly; keeping his knees slightly bent, he leaned forward and swayed to the right and to the left, undulating the whole length of his body. The movement of his head was especially pronounced. An Eskimo stood facing him; he held a small piece of wood—the *aviorut*—with which he followed Imina's beat; then he stopped, his eyes grew vague, and his arms dropped by his sides. Now Imina kept time, nodding his head. "A . . . aja . . . aja. . . ."

He was half naked, his bearskin pants fastened around his hips. As he leaned forward, he now pivoted from right to left, keeping his feet close together and motionless. He was trembling. The rhythm grew faster: the dance was taking possession of Imina. His muscles were taut; his eyes were vacant; his head was lifting slowly, but he did not move from where he had started. "Aja-a . . . aja!" His voice deepened; the words were largely smothered now, and indistinct. The sound was more like inarticulate breathing, the syllables running together, pouring out with incredible speed, as if he were suffering. Imina freed himself from his song by shouting twice, in unison with the man opposite him, who now turned the aviorut he held upright between his two forefingers.

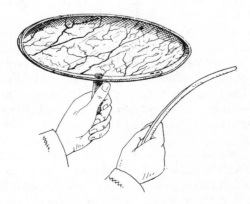

Qilaat. Siorapaluk, December 1950. (*Private collection*)

Tukuminguaq's song. 1909. *(Transcribed by Charles Leden, Med. om Gronl., 1952)*

It had become so hot that people took off clothes that made them uncomfortable. Some kept their shirts and nanus on. In a cloud of tobacco and oily smoke Inugteq was caught up by the fever. "Aja-ja-a . . . aja-a. . . ."[32] He rose and, with no one facing him, performed a solitary dance full of savage violence. The expression on his mobile face shifted between desire and guile. Several young men were now half naked. The watchers echoed the panting of the dancer. "Aja-a aja-a!" The man beside me stirred restlessly. A child ran out, crying.

It was two in the morning. One Eskimo was snoring in a corner. Others had collapsed along the wall. Conversation languished. An acrid smell of skins and sweat filled the room. We drank deeply from the bucket. . . . Well, the time had come to stop. People started to dress. Imina was the first to leave.

In the igloo, the woman was waiting. This was her moment. A step sounded. The door closed behind the man. He pulled off his boots and his nanu, and stretched out on the caribou skins that covered the wooden sleeping platform. The docile young wife waited, naked under the eiderdown. He pulled her to him; he desired her with his whole being. His fingers slid under the warm coverings, caressed her astonishingly soft and silky skin, lingering on her small, firm breasts. The platform creaked. The woman was very amorous tonight; she moaned almost inaudibly, and was answered by a sigh. Lying with all his weight on her, the man quickly brought the passionate drive of the dance to a sexual climax.

Awakened by the noise of their father's return, two of the children had opened their eyes for a moment. They were not at all surprised by an ordinary, almost daily act to which the promiscuity of the igloo made them indifferent; they promptly sank back to sleep in the soft, soothing light of the seal-oil lamps.

A Self-
Supporting Economy?

The pisiniarfik, the white man's store, had been playing a bigger role in native life year by year. If the Danish government had not turned Greenland commerce into a monopoly, theoretically the fluctuations of a free economy—the balance of profit and loss—would have determined each person's standard of living. However, the government could arbitrarily fix prices so that they did not hinder the natives' material and cultural advancement. The store, an administrative lever controlled by the Danish authorities, was the essential tool of colonization.

The cultural and economic emancipation of this archaic people had raised problems that were both delicate and difficult. The 302 inhabitants of the Thule region had been kept isolated from the rest of Greenland. By 1950, only two of them had been to Denmark—once. Fewer than ten had been to southern Greenland—that is, to the market town of Upernavik and points south.

Midway on the road toward a technological civilization, the Eskimo became demanding. His needs changed, and the native economy alone was no longer able to satisfy him. The European-style store generated new habits. The Eskimo became used to our practices; he modified his diet, consuming sugar, coffee, and tea daily, and biscuits, oatmeal, and milk occasionally; his domestic life-style was transformed by the frequent substitution of textiles for seal and reindeer skins, and by the use of wood, oil, and coal. And as he made such adaptations, the Eskimo manifested a true producer's intelligence. My detailed economic study of the Polar Eskimo group as a whole attempted to establish an overall picture of individual budgets, and my research showed clearly that the Eskimos' disbursements for equipment—that is, for "productive investments"—ranked high among all other categories. Almost one-fifth (19.8 percent) of the total budget was spent on weapons and tools (although hunters made up only one-fifth of the group surveyed); for the district as a whole, 23.3 percent of the budget went for food; 22.2 percent for clothing; 18.5 percent for tobacco; and 8.5 percent for household equipment. Taking all factors into consideration (personal consumption, operating costs, subsidies, taxes, debt amortization and interest), the average budget of an Eskimo family was—and this must be emphasized—larger than that of some peasant societies in old agricultural areas of Europe.

In order to earn cash and move into the modern world, as everything invited him to do, the Eskimo had one principal means at his disposal: fox hunting. Since the colonization of Greenland in the early part of this century, native life at high latitudes depended almost exclusively on this once-scorned animal.

Fox hunting was authorized by the Danish government for only five to six and a half months a year. Thule was certainly one of the districts in Greenland where foxes were most abundant. A few statistics will bear this out. From 1930 to 1939, the number of foxes killed by one hundred inhabitants on the southern coast of Greenland averaged 38; on the eastern coast, 20; on the northwestern coast (from Disko Bay to Upernavik), 15; and, in the district of Thule alone, 455. (In 1947–48 in Thule: 722 blue foxes, 212 white foxes.)

These foxes allowed the natives of Thule not only to buy what they needed but also to dispose of a substantial earned credit at the store. Let us look at some figures: during each winter month, an average Siorapaluk hunter in 1948–49 sold two to six foxes, which brought him about twenty kroner (three dollars) each; two to five sealskins, which brought him two to three kroner each —or one krone (approximately forty cents) per single unprepared sealskin, with a supplementary krone paid for an hour's work of cutting, cleaning, and drying.

Seal hunting depended on the market. During my stay, prices were very low. Therefore, seal was hunted only to meet the daily needs of the inhabitants or to feed their dogs. I estimated that the seventy hunters in the group caught three thousand seals that year. Not all the skins were sold. Skins had to be prepared, and this job was done (one hour's labor per skin) only when prices were high and skins were in fairly good condition. In 1948–49, a fox skin was worth ten sealskins.

The Thule tribe's prosperity lay in its having ready money. Together with Banks Island, in Canada, Thule was one of the very few areas in the Eskimo world that lived essentially from hunting and that, despite the very low prices paid for its furs, managed to keep its budget largely in the black. This was due to the group's archaic diet—its refusal to depend on whites for its food. In 1950 the prices paid for skins were revaluated, although the general level remained mediocre.

It is the migrating birds—the guillemots—as I have mentioned, which accounted for the high fox population in the region. In 1946–47, the people of Thule represented 1.3 percent of the population of Greenland, although they supplied 2.62 percent of the products acquired in all of Greenland by the Royal Society of Commerce. In 1950, Thule alone provided 11.7 percent of all Greenland products exclusive of fish.

Seventy-odd hunters in this isolated society of Polar Eskimos supplied, ad valorem, around $23,000 on the world fur market, or $330 per hunter per year. In return, however, this group received an average yearly income of only a little more than $12 per hunter, out of which had to be deducted the cost and depreciation of materials and tools (wood and thwarts for sledges, rifles, cartridges) and overall production costs.

These investments, which brought in a twenty-eight-fold return, were probably among the most profitable in the world. Yet the Eskimo got back about one-fifth of the wealth he produced. An economy would have to be exceptionally strong to support such a wide gap between production and income. By what sociographic processes did the Thule economy become so strong? And why were the Eskimos generally—a cohesive society, with a well-defined system of values—a poor society?

Since 1818, the Polar Eskimos have often been the victims of shameless bartering on the part of American and Scottish whalers, and of some exploring expeditions. Following in the footsteps of the whalers, Robert E. Peary, the civil engineer in the American Navy, an outstanding explorer, who led seven expeditions into this country, established a barter system that, thanks to the great profits he realized in the United States, enabled him to defray the costs of his expeditions.

The Peary Arctic Club is a private society and has not made its books public, but indiscreet remarks of members of Peary's expedition, and information collected by me directly from the Eskimos indicate the character of the bartering. It was an uneven exchange determined by the elementary needs of Polar Eskimos and the great demand on the American market for the products of their hunting: blue and white fox furs, walrus and narwhal tusks. Peary's competitor in his race for the Pole, F. A. Cook, accused Peary and his friends of having made more than a million dollars in fur trading over a period of twenty-five years. It is impossible, of course, to verify this figure, but clearly there was considerable profiteering—and on Cook's part as well: witness the fact that he accused Peary of having confiscated the stock of furs (two hundred blue foxes) that he had accumulated in Anoritoq through trade during the winter of 1907–8. Cook estimated its value at ten thousand dollars. That Cook could put together such a stock in the few months of his first wintering-over speaks highly for the productivity of Thule's sixty-odd hunters, only some of whom—ten to twenty men—worked for a few months on behalf of the explorer.

It seems that all the explorers of that period became businessmen, and at a time when the Eskimos, who were very low in supplies, had no store through which to trade, and when fur commanded very high prices on the market. What the Eskimos realized from these deals is not known. Looking at their standard of living in 1909, one would conclude that it was little.

The progress of the Peary expeditions had a great influence on the life of the Polar Eskimos. He recruited them in large numbers and depended on their work. Forty or fifty men, or about two-thirds of the group's hunters, were employed by the year. They, in turn, came to depend upon him for the products, weapons, and tools to which he introduced them. However, he came only every five years, and while waiting for him, for lack of ammunition, many Eskimos used to hunt with bone bullets.

Once he had fulfilled his ambitions as an explorer, Peary abandoned his repeated visits. The deprivation was such that the Danish government paid for a Danish boat to distribute the rifles and other tools by way of thanks for the help the Eskimos had voluntarily given young Knud Rasmussen and his companion Moltke when both were sick during the winter they spent in Thule, in 1903–4.

Having surmised that Peary would never return, Knud Rasmussen himself decided that it was necessary to provide this isolated, archaic people with basic necessities—knives, rifles, ammunition—on a regular basis. Initially his pur-

pose was philanthropic, later scientific. The Danish government refused officially, for financial reasons, to extend north of Upernavik the commercial
network that Rasmussen was suggesting be established in Thule. Young Knud
was obliged to found a Cape York Station society with private funds. By
degrees, the society came to function as a territorial government, and it did
so until Rasmussen's death in 1933. Rasmussen decided to use the returns
from his store to finance his scientific studies of the Eskimos. And so something
truly exceptional came to pass: an archaic society itself subventioned research
into its own history. Proceeds from the store were devoted in part to financing
seven scientific expeditions and the exploitation of their results; the balance
paid the salaries of Rasmussen and his colleagues.

Knud Rasmussen's sense of justice, his lofty vision, and his scientific
seriousness are evident. From the very first, he had chosen the Eskimos as his
lifelong companions; he was one of them, and they trusted him completely.
Rasmussen showed great respect for the human dignity and intelligence of
the hunters. Also, he was the first to acquire an overall view of Eskimo history. By funding the seven ethnological and archaeological Thule expeditions, as well as the admirable publications based on the expeditions, the
Polar Eskimos of Thule became the first patrons of Eskimology concerned
with an area that ranges from Alaska to the eastern coast of Greenland. Of
course, official financial support was added later, but I know of no other
instance in which a small archaic society has helped to finance a sustained
program of studies into its own history over so broad a geographical front—
nine thousand miles. Two hundred and fifty Polar Eskimos thereby helped
lay the groundwork of Arctic history for such powerful countries as the
United States and Canada. And it is to these modest Thule expeditions between 1910 and 1933, which were, I repeat, subventioned by the Thule
store, that Denmark owes its status as an important scientific nation in the
Arctic.

The Group
and Its Leader

Every Eskimo I talked with in 1950 knew that thirty years before, a dog's breath
made a denser cloud than now, a sign that the 1920 temperatures had been
lower during the winter, and the ice in March thicker and more stationary.
Waves had been more powerful then, which meant that winds were stronger
and were blowing off the glaciers (from the southeast), whereas winds now
blew in from the sea (from the southwest) and were less violent. Experienced
middle-aged kayakers were aware of all these things. They knew, too, that for
some generations prior to 1800, there had actually been a brief ice age (1600–
1800), and that for several generations before Piuli (Peary) came, in 1890, seals

and walruses had been scarce. Because seals were in short supply, there had also been few bears.

The harsh physical conditions in which the Eskimo has always lived fostered a social structure that is both communal and hierarchic. In an environment which poses a constant and direct threat to the community, everyone's function must be strictly defined. Traditions remained fully alive and vital because they embodied age-old or organizational requirements on which survival depended.

The main problem such a microsociety had to deal with was how to adjust the activities of the group—in the case of the Polar Eskimos, thirty families in 1800 and seventy families in 1950—to incessant fluctuations of temperature and humidity, which crucially affected the region's flora and fauna.

For example, when the climate was warmer, game was abundant. Eskimo society then encouraged an increase in the birth rate by lifting food, hunting, and sex taboos. The days when two out of three newborn females were put to death were long past. Taking infant mortality into account, the natural population growth rate was stable at about 1.5 percent. Only the sickly and deformed were killed. However, when ice and fog abounded, when snowdrifts persisted and turned into névé and then into small glaciers, causing the surrounding waters to become colder, Eskimo society turned Malthusian and prudently balanced the size of the population against their area's current resources. For a group the size of the whole tribe of Thule, forty or fifty fertile women were enough to guarantee demographic renewal.

As one can imagine in such a small group, this kind of planning was very complex: adjustments had to be made twenty-eight months in advance, since this was the average interval between births and since climatic forecasting was so difficult.

Accordingly, every effort was made to obtain an exact climatic analysis. These primitive hunters studied natural phenomena with the closest attention. They observed the flight of migrating birds; the movement and shape of clouds; the moon and its halos; the stars which were bright or dim depending on the amount of fog; the slightest nuances in early seasonal changes; the melting of the frozen tundra; the movements of shoreline and sea in relation to natural reference points—mounds of scree or stone caches. They took careful note of the depth of the thaw and of slides, changes in the routes of hares and foxes, a delay or advance in the flights of guillemots—all of which signaled warmth or cold. If there were no *illeraq* * and *eqalugaq* [33] along the coast and no birds hunting for them, clearly there would be no seal in the fjord that winter. Hunters studied the itineraries of the reindeer and musk ox with great attention because changes in their behavior reflected an entire ecology. If

---

*The illeraq is a very small fish the guillemot and whale feed on. The illeraq winters over, and it shines in the dark. The eqalugaq or Polar cod, is a small coastal fish and a food source for seals.

fewer guillemots than usual arrived at the spring gathering place, and if the thaw was shorter and less extensive, the hunters could predict a cold, foggy summer and a persistent ice field. They knew every detail of the morphology of every animal they slaughtered.

As people met and talked together, these signs were transmitted to the entire group, which could then assess them and, with the common good in mind, reach some joint decisions. No wonder the hunters seemed to listen so intently to me: they were literally soaking up everything I said; their reserved, seeming immobility contrasted sharply with their decisionmaking, which could be lightning quick.

Group life was also based on strict rules of social organization. The first principle was communism: the earth, the hunting areas, the sea, the more important tools of production—a boat, for example—and the igloos all belonged to the group. Only individual hunting gear was private property. Inheritance was limited to the transmitting of personal effects to the widow. If a man's sledges, kayaks, rifles, and dogs were not sacrificed and placed next to his grave, the Council of Hunters would distribute them—usually to his sons or his closest male relatives (brothers, uncles).

In this egalitarian society, which was opposed to the idea of accumulation and profit, the kill from a hunt had to be shared immediately. Women belonged to the group, and the purpose of exchanging women, which was ritually practiced during certain festivals, was to break the special bond that love created between a man and a woman and to remind the family that the basic and most important entity was the group. The widespread practice of adoption ultimately aimed at the same goal: it "broke up" the natural family. The family as the basic unit was only a temporary grouping for the sake of convenience. Sexual promiscuity favored procreation and also counteracted any tendency on the part of the couple to become mutually possessive and to exclude other people. Each of the partners belonged to the group and, all in a spirit of political unity, it was considered good for the couple to be broken up from time to time!

A second principle might be called the principle of inequality. There was inequality between age groups. A young man who was not yet marriageable or did not own his own dog team was not allowed to take part in discussions. He would stand in the doorway of the igloo, where the men had gathered, listening in silence with a feigned air of absence. The same obtained for old people who, like Pualuna, lived in an igloo or tent apart from the rest; it used to be that in hard times they were abandoned altogether. Unlike Indians, the Eskimos had no special reverence for old people. An old man was not considered a wise man, and the Council was not governed by elders. The old person was useless and lived out his life surrounded by indifference.

Then there was inequality between the sexes. Women ate by themselves and after the men. The order in which food was distributed after a hunt is significant; first the dogs were fed, then the children, then the hunters; lastly, the women.

DISCOVERY OF A STONE AGE PEOPLE

Discovery of the Polar Eskimos near Cape York on August 9, 1818, by John Ross. In the background, wearing the hat, is the interpreter Sakaeus.

Whaling ships in Melville Bay, off Cape York, 1818–1910. Drawing after a sketch by Kane.

A tupilaq. Ivory sculpture by Ussaqaq.
Siorapaluk, October 1967.

(BELOW) *Atisaq,* or jacket, made of
guillemot skins. Polar Eskimo, 1900.
(Berlin Museum; Dahlem).

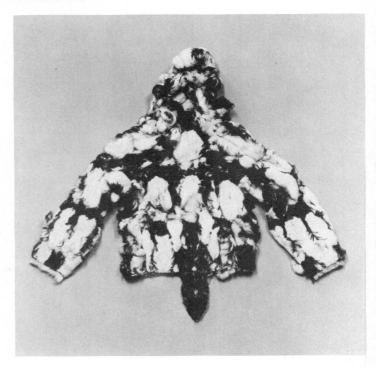

Sorqaq in Appat, August 1905. *(Bertelsen, Arktisk Institut, Copenhagen)*

Itukusuk and his sister Qaassaaluk, 1909. *(Arktisk Institut, Copenhagen)*

Qaassaaluk in her summer tent with her two children, Natuk and Inuteq, 1909. *(Arktisk Institut, Copenhagen)*

Four Polar Eskimo hunters. *(Bertelsen, August 1905; Arktisk Institut, Copenhagen)*

Woman from Thule with child in her amaaq. Uummannaq, August 1905. *(Bertelsen, Arktisk Institut, Copenhagen)*

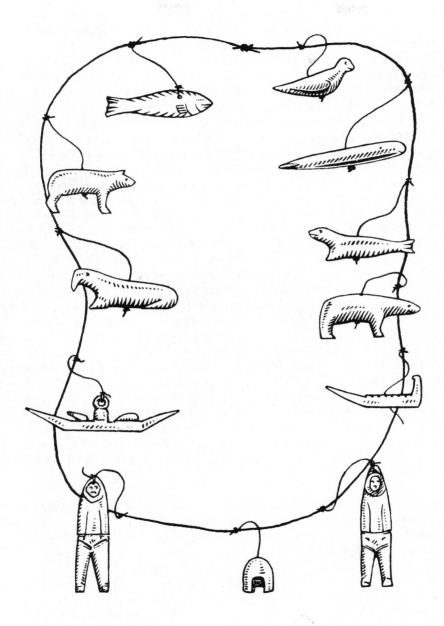

Necklace made of walrus or seal ivory. The subjects represent major elements of Eskimo life. Clockwise from bottom: igloo, Eskimo woman, kayak, walrus, dog, salmon, partridge, female narwhal (no tusk or tooth), seal, bear, sledge, Eskimo woman. Upernavik, 1950. (*Private collection*)

The producers were the ones who made the big decisions. The young, the old, and women as a group were very like what in ancient Greece was called the chorus.

There were "strong" people and "weak" or incompetent people. For an Eskimo, "Seqajuk! Lazybones!" was one of the most cutting insults. Parasites had to justify their existence by silently performing servile chores. They were recognizable by their bearing, tone of voice, and behavior; they acted either like clowns or like servants. Deformed or mentally deficient infants were killed at birth: the mother would strangle the child or smother it with a handful of snow. A child who grew up a weakling was usually killed by its family. But if it was allowed to live—and there were several such cases among the Polar Eskimos—it would be grudgingly accepted only as long as it did not become a burden. The scorn which a strong man felt for a weak one was sometimes expressed by acts of violence. When I was in Illulik, on Hudson Bay, in 1961, I witnessed a wrestling bout in which a "parasite" was pinned down by his opponent. To emphasize his strength and his disdain, the winner urinated on his victim.

Another story about violence shows how in a communal society, despite all intended correctives, the strong dominate the weak in moments of crisis. Two brothers were driving two sledges, accompanied by their father and the children of one of them. The brothers did not get along well. One was secretly in conflict with the other, who on this occasion was a little drunk. Unpleasant words were exchanged. One went for the other. The more violent of the two became frightened and made a move to protect himself which proved fatal: he grabbed his rifle. The drunken brother jumped him before he had a chance to cock the gun, broke the weapon, and bound him hand and foot. It was June, and the sea was still frozen. He slowly cut a round hole in the ice and threw his brother into the icy water. He silenced his old father with a glare, seized his brother's two little orphans, who were huddled near the sledge, and threw them into the hole for good measure. Officially, this was recorded as an accident on treacherous ice.

Lastly, in the communal society that was Thule, the different regions were recognized as unequal. Thanks to the region's diversity, it was rich in resources. The Polar Eskimos' unity was strengthened by kinship alliances cemented by exchanges of the surplus of each region, such as walrus meat, bird kiviaq, thongs made from bearded-seal skins, bearskins, narwhal tusks, meteoric iron, flint, and soapstone. The inhabited territory was divided into five complementary sections, of which Uummannaq-Thule was the center. To the north lived the Oqqorliit, the "people living north of Uummannaq-Thule"; to the south lived the Niggerlliit, the "people on whom the south wind blows." Each family lived in one section of the district from three to five years. In the course of the continual rotation from north to south, a head of family exchanged his stone house for someone else's; hunting grounds, as we have seen, were held in common and the houses were a *commune bonum*. Because homes were rotated this way, families could not become regionalized and it was impossible for one powerful family to appropriate a section of the territory. And the tribe remained unified.[34]

One essential fact: None of those who were discriminated against ever challenged the legitimacy of the discrimination—not the young man, or the woman, or the poor hunter; not the man without relatives, the weak man, the recently arrived Eskimo or the Eskimo who lived in a poor hunting area because his relatives were there; not the sick man or the scapegoat. This was because their social structure derived from conditions determined by the milieu and not by men. Produce, reproduce: where these two fundamental goals of Arctic life conjoined, the family formed the basic economic and demographic unit; it was the only one suited to fill all levels between what was too little and what was too much.

Collective hunting—for narwhal and walrus—always presupposed good relations among these groups and, by extension, required every man to respect the traditional rules that governed every phase of the hunt. At no stage did the individual as such exist: group law and group values were preeminent. The way in which public confession used to be made and forgiveness obtained is significant. The Eskimo would go out onto the ice field, turn to face the village, and confess his wrongdoing out loud; then he would be pardoned. Important as the role which the individual plays might be, his rights actually amounted to nothing, inasmuch as by himself he was incapable of solving the problems of his own survival. Though functionally aristocratic, sociologically the collectivity was communal.

The kinship community constituted a major organism that determined genealogical grouping but did so in sufficiently "open" terms for it to be extended beyond immediate blood ties to constitute also a unit or economic organization and regrouping.

One condition of an Eskimo's security was therefore genealogical. To be an orphan (*iliaruvoq, iliarsuq*) inexorably relegated one to the lowest level of

The orphan, or iliarsuq. Drawing by Aleralak. Illulik, Canada, August 1960. (*Private collection*)

society—unless one made extraordinary efforts to improve one's status. The orphan was literally nothing. *Iliarjupaluk:* poor little orphan! Since he had no parents, he was a burden on everyone. Therefore, he had to justify his existence by his physical strength, his endurance, and his high spirits. He proved that he possessed all these qualities by bringing himself up alone. He could not even be sure that, once the group hunting was finished, someone would lend him a harpoon or gun so that he could get food for himself. It used to be, at least in the Canadian Arctic, that an orphan was allowed to sleep only in the katak, the passageway that led into the igloo, until he was bigger and stronger, when he was allowed inside the igloo to mingle with the family. Was this a test? In the central Canadian Arctic, I once stumbled over an orphan. The poor shivering creature was huddled in the katak; he did not even have the right to share the warmth of family life inside the igloo, only a few feet from his bed. Sitting in the dark passageway, after the others had finished their meal, he ate whatever scraps they chose to leave for him.

In Thule, an orphan was also called *inulupaluk*—"poor little man." He was never allowed on the illeq; at best, he would sleep on the lower level of the igloo on the *ippat* where the oil lamps stood. Ululik had known an orphan when he was a boy, and he told me that this orphan was always ravenous. He was not allowed to join the hunt, but had to remain in or near the igloo, acting as a kiffaq—fetching water, lending a hand here or there, and so on. He was treated worse than the dogs and had a terrible time just staying alive. However, if an orphan overcame these trials, if he raised himself above other men, then he would be recognized as the best of men. Such is the orphan Kivioq—the great hero of Eskimo legends.

For those among the poor who had a mother or father or had been adopted, the collectivity was, in the sociological sense, communal. From earliest childhood, the Eskimo was aware of this. Père Mouchard, the French Catholic missionary and author in northern Canada, observed discerningly that when the children of the Caribou Eskimos on the Kazan River got up in the morning, they would visit neighboring igloos to ask for more food. According to custom, they could not be refused, and so there was an equalization of supplies which favored the youngest members of the community. "As soon as they receive the gift," Père Mouchard wrote, "they run home without eating it or saying thank you. I was told that the child must take the morsel of food to his parents. The parents pretend to eat it and then give it back to the child, who learns in this way not to be selfish."

Although blood relationships were binding, they did not determine everything. After all, in a small group in which kinship is bilateral, the genealogical family would include practically the entire population, and alone it would produce a diffuse, inert system. Through a genetic differentiation extending to the third degree, the global genealogical family was broken down into functional families in order to form definitive family nuclei and—even more important—economic units that structured society into active and responsible autonomous groups.

Marriage was the primary available means by which an adult man could strengthen or limit the crucial economic-familial nucleus on which his entire nature depended.

The Eskimo, always eager to cement alliances, has applied his ingenuity to inventing other kinds of relationships. Associations voluntarily formed helped to strengthen or extend the family network. The system of adoption, still widespread in the eastern Canadian Arctic in the 1960s although uncommon in Thule since the turn of the century, allowed a community to bring into its circle of relatives a family not allied by blood; or to strengthen blood or family bonds (bonds within the extended family were strengthened when the grandfather adopted his grandson, who would then call him *ataata*—"my father"—while addressing his natural father simply by his name); or to prolong temporary bonds (after an exchange of wives, couples often adopted any children who were born during this exchange and whose paternity was unknown).

The Eskimo's inventive genius led him to discover still other forms of alliance—by virtue of names, for example; two persons bearing the same name were considered to be related.

There were also certain forms of "godparentage," which I studied in 1960–64 in the central Canadian Arctic. As a child, the Eskimo was taught by his mother that certain very special bonds united him with a certain person, one of his more distant relatives. This person would be his *illora* or godparent. As long as he lived, he had to never pronounce this person's name, and his connections with him had to remain remote. *Illoriit,* being thus secretly allied, had to help each other.

Sakaeunnguaq told me how his life had been saved at Uinassuk, near Qaanaaq. He was walking on a dangerous patch of newly formed ice, and just as his harpoon sank through it, he was protected by the power of an old woman —his illora—who, at that moment, in the village, put her foot against the inside of the window in her igloo so that Sakaeunnguaq's foot would not break through the ice under his weight and he would return safe and sound.

The hunting relationship, which was no less singular, has been mentioned by the Canadian anthropologist Diamond Jenness as existing farther west, among the Copper Eskimos; it still existed in Illulik in the 1960s, but in Thule it had died out already in 1950. This relationship held only among men and, as far as I know, operated only in relation to the common seal. A hunter who gave part of a seal to another hunter established a contractual bond that was quite permanent. For example, if A gave B a certain part of a seal (say, the lower part or *kujak*), B now became the *kujaga;* the two hunters were henceforth *kujare.* The first chance B had, he had to give A the same part of another seal, and good manners dictated that the principle of this exchange be continued as long as possible. If, for lack of a seal, B was unable to cement the

Harpoon heads in the Thule district, 1950–51. The old form was called *sakku;* the new form, *tuukkaq.* The harpoon used in kayaks is called *unaaq.* The top center figure is a salmon harpoon *(kajujak).* Below, a bow drill, which enables the Eskimo to cut through a piece of bone. It was still in use in 1950. The bow drill serves to light a fire in the central Canadian Arctic, but not among the Polar Eskimos, who used to strike a flint or rapidly turn a stick on a piece of dry wood covered with cottony plants, which are kept dry next to the body. The embers were kept alive in dry peat.

alliance by returning the gift, he would be sure to offer a fish that was equivalent.

However diverse and flexible the traditional Eskimo group may appear, its core has been firm and its structure well ordered. Historically, this group has been more than an assemblage of people, more than a collection of families; it has been a tool, the consolidation of various survival techniques, all of which are informed by experience gained over more than a thousand perilous years. Tradition has expressed—and also provided a framework for—modes of behavior and techniques that have always guaranteed the safety of the group. Within the group, one man has served as the authority who interprets this tradition: in Foxe Bay, in Canada, he is called the *isumataq*. *Isuma* means "thought"; *isumataq* means "he who thinks a great deal"—a wise man. In Thule, he is called the naalagaq, although this term implies authority rather than wisdom.

In the past the naalagaq or isumataq had to be a skillful hunter; it was he who guaranteed the group a regular supply of food through his authority, his foresight, and his sense of organization. But the Eskimos' fear of permitting inequality to intrude on however small a scale meant that they would accept this authority only temporarily, for clearly defined and brief operations.

Today, as then, the naalagaq or isumataq should be more modest, calm, laconic, good-humored, and generous than other people. It is incumbent on him to be generous, but not to such an extent that generosity becomes oppressive. Whoever visited Inuterssuaq in Kangerluarsuk was always assured of finding an abundance of meat and fish there. "Qaa! Nerivoq! Go ahead—eat as much as you like!" But the very tone of this invitation, emphasizing as it did Inuterssuaq's power, reestablished his distance from the guest, who was put in the position of a person asking a favor. Therefore, when the best hunters visited Inuterssuaq, they preferred to remain as circumspect as possible: they did not want to benefit from his "generosity"; their dignity would have been hurt by the pleasure of eating together, which involved a certain amount of gluttony.

The naalagaq must also be laconic. Kutsikitsoq could never have been a chief: "He talks too much! He has no self-control, he brags like a child!" The naalagaq must have a certain bearing; his manner must put everyone at ease. And like Claudel's statues of saints, a naalagaq must "have a face that is in some sense ordinary." It is important that the naalagaq have roots in the country: although Kaalipaluk, Peary's Eskimo son, was an excellent hunter and an ingenious, agreeable, and generous man, he could never have been a naalagaq. He was too "individual," too "different." His mother, Aleqasina[35]—Peary's "friend," as the Inuit put it, and Inuterssuaq's mother-in-law—was well aware of this when she advised him to mingle with everyone indiscriminately so that his origins would be forgotten. But blood was stronger, and Kaalipaluk's behavior remained that of a white leader. His igloo was more like the hut of an American trapper than an Eskimo's igloo. The fact that he had a table and chair, that he took some care with its decoration, that he sorted his magazines and stored them in a trunk—such things evidenced an un-Eskimo way of thinking. "He's a white man!"—and it was true that he was never able to become the village spokesman, and no more than might his daughters, Paulina and Mikissuk, whatever their merits. The same was true of Anaakkaq, the son of Matt Henson, Peary's black servant.

The man who acts as an isumataq or the man who becomes a naalagaq through the forces of his personality—Nukapianguaq in Etah, Imina in Siorapaluk, Uutaaq in Uummannaq-Thule, Sorqaq in Qeqertarsuaq, and Gideon in Savigssivik—is constantly obliged to surpass himself. He is involved; he is swept along. He represents the sort of mysteriously strong personality chosen not only by the group but also by chance and the elements. He understands that in the eyes of his people his function is to organize vast undertakings and that the counterpoint to his special gifts is the achievement of great successes.

Although in the past the group's standard of living depended ultimately on the men's physical strength, prowess—their ability to provide abundant reserves of meat—this would have been pointless if the leader's intrinsic qualities had not ensured the group's vitality and inner peace, if safeguarding its social cohesiveness did not act to preserve its physical survival. The naalagaq-

Cutting up a seal. Drawing by Appalinnguaq. Siorapaluk, March 1950. *(Private collection)*

isumataq's generosity, and the hierarchic system by which game was divided on the spot or later, in the village, made hoarding or any differentiation on the basis of wealth impossible.

The naalagaq-isumataq saw to it that hunters not only shared the game but that they were mindful of the rules of solidarity. Once the men had returned to shore and divided the meat, I often saw the "captain" ostentatiously set aside from his own portion something for widows, old people, the destitute, and the disabled. In making these gifts, the leader acknowledged the fact that his power had, in a sense, been delegated to him, and in effect he was giving back to the collectivity goods which he knew he could accumulate only in proportion to the possibilities for action that the group had granted to him. The prestige and the authority were his; the benefits, in unequal shares, belonged to each member of the group.

"Naammappoq! He has done the right thing!" people said, and they smiled gravely. Or the gesture had, in fact, been too dramatic and individual to be well received:

"Look at our naalagaq taking himself seriously."

In the past, the naalagaq-isumataq was head of the family community; owner of the boat that enabled the hunters to undertake the arduous walrus hunt; unofficially the agent who handed out family allocations, old people's pensions, and other forms of assistance from the government; Eskimo delegate to the annual Danish-Eskimo Council (in all, the district sent three delegates); and on occasion, visiting nurse. In addition to these multiple responsibilities, he had also a religious function. In settlements that had not been assigned a catechist, the naalagaq-isumataq substituted as pastor. He was responsible for preparing the devotional lessons and for delivering the homilies.

To recapitulate, these are the requirements for being a naalagaq-isumataq: a great past, prestigious forebears, a family lineage, innate authority and wisdom, pride, a cheerful temperament, roots in the country, and a measure of good luck. The choice of such a leader, who always can be and always is challenged, is the answer to a need of the group, and the choice is a spontaneous manifestation on the group's part.

For the naalagaq derives his prestige from something over and beyond his personality and other circumstantial factors—from something more remote or, one might say, much higher. Through him, their leader and the master of their destiny, the people maintain contact, beneficial for one and all, with the supreme reality which lives in the hearts of all: "Inuit! Inuit, tikut! Eskimos! We, Eskimos!"

In the light of all this, would it not be ill-considered to assert that the Eskimos have no gift for politics and that their understanding of the problems of life cannot reach beyond the present? It is unquestionably true that for at least the last six hundred years the Eskimo people have had no history in the strict sense of the word. They have, however, a vivid memory of their past— a past in which the Eskimos were a strong, proud people, when those living near the forests of Alaska and Canada fought relentlessly against the Indians, while elsewhere others fought no less so against the Vikings. Every Eskimo carries within him the prideful awareness that his people have conquered their very surroundings—the implacable desert of ice.

The Thule Eskimos preserved their individuality over thousands of years by clinging to an anarcho-communalism that was at once supportive and constraining. The group was all-powerful, the individual never more than its mouthpiece. Each person's thought, each personality, coalesced with that of others in order to contribute to the good of all. One did not say "I think" but "the group thinks," thus suppressing one's personal ideas. I myself was gradually brought around to doing this; to behave otherwise would have seemed incongruous, inviting ridicule.

The sacred group had priority of claim on everything: the subsoil, the water, the hunting areas, the game belonged to it. When an Eskimo went out to hunt seal, he did not say "I am going to try to catch a seal" but "to have my share of seal." And for fear that a man become too possessively bound to a certain area, it was even provided that there be a rotation of dwellings every five or six years; a given igloo was never the permanent property of any one family. Authority as well could be accepted only on a delegated and temporary basis.

This collective spirit, then, obliged the members of this society constantly to rise above egoism and every individualistic drive. A competitive spirit might be expressed only as the wish to be best in service of the group. Curiously, it was the women, whose children are omnipresent witnesses—their eyes and ears perpetually on the alert, the igloos having no doors—who formed the chorus that ensured faithful observation of the rules.

(I think as well of the atypical people—often those sexually inhibited—the permanent expression of the opposition, forever on the outskirts of the group and yet, like royal fools, deeply respected by the group, as if they were the reverse of its own image. And what a reverse of that image!)

These men, violent though they were, feared their women. Was it due to the power that the women might acquire over them? Was it indeed women the men were fleeing sexually through the collective celebrations? Even the Eskimos' role-playing, as if they were perpetually onstage: was role-playing accounted for by their being caught in an oppressive communalism which their implacable milieu and ancestral fear of famine had enjoined on them for centuries?

Speaking for myself, it is a fact that I felt constantly protected by that great guardian shadow of the group; it obliged each of them to behave toward me in a way that was perhaps contrary to his own inner impulses—whether irritation, antipathy, violence, or affection and friendship—and always under the judgmental eye of that historical collective conscience embodied in the women. It was a rare thing to be a lone white man among them. I do know that all of them were grateful to me for having been in our daily life both actor and accomplice—like them—and also for having voiced on occasion the grandeur

Eskimo woman from Siorapaluk. Drawing by Appalinnguaq (eighteen years old). September 1950. (*Private collection*)

of their surprised self-awareness, for having sometimes made them comprehend the reality of it and thereby helped some of them to excel themselves.

But it is certain that this attitude on my part would not have had the same value in their eyes if, on the missions I made with some of them, I had not had the opportunity to know them on a one-to-one basis, to have shared their solitude and, sometimes, to have been the confidant of their inner distress.

They are, I believe, secretly grateful to me for their having been able with complete ease to express themselves briefly to me by signs—a flash of the eye, a gesture, a breath—which say more than words and speak for the second, most secret identity. This was something it would have been impossible for them to do within the group and especially in the bosom of the family.

But also and above all they knew that although they trusted me enough to allow me to perceive, in their brief moments of friendly abandonment, a little of their "hidden face," I judged their other face—the one reserved for the group—to be equally "real," however theatrical it seemed.

For the truth of a human being is found as much, if not more, in what he wishes to be.

What will the Eskimo become without his corseted half, from which he often used to suffer but from which he drew his grandeur, his dignity, and—who knows?—his reason for being?

When he is reduced to being no more than his secret shadow, what is the individual Eskimo going to become when he is enmeshed alone in a dominant, Danish-Greenlandic industrial society that is assimilative, indifferent to what is unlike itself? His ancient masks, sneering or impassive, have the face of the sphinx.

Daily Life
in a Peat Igloo

It was one of those nights when no one whispers even if he hears an Eskimo talking in his sleep, a night when the sexual act is silent and brief but the couple lies in a long, close embrace, a night when everyone snuggles up to keep warm. Bodies are naked under the animal skins. Heads are turned toward the center of the hut, feet toward the wall. Here a shock of frost-whitened hair, there a muscular brown arm is visible. The cold igloo begins to come to life around midday.

In the early morning, I rolled over onto my right side, then onto my left, and looked at the people who for the past week had been my hosts. The father lay in the middle of the illeq—his place both day and night—sleeping on his right side; with a master's gesture of authority, he had flung out his arm and cushioned his head on it. He had not moved much as he slept, but he had often been troubled by dreams and had muttered aloud. His wife lay to his right, near the wall where a tripod supported the oil lamp that she tended with the almost unthinking gestures of a vestal virgin. The small children lay between the parents. The old man was relegated to a place along the other wall, colder because it was on the north and exposed to the wind. Had there been an adopted child, it would have been next to him. And if the adopted child had been a girl, she would have been responsible for looking after the second oil lamp, located beside her.

Blood brothers and sisters bed down side by side until they are seven or eight; often they lie face-to-face, and play with each other's hands or sleep with their arms around each other. That night, in addition to me there were two other guests, a man and a woman. The man had bothered me all night: he kept yelping with fear because of nightmares. Later, he told me he had seen knives and monstrous men with enormous, misshapen five-sided heads flanked by rabbit's ears that stood straight up; their teeth protruded, and they lunged at him, trying to catch him in their little arms. Then, with legs apart, they would stand staring at him out of vacant eyes. His terror had been so great, he told me, perhaps by way of apology, that for part of the night he had been as if paralyzed, unable to touch the woman next to him or call for help. He was grateful for my friendly receptiveness, and talked on softly, describing his visions in detail; still very upset, he asked me whether white men also suffered from nighttime terrors. In a low voice, I explained that we do not believe in *tupilat*, but that we too are sometimes possessed by a mysterious inner demon.

We had been talking softly like this for perhaps ten minutes when the mistress of the igloo—the woman was always the first to rise—sat up and crossed her legs; her skin was creased and there were bags under her puffy eyes; her face was heavy and sad as, lost in an inner dream, she held her hieratic lotus position. Presently, she slipped into her kapatak, her hooded vest, straightened her legs, and drew on her foxskin pants; then, with deliberate movements, she bound her hair in a chignon.

She looked slowly around her: the igloo was half-asleep. One or two people were whispering; others were snoring. (Perhaps this is the very brief interlude when an Eskimo mother feels most herself, happy for an instant to recover the lost freedom of her girlhood?) Still seated, the woman reached out for her long white boots; their bear-fur cuffs had served as her pillow. The legs of the boots and the soles, which had been resting on the ground, were frozen. With gentle, resigned movements, she softened the skin, bending and creasing it; she had no time to chew the skin, which would have made it even softer.

Half-rising on the platform, she pulled on the cold boots and, walking gingerly, for the soles were still stiff, went to cut up some meat with quick blows of her hatchet; the pieces were small and would defrost, at least on the outside, by the time the men got up. She cut off a bit of gelatinous, pinkish white fat for the oil lamp. Some ten to fourteen ounces—a large handful—would last through the morning. With a root, she revived the flaxen wicks, separating them with some of the oil they swam in; they had been about to start smoking. The odorless yellow flame rose, but it was still ragged; the woman evened it all around the lip of the bowl. The heat rose and mingled with the musty night smells. Snuggling even closer to one another, everyone took wordless pleasure in this final brief moment of nighttime peace. Reveling in our tiny reprieve, we listened as the woman tended the lamp, broke the ice in the pan, chopped the meat, and peed abundantly into the communal pail.

Then, as if to assert their authority, the adult men began to clear their throats and hawk up phlegm. The guest blew his nose into his fingers. He swallowed the greenish mucus in one gulp. (As for the phlegm, it is considered good manners to send it flying into the can placed at the foot of the illeq for that purpose. Lying on his back, a well-bred hunter can spit into the air in a high parabola and hit the small opening of the can behind and below him . . . and less than a foot from the pile of freshly chopped meat!)

The men, adolescents, and children now began to stir under the animal skins. Half sitting up, the old man rubbed the rims of his heavy-lidded eyes and kneaded his armpits; his fingers were caked with blood and filth. The host scratched his mop of hair slowly, onanistically. A good half hour went by, while each person enjoyed being indolent in his own way. (This is the moment when an Eskimo examines himself, appraises himself. Therefore, he never gets up quickly. Yet if he lets this respite go on too long, a somber melancholy begins to steal over him.)

As if to cut the time short, our host called for something to eat: "Ti! Ti! Tuavi! Tea, tea, quickly!" The woman made a show of devotion by dramatically speeding up her movements. She took down the pan hanging above the oil lamp, lighted the Primus, and set the pan on it. She pumped fast to increase the pressure. The water boiled and steam filled the igloo. (All Eskimos like steam: it is a reassuring sign of wealth. Memories of warmth are stored up like

Louse scratcher made of bone. The wooden handle is topped by a tuft of bear hairs, which are said to attract *kumaks,* or lice. Thule, December 1950. *(Private collection)*

provisions against the hours of cold and stress.) The mingled odors of coffee and tea, whiffs of oil and sweat, and the murmur of the Primus were lulling the sleepier men and women into a new torpor. Without rising or even turning his head, our host stretched out his arm and the woman handed him his cup of tea. He turned over onto his stomach and drank it boiling hot. Floating on the liquid were bits of straw from the boots that had been drying above the lamp, and particles that smelled like coffee; since tea and coffee were prepared in the same pot, coffee grounds, tea leaves, and the tastes of both were all mixed together.

Apart from that "Ti!" no one had yet spoken aloud; only the children whispered as they rummaged about for their clothes. (The Eskimo values this silence. This is when, in his head, his day takes shape: "Will I go seal hunting in the bay?" he asks himself. "Or go to Tuluriaq for fox? Ah, but Kajoq, good dog, has a broken anu [breast strap]. Too late now to give it to the woman. I'll mend it on the way or, better yet, before I leave; I'll visit Imina. He has a little bit of everything—he'll surely give me a harness. After all, I gave him the hind leg of the walrus we killed together at Pitorarfik. . . . Ah! Supposing I go to Neqi? Taffinnguaq is so nice to me! . . . ")

Some such ideas were running through our host's head. He kept sniffing worriedly (the Eskimo's way of punctuating his thoughts). Meanwhile, the children—still abed although by now it was past noon—were amusing themselves by stroking each other's backs and scratching each other's heads.

Woman inside an igloo. Drawing by Ivalu (sixty years old). Qeqertaq. *(Private collection)*

The man continued to mutter to himself. Sitting on the illeq, he dressed without a word to anyone; one would have thought boredom was pushing him to go out hunting. Grumpily, he got into his sealskin anorak and half drew on his bearskin nanu. The woman handed him his kamiks,[36] which she had chewed to thaw them out and make them soft. Earlier, she had slipped into them the inner boots of hare's skin, which she had turned inside out the evening before so that they would dry during the night. With his boots half laced, and combing his hair with his fingers, the man went over to the igalaaq to take his first look at the weather.

Still grumbling, he turned his back, crouched, and peed into a little gas-oil barrel; then as he mechanically hitched up his nanu with his left hand, with his right he cut himself a piece of frozen walrus. His mouth was still full as he washed his face and dried it on an unspeakably dirty towel. At this point, he was just beginning to emerge from his half dream. He sat on a crate, carefully laced up his instep with a double thong, and tightened the laces around his calf. Then, still talking to himself, he noisily left the igloo. He squatted down before the outer door, his hands in his pockets, his body hunched forward. He breathed deep and long, sniffing out the weather that lay ahead: "Ieh! Yes!" he grunted after some minutes. Pivoting on his heels, he bent double, and, now totally taken up by his plan, hurried back into the igloo. One half-swallowed word— ". . . uriaq!"—let his wife know he was going to Tuluriaq. As he ate some more meat, he kept grunting "Tuluriaq," as if to convince himself that he had indeed made the right choice.

The woman, her head bowed, busied herself with the lamp and gave no sign that she had heard. The man's rhythm now changed abruptly. His gestures became quick and sure: in his mind, he was already on his way. Quick, quick —pipe, tobacco, pocket knife, reindeer-tendon thread, needle, snow-beater, file. . . . The man moved about the igloo with an air of authority, looking neither to right nor to left. He took short steps this way, that way, like a caged animal whose cage is about to open.

Now, playing important, the hunter began to speak very loudly, shouting about everything and nothing amid echoes from his admiring audience. At last he rushed out of the house and went to his sledge. After a short, calculated delay, the woman followed. (It is considered proper for a wife at this point to carry several small things out to her husband—she actually stoops under the "weight" of her load—so that the neighbors will say she is a good arnaq, a true "man's woman.") The packet was placed on the floor of the sledge and wrapped in layers of skins. Facing one another, the man and woman together tightened the sealskin thong which crisscrossed the sledge from front to back.

"Soo!" A pause. The Eskimo drew a long breath. He filled his pipe. The woman, who still had not uttered a word, walked ahead with a whip to control the dogs—now to urge them forward, now to hold them in check—as they negotiated the narrow passage over the hummocky coastal ice. Moving heavily, the hunter took his place on the sledge. The team had been waiting nervously for this moment; it took off like a shot and slipped skillfully along the passages between the hummocks. When the ice became smooth and flat, the woman began to run. She ran ten, twenty, thirty feet, then, suddenly, she moved to one side and the dogs broke into a gallop. As the man passed, without looking at her he grabbed the whip she held out, her face betraying as little expression as possible. He would be gone for forty-eight hours. The departure scene had been played to perfection: the hunter the strong one; the woman his humble, meek companion. She hardly had time to summon up a sad little smile before the man and his sledge were for her only a dark spot against the horizon.

Out on the ice, the man would keep up a steady five-mile-per-hour pace, shifting his position on the sledge now and then. Far from his family and village, he would feel that he had suddenly been set free. Quit of group constraints, he was himself again, sole master of his dreams—free. Some Eskimos have told me that at such times they feel as if a weight has been lifted from their chests.

Meanwhile, alone on the ice bank, the woman shivered in her *natserq,* her hooded sealskin jacket. (Such a jacket, made of fox, is a kapatak.) Shivered because it was too light . . . or perhaps to emphasize her inferiority. An igloo woman . . . she came back to the village, her hands tucked in her sleeves, her head bowed thoughtfully. Every movement of her body was controlled: she knew she was being watched. An Eskimo woman once told me that it is much easier than I would have thought to slip into this centuries-old role: it becomes second nature.

Four days had gone by. We were in the igloo, which was silent and peaceful. The only noises came from outside—the whistling of the wind in the *qingaq* (the igloo's ventilation hole), the faraway crack of a whip, the barking of dogs as they fought over an old bone, and the flapping of the dry skin over the window. The hours passed. Occasionally, someone coughed outside: some neighbor woman was announcing herself. She would stay for an hour or two of gossip. The woman of the igloo never tired of chattering, particularly in the company of one childhood friend to whom she had remained close. They talked about this man's love affairs, that man's impotence, how Olipaluk had been humiliated by a remark of Kutsikitsoq's and about that parasite So-and-So. . . . The woman did not stop working as she talked, but her friend was seldom asked to lend a hand. I noticed how tender their gestures sometimes were toward each other: one woman would take the other by the arm and sometimes put the palm of her two hands gently on the other's belly. With her feet close together, her body bent over the pan as if she were broken in half, the hostess never stopped talking as, with her ulu, she scraped the sealskin which was soaking in water. She scraped, washed, scraped, and washed again: forty minutes would not be enough to make one small sealskin perfectly clean and odorless, and then it would have to be stretched and dried in the sun. The women drank cup after cup of tea: nine or ten in the course of a day. The children, every Eskimo community's ever-watchful spies, ran in and out. In the husband's absence, I would not have ventured to stay inside the igloo unless

141

there was another visitor—a female visitor—present. No man would dare enter a young married woman's igloo alone when her husband was off hunting, unless he had an urgent reason for doing so.

A rumor started by the children burst on us like a bolt of lightning: "Ataata! Daddy!" Their father had been sighted four miles to the south, near the small northern tip of Cape Kangek. He was no larger than a dot, but he had been recognized. He must have made a wide sweep. The woman speculated about what he might have bagged. Everyone clustered around her in the igloo, including several neighbors who were determined not to miss seeing his return. The children had taken up positions by the door of the katak, to the left as one came, and there they stood, like statues. Their normally animated, happy faces were set and serious. They were actors in an ancient play that was to unfold in an almost liturgical style.

As she revived the flame in the oil lamp, the woman appeared more relaxed. She knew it was high time her husband returned with game. Indeed, on his luck and his skill at hunting depended the food for days to come and the fat for the stone lamp. The Eskimos rarely had more than a week's supply of seal meat in advance, not counting their winter reserve of kiviaq and walrus. And although it was a point of honor for them never to complain, she knew her children were beginning to be hungry.

Custom decreed that one appear indifferent, but the woman could not resist peering through the igalaaq. Was the floor of the approaching sledge flat or was it piled high? . . . The dot became clearer and clearer: it really was her husband. The steady trot of his dogs was slowly bringing him nearer and nearer. The sledge appeared to be loaded. With seals? Or with foxes? Or just with bags? Big or little bags? The neighbors were guessing what might be in them. Different opinions flew back and forth as they exchanged glances and whispered conjectures.

Now we could hear the hunter shouting, encouraging his dogs to thread their way over the torturous coastal ice foot.

It was impossible to tell from his voice whether his spirits were high or low.

Inside the igloo, each person had assumed a role from which he would not deviate. The woman acted busy. As if her husband could already see her, she humbly prepared water for him to drink and collected the last quarters of meat, taking care to put the most rotten pieces on top.

The man was now close by the igloo. He could be heard snorting, coughing, and stamping his feet to restore circulation, but he said nothing. (A hunter may be noisy when he sets out, but he must be silent when he comes back: he should be almost stealthy as he returns to the community.) The man set about unharnessing the team: two of the dogs whimpered with pleasure, prolonging their whines to attract their master's attention one last time; like the woman, they wanted to flatter him by exaggerating their weakness. Despite his extreme fatigue, the man took his time unharnessing them. He worked alone: no one went out to give him a hand because it would have been in the worst possible taste to help him and so deprive him of the pleasure of concluding the hunt with a long account of it which would prolong the adventure a little. If he let a few hasty words slip out when he arrived, it would have spoiled the suspense which is the storyteller's greatest joy.

The Eskimo finished attending to his dogs and piled the harness and his fur clothing in the katak. Finally, he hoisted himself over the inside door of the igloo, and we had our first glimpse of his face, blackened and hardened by frostbite. Shoulders hunched, he walked slowly to the platform and sat down in his place, which had been, as usual, left free for him. At first, he smiled wanly, exaggerating his immense weariness; then he stretched his legs wide apart, rested his forearms on his thighs, and gradually composed his features into the expression appropriate to a serious man burdened by responsibilities. Not one person among his family and neighbors had looked at him openly. Conversation had not stopped for a single moment. The custom was to feign total indifference. For several minutes, the hunter sat motionless, seemingly overcome by fatigue.

The woman, alert and poised to seize the moment when indifference should end, but still averting her head, handed him the bowl of water. Still without a word, he seized it almost brusquely, and, his hands wrapped around the cup, his eyes unseeing, he drank with voluptuous pleasure. He wiped his thick lips with the back of his hand. Only then, with lowered, half-shut eyes, did he prepare to begin his story. His first words were half swallowed; his voice was low and muffled.

So as not to disturb him while he sorted out his recollections, people continued to talk quietly among themselves. But gradually the tale was coming to life. Silence spread around the storyteller; all eyes turned on him, to help him release his memories. Yet for a few moments more, he pursed his mouth in an effort to travel back in time and maintain a measure of confusion that would preserve his trip in the fog of distance.

At last, his taste for suspense satisfied, his voice grew more nuanced and the story took shape. Punctuated by many taava's—"thens"—it began to slide smoothly forward, like a sledge over the ice. Descriptions streamed from him: ice conditions on the long slope at Innartalik, the great rock that was slipping down . . . many fox tracks at Tuluriaq, the fjord before Neqi . . . fresh fox and crow tracks around the big iceberg. . . . All sorts of observations were linked together: the color of the sky the first day, what he felt when he saw the iceberg, what he dreamed about lying beside lovely young Taffinnguaq, how his bitch suffered stomach gripes, how loudly his lead dog broke wind. . . . The adventure emerged by slow degrees.

The account was interspersed with self-criticism: "I'm an incompetent. . . . My dogs are worthless, completely worthless, no better than my runners on that blasted heavy snow. . . ." At one point, the story halted. "Hungry!" He stuffed the instantly offered chunk of frozen meat into his mouth.

Not a single comment had yet interrupted his monologue: there were only some ieh, iehs of approval now and then.

Arrival of the hunters. Drawing by Sarfak (eight years old), daughter of Ululik, Si-orapaluk, October 1950. (*Private collection*)

As he chewed and swallowed, he began little by little to reveal what game he had caught and brought home. After fifteen minutes, we knew he had killed several seals, two of which he had placed under stone caches at Innartalik. Then he added, casually, "Oh! I also trapped two foxes near Illulorsuit." The tension disappeared, and everyone dropped his mask. Faces brightened; people laughed and talked. The children, who had been so solemn and reserved, standing on either side of the door, began to circulate as if nothing had happened.

The hunter-actor, who had been dominating the entire scene, allowed himself to be jostled by his son. The boy wanted to get to the back of the platform near the wall where, behind old discarded skins, there was a big file he needed for his miniature sledge and team.

"Nerivoq! Puisi! Have some seal!" The pot was filled with meat brought in from the meat rack where the hunter had discreetly put it when he arrived. The whole village was arriving to share it. The brown water bubbled. The smell of fishy meat grew strong. Faces streamed with sweat. At last the woman smiled. What a good show! Piniartoq! What a fine hunter! Then, only then, did the Eskimo, proud of himself, glance briefly at his longtime companion.

Arnaq

After some hesitation, I have decided to write briefly about the traditional Eskimo women of Thule.

*Arnaq** . . . when she is young, her brownish black Chinese eyes look at you attentively and with inexpressible irony. She has long blue-black hair, pulled back and fastened in a bun, small ears with prominent lobes, a supple and astonishingly agile adolescent body, short legs, and small feet. She wears foxskin pants stitched with black and white patches that are rather daring. In her bearing, gentleness is mingled with a great reserve and melancholy.

It is hard to convey the quality of her presence, how light of step and quiet she is. An Eskimo woman's movements appear seamless, so smoothly and noiselessly does she go about her daily tasks.

She is extremely, touchingly sensitive, and capable of strong attachments. During even a brief separation, she immediately sends small gifts—a needle, three cigarettes, a hare's skin, a handful of caribou tendon thread, messages. She knows how to love passionately. She is private, the most discreet of women (in these villages everyone watches everyone else), and she practices the art of being a woman with finesse. Even in the igloo, apparently attracting no attention, she knows how to choose the right moment to give you a quick, bright

---

Arnaq literally means female. The term denotes both a human being and an animal, as does the word *angut,* or male.

glance or to wrinkle her nose meaningfully—either inviting you to go further or telling you to wait a bit. If she does deceive her husband, usually he knows about it, and she behaves so as not to make him look ridiculous. He must know about it, for an Eskimo husband and his wife have no secrets from each other. Her relations with her own man are deep, formed as they are out of a constant interdependence and cemented by the memory of shared hardships. Generally, a couple agrees about everything; the partners understand events in the same way, they act in the context of a sort of unspoken moral code, without express references to the rules that govern it. This moral code is betrayed only if the woman becomes seriously involved with another man—if, that is, she actually chooses another man. She knows very well, however, "how far she can go." The question of whether or not she has sexual relations with other men is unimportant—what matters is how much she gives of her inner self. If she does have other sexual relationships, she must have her husband's tacit consent (otherwise the worst would ensue). In such a case, the woman takes care to choose a man who is not too closely related to her, and to avoid too long a relationship: two or three days are considered without consequence.

Traditionally, the man makes the big decisions. The woman cannot and generally does not want to decide anything on her own. Say that you visit a camp when the men are away. The women will have hidden the provisions (the quarters of meat) so they will not be forced to lend you any without their husbands' consent. If the hunter is out tending his traps, the women at home in the igloo will be vague with a visitor when important questions or decisions come up. "You'll see when Inuterssuaq comes back. He knows!" Confined as she is by her demanding domestic life—caring for the children, sewing clothes and skin boots, cleaning house, coming and going to keep the water buckets full of ice, seeing to it that the oil lamp is supplied with seal fat, she entertains

Woman in profile. Drawing by Attanek. Illulik, September 1960. (*Private collection*)

a stream of visitors and she enjoys retelling legends and talking about the old ways. Some intimacy might allow her to know a few secrets about this or that person, but rarely more. Although she is amenable to decisions that are within the man's domain, the woman can be the stronger where little daily problems are concerned; this is her province. Her husband refuses to do something; she pretends to be languishing from an illness as grave as it is vague. He cannot set out immediately to hunt with his neighbor because his boots have holes in then! *Ajor!* (What a nuisance!) She hasn't one scrap of big sealskin left; or she has lent the reindeer-tendon thread to a neighbor; or her ulu won't cut anymore. . . . *Ajor!* Appearances to the contrary, in this area she is really the one in charge.

A woman is a man's constant support: she continually chews skins to remove all flesh and fat and to soften them;[37] she untangles the traces of the dogs, which are tied up near the igloo; she mends the garments of animal skins; she tends the oil lamp, which burns as long as it is filled with seal, walrus, or whale fat; and she prepares the food. She wants to accompany her husband on his long expeditions, and rarely gives up joining the spring hunting trips even if she is about to have a child—like young Atitak, whom Peter Freuchen describes during the dramatic birth of her child:

> Atitak was in labor.
>
> We tried to build an igloo for her, but the snow was so thin that as soon as blocks were cut they were worn out by the wind and blown to pieces. Somehow I got a glimpse of poor Atitak's face, and I saw on it all the pain and distress a woman feels under such circumstances. She seemed to expect me and Knud to do something for her. And yet what

Eskimo woman softening a fox skin with her teeth. Drawing by Sarfak (eight years old), daughter of Ululik. Siorapaluk, October 1950. *(Private collection)*

could we do? There was no question of building a shelter, and it was out of the question for her to undress.

It was a desperate moment and we had to employ desperate measure. We placed Atitak on the leeside of the sledge, and a number of men grouped themselves around it to break the wind. We split the woman's pants only as much as necessary. The bag of water had already broken, and I knew that the moment had come. . . . Qolugtinguaq, who had several children to his credit . . . pressed the baby out in no time at all. Atitak snatched up the child inside her coat, wrapped some skins around him—it was a man child—and soon had him warm and snug. The storm abated somewhat, we emptied the load from Knud's sledge and bade him drive Atitak across to Hege at once to get her inside a shelter. When we finally reached the village we found her well and gay, and the boy already slung in her hood.[38]

At the age of thirty-five, the Eskimo woman is changed beyond recognition. Her puffy eyes are yellowish white, rheumy, and almost lost in her swarthy, finely wrinkled face. Her small nose now looks even smaller; her negroid lips, blue inside, the lower one swollen, reveal teeth which have been worn down to the gums by her daily chore of chewing skins.

The Choice
of a Mate

In Thule, a young woman was apparently free to choose her own husband. And she did not lack men to choose from, because the high female mortality rate left more men than women. For their part, young hunters were eager to win the best women—the prettiest, the plumpest, the jolliest, and, above all, the best seamstresses. Women married early, at fourteen or fifteen. Before the man would marry, however, he already had to be a hunter, since he had to assume responsibility for his wife and even help her immediate family if it was in need. Generally he was twenty to twenty-four.

In the past, marriage decisions were made at birth. In the eastern and central Canadian Arctic, this was still the case in 1960–64. Many children were promised in marriage by their parents, who were anxious to ensure themselves of economic cooperation through the alliances of their offspring. At the time of my expedition to Illulik in 1964, I attended some arranged marriages. The father of the male child who was supposed to become the husband came to an understanding with another hunter whose wife was pregnant and with whom he wanted to cooperate; he gave the prospective father a present to confirm what would be a union if the children were of opposite sexes: the present might be a three-year-old dog, a rifle, some foxes, some cloth, or five packets of tobacco. Gifts were duly exchanged if their hopes came true when the baby was born. If not, there would be a change of partners; another pregnant woman would do just as well, provided that it was possible to marry into her group, and the man simply waited. So, very early in their lives, the children knew whom they would end up with. "Uinnguara! That's my little husband!" the little four-year-old girl would whisper.

Once a girl reached puberty she was said to be allernersuit, impure. A cluster of taboos was attached to the monthly periods. At the same time the girl was extremely free; she enjoyed a premarital sexual freedom not unlike that accorded to teen-age girls among those other desert people, the Saharan Tuaregs. When a visitor came to Siorapaluk, the young people gathered in a young bachelor's house, sometimes called "the youth house," where they learned to "keep company." They would play the game of putting out the lamps. These were petting parties, nothing more. Kissing on the mouth and, needless to say, the genitals was still—as always—taboo. Mere mention of it would have been deeply shocking. The young people caressed one another and cracked jokes.[39]

This is not to say that they were uninformed about sex. At seven or eight children became aware of sexual matters because adults made no mystery about them. People in the igloo openly used to tease Ussaqaq, the elderly bachelor who was "strongly sexed," and a woman who engaged in unsavory relationships. Did not such openness account, paradoxically, for the fact that young people were modest in their behavior toward one another? If you were to say something out of place to a girl, something that touched her personally, you would see her turn pale and her eyes would become clouded—signs of great emotion. This modesty characterizes all age groups. When a friend of mine was in Pelly Bay, in Canada, he took a picture of an old woman who was completely naked. At the time, the whole group was shocked. They still say, "That's odious!" Modesty has made it hard for the Eskimo woman to get used to medical procedures. For example, you could not even talk about the use of suppositories or rectal thermometers in Thule in 1950. The fact that everyone lived together in a single room was probably not favorable to the development of a voluptuous nature. Also, once he became a Christian, it became uncomfortable for the Eskimo man to approach his wife in front of an old father, the children, or an overnight guest.

This modesty sometimes extends even further. I know of cases in which young men engaged to be married hesitated to approach their future wives as if they were afraid of them, and would have preferred to go off hunting on the day of the big event. Young women were equally reserved, and the boasting that went on when men got together fooled no one. The Eskimo man is very inhibited, and he is vulnerable as well, for he knows he will have to take off the masks he wears. Anxious as he is to be comforted and, above all, to be treated with the tenderness he craves, he prefers to hide his sexual feelings from everyone. As for the young woman, she is afraid. Afraid of herself, afraid of the "human animal," afraid of leaving the confines of the magical world of stories and dreams where she has lived a sheltered existence with the girlfriends of her childhood. She is afraid of the man who will have absolute power over her. I came to the conclusion that in Thule, in 1950, a young Eskimo woman was usually a virgin when she first slept with her future husband. Except for a few well-known "loose" women, whose names were repeated from village to village so that men could make use of them when they traveled, most young women saved themselves for their future husbands. In a highly structured Eskimo society, group morality entailed self-censorship and was puritanical: the rules against the union of close relatives had to be obeyed, promises to marry had to be kept. The inhibition and the vulnerability of Eskimo men may explain the Eskimo woman's attraction to white men, who are freer. In towns where white men live, some Eskimo women do not appreciate Eskimo men: "They're rough, they don't know anything!" I have been told that an Eskimo woman is extremely gentle with a white man: she undresses him and caresses him expertly, wanting to be aroused by him.

In 1950, Eskimo women rarely became pregnant before the age of eighteen. D. B. MacMillan observed this about the Polar Eskimos in 1914: "Though she is married at the age of twelve, the young Eskimo girl is incapable of having children before she has reached the age of eighteen."[40] Since marriage took place only when the hunter was capable of supplying the needs of a family, the woman often stood before the pastor, her belly as round as a sealskin pouch. This assurance of her pregnancy was flattering to the hunter. Usually the "official" marriage took place in the spring. The groom went off with the young woman in a sledge. They lived apart from the others, alone in a tent on a fjord or cape. When autumn had come, the young husband moved in with his father-in-law for a year or two. Through cooperative work, he in effect "bought" his wife. However, there was no hard and fast rule about it in this essentially pragmatic society: often he moved in with the young woman's father, but sometimes with his own father; it all depended on social conditions —for example, the size of the two families or mutual liking.

A careful look at the tribes' demographic structure and its development up to 1950 indicates that the population, growing at the slow rate of 0.8 percent per year, had always been in a precarious situation. The number of childless couples had been increasing: out of fifty-one women who achieved a period of fertility, eight—or 16 percent—turned out to be sterile.[41] In order to understand more clearly this phenomenon—about which the Eskimos were very sensitive—it seemed necessary to me to calculate the average degree of "shared blood" or consanguinity (a characteristic of genetic homogeneity) and, to this end, to trace the genealogical tree of the white population for three or four generations.

On the basis of the facts I gathered—each of the Eskimos was interviewed personally by me, which required a great deal of moving about and long

Portrait of a young *niviarsiaq,* or girl, from Siorapaluk. Drawing by Bertsie. December 1950. *(Private collection)*

conversations of various sorts—a complete chart was drawn up after my re-turn.[42] This made it possible to calculate the average degree of consanguinity among individuals and couples. The results obtained were quite astonishing. Among the handful of men whose social structure had always been assumed to be very lax and tending to sexual promiscuity, one would have expected the degree of consanguinity to be high. It was not.

It is true that the average degree of consanguinity that we arrived at among Polar Eskimos was established only on the basis of relationship struc-tures. Perhaps that is the explanation. In any case, to everyone's surprise, it was *exceptionally low,* between 0.0002 and 0.0003. The rate is particularly low when one considers that the figure among the Ramah Navaho Indians (1953) was six, in the caste of Parsees and Mahrattas (1954) between seventy-five and ninety-two, and in Swedish parishes between 1890 and 1896, it was more than eight.

Sexual promiscuity in the form of exchanging wives probably counterbalances this high rate of exogamy among the Polar Eskimos. In any case, there were very few instances of deformity in this isolated group (four lame people, one hunchback, and two paralytics in the group of 302 Eskimos in 1950).

The remarkable situation of so few marriages between blood relatives in such a small and isolated group—isolated at least from 1600 to 1863, the date of the last immigration from Canada—this ability to control its demography by forbidding such marriage, can be understood only within the framework of a system and a history.

Census figures for the Thule population are dramatic evidence of their threatened situation: 124 people, according to the first census by Kane, in 1852–55; 200 in 1895, according to Peary's first census; and 302 in 1950, according to my own.

A policy of strict planning was the Eskimos' solution. My findings show that marriage between relatives closer than sixth cousins had once been forbidden.[43] This law had unquestionably proved to be the salvation of the group. However, when I questioned the oldest men, Pualuna, Uutaaq, and Imina, they could only remember the prohibition of marriages between first, second, and third cousins.

Despite the severity of the marriage rules, in 1950–51, 16 percent of the women beyond puberty were sterile. One wonders if this high percentage was due to the cumulative effects of consanguinity—despite the low rate of marriage between relatives—or to the secondary effects of repeated miscarriages brought on by difficult journeys by sledge in March and April, during which time the woman was violently bumped by the sledge on the bad ice—at a time when she was generally nearing the end of her pregnancy; or salmon fishing with spears in July (and, as a consequence, at the beginning of pregnancy), which requires standing in icy water up to the thighs.

The rule forbidding marriage between relatives closer than sixth cousins was not the only demographic arrangement that had been adopted by the group. Among other rules were: the interdiction on married couples from all sexual relations during mourning for close relatives, sexual taboos during menstruation or after a miscarriage, female infanticide (at birth) during times of hardship, murder of very young children if a widow could not remarry, and the exchange of wives to achieve maximum fecundity.[44]

The reason some families exchanged wives was most often a desire to become thereby related; at irregular intervals, it established or cemented ties between two couples. Like marriage itself, the exchange was governed by precise rules concerning consanguinity and alliances. Through the exchange the husbands became relatives. However, this relationship was ephemeral, lasting only as long as the exchange of wives lasted. On the other hand, the relationship of children born during the exchange was permanent: as long as they lived, they were obliged to help one another and might not intermarry. A sterile man would also lend his wife during a period when women were in short supply. Since remarriage was not allowed, this practice reflected the Eskimos' view of marriage as procreative.

Even the Eskimos' terminology suggests how terrified they have always been of too great consanguinity. In Illulik, for example, a woman calls her male first cousin *annigaa* (my brother); a man calls his female first cousin *nukaga* (my sister). In Thule, people say *ilagisapput:* they are bound to one another, they belong to one another, they are related.

Blood relationships have traditionally been supplemented by secondary relationships and especially the "created relationships" which Eskimos were so adept at proliferating. Thus, in Thule and Illulik, one might not marry a stepson (*ernissara* in Illulik, meaning one who serves as a son) or a daughter-in-law (*panissara,* meaning one who serves as a daughter), a brother-in-law, sister-in-law, one's adopted child, one's *illerioq* (chosen relative unknown to the group)—one of the partners in the very special guardian relationship (*illora*), known only to the two people involved, and so on.

There have always been exceptions to the rule, of course, but they remain exceptions. The Eskimo is above all a realist—don't worry about how you live, he says, just see that you survive—and he adapts his rules to fit the circumstances. The "exofamilial" solution was to marry outside the family altogether; this widened a man's choice of mate but also extended the obligations he incurred through his marriage to give financial help. The "endofamilial" solutions for the hunter who was a widower, isolated, and unable to find a second wife either among his relatives or elsewhere was to sleep with his own daughter and so ensure himself of a true partner. I know of such a case in northeastern

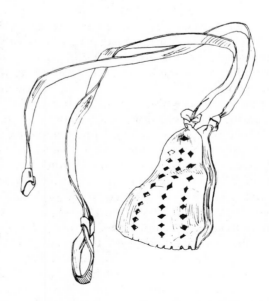

Woman's sealskin sling. Boothia Peninsula, Canada, September 1961. (*Private collection*)

Canada. The widower, who was a good hunter and who had many children, had spent two years in a fruitless search among neighboring groups for a new wife; only then did he decide on this course, provoking the silent disapproval of his neighbors and causing great sorrow to his oldest daughter, on whom his choice had fallen. His search had been useless, and no wives were to be had because the rate of female infanticide in the area had been very high between 1930 and 1940.

As I have said, the general rule against intermarriage was very strong—it had once extended to sixth cousins. More recently, Eskimos avoided marriage with anyone as closely related as a third cousin. In Thule in 1950, only marriage to a first cousin was prohibited. But even here, the rules were less strictly taken into account when the group was small and economic conditions were harsh. In 1950, there were exceptions even to the first cousin rule: three Thule Eskimo couples out of about one hundred actually were first cousins. This shows how the choice of a mate depends on historical, demographic, and climatic conditions.

With a data-processing method especially adapted for such work, Dr. Sutter and Leon Tabah used my genealogical data to establish how the degrees of consanguinity were distributed among all individuals in the group under the age of fifteen. Taking Eskimo rules into account, the choice of a mate was very limited—fewer than ten people for someone marrying within the extended family.

So, in 1950, the young people in Thule only *seemed* free to choose their mates. In fact their choice had to be made within the limits of rules that governed consanguinity and had to ensure good socioparental alliances with respect to hunting.

For many reasons, celibacy was really unusual. Among people over thirty in Thule in 1950, eight were single (four men and four women), three of them (one man and two women) because of some malformation.

In the old days, other marital customs were sometimes followed. The brother of a deceased man would marry his widow (levirate); or one man would marry two or more sisters, usually after the first wife had proved to be barren or had died (sororate). Polygamy and polyandry were common. In Rankin, Hudson Bay, I met a Padlimiok woman who had been polyandrous. Polyandry resulted from a dearth of women, which in turn resulted from female infanticide. In polyandrous households, it was always the mother who decided which man was a child's father. Usually the second husband was much younger—so that he could supply the hunting needs of the older couple. Cases of polygamy —and particularly of incestuous polygamy, in which father and daughter slept together while the wife was still alive—were not unknown. But as I have said, cases of incest were deplored by the group. In a polygamous household, the first wife was in the position of authority, although naturally the husband preferred the second—the younger—one. Among the Polar Eskimos before 1910, only the richest and most powerful hunters (the naalagaq or angakkoq) practiced polygamy. They sometimes had two wives, very rarely three. It seems that only the first occupied a position of trust.

Luki's wife (seventeen years old). *(Private collection)*

In 1950 little remained of ancestral marriage customs. A gift was made to the father-in-law, symbolically recalling the bride purchase. One could still find traces of marriage by capture: when a couple went off on their honeymoon, it was considered good form for them to leave the camp at top speed, accompanied by the cheers of the tribe.

Sexuality and Drama

Traditionally, the sex life of the Eskimos has been seasonal—being particularly active in late spring, June and July. It is also "normal"; that is, without refinements, not to say without unorthodox perversions. During the hunting period, which could last several months and which I observed in May and June as well, it never seemed to me that the hunter without his wife was distracted by any sexual frustration. Instances of homosexuality and bestiality (with dogs, seals, or dead caribou) have always been rare and severely frowned upon.

In 1950, a man's sexual life was relatively stable; apart from the time he slept with his wife, he occasionally slept with other women, though less often than believed. In 1950, out of a hundred women in the Thule district, there were a few "loose" married women—fewer than ten—and only four or five promiscuous unmarried women.

For the sake of a good relationship, husband and wife did not hesitate to anticipate the other's desire to escape if their particular circumstances justified it. In Siorapaluk, for example, a fifty-year-old Eskimo was well aware that he could no longer satisfy the desires of his young wife—his third—and he allowed her to look for some compensation elsewhere.

An Eskimo man was fairly easygoing about lending his wife if it was only for a short time. The popular belief among them held that casual relations (for one or two nights) did not result in pregnancy. If the affair lasted longer, the woman, who was more concerned than one might think not to have children by a man other than her husband, protected herself by choosing a time when she was not fertile—for example, when she was nursing a baby. It should be said that she knew nothing about temperature changes caused by her ovarian cycle or the days on which she was most likely to conceive. If the liaison had actually been a loan (lasting perhaps a few months, the maximum being two years), and if at the end of the affair a child was expected, it was always the woman who identified the father, and her opinion was usually accepted.

Although the practice of exchanging wives was rare by 1950, it still existed. In 1937, the Danish Eskimologist Kaj Birket-Smith noted that "the custom of exchanging wives for a short or long period is widespread, and far from being jealous of one another, the husbands feel that exchanging wives is one of the most effective ways they can enhance and strengthen a friendship."

From what I saw or learned in Thule, the exchange of wives lasted only a short period. It had once served to celebrate—and still did—some event that was auspicious for the group, such as the end of a period of mourning or a successful hunt. It involved only couples; bachelors and old men were excluded. Couples gave themselves up to it with all the more pleasure and intensity because they believed it could have no biological consequences, all casual relations being considered infertile.[45] Harald Moltke emphasized the festive nature of wife-swapping parties in Thule. The group exchange of wives which he witnessed took place after a five-day mourning period. A meal was organized, to be attended by everyone; the food was provided by a hunter who had left the village on purpose before the mourning-taboo period began. To celebrate the feast and the "liberation" of the village to the full, it was decided to exchange wives. Speaking as a witness, Moltke says that "the happy children were beside themselves. They ran from one tent to another, very preoccupied by their parents' arrangements." By 1950, group exchanges no longer occurred. Exchanges between couples, on the other hand, did take place occasionally during the winter I was in Thule.

In 1950 the Eskimos were familiar with several sexual stimulants, among them the liver and tongue of the seal, which were eaten only by adolescents, particularly by boys.

Meetings with the shaman followed by dancing and drumming also had sexual significance. The shaman used to bring peace to troubled souls disturbed by the return of tupilat—ghosts. "We are afraid," an Eskimo said once to Rasmussen. Songs relaxed and released these extremely self-controlled people. The whole group had to become excited before modesty and inhibitions could give way to a controlled exchange of women and to the sanctioning of temporary exchanges that would have been considered shameless had they occurred outside communal gatherings.

Explorers eager to create a sensation have told stories that reinforce the notion that Eskimos have sexual appetites verging on the abnormal. Eskimos *do* like to invest their behavior with a measure of theatricality. And I have to admit that, as a newcomer, I myself did not escape the impression that travelers passing through brought back with them: confound it, these men make love all the time! *Nuliarpoq! Kujappoq!* Eskimos *kujappoq* without stopping.*

In fact, at certain times, especially late spring they did seem to think of nothing else. Whenever I joined a group of men, they were talking among themselves about their most recent affairs, how many times they'd made love, how often this one had, how that one had had a bellyful, how So-and-So's *utsuuq*†—they attached great importance to this—was too tight for So-and-So; how this utsuuq was fragrant and responsive: it was good! Mammaraai! Mammaraai! Good!

Actual names were mentioned. When I heard the name of one woman, I observed that she was very young. "You're right," the men answered. "She doesn't finish. And she whimpers. But we've been passing her name around, and with practice it's becoming better all the time! She's getting to the point where she laughs at it."

I remarked to a forty-year-old hunter that a certain woman had the reputation of being promiscuous. "Well! That's not surprising! Her husband's usuk is no bigger than that!" He held up his index finger. "And no harder than that!" He took some damp clay, molded it, and tossed it away.

Two women who had been listening chimed in derisively: "The poor woman!"

And what about So-and-So? "Her utsuuq has no secrets from anyone! Many, many people pay it a visit on their way through here!" When I shook my head doubtfully, and objected that her manner seemed very reserved, another man retorted, "Ha, ha, ha! Don't you believe it! She's a hypocrite, a very cunning woman. Look, I'll draw her utsuuq for you if you like. There, that's the pubic bone . . . not much hair. . . . Here the hair is thick and black." As he spoke, he drew a moon in the sand, then the folds of the mons veneris. The two women watched with ironic attentiveness as the sketch developed, nodding their heads. Another hunter intervened to correct an anatomical detail near the anus. To this all the Eskimos present agreed almost solemnly

---

*Both *nuliarpoq* and *kujappoq* are terms used for sexual intercourse; *nuliarpoq* is the polite word, meaning more or less "to take a woman"; *kujappoq* is the normal, vulgar term. *Tigssarpok* and *annigsarpok* mean erection and ejaculation, respectively. There is no precise term for orgasm, except perhaps for the rather loose *kiakuvdluni* ("it's really hot").

†Pronunciation must be very exact in this area: *usuk* means penis; *utsuuq,* vagina; *ussuk,* bearded seal *(Phoca barbata).*

Statuette of woman made of walrus ivory. Thule district. (*From Holtved,* The Polar Eskimos)

until one man blurted out, as if in disgust: "She's no good! Last year she could very well have given us all gonorrhea."

This utsuuq—*commune bonum*—the sovereign usuk, the ussuk of the great hunts thrusting its head through the open water hole, enveloped by the misty warm breath of the water's depths. . . . I must say that there were many reasons why a white man new to this region would conclude that Eskimos were obsessed by sex, especially when he was assured that they really do lend and exchange their women.

However, I want to emphasize again that at least in well-established and organized groups the exchange of women complied with strict rules and controls, and with a whole group morality. The men made the decision in this area, and it was they who changed igloos, never the women. In fact, the exchange of women was a form of cooperation and in some cases a method of producing children, therefore the practice was necessarily limited. However, the Eskimo never explains these reasons; he jokes endlessly about wife-swapping and enjoys multiplying insinuations—in a word, enjoys flabbergasting the white man.

As I have said earlier, I shared the intimacy of their life in the igloo, and I can vouchsafe that no one is more modest than an Eskimo: he will not undress in front of you, for example. Also, an Eskimo will never be seen defecating in public. He will always find some concealment in the igloo or, out on the flat, deserted tundra, some nook or large stone or rise in the ground—even though only symbolic—which affords him privacy.

In the promiscuity of the igloo—which provides only twelve square feet per person—any sort of privacy could easily become impossible; discretion, therefore, is an innate part of the Eskimo's conditioning. For example, although he may sometimes belch, an Eskimo never farts; and while the igloo is filled with strong odors—of tainted meat, sweat, urine that has been purposely saved for various uses, etc.—the host would be extremely shocked by the sound and smell of a fart (which is a cause for losing face, as it was in ancient China): "Tipi! That smells!" he would say. This happens so seldom that *tipi* never denotes body odors.

Eskimo men and women do not have noisy orgasms: they do not cry out, they are not violent. They may perhaps sigh and breathe more quickly, but in the sleeping igloo, it is seldom noticed.

A new husband is so discreet that he prefers to have his first relations with his young wife away from the village, giving the excuse that he is going somewhere to hunt. It does seem that surrounded by the group he would find it impossible—or at least difficult—to make himself put aside his own masks (or inhibitions) and those of his young wife. Furthermore, the fact of being far away from his people and alone with the woman who has just become his wife is often not enough: he must beat the woman before he dares approach her, seize her, and penetrate her.

Here too, of course, I wish to avoid generalizations, but I know several very normal Eskimos who told me they acted that way on their "wedding nights."

When trust has developed over the years and an Eskimo is willing to talk freely and without playing a role, he will say, as X (from Illulik) said to me: "I caress her belly, her loins, her breasts, and her nipples." And he added: "As for kissing—kunik—always on the nose and the tip of the nose. It's very pleasant and exciting, and that's the way we do it—never on the mouth, which is disgusting. When we make love, I always lie on top of her or when she's pregnant, we lie on our sides. Of course I never touch her vagina or anus; my wife would strike my hand away. She would think it could kill her or make her bear deformed children. And I would be worried that I was the one to blame. We desire each other only at certain times of the year—especially in the spring." X specified further: "Also, I never feel desire while hunting. It's really as if hunting took away all desire—which is all to the good. As you know, the Inuit do not masturbate; it would weaken them completely."

Earlier I mentioned the relationship between men and women who have been married for a long time—the way, for example, they wrinkle their eyes almost imperceptibly in tacit understanding as they listen to people talk; the way the woman lights a cigarette for her husband in her own mouth, and affectionately hands it to him. Their interdependence is so great that a misunderstanding is intolerable. I have seen husbands become truly depressed in that situation and fall ill. The partners know each other profoundly. They have fought together against cold, blizzards, malicious gossip.

Only anger can make the Eskimo lose his habitual tact and serenity. Anger is great medicine. When a man feels that his wife loves him less than she did or if he loves her less, he beats her; this is true. He throws her out of the igloo onto the ice, drags her by the hair, arms, and legs, and sometimes he even

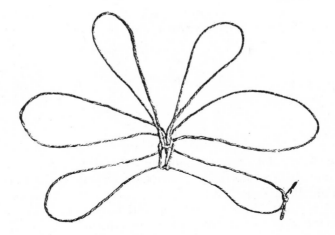

String game by Pualuna: hair knotted into a chignon and undone for the night. Siorapaluk, December 1950. *(Private collection)*

deliberately hits her in the belly, especially if she is pregnant by him. I witnessed such a scene one early morning in Thule, in North Star Bay. It lasted for no less than an hour, after the woman had been insulted and struck, sometimes on the belly, throughout the night. No one intervened, not even the village people who were watching from a distance.

Sometimes a hunter cannot endure his own anger. It is even more sharp and brutal if his wife is barren. After he has beaten the poor woman almost senseless, he thrashes his dogs furiously with a club, breaks up his sledge with an ax, and smashes his rifle.

But once his anger is spent, the feelings it has banished return: the man and woman draw near each other, and it is not unusual to see them afterward walking together tenderly, their eyes swollen, their clothes torn. Here again, the question is—as in all marital scenes, wherever they occur—how much arises from a certain connivance between husband and wife, how much from playfulness, how much from the taste for drama.

Occasionally, adolescent Eskimos attempt sexual arousal by suspending themselves with a leather thong from the edge of a low cliff; they secure the thong between two crates and squeeze their necks until they are nearly strangled, as if they could not achieve complete pleasure in another way. Hanging can indeed cause extraordinary genital arousal (hanged men are frequently found to have erections). The practice has caused a number of accidents in Thule, when the boy had no time or not enough strength to free himself. Eskimo hunters have assured me that this partial hanging sparks a sort of second sight.

Lastly, I should also point out that many young men do not have a chance

to sleep with girls before they marry. This could account for the few—very rare
—cases of bestiality with dogs or seals. They were mentioned to me only in the
eastern Canadian Arctic.

Childbirth
and Child Care

It is 1950 in Siorapaluk. A young mother gives birth in her husband's igloo.
For some days before the birth, visitors stop by to see her. During labor
children mimic the mother's cries and her contracted positions.

Delivery is quick. The first phase, up until the waters break, lasts from two
to six hours, the second phase ten minutes, and the third about twenty minutes.

During her pregnancy, the mother has been careful not to eat forbidden
foods (caribou tongue, marrow, and innards), which make women abort. Kutsikitsoq tells me that in the old days a pregnant woman was supposed never
to eat the front paws of an animal. "Qujapik was expecting a child. She did not
obey this old law. When her child—Anarfinnguaq—was born, the skin on the
baby's hands was the same color and just as rough as the skin of a walrus. These
taboos really mean something," Kutsikitsoq adds. "I've seen what it costs to
break them."

Since birth is clearly an extranatural event, it calls for special precautions.
Malformations and miscarriages must be avoided at all costs; until about 1930,
miscarriages were construed as a sign of rejection by "the powers." A woman
who had miscarried was considered dangerous: she was "infected." Because
she drove off game she had to take infinite precautions. For example, she might
not name the animals whose flesh she ate. She had to eat from a separate plate,
and her leftovers were given to the dogs; she had to eat without her boots on;
might not eat seal, fox, or bear meat; might not cut meat herself, or drink from
the same pot as the others; had to go for water herself; might not sew. Anyone
who talked to her about hunting had to use special words to designate the
animals that were seen or caught. These taboos remained in effect for one year,
and they were strictly obeyed.

A baby is being born; it is winter, 1910. The mother is confined not in her
husband's igloo, but in an igloo or tent set apart. The mother kneels on the
illeq, sweating under her furs. Visitors leave. An old woman grasps the arms
of the young woman, whose body is contracted. The delivery is hastened by
tightening a belt around her belly or by massaging it vigorously. If necessary,
the husband stations himself on the illeq behind his wife, grasps her torso in
his arms, encircles her loins with his legs, and forces her backward to facilitate
delivery.

With a mussel shell or a sliver of ice (by nature aseptic), the mother cuts the umbilical cord and checks the small of the baby's back for the Mongolian blue spot, a sign that he is a true son of the Inuit. Quickly, the infant is licked by the mother and wrapped in rabbit skins with the fur facing out, and then is cleaned more leisurely with dampened partridge feathers.*

The old clothes the woman wore during her pregnancy are thrown out. For one month, a number of interdictions set the young mother apart and protect her. For example, according to the ancient rites, once she has been washed from head to foot, she must remain outdoors, wearing her hood and mittens, for a given length of time, no matter what the weather. She must be barefoot when she eats. The first day she must eat only meat cooked in fat in a steatite pot.

It is said that the child cries as soon as he is born because he is demanding a name. Eskimos are still called by only one—traditional—name; they have no first and last names. Here are a few names:

MEN
Eqqorsuaq: big shit
Kutsikitsoq: with a socket at the hip joint
Iggiannguaq: throat
Taaferaaq: sea gull
Anarfiik: the place where people relieve themselves
Ammalortoq: he who is round
Angussuannguaq: little fat man
Angutikasik: poor man
Qalaseq: navel
Kigutikkaaq: he of the big tooth
Sorqaq: whale bone
Ululluik: the one with an ulu
Qisuk: wood
Sammik: left-handed man
Salluq: liar
Piuaittuq: the peaceful one

WOMEN
Putu: hole
Aleqasiaq: the rather nice older sister
Anarfinnguaq: the place where people relieve themselves
Aninnguaq: the unsympathetic one
Inalugannguaq: small intestine

---

*Twins are very rare; in 1950, the Thule group included three sets of living twins. It used to be that when twins were born, the parents were so frightened that they killed them. As far back as anyone could remember, there had never been a case of triplets or larger multiple births.

Meqqoq: the hairy one
Padloq: the one who stretches out on the stomach
Mikisoq: the little one
Aamma: again

The following are some male and female names from Illulik, Foxe Basin, Canada:

Tulukkaajuk: little crow
Alianakuluk: little misfortune
Arnatsiq: beautiful woman
Alaakkaatit: thick soles
Ijjangiaq: mild weather
Aluuluukkit: onomatopoeia
Maki: get up!
Paamik: longings
Utssuajuk: little-big (medium-size) vulva
Itikusuk: little anus
Naneruut: little flame

A relative, often the grandmother, gives the baby either the name of an important person who has died within the year or the name of an ancestor who has not dishonored his family. Several days or weeks before the birth, relatives discreetly mention a few possible choices. They note the reactions and so reach a decision. The name is tried out while the baby is being delivered, in front of the angakkoq if necessary. If the child comes out quickly, that name has a good chance of being the final choice, but it will be given to the child only two to eight days after birth, so that, like the child, it will be accepted by the whole community.

An individual has, however, several names at his disposal, and at his own

Three children. Drawing by a child from Savigssivik. January 1951. *(Private collection)*

discretion he may change his name when in a difficult situation or when something serious, such as illness, occurs. Kutsikitsoq, for example, had four names —Kutsikitsoq, after his dead maternal grandfather; Qumangaapik, after his paternal grandfather; Nasaitsorluarsuk, after a first cousin; and Avataq, after another cousin, his uncle's son. Old Avoortungiaq of Etah had three names, Avoortungiaq being the name of her father's sister, who died the year she was born. Iggianguaq, Kutsikitsoq's half-brother, had three names, Iggianguaq being the name of his father's brother, who died shortly before his birth. The Eskimos used to think—and in a rather confused way some still do—that the baby inherits the good and bad qualities of the person whose name he shares. In effect, the name is a sort of spirit which puts the newborn baby or the adult in direct communication with the dead person after whom he is named. Because of this, taboos and regulations of all kinds surround a name: one must not pronounce one's own or another person's name, one is obliged to help any person who shares the same name, etc. A name allies people; it is a bond. A child who bears his grandfather's name is not called "my son" by his father but "my father," even when he is very young. A girl may also be named after her grandfather, and she will also be called "my father" by her own father. Eskimos who are unrelated by blood but who share the same name are *affariik*—that is, two halves of one invisible whole—and are related by virtue of that tie, which obliges them to help each other. The child who bears the name of a dead person is the reincarnation of that person; the spirit of the deceased person helps the child during his adolescence. Therefore the child has two personalities, as Icelandic-American explorer Vilhjalmur Stefansson has explained—his own and that of the deceased. This might explain the way parents bring a child up. They may not criticize the child because the spirit of the dead person is perhaps acting through him. The child is considered an adult when he is twelve or thirteen, because it is thought that the spirit of the dead person leaves him at that point. What happens to the spirit no one knows. After this the child/adult can be given orders by his parents, whereas before, they could only make suggestions.

So long as a name has not been given, a crippled or sickly child must be killed by its mother. Soon after my arrival, in 1950, a premature child was put outside the hospital by its mother so that it would die.

News of a birth spreads through the settlement like the fire along a train of gunpowder. Everyone repeats the name or names given the child, and people congratulate one another. Word of the event and all related details are transmitted by sledge from village to village and within two months at most everyone in the district will know of it. Neighbors visit the young mother in her igloo, passing the little one from hand to hand. They make the baby cry; they cuddle and lick it.

If the infant whimpers, the mother immediately lifts up her jacket and offers the baby her heavy breast, and the baby seizes her dark-brown nipple hungrily. With her tongue, she sucks up his mucus, and delicately cleans his tiny soiled bottom in the same way. If he continues to whimper, she puts him to sleep by swaying back and forth and singing softly. She is always reluctant to leave her baby and prefers to carry him around for hours in her amaaq, the rather large hood on her jacket inside which the naked infant is carried, usually next to his mother's bare skin. The baby watches the world go by during his first few months, perched on her back like a little prince.

His mother shifts him to the right or left with a rather graceful movement of her hips. Undoing her belt, she leans to one side and pulls the baby out by his arms so that he can relieve himself; her timing is always perfect. When the child is older, he will wear a pair of pants with a vertical slit which opens as soon as he squats. No matter how heavy he is, he is there with her. But eventually even her infinite patience cannot withstand her weariness: at the end of the day, the weariest mother will say: "Don't cry, don't cry, don't cry. The big crow will peck out your eyes. Don't cry, don't cry, don't cry. Qaa, qaa, qaa, qaa, qaaa. Don't cry, don't cry; the crow will peck out your eyes."[46]

The Eskimo woman's abundant milk is proverbial. In 1907–8, Moltke cited the case of a mother of a large family from the Thule region who nursed her son until he was eight. In 1950, as far as I was able to tell, usually a child was not weaned until he was three or four years old.

Births follow a clearly seasonal pattern. During the five months of winter and spring, from February (the month in which most babies are born) to June, the igloos resound with the cries of newborn infants. Of the 140 known births in Thule between 1937 and 1950, more than half occurred during these months, the period of conception having extended from the previous June (the month with the best light) to October. It seems that as with the Canadian Eskimos, conception generally takes place in late spring: the sun has returned, resources become more abundant, and the Eskimos are again on the move. Sexual excitement peaks around the middle of June. On the other hand, in this population group, the months of lowest fertility are very clearly December to February, the dark months when food supplies are low.

Other factors affect the childbearing of the Eskimo woman: her isolation, ethnic origins, the harsh climate, her diet. In 1950 a pure-blooded Eskimo woman generally had a child only every three years or so, although she used no contraceptive devices. Statistics for 1940–50 show that out of 106 intervals between births, the average interval was 31.8 months. In 1950, menstruations were regular all year long but notably light during the winter; a little reindeer fur or dry grass absorbed what flow there was. Sixty years earlier, menstruation was exceptionally light or stopped altogether during the winter.

If there was one place in the world where the male child was king, it was among the Polar Eskimos. For the Eskimo man, his son came before hunting, before his dogs; he was his only real pleasure. In the igloo, the boy received all his father's tender attention. The only time the Eskimo, who was otherwise always acting, masking his feelings, seemed really free and at ease was with his young

The child-king. Drawing by Inuteq. Illulik, September 1960. *(Private collection)*

son. He talked baby talk to the child and, addressing only him, told him about the hunt from which he had just returned.

"Kinaana? Well, who are you? Kinaana?" The child would look down and say in one breath, "Masserannguaq!" Everyone would then admiringly repeat: "Masserannguaq," imitating the boy's tone of voice.

To chastise or strike a son who was making a nuisance of himself was a very nearly scandalous thing to do. The child was brought up in the greatest freedom, and once he had passed beyond babyhood, a child in the village was very rarely heard to cry or scream because of something his parents had done. It was as if his father were anxious to let him be perfectly happy before he came to know—as he would at a very early age, when he was eight or ten—the harsh law of the tundra, the intense cold and privations of the hunt.

While growing up, both Eskimo boys and girls learned from the facts of daily life around them, from the comments people made about good and bad hunters, from stories, from certain tones of voice. Mothers, fathers, and grand-fathers taught them early on who their relatives were, some of whom were secret ones (the godparent connection, or illora). As we have seen, these relationships could be very complex, so that a boy might be the son both of his father and, by adoption, of his grandfather; both the cousin and the nephew of another man; and the half brother of someone else who was no relative but merely had the same name. In addition, relationships changed from year to year. Like Jewish children learning the Torah by heart, at an early age the Eskimo boy and girl sharpened their minds on these subtleties and on the effort of memory they had to make to acquire a thorough knowledge of taboos and legends.

Children's toys were crude and in the main, practical: for the boys, whips, puppies, and knucklebones; for the girls, skin dolls and miniature igloos. At the age of eight or ten, boys accompanied their fathers while hunting. For the most part, the novice hunter's instruction was wordless. Everything was taught by example, by reference to an authentically Inuk type of man who was dependent on no one and who was loyal to the group. The boy's education was rooted in extreme respect for the father who for so long as he lived, no matter what he might do, might never be judged by his son. When a boy spoke to his father, he lowered his eyes or looked away. I remember one father who was an alcoholic. He could be at his very worst, but his children, playing nearby, would behave as if they noticed nothing.

Very early, when a boy was about eight, he had to learn to walk long distances—twelve to eighteen miles a day; find his way in fog; go with little sleep; aim a rifle accurately; identify with the game he was hunting so that he could find it wherever it might be; and finally, he had to be prepared to help his neighbor in case of need. If the boy rested on the illeq for more than four hours at night when the group was sleeping over somewhere—while hunting or moving from one place to another—a few rough words from his father would bring him down to earth. Brief orders issued in a dry voice reminded him that he had to be a man. But this was rarely necessary. Fear of the stinging monicker *seqajuk*, lazybones, brought even the laziest boy to his feet. And the desire to emulate his elders induced even a backward boy to surpass himself.

Young Eskimos were integrated into the group little by little and in various ways. Before the father went off to set fox traps, he would pick out two traps which would be his son's. If foxes were caught in both, they belonged to the child. If the father returned with fifteen foxes, he would say, "I have thirteen foxes," since thanks to the traps, two belonged to his son. Similarly, if one of the ten dogs in his team had been given to his son (who might do whatever he liked with it—lend it to his father or to someone else), he would say, "I have nine dogs."

"The children do not help themselves to food," Père Mouchard observed at Baker Lake, Canada "They ask, and if they don't ask, the father or mother will give them a morsel." Usually, men and women would eat separately. Children ate with whichever group they chose. But generally the boys ate with the men and the girls with the women.

One man from the southeastern coast of Greenland, who had lost his son and whose wife had just given birth to a daughter, used to sing this song:

> *That is my first-born son . . . as we say!*
> *That is his younger brother . . . as we say!*
> *That is the son I wanted to make again*
> *But I did my job badly . . . as we say!*
> *And I must sharpen my tool again!*
>
> *Ah, that is my first-born son!*
> *Whom I tried to make again! . . . as we say!*

Inspection of stone fox traps. (*From Hayes,* An Arctic Boat Journey)

But I made a real mess of it . . . as we say!
If I sharpen my tool again

There'll be another one in the sack . . . as we say!
I made a mess of it only once, as I said.[47]

For these primitive people, to have children answered an absolute need. Life seemed meaningless to a sterile woman with no offspring. An igloo in which there were no children was shunned by everyone; it was lifeless. An old people's igloo, people said, a useless family—an igloo of death! It was not surprising, then, that anxious as Eskimos were to have a tightly knit community, adoption of children was a widespread practice. How widespread depended on how communal the group was. However, if a widowed mother could not support her family, she could be sure that each of her children, no matter how young or old, would find another home and that the group would feel he had a rightful place. His status would depend on his age at the time of his adoption.

True adoption took place when the child was very young—less than a year old. It could also be prenatal: the pregnant woman promising her baby to someone else. Most often, adoption took place a few days after the baby was

Little person. Drawing by a child from Siorapaluk. October 1950. *(Private collection)*

born. This system allowed a community to take in as part of its larger network of relatives a family with which it had no blood ties, or to strengthen blood and familial ties, or temporary ties. A special bond united the natural and the adoptive parents: the child was the guaranty of familial closeness, of a new alliance. Adoption at a late age created no ties between the two contracting fathers, and the child remained a stranger to his adoptive family.

Kapuivik (Illulik, Foxe Basin): in the tent belonging to Piuaittuq, head of the walrus hunters' camp, a young girl sat on the illeq to the far right of Piuaittuq; her head was bowed and her expression was contrite and rather defeated. Ever since getting up, she had been sewing or rubbing the same piece of skin. Now and then, unpredictably, she would get up and go to the door, her head still bent, seeming preoccupied. She would walk back and forth along the shore, looking at no one, her thoughts obviously elsewhere; then slowly she would return to take her place in the tent again. She was a *tiguaq,* an adopted child.* I was Piuaittuq's guest for the week. I slept between this girl and my host. During my entire visit her behavior did not change. Her head was always bowed; she kept her eyes on her particular household tasks: fetching water, preparing the meat, mending the kamiks. The moment she felt she could help, she anticipated our gestures and got up. I never saw her take part in conversation; she was a kind of au pair, and her silent presence was barely tolerated. "She has no family left," Piuaittuq told me. "Her father, whom I was very fond of, died four years ago while he was hunting walrus—fell through a hole in the ice. She was an orphan with no close relatives, so I took her in. But she was already pretty old—she was eleven."

Adoption is an ancient mechanism. It was practiced in Sparta, for example, where the tiny minority of Spartiates lived in constant danger from the huge numbers of Perioeci and helots, a situation somewhat akin to the isolation of Eskimo society in the menacing Arctic environment. Not only can adoption help to correct a manpower shortage but also in this society, where isolation is dangerous, where people seek alliances, it creates and even imposes familial bonds between the family surrendering and the family accepting the child; it

---

*In Thule dialect, a *tiliarnuk.*

169

thereby confirms that the imperative need to survive takes precedence over the importance of blood ties and that parental structures are less a determinant than they are a product of a way of life.

Short of an overriding need for economic alliances, people are reluctant to give their children for adoption to sterile couples, who because of their sterility were reputed to be "cold." Qaaqqutsiaq and Padloq, Nassapaluk and Avoortungiaq were two couples who had the greatest difficulty in adopting a child, and the latter pair was able only to adopt children who were already quite old; Kaalipaluk Peary would not give up his son Peter to Nassapaluk until the boy was five years old.

When the child was adopted very young, his blood ties were broken and he knew only his new family. In Neqi, Taffinnguaq adopted Igaapaluk when the child was three. The mother had just died, leaving numerous children; the father was a poor hunter. Countless times I saw the stepmother playfully and without malice incite Igaapaluk to mimic his natural father, Qipisorsuaq, who as a widower had become dirty and sullen.

A father's instinctive reactions could sometimes surface abruptly: people do not forget a tragic occurrence on King William Island (Canada), when an adoptive son who was playing with an old loaded rifle accidentally killed the oldest natural son of the family. When the father, Umittuualuk, returned from visiting a neighbor family, he flew into a pitiless rage. At the back of the tent, before the eyes of Roald Amundsen, he snatched up the poor tiguaq, killed him with three knife blows to the heart, and kicked the body until it rolled away. He had the adopted son buried with scant care—buried only in a manner of speaking: since the earth was frozen, the body was left above ground and merely covered with stones on which the man lay a worn pair of gloves. The corpse of his natural son he had sewn up in a reindeer skin and interred together with the boy's bow, arrows, cup, and his new gloves. In this way, the father's vengefulness pursued his clumsy adopted son even beyond the grave.

Sounds and Speech,
Signs and Silences

Two Eskimos meet: standing fifteen or so feet apart, gravely and ceremoniously they scrutinize each other, each with one arm raised as if he was on guard against some act of treachery. Slowly, each man's eyes turn to the other's boot or the sleeve of his *qulitsaq,*[48] where a knife may be hidden.

No feeling is more deeply rooted in the Eskimo than the fear, blended with curiosity, that he feels toward a stranger, whoever that stranger may be—an Eskimo neighbor, an unknown Eskimo, or a white newcomer who arrives bringing chicanery or trouble with him. A few casual remarks are exchanged —almost hissed between the teeth. The two men move closer together and at first in silence—by signs—and then in a few words, they begin to exchange news. If they are in no hurry, they bivouac and have some tea together. If the atmosphere is even more friendly, they pitch a tent where they meet or find a more suitable place nearby; or if the weather is good, they simply place the sledges against a snow wall that shelters them from the wind, or they stretch a canvas overhead to protect them from the sun. If the atmosphere is really excellent, they prolong their shared meal in order to pursue their conversation as long as possible, and sleep side by side.

What do they talk about with such wariness and reserve? About hunting, in minute detail. Men visibly enjoy reliving their pursuit of game; it is almost as great a pleasure for them as the hunt itself. The tone of voice varies according to ups and downs of the chase: if the speaker is a visitor from another camp, at first his voice is monotonous and muffled, his words are half swallowed, and he stares fixedly at the ground. If a woman speaks up, she will sound self-conscious and her tone will be peevish and critical.

When an Eskimo believes that he must exchange some information, his entire effort is bent, as he speaks, on reading the thought or response of the person with whom he is speaking; the purpose of this is to adjust instantly what he believes he should, in the name of the group, transmit. Speech is precise and brief when it deals with technical matters, sententious and circumspect when in the affective realm, wordless and gestural when it has to do with moral evaluation. When the Eskimo is imparting information or relating a story, he keeps his eyes lowered and relives, as if in a mental travelogue, what has happened to him. In order to make his accord more evident, the person to whom he is speaking will support the narrator with intermittent ieh . . . iehs of approbation; this serves also to help the speaker in his effort to remember.

I can tell just by the timbre of an Eskimo's voice whether he is talking to a white man whose help he needs. In that case, his voice will be soft and smooth —he becomes humble and awkward, and he speaks a slow "pidgin" Eskimo—

Sketch of Eskimos, by Appalinnguaq. Siorapaluk, November 1950. (*Private collection*)

as the white man does—with mistakes, hesitations, and silences; he will use words the other knows, and as he talks he will be examining and sizing up the white man.

As Kaj Birket-Smith has written, Eskimo is an incorporating, polysynthetic language because an endless chain of ideas can be linked together in a single word, a word with a thousand feet. For instance: *taatussimatsianngilagut*—that is what we did not understand; *ahiningark'suahadekukahyo*—the full moon. These are relatively short examples. If you are dubious, a glance at an Eskimo newspaper from Godthaab, Greenland, or Churchill, Canada, will convince you.

Here is one simple example of verb construction: *tiki*—to come; *sa*—often; *r*—movement; *poq* denotes the indicative mood; ergo, *tikissarpoq*—he comes often.

In this language, everything depends on context and on suffixing, together with the stress given to different syllables. Length, accentuation, and intonation are employed to change meanings. When Eskimos are talking among themselves and do not want to be understood by their neighbor—particularly if he is a white man—they use a special language or, more accurately, a special accent: the voice is heavy and nasal, and most words are swallowed. However, when they speak publicly, the voice is deep and the speech distinct. The language of the shamans has its own characteristic and secret words. When women are under taboo, among other cases, the names of animals must be changed by hunters speaking in their presence. A special vocabulary is used on these occasions. In some tribes—the Tchligit, for one—women and men have different languages. This is not the case in Thule.

In certain areas, the vocabulary is very rich. The grammar is difficult. There are assonances that must be respected and numerous declensions: *siku* (ice bank) is an ablative; *siku-mit*—coming from the ice bank; locative, *sikumi* —on the ice bank; *siku-mut*—toward the ice bank; *siku-kut*—across the ice bank; *siku-tut*—like an ice bank, etc. Verbs are conjugated: *aallarpunga*—I go away; *aallarputit*—you (singular) go away; *aallarpoq*—he goes away; etc. Eskimo is a musical language; it has precise rules and it is taught. Identical in structure from Alaska to Greenland, it was diversified during prehistoric times (1,400 years ago) into forty languages and dialects.

The Thule and Angmagssalik dialects differ from the Greenlandic spoken on the southwest coast. In Canada, the language spoken in the east—Baffin Island—is very different from the one spoken in the west (Caribou and Mackenzie). Dialectical nuances can be grasped only after one has spent considerable time among the people.

There are two large language groups: the languages of the Bering Sea area, called Yupik, and those of northern Alaska, Canada, and Greenland, called Inupik or Inupiat. Speakers from certain groups find each other absolutely incomprehensible. (For example much of the Thule dialect was incomprehensible to the more southern Greenlanders, since my Polar friends retained words and speech patterns which had long since died out in the more assimilated regions.) Today, newspapers and the radio tend to recast these clusters of languages and dialects into larger shared languages: Greenlandic, Canadian (eastern and western Eskimo), Alaskan (Yupik and Inupiat).

Two examples will convey some idea of the delicacy of the language: *Siutitaq,* or interpreter, means literally "the ears, I take them"—the ears, by implication, belonging to the one for whom I translate. *Uqarti* means literally "the one who speaks," or police interpreter. There are also very rich and varied nuances in the terms having to do with family relationships, geography, snow, hunting techniques, etc.—the essential concerns of this society. The Eskimo language is not related to any language family in the world.[49]

As for myself, I achieved most of my progress in learning Polar Eskimo during the long winter nights in Siorapaluk by making rough translations into French of the work written in Eskimo by Knud Rasmussen about his first stay in Thule: *Avanqarnisalerssarutit Okalualat (Legends of the Men of the North).* I was aided immeasurably in this endeavor by my Greenlander friend John Petrussen, the catechist, and by the Polar Eskimos. The Eskimos were particularly helpful in explaining—often in long paraphrases or in pantomime—a number of words and expressions totally unknown to me.

Siorapaluk: propping his elbows on his knees, a hunter began to speak in a clear voice, modulating it to suit the events he was describing. Because he was in his own home, he figured prominently in his tale, whereas a visitor would be laconic and stick to facts. In a confidential tone, he launched into a long recital which was interspersed with personal reflections and punctuated by silences. Yet there was no hesitation in his delivery. Sentences flowed easily, and inflections varied. His voice was dry and hard when he spoke of difficulties, grave and theatrical during the moral passages, bright when the work described yielded results. When the story evoked religious forces, spirits or signs, the speaker lowered his voice. It became even sepulchral when dead people or ghosts were mentioned; then it was reduced to a mere breath, sounding as if it were flowing out at his feet.

When narratives are very technical, they always go to the heart of the matter and do not get lost in digressions. The only time a hunter will let some geographical detail jog his memory and set him to reminiscing is when he is on the trail and if he is in the right mood; practically never does this happen in front of a group of people in his igloo.

Death is a constant theme. *Toquvoq*—the death of this or that person, the imminent end of the speaker himself, the precariousness and futility of life, destiny's sign. Although he does not say so explicitly, the Eskimo quickly harks back to his belief in the tupilaq (or qivittoq)—the evil spirit that takes possession of the soul and brings misfortune.

If briefly and with restraint, the Eskimo evokes dangers he has encountered, he never hesitates to describe the fear he has felt. If he is speaking about an old person or an incompetent, his voice and mouth become scornful: his eyelids close and he lowers his head: "Toquvoq una, qujanaq! Let that one die. Good riddance!"

Now and again, depending on the men's characters (and here—as elsewhere—men are variously modest, reserved, or indifferent, and some are sanctimonious hypocrites), their talk will turn to utsuuqs, with precise descriptions of the structure, shape, emptiness, and lubrication; to usuks and their varying dimensions; and to intercourse and the frequency thereof. Then the men's voices become bright and merry, but never lecherous; I must say that very soon there will be only one voice continuing a monologue that becomes tiresome if it dwells long on this topic.

Once married and up to the age of forty, Eskimo women discuss sexual pleasure constantly and very openly, but without any lewdness. It is gossip rather than erotic talk. Ann Sofia and Sophie used to come often to my house, one on the heels of the other as if they were keeping tabs on each other. They would sit down, straddling two crates—a position that showed their long and magnificent white boots to advantage—and would commence with spiteful comments about various men in the village, then proceed to stories about the current nuliarpoq-kujappoq.

A meeting with this or that person is recalled in detail: the circumstances in which it took place; how many dogs were pulling the man's sledge and how strong they were; how big was the load on his sledge; details about his life and aspects of his character; the health of his wife and children; and the tiniest events in his hunting adventures. Everything has been observed and remembered. The story is punctuated by accounts of advantages that the narrator either anticipated or actually gained, and by descriptions of goods exchanged: leather thongs for a complete harness given in exchange for a knife; half a walrus for a kiviaq; a very good two-year-old dog for a rifle. . . . The men always prefer to hear about sons, and as they listen they assume a virile pose. When the story concerns a daughter, on the other hand, their expressions soften and are faintly amused. The smallest scrap of information about the feelings of marriageable girls or about boys' inclinations is attentively noted. Eskimos reminisce also about copious meals of walrus and mattak, but only as parentheses within the tale they are telling.

Eskimos have many different cries and exclamations. The following, which were heard in Illulik, will give the reader some idea. *Qiluausuq:* that does something to me down there (that is, great surprise makes their sex tingle); *usunnguaq:* big prick; *utsunnguaq:* big cunt; *nujannguaq:* that makes my hair feel funny; *anariarit:* go fuck yourself; *isumarartjuaq:* little leader; *uqassalaitteq:* blabbermouth! fool![50]

Certain kinds of specific statements are never doubted; they are accepted as absolutely true: for example, statements about ice conditions; the absence of seals in this place or that; the presumption that such and such a woman is pregnant; or word of disease—received with terror as a fateful portent. Such news is transmitted by word of mouth, by the women who have heard it from the children who pick up and repeat everything they see and hear. Whenever

Sketch by a child from Siorapaluk. December 1950. (*Private collection*)

a sledge or kayak passes by, news is briefly told—the Eskimo has mastered the art of summing up the most complicated situation in a few words—and is accurately passed from camp to camp. For practical reasons having to do with hunting as well as with family life, a report is always considered exact. "Sallutooq!" (Liar!) is the worst insult one can receive.

I should point out that a distinction is made between a pledge and a promise. A pledge must always be kept exactly and punctually; a promise is understood to be a fragile thing. A promise holds good for the moment when it is made but not necessarily later. When the desire which gives rise to the promise fades, the promise no longer holds good; if the promise is kept, it means that the desire is still there. Eskimos are pessimistic by nature and attach no importance to promises: "Tomorrow is another day. Immaqa! Maybe!" What was said is assessed according to the circumstances in which it was said. And the Eskimo is wise enough to measure the fragility of the promise. . . . And so, resolves change with the weather, the condition of the ice, or a person's mood. An agreement, on the other hand—a solemn commitment—is held to be such, for it is rarely made and is deemed timeless, especially if it has been made with a white man.

I was able to observe that under the most favorable conditions for transmitting news—in April and May, when many sledges are traveling about—a piece of news reached everyone from north to south of the 300-mile-long district within three weeks. During the months of isolation, July and August, when the open sea cuts the camps off from one another (kayaks never venture long distances), it took six weeks, at the most, for a piece of news originating in Etah to be brought by a hunter to a camp and then to be transmitted by kayak or boat down to Savigssivik. As an illustration of how the most intimate details were passed along to the whole village, I will describe what was considered to be a very scandalous affair.

A young Lutheran catechist from Greenland who was a bachelor and a very agreeable man was living in the small hamlet of X. The one time I visited him, I got along with him very well. Clearly, he was friends with everyone, and the guardian father of the camp; for the Eskimos, he was *ajoqirput*—"our little catechist." Time went by. It came to pass that because he was so isolated, the *ajoqi* slept with the wives of two hunters. People laughed when they spoke of it: "Tupilak una! He's an odd fellow!" But then suddenly the two women found that they had gonorrhea—and had infected their husbands! The two hunters were worried about their swollen genitals, which burned when they peed, but at first they said nothing to anyone for fear of being ridiculed. The two women, however, made discreet inquiries and discovered that the catechist had slept with every woman in the camp except two (one old and the other feeble-minded). After discussing the matter together, they decided to go see the doctor in Thule the first chance they had and, meanwhile, to ask their husbands not to sleep with them. The husbands were furious and beat them. "Kina tupilak? Who is the rascal?" they yelled. "Who? Who?" they shouted, beating their wives black and blue the while. "Ajoqi! Ajoqi! The catechist! The catechist!" the women answered in unison. Armed with sticks, whips, and axes, the two men set out with their neighbors (who had known about the mixed-up affair for quite a while) in a tight, angry group headed for the church.

Luckily for the poor catechist, he had been informed of what was going on by some friendly person who wished him well, and he had already fled up into the mountain. The inside of his house was demolished from top to bottom, and the group vented the balance of its anger in furious curses.

Several days later, Thule was informed and the authorities dispatched the senior regional pastor to soothe people's feelings. He went to look for the catechist up on the mountain, where he was hiding out with a peaceable old Eskimo, and arranged to have him quickly removed. At the clinic in Thule, the *ajoqi tupinara* (the odd catechist) was examined and found not to have gonorrhea, so it had been some other more discreet rascal who had made all the trouble. The authorities suppressed this scandal in the Eskimos' complex private lives and assigned a less attractive ajoqi to the hamlet—a man with a wife and numerous children. He arrived from the south of Greenland by the next summer boat.

In this society, which was obliged to be cohesive, speech was a tool of constraint which required a man to act only in accord with tradition, to disregard himself. Group society was repressive; Eskimo speech, expressing the view of the group-arbiter (the Eskimo never said "*I* think" but "the Inuit think"; the "I" was proscribed even in their thoughts), was a powerful weapon. The Eskimo might never say what "he" personally felt but what the entire group felt. Eskimo thinking was, therefore, like the smallest common denominator shared among these various family groups or, sometimes, collections of individuals. Speech acted via conversation and gossip to correct situations and set things straight. The slackers, weaklings, parasites, and cheaters were criticized as they are in a communist society; poor workers were singled out and held up to public contempt: "They bring us trouble, they don't respect the rules, they scorn the taboos. . . ." With extraordinarily cruel epithets, the faults of these atypical individuals were denounced throughout the territory. If the wrongdoer did not humble himself by acknowledging his weaknesses or his impotence—and he had need to do this before only a few witnesses—he would have to go off and live by himself in isolation. The atypical person could never exert influence by example but only by speaking within the group; the group would then digest and adopt what he said, or reject it.

In 1950, I encountered a case of such banishment. In Nunatarssuak, Sauninnguaq and her husband had been excluded from the group. They were kleptomaniacs: people said they robbed traps and showed no remorse for doing so.

One last remark: the Eskimo detests long quarrels, the kind that are never settled. He finds continual bad humor *(kamappoq, kamajavoq)* intolerable; ergo, his rages, especially his verbal outbursts, are all the more spectacular because he knows they will have to be very short. An isolated community cannot afford to be a preserve of contentious members.

The Harshness
of the Eskimo

A young white man who was both poor and poorly equipped planned to go from Thule to Savigssivik to take some scientific measurements. I was in Savigssivik at the time, on one of my more recent expeditions.

An Eskimo hunter agreed to take him to Savigssivik. Out on the glacier, the two men were soon overtaken by a storm. The qallunaat, who knew very little about conditions in the Far North, had been so improvident as to take with him nothing to eat but chocolate bars, vitamin-enriched biscuits, and other inappropriate food. The Eskimo scornfully watched him "nibble" while he himself tore into his frozen meat with his few remaining rotten teeth. From bivouac to bivouac, he cared for his passenger most "affectionately," protecting him from the wind, seeing that his qulitsaq was in good condition, that his hands were not cold—in other words he was both diligent and attentive. Was he not, after all, the guide? Yet strangely enough, he paid no attention to the kamiks the unfortunate young man was wearing. After an arduous round-trip journey, they returned to Thule-Uummannaq. From the hut where I was staying with the Eskimo members of my team, I saw the young fellow wandering miserably along the shore as though he had been abandoned. I sent someone out to fetch him. When I heard his story and saw the condition of his kamiks, I became suspicious and asked him to show me his feet immediately. I helped him take his boots off; it was not easy, because this boy, who was no coward, was clearly suffering intensely. It was lucky that I checked: several toes were beginning to freeze. Nobody had told him to put hay between his inner sole and his boot—a rule that no one can afford to ignore in an Arctic climate.

The Eskimo had actually made a point of not getting him hay and of not telling him he must put it in his boots. Although he changed the grass in his own double boots at each bivouac, he did not protect the poor man, but let him walk virtually barefoot on the ice.

First, I brought the blood back into his toes by massaging them, then had a tub of warm water prepared for him. Fortunately, these measures were not too late. Within a few hours, the patient had learned a lesson on the job: science begins with basics.

Later that day, I came upon the Eskimo hunter at the edge of the ice field, harnessing his dogs for his return trip north. I took the opportunity to talk to him, all the more frankly because we were alone. "We've known each other a long time." I said, "The way you treated the young qallunaaq is inexcusable, and it concerns me very much. You know that in the Arctic all qallunaat are brothers." The Eskimo was quite brazen: "But I didn't do anything to him, and anyway here he is, as you can see, very much alive." When I spelled out my complaints, he looked at me sideways. "Listen," he said, "that little fellow is a pitiable creature, and we don't know him. It goes against the grain when we Inuit have to suffer for these youngsters who know nothing about our country! Qallunaat are surely rich enough to give them the money they need, and it's not up to us who have nothing to take care of them. Thank you, they say, and that's the last one sees of them. With you, it's different. You've been with us a long time, you have your own team, you know us and understand us. Sure, I knew he had no straw. Sure, I saw him stamping his feet on the ice. What the hell! It'll put some red blood into him! Ha, ha, ha!"

During my first trips from Illulik, north of Hudson Bay, to Kapuivik, I shared a sledge with S——, yet he did not hesitate to treat me like a total stranger.

He was up front, three-quarters seated; I was in the rear, also three-quarters seated but facing backwards. Hours went by. The Eskimo was entirely absorbed in watching the landscape and in his own thoughts; he never once opened his mouth. We were traveling about two and a half miles an hour. At one point, I had to pee and I slipped off the sledge—without a word to him, of course; he would have stopped the sledge with ill grace and wordlessly made me feel the full weight of his superiority. You might ask, in this situation how was he superior? The answer is that an Eskimo has plenty of "superiority" in reserve for whatever situation! So, I calculated my time, peed quickly, and prepared to catch up with the sledge, which was then some fifty yards ahead. I started to run, but the mocking Eskimo—who surely had eyes in the back of his head and had seen everything—began in a low voice to urge on his dogs. I was not going to be able to keep that pace very long. I controlled my breathing, which was growing shorter by the second, and yard by yard I negotiated the space separating me from the speeding sledge. The Eskimo was waiting, of course, for the delectable moment when I would lose face by humiliating myself and calling out after him. I managed to deny him this

Drawing by Sespalik. Illulik, August 1960. *(Private collection)*

pleasure, even though the team was being deliberately made to trot faster and faster. I caught up and, completely out of breath, collapsed onto the sledge. The Eskimo had not budged; his broad deerskin-clad back was still innocently turned to me.

We continued on our way for two more hours without a pause or a word, and not once did the Eskimo turn around. When we reached our stopping place, he looked at me as if nothing had happened.

Four months later, I met him again. We had got to know each other pretty well, and had even formed a kind of friendship. He talked to me about his problems with this and that person, and about his carefully programmed sex life. Counting on his fingers, he said, "You see, with my wife it's first every three days, then every two days, then every day—but rarely twice a day. That would wear out my knee joints, which is not good for walking—that's what the Inuit say—and then it's every three days again. . . ." Everything was fine; I had all but forgotten the "sledge incident." We were returning from the village of Utsuutassut (which means, literally, "the place where there are many vaginas"; the men there had apparently been massacred in a war between villages), and were crossing the ice field from Foxe Basin to Kapuivik, on Jens Munk Island.

We were very tired, having run into a storm, and our meat supply was low. The Eskimo told me he was related to a hunter who lived in a village nearby. "I know he'll give me some grease and fat. We've always helped each other even though we don't see each other often. And of course he'll invite me to sleep at his house." I answered that, as for me, I would stay with Piuaittuq, as I always did when I came that way. Piuaittuq was the elderly head of this camp of walrus hunters, and he was a loyal friend of mine. Huddled on the sledge, we talked about how pleasant it was going to be to see this man or woman again, and I thought to myself how important relatives were, even more so than friends, in the organization of trips in the Arctic. At every hamlet we had come to over the past few weeks, my companion had sought out some cousin or other relative (relative by blood or adoption, name sharing, or hunting alliance), in order to obtain meat for his dogs; otherwise, we would have had to hunt, and being at the mercy of the itineraries of the walruses or seals, our trip would have been prolonged by several weeks. There was something festive about our arrival in Kapuivik. After many long hours, we had finally arrived in front of its five igloos. With one final heave, the barking dogs climbed the slope from the ice field right up to the igloo where the old chief lived. He welcomed me in his usual friendly way.

S——, who prided himself on his assertive personality, greeted the old man in a deliberately offhand way and left us to go find his relative (who, as it happened, was an opponent of the old chief). My arrival was, naturally, the occasion for some feasting. We were about to go to sleep when my traveling companion very cautiously pushed the door of the katak open and thrust himself through. He walked into the single room and stopped. He stood there, hunched over, his eyes lowered; he was carrying a caribou skin slung under his arm.

Piuaittuq was seated on the illeq, looking important. He continued to address his remarks left and right without seeming even to have noticed that S——had come in. A good twenty minutes went by. S——stood there, embarrassed, holding his caribou skin under his arm. If he had wanted to speak in order to call attention to himself, a cutting laugh would have immediately punished his lack of tact. It was Piuaittuq's intention to talk or, rather, to sound off, until he felt like stopping, as was appropriate under the circumstances for someone of his rank. Because I was a guest, it would have been completely out of place for me to intervene in the matter, which did not concern me. Then everyone went about preparing to bed down, as if S——were not present. It was not until we were pulling our boots off and starting to undress that Piuaittuq glanced obliquely at S——. He looked him up and down without saying a word, thus haughtily letting S——know that he would be allowed to sleep only in the most humiliating location—on the floor. S——immediately and gratefully lay down, losing face both with Piuaittuq, whom he had treated so casually when we arrived, and also with me. But he had no choice. To sleep in this igloo, even if on the floor, could still be considered a privilege, since his relative, who must have held some old grudge against him (no doubt a

The interior of Piuaittuq's Eskimo tent, in the region of Illulik (Kapuivik, on Jens Munk Island). To the left is the bench for guests, in front of which a few scraps of meat have been placed on a board. On both sides of the illeq, on flat slabs, are two oil lamps and a few ulus. In the foreground, far right, are buckets for dirty water and boards on which salmon are laid. At the back of the illeq, which is covered with an animal hide, are an accordion and a gramophone. Outside the tent a sealskin is drying. Drawing by Lea (sixteen years old). September 1960.

legitimate one, I thought, judging by my own experiences with S——), had refused to let him stay. To be turned away from a second igloo would have been terrible: indeed, there would have been nothing left for him to do but to sleep under a tent like an outlaw, and this would have been the ultimate insult.

The Eskimo long remembers anyone who has wronged him, and is unforgiving; in his own time, at his convenience, he will make that person pay dearly for it.

A year after this incident, I arrived at Back River, an estuary of Chantrey Inlet, in the central Canadian Arctic, where there were four snow igloos. The Eskimos of this region, whom the English explorer George Back discovered in

August 1833, are considered among the most primitive in the Arctic; they live only in snow igloos which they practically do not heat. The Utkuhikjalingmiut, as they are called, had not had an extended visit from white men in their camps for a long time. I was one of the first scientists to stay there since Rasmussen in June 1923. My brief visit, with two sledges of Netsilimmiut Eskimos (their nearest neighbors), and one mounted policeman—forced on me this time as aide in this area—was unquestionably quite an event. The Eskimos seemed to remember Rasmussen's six-day visit as if it had been yesterday. "He came from that direction . . . he left heading that way . . . he asked us. . . ." It fascinated me that despite a lapse of forty years, what they told me corresponded for the most part to what I had read in Rasmussen's published report. I had brought that report with me so that I could compare it to the then current facts, and I discussed it with them line by line with the aid of an Eskimo interpreter.

At the time of my visit, the thirty Eskimos who made up this endangered community were recovering from a famine which had killed several members of the group the previous winter. I arrived at the coldest time of year, around the end of March. It was −40°C (−40°F). We had just eaten our last haunch of bear meat when we came on the Eskimos' abandoned camp—four igloos that had been deliberately staved in as a sign that their occupants had left. We were uneasy because we did not know where to find them. As we were discussing the situation, we saw a man walking toward us from the far end of the lake. The dogs leaped forward; when we reached the man, we took him with us on one of the sledges, and half an hour later arrived at the four new igloos, to be greeted by the wild barking of fifty dogs.

The men were lined up a few feet in front of the *torssuqs* (front entrances) of their igloos, their arms crossed, as was the custom. Their women and children were clustered behind them as if for protection. They had slipped their arms out of the sleeves of their qulitsaqs to keep their hands warmer in their armpits, and the empty sleeves dangled at their sides.

We halted the customary thirty yards away from them. This is the range of a harpoon or a small bow and arrow; at this distance, a man can avoid being hit by an arrow. The usage is a holdover from the old days, for now the Eskimos have guns. The two Netsilimmiut Eskimos from Gjoa Haven who had accompanied me stood, whips in hand, in front of their quiet dogs. Brief remarks whistled through the Eskimos' teeth, as the two groups watched each other intensely. Of course they had some slight acquaintance, but since they came from different tribes, they were obliged to show mistrust.

After five minutes of preliminaries, they shook our hands and, with arms held high and smiling eyes, let us know that we were welcome. To lighten the atmosphere, I then remarked that I would be crazy to pitch my tent in a village where several igloos seemed to be waiting for us! The response was a polite although rather tense laugh. But how was I to choose the most hospitable igloo? When you arrive in a village and are made welcome, the custom is immediately to invite yourself into one of the huts. The choice you make is taken as a sign of respect, a considered sign of respect. . . . "Choose whichever one you like!" But you will be judged by the choice you make, and your authority will be either increased or diminished thereby. (One is wise to avoid a poor igloo belonging to old people. Usually it is freezing, because the only heat comes from human bodies, and the older a person is, the lower his body temperature.)

In a situation where it would have been in the worst possible taste to appear hesitant, a quick and happy inspiration made me choose an igloo buried in snow, the interior of which I glimpsed through the bottom of a door. This was a special igloo, a double igloo! When I went in, my hosts immediately dispossessed a bitch and her puppies so that I could use the second room. I set up my tent in it so as to have a more comfortable shelter. Every morning, I awoke in the glacial cold of the unheated igloo, got up, and placed tea and tobacco in the hood of the nearest person in the adjoining room of the double igloo, usually a young married woman. Her crinkled eyes would smile at me contentedly. Like my hosts, I ate nothing but frozen raw salmon every three or four hours. Life went on that way, pleasantly interrupted by conversation and interviews.

There was a boy of about ten living in the igloo, who was related in some way, whether by adoption or not I unfortunately never bothered to find out. A few days after I arrived, this boy began to have attacks of what seemed to be hysteria. He trembled, became rigid, flung his arms forward, beat his fists together, and stamped his feet; his teeth chattered, his face became livid and his eyes haggard, and presently he would lose consciousness. No one did anything except the "head" of the igloo, who would grasp the back of the boy's neck and his wrists and squeeze them with all his might. The first day, the attacks lasted a few minutes; the next day, twice as long; and the day after they began to occur more often—the boy had eight convulsions. Between attacks, the poor shivering thing would sit down to rest against the snow wall in a state of extreme prostration. The people around him were indifferent, perhaps even scornful.

Thinking that my sudden appearance in the village might have been in some way responsible for the boy's attacks, I tried to help—at least the poor boy could have crawled into my sleeping bag to get warm. But the "head"— the resident Eskimo who had say in these matters—categorically refused to allow it. To my amazement, he said, "A long time ago, orphans ate and slept in the passageway. If someone had an orphan living in his house, you saw him because you had to step over him to enter. He ate leftovers, but otherwise it was up to him to hunt for his own food. This was the way men were brought up here—the hard way, everyone according to his status. This 'sick' boy is lucky —he sleeps on the illeq with us, he lives just the way we do. You'll see how I plan to treat his illness. Don't interfere, krabluna!* This is the country of the

*The Canadian term for *qallunaaq* or white man, often rendered *kabloona* (as in the famed book by Gontran de Poncins of that title).

Eskimo igloo in the Thule district in 1853–1856. Top drawing: the katak, or passage-way, with two "lengths" and two "heights." In 1967 this type was still found in Illulik, in northeastern Canada, during severe cold. The widespread practice was to have no doors, in order to permit ventilation. The less hardy Eskimo of 1950 provided himself with more protection: two doors were used, even though the winters are slightly less cold than they were between 1600 and 1860. Above, right, a standing figure is recogniz-able as a woman because of the high boots.

Bottom drawing: Notice the Eskimo woman on her hands and knees—recognizable because of her foxskin pants and high boots—preparing to enter the katak. To the right, a man returning with his harpoons from hunting. In 1950–51, the entrances to some igloos in Thule were hardly any higher than those shown here. (*From Kane*, Arctic Explorations)

Inuit and you are not an Inuk. In fact, I'll show you right now how I plan to cure him!"

At that moment, the boy was recovering from an attack. Even though he was shivering from cold and fever and clearly suffering deeply, an old man from a neighboring snow hut asked him to go with him on foot across the icy lake to the old caved-in houses, where they had left a small pile of frozen fish. This meant walking a good distance, returning against the wind—all in a temperature of −30°C (−22°F).

"If he comes back," the old Eskimo said to me, "and you'll see, he will come back—that will prove he's not sick."

He actually did come back.

"You see how we cure people here. What you call 'this poor sick boy' was pretending to be sicker than he was. Outside in the cold, the sickness would go back inside his body. In the igloo, which is warmer, it would come out again. So it was no very serious illness. The Inuit have learned to cure this sort of faked sickness which sly people claim to suffer from."

Shortly after that, the boy was taken away by plane and treated for what turned out to be a nervous ailment.

Contrary to what it may seem, the Eskimo was not cruel because he enjoyed being cruel but because he had to be. From an early age he had to kill in order to survive. In the Arctic, harshness was synonymous with life-force. If a mother died in childbirth, the father would kill the infant unless he could find a family in the neighborhood willing to adopt it and have it breast-fed. The father was obliged to kill the newborn baby either by strangling it or, more often, by putting a little snow in its mouth, thus smothering it. Another reason for infanticide used to be the death of the father: custom required that fatherless orphans under the age of three be killed by the mother. In periods of terrible famine, there had been cases of people cannibalizing adults and even children.

Cruel as the Eskimo's harshness may seem, it was never gratuitous or sadistic; he simply liked to see others suffer as he himself did. In fact, suffering seemed to him necessary in that it obliged him to surpass himself. Harshness became an example to emulate. The weakest member of an Eskimo group, who had to be supported by the others, also had to give as much of himself as he could.

There is no known instance of an Eskimo abandoning a companion less fortunate than he while hunting. Without exception, all strong, healthy men had to help one another. Everyone was so aware of how important this system of mutual aid was for the survival of the group that formerly an unproductive member or an incurably sick person who was incapable of repaying the services performed for him would either voluntarily do away with himself or persuade someone else to kill him. And as I mentioned earlier, when old people became too much of a burden, they, too, were always prepared to kill themselves for the sake of the group's survival.

Danger, the daily fight to survive, misfortune, and very ancient customs that reflect terrible privations made these men implacable. Life was a struggle; death and the suffering that precedes and follows it confronted them daily. The Eskimos were cruel to people who pretended to be sick as they had been hard on themselves for the sake of all.

To illustrate these generalizations, I will describe three more scenes. I mentioned earlier the inflexible old rule that once governed the choice of children at the time of birth. In hard times, no Eskimo could keep more than two children, preferably boys. A minimum number of girls—the very strongest— were allowed to survive within the group.

Kajarsuaq's daughter-in-law, who lived in Kapuivik, near Illulik, was on her deathbed. She had been sick for a long time, and no one in the village, which stood by itself on Jens Munk Island, had thought of notifying the station at Illulik. Only two days' journey away, Illulik had a radio and the missionary there was qualified to act as a public-health nurse. By mere chance, this French priest happened to hear that the unfortunate woman was dying, and he went to her immediately. It was obvious that the people of Kapuivik were not happy to see him. Usually, the group was very friendly toward him when he was acting as nurse; now they stood around him in a circle, silent and almost hostile. The missionary decided to remove the sick woman. As soon as she was away from her people and felt less pressure from them, she relaxed and began to smile at the priest, who asked her why she had been neglected like that. "Annerijaujuunngilaq! . . . I was not chosen when I was born!" she exclaimed. Then she explained: "I was born when there was a famine. Because I was a girl, it was decided that I should die. Then something unforeseen happened—a sledge from a neighboring village arrived with some food. My father's mood changed and he let me live—against the will of the group. Now fate, which was thwarted then, has showed its will again by making me become sick. Everyone thinks you should not have interfered now, when affliction chose to strike. Because now the whole group may be afflicted. And since they cannot know when this may happen, the Eskimos of Kapuivik will live in fear from now on. . . ."

A hunter is bound—very closely bound—to his dogs, but if one of them is hurt and is unable to work, his fate is sealed. The following happened one winter. I watched as a fellow from the Thule area fired at one of his eight dogs. He had owned the animal for five years and it was one of his favorites. The dog had been limping for some time. A few days earlier, the man had said, "He doesn't deserve to live anymore. At least this way I'll be able to use his skin!" The animal was wounded in his rump; leaning to one side, he dragged himself toward the ice field, yapping weakly and looking at the Eskimo with an expression of mingled desperation and resignation. Smiling, with teeth clenched, the Eskimo shot six carefully spaced bullets, only the last of which was aimed to kill. For weeks the Eskimo had been irritated by the limping dog. Now he was taking his revenge; it excited him. Later, he would skin the animal as he had said—not to save the skin, which had been ruined, but so that the carcass would be edible for the other dogs; dogs will rarely eat a dog teammate if they recognize its smell. The hunter went back to his igloo. He would let the carcass freeze on the ice bank, neither too close to nor too far away from the team. When the time came, he would chop it up.

Some years later I visited Naajaruluk, a hamlet northwest of Illulik: three tents inhabited by people in great and evident poverty. I was the guest of Ava, whom I had met before. His wife had an attractive face, and she gave me a warm welcome. We talked about one thing and another, and I mentioned the coming winter, which promised to be very difficult for Naajaruluk. Everyone was already worried, because this village of hunters was in a bad location: there were seals here, but apart from them only gulls, as the camp's name implied (naajaq means gull). Meat was abundant farther east, at Kapuivik, where walrus hunters lived. However, in this region the structures of Eskimo society had already been greatly changed by the influence of the white man and there was already less interterritorial solidarity within one group than there had been.

"Every winter it begins again," Ava explained. "X holds the moral authority in our group, but he has made almost no preparation for dealing with the cold, and we are uneasy. Each family is using up its summer reserves—ten to fifteen seals—and we have no fat at all left, and very little oil, because we haven't caught enough foxes to exchange them at the H.B.C.[51] trading post in Illulik. Every January we begin to shiver. Then we decide to do what we always do. The walrus hunters live four days away from us. They'll help us, of course, but they'll make us pay for it!

"Our elder once wrote a letter to Kapuivik, but they would accept the letter from no one but his youngest son—an eight-year-old! The poor boy had to go there all alone by dog sledge; four days of traveling through bitter cold is very hard on a child that age. They wanted to humiliate us in this way and show us that we were wretched, incompetent seal hunters.

"They made the boy wait for a whole day before they let him enter the village. All day long, everyone in Kapuivik saw him waiting, his nose frozen, huddled in his worn qulitsaq, but no one raised a finger. At last, when they thought the boy—and all of us—had been sufficiently humiliated by this treatment, they allowed him to load his sledge with quarters of walrus meat; while this was done they didn't say a word. Once he had arrived home—and only then—could we men go over there too, to hunt walrus. That's how the people of Kapuivik make us pay; they know we have nothing to offer them in return."

Fighting and War

Historically, the various Eskimo groups have often been at odds with one another. Unrelenting battles have put individuals, families, and whole tribes at loggerheads. The larger and richer the groups, the more intense the battles. On the Bering Strait, on the Alaskan and Siberian coasts, where large populations lived, actual military confrontations took place among these wealthy collectivities of whale hunters, also between the Siberian reindeer breeders, and the Siberian whale hunters. Organized troops were used in these battles. On the other hand, when Eskimos engaged in combat in central and eastern Canada and in Greenland, they were always extremely careful to keep the number of casualties down.

These wars and murders were often vendettas, successive acts of revenge that the family groups of successive victims carried out against one another. Orphans or solitary men with few relatives often hesitated to kill anyone, knowing they would have no support in the vendettas that would inevitably follow. Moltke, Rasmussen's companion, tells how in 1905 Ulloriaq killed a sorcerer in Thule who came from a large family. Ulloriaq wanted to murder the sorcerer's brother, too, before the brother murdered him. He approached Moltke—a Dane—and asked him to kill the man. He had few relatives and feared that by himself he would not be able to cope with the vengeance of the family group he had wronged.

One should remember that the Eskimo first shows hostility in the form of humor or silence: *Erininartorlu*—one feels uncomfortable.

A visiting neighbor is staying too long, let's say. He will be indirectly asked to leave by a series of jokes. On the east coast of Greenland, in humor contests —joking matches—each of two antagonists tries to win the laughter of the assembled community. Although the custom has not become institutionalized, the same thing takes place in Thule when people meet in the igloos.

In the central Canadian Arctic, disagreements are decided through fighting exercises and endurance contests, in which one man, tensing his muscle the better to endure the pain, allows himself to be hit repeatedly on the same spot on his upper arm.

Disagreements are also settled in single combat. The two antagonists passively allow themselves to be struck, turn and turn about. They hit each other as hard as they can with their fists. Usually they aim for the face, in particular above the eyebrows or on the temples. The village men form a group around the fighters. There is no referee. A blow "below the belt" is unthinkable. Occasionally there used to be public knife fights in northeastern Canada. If a man was provoked, he would stand up, his chest thrust forward. He would respond only after he had been wounded.

Near Pelly Bay (south of Boothia Peninsula, in the eastern Canadian Arctic), people still remember a confrontation that resulted in the death of both men. "Give me back my honor!" was more or less what they said to each other as, with the tips of their knives, they searched deeper and deeper for each other's heart.

The scale of punishment for different crimes varied. In Gjoa Haven, King William Island, Canada, a woman kept stealing small objects. The men in the village caught her and pulled out every hair on her head one by one: *Nujaatok!* No more hair! The woman was bald for some time, and she wore a hat to hide her shame.

In Ungava, in northern Quebec Province, there was a hunter who pursued women so avidly that he no longer even left the camp. The husbands of the women wearied of the adversity this entailed for them, so they forced the man to build a snow igloo outside the camp and assigned it to him as his residence. One evening, the hunters surrounded the igloo and in absolute silence cocked their rifles. A signal was given, and they all fired.

The Eskimos' cruelty could be implacable. If a man caused a neighbor to lose face—by making an offensive joke at his expense in public, by stealing a trap, or by raping a woman (the worst offense of all)—the neighbor would take his revenge, usually in a treacherous manner. After some time had passed— anywhere from a month to several years—when the right moment came along, he would kill his enemy by stabbing him in the back with a harpoon or a knife. This climate of suspicion and this constantly vengeful mind-set explain why in the past (and even now) the Eskimo always has carried a knife within easy reach, often slipped into the top of his boot.

During those days of widespread fear, which fortunately are behind us, a stranger was received by the village with extreme caution. To avoid the risk of being robbed, the villagers used to scatter their possessions—meat, pelts, harnesses, etc.—and hide them under stones and snow.

Recently I was told a story which illustrates how the Eskimo used to be capable of cruel acts of revenge that were carried out after a lapse of time. The story took place some time between 1900 and 1922, again in the eastern Canadian Arctic. A camp was being decimated by severe famine. One old man and his wife were finding it hard to stay alive. Then their son-in-law, daughter, and granddaughter arrived after a long journey. In Eskimo fashion, the son-in-law immediately asked for a drink of water. Then he announced that he was going to build his own igloo. He and his wife went out to begin working on it. He left his child in his father-in-law's igloo so that she would not be exposed to the cold wind.

The old man was hungry, extremely hungry. He wantonly killed his grand-daughter, chopped her into pieces, and cooked her in his stone pot. Forty or fifty minutes later, not a trace of her was left.

Outside, the new igloo was nearly finished. The young mother had been helping, but it was so very cold that she went back to her father's igloo. She saw instantly that her child had disappeared.

A spear made of a narwhal tusk. Seen by E. K. Kane in 1854. It is very heavy and can be thrown only a short distance. (*From Kane*, Arctic Explorations)

She did not say a word.

For a while she sat, inscrutable, with the old man; then she went out. The day ended. The night passed. The next day, the camp set out to hunt seals. One week, then two weeks, then three weeks went by. Not one reference was made to the incident.

One morning, the son-in-law called on the father-in-law. There was a long silence. The old man sensed that something was brewing. So what! As he had yesterday, and all other days, he joined the group of hunters going to their allut (seal breathing holes) out on the ice. It was bitter cold. That morning, they walked with the wind behind them. It was blowing harder and harder: the return would be cruel.

The Eskimos scattered to their respective allut. Suddenly, one caught a seal. "Uutto . . . o . . . o . . . o . . . oq." His long-drawn-out cry announcing the first seal of the spring could be heard far away. In keeping with tradition, everyone went over to the lucky hunter and shared the liver to celebrate the event.

The old man was among them. He leaned down to cut himself another piece of liver. This was the moment they had been waiting for. One man sprang on him, held him down, and in total silence he was quickly stripped naked. He was desperate as he started back to the camp to seek help from his wife or his daughter. Little by little he was freezing in the wind. At the end of his long walk, he passed through his katak and leaned down to enter the igloo; at that moment his frozen spine snapped and the man died at the foot of his own illeq.

Among the Paadlimiut, who are very poor Caribou Eskimos living in the central Canadian Arctic, war was limited to single combat.

Two groups of men—women here, as elsewhere, did not take part in the fighting—faced each other with their arms raised. Two hunters, one chosen by each camp, stepped out of their groups and walked forward. After an initial feint, they tried to kill each other. When one died, a man came forward to replace him. After three or more men had been killed, the winning side discussed the conditions for peace. Occasionally a confrontation could end in total extermination.

In 1963, in Rankin, on Hudson Bay, I was told a story about the Netsilik Eskimos by an old Paadlimioq woman named Qalalaq. It is another illustration of the kind of fighting that used to go on among the Eskimos.

"A long time ago—before my grandfather—there was a tall mountain at Arveraq, and a large lake [Tasersuaq], and an igloo near the lake. A young hunter, Ersaujuk, lived there with his wife and his mother. Ersaujuk's father had been killed by the Netsilimmiut. The young man and his family wished only to be forgotten. Indeed, they had no relatives to help them take revenge, and they lived off by themselves because they knew others feared they would seek vengeance, for this was the sacred duty of any well-born Eskimo. Now, of course, the best way for the Netsilimmiut to get rid of this threat was for them to wipe out what remained of the family.

"One spring, a large number of men—Netsilimmiut men—appeared at the lake. They were armed with bows and seemed to be carrying many arrows. They stopped at the shore of the frozen lake. They chose a young child of ten, an orphan—one of those poor iliarsut—to be their emissary. His task was to tell the three living in the igloo that the time had come for them to suffer the same fate as the young man's father. The Netsilimmiut would no longer tolerate a single member of the family's remaining alive. So the iliarsuq set out, trembling with fear. He fully believed that he had been sacrificed by the tribe and would be killed by Ersaujuk.

"He stood facing the igloo. Ersaujuk stayed inside to listen to the message. He answered the orphan, urging him not to be anxious. 'I understand completely! Come here! I'm inviting you to come in!'

"The group was advancing and drew near, making a great deal of noise. But then it stopped and set up camp. There was a long silence, followed presently by a cheerful din—a mingling of shouts, songs, and dances.

"Ersaujuk prepared to leave his snow igloo. He was carrying his bow. 'I'm going out, all right?' he said to his mother. 'Ieh! Yes!' Then he turned to his wife, who was sitting to his right on the illeq. She was expecting a baby, and he had decided it would be given the name of its maternal grandfather. 'If I am going to die,' he said, 'my child will not move. If I'm going to be safe the child will tell me so. He will move.'

"He put his hand on his wife's belly. The child moved. That was enough. Now the man knew he would not die.

"So he went out of the igloo and shouted to the group on the lake, 'I'm ready! Let your arrows fly!' And the arrows flew. All of them missed him. The man's two dogs—a male and a female—ran out and with their teeth broke the arrows lying on the ground. Then Ersaujuk let fly an arrow and hit a man in the stomach, then a second man in the stomach, and a third in the throat. Every time he let fly an arrow he killed someone. So the Netsilimmiut went away. Ersaujuk gathered all the corpses in one place and covered them with stones.

"Both summer and winter passed. One day the following spring, the family heard a noise far off on the lake. The Netsilimmiut were coming back to take their revenge. They halted at the shore of the lake and sent a messenger, this time an old woman, a widow. The men danced and sang while the old woman fearfully made her way to the lonely igloo. The old woman told Ersaujuk that the hour had come for him—and doubtless for her, too—to die.

"Ersaujuk went out, paying no attention to her. The hunters all fired at once. Ersaujuk was wounded: arrows stuck out all over his body. He pulled them out with no trouble except for one, which was stuck fast in his stomach. It was barbed and had gone in very deep.

"The Netsilimmiut went off with their messenger. With great difficulty, Ersaujuk's mother and wife dragged him into the igloo. They laid him down on the illeq. For many days he rested there. It did not seem possible to remove the arrow without killing him. Ersaujuk knew he was going to die. Solemnly he asked to be carried to a knoll where the rock was clean and free of sand. And there it was that he breathed his last."

When Qalalaq had finished telling me this story, she said that she had seen his tomb. Ersaujuk still had beads around his head. The village children, who believed that his guardian spirit was protecting them, continued to fill his great headband with beads.

Approaches to the Psychology of the Eskimo

Eskimos are by nature complex and changeable; they are at once hard and sensitive, and they habitually mask their feelings. We white men often find them elusive. Of course, as Montaigne observed, "Every man calls barbarous that to which he is not accustomed." It is difficult to find precise words with which to capture without congealing the reality of these people because—like their expressive, mobile faces—they are altogether unpredictable. Actors playing Eskimos—this is probably the principal memory I have of them.

When the native first sees the white man arrive, loaded down with the wonders of the world, he assumes an attitude that is a little like that of an animal at once curious and agitated, proud and wary.

"Tame me," the Fox said to the Little Prince—this situation is the same. As you leave the ship, they look at you out of the corners of their eyes:

"Qallunaat. Hmm . . . hmm . . . sunaana!"

Out of a kind of basic pride, they do not wish to appear either surprised or admiring. With these few words, they go away in silence, as if lost in endless speculation. After a few days, people begin to invite you to their houses. You are assailed by cordiality, and questions both varied and precise are put to you. People give you presents. You are tempted to think you have been accepted. Not so fast. True acceptance requires much more: this is only amiability and a kind of cunning—after all, you have sugar and Nescafé, and perhaps other things.

I happened to leave a family I had been living with in Godthaab, in southern Greenland, when our relations had reached this stage. With the greatest politeness they refused the payment I offered. Smiling, my hosts escorted me back to the boat. Months passed. From Paris I sent them a package of various things, including perfumes, which won me this astringent response:

"Thank you, but we would have preferred a Dior gown!"

They had undoubtedly found someone to translate the latest issue of *Vogue* for this dig at me. Obviously, I had not succeeded in taming them.

Like a chameleon, the Eskimo leaves the person who observes him with complex recollections, with impressions as numerous as they are contradic-

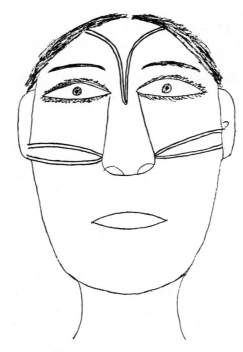

Drango, born at Pond's Inlet, inhabitant of Illulik, August 1960. *(Private collection)*

tory. Watching him live, one thinks one is looking at an amazing kaleidoscope. He is both spontaneous and an actor to the tips of his fingers; he tries simultaneously to play the role assigned him by his place in the small group and to satisfy his personal desire of the moment.

Rarely does a rational thought enter his mind and influence him to temper or change or abandon whatever it is he has impulsively set out to do. Often his impulse can be supplanted by a new and irresistibly enticing desire. Not to satisfy his desire "diminishes" the Eskimo, and sometimes makes him really ill.

This is your initial impression. But soon you realize that in serious situations the Eskimo is capable of controlling his actions. Group life has taught him this. He imposes limits on his impulsiveness.

It was Christmas, 1950: for my entertainment, Igaapaluk was mimicking the lame Asarpannguaq "making love"; it was grotesque and odious. Imina wrapped himself in some black cloth and for his own amusement "aped" the *palasi* devoutly reading the Gospel. He dropped his jaw and imitated the way I fired a gun. Everyone laughed. I prepared to mimic my host in turn—but cautiously; the Eskimos may have a sense of humor, but they don't like the laughter to be at their expense. When an Eskimo is irritated, in a matter of seconds his resentment can turn to anger, and his anger to enduring rancor.

The Eskimos take pleasure in giving one another nicknames that are used only when the person in question is absent. Unarsuaq: Bloody Nuisance; Unakasik: Little Nothing. No one takes offense: others have merely sized a person up. But the system of measurement here becomes very complicated: the nickname may stick, but its initial significance is forgotten or changed. For example, *eru*—shit; *eqorsuaq*—big shit; an epithet has become a name—it denotes a man who has compelled recognition and by now it is a term of respect. Not one of the important explorers, however rich they were or however prestigious their titles, could avoid being given a nickname. It is useless to try to defend oneself or try to explain anything. The nickname sometimes seems to emerge from the depths of the Eskimos' unconscious, so that often they themselves are rather surprised by the epithet which rises to their lips. People here hardly ever reason—they feel. Intuition often takes the place of thought.

Three × 2 = . . . 6; 10 + 10 = . . . 20. Imina was doing his accounts. He was having a hard time. As he tried to follow the numbers his mind wandered. He would have a headache that evening, for sure. Eskimos do not like arithmetic. In fact, there are no words in their language for numbers higher than twenty. Two times ten represents a complete man: the four sets of five fingers and toes. Beyond twenty, they speak in terms of mass, of volume. They use guesswork. Their way of counting from zero to twenty harks back to our old ways of counting, when man used his own body as his unit of measure: a fathom was six *feet*, one foot being twelve inches or *thumbs*. Of course, feet varied in length from one region to another: a foot was 12.48 inches in Paris, and 10.14 inches in Naples. The same goes for weights: among the Eskimos they are measured in "armfuls," just as in France before the metric system a *livre* (pound) was "what one could take in one's hand in order to *deliver* it."

The Eskimo cannot tell time exactly, either. Past time is told by the movement of the sun, in winter by that of the moon. Because of the lunar cycle, then, he divides the year into months and, as I have said, has given a special name to each month of the year.

As with a fraction, Imina would draw a similar blank when confronted with a northern Greenland newspaper published in Disko Bay, the *Avangnamioq*. "Democracy," he would read slowly aloud, "is government of the people by the people. The Scandinavian kingdoms are democracies." From boredom, he would let the newspaper fall from his hands.

But if I talked to him about hunting, animals, the weather, the geography of the North, the history and prehistory of the Arctic, or the habits of animals, he came to life. Only the concrete events of life—and especially the life he knew at first hand—filled him with enthusiasm. My studies of the erosion of sands and clay by torrents, the deep or superficial splitting of rocks by the frost, the timetable and topography of the melting of the snow, the rising of the glacial continent once it was unburdened by the melting of the glaciers—all these matters excited him and elicited precise answers from him.

"Here, look at this rock," Iggianguaq would say to me. "See how red it is—like savik, iron, eaten away by water. Do you know why? I don't."

He listened obediently to the explanation, with a slightly critical look. A moment later, he was off exploring.

The Eskimo's eye grows bright and intent when he is given information about other Arctic peoples, particularly other Eskimos. I have always been amazed by the confidence with which they adapt to what interests them: they could read my maps, no matter what the scale was, and were able to add details about things that have not yet been mapped; for example, they would mark down ocean currents, using their own direct observations of the movements of icebergs and the ice field. The same was true for the location of birds' nests, archaeological sites, hunting areas, etc. But theirs is a society of hunters, and Eskimos are notably incapable of dwelling for very long on an idea that is unrelated to problems of hunting. Music, painting, politics, modern technology—these and other general ideas do not hold their attention. It is not that they do not think these things are important; they simply are not interested. Of course I used to talk to them about what the rest of the world is like. But certain subjects—our music, our technology—were almost never brought up by them, and except for Inuterssuaq (Peter Freuchen's friend), Imina (out of almost fatherly affection for me), and Olipaluk (a métis who had emigrated from Disko, in the south of Greenland), their interest was usually merely polite. Still, how can anyone know another person's secret thoughts?

They observed what I did and the modern equipment I used (radio transmitter and receiver, photographic equipment, mapmaking apparatus) very intently, but with an evident desire to keep their distance from these tokens of another world—a world they admired but whose limits they were aware of. They had seen too many white men on expeditions from America or other countries experience difficulties in coping with Eskimo territory, and they had some idea of the human weaknesses that existed within our technological society. Perhaps this explains the indifference or slight scorn they showed for the modern equipment I carted along with me. When an Eskimo has the support and solidarity of his group, I have always sensed that instinctively he feels that by using his own methods and in his own time he can always outstrip us.

The Eskimos' sense of direction is remarkable. The slightest signs observed in due time—a mark in the snow, the slant of vegetation, the dampness or dryness of rock walls, the movement of clouds, the leaden or other color of the sky, the positioning of stones in stream beds, the relative depth of the thaw—are interpreted by the hunters as aids in helping them find their way when lost in a storm.

In 1923, Birket-Smith felt that Eskimos were incapable of abstraction. He related how Knud Rasmussen had once asked a Netsilik (from the Canadian central Arctic) which of two paths was shorter. "Even although the man knew the two paths very well and could say how long it took to travel each of them, he could not hold them both in his mind at once."

On the other hand, thirty-two years later, in 1955, a Canadian Eskimo

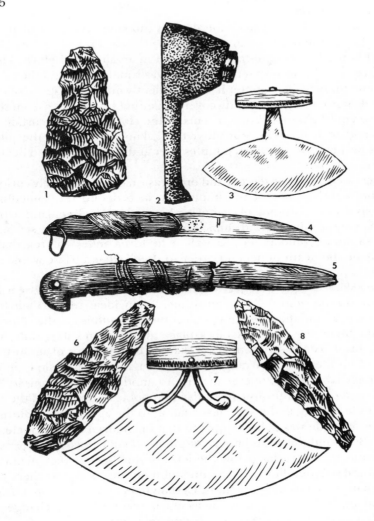

Various types of hatchets, knives, and sharpened stones used over the ages by the Polar Eskimos. Having no wood until the early nineteenth century (when some began to be obtainable from European whalers and expeditions) and no iron except for the meteorite at Savigssivik and objects of Norse origin obtained by barter beginning in the twelfth century, the Polar Eskimos of Thule displayed extraordinary ingenuity in making these indispensable tools. From top to bottom, left to right: Fig. 2 shows meteorite iron shaped for use as a knife. They obtained these pieces by chipping away at the mass. When meteorite iron was not available, the Eskimos used sharp stones, bear's teeth, deer antlers, and shells. Figs. 3 and 7 show knives (ulus) with ivory handles, used by women of Siorapaluk, 1950–1951. Pieces of flint (Figs. 1, 6, and 8) were shaped for heads for harpoons and arrows. Figs. 4 and 5 are knives obtained by bartering with whalers, and repaired from generation to generation. (*Sharpened stones and knives from Holtved*, The Polar Eskimos)

showed an astonishing capacity for abstract thinking. The pilot of an airplane had got lost in the fog over an area of Canada near Frobisher Bay. On board was an Eskimo hunter who had never been in an airplane before. They were flying directly over his own territory. Fuel was running low and the pilot asked the Eskimo for help. The hunter had been silently noting the speed of the plane and the distance they had already covered, getting his bearings from reference points he could glimpse through rents in the clouds and the curtain of mist. Calmly and with no great difficulty, the Eskimo reoriented the pilot, who brought his plane down fifteen minutes later at the airport he had been unable to locate.

These people are observant and on occasion can be infinitely curious: they will unhesitatingly attempt the impossible in order to see something new. Peary tells a story that took place during his first north Greenland expedition, when his young wife was with him. An elderly Eskimo woman set out in the middle of winter, undaunted, to walk a hundred miles—a trek that would probably be the death of her—in order to "see" what a white woman looked like.

The Eskimos' logic is subjective and affective. According to Roger Buliard, missionary in the central Canadian Arctic, "their ideas reflect their thoughts of the moment, and their thoughts reflect their emotions . . . the color of what is around them. . . . All this takes place abruptly and illogically, through superimposed scenes—without the Eskimo's being aware of it, so to speak. Instead of his ideas being arranged in an orderly way in his mind, they follow one another laboriously, one giving rise to another or banishing it."

I carried out the various City of Paris school tests on most of the children in the Thule district, and it was clear that up to the age of ten or eleven, their scholastic aptitude was at least equal to that of children in French elementary schools. But—and this is an important point—their scholastic *performance* was often mediocre, falling far below the level of intelligence they manifested in their natural surroundings. It was undoubtedly up to the teachers to make radical changes in teaching methods. Certain people both in Copenhagen and in Greenland had been emphasizing as much, recommending changes in programs that were, in many respects, completely absurd.[52]

Schooling dulls the native mind. The proof is that in the old days, the Eskimo's powers of observation and of recall were so acute that they had only to look at a landscape or hear a piece of news for the related facts to be engraved in their memory forever, whereas of what they were learning in 1950 through books they retained nothing or very little. By 1950, Danish had been taught in the schools for nearly twenty years, yet no Eskimo spoke it; one would have ventured to say that literacy advanced to the detriment of that mental writing we call memory.

Alert as he is to nature, the Eskimo has an amazing ability to fix things in his mind and sensory memory. Undoubtedly the vibrancy of his perceptions goes back to deep stimuli which have left indelible traces. And because he gives expression to these sensations in behavioral patterns rather than in words, they remain unchanged. The many interpretations of sensation which intelligence could provide would weaken its original force. The Eskimo must be dimly aware of how important it is to protect this fund of propulsive drives because when he speaks he is noticeably intent on masking his deeper perceptions. To modify Stendhal's notion, I would say that the Eskimos' speech is meant not so much to disguise their thought as to protect their sensory experiences. So true is this that although in the great shamanic gatherings the Eskimos are as noisy as they can be, their noise is rhythmic, as if it must not affect the medium's power.

Another interesting fact: like all ancient hunters in the North, the Eskimos possess a particularly marked brain formation. Their paleocortex has been noticeably sharpened by their activities as hunters; their sensory reading of their environment occurs to the detriment of—or to one side of—their little-used neocortex. Thus they retain their ancient powers over nature because of their particular schizo-physiology.

For the Eskimo everything is a sign. Alert, ever on the lookout, they sniff the breeze, the smell of peaty earth steaming in the summer, the scent of air blowing from far away; they appraise how dry is the sound of cracking ice, how damp the blanket of snow in warmer weather; they interpret the mood of animals, the halo around the moon, and the vibration of the air. These thousands of signs are translated into their very rich language; they are so many letters in an age-old alphabet whose characters the Eskimos can readily decipher. Like the rainmaker Valet in Hermann Hesse's *The Glass Bead Game,* the Eskimo "had more to learn through his senses—his feet and hands, his eyes, his touch, his ears and his sense of smell than through his understanding. . . . He learned how to be watchful, to listen, to make a furtive approach, to

Hunter in the act of harpooning. Drawing by Imina (fifty-four years old). Siorapaluk, December 1950. *(Private collection)*

observe, to be alert and wide awake, to spot signs with his nose and his eyes.
. . . They did not try to penetrate [nature's] secrets by violence; they never
fought it or were hostile to it, they remained one of its elements and cultivated
a devotion to it that was full of respect."

When the Eskimos meet in the evening and are all together, the collective
consciousness of the group, like a giant computer, reinterprets these signs.
One proof that they think better and more searchingly as a group is the fact
that these men, who as individuals are definitely but not exceptionally intelligent, and who are technically ill-equipped, have been able, on various occasions, to predict far-ranging changes in climate several years in advance. It is
significant that like "human animals" with an organic intelligence, they have
adapted their demography, their way of living, to natural conditions—icing
over, fog, cold—of which they have a presentiment.

Therefore, when away from his tribe the Eskimo rarely manages to express
his deeper thoughts. It is not surprising that he has a pronounced tendency
to be subservient. "It is hard for the average Eskimo to assert himself," Birket-
Smith observed. "As a consequence, he has a certain mental inertia." He
accepts without question the opinions of the person in whom the group has
invested authority. The effect of tribalism, it's true, but usually the Eskimo
recognizes these opinions as his own, and as more fully elaborated than he
would have been capable of doing.

I noticed this on many occasions, but never as distinctly as one time when
Inuterssuaq came to Siorapaluk to solicit that settlement's opinions in advance
of a district council meeting.

Inuterssuaq was the northern regional deputy to the Thule District Council of Hunters. He had a strong personality and was one of the six or eight
leaders of the tribe. Every year he held a meeting with his "constituents" to
find out what the wishes of one camp or another in the north region were; these
he would support effectively before the Danish administration, which was
based in Thule and consisted of three Danes—the district administrator, the
doctor, and the pastor—and three Eskimo deputies, one each from the north,
center, and south of the district.

My Eskimo neighbors had been talking about this meeting for weeks
beforehand; everyone was quibbling and making demands in advance even of
Inuterssuaq's visit. Whoever spoke up loudest carried the day. Some let on that
they did not intend to agree with Inuterssuaq, whom they may have envied, and
these people gathered around Imina, who was himself a former deputy to the
Council of Hunters. But then Inuterssuaq arrived. In his new bearskin pants
and his beautiful qulitsaq, he did look truly noble. The meeting was held in
the church school. All the men sat quietly on benches. They had had to run
to get here on time, and they wiped their sweaty faces with the backs of their
hands. Although the women had voted,[53] they did not take part in this meeting,
and were waiting for the men at home, with much sneering laughter and
gossip. Silence fell over the meeting. Then Inuterssuaq began to talk . . . and
he talked. . . . An hour later, he was still talking. His listeners' eyes were all

Arrival of Inuterssuaq and his wife in Siorapaluk; the sledge hugs the ice foot, separated from the ice field by a small barrier of hummocks. The igloos of the bachelor Jaco, Inapaluk, and Iggianguaq are shown. In the background, the big slope cut by a torrent. Drawing by Appalinnguaq. Siorapaluk, June 1951. *(Private collection)*

that spoke for them. The anticipated discussion had been reduced virtually to a monologue by the deputy. Later I asked Imina, who had been one of the most aggressive the evening before, "Why didn't you interrupt him?"

"My tongue suddenly became very heavy," he answered. "My mind was filled with a real fog. And then, you see . . . what would have been the use? . . . He was saying everything I really believed. True Inuit ideas. . . ."

As soon as there is a problem during an expedition, the Eskimo wants everyone to consider the whole situation together. Everything must be repeated before the assembled hunters, as if each man feels he can think better and more accurately as part of a group. It is not that he cannot express himself alone: when an Eskimo is questioned about a situation he is thoroughly familiar with, he usually makes a brief, clear, and relevant statement containing only what is essential. But he will never express a truly personal thought. Only the group opinion will be fully satisfying to him, will in fact be really "his own."

Since the Eskimo is extremely observant and very skillful with his hands, he can be an incomparable mechanic. A boat's engine breaks down? He will take the engine apart in the midst of a blizzard, with the cold freezing his fingers, and having understood the function of each part, will unhurriedly repair it.

I can testify particularly to his skill, demonstrated in an incident that took place in the Canadian Arctic at Kapuivik in 1964. The bottom screw of the lever which advanced the film in my camera was broken (it was an Alpa, with a very complex mechanism). The same lever was used to change the speed: $\frac{1}{15}$, $\frac{1}{30}$, $\frac{1}{60}$, and $\frac{1}{100}$. I was using only $\frac{1}{60}$ here, which is the speed used most often for outdoor photographs. I was sitting in the tent of some walrus hunters from Kapuivik. I am clumsy with my hands, so I promptly handed the delicate instrument to a young hunter who had accompanied me on an earlier trip. He had often seen me take pictures with the camera but had never actually held it himself; however, like all Eskimos, although he had seemingly paid no special attention, he had "perceived" most of my movements and the mechanical operation of the camera. He had seen me change film and try out different speeds when the camera was empty. Honored that I should entrust the repair to him, since there were several others in the tent, he wordlessly bowed his head as he took it. (I should add also that he had never owned a camera himself.) Without stopping their conversation, the group watched what he did.

The Eskimo rummaged about in his tool box and found a file and an old screw; he cut a fresh thread on the screw, laid it on the caribou skin, studied the camera for a bit, and then carefully fitted his screw into the camera, after casually checking other screws for tightness. Then he compared the different speeds by listening to them. As he handed the camera back to me, he excused himself for his clumsiness. I continued to use the camera, set at the usual $\frac{1}{60}$, which he estimated was close to what he had most often heard me use. When I returned to Paris four month later, the hunter's observation and his repair work proved to have been accurate. He had replaced the delicate lever of the shutter back to within $\frac{1}{25}$ second of where it had been, and thus enabled me to go on taking good pictures (allowing for the tolerance of color emulsions) during the rest of the expedition.

The Danish government was patiently trying to teach the Greenlandic Eskimos to save money. Its policy of raising their standard of living depended on this. To this end a small bank was established even in Thule. The bank paid interest on deposits and made loans. But while the Eskimo might have had a savings-account bank book, he did not know how to save. (There were exceptions, of course, including Inuterssuaq, Anaakkaq, Kaali, Inuteq, Sorqaq, and others— at most, ten hunters out of seventy—but they had only small sums on deposit: between one hundred and five hundred kroner each, or sixteen to eighty dollars.) His firmly anticapitalist turn of mind, his wish to share everything, conflicted with it. As did his taste for celebration and ostentation: did misers give parties?

Take Ululik, for example. He was giving a birthday party in honor of his son, who had just turned five. Ululik's prospects were good. He was rich. November had been a good month for hunting; his fox skins had sold well. The Siorapaluk women were saying that he might acquire a boat, but other people thought he would buy lumber for a new house. I arrived at his home around four o'clock. I stopped on the threshold, dumbfounded: before me I saw the most wonderful igloo an Eskimo Peter Pan could have imagined in his wildest dreams. The walls were studded with multicolored candles; the ceiling was hung with colored streamers. In the middle of the room, pans of milk gave off a fragrant steam that mingled with the steam from a kettle of coffee; heaps of seal meat and narwhal skin—mattak—and buns were heaped in one corner; chocolate and tobacco everywhere.

Alone on the platform bed sat Aqqaluk, Ululik's son, as if on a throne.

He was wearing party clothes, and seemed both stunned and enchanted. As if he were a stallion at a fair, someone had put a red ribbon around his neck. Saliva drooled over his lips; his beautiful white anorak was already spotted with chocolate. What did it matter! The presents—a knife, cloth, ivory teeth, soap, a cup, a whip—were already piled on the floor at his feet.

When Ululik saw me walk in, he came over and took me by the arm, saying:

"You see, in Ululik's house coffee, milk, and everything else run like rivers!"

People had come from thirty miles around; my host was blissful; his round face was creased with satisfaction. He strutted up and down, shook people's hands, and bustling about, played the Important Person to his heart's content.

He was now ruined for a whole month, but never had he been more sincerely happy.

In the traditional Eskimo community, sharing was the very basis of society. There was never even the question of eating the smallest scrap of seal by oneself. Stealing was extremely rare. Until the integration of Greenland into Denmark as a province, there was no prison on the island.

The Eskimo's generous hospitality was traditional: the host would welcome me standing on his doorstep with his hand outstretched:

"Nuanninnguujuk!" he would say. "How much pleasure your visit gives us!" Once inside, I was immediately considered one of the group, and they set before me everything they had—and everything their neighbors could give them—in the way of bedding, blankets, meat.

But what most justified the proud name of Inuk—"the best of men"— which the Eskimos took for themselves was their extraordinary taste for adventure. They actually did seek it out. For example, in 1950 Ululik was supposed to leave at four in the morning to go fox hunting. But no one woke him until eight, whereupon the hut was turned upside down. The children shouted; they peed on the skins. Nothing was ready. However, this sort of improvisation just added to the attraction of the trip.

Ululik grunted, but with contentment. He came and went; he gave contradictory orders. The door kept banging. Where was the coffee? The sugar, the matches . . . and the knife? Sent by his mother, a young boy came looking for the anu, the harness, so that she could mend it.

On her bed, Ululik's pretty wife, Aqatannguaq, stretched lazily; she was half naked, and her breasts hung down like pears; she yawned and muttered something. "Seqajuk! Good-for-nothing!" Ululik said, laughing at her. No one knew what he was taking in the way of provisions. A new shirt was torn up to reinforce the ties on a bag. A neighbor woman was called in to mend a kamik. By now the whole camp was awake and come to witness the departure. People chattered and the dogs, who had been ready since six o'clock, barked. The kitchen stove smoked. The children started to shout again.

"Allarpunga! I'm leaving," Ululik said at last.

The women worked faster but with a certain smile, for they knew that they were actually the ones controlling the event. The bags were divided up. Coffee, noodles, sugar, and pepper got all mixed up. No matter; on the trail the hunter would spend his evenings in his igloo sorting them out.

"Aallarpunga massakkut! I'm leaving this minute!" Ululik said again, and moved toward the door.

At that moment, his bearskin pants ripped at the seam. Furious and streaming with sweat, he took off his pants in front of everyone. With bare backside and whip in hand, he waited for his pants to be stitched (which Aqatannguaq took her time doing). Meanwhile he joked and laughed with his friends. What a fine departure! he boasted. Ululik, in this situation, waxed all the more theatrical for being manipulated by his wife. And he was even prouder of this shambles of a departure since, to his way of thinking, virility went hand in hand with a certain disdain for order.

When adventure does not come to him, the Eskimo goes in search of it. In 1906, a group of eight families whom Peary had taken aboard his ship left it one day because they found the monotony of life on board oppressive and its comforts upsetting. The excuse they gave for leaving was a misunderstanding with Peary which arose over a slight reduction in their daily rations. After wintering over in the desolate region of Lake Hazen, on Ellesmere Island, the families spent eight months traveling on foot over the hundreds of miles that the ship covered in twenty-two days. Their trip was in many ways dramatic. The families suffered cruelly and often came close to death. When they reached Etah, they had only a few half-starved dogs; several pregnant women were dragging themselves along with great difficulty; mothers were holding their children by the hand—but all of them were ready to start out again. How can life be worth living if it offers no surprises, no adventures?

That the Eskimo is an explorer is beyond question. The next-to-last migration of Canadian Eskimos to Greenland, in 1860–63, is an amazing example of this character.[54]

During a magic séance one evening, Qillarsuaq, the famous sorcerer from Baffin Island who probably lived in the region of Illulik or Pond Inlet, was seized by the prescient certainty that farther north, much farther north, there lived other men who were as yet unknown to his people.

Rumors spread by the Pond Inlet whalers confirmed him in his plan. "There are Inuit like us up north. It is certain," he said to anyone willing to listen. "We must go see them. Right away!"

His enthusiasm infected the camp. People became excited and plucked up their courage; their imagination took fire—they should leave forthwith.

When the sun returned, the sledges were organized and they set off for unknown lands. Thirty-eight people went. Women and children—some of them still at the breast—perched on top of the luggage. They had no map, no compass, no guns. As they drew near to the Pole, they had to cross vast deserts where no man had ever set foot, had to travel over mountains, glaciers, and seas without losing their courage. Two winters went by this way. Then, worn and anxious, some people began to doubt the truth of what the sorcerer had said.

"This Qillarsuaq doesn't really know much. You'll see. Ajoq! We'll all die here. Ajoq! Ajoq!"

There were discussions and more discussions. Sharp words were exchanged. Five sledges decided not to go on, and headed back south. With fierce determination, the sorcerer and the fourteen people who had faith in him persevered; the sufferings they endured were inhuman, indescribable, and if Qillarsuaq's white hair had not been haloed by a nimbus of fire every night, the group would certainly have lacked the courage to go any farther with him.

At last, at long last, during the sixth or seventh spring, battered and famished, they reached Ellesmere Island. They rounded Cape Sabine; a blue-green coast appeared on the horizon. It was Greenland—Inglefield Land. With astonishing authority, the sorcerer announced that there they would find men. And indeed, after they had crossed the sound, they found empty igloos and animal bones near Anoritoq; then all of a sudden, at Taserartalik, near Etah, two sledges hove into sight. "Inugpagsuit! Lots of men!" It was an extraordinary meeting! After being separated for hundreds of years because of a widespread cold spell that began during the seventeenth and eighteenth centuries, two peoples who belonged to the same race had found each other again. They shouted words of peace to one another. As proof of their good intentions, they threw their harpoons down on the snow. After making themselves known, the sorcerer and his companions accompanied the two men to their camp. One of them, Aqattaq, had a wooden leg, which the whalers had gotten for him; such a thing had never been seen in Baffin Land. Farther south, near Siorapaluk—at Pitorarfik, apparently—they spent five or six years together, exchanging practical knowledge and mingling legends.* It was from this Canadian group that the Polar Eskimos learned—or relearned—how to use the kayak, the bow and arrow, how to hunt reindeer, and how to fish for salmon—none of which they had known when John Ross visited them in 1818; these practices had been known earlier but had been forgotten after 1600. The immigrants taught the Polar Eskimos a better way to build their snow igloos. "We showed them many things," one of the six descendants told Moltke, "especially how to make igloos with a long corridor and the entrance below. Igloos built this way have no drafts. They knew how to make igloos before we came, but they didn't know

---

*According to my genealogical study in 1950–51, 14.5 percent of the Polar Eskimos were descendants of these Canadian Eskimos; Polar Eskimos presumed to be pure-blooded (from within the Thule group) represented only 19.2 percent of the current population. The others were of mixed Eskimo blood.

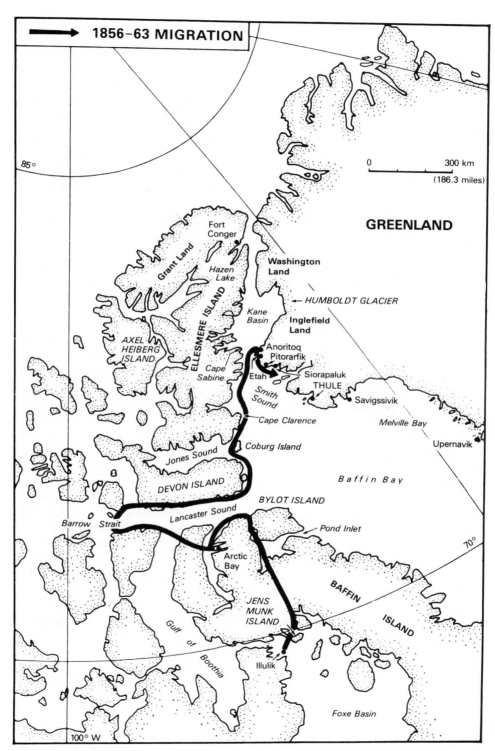

Map 4. Itinerary of Canadian Eskimos from Baffin Island toward Greenland

you have to dig out the katak, or tunnel, below to make it easier for pure cold air to replace the warm foul air. We taught them how to hunt with a bow and arrow. Before we came, they didn't hunt reindeer, though there were many there. . . . We taught them to build kayaks and to hunt on the sea that way. Before we came, they hunted only on the ice and they had to kill enough seal, walrus, and narwhal during the winter and spring to last them through the summer when the ice was gone. In the summer, they camped on the islands, where there were birds. . . . They told us about a pernicious disease that had killed off the old people; the young people no longer knew how to build kayaks, and the existing kayaks had been buried with their owners."

This was what the one-eyed Meqorsuaq, a descendant of the Canadian Eskimos, said. Even though Canadian Eskimos would be leaving children behind at Thule, they were overcome by a desire to see their own people again, to be buried in Canada near their native igloos. So one spring, they left for home. Unfortunately, shortly afterward, the sorcerer died en route. Without a guide, the group wandered aimlessly for a while. Soon food became scarce. Quarrels broke out. It was the beginning of disaster—a dreadful famine. "Let us not separate again! We have been in great trouble!" As is the Eskimo way in such a situation, they regrouped. But their situation worsened; people who had recently died were eaten, then the stronger killed the weaker in order to survive. The details of these cannibalistic scenes are horrifying.

Eskimo in a kayak. Drawing by Kigutikak (fourteen years old). Thule, June 1951. (*Private collection*)

The few survivors retreated to Greenland. Old Tornit, Padloq's father, was one of them.

During the winter evenings, while the wind blew and whipped around the igloo, the old people told stories like this, while the young talked about their hunting adventures. The language was very specific as they relived their difficulties. Reality became a tale. The "truth of impression," as Jean Cocteau called it, emerged from the scene. The familiar demons of the night—the age-old fears and agonies of this people of the cold—in his waking state the Eskimo reassembles in legends.[55] Thus they had more control over them; at least this is what they hoped. Mythic time, which has its permanencies and is without relation to historical time, reentered everyone's unconscious through these impulses.

Look at that man! A moment ago, he seemed prostrate, yet soon he showed himself to be an ironic storyteller; then gradually, an inspired storyteller, a seer who made the heroes and victims of a terrible mythology appear vividly before our fascinated eyes.

Religion and Death

Basically, the Eskimo is a depressive; as he lies on the illeq in the morning, after awaking often in a tormented state of mind, morbid thoughts insidiously take shape and haunt him. He allows his mind to wander during these periods of somnolence, which can quite easily last as long as an hour. When the weather is bad his thoughts are particularly black, especially if a squall confines him to the igloo.

Days go by without the Eskimo's giving voice to his true feelings, but when he does let himself go, what he expresses are almost always dark thoughts that center on sickness, hunger, the dearth of game, the physical inability to hunt, abandonment by his family, the baleful actions of evil spirits. An out-of-the-ordinary event is enough for fear of the tupilak, the spirit of evil, to overwhelm him. Such states of mind can lead to a feeling of desperation, especially if one of his family has died. But he fights with the energy of despair against his tendency to surrender to depression, because he is even more violently afraid of the soul's loneliness and emptiness. So, he pulls himself together and plays the role of the "happy Eskimo" he would like to be, whereupon life quickly assumes a normal aspect once more.

He seizes eagerly upon specific technical concerns having to do, first, with hunting, with the pursuit of game: "Where are the walruses? How are the dogs doing? The meat caches must be restocked. . . ." For the moment, this project represses his dark thoughts. Food does the same: nothing cheers the Eskimo up, nothing takes him out of himself, as much as being and eating with other people. To mill around in a group, to be close to other people, is his best defense against his familiar demons. In a group people laugh, they make fun of one another, they unwind—and this is just what is needed. A long, difficult hunt followed by such gatherings is what an Eskimo considers the good life. Food always takes precedence over women who are associated with sex and sentiment, and who belong to his private life.

But if a member of the group dies, the Eskimo's secret terrors suddenly return. Somber, hardened, and withdrawn, he takes refuge in crying; probably his tears serve as some sort of exorcism. Without apparent effort, men and women weep copiously whenever they wish. How is one to explain this capacity for demonstrative emotionalism unless it is that the Eskimo is so superstitious and so afraid of the demons and phantoms that inhabit the sleep of so many of them? The Eskimo needs merely to recall the evil spirits that visit him some nights for him to lose his pride and look like a frightened child, his eyes dimming with tears.

Death. . . . "Toquvoq!" He's dead! Why do tears have this exorcizing power? Who is it one cries for when a close person dies? Is one crying for one's own death, which has been forcibly brought to mind?

Or do the tears have some propitiatory power? In a public act of humility, the Eskimo crouches down and makes himself small, the better to ward off suffering and death, those universal forces that are ever on the prowl nearby.

Siorapaluk was mourning a young hunter, Nipittoq, who had fallen from Inuterssuaq's boat. He had drowned off the tiny headland of Kangek, the cape I so often admired from my window, his lungs congested by the cold. The crew had been asleep, and Nipittoq, who was eighteen, was standing watch. He must have caught his feet in some rope and tumbled noiselessly into the sea.

The memorial service was held five days later. Summoned by the bell, the villagers gathered at the church. Several men were dressed in white anoraks; only the old people wore kamiks. It was the summer of 1972.

A slow, solemn hymn was sung; the words *Gutip Ataata* (God the Father), *dark* (night), *Gutip, toqusoq makitoq qilaliartoq* (God, the dead and resurrected Son), kept recurring.

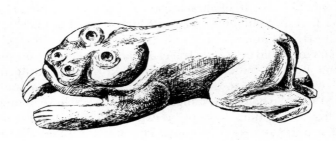

Bone tupilak sculpted by Pualuna. Siorapaluk, December 1950. (*Private collection*)

Fifteen minutes later, Inuterssuaq took up a large wooden cross, which would be set at the head of the symbolic grave. He rested it on his back and led the way to the cemetery, which stood on a rise a hundred yards away. The bell tolled, with long silences between peals. The village dogs began to howl mournfully, their muzzles pointed skyward. Several were loose and mingled with the crowd, which walked silently, both men and women in tears. Slowly they climbed the slope which faced the mountain, over which the great glacier towered. When they reached the cemetery, everyone communed with himself; then, under a rain mixed with snow, Inuterssuaq bowed his head and began to speak in a low voice.

Qaarnaaq, a hard-bitten hunter who normally showed compassion to no one, was among those present. He stood firmly planted on both feet, with his hands clasped; big tears rolled down his cheeks. Asarpanguaq's heavy features were closed and somber, as always on his bad days, but he, too, was sniffling discreetly. Qulutanguaq, Imina, the old people, looking like grieving elders, had clustered around the symbolic grave—a rectangle of stones pointing east, like most of the other graves. All wore suitably sad expressions, yet there was not one among them who had not been capable of speaking harshly of the unfortunate boy when he was alive: "Nipittoq is a good-for-nothing; he is forever a burden on this one or that one!" Now "this one" and "that one," hard, calculating, and implacable, together with their wives, were weeping in public.

They stood there a long while, motionless. Were they crying for themselves? They were bowed under the weight of the mystery and infinity of death. Presently, they left; their heads were bent as if in some sense they felt wounded, guilty, and resigned.

All evening long, their voices were grave and restrained; a few people cried a little; now and then, someone briefly mentioned the accident. In a few days, the affair was a thing of the past; no one spoke of it anymore. Nipittoq was no longer a tragic figure; once again people thought of him as the good-for-nothing, the parasite he had always been. Yet the memory of how he had met his death and fear of provoking the dead kept people from making sarcastic remarks about him as they had when he was alive.

The Eskimo inhabits a world of miracles: nothing astonishes him. His ancestral religion puts him in communication with his personal familiar spirits, who counsel, support, and guide him. To him, it seems normal that within a few seconds a shaman should be able to travel under the waters to consult Nerrivik, or to visit the moon or other faraway places. In times of misfortune, great angakkoqs have been able to do such things: all Inuit say so, and the Inuit cannot be wrong. "We believe our angakkoqs, and we believe in them because we want to live a long time and not be exposed to the dangers of famine," Uutaaq told Knud Rasmussen in 1907. This was the same Uutaaq I knew, Kutsikitsoq's father.

Uutaaq added, "We keep to our old customs in order to hold the world

209

in balance, for these powers must not be offended." Forty years of Christianization had not been able to uproot the Eskimo's reliance on secret, omnipresent forces. By 1950, the power of the angakkoqs was unquestionably less in evidence. However, let calamity strike, and the belief in magical forces immediately reemerged unchanged, coexisting with Christian beliefs inculcated by the white men.

In fact, the Eskimo lives in terror of making a mistake, of blundering in a way that might interfere with the natural order of things. He is convinced that death is only a transition; he thinks that the spirit of the dead person prowls around the living, and that it can suddenly assume a grotesque shape or that of a completely familiar animal. Thus, the seal he is hunting can very well be inhabited by someone long since dead. If he kills an animal, he must act with extreme caution: it could be a dead person or an evil spirit, one of the *toornat* that exhaust the hunter and then, after they are harpooned, cause him to slowly decline and die. It is up to the hunter not to make a mistake and annoy a *toornaq* wandering about disguised as a seal. The hunter must (or so it used to be) always consult his personal spirit before acting. "In 1930," Sakaeunnguaq told me, "Olipaluk and I left Etah by sledge, heading for the fjord near Nullit [Granville Fjord]. This was toward the end of spring—it was almost summer. One day we were sleeping on the shore. When we woke up, we saw that a catastrophe had happened: our kayak was gone. We had brought it with us on the sledge, and when we'd taken it off, we had moored it on the shore with stones—but evidently not securely enough. We had lost not only the kayak but everything else—our harpoons, our guns. We were prisoners: we could not go anywhere. We tried living on roots, but we were tormented by hunger and had to eat our ten dogs; we used some of their fat and flesh as bait in ten traps we found nearby. One day I went up the mountain alone. I was famished. I prayed to Guuti [God] and also secretly—very secretly—to my familiar spirit, the one my father, Nukapianguaq, had taught me to respect. 'Make hares come to me!' I said to him. Then I looked up, confident and yet a little uneasy. At that very moment, a white hare ran up in front of me, although for weeks we hadn't been able to find a single one. I killed it and we ate it. Days passed, weeks passed: we were more and more cruelly tormented by hunger. Not one seal, not one hare, not one bird. On top of this, the weather worsened and grew colder; the wind gusted and snow fell. Winter was nearly there, but the ice field—which would save us because we would be able to cross the sea—had not yet formed. There was no way for us to reach the settlement.

"Then I leaned against a cliff, and for the second time I prayed to Guuti and also secretly—very secretly—to my familiar spirit: 'Make ice form on the sea tomorrow, so that at last we can get to the meat caches the Inuit left on the neighboring islands.' I went to bed feeling more calm and full of hope. When I woke up, the miracle had happened: I saw Olipaluk already walking on the new ice. I ran and caught up with him, and we set out for the three islands. Saved! Soo Guuti! Thank you, God! And many thanks to you, my familiar spirit!"

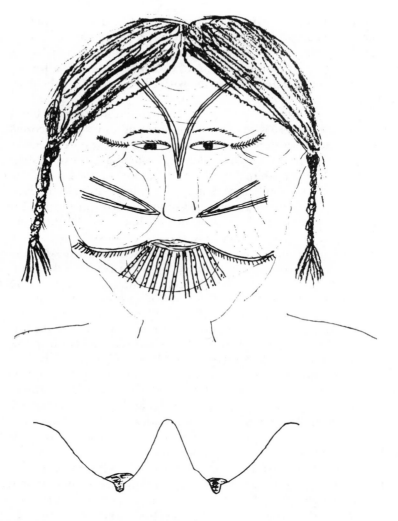

Eskimo tattooing from north of Foxe Basin (Illulik). This is Tasser's mother as seen by her daughter-in-law in May 1961. Women in particular were tattooed—on the face, chest, arms and hands, and the front of the thighs. In general, tattoos were related to a magic theme, the motifs varying from tribe to tribe. They were done by a female relative shortly before the girl's marriage. In Thule tattooing was done with a bone needle and a thread blackened in the soot of a stone oil lamp. It is called *kakiorneq*.

At the time of their discovery, the Eskimos of Thule were distinguished from the Eskimos of central Canada and eastern Greenland by a complete absence of tattooing. The Canadian Eskimos from the Illulik region who immigrated to Thule in 1867 shocked the whole population with their tattoos, which were probably similar to the one shown here. Some Thule men—Kutsikitsoq, for one—and a very few women still have three tiny blue dots in a triangle on the back of the left hand, above the thumb. (*Private collection*)

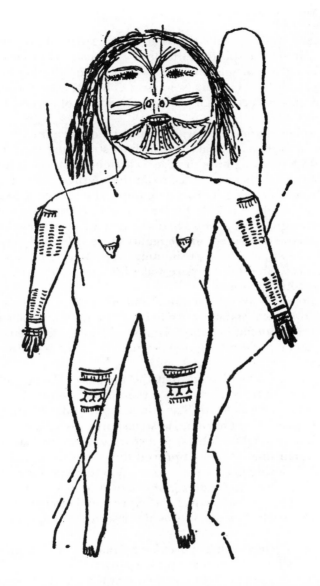

Complete tattooing of the body among the Netsilimmiut. This is a drawing of the
mother of the hunter Equalla, as seen by Equalla himself. Thom Bay, Boothia Peninsula, Canada, September 1966. *(Private collection)*

The Eskimo feels it is certainly a blessing to have been born: he appreciates
life and deeply enjoys the happy moments it brings.

He does not wish to die precisely because he profoundly loves life, but he
does not fear death. "Why worry about whether it's the end of all life or leads

to another life?" Uutaaq said to Rasmussen in 1916. To repeat, what the Eskimo does fear are the spirits of the dead or evil spirits—toornat or tupilat —which can bring misfortune and the most terrible suffering before death. Tupilat, who usually have big ears, some sort of horns, large protruding teeth, and enormous clawed feet, much prefer the medium of dreams to announce their imminent visits.

As did another Eskimo I knew, Sakaeunnguaq once described to me the nocturnal visit of a dwarf tupilak. It had short straddling legs; a small head made smaller by a receding brow; a nose so flattened that it was no more than two holes; square teeth that protruded so far they pushed its lips up to the level of the ears, those ears being inordinately tiny. All night long, Sakaeunnguaq told me, he had fought this little monster, which, in fact, often haunted his nightmares. His wife, Bertsie, described to me how Sakaeunnguaq tossed and turned like a person demented on the nights these visits took place; his arms and legs flailed about, and he kept shouting, or muttering broken, incomprehensible sentences. She did not dare wake him, no doubt because she was afraid of displeasing the tupilak.

These expressions of "superstition and witchcraft" actually reflect the religious rules by which Eskimos once lived. In Latin, *religare* means "to bind together, to join." By definition, the Eskimos' religion joined men to the forces of nature; for them, the meaning of existence was to be in harmony with all of these forces.

At first glance, it would seem that the people of Thule rather quickly allowed themselves to be converted to certain ideas of Christianity. The first missionary disembarked in North Star (Uummannaq) Bay in 1909. He was a Greenlander, Gustav Olsen, born in Holsteinsborg. His salary was only about five hundred kroner (eighty dollars) per year, and he lived by hunting. An excellent kayak huntsman, Olsen improved the construction and refined the lines of the kayak during his ministry, from 1909 to 1927. He was succeeded by his brother Jens Olsen in Qaanaaq, who served from 1927 to 1947. Within twenty years of Gustav Olsen's arrival, the entire population of Thule had been baptized; my friend Nukapianguaq was the last adult to accept baptism, in 1934.

What was this religion that the Polar Eskimos at least seemingly abandoned so quickly in favor of another? We know something, though little, about the rituals of this complex religion, certain features of which were the same from the Bering Strait to the east coast of Greenland.

The Eskimo must endure forces unleashed against him by the weather and the ice. His environment, his surroundings, have had a decisive influence on his psychology. He has resented and feared his helplessness and has tried to protect himself by getting to know and learning to cope with the mysterious shadows that surround him and people his dreams. He has lived in a "prelogical, mystical" state of mind. The manifestations of his religious impulses were as numerous as the manifestations of his faculties of sight, hearing, and intelligence, and they were no less exceptionally precise and imperative.

According to the Eskimos, life, the transmittable vital force, found different forms of expression—human, animal, and geographical—and custom required that they be respected in all their transformations. For example, after an animal was eaten, the bones of its paws or its hooves would be gathered up, placed where the dogs could not eat them, and reassembled according to their original pattern (this applied especially to seal claws and reindeer hooves). Similarly, the heads of foxes, seals, hares, and birds were placed sometimes in crevasses in the sea, sometimes on the snow beneath stones.

In the Eskimo's life, everything exists in the supernatural, in *sila,* the vital force. One evidence of this: in the winter of 1941, an Eskimo saw a haggard hunter come up the Kangerluarsuk fjord shouting: "I have just met a qivittoq!" A qivittoq is one of the evil spirits that live on glaciers and come to visit Inuit who do not respect the principles of life. The hunter described the evil spirit in detail. "This hunter never lied," the Eskimo said. "Yes, he really saw that qivittoq. And, in fact, he died that same winter." If you have seen a spirit, the most important rule is not to mention it by name; if you do, you restore life to it and the spirit will steal away your soul, absorbing it little by little.

There is no cause for surprise, then, that innumerable taboos, or allernersuit, arising from the Eskimos' demography, economy, and also from his ecological concept of the world in which man and the earth are closely allied, governed the events of daily life. The following description of the old taboos is based essentially on Rasmussen's *The People of the Polar North.*

When a man died, Rasmussen wrote, all the members of a family used to plug up their left nostrils; then, within the prescribed time, his close relatives —and no one else—removed the body from the igloo through a special artificial hole, which was quickly filled in so that the spirit of the dead man would not reenter the igloo. The body was dragged feet first, everyone present having at that moment both nostrils plugged with fur or straw; children had to keep their hoods up and wear their mittens. The corpse, its eyes closed, had been sewn up in a skin; now, lying on its back, it was buried beneath stones, with its head turned toward the sun—that is, its feet toward the east.[56] In ancient graves, like the one in Olrik Fjord which was described to me, the man would be sitting up in a stone igloo, his legs stretched straight before him. He would be wearing his qulitsaq and gloves. A miniature sledge and tip of a harpoon would be lying by his side. In some graves, the man would be seated with his chin on his knees.

For five days following the burial, the family group was not allowed to hunt, and the dead person's nearest of kin, hooded and mittened, were supposed not to go out, speak, lie down, or prepare any food whatever. Sledges were upturned on their stanchions so that all—especially the forces of nature —would know that no one was hunting out on the ice field. If a man absolutely had to go hunting in his kayak, he would wear his hood and mittens. For five days, one might not cross the tracks of those who had dragged the body away. Women were forbidden to sew. But if they absolutely had to sew, they had to first blacken their eyes with soot from the oil lamp. In times of famine, these regulations—more or less strict, depending on one's age and relationship to the deceased—could be so disastrous that when a certain person's death was anticipated, some families would leave the village so that they could continue to provide for themselves. In some instances the angakkoq, wishing to spare the village the observation of these various taboos, would take an old man who was expected to die far away from the settlement. After the five-day mourning period, a magic formula would be pronounced before stepping onto the sea ice. In summer, the kayaker would do the same. These examples show how the mourning period involved locale, too.[57]

For a full year and sometimes longer, people would visit the dead person, talk softly to him, and relate for his benefit the main happenings in the village. As they talked, they would walk around the grave three times in the direction of the sun's rotation. It was forbidden to speak the name of a dead person until he was reincarnated, so to speak, in the body of an infant born that same year who would bear his name. (Even nowadays, a deceased person is referred to obliquely; his actual name is pronounced only with extreme misgiving, in a low voice and with eyes downcast.) For one full year, a child who had lost his father was not allowed to cut snow or ice, build an igloo, or fetch water. A neighbor had to perform these chores for him, and even give him water to drink. He had to follow very precise rules that governed his hunting. He was not permitted to eat a female hare until he had killed a male hare. When he was hunting walrus, he had to wash his hands after harpooning the animal. Once the mourning period was over, one of the elders had to pronounce sacred angakkoq words before the orphan was allowed to touch snow, ice, or water again. When a death occurred, close relatives were prostrated not so much from grief at having lost someone dear to them as from terror that the dead man's spirit could take revenges on them that he had not carried out while still alive. The dead man became—and he continued to be—the great administrator of justice. During the awesome passage from life to death people's social conscience was reawakened: everyone remembered taboos or moral rules that had been slighted, murders that had been committed, dirty tricks that had been played on the family of the deceased. (This is still true.) Close relatives could become so heartsick that they lost their taste for living. The aim of ritual was—and in its Christian form still is—to drive away these malign forces, to help free people from fear that was almost always with them and that became particularly intense in times of bereavement.

A large body of prescriptions recalled woman's original state of impurity. For her the period of mourning was longer than for a man; she was allowed to urinate on icebergs (sons of the land) but not on the ice field (daughter of the sea), where she was not allowed even to walk; in certain cases, she was forbidden to drink water that came from the land (glacial icebergs or lake ice), and in this case she had to make do with snow.

While menstruating, the Eskimo woman had to wear her hood outside the house and walk at some distance from the igloos, especially if animals had been brought in from the hunt; she was forbidden to walk in the space between the igloo and the ice field. In the tent or igloo, she was not allowed to look through the little hole in the window if animals were reported outside or to pronounce certain words—for example, *nanorsuaq,* the great bear, and *aaversuaq,* the great walrus. She was supposed to refrain from eating certain foods; she might eat only from her own bowl, and a child had to hold her hand as she cut her food; she was not allowed to carry water and had to use her stone for melting snow apart from the others. In brief, she had to redeem her fall from grace by performing a group of penances. It could happen that one of these taboos might be lifted if the woman chanced to see a crow.

When pregnant, a woman was considered to be full of uncontrollable forces which threatened the continued good rapport the group strove to maintain with the forces of nature; of her own accord, therefore, she would stay away from the others. For one year after delivery, she was not allowed under any circumstances to eat young seals, eggs, or animals' entrails. A woman was not allowed to have sexual relations for three months following the birth of her child, and the same interdiction obtained during menstruation and periods of mourning.

A woman who had given birth prematurely to a stillborn child was placed under the most stringent taboos, or allernersuit. Besides the other taboos that narrowly circumscribed her life, such a woman was not supposed to turn the meat in the stone plate herself at the risk of aborting again and provoking untoward natural phenomena (ice at the wrong time, storms). Another woman had to hold her hand while she turned the meat. According to Ava, in Illulik, she could not cut fat except with her feet. She must not mention by name the animals she was eating, and while eating she was supposed to take off her boots. Her husband was not to describe the hunt in her presence without using disguised terms for the animals he had killed. If she saw a sledge on the sea ice or a kayak in the distance, under no circumstances might she alert the village; if she did, via her voice, she would be establishing an unpropitious communication that would be a threat to everyone. She was supposed to return to the igloo as fast as possible and remain there in silence. Similarly, when traveling she was supposed to sleep in a separate snow igloo and not remove her clothes. In extreme cases (the group having no game to hunt, say), a woman who had had a miscarriage and had not reported it immediately ran the risk of being killed. This happened to old, one-eyed Ivalu, around 1900: according to Rasmussen, she was shut up in a snow hut and left to die of hunger and cold.

The three sources of impurity in a woman, then, were menstruation, mourning, and miscarriage. These also entailed the strictest taboos. Taboos remained in force for a few days or longer, and in the case of a miscarriage, for a year, when the sun would have returned to the position it had been in when the miscarriage occurred. After a taboo was lifted, the woman could not sleep with her husband again until she had cleaned herself thoroughly while entirely naked, and had thrown away the clothes she wore during her period of penitence. A woman was also restricted by special taboos during the hunting of the white, or beluga, whale.

A marked discrimination between the sexes is evident; periodic chastity was enjoined on the woman, but never on the man, who was always free to be sexually promiscuous.

There were also taboos regarding food. A given order governed the eating of meat—a hierarchy based on the kind of animal, and on the age and sex of the individual. If by mischance a man ate a heart or boiled viscera, he was sure to find his virility rapidly diminished. A young man or young woman was not allowed to eat reindeer meat, hare, ptarmigan, eggs, lungs, young seal (before the first snowfall), or bear. A young husband was not permitted to eat partridge, and a woman who had not yet borne four children was not to eat birds' eggs. The oldest child in a family was not supposed to eat the liver of any animal. A small child was absolutely forbidden to eat seal fetus, eider eggs, bear or narwhal meat, entrails, heart, lungs, or liver. No Eskimo was allowed to hunt small animals unless he had already hunted all other animals. When in mourning for a very close relative—husband, child, or brother—one was forbidden for five years to eat hare, bear, guillemots, eggs, male duck, etc. Hayes observed that for one year a widow was not permitted to eat walrus meat; unlike her neighbors, she was reduced to eating birds. On the other hand, children whose father had died could eat everything. (Childhood was construed as lasting until about the age of fifteen.) Taboos varied from one family to another, from one situation to another, and could even be contradictory. A complete list would be very complicated to draw up.

If a member of the community failed to abide by one of these prescriptions —if, for example, a child broke a taboo before an elder had taken the forbidden meat in his own mouth and then slipped it into the child's—his only recourse would be to ask the angakkoq, or shaman, to intercede for him, particularly with Nerrivik, the goddess of the waters (and of food), so that she could wash away the sins which "stuck to him like excrement in his hair." Imina and Kutsikitsoq told me that as boys they had greatly feared their elders and the constant surveillance the group exercised over each person through the women and children. When someone failed to respect a taboo, he had to confess or else the whole community might suffer, and the penalty for the guilty party was severe. Imina admitted to me that, in spite of this, he had often eaten hare and eggs secretly, although they were forbidden him.

The angakkoqs-doctors used to examine a sick person and decide whether or not he was going to live. Their judgment was awaited with dread. Feeling psychologically abandoned—in effect, condemned—the sick person would allow himself to die. Angakkoqs-doctors practiced *qilavoq,* the operation that enabled them to interpret omens. When someone was sick, it was they who consulted the forces of the outer world. They seated the patient on the platform, attached a rope to one foot, and then tried to lift it. If that proved difficult, the foot seeming to be heavy, the patient was seriously ill; if his foot was easy to lift his recovery was imminent. The same procedure was carried out with his head. The angakkoq could try to exorcise the evil spirit that had taken possession of this or that part of the body.

When the Danish explorer Moltke fell seriously ill in Thule, in 1904–5, no doctor was attached to Rasmussen's expedition. Since Moltke was dying, the angakkoq was consulted. After a session with the shaman, these ten prescriptions were laid down: (1) the patient should eat seal and walrus meat in quantity, but from male animals only; (2) he should not cut the meat with a knife but tear it apart with his teeth; (3) any women visiting the patient should sit not on the main bench but only on the side benches; (4) the patient could eat reindeer meat only if he ate seal meat first and walrus meat after; (5) smoke was harmful, so the oil lamp should be watched; (6) the patient should never prepare his own food; (7) the patient should not have sexual relations; (8) the patient should show constant gratitude to the shaman; (9) he should give the shaman a large dog; (10) he should also give him a good rifle.

The Inuit believed in the existence of a soul (or, rather, a "breath"), and even in more than one. They believed, no doubt confusedly, that the life principle was eternal. Every man had a guardian spirit that could help him in difficult periods of his life. Subject as the Eskimo was to strict taboos, if he was in great, immediate danger he could have recourse to a charm (a sacred word learned from the shaman) that would allow him to act despite the allernersuit, or great taboo. Eskimos had some notion of purifications: they believed that the breath —one of several breaths they recognized—must suffer, must mortify itself before it deserved to attain a sort of paradise where abundance reigned and everything was easy. They were not far from having faith in a real hierarchy of rewards. The breaths of those whose bodies lay on the earth went to the "sky," a cold place abounding only in birds and insects. The breaths of those whose bodies were thrown into salt water lived on underground in a territory rich in hunting terrain and containing mountains of meat. (This distinction was not recognized everywhere, however.) On the Chukchi Peninsula in Siberia, the land of the aurora borealis, a sort of paradise was reserved for Chukchi who died a sudden or violent death.

Amulets, or *aarnquaq,* were worn, especially by men. Rasmussen mentioned in particular that the skin of the upper jaw of a recently killed bear endowed a man with courage; the skull of a fox imparted cunning. The animal whose good qualities a man wished to possess must not die by his hand. Girls often carried small eggs of the snow bunting so that later their labor would be easy. Rasmussen noted that both men and women usually wore a shard of an old oil lamp, which symbolized the warmth of the human hearth. He said that even dogs were protected by amulets, which made them fierce when attacking bears, high-keyed when pulling the sledge, and silent on the trail when their master so wished.

There were also *seratit,* or spoken charms, whose wording went far back into the past, to a time when men could still make themselves be understood to animals. "These charms were chanted softly," Rasmussen stated; "each word, repeated twice, contains a tangeq [an intrinsic power]. If the words are heedlessly spoken, they immediately lose their power." The angakkoq had to beware of certain forms of expression that might offend these tangeqs; if he did use them, he had, for example, to hold a knife in his hand for five days thereafter.

These charms, which were secretly passed on from one angakkoq to another, undoubtedly derived from an archaic proto-Eskimo language. They came from the depths of time, when hunters could speak to animals and the daughters of the Inuit were impregnated by dogs and gave birth to the peoples of the world. Some of these expressions were comprised of untranslatable words, like the salutation still currently used in addressing strangers: "Sainang sunai! Greetings to you!" Without question, paleolinguists could undertake fruitful research into these shamanist formulas and the vocabulary of the legendary Tunit.

The most important principle of the Inuit set of beliefs was never to oppose the flow of the vital force (sila) in its multiform aspects. For example, Rasmussen reported that Nuna—the Earth—was deeply sensitive. Nuna was composed of living matter and was grieved by death. Because the village was bound to the earth, for the sake of order it was fitting that the skins of dead animals not be laid directly on the ground except on islands or in areas separated from the village by a glacier; if this rule was not followed the spirits of the dead animals would afflict the earth.

Another rule was that of hospitality toward captured animals. The bear and the seal were not "really" killed when they were harpooned. To the hunters' way of thinking, the animals let themselves seem to be killed so that they could visit their human brothers and help them. Therefore, in the igloo everything possible must be done to show them respect and amuse them. Songs were sung to them softly and certain words like *knife* were carefully avoided. A seal needed fresh water; fresh water was brought to him in a bowl. The severed head of the bear had to be turned inland so that the animal would not have too much trouble returning home, Rasmussen related, and added that sometimes the bear was even provided with hunting gear because in case of need he was capable of assuming human shape.

In Alaska, on St. Lawrence Island, people went even further. Knowing that the bear liked to smoke, they would light a pipe for him and put it in his mouth. An old hunter from Savoonga told me that his father always did that. Various tools were made for the bear that no one else was permitted to use later: a bow drill and a curved knife for a male bear, and a scraper and a needle for a female. Only four days after the death of a male bear or five days after the death of a female did they deem that the animal had "rejoined its own kind" and that the taboos could be lifted.

All these rules establishing "what is suitable" were intended to avoid thwarting the will of sila and its diverse manifestations. Now, a great deal of attention had to be paid to the evil spirit, *perlussuaq*, who wished all living creatures ill and who stole breaths and took possession of them forever. "When perlussuaq has possession of you," Rasmussen wrote, "there are signs that indicate it clearly: first, you have a fever, then you are overcome by lassitude and finally by prostration. If the angakkoq does not manage to snatch the victim from the claws of the Evil Spirit, he will be lost. His share of sila will be sucked away and he will die."

"The Inuit perform rituals because the dead, who possess enormous vitality, are infinitely powerful," Uutaaq told Rasmussen in 1907.

One of the Eskimos' great fears, as I have said, was that a dead man who had been deceived or ill-treated during his life on earth might return to plague his tormentors. This fear was so strong that it could drive an Eskimo to kill a man twice over if he feared his vengeance after death. In this connection, Rasmussen recounted the story of an old woman who had killed the murderer of her son. To deprive him of his newly acquired supernatural power, she scalped him and turned his eyes, mouth, ears, and genitals inside out, the better to kill him once and for all. I heard the same story, almost word for word, on Diomede, in the Bering Strait.

After 1909, the principles of Christianity were superimposed on the old ancestral beliefs. According to Sakaeunnguaq, for example, a sort of local Mount Ararat came into being as a result of the Flood; he believed that the Flood created, among other things, the stranded beaches, and Ararat was supposedly located somewhere in Washington Land, north of Cass Fjord.

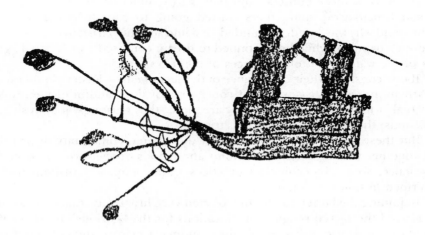

A *toornaq,* or evil spirit, has harnessed himself to a sled, in spite of the driver, in order to drag it off to a diabolical world. The driver is about to hit him, while his wife—who has an infant in her amaaq—holds back his arm. Drawing by the Eskimo Samik. (*From Steensby,* Contributions)

Undoubtedly the explorers helped to pave the way for the missionaries. Thus in Thule, which white men visited in the nineteenth century, often remaining for months at a time, shamanist beliefs gradually weakened. During the expeditions of Kane and Peary, certain questions must have been asked and answered in the intimacy of the camps. And if the Eskimo continued to practice his customary witchcraft when he returned to the igloo, it must have been because he respected or stood in awe of a tradition thousands of years old.

At the beginning of the twentieth century, the Thule Eskimo underwent a sort of psychological crisis and felt a confused desire for less empirical practices. Nonetheless, in 1909 he was still following his ancient rituals. The accounts of Peary, Cook, and the millionaire hunter Harry Whitney attest to this, especially with regard to funeral rites. It was at this moment (1909) that the preachers of the gospel arrived.

The Inuit finds doubt and worry painful, depressing, even intolerable.[58] In his world, the white man acquired great prestige, partly because of his material strength. Because the Eskimo was open to outside influences and seemingly filled with a lively desire to understand, he paid close attention also to the missionaries' message. He was quickly won over by the preaching of a qallunaat religion which, like the angakkoq's, depended on miracles and prodigious occurrences. Why would he hesitate?[59] The white men insisted that theirs was the true religion and criticized or ridiculed the Eskimos' ancestral beliefs. "Would the white man be wrong about this? It seems unlikely." The white man ordained beliefs from on high which seemed to be universal. A confused idea about a transcendent unity among religions began to take shape in the minds of these hunters. And that is why Imina (in 1920), Uutaaq and his son Kutsitkitsoq, and others started going to church in their Sunday clothes, and why the "modern-minded" Eskimo sought Christian names for his children's baptism, while he continued to dream confusedly of Nerrivik, goddess of the waters, and of the forces of darkness.

If one considers their observance of the sacraments—Easter Communion, confirmation, marriage—one must conclude that this handful of men follow the rituals with great good will. They are pious; they trustingly join in singing the hymns; they are good Sunday Christians.

But these good intentions have cost the Eskimo community dear: it has lost, together with its codex of customs and taboos derived from reason and experience, sound bioecological practices whose empirical wisdom will be reaffirmed in times to come.

In joining the larger community of men via Christianity, this small society abandoned the sacred religious justifications for the "curious" practices that served over centuries as its social and economic armature and imbued it with the will to fight and resist.

The angakkoq was shaman, priest, intercessor, interpreter of signs. *Anga* means "he who has precedence," "the elder who commands respect." The angakkoq was the arbiter and the guardian of traditions. In adopting completely foreign forms of civilization, the Eskimo gradually became incapable of understanding or reading his own alphabet.

Yet even if he no longer has a shaman, the Eskimo is too much his own man to forget entirely his forefathers' fears and faith. In his heart of hearts, he still believes in his traditions, even if he returns to them only in his final moments. In 1971, as the beautiful Sauninnguaq, "the sweetheart from Neqi," lay dying in a Thule clinic she sang *ajajas,* desperately calling on the cherished familiar spirits to help her. When the Eskimo is in good health, undoubtedly he seems to be a docile pupil; or at least he is a good actor, as he performs the rituals of the people on whom he is dependent. I am convinced that the Eskimos' Christianity is more superficial than one might think.

I would certainly not presume to criticize anyone's right to think of himself as a Christian. But evangelizing Judeo-Christian concepts inevitably violate the Eskimo conscience. Eskimo society is a fighting society; if it finds much that is compatible in the principles of charity and renunciation of the world, it also finds much that is alien. The Bible says, "Blessed are the poor in spirit: for theirs is the kingdom of heaven." Eskimo law says they must be done away with because they are parasites; it tolerates them only as scapegoats or clowns. The place of honor belongs to him who produces! "Blessed are the meek." For the Eskimo, the social struggle is unceasing, whether muted or extremely violent. Necessity makes the law! "Blessed are the merciful!" Eskimo law is a law of retaliation. *Do ut des:* I give to you so that you may give back to me. Rigorously construed, Christian doctrine can be meaningful only within the framework of a society which has outside "assistance." For the Eskimo, that would be Denmark's social welfare assistance.

For the Inuit the new religion has been primarily a liberation from the powers that a malefic world held over their minds. "We were so poor and we were afraid! We lived in fear of forgetting a taboo, of not doing right according to the rules. Christ has brought us peace. Because the white man came to help us." This is how the qallunaat's religion appeared to the Eskimos—rich, powerful, and materialistic. For them, the white man's society was efficient, technologically operative, seductive.

But after a while a new problem arose. When, in the light of Christianity, the Polar Eskimo compared himself to some of his cousins in southern Greenland who had long since been converted, the still primitive northerner became even more confused. Although living in the same kind of milieu, the southern Greenlander, who had been a Christian for a good two centuries, had also been detribalized and Europeanized, and in the process he had lost a fair number of the good qualities his Thule neighbor still possessed.

"Let others judge," they say. "We never used to steal and we still don't." (In their communal society, the possessions of each were protected by all.) "We don't lie." (Each item of news, each scrap of information a hunter imparted, had both practical and moral value.) "And now we no longer turn to witchcraft or taboos." (The old angakkoqs Uutaaq and Pualuna hardly dared admit, with a smile, what their lives had been like before.) "We have only one wife." (Demographically necessary here, since the choice of mates is very small.) "We get along together very well." (Mutual aid is essential; one man cannot survive by himself in this society.) "We have always obeyed the government regulations." (The Danish government was particularly attentive to the interests of natives until June 5, 1953, when Greenland was constitutionally integrated with Denmark; this policy, although conceived in a generous spirit to promote development, falsified and complicated relations between the government and the Eskimos.) "We attend church services and receive the sacraments." (The church has replaced the *qaggi*, or house of the hunters, where they used to meet under the authority of the angakkoq to sing, dance, and, on occasion, "invoke the spirits.") "We no longer abide by our ancient taboos." (Why should they? Their security is now guaranteed. Famine is only a memory; the white man's help makes it useless to interpret the signs.)

The first missionaries were Greenlanders who lived as true apostles among the Eskimos, adopting their rough way of life and hunting with them for their own food because their own resources were so modest. Certainly their example impressed the Eskimos and left correspondingly vivid memories. Inuk Christiansen, a Greenlander catechist whom Rasmussen brought to Thule from Disko in 1910, talked to me about them many times when he was living near me in Siorapaluk. However, the recollection of such long-ago men is fading and means little to the younger generation.

The pastors in Greenland since 1950—many of whom I have visited and enjoyed talking to—are all civil servants and therefore well and regularly paid. Some of them are quite engaging men. But their teaching and spirituality really should be matched by a materially more modest-seeming way of life. Well paid as they are, the pastors flaunt an affluent, comfortable life-style which in these poor communities is all the more shocking in that the gospel they preach urges even greater renunciation.[60]

Naalagaq Gutip; ataatak. My Lord, Father. Qilammiusutit. Those who dwell in the sky. . . . The bell has summoned everyone to church. The pastor, dressed all in black except for a white ruff around his neck, steps out of his warm house with all its middle-class trappings. The service in Thule begins with the Lord's Prayer. The men and women who have gathered together recite it aloud. After the prayer, the pastor preaches the word of Jesus Christ to the Eskimos, who have come from their cold igloos to hear him. What does Christ say? That it is easier for a camel to pass through the eye of a needle than for a rich man to enter the kingdom of heaven. . . . "Turn your back on wealth!" "God will not forgive the rich!"

"Whose leg is he pulling?" more than one Eskimo has asked me. "It's the white man who has everything—house, food, money, credit. And here is the church speaking out against misers! Whom is he talking to? To us, of course, since the qallunaat are never in church on Sunday. Come on! Come on! *Tupinara:* that's hard to swallow. Whom are they making fun of?"

Qaammaliaq:
The Month
of the Moon

Qaammaliaq: the month of the moon (January).
Seqinniak: the sun appears (February).
Ulluujuarsaat: day returns (March).
Aqqajursivia: the sun is warm (April).
Appaliarsuit tikitaafiat: the birds return (May).
Timmissat erniviat: they lay eggs (June).
Innanit aarsarniartalerfiat: the newborn birds fly south (August).
Tatsit sikutoat: the water in the lake freezes (September).
Tutsarfik: we listen (November).
Qaumasigssoq: the very luminous one (winter solstice).

As the Eskimo puckered his eyes and in his concise language, replete with infixes and nuances, recited his ancient calendar, I thought back on the main events that, for me, had marked the weeks since I arrived in Siorapaluk. In a few days it would be Christmas.

Christmas here was not only a Christian holiday but also a traditional holiday celebrating the midpoint in the long darkness of winter, the winter solstice, Christmas, midnight . . . . Large fires had been lighted down by the edge of the ice, while boys made up as qivittoqs or spirits—their faces were smudged with soot from the seal-oil lamps—wandered along the shore looking for victims. In the igloos, the people who had "escaped" the qivittoqs were feasting amid light and laughter.

"Aammalo! Aammalo! Again. . . . Again. . . ."

A drum sounded, the signal for everyone to fall to eating again. In the space of a few days, Siorapaluk, a village of nine igloos, had become over-populated. Fifty-five people were spending the holidays in Siorapaluk, which normally had thirty-four inhabitants. People had arrived from more than sixty miles around. Normally, the station had sixty dogs; now it had almost a hundred and fifty, and there were nine more sledges, some of which had carried women and children. Despite the influx, only one snow igloo had been built, to accommodate a family that had no close relatives here. The other fifteen visitors were divided among the eight local families according to family relationships. Invitation after invitation was extended from igloo to igloo; families crowded in together and sweat to their heart's content.

"Nuanni! How agreeable life is!"

The guests were offered kiviaq, the birds the Eskimos were hunting along the cliffs the day of my arrival.

On New Year's Eve, I heard singing outside my window. Following a recent custom, I immediately set candles in front of the double pane to show that I was listening. Young Eskimos were singing in −30°C (−22°F) weather; at moments, their song was snatched away by the wind. Then they fired some salvos toward the south to salute the new year. My door opened and in they came. The few hairs on their chins were frosted, their eyebrows were white, and they were bent way over from the cold. It was Arnarulunguaq, Jaco, Appalinnguaq, and Ululik. They crowded around the heater, massaged their fingers until the blood came back, and then left to visit the other igloos. The salvos sounded all evening long.

"Illit! This is for you!" one of my visitors said, putting a large matchbox in my hand. I opened it. Inside was an *ajagaq*—a cup-and-pin game made of walrus tusk. This was his present, and I put it with my other gifts: twenty-four aaveq (walrus) teeth; three fox tails; two sealskins, one of which was worn; three dog harnesses, and one frozen fish.

These were happy days.

In early January, an even greater surprise was in store for me. The Eskimos were disconcerted and somewhat downcast to see me live all alone in my hut, and they decided to find me a wife. How should they go about it? Whom should they choose?

The previous November, on my journey to Kangerluarsuk, I had spent part of a morning in a small igloo in Qeqertaq. I had arrived late the night before with Iggianguaq. The Eskimos were asleep, and after quickly eating some frozen narwhal, we both slipped in between the people bedded down near the illeq. In the light of the oil lamp, which burns low at night, how could one know who lay to the right, who to the left? In the full light of morning I half-opened my eyes, which were bleared with reindeer hairs: the hunters had already gone, and the igloo was peaceful. Outside, the children were playing at being grown-ups. I was alone . . . and yet I was not alone. I turned by head. Seated to my right, Aamma, a young Eskimo woman, was chewing on my kamiks, which had frozen during the night. She smiled and lowered her eyes. There was no mistaking the gesture. Before I even had time to answer the message in her laughing, flashing eyes, the katak resounded with shouts: "Puisi! Seals! Ten of them! Qepisorsuaq has killed ten seals." For hours thereafter, the igloo was filled with talk about the exploit and the sound of people chewing. That same evening I left Qeqertaq.

Without a word to me, the Inuit had decided to follow up on the look Aamma had given me. Unbeknownst to me, Inuterssuaq let Aamma know that it would be a good idea for her to join me. "Ieh! Yes!" she said. "Massakkut, right away. Qanortoq! I want to very much!"

She was pretty, out of the ordinary, skillful with her needle, but . . . she was thirty years old and responsible for two children fathered by two brothers, neither of whom, curiously enough, had married her. One of them, I knew, she had turned down.

In early December, I received a note from Inuterssuaq: "Aamma is waiting for a sign from you," he wrote. "Make up your mind!" At first, because I was lonely, this sudden invitation to become part of the tribe, with its network of complex relationships, was very attractive. "But send two reindeer skins!" the note went on. "It's a cold trip by sledge from Qeqertaq to Siorapaluk and she has nothing to put on her or the children either! One word from you, and she'll be with you by the first sledge that goes by." For one evening I hesitated. I consulted one or two Eskimos, but they were like stone. . . . Was there a hint of disapproval in their impassivity? Like a leitmotiv, a masked response: "Qvanga! When?"

Two days later, I gave a letter to a hunter on his way to Kangerluarsuk. My answer was no. Olipaluk seemed amazed that I had refused. "Why don't you want to have a woman share your hut? It's not good to be alone. You're young and strong. You need to have your clothes mended. Who will tend your oil lamp for you? Peary had Aleqasina. And then, Aamma would have talked to you, since you want to know everything about us. We thought it would be a good thing for you. . . . And you would have been helping the Inuit, too. Aamma is alone, she's poor. . . . Well, maybe you're right. You don't treat our girls the way other white men do; they take up with them and then leave them behind. And you want to be independent, too! Qanoq illit! As you like! We'll come see you more often, or you come visit us."

I have often wondered about my decision. I detest colonialist behavior; besides, I was going to be embarking on a difficult expedition in the spring, and I did not feel strong enough vis-à-vis the Eskimos to deal with the currents of jealousy that would inevitably have been set in motion had I joined one family group rather than another. I was more closely associated with the group that included Pualuna, Sakaeunnguaq, and Bertsie, even though, to all intents and purposes, I was independent. The women—so important in this so-called male society—kept a close eye on me, and in the context of my work I had to be in control of a whole ensemble of relationships and reputations that were as changeable as the weather. Also, how would I ever really know the women's true feelings, even although the proposal had come from them, too, and how would those feelings change? Very likely, they themselves hardly knew. Yet, because I was so much a part of the life of this group, there were days when I regretted my decision, days when solitude weighed more heavily on me . . . without Aamma, whose name—in Eskimo, "again," in Latin, "to love"— bore a double significance!

7

ON
THE WAY
TO THE
SUN

*The February
Trip to Savigssivik*

Early in the new year, I decided to take to the road again and to visit the tribe's southernmost camp, Savigssivik. Savigssivik, which means "place where iron is bought and sold," took its name from three meteorites which providentially fell on the glacier there. Since the Polar Eskimos have no wood (even driftwood) or natural sources of metal, they traditionally had to rely either on flint from several small quarries in the north and south of the district or on the metal they chipped off these meteorites. By striking the meteorites with stones, very small flakes they broke off, no larger than a fingernail.

The distance from my base in Siorapaluk to Savigssivik was some 250 miles one way, and I planned to stop at all the camps that lay en route and study them. I was accompanied by the son of the great Uutaaq, Kutsikitsoq, whose manner and sense of humor I had instantly liked when I met him on the glacier in November. For some obscure reason, it was decided that his wife, Natuk, would not go with us.

"It's better this way. . . . Once we get there you'll understand, I'll explain everything. Here they're ugly as sin, but there . . ."

In short order, we gathered together the equipment needed for a two-week trip, harnessed a team of sixteen dogs, and set off. In the twilight night of early February, we traveled over the ice field quite easily. We crossed fjords and sounds. . . . Our route took us over the Politiken Glacier, nearly three thousand feet high. Here the crevasses made crackling sounds, the weather grew threatening, and snow fell from the edge of the cliffs. Every evening my friend's spirits became brighter. We took turns running before the dogs. After twelve to fifteen hours of travel, we would pitch the tent, stretch out side by side by the stove, and spend a long time telling stories. How many stories! . . . every detail along the track tells us something.

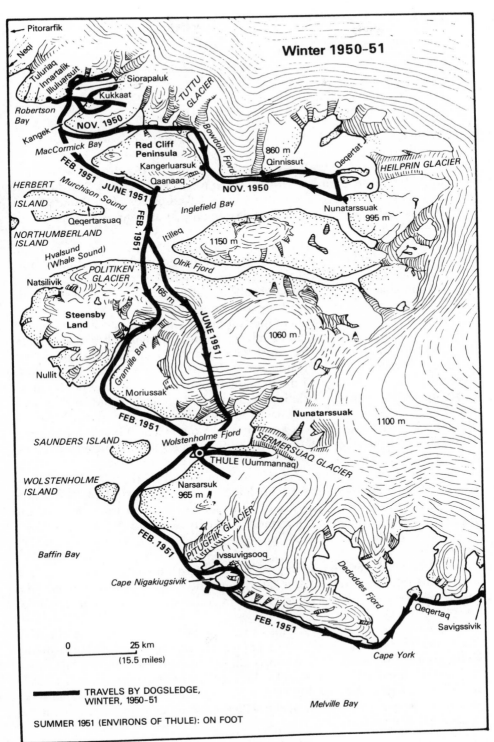

MAP 5. My Winter Trips

The Adventure
of Usukitat, the
"No-Good
Little Penis"

"... You see ... over there, about three hundred feet away."
Kutsikitsoq was pointing to an area striped with crevasses.
"You see that? ... Well, Usukitat was trying to cross the glacier on foot,
and he fell into an enormous hole. He stayed there for ten full days with
nothing to eat but lice; to quiet his thirst he licked pieces of ice, which he cut
off with his savik, his knife. It must have been just as cold as it is now. ..."
It was −40°C (−40°F).
"Usukitat, he stutters—nallinaaq! poor fellow!" Kutsikitsoq said, and he
sighed. "He speaks by imitating the sounds of things, and he helps himself with
lots of gestures. He's got a vocabulary all his own. He's very poor, and he wears
nothing but shabby pants of scruffy yellow sealskin and a worn dogskin quilit-
saq. It startles a person to see how thin he is."
Kutsikitsoq tried to translate the stutterer's language into Eskimo for me
as he went along. " 'Puppä ippick' means qallunaaq savik, white man's knife.
Usukitat told me his story like this: 'I left Natsilivik on foot without telling
anyone. I wanted to go to Uummannaq. There was hardly any light; it was
the end of the winter night. I didn't want anyone to see me ... I hadn't taken
anything with me—just a little ippick. I had had enough of the Inuit of Natsilivik. In the crevasse of the glacier there was a translucent glow. Suddenly,
not far away from me, I saw a kind of enormous magical black dog digging
in the ice with his claws. I was terribly frightened, and I curled up into a
ball!' "
Poor Usukitat, always a burden to someone or other! As his name—
No-Good Little Penis—indicated, life had hardly been kind to him. "... 'It was
some Eskimos who were passing by in a sledge who heard me,' he told me
himself a few days later in Qeqertaq," Kutsikitsoq ended the story.
"That No-Good Little Penis is a true Eskimo, part of the bastard race of
the Kivioq!"
(Kivioq is a legendary figure, the Eskimo hero who as an orphan suffered
a sad and lonely childhood but later confronted the greatest dangers and
overcame them with remarkable ease, and sometimes came to the rescue of
people in danger.)
Between stories, between cups of tea, we drew closer to our destination.
Two *siniks,* or "sleeps," from where we had started, we saw little lights winking
to the south of us. It was Uummannaq, the almost entirely native village which
Rasmussen renamed Thule—or Toollay, as the Eskimos say when, as rarely
happens, they call it by this alien name. *Uummannaq* means seal's heart; a small
mountain stands out in front of the village, and its tabular mesa gives it the
shape of a seal's heart.

PEARY AND COOK

Copy of the note by Cook, the original of which he supposedly deposited in a tube at the North Pole.

Dr. F. A. Cook (1865–1940).
(*From* My Attainment of the Pole)

Cook's return from the glacial ocean to land and to life, 1908. *(Cook)*

Cook expedition 1907–1909. Polar Eskimo and his wife who helped Cook. *(Cook)*

(LEFT) "FREE LUNCH: Unaccustomed to the bountiful menus of the *Roosevelt*, the Eskimos rejoice at the free lunch offered them generously by Peary." *(From the French edition of Peary's* Nearest the Pole, *Paris: Laffitte, 1911)*

(BELOW LEFT) "THE ESKIMO VESSEL: The Eskimos quickly adopt civilized customs, as this photograph shows." Peary is at right. (*From the French edition of Peary's* Nearest the Pole)

On the left is Uutaaq (seventy-three), conqueror of the Pole, with Jean Malaurie and Inukitsupaluk (sixty), companion of Peary, Rasmussen, and Lauge Koch. Thule-Uummannaq, July 1950.

Kaalipaluk, of Uummannaq-Thule (born 1906). According to the Polar Eskimos, he is Peary's son. Qeqertarsuaq, 1967.

Ussaqaq, of Savigssivik (a mulatto, born February 8, 1937). According to the Polar Eskimos, he is the grandson of Marripaluk—Matt Henson (born 1906). Savigssivik, 1969.

Hunters ran ahead of us, carrying storm lanterns. Doors banged. . . . The word was already spreading.

Avannaamiut . . . qallunaato! Men of the North . . . a qallunaaq too!

All that evening and the next day I went from one man to the next, shaking hands and telling the story of our summer for the nth time. We did not leave this haven for several days, as much to give our dogs a rest as to give me a chance to begin my investigations into the resources and the demographic organization of these families.

The Meeting
with Uutaaq, Who
Went to the
North Pole with Peary

Reading line by line the travel notebooks of Peary, following him on his sledge along thousands of miles of ice field, one cannot but be impressed by the sort of quiet madness that inhabited the man. Particularly during his second expedition, from 1891 to 1902, when everything seemed to go wrong—problems with his wife, who was otherwise his loyal ally and inspiration until the end; failure of his first marches toward the Pole; the amputation of nine of his toes—in all this difficulty, Peary pushed himself farther into the North, on march after countermarch. His life was infused with a force, born of the ice, that would eventually push him to the achievement—whether real or not—of that singular ideal: the conquest of the Pole. Peary, haunted by Cook, driven by his own vision.

I was happy to be able to find old Uutaaq, Kutsikitsoq's father, in one of the igloos in Uummannaq. Except for Peary's black servant, Matt Henson, this elderly Eskimo was the only man still living who had been one of the conquerors—or false conquerors?—of the North Pole in April 1909. As his finger traced routes in the air, he described for me, in his cracked voice, "Piulissuaq's" various attempts to reach the *pool*. Recounted by that man in that hut, the story began to assume an almost fabulous quality.

Uutaaq was Peary's favorite guide and main Eskimo associate; he was the leader of dozens of Eskimo hunters and an important companion on the successful Polar expedition. When that expedition left Etah aboard the S.S. *Roosevelt* in August 1908, it included seven American explorers and eighteen Eskimo hunters (a good portion of all the hunters in the region), as well as many Eskimo wives and children. This large party wintered in the vicinity of Cape Sheridan. The slightly smaller group of five Americans and ten Eskimos set out for the Pole on February 28, 1909, with ten sledges and one hundred dogs. For the final dash to the Pole, Peary selected four of the Eskimos, including Uutaaq, and Matt Henson. He sent the last of the whites back to Ellesmere Island on April 1, and he and his small party set out for "the big nail." According to Peary, they reached the Pole on April 6, 1909, stayed approximately thirty hours, then turned back, arriving at Cape Columbia some sixteen days later.

When Uutaaq returned to Etah from the North Pole in August 1909, after working for one year, his payment was one rowboat, one rifle, one knife, one sledge, some anorak canvas, underwear, some "white" food, and tobacco. As a reward, Peary permitted him to hunt walrus from his cutter. In line with Peary's rules, he himself took the tusks, but he gave the walrus meat to the hunter as supplementary payment. "We left all of them well provisioned with everything necessary for life in the Arctic, better off than they had ever been before," Peary said. ". . . they became like millionaires of the far north." In fact, if Rasmussen had not established a store that same year these people would have had very hard times ahead.

"Tatsekuuk, Tatsekuuk!" Dr. Frederick Albert Cook loomed large in Uutaaq's narrative. As a matter of fact everyone in Thule was still talking about Cook and Peary. Cook had once served as doctor on two of Peary's expeditions, in 1891–92, and in 1901. At that time Peary praised his exceptional qualities both as doctor and as explorer, though his attitude would change. The reason: Cook claimed that he had reached the Pole one year before Peary. Dr. Cook set out from Anoritoq, an Eskimo village north of Etah which was then inhabited, on February 19, 1908. He was bound for Cape Stallworthy, to the north of Ellesmere Island, with eleven sledges, a hundred and five dogs, and nine Eskimos, including Pualuna. The expedition was carrying four thousand pounds of provisions and other necessities for the trip across the Polar ocean, as well as two thousand pounds of walrus meat and fat, making three tons in all. He left Cape Stallworthy (formerly Cape Svartevoeg) for the North Pole on March 18, 1808, with two Eskimos who were only twenty years old. One of these two men, Aapilaq (or Ahwelah, as Cook called him), was the father of Ussaqaq and the brother of Inuteq, who had danced so well the night of the price increases. The other Eskimo, Itukusuk, was the brother of Ivalu, the old one-eyed woman who helped illustrate this book. The two Inuit went with two sledges, each carrying a load of more than six hundred and fifty pounds, and twenty-six dogs. Allegedly the expedition reached the Pole thirty-five days after it left Stallworthy, on April 21, 1908, and remained there until April 23. Their average speed crossing from Canada to the Pole was a good nine miles a day. After they left the Pole, it took this three-man expedition twelve months—filled with indescribable adventures—to make the return trip from the Pole to Anoritoq. By Cook's account, he got back on April 18 (or 15), 1909, exhausted and starving, with the two Eskimos, one small sledge, and no dogs. The reason for the uncertain date is that, in the fifteen months that Cook was away, he lost three days in his calculations. He kept a journal irregularly during his expedition.

Cook had returned to Anoritoq seven months after Peary had left the Thule area on his last effort to conquer the Pole. Peary had heard rumors of Cook's attempt before starting his own, and after he returned to Etah in August

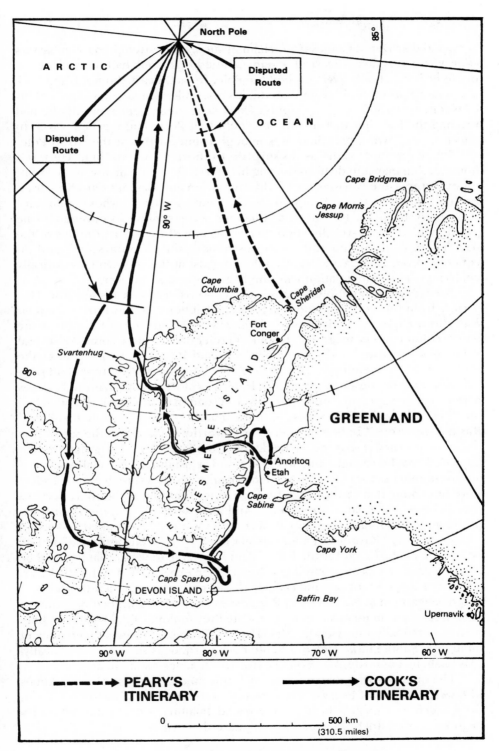

North Pole

85°

ARCTIC

Disputed
Route

Disputed
Route

OCEAN

Cape Bridgman

Cape Morris
Jessup

90° W

Cape
Columbia

Cape
Sheridan

Fort
Conger

Svartenhug

80°

E L L E S M E R E   I S L A N D

GREENLAND

Anoritoq
Etah

Cape
Sabine

Cape York

Cape Sparbo
DEVON ISLAND

Baffin Bay

Upernavik

90° W   80° W   70° W   60° W

- - - - ▶ PEARY'S
        ITINERARY

━━━━▶ COOK'S
        ITINERARY

0 ————————— 500 km
              (310.5 miles)

MAP 6. Itineraries of Cook and Peary

1909 and discovered Cook's prior claim of success, he attempted to embarrass —or worse, disgrace—his rival. He maintained that Cook had no evidence to prove he had actually ever reached the Pole. In fact, Peary did not bring back much more proof of his claim than did his erstwhile companion Cook; and his own statements left room for doubt. Cook kept calmly repeating that he had reached the Pole but that he did not doubt that Peary had reached it too. In effect he was saying that there was enough room for two at the North Pole.

Peary's attitude came as no surprise to those who knew him. He was a domineering man and disliked sharing his glory. Therefore, many of the greatest explorers—the Norwegians Roald Amundsen and Captain Otto Sverdrup, and the American Major Adolphus Greely, supported Cook, whose endurance and ability to adapt to different situations were generally conceded to be prodigious. In 1909–10, the controversy was one of the great scandals of the day. There could be no end to the discussion, since ice does drift and no concrete proof of such a journey could still exist at the site. Only by critically analyzing the documentation can one begin to find an answer.

Nowadays many people—though not all—consider Cook an impostor. This is clear from the excellent studies by Russell Gibbons, D. Rawlins *(Peary at the Pole: Fact or Fiction?)*, Hugh Eames *(Winner Take All)*, and the 1951 dispute in the letters column of *Life* magazine. Here I will refer only to the accounts of several Eskimos who trusted and spoke freely to Knud Rasmussen shortly after the return of both expeditions. In an article dated September 25, 1909, and published in *Politiken* on October 20, the Danish explorer wrote that the Eskimos whom he had personally interviewed were certain that Cook really had reached the Pole. "It was the Eskimos' opinion that Cook had been at the Pole," Rasmussen wrote. "I am informed by trustworthy members of the same tribe that their journey across the ice field away from land was so long that the sun appeared, reached a high point in the sky, and at last did not set at all and it was almost summer before they reached land again. . . . So it is sure that the travelers were not compelled to turn back because of ice hindrances, but only because they believed the goal was reached." And after seeing Cook, the Danish explorer added, "His attitude toward all criticism was one of dignified and proud superiority. . . ." Rasmussen made it clear that he had seen Cook also in Etah, before the explorer left for the Pole: "And I was able to verify that it would be hard to conceive of a more intelligently equipped expedition than his."[61] Later, after Cook lost his journals and came under an orchestrated attack by scientists and businessmen allied to Peary, Rasmussen somewhat modified his point of view, but he was in no position to invalidate the opinions of the Eskimos whom he had personally interviewed. Mrs. Dagmar Rasmussen (an acquaintance of mine) was quoted in *Le Matin* of September 5, 1909, as saying unequivocally, "My husband has no doubts about the truth of Dr. Cook's statements."

The opinions Rasmussen reported at this time were those of the Eskimos who were not part of Peary's "clan" or who were more closely associated with Cook, such as Uutaaq's brother, my friend Pualuna. Uutaaq himself and a majority of the other Eskimos did not share their views:

"Piuli was"—Uutaaq paused to think—"a great leader. Tatsekuuk was a very likable man, and he drove his dogs like an Eskimo. . . .

"Isumaarliorpunga . . . Tatsekuuk!" Utak continued. "I think Cook was a liar! Not one Eskimo believes he conquered the Pole. Ajornarpoq, it's impossible. . . . Piuli kissianni! Only Peary went there! Piuli-Suaq—the Great Peary!"

Of course, Uutaaq had worked with Peary, and trusted him. Since, however, Uutaaq had no knowledge of navigation, he could not vouch for the fact that Peary had really reached the Pole. (Nor, for that matter, could Cook's Eskimos.) Reading Peary's report on his expedition, and paying particular attention to his account of the last eight stages, from 87°47′ north to the Pole and back, we must conclude that it is not at all clear that Peary really reached *the* Pole. The time the eight stages took is too short. If one accepts his account, the average distance traveled daily for the last eight days, not including detours, was 43.49 miles. This is considerable, if not impossible, given the contrary drift of the ice and unavoidable deviations imposed by the terrain even when it is not notably rough. In 1968–69, during sixteen months on the ice, the British explorer Wally Herbert only once managed to cover 26.4 miles in a day and even then "this performance was the result of being steadily on the move for fifteen hours, over excellent ice-pack surfaces with strong dogs and light loads."[62] The Norwegian Dr. Fridtjof Nansen's best performance over a span of 450 miles was 28 miles a day, his average being 23 miles. Dr. Cook, by his own account, only twice covered more than 29 miles per day on the Polar ice bank, including detours. We now also know that because of frequent fogs and the constant and contrary drift of the ice, *exact* siting by plane is necessary and must even be carried out *at frequent intervals* as one approaches the Pole. Wally Herbert (on the British Transarctic Expedition, 1968–69) and Guido Monzino (on the Italian Expedition to the Pole, 1971), who were traveling by sledge, had the greatest difficulty in getting their bearings without the help of airplane or radio; Herbert's best guess was seven miles off, and Monzino's about six. Dead reckoning together with interpolating can mislead one: the ice drifts in the opposite direction, and rarely is there any sun. If navigators in the second half of the twentieth century still make mistakes in spite of all radio equipment at their disposal, how much more true this must have been for Peary or Cook in 1908 or 1909! Peary rarely used astronomic positionings after the 87° 47′ point, and his positioning by longitude was especially imprecise. He did not produce *scientific* proof of his presence at the actual Pole. (Neither did Cook.)

The matter was so unclear that the Naval Affairs Subcommittee charged with investigating the matter made the following observations in front of Peary: in the words of its chairman, Senator Thomas S. Butler, "We have your word for it [that you explored the Pole], and we have these observations to show that you were at the North Pole. This is the plain way of putting it, your word and your proofs. To me as a member of this committee, I accept your word; but your proofs I know nothing about at all." The committee did accept the so-called Peary Law, which recognized that Peary had reached the North Pole, but by a vote of only four to three. One senator who voted against the law stated: "The more I investigated and studied the story, the more thoroughly convinced I have become that it is fake, pure and simple." It should be pointed out that for obscure copyright reasons Peary refused to show his astronomical documents to the Naval Affairs Subcommittee. As the Berlin astronomer Professor Gustave Galle points out, "None of Peary's methods was dependable. Even if he had reached the Pole, he would not have known it."[63]

Personally, I believe that the respective behavior of Cook and Peary toward the Eskimos may throw some useful light on this dispute, which will likely never be settled.

Even though he is dead, in the minds of the Eskimos Peary is still almost as fearful as he used to be. An old Eskimo came to talk to me about Peary one evening in August 1967 in Siorapaluk. He was still so afraid of the American —this Eskimo used to call him "the great tormentor"—that even before he began to evoke his memories of Peary he went out to make sure there was no one around our cabin. Who knew? Perhaps the ghost of Peary was prowling about? I had never seen the man so agitated. "Piulissuaq? . . . People were afraid of him . . . really afraid . . . like I am this evening. . . . His big ship . . . it made a big impression on us. He was a great leader. You always had the feeling that if you didn't do what he wanted, he would condemn you to death. . . . I was very young, but I will never forget how he treated the Inuit. It was in Uummannaq [Thule], in July 1908, and this voyage was to be his last. His big ship arrives in the bay. He is hardly visible from the shore, but he shouts: 'Kissa Tikeri-Unga!—I'm arriving, for a fact!' The Inuit go aboard. Peary has a barrel of biscuits brought up on deck. The two or three hunters who have gone out to the ship in their kayaks bend over the barrel and begin to eat with both hands. Later, the barrel is taken ashore, and the contents thrown on the beach. Men, women, and children hurl themselves on the biscuits like dogs, which amuses Peary a lot. My heart still turns cold to think of it. That scene tells very well how he considered this people—my people—who were, for all of that, devoted to him." To Peary, the Eskimos were "primitive."

According to the Eskimos, Peary had two sons by Aleqasina, Inuterssuaq's mother-in-law: Samik and Kaali. I talked to Kaali, or Kaalipaluk, the only one still surviving in 1950. Under Danish civil law his official name is Peary; he looks just like his father. "I never heard a word from my illustrious father," he said, "nor did I ever receive any money. All I have of his is a photograph I cut out of a magazine. Yet I remember him very well. We lived on his big ship with our mother, and he was nice to us."

In 1897, Peary took back to New York one of the four meteorites that, from time immemorial, had belonged to the Thule Eskimos—a people who, lacking iron, had used them to make their knives and harpoons. Eventually, the other three meteorites were also shipped to the United States and to Denmark. Peary had chosen the largest, shipped it on the S.S. *Hope,* and sold it to the Museum of Natural History, in New York, through his wealthy patron Morris Jessup. Naturally, the people of Thule, living at a subsistence level, did not receive a cent. The same traffic standards characterized the sale of ethnographic collections to the Chicago and Berlin museums, but then, such transactions were common in the nineteenth century.

In the same year that he took the meteorite, in 1897, Peary also embarked six Eskimos for various "exhibitions" in the United States. Within a short time, four of them had died of galloping tuberculosis. Peary gave (or sold) their skeletons to the Museum of Natural History. Of the two survivors, Minik stayed on in the United States for a period and Uisaakavsek returned to the Thule area. There is a depressing sequel to the Uisaakavsek story.

"When Uisaakavsek slept in the same igloo with Peary, the Eskimo would not take off his clothes," Moltke, Rasmussen's companion, has told us. "He probably wore an amulet that made him invulnerable and immortal, just in case Peary should become violent." According to Peter Freuchen, another of Knud Rasmussen's companions, Uisaakavsek eventually abducted a woman and was in turn killed by two of the Eskimos who had conquered the North Pole with Peary: Sillu, the husband of the abducted woman, and my friend Uutaaq.

Cook's personality and ability to approach the Eskimos on their own level stands in marked contrast to Peary's. While I was in Thule, Imina showed me a whetstone that Cook had given him; his memories of Cook were just as friendly: "He had charm, and his two young companions, Etukishook [Itukusuk] and Ahwelah [Aapilaq] would have done anything for him. He knew how to lead us and handle us—by charm and by example, not by threats, coercion, and the power of his authority, like Piuli, our great tormentor."

Cook had a guarded yet generous nature, and was quite daring. He was a skillful physician, he spoke the Eskimo language fluently, and his ethnological observations were sharp. *Return to the Pole,* Cook's account of his exploration of Ellesmere Island and of his extraordinary, almost unbelievable experience at Cape Sparbo, where in order to survive he returned to a prehistoric way of life, seems quite true on final analysis. His technical preparation was always a model of boldness and precision.

By contrast, the many works of Peary show him to have been prepared to use any methods at his disposal to attain his goal. His lack of understanding of some aspects of the Eskimos is surprising. He called them "my Eskimos" and treated them like children. He was unable to speak their language well, after living among them for twenty years, and had rough manners. I am astonished not only that the scientific results of his seven expensive, showy expeditions are so mediocre but also that often he made errors in geography and cartography. By way of example: Peary Land is not, as he says, an island, but is indeed attached to Greenland; therefore, Peary could not have explored Independence Fjord thoroughly, yet he did not hesitate to extrapolate from the little he did see when he was there; and the land he discovered on his way to the Pole—Crocker Land—existed only in his imagination. What's more, he did not produce a single good ethnographic or archaeological study, even though he claimed he had "studied" the Eskimos for eighteen years, starting in 1891. He dared write, "To put it plainly, the Eskimos have no religion"! In the Marvin census of 1906, published in his *Nearest the Pole* (1907), Eskimo names were incredibly butchered; the count itself was arrived at by the most rudimentary statistical methods.

Peary was not rigorously scientific, and his system of ethics was all his own. His differences with the millionaire hunter Harry Whitney and with Otto Sverdrup are a matter of record, as are his efforts to forbid "his" Eskimos to work as guides for the Norwegian explorers or for Cook. It is also well known that he was anxious to monopolize the lucrative trade in walrus tusks and foxes in that region.

What happened after Peary reached 87° 47'—having heard by then of Cook's claim—will probably never be known. There he was, about a hundred miles from his goal. Before starting on the last stages, he sent Bartlett back south and proceeded onward with his Eskimos and his black manservant. Bartlett, the one man entirely capable of verifying his position, was left behind.

The debate is still open.[64]

A Blizzard
in the Night

Several sledges joined Kutsikitsoq and me on our journey from Uummannaq to Savigssivik. After we had passed Narsarsuk, we encountered some Inuit coming from Wolstenholme Island, where they had harpooned five walruses. Their sledges were heavily laden with meat. The Eskimos had been hunting out on the ice field near the open sea, on the newly formed, thin ice which walruses prefer. Their faces plainly showed the suffering they had endured. Their frost-whitened eyebrows stood out against the grayish skin of their foreheads; their cheeks and chins had been blackened by frost; the tips of their noses and the wings of their nostrils were peeling, and the flesh there was raw and red. Some of the men tried to protect themselves from the frost by carrying a fox's tail between their teeth. It was the coldest period of the year, −40° to −55°C (−40° to −67°F), and strong head winds created a wind-chill factor which lowered the temperature even further, from −60° to −70°C (−72° to −94°F).

At our first stopping place, we camped by the Isugigssok Fjord. Kutsikit-soq and I pitched our tent at the mouth of the fjord, but the rest of the group went farther up into it. We had settled on the sea ice in order to be less cold, but at a judicious distance from the cliff to avoid the risk of being crushed by large boulders the frost and wind might work loose from the plateau above.

"Innaq naammanngippoq! There's nothing good about a cliff!"

Each of us automatically did certain jobs. The dogs had to be attached to a spur of ice a length and a half away from the sledge, or else they would gnaw the skins right down to the wood; they were tired, and once they were fed they would quickly lie down in the snow and curl up with their noses under their tails. If fresh snow fell, the next morning they would be completely covered by it. In the space of fifteen minutes, many things had to be done quickly: unload the sledge; pitch the tent over it and secure it firmly; spread skins over the sledge, which would serve as our sleeping platform; set aside what we would need that night—a supply of snow for water, the Primus stove, food, lamp, knives. Feeding the dogs took another twenty minutes. By then, the Primus was already purring; we lighted a candle and relaxed at last, savoring the oil-scented warmth of the tent. Kutsikitsoq told me how, if he had wanted, he could be very rich. All he would have had to do was agree to what a certain Dr. "Uvé" from the Museum of Natural History in New York had once suggested to Imina (in 1906?): spend several years in America as a museum exhibit.

"I would have sat on a little chair, dressed in bearskin pants—my most beautiful qulitsaq. As Uvé used to tell Imina every time they stopped—this was when Imina was driving him back to Upernavik in the sledge, all wrapped up in a kind of tent to protect him from the cold—I would have held a large harpoon in my hand, and all day long well-dressed, perfumed qallunaat would have filed by in front of me. I'd have been well paid. Tollar amerlaqaat—bundles of dollars!"

Not just a mannequin but a real live display: what a godsend for a natural-history museum! It reminded me of the painter George Catlin's Indians, who were put on exhibit that way in England and in France, where they appeared in the Tuileries before Louis-Philippe during illustrated lectures.

"We could all be rich, you see," Kutsikitsoq concluded. "For the Inuit, sapinngilaq, nothing is too hard. But not one of us agreed. That's not fit work for Inuit. . . . Barely fit for kiffaqs. And yet, and yet, Piulissuaq certainly managed to drag us down there. How could you say no to such a great leader? Six Eskimos left with him on his big boat. Only two of them ever came back—Uisaakavsek and Minik."

We were chatting like this when a sudden gust of wind blew the door open. "Nigeq! The south wind!" Kutsikitsoq muttered.[65] We hurried out and, covered with snow, checked the four corners of the tent to make sure it would not tear. Then the wind died down. For some reason, perhaps because we were so tired, we were not very mindful of the movement of the ice floe; far out, the storm had stirred up the sea, and the swell was dislodging the ice. Kutsikitsoq, who had a good sense of humor, told me how a cousin of his had been set adrift this way. The man thought he heard the ice crack, but he was not quite sure. Several minutes later, he stepped out of his tent to discover that the current was carrying him out to sea. For more than a week, the Eskimo drifted over Baffin Sea Bay. Half dead with hunger, he ate his dogs one by one. His ice floe was being nibbled away day by day. Luckily, a westerly wind pushed it toward land and saved his life.

Kutsikitsoq had scarcely finished his story when we felt an unmistakable movement of the ice beneath our feet. The violent pressure of the wind pushed the tent door open again. The candle was blown out. In the dark, we leaped up and went outside. Kutsikitsoq dashed over to the dogs to make sure they had not been swallowed by a crevasse. I quickly assembled our equipment. Three minutes later, seated on the sledge, we were rushing toward land. Once again the wind died down. We laughed at our fear. But not for long! A gust of wind beat down, swept over the surface of the ice, and enveloped us in whirlwinds. The snow stung us, blinded us. Kutsikitsoq confronted an infuriated Nature with calm and deliberation. He moved precisely and efficiently.

"Over there!" he shouted in my ear, pointing in the lunar night toward a trembling curtain of snow. We pushed ahead as far as we could, but the wind was raging even more violently. We were forced to abandon the sledge and continue on foot. Each of us took his snow knife. I tied my notes up into a package and Kutsikitsoq took the Primus stove. Everything else we sacrificed.

We walked on single file, heads down, teeth clenched. Kutsikitsoq managed to get his bearings, how I'm not sure. We felt we were saved when we reached land, but we had still to find the shelter where our companions had no doubt taken refuge. And find it fast, for such exertion could not go on much longer. Holding on to one another, we walked in single file, for one yard, five yards, ten. . . . I stopped, lowered my head, and turned it to one side to shield my face from the wind; moving on again, I reached out to take hold of Kutsikitsoq. There was nothing. Emptiness. Kutsikitsoq had disappeared in the snow. I took a few steps forward, then to the right, then to the left. Nothing but that entrapping wall of cotton. Oh! How stupid of me. After passing what must be a large rock, he surely had turned to the right. I ran, fell, got up, fell again. I took a few stumbling, uncertain steps, only to find myself back where I had started from. Might he have gone back to the coast? I ran there. . . . No, no one there. . . . I was about to set off into the darkness again when I bumped into a heavy mass bearing down on me. Kutsikitsoq! We could not make ourselves heard above the howling tempest. Once more we set off. For a while we inched forward on our knees, along what seemed to be a slope. Then the land flattened out. I stumbled over a dog curled up in a ball and buried beneath the snow.

A dog . . . that meant men could not be far away.

A minute later, we plunged into a hut where six Eskimos lay huddled together, dozing and shivering; the air was damp and cold, and smelled of mildew and wool grease. A mournful eye surveyed me from beneath a frosty, shaggy eyebrow; then, rather like a pillowcase, eyelid closed over eye. I elbowed my way into a tangle of arms and feet. A small female voice cried out on my right. I struck a match.

"Kinaana? Who's that?"

I saw a face pinched with cold. We recognized each other and laughed. It was Paulina, a sixteen-year-old girl who, according to the Inuit, was the granddaughter of Peary and Aleqasina, the daughter of Kaalipaluk. Outside, the wind whistled. It was blowing so hard that the snow sifted between the boards of the hut and dusted over us. We were shut up in that hut for two days. We kept rubbing our feet together. We kept all our clothes on, including gloves and hoods. At the first lull in the wind, Kutsikitsoq and I hurried to see whether the storm had carried off our sledge. No. The ice had held and the dogs were still there.

Since the ice had been dislodged near Cape Nigakiugsivik, we decided to continue our journey by way of the mountain. But before going on, we had to hunt for food for the dogs in the water holes the storm had created.

It was not until February 13 that we climbed the ice cap. Day came slowly. Far, far to the south, a glow seemed to be rising as if from behind a stage set. A cold, wide horizon disengaged itself from the wintry monochrome that hung over the shadowed earth. The dominant blue and gray was suffused with yellow, carmine, and green, giving the clouds aquariumlike sea-green reflections. In the damp air, the opaline ice was tinted by underwater colors. These were hues and lines for an acute sensibility that gives thought to the nature of water and has an intuitive feeling for the momentary. A landscape of the outer limits of the real for a Nicholas de Staël.

As we were laboriously pushing our sledges up the slope, an enormous dead-looking purple sun lifted—at last, for the first time—above the ridge. The disk was perfectly round. An immense shout arose instantly from the group.

"Sainang sunai seqineq! Greetings, sun! Seqiniliaq! The sun is appearing!"

In keeping with the old tradition, we bared our heads despite the cold and tossed our gloves into the air, shouting again. The Swedish explorer Thorild Wulff made fun of these beliefs: in February 1917, he neglected this ritual and, as the Eskimos feared, he died within the year, in September, during the Second Thule Expedition.

Our shouts were lost in the wind and snow; we shivered. A fresh storm was threatening. What did it matter, since the night and its pale moons were retreating; the cloudy, frosty light would be succeeded by a new and triumphant season. But we had to be patient. The Arctic is pure paradox: this return of the sun was followed by the onslaught of even more bitter weather; a few days later, the temperature dropped to its lowest point in the whole year. When the wind was blowing, it registered between $-55°$ and $-60°C$ ($-67°$ and $-76°F$).

"You ought to carry two or three stalks of grass between your teeth, as the Inuit used to do," Kutsikitsoq advised me. "That way, the skin around your mouth won't freeze."

And it really did work.

The Legend of the Sun and the Moon

It will come as no surprise that, living as they always have lived in such solitude and in such an extraordinarily austere milieu, the Eskimos have sought an explanation for how their world came to be. They have developed a cosmogony whose basic tenets are still passed down from generation to generation: this is "the expression of external life in legend." Do men devise moral tales in order to protect themselves? Are they remembering primal things? . . . To guard themselves against the forces of nature, these people have attempted to draw close to those forces by endowing them with familiar appearances, by imagining that their origins are human. For the Inuit, these are not gratuitous fictions. They are more or less vivid realities—how can we know, exactly?—which alone are capable of giving their hard daily life a meaning. Their myths are perceived by them as explications of the world which have been proved by many centuries of experience. The only way the Eskimos can apprehend their identity is by placing themselves in a larger context that can be understood only in the perspective of genuine dramaturgy. The time is not so long past when men and animals were not completely differentiated, when they were able to speak to one another. (The Eskimos still know a few sounds that seals and bears respond to.)

The influence of Christianity notwithstanding, the power of their myths remains so great that Eskimos live in quite a natural relationship with the supernatural. A universe of giants, of all-powerful spirits, both good and evil, of animals which change into men and vice versa, is as familiar and almost as present to them as the daily seal or a cup of tea or a dog dropping turds.

Oqaluttuarpoq! Someone is telling a story! In this instance, the story is being told on Kutsikitsoq's sledge. Usually stories are told in the family igloo: people lie on the illeq, heads toward the center of the igloo, feet toward the wall; their breathing becomes peaceful and takes on the rhythm of nighttime; two people, their heads close together, tell each other their secret thoughts in low voices. Their soft murmuring does not disturb the solitary man who is slowly sinking into a half-dream. The soothing flame of the oil lamp is lowered. It is then that the mother begins to tell the story, slowly, in a low voice. Everyone listens in silence. The next morning, when the children wake up, they will ask questions about some details, and difficult sentences they will repeat several times. Someone will correct them. And that is all: they will remember the story forever. The people possess a body of some two hundred myths— history transposed into legends and stories the essentials of which are well known to adults, although only five or six storytellers, men or women, know by heart, word for word, the texts which have been transmitted orally for centuries. When transcribed, some of these legends fill four handwritten pages.

Kutsikitsoq was sitting in the front of the sledge, facing forward but leaning back against me, who sat facing the back of the sledge, huddled against the cold. He turned his head to one side to avoid the north wind, and between jolts of the sledge, he told me in snatches that old and ever popular legend about the sun and the moon.

"A long, long time ago, in order to amuse themselves by making love in the dark, the Inuit used to set their oil lamps out in front of their igloos. One

girl who joined in this game every evening began to suspect that her own
brother was making love to her.

"In order to make certain, she had the idea of blackening her fingers with
soot. After rubbing them over her lover's face in the dark, she ran outside.

"There she snatched up a torch[66] and turned around.

"The man pursuing her, his face all smudged, really was her brother.

"He had taken up a torch, too, so as not to lose her in the dark.

"For a long time, they ran on, faster and faster, faster and faster. . . .

"At a place called Saviusartorfissuaq, the girl cut off one of her breasts and
threw it to her brother, laughing and saying: 'Eat that, since you desire me so
much.'

"As the young man leaned down, he had the bad luck to drop his torch,
which almost went out.

"Yet he ran on, his torch barely glowing.

"And faster and faster, faster and faster, they chased one another.

"Presently they began to rise, running in higher and higher circles, higher
and higher . . . and since they had one double igloo in the sky, they never
stopped . . .

and the girl, warm and shining,

became the Sun

and her brother, dark and cold,

became the Moon.

"During the summer, the sun comes out of the house. It is warm day and
night, and the moon stays inside. During the winter, the opposite happens.
The sun stays in the house and the moon stays outside; the moon disappears
only when it goes to look for animals for men to hunt. That is why when men
see the new moon they cry, 'Thank you, thank you, you have brought us
game.' "

The sledge was carrying us forward, gliding toward the ice field. Our legs
dangled over the side. Kutsikitsoq was pleased with the effect his story had
produced, and proceeded to a new topic: "The reason I am going to Savigssivik
with you is not to get iron for our harpoons, as I did before. I'm not going to
finish breaking apart the rest of that seated woman whose head the Eskimos
of Pitorarfik took off long ago so that they would not have to depend on the
good will of the Inuit." He was referring to one of the Savigssivik meteorites,
which was shaped like a woman.

"So, why am I going to Savigssivik? I'll tell you. My wife, Natuk, is up
north. I love Luisa, and Luisa lives in the south: I was young at the time and
decided to wait until we could live together, but I wanted to be rich. . . . It was
the terianniaq, the fox, that made me miss out on everything. . . . I left
Savigssivik for the north. Somewhere along the coast near Etah, where there
are lots of foxes, a bear hunter told me Luisa had gone off with Gideon.

"So I married someone else . . . Natuk, Ulloriaq's daughter. Inuterssuaq,
as you know, is my brother-in-law. When I go south, the pastor in Thule must
think that I'm a dirty old man. . . . But what does he know?"

". . . Let's forget it, all right? We'll talk about it tonight when we get there. Anyway, so many unexpected things happen on trips. Maybe some surprise is waiting for us . . . who knows? We Inuit spend our lives in the midst of extraordinary things. Maybe you'll meet a white man, the son of an Eskimo. For many generations, we have kept a tradition that says a white child who was with the crew of a whaling ship survived when the others were massacred near the Big Island [Northumberland]. This child was brought up by the Inuit. One day he took off and disappeared, Who knows where he is? Also, when you visited the beautiful Sauninnguaq in November, you saw Nulioqqaarfik Island near Nunatarssuak and not far from Qeqertaq. Did you know that the Inuit say that's where an Inuit woman was mounted by a dog and that's how the first men came to be? Speaking of strange things, in the course of your travels did anyone in Siorapaluk tell you how odd the Eqqili are, who live inland? Their anuses and their mouths are the same. People have also seen them urinate through little holes in the insides of their hands. They don't stop walking when they copulate, so they kick the women in the belly. The women give birth through their stomachs, which must be opened. Never in the normal way. These men—and I hope you never meet them—are extraordinarily fast; people say they can overtake a running hare. Their footprints are like the footprints of both men and dogs.

"We also know of other men who are very big and strong and even more formidable: the Tunit. They lived on this earth before the Eskimos and had no dogs. The Tunit were terrifying. They had no bows and arrows and no kayaks. They hunted reindeer and lived in large houses. They had the powers of the angakkoq and could disappear into the depths of the earth: some people said their wives' vaginas were like the vaginas of bitches. Since they were very aggressive people, these Tunit were well known to the Inuit, and sometimes they lived on good terms with one another. . . ."

The existence of the Tunit (singular form: Tuneq) was attested to by others as well. According to Nukapianguaq and his son Sakaeunnguaq, who were very vehement about it, when the Etah glacier lay farther to the east—more than a century ago, I believe—the land between Lake Alida and the glacier was inhabited by very strong men who had neither kayaks nor dogs. Their houses—Nukapianguaq or his forebears allegedly saw the ruins of them at the edge of the glacier—were built by the Tunit.

"A long time ago, a very long time ago, the Tunit visited an Eskimo camp near Illulik.[67] The men were not there; they had gone off hunting. The Tunit raped all the women. When the hunters returned, they resolved to take revenge for this horrible insult. They left immediately, knowing that the Tunit would be in their camps sleeping, as all men sleep after a long trip. The Tunit were indeed in their igloos. Their bows were hanging outside their stone houses. The Eskimos crouched in the doorways and waited. Then they made a huge noise. The Tunit immediately jumped up and prepared to go out and get their arms. The Eskimos wounded them with their harpoons; they took pleasure in killing the powerful but unarmed men by piercing their skulls. The Tunit spoke only one word as they died: 'Nakâkâ!' What does that mean? I've no idea—naturally, no one knows how to speak Tunit. They must all have died out by now. Only two children, a brother and sister, escaped. They pretended to be dead. The brother took an Eskimo as his wife. One day someone asked him if he would harpoon a dog on the other side of the lake. They knew that, like all Tunit, he was strong enough to throw it a great distance accurately. The boy hesitated a long time. Then, since they insisted, he threw the harpoon all the way across to the far side of the big lake. And he hit the dog he was aiming at.

"This exploit was greeted by a general silence. Everybody watching was dumb with fear. The Tuneq thought that silence indicated disapproval. He was terrified. He ran off immediately and no one ever saw him again."

"In our country," Kutsikitsoq went on, "we knew the Tunit well. In Natsilivik, for example, the Inuit and the Tunit lived together for some time with no serious troubles. Then, I don't know why, the Inuit killed most of the Tunit and the survivors escaped by boat to Canada.

"My father, Uutaaq, told me how an Eskimo named Niroqaq married a Tuneq—a woman by the name of Navaranaaq. Navaranaaq had no big sealskin boots. She used to go out wearing only a pair of gloves. She had some brothers but no sister. One day, Niroqaq got angry at his wife. With a drill—without a bow—he made a hole in each of the bones above her knees. He guided the drill by holding a square piece of bone in his mouth.

"Navaranaaq said, 'I have many brothers!' 'Well,' Niroqaq retorted, 'let them come!' A short time later, ten Tunit appeared. Niroqaq's brother, who was in the igloo, said, 'The Tunit are coming!' Niroqaq got dressed, went out, and then hurried back inside. The Tunit began to pull down the house. One Tuneq was walking on the roof. He made a misstep and his leg went down into the *qingaq,* the igloo's ventilation hole. Niroqaq cut off the leg with his knife. 'Erdlaqaaunga!' the Tuneq cried, which might mean—though I don't know the language of the Tunit, so who can tell?—'My leg is gone!' Niroqaq ran off. The Tunit shot arrows after him. He quickly climbed up the big rock which everyone in Natsilivik is familiar with and where you can still see the steps. Navaranaaq's brothers surrounded the big rock and laid siege to it. They shot all their arrows. But Niroqaq did not shoot. He gathered up the Tunit's arrows. The Tunit had no arrows left. He killed nine Tunit. One Tuneq and Navaranaaq were left alive. Niroqaq said, 'Clear out!' The Tuneq left with his sister. . . .

"The reason we distrust the Tunit so much is not only because of their constant aggressiveness toward us but also because of their powers as angak- koqs. I was once told," Kutsikitsoq went on, "that one of our Inuit went seal hunting and saw another kayak out on the water. He looked at it carefully. He said to himself that the man in it had to be an Inuk, since he had a kayak. He approached and touched the kayak. The man in it sat up: it was a terrified Tuneq, who hastily said 'Siku! Siku! Ice bank!'" and the kayak turned to ice.

So the Tuneq, who certainly must have been a very important angakkoq, went back to his country on foot.

"We can never be sure of them. Two Inuit wanted to go find a Tuneq who had killed an ussuk, a bearded seal. Loaded down with his seal, the Tuneq went up into the mountain. That was where he lived. The Inuit followed him and at last saw his house. It was a double igloo. They approached it quietly and with the greatest caution. There was no one outside. In the katak there was a dog. They looked down the katak. Inside the igloo they saw a Tuneq woman. She was naked. Facing the katak, she was straddling an ussuk on which she was working. The two Inuit, who had moved through the passageway, looked between her legs as if spellbound, and then laughed. 'Who is laughing?' the Tuneq asked. He was lying on the platform. Not understanding who had laughed, the Tuneq, who was an angakkoq, used his power on the two Inuit as they were running off. Suddenly they lost their strength. The only way they could get away was by walking backwards. And when they got home, they had temporarily forgotten everything. They could not even speak."

While Kutsikitsoq talked, we came upon a Qeqertarmioq, an Eskimo from Qeqertaq, on the ice field. He was dressed in worn skins that were rubbed bare in front and torn at the knees and elbows. He looked miserably poor. His team consisted of only three dogs. He had no kayak, only a fifteen-year-old rifle. He had two bullets. He shared his igloo with someone else, which was unusual here. He was one of the poorest hunters in the hamlet. Although he was forty years old and married, he had no children.

He appeared to be extremely happy, but it had nothing to do with our arrival. He was jumping up and down, as much to warm his feet as to show his pleasure. His eyes, rimmed by frosty-white lashes, were smiling as he showed us the four large seals lying on his sledge which he was about to take back to his hut. For seven weeks, the three igloos in the hamlet had been suffering terribly from lack of food. He advised us not to visit his camp on our way back. He was sorry, but there was nothing to eat there. Nothing but kiviaq, and awfully rotten kiviaq at that.

The Black Eskimo

Several hours later, in Savigssivik, I met a black Eskimo.

His name was Anaakkaq, and he was the son of Peary's black servant, Matt Henson. Anaakkaq—"the man who empties his bowels quickly"—was tall and extremely well built. His skin was dark, his nose was flat, and his hair frizzy. He had his father's eyes—brilliant and lively. Laughing heartily, he came up to me to shake hands. The next day he questioned me eagerly about "Marripaluk," who the Inuit said was his father.

Savigssivik. Drawing by Mikissuk (seven years old). Savigssivik, January 1951. *(Private collection)*

"Have you seen him? . . . Is he happy? . . . If he isn't rich—and you tell me Piulissuaq gave him hardly any financial help at all; ajorpoq! What a misfortune!—then let him come here, and I'll take care of him in his old age. . . ."

Matt Henson, whom the Eskimos called Marripaluk, was born in 1866. He worked as Peary's servant and companion in the north of Greenland from 1896 to 1909 for a monthly wage of fifty dollars. At least twice he saved Peary's life. He never returned to Thule after Peary's last expedition in 1908–9. Back in the United States, apparently he was not as well off as he might have expected to be considering his faithful service to the man who later became Admiral Peary. Though at least officially he had conquered the North Pole with Peary, the only work he could find was as an employee in the customs bureau in New York. He died in 1954 at the age of eighty-eight.

Apparently he never sent any word to the son he left behind in Savigssivik.

I stayed in Savigssivik almost one week. To my amazement, every night Kutsikitsoq joined me in the igloo where I was staying. He begged me to go with him to see his friend Luisa.

"But after all, Kutsikitsoq, you don't need me!"

Alas, yes, in fact he did; Luisa's husband was away and under the circumstances, convention did not countenance his going to see the woman alone.

Her hut was small and buried under snow. Kutsikitsoq followed me like a child. I pushed open the door and entered a long passageway piled with meat. We coughed to announce ourselves. I went into the hut's only room, which was clean and warm. Luisa, a small, plump, pink woman, nodded to me. She was sitting alone far back in the room. I took my place in a corner. Then Kutsikitsoq went forward; he sat down at his friend's feet, took her hand with a sad smile, and stared at her without a word. The visit had not lasted more than fifteen minutes when my companion was ready to leave. His dearest wish of the year had been fulfilled.

PART THREE

ONE THOUSAND MILES OF EXPLORING IN INGLEFIELD LAND, IN WASHINGTON LAND, AND ON ELLESMERE ISLAND

8

THE PURPOSE OF THE EXPEDITION AND THE PREPARATION FOR IT

I had arranged with Kutsikitsoq that around mid-March I would leave my base in Siorapaluk on an expedition through uninhabited regions to the north and west. My plan was to travel first to Inglefield Land, on the eastern shore of Kane Basin, push farther north to Washington Land, then return southward to cross Smith Sound, to Ellesmere Island, the most northeasterly area of Canada.

I estimated that three sledges would travel the whole itinerary, carrying heavy equipment, provisions, and four people: Kutsikitsoq and his wife, Natuk; Maassannguapaluk, a young half-Eskimo from Thule, and myself. In addition to these three sledges, I would have to find a few more to help us transport supplies to be stored in Etah or wherever our main depot would be; once the transport had been made, these teams would be sent back to their respective camps. I had no sooner returned from Savigssivik than the rumor that I would presently be setting out spread among the Eskimos. Men began coming to see me; the money was attractive, and even more so the prospect of adventures and unforeseen encounters.

I had set March 20 as the date for my partners to join me in Siorapaluk. Early in the month, I began my preparations, checking the condition of my equipment and assembling the necessary provisions. This work was easy and went quickly; in fact, it meant simply opening crates and taking out what I had long before decided would be needed. So, on this score, I had nothing to worry about. Then it appeared that there was not enough oil for the Primus. A minor matter. In −30°C (−22°F) weather, I set off for Thule. It was a 125-mile trip with five sounds and a 3,000-foot glacier to be crossed. I made it in three days each way, scarcely pausing to catch my breath. The sledge was damaged because it was carrying so much weight, and the terrain was so rough. I was done in, my nose and cheekbones were blackened and frostbitten—all one needs on the eve of setting out in search of adventure. But I had brought a 500-pound supply of oil!

9

DELAYS

Siorapaluk, March 16: Our supplies had been packed and labeled; the expedition was ready. Every day, at noon, the sun rose a little higher above the horizon. The barometer had stabilized. The thermometer registered −30°C (−22°F). The time had come to leave. Then, without warning, one partner dropped out. On March 18, an Eskimo who had left Thule several days after me arrived at my hut. He was carrying an "express" letter, dated March 14, from the Danish administrator, Torben Krogh, who wrote that an epidemic of perlerorneq had broken out among the dogs in Thule several hours after I left. Maassannguapaluk had told him that his animals were too sick for him to leave. "It is not bad will on his part," Krogh assured me, adding that he had gone to see the dogs himself. They were indeed in such a state that they certainly would not have endured the hard work that lay ahead. Maassannguapaluk, reputedly the grandson of Peary through Samik, had the beautiful face of a métis. He was a popular man, and word of his decision not to go spread quickly. A few mornings later, an Eskimo I was counting on for the short trip to Etah told me that, after all, he would not be able to go either. His wife had a cold, and his bitch was whelping. In point of fact, the man would rather stay home and hunt bear than work with a qallunaaq. Came March 20, the day we were supposed to leave. Kutsikitsoq, who was away, had not shown up.

I was not unduly worried; in the Arctic, a delay of one day is not serious. March 21 and March 22 came and went; still no sign of him. Eskimos dropped by to ask mockingly for news. Sakaeunnguaq visited me twice, but he was moved by feelings of friendship. The attachment was mutual, actually, and later it proved to be strong and loyal in many difficult situations. (As I have said, the Eskimos always considered me associated with Sakaeunnguaq's family group on the side of his father, Nukapianguaq, and his father-in-law, Pualuna. When I stayed over in other villages, I was immediately adopted by his relatives. This had its advantages—an igloo to sleep in, meat for my dogs, information, and so forth.) Sakaeunnguaq wanted to go with me. We had talked about it in a friendly way, but I did not come to any decision. March 23, and still there was no sign of anyone. I decided to set out to meet Kutsikitsoq or, if necessary, to go as far as his camp. Shortly after leaving, I saw two sledges headed north on my route. I took out my binoculars, adjusted the lenses, and made out the dim, wavering image of Kutsikitsoq cheerfully running by his dogs. . . . In no time, he drew near. He was truly a sight to behold. He was wearing his best bearskin pants, his long-furred boots, and his large caribou jacket with the fringe trimmed Canadian style. The man was impressive: now the owner of eighteen dogs, he was not adverse to putting on side, but he carried himself easily, with the liveliness of a free, young animal. His ironic eyes lent light to a face as brown and dirty as an old tile shard. When he reached me, he leaped from his sledge, passed the whip to his wife, Natuk, and came toward me with outstretched hand.

"Qvanga angalavoq? Ullumi? When does the great departure take place? This very day? As you see, I'm ready."

Confronted by his magnificent equipment and regal appearance, I would almost have forgotten how late he was if shortly afterward he had not said to me, "We've been at Kangek for two days—over there, just opposite, on that deserted cape—with my old friend Qaaqqutsiaq and his wife." The couple was standing a little distance away from us. "You see?" He pointed. "Behind Kangek. We liked each other so much, the four of us, that we couldn't resist spending some time together. You know, we weren't far away . . . just over there, on that little bit of headland, that tiny little headland. You couldn't have seen us—we were hidden by a fold of land—but we could see Siorapaluk clearly! Oh, we did have some good times! We changed women every evening."

As he spoke, Padloq came over to him, and he stroked her neck. "Nice Padloq," he said, "as strong and lively as a salmon. Natuk, pooh! . . . And what about you? You weren't too worried, I hope?"

Giving me no time to answer, he continued, "Do you know Qaaqqutsiaq? He's been hunting near Natsilivik for the past three weeks, and he's on his way back to his igloo in Etah. Would you be willing for him to sleep with the rest of us in the hut? Padloq too, of course. If you like, he'll carry some equipment to Etah for you."

Qaaqqutsiaq nodded. I agreed. What else could I do but, like an Eskimo, swallow my feelings? Later, when I was calmer, I would know better how to react. Our agreement was confirmed by drinking a cup of tea, which the women had prepared while we were talking, and as we stamped our feet on the ground we celebrated our meeting with good humor. As I said, I postponed having it out with Kutsikitsoq about his strange little story. Like the Eskimos, I too could wear a mask.

Our noisy arrival in the village sparked a flattering hubbub. Women and children came running up from all sides. Delighted, my companions played their roles seriously. Their voices changed, became slow and deep. Kutsikit-soq's bearing was positively magisterial. They did not linger to greet everyone individually, as is the custom, but, with an air of self-importance, went directly to my hut. The five of us settled down in the largest room. The door kept opening and slamming shut. All winter the house had been very quiet, but now it soon resounded with shouts and laughter. Kutsikitsoq moved slowly from group to group, shaking hands and speaking with authority. He and his gang were a rousing success. Eskimos rushed in breathlessly for news: "When are you leaving?"

A small crowd was sitting there in disorder before me. I told them how glad I was to see them all together at last; I told them about the few recent problems—people dropping out, lack of oil—and the problems that lay ahead of us. Quickly I sketched the scientific purpose of the expedition: to draw up a precise map of the area lying beyond the inhabited environs of Etah—the geomorphologically unmapped plateaus of Inglefield and Washington lands. As I emphasized these points, I sensed their steady attention. For all primitive people, to reproduce, to depict, the earth has something sacred about it. I reminded them that I was going to Canada especially to measure the beaches and determine whether they are higher there, in the country of the *umimmak* (musk ox), than in Washington Land.[1] When relieved of the weight of melting glaciers ten thousand years ago, did the surface of Ellesmere Island which had thawed earlier rise 500 to 600 feet above what was then sea level, as had happened in Inglefield Land? (These are called isostatic movements.) I explained that comparative measurements of two shores of a large sea basin, like the Kane Basin, were of great interest. They would tell us how thick the glaciers originally were and how fast they had melted. Addressing particularly those present whose relatives had taken part in the expeditions of the Danish geologist Lauge Koch twenty-nine years earlier, I made it clear that the work now planned was of the same sort as his and that we would have to bring back pebbles (geological samples) and small marine animals deposited in concretions of white limestone. All the men present were familiar with the fossils found in the sand of ravines and understood their general history. Sharp-eyed hunters like them would be good collectors, I was sure. My talk had been a bit long-winded, but secretly the men were grateful because it solemnized our departure by emphasizing that the success of the expedition depended on each of us—on the four or five who would make the entire trip with me as well as on myself.

"Does anyone have any questions or any comments?"

The men—they looked so fat, bundled up in their animal skins—were embarrassed. They cleared their throats and shifted about uneasily but said not a word except for ieh, ieh (yes, yes), and asukiaq (I don't know) and other banalities. They were thinking, mulling things over; their technical questions would come later, once we were on our way. But I was aware of how exacting they were and realized that these introductory words of mine were not sufficient. From experience I also knew that the very fact of their being present at the meeting gave them a stake in future decisions; this was their custom. But at that moment, their ieh, iehs were mere civilities. I had to go further, enlarge the "soviet." So we began to talk about "practical" things—the number of dogs, the weight of our cargo, the condition of the ice, the length of the laps we could cover daily in late March and early April, a period when seals are hard to find and the load of meat to be transported would therefore be particularly heavy. They began to talk among themselves, exchanging brief asides; then gradually the circles opened and then re-formed in one group which included all the Eskimos present. By withdrawing from me, the men were in a better position to come to a group decision, and imperceptibly, they were doing so. It was up to Kutsikitsoq and me to orient the process delicately by a word, a laugh, an expression of concern, taking care not to contradict the unexpressed thoughts of anyone present. The men watched one another, evaluated the silences, the glances, and the tacit agreement they implied. My four partners had to have the approval of the men who would be helping us carry the loads as far as Etah and also of the village as a whole, acting as a group-arbitrator. Without a general concurrence, Kutsikitsoq and whoever else joined me would, within a week or two, perhaps even sooner, abandon me for fear of being conspicuously different.

Masaannaa and Qaaviannguapaluk were the first to express an opinion that showed they were committed. They were tight-lipped and they stared fixedly at the ground: "That's right, that's exactly what we were thinking. We'll leave after you, but we'll help you as much as we can." They had spoken up in front of everyone; a resolve had been voiced.

The atmosphere immediately brightened. Only now was I included in one of the shifting circles. The two young men had spoken for the group of hunters who would accompany us to Etah and had endorsed the plan; their satisfaction was all the greater because Eskimos hate prolonged indecision. After some casual conversation, I decided to postpone our departure until the afternoon of March 29.

My one reason for doing this, I must admit, was to puzzle these men who were oversure of themselves and somewhat unpredictable; creating a mystery would give me a better hold over them. My announcement caused much comment, and amid some hubbub each man went out to his sledge. Telling Kutsikitsoq to join me, I went "home"—into the small room that adjoined the one where the meeting had been held. I had no sooner sat down than Kutsikitsoq came in—a changed man, twisting his gloves between his fingers, awkward, craftily worried.

"Well, asasara Kutsikitsoq, my dear one! I'm no fool—I know how much you enjoyed making me wait while you stopped off for a few days on the beach over there."

"Ieh, ieh! . . ."

"As members of a scientific expedition, we are now angalasoqs, we are all researchers on a journey. . . . It is hardly worthy of a son of Uutaaq not to be at the rendezvous."

I had struck home: Kutsikitsoq's pride was touched to the quick.

"Utoqqatserpunga, you're right; I was wrong, especially in the eyes of the others, who are watching us."

And he shook my hand. One never appeals to the pride of these men in vain.

A month later, we smiled at the memory of this exchange. I had not been mistaken; I had done the right thing. An authoritarian attitude has never been worth anything here. "Kamappoq una! Ajorput. He's angry. That doesn't sit well with me at all." Eskimos, like everyone else, find stiffness and bad temper intolerable.

Later, I learned that the sardonic comment was fairly common. Some Eskimos went even further when they were exacerbated by nervous white men perpetually in a hurry. When a white man asked them to drive him to this or that place and fast, they would set out and, with an air of great diligence, drive him around in circles for a few days while the blizzard raged.

"Well, Kutsikitsoq, do we still agree about this? We have just a month's supply of provisions for a two- or three-month-long expedition. If we want to go far, we can't carry more than that. And as you know, we have far to go."[2]

"Ieh, I know. . . ."

"So, essentially everything will depend on hunting. There won't be many seals lying on the ice in late March and early April; it's too cold. We'll have to kill them at the allut. I think those weeks will be the most difficult. If it doesn't take me too long to draw my map, I expect that we will have arrived at Inuarfissuaq by then. It seems that there are lots of seals up there from the end of April on, and that that's when they begin to lie on top of the ice. That's what Qisuk and others told me."

Kutsikitsoq interrupted: "But the Inuit have their meat depots in Etah."

"Of course, I'm counting on that! But we've had no news from Etah for a long time. We have enough cartridges, don't we?"

"Ieh," said Kutsikitsoq, "you've got boxes and boxes full, amerlaqaat. I can't even count them all.[3] But if we're going to be warm enough in the tent, really warm, we'll have to keep the Primus going all night. For that, we need oil, lots of oil. Eskimos don't like to be cold."[4]

"If the 'Eskimos' want to keep warm at night, like women, they can bring their own oil."

Kutsikitsoq smiled.

But Maassannguapaluk's having dropped out disappointed him greatly.

"There isn't a better hunter among all the young men. . . . And you, well, obviously you're in good shape, but I'm getting old. My legs are no good, my heart's petering out. . . . We've got to find a young man with some energy. . . . It won't be easy, since we're going all the way to Canada. We're sure to run out of food—but I have every intention of making it back. . . . You know the story about the Americans: Grilissuaq [Major Adolphus Greely] and his people almost all died of hunger. They were eating each other. They even baited their lines with flesh from dead bodies! That's what the Inuit say. What's more, if we're going to spend the winter on Ellesmere —the island is uninhabited, the cold is terrible, and the allut are useless—the ice is too old and thick because of the Pole current and there aren't many seals. Ululik said that oil freezes there. It's a real white-porridge of a place! If the ice field breaks up between us and Greenland . . . and it very well may —one summer a few years ago, the water was free of ice all the way up to Washington Land. So we shouldn't be hanging around on the other side as late as June. What would we do then, without a boat? Huh! You've no idea. . . . But whatever you want we'll do. We Inuit are always prepared for the worst. How would you make out in the wintertime over there, in that unin-habited island in Canada? You'd have nothing to eat but what you hunted, and you'd have no kiviaq for months and months. . . . We can't carry a year's supply of cartridges with us, for sure. . . . So we could use harpoons. The qallunaat of your country certainly wouldn't come to our rescue. And you don't want to take your radio.[5] Ah! It's too bad that Maassannguapaluk won't be there."

"And Sakaeunnguaq? What about him?"

"You haven't seen his dogs. They wouldn't last ten miles. . . . There's always old long face Iggianguaq—but you don't like him."

Whereupon the theatrical Kutsikitsoq leaned on my map—one elbow on the Pole—and buried his head in his hands.

Mentally I struck Sakaeunnguaq off the list. That modest, troubled man did not get along with Kutsikitsoq, whose dogs were unmatched. In my head, I was reorganizing my teams. I knew in fact that I would have to approach "old long face" Iggianguaq and did not relish the prospect—ever since when, on our trip south last November, he had forced me to play "catch-up" with his sledge on the ice, my relations with him were not of the best.

"Oh, well, I don't see anybody for the job except Qaaqqutsiaq. . . . Why don't you want to take Padloq?" Kutsikitsoq slipped the question in casually.

If Qaaqqutsiaq went, he could not leave his wife behind, alone in the camp. It seemed that the Inuit kept her at a certain distance. It was an old story and not too clear. Years ago, Padloq had grieved because she had no children. . . . She adopted a little boy and became fiercely attached to him. At the age of four, however, he was still wetting the bed. She was so annoyed that, not knowing what else to do to cure him, she began giving him less and less to drink. That way, she thought with implacable logic, at least he won't pee so often.

The Inuit did not agree.

"Ajorput! That's not good!"

But Padloq had always done as she wanted. Whether because of his diet or for some other reason, the child died. Padloq was desperate, but the Inuit would not forgive her for ignoring their advice, and ever since she and her husband had led a fairly solitary life.

Although I was trying my best to avoid taking another woman in addition to Natuk, it was certainly not because of that story, which I had always doubted. My calculations had been very exact, and I was afraid I would not be able to feed another partner. I had Qaaqqutsiaq come see me. From the outset of our conversation, he was very tactful and gracious, but he was unwilling to leave Padloq at any price. We agreed that they would both come if I could not find an available unmarried man.

The next morning, I was too busy to attend to the problem first thing. My time was taken up in checking the sledges, packing provisions and equipment, and getting our gear in order. The Eskimos' questions about practical matters had to be answered—about teams, extra dogs, what equipment to take—this and not that, bring this, leave that, pack that. . . . Not fragile, no . . . but careful of that one! Upturned sledges lay around my hut; the drivers were energetically polishing their steel runners with heavy files so that they would slide more easily.[6] The men were sweating, and in spite of the cold, some had taken off their qulitsaqs. There were dogs everywhere. To keep them high-strung, they had not been fed since the day before; sensing that we would soon be leaving, they howled aggressively when anyone went near them, and at times the noise was deafening. It was just as bad inside my hut. Using a hammer as a lever, Qaaqqutsiaq was prying open all the crates that had served as a bed that winter. I did not want to burden myself with them, so I was adopting the tried and true local method of carrying my few cans of meat and stewed fruit and my biscuits and margarine in clearly marked canvas bags.

While this work was proceeding, I left to meet Iggianguaq, even though it cost me something to do it. For the sake of the group, I would put aside any personal feelings and ask this man to join us: he had an excellent team and usually he traveled without his wife. As I stood outside his hut, I looked through the half-frosted window into his one room and saw him crouching there, his elbows on his knees. His wife and an Eskimo woman from the neighborhood were huddled together in a corner near the lamp. Their heads were bowed, and they were pretending to sulk: they had already seen me. I coughed to announce my presence, as was the custom, and went in. The stench of poultry and gamy, rotten meat filled the room. The welcome I received was reserved, barely polite.

"We were dropping with sleep when I thought of going to invite you to the little party I gave for my son's birthday. . . . Anyway, you didn't miss anything. It smelled terrible."

Indeed! . . .

Scattered all around me on the floor were the remains of food, scraps of unplucked birds, beaks, and claws. In the corners were little heaps of gnawed bones, shining and obviously well licked; the smallest had been broken, as I have described earlier. We talked of one thing and another, but it was impossible for me to speak freely in this hovel. Iggianguaq's wife was observing me out of the corner of her eye; she had never liked me, and I had the feeling that her neighbor was lingering merely in the hope of overhearing some unpleasant talk which she could spread around. The child abruptly began to cry, as many Eskimo children do when they see a qallunaaq.

I gestured to Iggianguaq that I wanted to speak to him outside. He pulled on his caribou jacket.

"Sunalikiaq? Sunalikiaq? What is it now?" To be even more of an Inuk, he lowered his voice and aspirated his syllables.

He also winked at his wife.

As soon as we were outside, the man became small and wary. Without preamble, I asked him to go with us; I took pains to underscore the honor and prestige that would redound on him and his family from such a trip. . . . But then, for sixty years white men had been talking that way to the natives. In the space of a second, an almost imperceptible smile of satisfaction spread over Iggianguaq's face. The man felt wanted; he knew I needed him. For several minutes he answered my different questions with a series of excuses.

"My dogs are no good. . . . My wife will be unhappy. . . . I don't get along with Kutsikitsoq. He hurt my feelings with his mockery. . . . I'm tired. . . . You might have to spend the winter completely isolated in the country of the umimmak. . . ."

In exasperation, I finally begged him to answer me yes or no. We were standing no more than a yard apart, both shivering in spite of our furs. I sensed that other Eskimos were watching us. Keeping his eyes fixed on the ground, in a calculatedly soft, measured voice Iggianguaq at last gave me his answer:

"Immaqa naamik. . . . Perhaps not. . . ."

Immaqa naamik!

I quickly shook his hand and we left each other. I was not to see him again until several long months later out on the ice field. His wife was far away, and we were both happily following the tracks of a bear.

Back in my hut, I found poor Qaaqqutsiaq sweating away. He was on his knees amid a quantity of precariously stacked cans which he was carefully itemizing.

"Ataaseq: one stewed fruit. . . . Marlluk tiit: two teas. . . . Arfineq-pingas ut sukku: eight sugar. . . ."

"Hey . . . Qaaqqutsiaq!" Absorbed in his counting, he turned to look at me absently; a lock of hair had fallen over his eyes.

"Qaaqqutsiaq! You're coming with me. It's all settled. . . . Padloq too, of course."

"Qujanaq, thank you," he said simply, a can of spinach in his hand. Then he smiled.

"Don't worry about Padloq. She doesn't eat much."

10

THE ROUTE
TO ETAH,
ULTIMA THULE

In keeping with custom, the night before we left I invited every resident of Siorapaluk to spend the last evening with us. Among the first group that invaded my hut, I caught sight of bushy-haired old Pualuna. He was feebler than ever, but he had not wanted to miss this departure; he enjoyed the chance to reminisce again about his expeditions with Peary, Cook, and MacMillan. Imina and Ululik entered stiffly in their Sunday best.

"See," murmured Bertsie to three children who were staring at me out of little round eyes, "that's him, the naalagaq, the leader of the expedition. . . . And your cousin over there"—she pointed to Ussaqaq—"is going too—far away far away in the north, avani, avani, where it's very cold, where Aapilaq and your father, Itukusuk, spent more than a year with Tatsekuuk, Dr. Cook. Maybe they'll see umimmak." Our eyes met; she smiled at me and blushed.

Natuk and Padloq passed around cakes and coffee until midnight. I gave everyone some dried cod, which they were quite fond of. At one point there were almost fifteen people in the room. Each of them was eager to talk to me warmly about the expedition, to express specific good wishes, which were as diverse as they were unexpected. It was moving to see them standing in single file, waiting their turn to say good-bye to me personally and to wish me well.

"We will miss you," Imina said to me, almost crushing my hand. "Every morning I'll be watching for you to come out of your hut here in Siorapaluk. You know, you shouldn't think . . . well, we all feel pretty good. . . . You're just like an Inuk. Pissortut—of course—you're almost one of the group. We share memories, you've eaten kiviaq, you have your dogs. . . . It isn't like in the beginning, in August, when you lost them on the sand beach and all of Siorapaluk had to go find them for you!"

"Have a good trip," Ann Sofia whispered. "Here, take this." She slipped into my hand some thread made of caribou tendon, which was almost impossible to find and which had taken her a long time to make.

"Now Natuk, too, will be able to sew your buttons on," she added.

The hubbub increased; moving among the different groups, I overheard snatches of conversation:

"I have plenty of confidence in Qaaqqutsiaq," one man was saying.

"But he hasn't finished explaining the atomic bomb to us," Olipaluk reminded him.

I was overcome by a host of emotions and memories. I was surrounded by real friends, some of whom had waited until this evening to show how they felt. The next day, when I embarked on this adventure, I was to feel almost as if the people I was leaving were my own family.

The rest of that night was brief. The Eskimos were on edge because of their responsibilities, and they stayed up talking softly, almost reverently, about their families and the people they were leaving behind. In my alcove, which served as an office, I mentally reviewed what things and what papers should not be forgotten; I reread directions I had written that were to be sent if necessary to the Danish administrator in charge of northern Greenland; he was stationed far to the south, in Godhavn, on Disko Island; with the directions were enclosed a sum of money and precise instructions which would enable him to send a rescue mission after us if we had not returned by a certain date in the fall. He would receive these papers by boat in August or September. I could not get to sleep until three in the morning.

In the early daylight hours, people began moving around inside the hut. The drivers came and went, each stowing his share of our cargo on his sledge. The loads were apportioned according to the strength of each team. They averaged from 400 to 600 pounds. One dog is strong enough to pull about 80 pounds, and when running on good, smooth ice at the rate of three to four miles per hour, a first-rate team can cover thirty or thirty-five miles per day, pulling about 800 pounds. (A reindeer can pull about 200 pounds, a horse about 500 pounds.)

Over long distances, however, it was safer to allow considerable leeway. Because Kutsikitsoq was proud of his eighteen dogs, he was not afraid to take on crates the other drivers could not handle, and his sledge was already stacked more than three feet high.[7] As the load grew higher, Kutsikitsoq swelled with pride and became expansively sarcastic.

"Look at my qamutit, my sledge," he said to me. "It's as high as a qallunaat's house. . . . My eighteen dogs, now there are some real dogs! Just look at Ussaqaq's—what a pathetic pack!"[8]

I arranged to have the boards and straw from the crates, some paper, empty tin cans, and what coal I had left distributed among people in the camp. Here everything was precious, even a mere nail. I gave Sakaeunnguaq my winter furniture, my lamps, reinforced window panes, and some tar paper. Finally, in my hut I left some provisions which could prove useful when we returned in three months. As was the custom, the door had no key: the store of provisions was left in the care of the group, and of Sakaeunnguaq in particular.

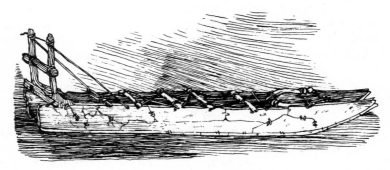

The traditional sledge—nineteenth century—was made of several lengths of whalebone joined together by supple thongs of sealskin. Rivets and nails were never used. The runners were made of bone—whale, seal, or walrus. This kind of sledge used to be handed down from generation to generation. The sledge of today—with wooden thwarts—is larger, but is constructed in virtually the same way. Every Eskimo makes his own sledge as well as his hunting tools. (*From Kane,* Arctic Explorations)

It was March 30, 1951. In a moment we would be leaving, but first we ate one last time at the camp. The meal was commonplace enough and we were simply sitting around on bags and bundles of paper, yet everyone was a little more grave and reserved than usual. One by one I looked at these four faces, which I would be seeing for many hours and days. I could count on the two women, Natuk and Padloq. They would be good and useful companions, adapting to circumstances without demur. They would never take part in the men's discussions, no matter how lively those discussions might become; they would remain in the background, waiting. Their attitude is hard to define—it is neither critical nor impatient, nor mocking; the women's eyes, their expressions, are absent. Qaaqqutsiaq I trusted. That left the handsome Kutsikitsoq. What was the meaning of that sulky look which he invariably turned on me, but which his laughing eyes contradicted? By now we had spent months together, running behind a sledge, sleeping side by side, enduring blizzards, yet I swear I knew him no better then than I had before. The man had too many facets. Perhaps he was concealing his inability to win recognition as "a leader."

"Your dogs are ready, Malaurie," he said to me.

We went out together. Qaaqqutsiaq was already on his sledge. I shouted to him that he could start off, since he would be at the head of the group. I was to follow him. Kutsikitsoq would bring up the rear.

Qaaqqutsiaq moved off briskly, firing into the air several times to salute the beginning of the expedition.

My dogs, restless from waiting, were looking at me. The trail lay before us, white and well defined. They started down it, then fanned out and, with growls of joy, plunged north toward Etah.

The snow was good. The shore passed quickly before my eyes, and the igloos soon disappeared behind a headland. Everything was going well. I was pleased to see that I was beginning to gain on Qaaqqutsiaq, when suddenly my team began to slow down. From a fast trot the dogs went to a slow trot, then to a walk; they were panting and their tongues hung out. Even Paapa, the leader, my beautiful Paapa with the tawny fur. I was dumbfounded to see that his belly was slightly distended. He was dragging along, leaning to one side. I whipped them and yelled, but nothing happened. Nothing worked.

A shout on my left: "They must have eaten a little too much!"

It was Kutsikitsoq, who was passing me with a brilliant display of whip-cracking. They must have eaten too much! I bet they did—that joker! Later, he told me that the night before he had deliberately stuffed them to make sure that his departure would be an impressive, triumphant success—at my expense.

So it was only after half an hour that I rejoined the group, near a large iceberg off Illulorsuit. Kutsikitsoq came over to me.

"Your dogs must be pretty sick. It's probably all rotten inside there," he muttered, patting their stomachs. "Dogs of a qallunaaq!"

Without a word, Qaaqqutsiaq took several bags off my sledge to lighten the load. I contained my anger, Eskimo fashion. Later, later. . . . It was already late in the evening when we pitched camp on the ice field at Tuluriaq, within sight of Neqi. I assigned each person certain duties that would remain unchanged throughout the expedition. While the men pitched the tents the women would unload the sledges and finish setting up camp. After taking care of the dogs with Qaaqqutsiaq, Kutsikitsoq occasionally helped me cook. That first night was very cold. We had quickly established where everyone was to sleep in the tent. Two men (of which I was one) on the outside, the two women between us, with one man in the middle.[9]

The next day, when we got up, our hair whitened by frost although the rays of the sun were touching the roof of the tent and melting the frost on its inner canvas, our team began to really feel like a team, to shape up like one. On the Primus the women prepared a big breakfast which, as was customary, would be our food for the whole day. I had my inevitable porridge; my companions preferred several large, fat chunks of frozen seal.[10]

"You'll see that you'll come around to it. It's the only thing that keeps your body warm. It's fat, it melts in your mouth. That pap"—Kutsikitsoq pointed to my milky plate—"won't give you strength or heat your blood. Your spinnaar, your spinach, is nothing but grass and water. I saw one of those cans at Ululik's. For an Inuk, the only thing is neqe, meat." (Actually, except for coffee, tea, and hardtack, I was soon eating nothing but seal meat like the Eskimos, and continued to do so all during the expedition.)

The atmosphere was good. We were gathered around the stove, holding our bowls of coffee. Qaaqqutsiaq dug into the "marmalade" bag and pulled out a jar of jam that we could open at last; we hesitated over the choice of beautiful Lenzburg labels:

"Those big red things," Kutsikitsoq demanded.

"No," Natuk whined. "I want the yellow ones."

The moment the lid was off, fingers and knives plunged into the jar and daubed the hunks of meat with frozen jam. The jar had been supposed to last three days; it was scoured clean within ten minutes, which led me to reflect on the futility of planning rations for "Eskimo explorers." The tent was full of noises—belching, chewing, loud laughter.

"Mammaraai! It's good!"

We ate, drank, ate again, and arrived one hour late at Neqi.

Neqi: Four igloos standing at the mouth of an ice torrent, lost in the vastness of the snowy landscape they looked out on. To someone approaching the tiny village from the south, it seemed crushed by the cliff above it. Seeing its four small igloos made one wonder why nature, which is so hostile here, would allow this weak echo of human activity to exist, and how it could resist the tide of forces leagued against it. Neqi—meat, as its name indicates—was a place where walrus were hunted. Neqi is next to Pitorarfik, which might better have been named *Pitorarpok*—"they [the whale and walrus] are sticking their heads out of the water." The waters hereabouts were so full of game that hunters did not hesitate to travel one hundred or two hundred miles to reach the area. This minuscule village, known from Savigssivik to Etah, had always been a meeting place for the tribe.

In front of the igloos I saw two thick black columns three feet high and five feet in diameter, built of small sandstones.[11] Usually they were loaded with meat dripping white and ocher fat, but that day, because the winter had been so hard, they were quite bare.

As was the custom, we stopped our sledges on the ice field a short distance from the shore. Our arrival set off a concert of barks. Eskimos appeared on all sides. Standing beside our dogs, we waited, as usual, for our hosts to approach and welcome us.

But the stiff, distant inhabitants of Neqi lined up in front of their doors, men to the fore, women and children to the rear, and were examining our group with feigned caution.

"Sunaana? What does this mean?" Kutsikitsoq growled. "They're not very friendly here. . . ."

It is customary among nomad peoples that initial contacts be reserved, yet Kutsikitsoq was always irritated when an exception was not made for him, the son of Uutaaq, for the great hunter with sixteen dogs, the angalasoq, or "partner on an expedition," the lover of women. . . .

The women here were awkward and shy; they kept their distance, and their children clung to them, clutching their long white boots set off by bearskin cuffs, or their blue and white fox-fur jackets. At last, two men stepped forward solemnly to meet us. We moved to meet them and silently shook their un-gloved hands. We looked one another in the eye. Minutes later, the ritual having been duly performed, we were noisily invited into the only two inhabited igloos. I had planned to make no more than a brief stop here, but tradition demanded otherwise. I had to visit the families one after another, receive the usual compliments, and eat whatever was offered me. Within one hour, I had drunk ten cups of coffee and consumed both kiviaq and seal. Eating cements a friendship immediately. To strengthen my team, I bought an extra dog from a lame young Eskimo, Asarpanguak. Near a stake I had seen a carcass covered with mixed black and yellowish fur: "that" was his dog. The beast was so emaciated that my friends forthwith named it Atitak, after Pualuna's wife, that broken-down, stunted old woman. The dog's appearance was misleading, for he turned out to be one of the best of the ten in my team. I acquired some extra meat from the stone caches and we loaded it onto the sledges. Kutsikitsoq and Qaaqqutsiaq were also transacting a little business: one file exchanged for a harness, twenty-five frozen salmon for one sealskin.

Our group was joined by Qaaviannguapaluk and Masaannaa, who were going to Etah to hunt bear. They had not intended to leave for several days, they said, but Eskimos find it hard to resist the attraction of a grand departure, and many times I noticed that as we passed through camps we set off a chain reaction. It's more pleasant to travel in ten than in two. To our amazement, the young men brought their women with them. Masaannaa had been followed this far by his young girlfriend, Ulrikka, who was five months pregnant and anxious not to let him out of her sight as long as he refused to marry her. Ulrikka was fifteen. Inapaluk was the same age. She accompanied her husband Qaaviannguapaluk for several miles, and then suddenly she jumped off the sledge. Forcing herself not to look back, she walked alone through the snow toward the camp. We passed her, but when we greeted her, she did not bother to answer. She kept her eyes lowered. She was alone, I said? Not at all. As she walked, hips swaying, we could glimpse the head of a fat baby tucked in her hood; he, too, had had to be present at the departure, no doubt as a symbolic reminder to his father, before he plunged into the dangerous pleasures of the hunt, that his life was doubly precious.

As we threaded our way between frequent icebergs, our column stretched out; the pace was very slow. Although our sledges were less heavily loaded now —the bear hunters were so anxious to protect their freedom and to avoid being bound to an expedition that they had willingly agreed to carry part of our load as far as Etah—we still did not cover more than one or two miles an hour. The dogs' breath made haloes of steam, and a driver had difficulty seeing his own team up ahead and the one behind him. Each man kept his eyes fixed on the silhouette of the sledge in front of him. Perched up high on the bags, we sat sidewise, turned to the right or to the left depending on the direction of the wind. The thick snow muffled all sounds. An indication of our speed was the whistle of the long lash of the driver's whip, which he let hang behind him— the handle held almost horizontal—ready to strike. Pssssi . . . Pssssisisisi. . . . Added to this sound, but distinguishable from it, was the low, rather flattened squeak of the steel runners as they cut through crystalline snow and then pressed it down as the sledge passed heavily over. Preueueueueueueueu- tok! Preueueueueueueu . . . eueu . . . eueu . . . eueueu. . . . Sitting alone for

265

hours on end, a driver falls into a reverie pursuing some thought that eludes him. Weariness, the monotony of the routine, the smell of musk from the skins he wears, the reflection of the snow, gradually plunge him into a state of mind that borders on clairvoyance. The dogs, who are extremely sensitive, share this experience: as they trot on, they become "bound" together. Each loses himself in a single unified motion that carries them all forward; now their ears are laid back, their plumed tails no longer wave to left or right, and their panting is regular. The team has become one single body moving forward on many feet.

This had happened to our group when suddenly up went the ears, and tails trembled: ahead of us, one of the hunters was waving his arms. A minute later, in indescribable disorder, we were all milling like idiots around the footprint of a bear!

Nanoq!

Standing before his dogs and pointing with his whip handle, Qaaqqutsiaq tried soberly to decide how old the broad, almost square print was, and whether it was male or female.

The Inuit discussed the question briefly. A hunter stepped out of the group, fitted his foot in one of the prints, and by rocking back and forth delicately from toe to heel, was able to estimate how compact the snow was and how hard it was frozen.

"Ippassigami," he guessed.

"Ippassigami," the others sadly echoed.

The animal was a female; she had passed by two days before. Without further comment, we struck out again.

We did not reach little Sonntag Bay until late in the evening; it was completely dark, for the quarter moon was hidden. The campsite we chose lay at the base of steep sandstone rocks that offered protection against the wind, which was rising again. Quickly we tied the dogs up some distance out on the ice field. Several of us pushed the sledges down to the shore. Two of them, placed side by side, formed a floor, over which we then pitched a tent. In this way, we had large and comfortable quarters. Short, gruff remarks flew back and forth in the dark.

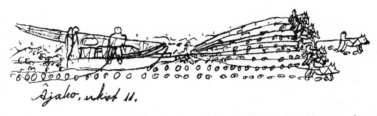

Drawing by the eleven-year-old Ajako, son of the mulatto Anaakkaq. A kayak can be seen on the sledge. The Eskimo often travels this way, so that he can move more freely: when the ice breaks up, he unloads the kayak and in it follows the seal or walrus that has eluded him on the ice. Dog tracks in the snow are also visible. Savigssivik, January 1950. (*Private collection*)

"Qaa, Natuk! Massakkut! Give it to me right now, Natuk!"

"Soo. Thank you."

"Malorinnguaq! Saarullik qassit? Malaurie, how many cod per person?"

"Marlluk, two."

"Pissortut. You're right."

We called to one another as each worked quickly and efficiently with his own baggage, but lending a hand wherever it was needed to fasten down a tent, carry oil, or fetch someone an ax. The men fought against the penetrating cold as best they could. One blew on his numb fingers; another jumped up and down; another stamped his feet. The storm lamps were lighted, little flames wavering in the wind. They flickered every which way, as if brandished by gnomes. Within fifteen minutes, we had carried everything we needed for the night into our shelters: caribou skins, sleeping bags, and, above all, the essential, invaluable Primus stove which would quickly heat the interiors of our tents. That evening, the temperature was −36°C (−32.8°F), and in the hours to come it was quite likely to drop even lower. The tents soon looked like little fortresses. We made ourselves snug, careful not to let an iota of warmth escape. To get in and out was not very easy; we had to crouch down on hands and knees to pass through the little flap. And it was deemed bad manners, once you had settled down inside, to decide to go out for some fresh air.

The men undressed rapidly; they were sweating. After a whole day spent in intense, damp cold, a temperature of −5°C (23°F) makes one perspire quickly. We were three or four to a tent, and we took our places without thinking about it. I expected that my partners, who had been tired out by these first few days, would surely drop off to sleep at once. I was wrong. Suddenly I heard shouts outside to my right. Ussaqaq—as usual—wanted more tobacco and more fish. I sent Qaaqqutsiaq to pacify him with a chunk of walrus and some cigarettes. Conversation died down at last, and an hour after we had arrived the lights in the tents went out one by one.

At two in the morning there was a little drama. Qaaviannguapaluk, the young married man from Neqi, had lingered behind to check his traps during the afternoon. Now, in the middle of the night, he had caught up with us, setting off a terrible din among the dogs. He was the happiest man in the world: he had caught one fox and two hares. How he managed to find my tent in the dark I don't know. His flat, yellow, good-humored face peered through the flap.

"Qaa! Take!" he said to me.

He was determined to give me the fruits of that first hunt. I invited him to sleep in my tent, along with Kutsikitsoq and Natuk. His entrance offered the immediate opportunity for a renewed and endless bout of eating. We bestirred ourselves, yawning. The Primus was relighted. The three Eskimos were delighted: here one never refuses to eat. And so for a good hour there was much cutting and hacking. Bones cracked; blood and fat ran down our chins. We washed everything down with several more cups of coffee. Not before three o'clock did we get back into our sleeping bags.[12]

But by eleven the next morning we felt completely rested. It was a big day: in theory, we were supposed to reach Etah. The weather was in our favor. After some problems along the ice field by the cliff, our group and its small escort arrived with no further difficulty at the foot of Storm Glacier, which we had to climb. (The route over the ice field off Cape Alexander was closed to us, because the sea ice had broken up a few days before.) With our heavy loads, we would need nearly three hours to climb the 600-foot glacier; usually, the climb took forty minutes. We shouted at the dogs; we doubled the teams, putting one nine feet in front of the other. Still it was not enough. On the lower slopes, the dogs, who were terrified by the way the central leash shook under the blows of the whip handle and who were afraid of being beaten, leaped forward, pulling briefly with all their might; they braced themselves by digging their claws into the ice, barked, and turned their heads back toward the driver, looking for a clearer signal. Again, we beat the central leash, but the panic-stricken dogs scattered. We had to dash forward and either reassemble them or lead them forward. "A', A', A', A'. . . ." Then we ran back, braced our shoulders against the sledge and pushed to unstick the runners, ran forward again; harnessed ourselves, in effect, by pulling from the side on the leash between the two teams; whipped the forward team; relieved the strain on the leash between the sledge and the back team; then ran back to the napariaq: this running back and forth was exhausting, but it was the only way we could make the sledges jolt to a start and continue with our provisions up to the saddle of the glacier.

When we reached the top, what a reward, what joy, awaited us! Breathless from our efforts, we looked down in disbelief: below us, reflected in the open waters of Smith Sound, lay Canada and the still unscaled peaks of Ellesmere Island.

The descent from the glacier, which ended in a sheer precipice at the water's edge, was extremely steep. At places, the angle of slope was twenty-five degrees; there was no snow whatever and the ice was deeply rutted. In order to slow down our heavily loaded sledges, we put not only thongs but also chains in front of our runners; the dogs were hitched to the back, naturally, to brake the sledges even more. As an extra precaution, two of us worked together—even three in the case of Kutsikitsoq's large sledge: one stationed at the napariaq, another keeping the dogs back with his whip, and the third pushing against the front of the sledge with both hands as he braced himself with all his strength against his heels. To avoid the precipice at the bottom we cut diagonally across the glacier. Then, at the foot of that formidable wall of ice, we looked out on a fantastic, luminously white world.

The Crystal Palace. . . .

A silver-blue and sea-green halo. . . . Sitting on my sledge, I watched the most unimagined assortments of architectural shapes march by before me. The wall of a cathedral carved out of opaline glass leaned against a medieval castle whose turrets and crenellated, worn curtains suggested a fortified town of the Nibelungs. Clustering nearby were pinnacles and gargoylelike forms and heavy ice masses perforated by gaping holes. Crystalline particles in a liquid white fog glittered in the sunlight; abstract geometric forms reared up, sparkling as though set with diamonds and emeralds. The spectacle was so dazzling that I soon closed my eyes, unable to endure the glare any longer. But the dull sound of grinding ice, the sharp reports issuing from the crystalline glass, reminded me that this fragile palace, formed by the whims of weather and chance, was undergoing a continual metamorphosis. Reduced by pressure and melting, it would presently become just one more anonymous iceberg wandering over the sea.

Three hours out from Foulke Fjord, I noticed some barely visible specks, no larger than pinheads, on the ice field far off our route. They grew bigger as I watched, until I made out the silhouettes of dogs, then the silhouette of a man seated on his sledge. He had caught sight of us and was hurrying toward us.

"Una! That one!"

My drowsy companions roused themselves and began excitedly to shout and point. A man!

Our orderly line broke up as drivers urged their dogs on, cracking their whips and shouting "Qaa! . . . Qaa! . . . Qaa! . . ."

Each man was striving to be first, and I whipped my team vigorously. We churned up clouds of powdery snow. When, dazed by the mad dash, I reached the man at last, he was surrounded by a hundred howling dogs. We shook hands heartily. He was as breathless and as pleased about our meeting as we were. His cheekbones and nose were blackened by frostbite; his eyebrows and lashes were frosty white against a dirty old face alight with laughter. It was Nukapianguaq.

Nukapianguaq had taken part in the largest Danish expeditions into northern Greenland. He was the only man still living who knew the coast of the vast island of Ellesmere quite thoroughly from having covered part of it on foot and by sledge. He had crossed the ice cap with Lauge Koch as far as Peary Land. Now fifty-seven years old and still vigorous, he had just married for the fourth time. His bride was the charming young Nivikannguaq. I observed him with particular interest because he was the father of my friend Sakaeunnguaq.

We exchanged the usual courtesies, and while Padloq and Natuk passed around bowls of tea, he wordlessly examined my equipment—binoculars, rifle, and topographic chart—with a rapid, inquisitorial eye; then, as if he'd done no such thing, he proceeded to give an animated account of how only yesterday he and Maassannguarsuaq had succeeded in killing a large bear very near the Crystal Palace we had just left. He was listened to closely. The Thule Eskimos had the greatest admiration for the four families who had settled in Etah, so far north in their country—who indeed lived in the world's northernmost settlement. Ultima Thule. . . .

What he told me about the meager meat supply in Etah was devastating, and his account was to be confirmed a few hours later. As we approached the settlement's five igloos, we met two residents who immediately abandoned their unproductive hunt to return home with us. And so, at eight o'clock in the evening, attended by an escort, we reached the famous camp. It lay at the end of a long, narrow fjord dominated by the Brother John Glacier and its wind tunnel, and it was surrounded by massive scree slopes of pink sandstone over which towered twelve-hundred-foot-high precipices. Situated between the frozen sea and a small lake, clinging to its pebbly beach, Etah was a cold, gray camp swept by almost constant winds. Home of the blizzard.

We divided our group as best we could among the peat-walled huts. The Etah Eskimos had evidently not known exactly when we would be arriving, but they welcomed us warmly. They knew what my arrival meant. Many Polar expeditions had passed that way; although there had been no previous French group there had been many British and American expeditions, including those of Peary and Cook, and a German one.[13] They could guess what our problems might be and had a good idea of the risks we were taking. We could be sure that if we needed it, this isolated little group of people would give us effective support.

I was Qaaqqutsiaq's guest. I had just gone into his modest igloo to unpack my bags when the very bad news we had already heard was confirmed; it meant that to continue on my expedition could be perilous indeed.

11

THE STORM

Nassapaluk was a hunter whom I knew and trusted, and it was he who came immediately to tell me that I must not count on large reserves of meat. He was very sorry, but he had only two or three seals to give me. I needed more than twenty.

"During the past winter, Etah has suffered a terrible famine," he explained. "The wind blew constantly. Because it was so cold the ice grew too thick and the seals left the fjord and the bays nearby. . . . Ajor! I haven't seen anything like it for years. . . . We don't have many dogs left. Almost all of them died, one by one. Toquvoq! Ajor! Yes, they're almost all dead and some of them we ate. It is a tragedy."[14]

Hunting had resumed two weeks before, with the return of the sun, and none too soon. The situation was threatening to upset even these Eskimos. And then, during the night we arrived, the problem worsened. A real tempest burst over the fjord; seventy-mile winds tore down the glacier. There could be no question of hunting; our dogs would have to be fed from our reserves. For the moment, they had taken shelter behind large rocks. The hair along their spines was lifted by the icy blasts; their muzzles, protected by tail and paws, were buried in the fur of their rumps. The shore was swept clean of snow, and the ice field was as smooth as a skating rink. The wind played with every object that had not been secured to the ground. As it rushed by, the rocks it scattered slid and spun around like grains of dust. The sight was a warning to be cautious. How often had they seen sledges and teams blown over and rolled along by the wind.

My companions were worried. The safety margin I would have until June was very narrow. For the forty-three dogs in our permanent group of three sledges, I had only four to five (sometimes two) days of food in reserve, because the expedition was traveling light in order to move fast. During the days of inactivity the storm caused, this margin became even smaller. Four days was ample time in which to transport our stores and reach the uninhabited area of Inuarfissuaq, which was rich in game; but the Arctic is unpredictable. The wind did not stop blowing around our huts; at times we heard it whistling, and it hummed steadily in the igloo's ventilation hole.

It might be objected that it was reckless on my part not to have brought along a supply of pemmican; one pound per day of this concentrate of beef, fat, and fish would have been enough for each dog. The fact is, at first I had very limited means at my disposal.[15] I had decided that in order to leave enough money for the spring expedition, I would allocate what little I had mainly to wages for the men, and to the purchase of cartridges, oil, and other equipment.[16] Beyond that, we would have to rely on finding enough game in this white desert to feed five people and forty-three dogs for three months or even longer. It was hazardous but not impossible. Few Polar expeditions had carried out their projects in such straitened circumstances, living as the Eskimos did; one had been Rasmussen's Second Thule Expedition, which came to a tragic end. But if I wished to complete the scientific program I had planned, I had no other choice.

Without question, the lack of funds was a handicap throughout the expedition. My partners were to suffer from it particularly, since they would have to make up for our food deficit by hunting—first, for walruses[17] and then for seals, the latter often daily, and in very harsh, even cruel weather. During our first few weeks together, I was to pay for this in the form of personal problems with some of them, especially because the meat, even when boned, was heavy. The bear hunters had helped us transport our cargo as far as Etah. Thereafter, as we headed farther north, we would have only three sledges. With our inadequate reserves, it was imperative that we hunt here in Etah, and during the coldest month; walrus and seal were again relatively abundant here, while to the north, as far up as Inuarfissuaq (which my research program would not allow me to reach very soon) the ice was too old: there were no allut, no holes in the ice, enabling us to hunt seals.

It was thanks only to everyone's good will and determination, to our exceptional luck in hunting, and to my good humor or, on other days I must confess, my fierce will that the expedition was ever carried out.

For the time being, we had taken refuge in a dark, overheated room. We crowded around a stone lamp filled with seal oil; it cast a melancholy yet soothing light. Our every move was projected in outsize shadows on the walls, which were covered with newspapers. In the wick's dim light, one could make out the large headlines. In this northern latitude, the ads made one smile: "The perfect refrigerator for everyone." "The soft breezes of Florida are waiting for you. . . ." "Jolie Madame is more than a perfume: it is a presence. . . ." And so on. For us, a storm was roaring outside, forcing us to remain inside and idle.

Morning was generally a lazy time: there was tea in bed for the men. The air stank of the night's urine that filled the cans and of the oil in the Primus, which was going out because the pressure was too low. Our bearskin pants hung from the ceiling on a "clothes dryer" improvised out of strips of skin. My bare-chested friends lounged around for hours: one man lay on his stomach, his head raised like a seal; another crouched barefooted on his boots, whose double hareskin, the *alersit,* had been carefully turned inside out so that the fur could air. Several men scratched themselves, heads bowed, eyes vacant. With his square, black fingernail, Qaaqqutsiaq cleaned his toes; his feet were high-arched, like an animal's; his big toe stuck out beyond the others, pale, hairless and fat as a wart. Good manners required us to make occasional vague remarks in a serious manner, although no one paid any attention:

"Soo . . . soqutaanngilaq! Well. . . . It's quite unimportant. Suna? What is it?"

On one such morning, an Eskimo, who had wearied of having nothing to do, belched, groaned softly, and then got dressed with his wife's help. He gave a big yawn; he stretched—the better, it seemed, to clear his throat. He walked over to the pan of meat, cut himself a piece, took two bites, continued on his way to the opposite corner where the bucket of ice stood, and sucked up some water through a hollowed bone. For one morning, that was enough exertion. He picked up his pipe, snuffled, and, in his restiveness, came over to assail me with the most preposterous questions.

"You'll inherit? How much? . . . You rich? How rich? How many kiffaqs you had? Your house, how high? Two igloos, three igloos?"

Enforced idleness does not bring out the Eskimo's better side. He is at the peak of his powers only when he is on the move, when he is hunting, which is what he does best. When bad weather immobilizes this vagabond, he loses all resiliency. When he is forced to stay put within four walls, he is filled with a sometimes intolerable unease.[18] He eats, he sleeps, he sleeps some more. . . . But is he not really thinking even as he dons his mask?

Kutsikitsoq was slumped down, playing with bits of skin and string; then he raised his head and, for the *n*th time, slowly plucked hairs from his smooth face with his fingernails.

Suddenly his mood changed and he tried to make people laugh by poking fun at himself, telling how he'd gone hunting once and caught nothing. But he and Qaaqqutsiaq, visibly bored, were tired of their continuous mimicry, tired of their wives, tired of the storm that never stopped.

"Pulaartoq! Visitors!" Natuk cried happily.

Indeed, someone was outside, coughing. Instantly everyone straightened up, then assumed an attitude of indifference. It is certainly pleasant to receive visitors and to be received, but it is good not to show it too much, for fear of appearing to seek guests. Nassapaluk came in, bundled in his qulitsaq; his manner was cold and stiff, and he looked at no one.

"Ikkii! It's cold!"

He made a show of going to sit in the dirtiest corner of the hut so that with a glance his host would be obliged to invite him to take a better place. The guest's place was to the left of the door, a small crate opposite the pan of meat, which was placed on the ground.

"Soo! Uunarpoq. Thank you. It's warm here," he muttered by way of thanks.

No one pretended to pay any attention to him, so he took it upon himself to sit down on the small crate. As he sat hunched slightly forward, with his elbows on his knees and his forearms dangling, he complacently emphasized what was most neanderthal about himself: lower lip thrust forward, jaw clenched. Nassapaluk was not pleased to be ignored; with no difficulty he was able to convey that he was becoming bored, and that soon he would begin to find that annoying. Kutsikitsoq bestirred himself, finally, and handed him a page from a magazine; he stood beside the man and commented on the illustration. It happened to be an advertisement for brilliantine: in it, a sophisticated Hollywood starlet was praising the virtues of a brand called Roja.

"Look," Kutsikitsoq said, pointing to the woman's lips, then her long eyelashes, "she must be pretty nice! . . . Well, well, she has no eyebrows. She must shave them. . . . Look at that! Her hair shines like the fur of a bear just out of water."

The people sitting around idly glanced over indifferently and then went on with their busywork—folding a piece of dirty paper into sixteen squares, cleaning an old black comb.

Nassapaluk ran his thick fingers over the movie star's shoulders and bosom: "Hmm! They're very pointed—high, too! Takkuut! They're so small, mikisunnguit, that I could easily hold both in one hand. . . ."

Kutsikitsoq was chewing on a slice of seal. He nodded. The conversation died. Whoever talked about native imagination? What about all those indigenous Eskimo games—ajagaq or *nulluttaq,* a game in which a perforated bone is hung from the ceiling and the player tries to jab another bone through the holes with an awl; *inukkat,* a version of knucklebones in which the ossicles of the seal are used; *attortoq,* a game played with a soft ball made of sealskin and filled with sand; *amarotoq,* a wolf game, a form of cross tag; hangman games; games of skill, played with walrus ribs and a ball made of bone; and games of strength. This group of people behaved as if they were struck all of a heap; now that winter was over they no longer took the slightest pleasure in the string games that were so popular during the dark months. People's eyes were vacant; apparently each pursued his own dream. Our guest was now very much at ease: he was cleaning his fingernails with an iron nail and plucking odd hairs from his face; his eyes were fixed on some distant point; his mouth hung half open. The man was waiting for something to happen, some event that would become a temporary focus for his restless mind, which demanded constant distraction when he was not hunting.

The dogs howled. Someone was coming.

"Kinaana? Who is it?" everyone wondered. The door opened; a current of cold air flowed in.

"Matu! The door! Umippigik! Shut it!"

There, covered with snow, stood Nivikannguaq. She was Nassapaluk's daughter—his *pania*—nineteen years old and not yet married. The excitement

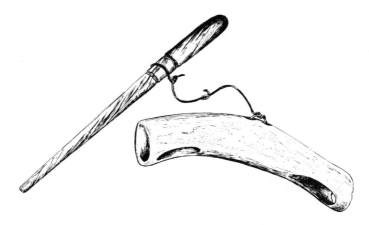

Ajagaq: walrus ivory game. The smaller orifice represents the anus; the larger, the vagina. The awl should be aimed toward the bigger hole. This group game, which was played during the winter of 1950, has many rules and penalties. For example, one must aim twenty times in a row. After doing this without missing, with great sensual gusto, the winner moves the stick in the hole and shouts "Nanoqsuaq!"—the victory cry of the bear hunter. In my opinion, this game of ajagaq is to be related to the tradition reported by Holtved's *The Polar Eskimo* that "in the middle of the winter men should kujappoq hard" so that game will be plentiful. The victory cry of *Nanoqsuaq* (the big bear) underscores the genetic and hunt-related nature of the game of ajagaq. Siorapaluk, December 1950. *(Private collection)*

subsided. Her gossip was all too familiar. The only thing we gleaned from her visit was that it was snowing.

"Soo!" Nassapaluk grunted. The word had been spoken, the signal had been given: he had paid his visit. "Aallarpunga! I'm off!"

He picked up a slab of meat on his way out, stuffed it in his mouth, opened the door, and disappeared into the night. He would visit like this three times a day, judiciously interspersing his visits to us with his visits to other houses and with the visits other people paid him in his igloo.

Neighbors kept stopping by for news. Kutsikitsoq kept on muttering. The tension between us was mounting. Whenever I looked at him he would turn his eyes away. On our second evening in Etah he announced to no one in particular that he was old, too, and all things considered, hardly suited to such a hard life. Given his penchant for the theatrical, Kutsikitsoq was disappointed to be part of an impoverished expedition. In exasperation, I answered his muttering by saying that, all in all, life wasn't so bad at the moment. "Right, Kutsikitsoq?" Abruptly he poured himself a brimming cup of my good coffee. Softly, as if talking to myself, I added that like so many other expeditions into the same regions, this one depended particularly on hunting, that pemmican

275

was an easy but also an expensive solution, and that if I had wanted to bring along a supply of it, I would no doubt have done without his, Kutsikitoq's, services. In enterprises like this one, I added, there were always good days and bad days, and surely it was a pity that the rumors about his tendency to become depressed in difficult situations was being proved all too true this evening. I reproved him by reminding him of the heroism of two of his forebears on the Rasmussen-Koch expeditions, some thirty years earlier.

"Kunuk [Knud Rasmussen] and Kuukkok [Lauge Koch] were hardly any richer back in 1917 and 1922. Look at Borseman, or Inuteq! They would laugh at you—you haven't stopped being angry for two days now. Bad humor is tiresome. Ajorput! It's no good!"

The hut was hot and stuffy. I could not endure looking at those secretive, cunning faces one minute longer.

Abruptly picking up my gloves and qulitsaq,[19] I left the hut and went out into the night. The storm was raging; in the blue-green moonlight, shadows crept along humped rises in the ground. In order to walk I had to bend forward. After a few yards, I felt surer of myself and believed I could stand up, but a veritable tornado blew up on my left. The ground shook. The snow lashed the ground wildly in parallel streams, twisted by the wind first in one direction, then in another. Now its frozen crystals needled my face. Whirlwinds spiraled up in the snowy light. Behind me I heard a mournful whistling. The modulations of the wind had tragic accents; it hissed unceasingly, and before every new intake of breath, its rattle was loud and sibilant. Several yards away a gust of wind crashed down like a solid mass. Sucked up, compressed, the wind returned, receded, and attacked our morainal hill, burrowing into it, penetrating its slightest folds. Sky and earth were one; through frozen slitted eyelids, I saw a milky screen before me in which everything was drowning. . . . Snow was sifting into the sleeves and under the collar of my qulitsaq. Exposed rocks as big as a man's fist rolled and bounced around me, and then were hurled far off. I had kneeled down the better to withstand the wind. I was still too tense to feel the violent bite of the cold.

Someone touched my shoulder. Surprised, I turned around. It was Qaaqqutsiaq. With his back to the wind, he too hunched over to brace himself.

"Ujarak? You're looking for stones?" he shouted in my ear. "I just saw a beauty. Look, here it is . . . unauvoq, this one!"

I felt him put a round piece of shingle in my hand.

"Don't you find it's a little cold? As for stones, the wind will certainly leave you a few."

Qaaqqutsiaq's voice was not mocking. His semblance of detachment masked lively emotion. His story about stones did not really conceal the genuine uneasiness my suddenly going out into the darkness had caused him. White men had been known to try to kill themselves during difficult periods of the winter.

The blizzard finally began to die down. Qaaqqutsiaq and I walked a little way together. In a more serious voice, he said: "You know, as I've told you, you can count on me. . . . Padloq and I will go wherever you like whenever you like. Natuk will too, but she doesn't dare say so."

We moved slowly. Kutsikitsoq was standing on the doorstep, his face striped by the flame of the storm lantern he held. He glanced obliquely at us and then, without waiting, disappeared into the igloo.

There were decisions to be made. Our difficulties sorted themselves out in the order of their importance, and problems that an hour before had seemed insoluble now became simple.

The door creaked. We entered the room, one behind the other. The hum of the gusting wind through the qingaq was muffled now, and the protection of the four walls soothed my nerves. I sat down as though nothing had happened. I drove all thoughts out of my mind and assumed an attentive smile. Was I turning into an Eskimo? Kutsikitsoq's head was bowed over a walrus tooth that he was working with his knife; he was sitting alone with the two women. After a long silence, I began to tell a story about Paris; I related it in a playful tone of voice, acting it out. I recalled the story of the incestuous love affair between a widower from Thule and his niece. The atmosphere in the igloo brightened. We caught ourselves looking at one another again. Kutsikitsoq had been amused, and now his mind was on something or other. Finally, shaking off his apathy, he started to tell a story.

"Aallarnerpoq, aallarnerpoq, itsaq, itsarsuaq, itsarujusuaq—a long time ago, a long, long time ago, a very, very, long, long time ago, a man and a woman lived together alone and very far from everything. Soorlo Sauninnguaq —you know, you saw her in Nunatarssuaq. She had once been quite beautiful and had had some wild times, and she would talk to me a lot when I passed by there. Her husband was killed by a rival who harpooned him in the back while they were in a kayak off Neqi. When she spurned the rival, whose name was Orfik, he killed himself and was found hanging from a cache of meat. Sauninnguaq left Neqi for Kangerluarsuk with a new husband, then went to Nunatarssuak, where I discovered her last November with two men, the husband and a young man. . . .

"In the daytime during the summer," Kutsikitsoq went on, "and don't misunderstand me, this time it is a legend, the man would go out on the water in his kayak. His wife always told him that while he was gone she stayed home. What a great little liar! In fact, she also went out. And there happened what had to happen. One day her husband came back early, and he found that his wife was not in the igloo. This happened again and again. The wife kept turning up after her husband had returned. He was intrigued, and one day he pretended to be leaving for a long, long time in his kayak. Of course, it was a trick. He hid behind a slight rise nearby in order to spy on his wife. He did not have long to wait. She came out of the igloo and walked straight —as straight as my whip handle—inland. He followed her the way one does when hunting an animal; he walked on tiptoe so that she would not hear him. He followed her for a long, long time. Presently she came to a small lake, and as she stood on the shore, she cried: 'Usuk! . . . Usuk! . . . Penis! . . . Penis! . . .'

"A large penis rose from the lake and began to serve her.

"This sight thoroughly disgusted the man and, without betraying his presence, he returned home. He was too restless to stay there, so he took his kayak and went out on the water. The farther he paddled, the greater his hatred for his wife grew.

"He was so disgusted that it was some time before he went back, and as he reached home his wife returned, too. He went off alone toward the little lake. He walked for a long, long time, and when he arrived, he too cried:

" 'Usuk! . . . Usuk!'

"And after a while, the penis indeed appeared.

"He immediately began beating it with a stick with all his might, and he killed it. When he had killed it, he took it back home. His wife was asleep. The man cooked the penis, and when it was thoroughly cooked, he woke up his wife.

" 'If you like,' he said in his gentlest voice, 'here's a little something for you to eat.'

"His wife began to eat, and when she had eaten a little, she exclaimed: 'Mmm! Mammaraai! . . . This is good! What makes it so good?'

"Then he answered her: 'It could be because it's your lover's usuk!'

"At these words she fell into a dead faint.

"Then he went in search of various animals—I won't list them, it would take too long—laid them on top of her, and wrapped her and them together in a large animal skin. Slowly, from all sides, the animals devoured the woman. The husband calmly set everything on fire, took his tent, and went off in his kayak. . . ."

"Shall I go on?"

The igloo was quiet now: heads were bowed; everyone was making an effort to seem absorbed in what he was doing. With her back to Kutsikitsoq, Natuk was sewing a sealskin. Qaaqqutsiaq was whittling the tip of his whiplash to a fine point. Young Padlunnguaq, who had just come in, was stroking her fox-fur trousers voluptuously with her fingertips.

"I'll go on," Kutsikitsoq said. A low, collective ieh was his answer. "What about thunder?" he asked, addressing me. "Do you know where thunder comes from?

"One woman, two children—a boy and a girl. They had no father anymore, only a stepfather. One day when they were playing instead of sleeping, their stepfather was so annoyed to hear them laughing that he shouted: 'You two, go play farther away! I know someone who is fed up with hearing your noise!'

"When he had spoken this way, the two children ran off far, far away.

"They had taken with them only a flintstone and a dogskin to sleep in."

"When they had gone as far away as possible, they asked themselves what they could try to change into."

"And they talked about this transformation, talked about it endlessly."

"At one point, the boy said, 'Let's change into walruses!' But his sister, who was older, refused."

"The boy enumerated by name all the animals living on the land and in the sea, but the little girl always answered, 'No, no.'"

"Finally the boy cried, 'Let's become the thunder!'"

"And this time his older sister agreed."

"So they began to change themselves into thunder."

"Over and over, the boy kept repeating, 'Let us become thunder! Let us become thunder!' and the little girl would answer, 'Yes, yes!'"

"Then little by little they began to rise into the sky. The older child kept ordering, 'Piss on this! Piss on that!' and as they pissed on this and that they made sparks fly, and little by little they really turned into thunder."

"Meanwhile, in the igloo, their mother began to worry. She became so very much worried that the Eskimos gathered together to call upon the spirits."

"Among them there was a woman carrying her little child in her hood. She left the others to go back home, waving the string which fastened her hood."

"When she got home, she saw the two thunder spirits appear before her. To conjure them away, she cried to them, 'Here, I have two breasts full of milk for you.'"

"But the two spirits would have none of that and, going on into the men's house, they loosed their cry."

"At that very moment, the Inuit were struck by lightning."[20]

Although they seemed taken up with other things, the three Eskimos had followed every word.

"My uncle Pualuna told me those stories, and so did Uutaaq. They are old, old legends. We know them all well."

Then, with some ostentation, Kutsikitsoq came over to me to speak to me privately. But I wanted no "private" conversation that—just because I agreed to talk—would turn into a "negotiation." This was a habit of Kutsikitsoq's. Since the winter, I had got to know him well. He was a sly fellow; he used tricks and stories to wear the other person down and assume the role of privileged confidant. To listen to him, we would have to wait two weeks—until the weather grew warmer.

"We'll listen to what you have to say later. First of all, let's take a look at our situation *all together*," I said to him in a loud voice, turning toward the others and emphasizing the last words as though seeking support.

The atmosphere was favorable. It was time, I thought, for me to assert myself as a qallunaaq.

"This is the situation," I said. "There are no reserves of food in Etah, and this long storm means I'll have to change our plans. Soqutaanngilaq! It doesn't matter! The forty-five miles between here and Uunartoq we'll cover later. We will reduce our loads as much as possible. We'll get rid of our qallunaat cans of meat. I've talked to Avoortungiaq and Maassannguarsuaq about that. They are interested in having them. In exchange, they will give us seal for the dogs. As soon as possible, they will go out hunting with us. From Etah to Uunartoq the three of us will be able to manage the transportation, and in two trips— well, we'll see.[21] Four or five siniks. [Traditionally Eskimos counted time in siniks, or "sleeps."] That much will involve all of us. Immediately afterward, you will leave me there alone, on the coast north of Etah, so that I can begin working on my topographical map and my geomorphic survey. I don't want to lose any time. Once you're back in Etah, after you've transported part of our supplies, you'll go hunting together to get the rest of our meat preserve. You won't rejoin me until you've caught enough for us to continue our journey in safety. Natuk and Padloq will stay with you. I don't need them. To save peat, fat, and oil, they can stay with Avoortungiaq and Nukapianguaq. I'll manage very well up there in a snow igloo. I've talked to Maassannguarsuaq and Nukapianguaq, and they say that at Ullerssuaq, at the mouth of the big fjord, there are lots of walruses sleeping on the ice floes or in water holes the storm has opened up. The re-formed ice is still too thin to get close enough to them. But in two or three days, if there is no wind, you'll be able to go hunting there, I believe."

The four Eskimos had listened to me without a word. Qaaqqutsiaq, look- ing sideways at his neighbor, spoke up first: "I repeat, Padloq and I will do exactly what you want."

There was still no reaction from Kutsikitsoq.

"And what about you?" I asked, turning to him. "What do you think about it?"

"Ieh . . . ieh . . . Of course. . . . Hunting. . . . You could be right! Four or five days, if everything goes right, that could work. Ullerssuaq? . . . Qaaqqut- siaq knows the place. It's always full of walrus and seal, the Inuit say.

"But what about you? . . . Of course you can do whatever you want, to live alone there. But . . . I don't know how to say this to you: it scares me just to imagine you there, the way I can see you now when I close my eyes. You know, there may not be any people living there anymore, but there are still bears."

With this sanctimonious speech, this false show of solicitude, delivered in a gloomy voice, Kutsikitsoq was trying to regain his role as adviser, which his mania for criticizing had caused him to lose somewhat among the Inuit.

"It's just that it's cold up there—and I know. Your lungs could freeze, and then there are storms. People get lost there. We've seen that happen. . . . Hendrik [Olsen], who was on an expedition with Knud [Rasmussen], he never came back. Neither did Amaroq [Thorild Wulff]. . . . What will you do up there by yourself? Have you thought about what if the ice breaks, the way it did at the last moon near Littleton Island? It might be weeks before we could join you. . . . These regions are not made for qallunaat! Ajorput! It's no good for you! It hurts me already, here in my heart, to see you leave. . . ."

Kutsikitsoq stood up. His face, as tanned as a piece of old leather, puckered up; his almond-shaped eyes became mere slits, through which a gleam of anger filtered:

"And you do understand that if anything happened to you . . . well, I'm the one who would be blamed by the white men down there. We've seen that happen, too. . . ."

I thanked Kutsikitsoq for his advice and comments, but said that as far as I was concerned my mind was made up and I would not change it.

"No one should be left alone in the Arctic, if it can be avoided. There are so many problems which can seem almost insurmountable to one man, though they would turn out to be utterly negligible for two men." These words, from Peter Freuchen's *Arctic Adventure,* were to come back to me later, and with good reason.

The next day, although the storm had abated somewhat, it still kept us confined to the camp. The dogs had had no food and the temperature the night before had fallen to nearly −40°C (−40°F). It was urgent that they be fed. Qaaqqutsiaq and I chose two seals from our reserves and spent the whole morning chopping them up. The dogs, covered with snow, saw us at work and strained toward us, pulling violently on their chains.[22] We hacked away at the frozen carcasses with hefty ax blows until twenty pieces of meat as big as my fist lay in a pile at my feet. I began throwing them, one by one, to my dogs. Some caught their pieces in midair. It was startling to watch those half-wolves as, eyes flaming, fur bristling, they hurled themselves on chunks of meat as hard as rocks. It takes them twenty-four to forty-eight hours to digest their food. So, as Freuchen points out, even dogs that are fed every third day often feel as though they have just eaten, and therefore tolerate hunger better.

Anxious not to miss a single piece, our dogs swallowed the black chunks of meat whole, taking no time to let them melt in their mouths or chew them. If a piece was too big, they stretched out their necks and jerked their heads back, forcing it down in a sort of hiccup. A few big licks over the snow to gather up any last scraps, and they had done. Their distended bellies were evidence of how much they had eaten—enough for four or five days. On the trail, however, the same amount would last them only two to three days.

This bit of exercise had put us in a better mood. We were both glad for the break in our devastating inactivity. Once back inside the igloo, we began eating again. Nukapianguaq had come by for news and had brought some of his bear meat. We talked cheerfully about new plans, and thus I learned that the Etah Eskimos were preparing to leave for the south. They had no meat left to feed their remaining dogs.

During the night, the wind died down. It was essential to take advantage of the lull. We made our decision: the next day we would leave as early as possible.

It was the first of April. After some quick trips back and forth, our three sledges were loaded. We were making one last check when, suddenly, voices rose on

all sides. Near me I first heard Natuk and then the whole camp screech:
"Qamuti-i-i-t! Qamuti-i-i-t! Sledges! Sledges!"

It was a moment of high drama. Three sledges, coming in all likelihood
from the south, had loomed into sight far to the west, at the entrance to the
fjord. Excited by our voices, the dogs began howling. Excited children began
running about. A door slammed. "Qamutit!" people yelled at the top of their
lungs, looking at one another with fiery eyes. The sledges were getting bigger
by the minute.

"Kinaana kia? Kinaana kia? Who is it? Who is it?"

"Nakorsaq qamuti-i-i-t! Nakorsaaaq! The doctor! The doctor!"

The din grew even greater. I could not believe a word of it. The doctor
here? At the beginning of April? Incredible. Yet it really was he. A few minutes
later he stood before my eyes. His El Greco-like face, shrunken and battered
by the cold, his chapped and gray-blue lips, were painful to look at. He had
been traveling bravely for two weeks. During the storm, he and his Eskimos
had been on the glacier and had taken what shelter they could find.

The doctor had been an even better friend of mine since last summer in
Thule when he had offered his consolation about my loss of maps to the
captain who shouted "Raus!" He came up to me and asked, in English, if I
knew of any place in this damned countryside where a man could find a warm
corner to sleep in. I pointed, and, leaving his team to the Eskimos, who took
the dogs in charge, he followed me toward the igloo I was staying in.

"My goodness!" He raised his big arms to heaven. "Your letters!"

He ran back to his baggage, rummaged through it, and, after much praise-
worthy effort, fetched out two little letters—the two very small letters that he
had vowed he would deliver to me personally. A sorry batch of mail! One of
them, dated the previous July 16, was from an elderly aunt who complained
once again about her troubles, including her bouts of rheumatism, and reminded me in particular to give daily thought to the task of bringing those poor
"savage Laplanders" into the way of "the Truth." The other letter, more
recent and much briefer, was a final notice from the revenue office of the Sixth
Arrondissement in Paris, requesting that I be so good as to remit the taxes I
owed to the most convenient revenue office, and at the earliest possible moment, or risk incurring the full penalties under the Law. . . .

Everyone in Etah was healthy. Not one invalid, not even a tooth to be
pulled. . . . Poor Doctor B——! In the Eskimos' somewhat simple view of the
matter, a nakorsaqssuaq's* fame depended less on his skill in curing sick
people than on his luck in finding any to treat. It was a terrible job. . . . He
had not only to find people who were already sick but also to discover which
ones were about to fall sick. Because nothing worse could befall a nakorsaq
than that someone should die several days after he had passed by.

"Takkuut! Look!" Nukapianguaq whispered to me. "A nakorsaq frozen

*Suaq means "great," therefore nakorsaqssuaq means "the great doctor."

stiff! It hurts to see him like that—so thin, with no work to do. It almost makes me want to get sick just to make him happy."

Worn out by his hard trip, Doctor B——lay down to sleep for several hours. The Eskimos discussed him anxiously, though not without smiling a little:

"Do you think he's sick? Will we have to take care of him?"

No. Very pale and dignified, he emerged presently from the igloo. He had just been told that no one was sick.

"It doesn't matter."

And with his stethoscope around his neck, carrying his towel and instruments, he went off to examine the six resident families of the area. After some vague conversation in each igloo, the Eskimos unfailingly asked him for aspirin. Easy to take, and potent, this universal pill represented to them the full range of possible therapy. B——really had no luck.

"Impossible," he answered wearily every time, in his broken Eskimo. "Impossible. I have only forty tablets to last all of you five months. Orders from above."[23]

The Eskimos would ask him to repeat what he had said, and they looked at B——with round eyes and incredulous smiles.

"What!" they would say. "Four hundred miles of dreadful trails, in the lowest temperatures of the whole year, just for forty tiny little tablets!"

After that, how was one to explain or extol qallunaat seriousness and logic?

"Ajorpoq! . . . There's obviously nothing to be done!"

12

MY EXPERIENCE ALONE AT QEQERTARAQ

On Monday, April 2, after the doctor came, our three sledges finally left Etah at about four in the afternoon.

The weather was calm. At the far end of the fjord, behind the icebergs to the west, a hazy, red sun was setting in a sky striped with tawny wisps of cloud.

"A long time ago, someone would have looked at that sky and said either a man was dead or he had a good chance of dying," Kutsikitsoq remarked casually, giving fresh proof of his knack for the timely comment.

It was hard to believe that only two nights before, a storm had been raging over this countryside. The silence was extraordinary.

Because the ice field had been swept clear of snow, our sledges made rapid progress.

Off Taserartalik, *qilavik:* the sea—real open sea. We kept as close to the coast as possible so that we could follow along the ice foot, the ledge of sea ice fringing the coast which does not melt until July or August.[24] We advanced single file along the ledge of ice because it was barely six feet wide. To our right, a wall of rock. To our left, hostile, black water, strewn with chunks of ice. We could hear the waves booming under us, feel the water lapping under our feet. We proceeded with the greatest caution, keeping a good distance between the sledges so that the bridge of ice supporting us would not suddenly give way under the weight of our loads and the hammering of our footsteps. Each driver held onto his *napariaq*. We had to guide the sledges between stones that had fallen down from the mountain onto the narrow coastal route. This was my first encounter with an ice foot. I guided my dogs more with my voice than with my whip. My sledge was in the middle; Kutsikitsoq was in the lead; Qaaqqutsiaq was bringing up the rear. I had left the two women behind in Etah to prepare new harnesses. To walk and slide along this "sidewalk" called for skill and a quick eye. The dogs, squeezed together because there was so little room, were nervous. They kept stopping. Their harnesses got tangled up. At one crucial moment, I remembered a story Qaaqqutsiaq had recently told me—it is always at such times that one remembers such things. He was on an English expedition; the ice foot had broken under his sledge, which was loaded with pemmican, provisions, and ammunition. He hardly had time to whip out his knife and cut the team's leashes before his cargo slid into the sea. His dogs managed to flounder through the water to shore, but his sledge sank like a stone.

I saw the tip of the small island of Littleton, famous in Polar history for having served as "postbox" for many Arctic expeditions, starting with Kane's in 1853, and famous also among the Eskimos because once it was frequented by sea elephants, who gathered there to sleep in peace. Since prior to 1863 the Eskimos had no kayaks, they used ice floes as rafts to go out and harpoon them. . . . Qaatanguarssuaq . . . Qaqordleq . . . the coast and its deep bays slid by us. In the distance, the dark promontory of Qaarsorsuaq. . . . We were about to move around Cape Olsen when Kutsikitsoq gestured wildly at me and stopped his dogs:

"Paaralugo! Paaralugo! Aaveq! Watch out! A walrus!"

Qaaqqutsiaq halted too. With some difficulty we quieted our dogs so as not to awaken the animal. Then, in a nasal, somewhat sarcastic voice, Qaaqqutsiaq exclaimed: "Ajornara! It's useless because of the wind."

Kutsikitsoq agreed. The animal was within our range, but there was no point in firing at it because, wounded or killed, it would be carried out to sea by the wind. We went on, and in the very early morning arrived at Cairn Point, where our first depot of provisions would be located. We set it up securely on a rock under slabs of stone which would protect it from possible incursions by bears and foxes. Then we slept for six hours. The next day, the Eskimos would be returning to Etah for the second load. (They brought it up to the same site without difficulties; it would take another eighteen days before the whole cache was moved to Uunartoq, or Rensselaer Bay.)

En route to this point, I had noticed in the distance three valleys lying between Littleton Island and Cape Hatherton. One of them was quite wide and might, I thought, make a good work area: large sandstone plateaus fringed with thick scree slopes, a narrow coastal plain, two frozen torrents leading to the ice cap some eight miles distant. I immediately headed toward one of these valleys and a group of small islands—a lowland area called Qeqertaraq. Here, on the shore of one of the islands, which was linked to the coast by a narrow strip of ice, I decided to set up my base.

I would be staying alone in this great setting of rock, snow, and ice for about a week. Having returned to Etah, the Eskimos would be making sure that we had sufficient food for the dogs by hunting in the now open water to the west of the Etah fjord, as I had decided during the storm. On our way up we had passed this sea: it is the northern part of the large polynya, or area of open water, called North Water. This vast stretch of free water off Pond Inlet remains unfrozen, for various hydrographic reasons, even during the most severe winters. Beyond this polynya, still farther north, lies the ice field which extends all the way to the Pole; to the south of the polynya lies the Baffin Bay ice field. As we were continuing on our way in the sledges, I had hesitated over a first possible site but then, for geological reasons, had opted to go farther up. Once we reached Qeqertaraq, I looked the place over quickly and decided it was a good choice. The dogs lay down on the ice and we set about building my igloo—or, rather, illuliaq, a snow shelter, never used here as one's main dwelling. We intended to construct it on solid ground a few feet in from the frozen sea and facing the mountain and the glacier, so that the rocks would protect it from the west wind. Energetic as always, Qaaqqutsiaq tested the snow on the beach with his harpoon. Not too soft, not too hard. Naammappoq! Just right! A few yards off to one side, he opened a quarry from which we would saw blocks of ice. Then, retracing his steps to where the illuliaq would be built, he outlined its circumference with one large sweep of his knife. We could now begin work. Taking turns, Kutsikitsoq and I cut out about fifty rectangular slabs of ice in twenty minutes. After beveling the upper surface, Qaaqqutsiaq, working on the inside, sawed the semicircular dome close in above his head. One more block, as large as possible, and the structure would be complete. With a single clean thrust of the knife, an entrance was opened at the base of the wall. This would be the door; there would be no katak. Half of the snow floor of the illuliaq nearest the entrance was cut into blocks and the blocks shoved outside to serve as a windbreak in front of the opening. Inside, the remaining half floor now formed a raised platform. Nimble as a monkey, Qaaqqutsiaq scampered up onto the roof, evened off the qingaq, the central ventilation hole, or nose, of the illuliaq, and built a small protective wall around it. Soft snow was stuffed into the joints yawning between the ice blocks, a pathway was made around the base of the illuliaq, and the job was done. We could be confident that within a few hours the whole structure would have frozen over and become firmly established for many days.

Next, the inside had to be arranged. The illeq took up the back half of the

Building an igloo. Drawing by Ivalu. Qeqertaq, November 1950. (*Private collection*)

illuliaq and stood a foot and a half high. Since it was a block of snow, for insulation two sealskins were thrown over it, then a caribou skin and two blankets, and finally my sleeping bag. To the right of the door as one entered were my provisions and Primus stove; to the left, a supply of snow for water, a broad-bladed knife, a saw, and an ax. My storm lantern stood on a narrow ledge of snow. Lastly, stuck into the wall were the *tiluttut*—the wooden knife used to beat the snow off one's clothes on coming back to the igloo—and some long needles (used for cleaning the clogged stove) on which gloves or handkerchiefs could be hung to dry. My rifle leaned by the entrance, which would be closed off by a large block of snow.

In a few moments I would be sending Qaaqqutsiaq and Kutsikitsoq back to Etah. My dogs would be of no use to me here—I would get around on foot —and I had given all but one to the two men. After a last cup of tea together, we shook hands. A whip cracked; the dogs yelped. Sitting on a jerrycan at the edge of the ice field, I watched rather stupidly as they grew smaller in the distance. The cold gradually penetrated my clothing, and my mind, which had been filled with doubts and forebodings, became calm again.

How relaxed—my God, how peaceful and relaxed I felt! I was quit of the weight of those people who watched every move I made. I can still visualize myself pushing boxes around, shifting a can to the right only to replace it on the left, checking and tightening the laces of my kamiks a dozen times over, chewing on a piece of frozen meat. There was not one sound around me. Not the slightest echo. I noticed that the air seemed to have no volume. At that moment I became fully aware of my situation. I had achieved what I had longed for for years, what some people would envy me: total isolation in the Ice Age. Having shared Eskimo life as part of a group, I was about to attempt a new experience —living that life alone.

What had driven me to do this? My Scottish-Norman ancestry perhaps, my attraction to deserts, to vast spaces, rugged, virgin spaces, a constant personal need for silence and solitude, a desire for a more rigorous way of life? But I want to eschew any hint of affectation. The hunter in the North, for whom fear and courage are interallied, would smile if one talked to him about heroism. (And in what language? There is no word for heroism in Eskimo.) The one effort I had to make in relation to myself was to adapt: to the cold and to food that was increasingly limited to the native diet; to train myself in certain techniques—handling dogs and sledges, orienting myself in fog and in the four-month-long darkness of winter, hunting, predicting the weather, etc. In my view, effort and risk are not justified unless accompanied by meaningful work; I was drawn to the idea of "exploration" only insofar as it served and supported my research. André Malraux put it correctly: "Risk alone does not qualify something as an adventure." In this connection, I remembered the question an eminent French geologist, my teacher and friend Conrad Kilian, had asked when I returned from one of my trips to the Sahara. I was telling him about my various troubles there—heat, thirst, exhausted camels, complaining natives—and he said: "Good enough, good enough, we've all been through that. Now, tell me, what have you got to report to us?"

A moment ago, I alluded to the wish to commune with oneself. But in such precarious living conditions as obtain in the Arctic, is this actually possible? When one is alone in this pitiless country, the manifold practical tasks one is required to perform make true reflection impossible. I was stunned by stories my friend Gontran de Poncins told me about Père Henry of Pelly Bay.

Père Henry, the first Catholic missionary to go to Pelly Bay, in the central Canadian Arctic, was a Breton monk. His ascetic ideal led him to live for a long time not in a snow igloo, which can be relatively warm: −12°C or 10.4°F, but in a "rough ice cave which the Eskimos had hollowed out on the side of a hill in order to preserve the seals caught during the summer. . . . Because the earth was frozen to a depth of more than one hundred feet, the cold it exuded was so intense that one could hardly bear to touch one's hand to the ground."[25]

This manifestation of faith on the part of a missionary in the Arctic is exceptional—I would say even unique. I well know how the mind must attend to pedestrian matters and how restrictive such preoccupations become—and how vitally necessary they are. Woe to the man who is inattentive, who miscalculates his ration of oil and finds himself alone in his tent on the ice field with an empty Primus—in −50°C (−58°F) weather. The act of reflection demands a measure of security to function freely; one could even say, taking the anchorite as an example, that mysticism is linked to the sun. However severe the Syrian winter may be, I find it hard to conceive of Simeon Stylites living in the Arctic as he did near Aleppo. Seated atop a column seventy-five feet high, on a twelve-foot-square pedestal, Saint Simeon lived for forty years without once coming down; his only clothing was an animal skin, which he wore in winter and when it rained; once a day, a disciple hoisted a basket of food up to him by a rope.

I had been walking along the ice field for a little while, mechanically tracing large lines in the snow with my knife. The igloo, my dog Caporal, and I were becoming as one in that extraordinary silence. Slowly the cold began to penetrate my body. By now I would have welcomed the slightest noise as a blessing. It was growing late and dark. I crawled back into my shelter and carefully closed off the entrance with a block of snow. I lighted the lamp. In its yellow light, my refuge looked white, clean, and anonymous. A few drops of oil, the scratch of a match, and the heater, that daily temptation, began to purr. As the surface of the lusterless walls warmed, they began to sparkle. In a few moments, I changed from a −35°C (−31°F) outside temperature to −5°C (23°F) inside, and the grateful warmth continued to rise. Had it not been for whiffs of oil, I would gladly have given in to the gentle torpor it induced, but yet one more effort had to be made. I must eat! A saucepan must be readied; snow must be whisked about in it as it melted so that it would not smell; some frozen seal must be chopped with the ax. In the midst of these chores, I paused to savor a slice of frozen raw salmon as it melted in my mouth.

A pinch of tea, a little powdered milk, and a portion of seal sufficed for my dinner that evening. In one spot, the roof began to melt. I took a handful of snow and slapped it over the little drop, which instantly froze. The ceiling was spotted now with different colors—patches of dull green-gray and pitted, porous white. I wound my alarm clock; its steady, friendly tick-tock helped make my surroundings seem intimate. Sitting on the illeq, I took off my nanu, made of rough bearskin which scratched my thighs, then my qulitsaq; I slid my double sealskin boots into my sleeping bag, taking care first to remove the summer grass—gathered on the slopes of Siorapaluk—from between the two soles so that it could dry. The Primus sat within reach, with its ration of matches; my rifle was also at hand. Propped against the wall, I wrote briefly in my journal. I looked at my watch and then the alarm clock, comparing the times. It was ten-thirty: one day was over. I buried myself naked in my double sleeping bag, curled up while I waited for the air inside to grow warm from contact with my body. As I tried to fall asleep, I heard the walls crack from the freezing cold, the wind prowl around the illuliaq, and my dog outside scrape against the wall and growl as he moved about. The cold penetrated from everywhere—down through the qingaq, up through the ground, in through the walls. The ice field made long grinding sounds as it swelled under the thrust of the tide and the lips of its crevasses rubbed together; the sound was "the weeping of those who live beneath the earth," Kutsikitsoq had told me. I struck a match to make sure I had not forgotten to mark off the day on my paperbound calendar. One such lapse could have drastic consequences. For two or three minutes, I mentally reconstructed everything I had done. "No . . . oh, yes, I have already crossed out the date. Yes, of course, now I remember. I was sitting in that position when I crossed out the date." I hid my head in my sleeping bag and hugged myself more tightly, having carefully blocked every possible leak. The cold covered me like a cloak.

In the early morning, the light filtered by the igloo walls was soft and milky. Stalactites formed by drops of steam frozen in place hung from the ceiling, which was stained with black streaks. In the daylight, I saw that I had aged twenty years. My hair and eyebrows were white with frost, my nose was red, and my skin was soft and dirty. Automatically I looked at the alarm clock. No point: the hands had stopped at ten minutes past midnight. Frozen, no doubt. I looked up. Through the hole of the qingaq I caught a glimpse of sunny, blue sky. Here inside was death; life was outside, in action and movement.

I shook myself. Shook the Primus, too, before lighting it, until the frozen oil began to change into a white slush. Three interminable minutes dragged by before the heater started to purr again. I got quickly out of the warm sleeping bag and kneaded and softened my boots and my pants, which had become damp from contact with my body the evening before and during the night had frozen. Shivering, I got dressed in leather that felt old already, and I crawled outside. I patted Caporal and he growled with pleasure. A new day was beginning.

My intention was to improvise a small station for meteorological observation (of temperature, wind directions, and atmospheric pressure) which, within the limits of the possible, would continue to function for as long as I was here. I took up my pack and off I went. The weather was fine. The crystalline snow crackled underfoot. As I strode along, I felt my muscles relax and my lungs expand; after the long, dark days of winter, my whole body came awake and quivered in the light. That afternoon, pencil and map board in hand, I walked from one knoll to the next. As I went, I chatted and debated with myself—sometimes out loud—over Lauge Koch's very summary map of the coast, which I was relying on for some guidance. I stopped often to take sights with my compass or along my rifle, to make a sketch, or to read and verify altitudes on my aneroid barometer.[26]

What pleasure is there in drawing up a map? Every topographer knows the answer. At the end of a survey trip, you feel real satisfaction to see that the essential features of a landscape that the day before was unknown or misunderstood have been organized and recorded on paper: "This stream . . . this knoll . . . opposite that rise. This island is too far north. . . ." And you erase and you sketch it again.

During this period I covered seven to ten miles a day, sometimes more. I walked over gravelly rocks. Here "nothing attracts you and yet everything holds you." Is it because this harsh country can change with such unpredictable suddenness—one moment so hostile, so friendly the next?

Professional training led me to pursue my familiar demons: I noted the size and polish of rocks within a given area, and the number of cracks they exhibited; the volume and nature of torrential alluvial deposits from the farthest point downstream to the midpoint, thalweg by thalweg; also, the heaps of talus—their shape, cut, internal structure. In snowy landscapes like this one, color is dazzling. For a while, I let myself register the tiered planes, the cubist visual effects created by the frozen light, until gradually my eye sharpened. The massive, bare reliefs asserted themselves, and I tried to grasp the configuration as a whole. Balances and relationships emerged. I observed cuestas and plateaus. In geometric lines, straight and angled, and with the eye of a cubist, I reconstructed the landscape—first in my head, then on my sketch pad; a landscape was becoming a real place. The joys and that "little feeling" of Cézanne's come into play for the geographer also. My eye, less interiorly directed, was constantly verifying Delacroix's great observation: "There are no parallels in nature." I tried to account for the rounded contours of the reliefs, and for faults and fissures. I tried to identify the effects of this or that climatic period, to determine what dated to the postglacial erosion eight thousand years ago and what dated back even earlier; what effect frost, wind, running water, névés, and snow had had after the plateau thawed. During the months spent in Siorapaluk I had patiently taken such geographical measurements area by area, either applying precise indices or inventing ways of observing geodynamic processes. The question was, when this geomorphological reasoning was applied to a much wider terrain—to one as vast as these enormous Inglefield plateaus—would my overpunctilious measurements prove to be justified? And so I went on calculating, visualizing things in my mind. . . . The jagged outline of some rocks caused by icy winds made me stop short; I took out my notebook and jotted down the detail. And so I continued to measure, to record, to calculate, to analyze—in a word, to draw a map. . . .

The dog was always at my heels. I liked his reddish brown fur. I had deliberately chosen Caporal when, in September, a good bitch produced a litter of eight pups for me. He was the only one that lived, which was one more reason why as the weeks passed with all their ups and downs, Caporal and I had become close companions.

Now, he followed me on my daily treks. When I stopped, he stopped. He would burrow into the snow, bury himself, and go to sleep. After a moment he would lift his little pointed head, and his caramel-colored eyes would study me mildly: "Now we are going on . . . ?" If I made the slightest move, he would leap up joyously and rush down the slope, helping. Caporal was happy: he ran through the snow, "exploring" to his heart's content.

The days went by. The sun was now rising three fingers above the horizon. I was caught up in the routine of work and preoccupied by the harshness of life in the open, now that I was coping with it entirely on my own. Like some worried farmer, I kept sniffing the air for clues to the weather. This land was mine alone: at sunrise, in the still, frozen air, I rejoiced in the freshness of the steaming earth and the fleecy mist that rose from cracks in the ice field. The smallest noises were eloquent. A dull thud? A rock had broken loose and fallen from the cliff. A dry crunch? Segments of the ice field were grinding against each other under the multiple pressures of the currents. A low, muffled echo? A section of snow had slid down some slope. A patch of shining névé? Better skirt it, because there the snow was soft. Black ice? Avoid that, too, for it would give way under me. White ice? Good, thick; trust it. By now, I was hearing the call of the snow bunting and the sinister croak of the tulugaq, the crow. Soon the qarsaaq, the duck, would be uttering its strident squawks. A little later, I would hear the throbbing whistle of the taatseraaq, the gull, the piercing cry of the gyrfalcon, and the nasal call of the tern.[27] The white-fronted goose and the barnacle goose would be cackling along the coast. I wandered from peak to peak in loving pursuit of partridges. The air hummed. Spring was nearly here. Nature was tumultuously "setting to work."

The slopes were still covered with snow, of course. But already spots of uncertain color could be seen here and there. The worn snow was spoiling. On all sides a kind of leprosy was nibbling away at it. At the edges, and where it was thickest, black gutters were being hollowed out on the south side of the largest rocks. In this part of the world, more than any place else, spring is a light-filled renewal, a metamorphosis. The scene can change completely from one week to the next. The sheet of ice on the rocks still made them shine in the sunlight, but the ice was melting slowly and trickling down in thin rivulets.

Only a little longer and the movement of water in streams and thousands of lakes would restore to the landscape the perspective, the contrast, the poetry it had lost in the pervading semidarkness of winter. The light of spring here is diaphanous and spangled. Who knows how to reproduce it for us? The Arctic has yet to find its painter.

This spring was particularly surprising to me in that I could detect no smells in the air—not the whiff of a scent heralding the coming season. Yet under the film of snow, many flowers were preparing to come to life again: the hersperis; the dryas and the *niviarsiaq* or willow herb *(Epilobium angustifolium);* the saxifrages with their mauve blossoms which huddle together as if in self-protection; the campions with their purple corollas and leaves; the drabas and cochlearia and the tiny phanerogams; the dwarf willows, which trail over the ground; and even the wretched lichen, woolly and black when gripping the face of rocks, rust-colored and pustular when tucked in their fissures, white and yellow and stringy when lying loose on the ground. Long, coarse, anemic grass was having its first taste of water in clumps of muddy turf. In hollows here and there, nature was skillfully coloring a few chosen clusters with the rarest tones—a profusion of fiery brown, steel blue, and yellow green. In a few weeks even the most timid flowers would unfold at last. A world of color would open to the sun: the violent red of poppies, the golden buds of buttercups, the white corollas of daisies, beds of green moss pricked with white. Then the season would pass and the tundra, swollen by the heat, would turn a uniform tawny rust against a steely background. And all the while, out in the choppy sea, icebergs freed by the sun would continue their majestic march southward.

Thus I daydreamed. But it was still only April. *Aqqajuersivia:* the sun is hot. The animals around me were certainly coming to life. Partridges emerged from their holes and cocked a startled, blank eye at the vast expanses of white. The snow tunnels appropriated by the hares during the long winter were melting and gaping wide open. The beach was densely imprinted with the tracks of early-migrating birds and vacationing foxes. At any moment, hopping from rock to rock, the cheerful *qupannaaq*—snow bunting—would begin his chirping. One morning I had seen three white hares running and capering about on a talus, drunk with warmth and light.

How tempted I was to abandon myself to these ephemeral and luxuriant hours, to these first days of spring!

But these moments soon passed. One day, to the south, the sky became leaden and low again. A southeast wind swept over the edge of the cliffs. These were bad signs. In the direction of Littleton Island, I caught a glimpse of open sea. Over an area of some twelve square miles the ice field had broken up; dislodged floes had drifted off into the vast North Water. And I had sent Kutsikitsoq and Qaaqqutsiaq to hunt there! I should have been more cautious. All morning long, I worked in a small deserted bay called Life Bay Cove, where the survivors of the famous ship, the *Polaris*—Captain Sidney Budington, Dr.

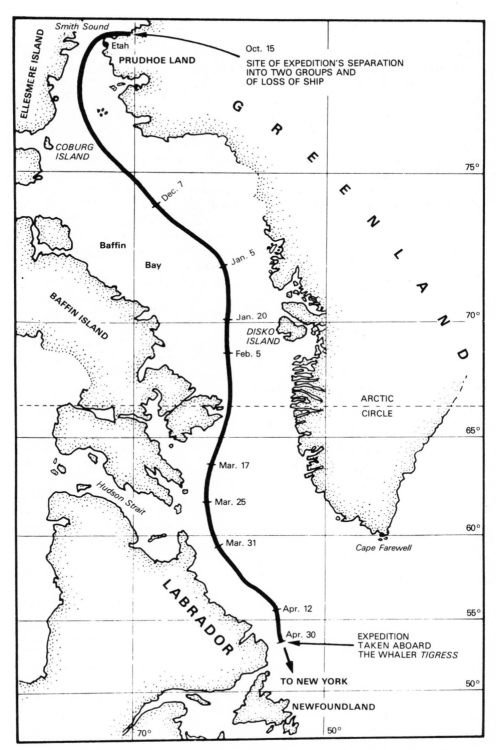

MAP 7. Drift of a Shipwrecked Group from the Polaris Expedition

The loss of the *Polaris* off Etah, October 15, 1872, and the separation of the expedition into two groups. (*From* The Narrative of the North Pole Expedition Polaris)

Emil Bessels, First Mate H. L. Chester, and others—spent the winter of 1872. At the same time, nineteen other members of the expedition (including the south Greenland Eskimo family of the famous Hans Hendrick, who was to save the shipwrecked survivors by dint of building snow igloos, catching two bears and many seals, and devising various technical contrivances) were marooned on an ice floe some four miles in circumference. On October 15, 1872, at the very beginning of the Polar night, the ice floe began to move, and thus commenced the most dramatic drift in the history of Polar adventure. It lasted for thirteen hundred miles, in the course of which a baby—Greenlander, female—was safely delivered. Finally, the group neared the coast of Labrador, where, on April 26, 1873, they were rescued by the *Tigress*. (With the permission of the Danish government, I named the main river in this area Polaris River, in honor of the memory of my brave predecessor, the American Charles Francis Hall.)[28]

Now, almost a century after those events, in Life Bay Cove,[29] I was examining an iron bar and a machine axle from a historic pile of iron objects that I had uncovered beneath the snow, when abruptly the weather began to change.

I was two hours' walk from my illuliaq. I absolutely had to get back to it. I had been walking for fifteen minutes when the gust became a gale and the gale became a storm. I could not see clearly or even get my bearings. The best I could do was to follow the shoreline, groping my way from stone to stone.

Under me the ice field, lifted by the waves, heaved in large undulations; I was surrounded by the sound of grinding ice. The ice field was breaking up. In places it was already working loose from the shore. I kept raising my gloved hand to my face, to protect it from the wind. The skin on my cheekbones and chin and above my eyebrows was stretching and cracking like old leather. Every twenty yards or so I had to turn around to catch my breath and keep my face from freezing. Howling by fits and starts, the wind began to sound like a human voice. I got lost among the hummocks. That made me anxious and I tried to make my way back to an earlier point of reference. I couldn't find it. Under my hood, sweat was running down my scalp. For a moment I was frightened. I managed to find another landmark and methodically checked the area around it in all directions. But it was by pure chance, thanks to a momentary clearing of sky, that I finally recognized my route. I sat down, with my back to the wind, uncertain whether I should go on, because the storm had again become so terrifying. What if I built myself a shelter right here? I thought.

But when I tested the snow with the handle of my geologist's knife, it was no good. Not thick enough for building an illuliaq. I had a moment's hesitation, then I pushed ahead. It was a good thing I did. The storm was to last two days without letup. With no fuel or provisions, I would have paid dearly for a brief failure of will. Keeping a close eye on my watch, wary of overshooting my shelter, I moved on, leaning into the wind; often I wheeled around to walk backward. Every step was an effort. Caporal kept bumping into my legs. I estimated that I was still ten minutes away from my shelter when suddenly I had the good luck to come upon a fresh, frozen dog turd. A few yards more, and I crept into my shell of snow, dazed and exhausted.

All that night and the next day the wind beat down violently on my shelter. The gusts seemed to smash against the wall. Exasperated by the noise, I stuffed one of my gloves into the qingaq.

The second morning I did try to go out. My survey of Qeqertaraq was completed, in the main, but I wanted to clear up two or three doubtful points near the main valley, carefully record the height of the "stranded beaches,"[30] and collect fossil shells on the way. However, the wind was driving clouds of snow before it. The flakes clung to my eyes and nostrils. With the best will in the world, there was no way for me to accomplish anything worthwhile that day. In the warmth of the sun, the snow melted and soaked through the paper, which then stuck to the map board. The mark of my pencil strokes drowned as if I were writing on blotting paper. Had I persisted, the paper would have reverted to pulp. For all my efforts, my one accomplishment on this outing was to determine the altitude of two little beaches. I went back to the illuliaq, worn out. I threw myself on my bed and lay there, leafing through the yellowed pages of notes I had taken during the winter. Then, as I traced over my sketches with pencil, checked my past week's observations, and corrected my map, I began to realize how big a job remained to be done. How would I ever have enough time? The work I had wanted to do suddenly seemed out of all proportion to the way in which I had chosen to do it. Was it not ridiculous in the twentieth century for anyone to depend on arms and legs in making a topographical—and especially a geomorphological survey—of a country as vast and difficult to traverse as this? Within ten or twenty years a map of these immense plateaus would be drawn up on the basis of a photographic survey made from an airplane in a few hours, I had no doubt of it. The geomorphological map I was establishing, my notes on stranded beaches, my erosion measurements, the fossils I had collected, my firsthand observations, the papers accumulating daily in my bag, masked my sense of futility but did not erase it. Of course, one had always to take into account the factor of detailed observation: for the trudging naturalist (which is what a geographer essentially is), glued to the ground like an insect, is irreplaceable. And who would take my place here, measuring things, seeking explanations on the spot?

I spent some bad moments. When you are alone, your work can suddenly begin to look very unimportant. But I kept telling myself that the geology and geomorphology of the Arctic regions I was groping my way through, with their intense, dry, cold, were practically unknown. Reliable data would be very useful to both Eurasian and American paleographers. Besides, the correspondence I had had with American, Russian, and Danish experts before I set out—as well as my own training—had convinced me of this, or I would not have been here.

My spirits somewhat bolstered, I sat down and began to eat—with my fingers, taking something of everything, a little bit at a time. How fragile is the margin of civilization in each of us once we are no longer part of a group! My daily rituals I kept faithfully: before bed, I filled the Primus, put matches within reach, wrote the daily diary entry, crossed a day off the calendar. . . .

It was two in the morning and dark when I awoke. For several minutes I lay still, sensing an unusual tension about me. I listened. Wasn't someone moving outside? I felt uneasy and struggled partway out of the sleeping bag to have a look around. No, nothing unusual. I was about to cover up again when I heard Caporal barking outside somewhere, to the left. A mighty growl answered him. Then I heard heavy steps perhaps several yards from my frail wall of snow. A bear! I leaped up. I had to get out of my insecure lair at all costs. If the bear were attracted by the seal meat and so much as brushed my shelter with his tremendous paw, it would collapse like a house of cards. I was shivering—you get used to everything in the Arctic except the cold when you first get up—and pulled on my boots and nanu, which were already a little stiff. In two minutes, I was outside with my rifle and storm lantern. The wind was coming from the southwest, moist from passing over the North Water, and it stirred up eddies of snow. My lantern went out, but not before I had seen some enormous paw prints. It was a bear for sure. But where was he? I heard nothing but silence, yet it was a tense—an inhabited—silence. I held my finger on the trigger. I turned in every direction, but could see nothing. The only sounds were the whistling of the wind and the crunching of the ice field. I kept expecting something to tap me on the shoulder at any moment, like an old friend.

Suddenly, quite close to me, the dog barked again, and was answered by a growl which seemed to be moving away. I fired the rifle blind several times in the direction of that growl, aiming several feet above the ground to avoid hitting the dog. The shots were wasted, no doubt. I started to go after the bear, which was a foolish idea: in such weather I would accomplish nothing and had every chance of getting lost. I stopped myself, turned around. I went inside and turned up the Primus again. Half an hour later Caporal was back, wildly excited. His eyes were on fire. He yapped and, full of demonstrative affection, ran between my legs and licked my bare hand with his warm tongue. Relighting my lantern, I discovered that the bear, attracted by the smell of my walrus and seal meat—and probably drawn by curiosity, too—had circled the illuliaq until he blundered upon my young friend.

I lay down again, but could not fall asleep. I tossed and turned, pulled my head into the sleeping bag, and poked it out again. "Suppose he comes back? . . . maybe this time with one or two others?"

The most fantastic of Jules Verne's Captain Hatteras stories came to mind. Still in the grip of considerable tension, lying fully dressed in my sleeping bag, I began to eat. I ate seal, salmon, noodles, and I drank some tea. I was full, and toward dawn I dozed off. I learned subsequently that three days later an old male bear was killed by hunters crossing the sea off Anoritoq, ten miles from where I was. Who knows? Maybe it was "my" bear.

There followed two days of good weather and intense work, and then, on the morning of April 8, the weather once more turned bad and Caporal, who was again sleeping out of doors, was completely covered by snow. I settled down to read; I kept on turning the pages, but could not concentrate on what I was reading for a single moment. My mind kept wandering off . . . to Etah. Eventually, my provisions and oil would run out. I had to decide when to leave my lair if my partners did not come back soon. The day was gray and gloomy —one of the most threatening I had yet seen. One problem after another kept cropping up. It was so cold that I had retreated into my sleeping bag; barely fifteen minutes later, the Primus stopped. "Must be a bit of dust," I said to myself. "I'll have it going again in a second." I inserted a needle into the feed pipe but—a stroke of rare bad luck—the needle jammed and stuck. This was serious, and must be repaired at once. I got up and groped in my bag for a pair of pliers. I dismantled the Primus. In spite of my fur clothes, my whole body was freezing. I knelt, thinking to be more comfortable. The pliers fell from my numbed fingers. Grease spattered over my notes. I began to breathe heavily. A tiny adjustment was taking an infinite amount of time. The dry, peeling skin on my fingertips kept sticking to the metal. I had to stop repeatedly to warm my hands against the storm lantern.

Twenty minutes later, the reassembled Primus was purring away. The time had come to prepare dinner. I sat down and picked up a pot. My supply of snow had been used up! I put on a qulitsaq, and crawled through the "door," staggered in the wind, and returned with an armful of snow; I made several trips, taking care not to let the dog get in. If I were unmindful of that, he would eat up every scrap of my remaining provisions and even the seal and caribou skins, which he would tear to pieces. I washed the dishes from the day before; the smell of hot soup began to pervade the illuliaq. At last! I sat down, blew on my fingers, and spent a good ten minutes over my notes. But it was getting awfully warm! I pulled off one sweater, then another. A little cloud of steam was encircling me. Plip, plop. Drop by drop, my ceiling—my very shelter—was melting. I got up again, turned down the Primus, widened the qingaq with my knife, patted fresh snow over the wet joints in the wall. The temperature dropped rapidly. Again I pumped the Primus, taking care to keep the mantle sitting level, and filled the container, which had gone dry. And so the hours passed.

It was nine in the evening. My experiment in living alone was proving to be one continual struggle. Outside, the voice of the wind was hoarse and thick.

It was different from the prolonged whistling of the night before; this was a congested sound, a warning that a fresh storm was imminent. Indeed, almost immediately the wind began gusting and circling around my walls again.

The heaviest blasts shook the illuliaq to its very base. I could hear the muffled blows of crashing sea ice. Are they ever going to come? I wondered. I tried to remember what they looked like, some of their expressions, details of their faces—moles, wrinkles. I tried to dismiss the absurd thought that they had abandoned me. But after an hour, I was somehow convinced that they would not be back.

It was 6:00 P.M., April 8. Outside, there was a great hubbub: I heard Kutsikit-soq's loud, cheerful voice as he tied up his dogs, but the wind smothered his words. He called out again, but I purposely didn't answer. Natuk spoke quickly with her husband. They were too far away for me to understand them. Kutsikit-soq rushed to the illuliaq and smashed in the snow-block door with one blow of his fist:

"Qujanaq! So much the better!" he said to himself. "Sainang! Hello! I knew it was only a joke! Pissortut, obviously," he muttered, "you wouldn't be outside in weather like this. Qujanaq!"

I looked at him. His face, powdered with hoarfrost, was marked by frost-bite and in places was black.

"Natuk really thought you were dead. So did I . . . but only a little bit!"

Natuk, good woman that she was, hurried in. She tidied up the illuliaq, and we sat down on the snow sleeping platform. My two friends were extremely tired. They had traveled all night in order not to miss our rendezvous. While they ate the last of my provisions, they told me the news:

"Terrible . . . the storm at Etah. The igloo shook. And here? Everyone said the qallunaaq must have frozen to death. . . . Etah has the flu. They think that when he brought the mail from Upernavik, Inuteq must have infected Uummannaq.[31] We caught the flu from him in Uummannaq and carried it up here. At least, that's what the Inuit say. Ajorpoq! Ajorpoq! What a nuisance! . . .

"Nukapianguaq went back down south to his son Sakaeunnguaq, in Siorapaluk, to buy dogs. The hunting has been good. . . . But aside from ours, Etah has hardly any dogs left. And because they have no fat, some people keep warm by burning dried *issoq* from the walls.*

"Pissortut. Of course! Ready to be off again?" Kutsikitsoq exclaimed. "Angutit pissortut—aren't we men?"

Quickly I reported to them on my work and handed them the maps I had sketched. They trailed their thick fingers over the graph paper, following the contours of the shore. Intense concentration. No comments.

"We'll leave for Etah right away," I said, "to get the rest of the baggage. I'm afraid another storm is brewing. The pressure's very low." I showed them my barometer. "We'll leave Etah immediately, taking all three sledges, and go to the little cache we set up halfway—there's nothing left to eat here."

They had arrived only two hours before, yet with no fuss both Eskimos were willing to travel that awful route again, despite gusts of wind that were soon to turn into really bad weather. And so the three of us left on one sledge. The whip cracked, and I looked back, smiling a little sadly: I felt that shadow of regret one experiences when leaving something one knows one will never see again. While I was still able to see my illuliaq—Kutsikitsoq had staved in the dome before we left, in keeping with tradition—the days I had spent at Qeqertaraq were already taking their place in my memory among the episodes in my life which I was sure I would look back on with pleasure.

We made part of the return trip by taking a shortcut over the mountain. We crossed frozen torrents the position and dimensions of which I duly noted one by one—and with what effort! The dogs were keyed up and pulled well, and we struggled to make progress through that powdery snow. I doubt that it would have been possible to follow such a bad route in a blizzard without an Eskimo who knew the country. There were outcropping rocks everywhere. The sledge scraped over the stones like a low-slung cart. We had to descend a talus 450 feet high that sloped at an angle of nearly thirty degrees. I would much rather have tumbled down into the fjord. Surrounded by whirlwinds of snow, we pushed on the napariaq, freed the leashes, which kept getting stuck between rocks, restrained the dogs one by one when they had to travel behind us, and braced heavy stones that jutted out above our heads so that they would not work loose and carry everything, us included, down to the foot of the mountain. At last we reached the ice field. All the

---

Issoq is peat cut into slabs by Eskimos living in the few districts where it has been forming over the last five or six thousand years. A wall made of peat is raised alongside the walls of an old igloo built of juxtaposed stone and peat.

snow had been blown away: it was like a skating rink, with blue glints and tiny iridescent white veins. The dogs' claws could not get a grip on the bare ice, and they were knocked down by the northeasterly wind. They would roll over, jump up, and pushed or pulled by the skidding sledge, start off again, jigging up and down restively as if the icy snow were matting their fur. To prevent the sledge's being upset also, we took turns riding on it, but were careful not to weigh it down too much.

After quite a few adventures of this sort, we arrived in Etah on the morning of the ninth, congealed but cheerful.

Pissortut Inuit!

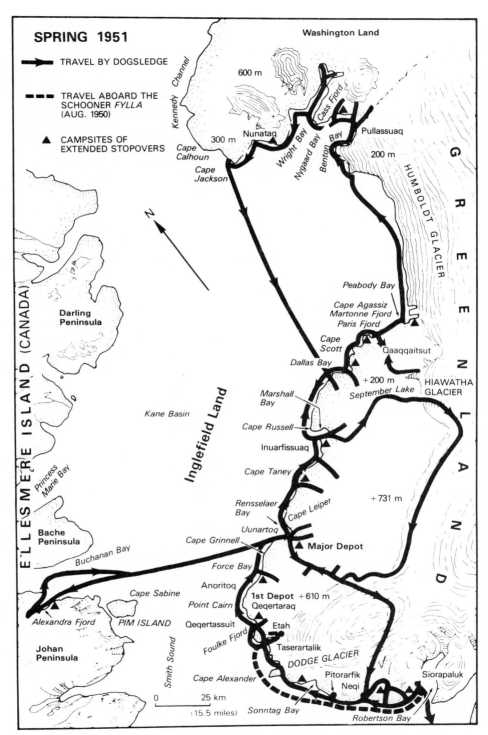

MAP 8. Itinerary of Our Spring Expedition

13

TOWARD THE
BAY OF THE
GREAT MASSACRE

Several days later, we left for the north again, this time with no plan to return to Etah. I stopped again at Foulke Fjord, where the American astronomer August Sonntag is buried. Sonntag was part of the mid-nineteenth-century American expeditions of Elisha Kent Kane and Isaac Hayes, and he died here in tragic circumstances—some say murdered by Olipaluk's grandfather.

The Eskimo who accompanied me looked at me curiously. The foggy day and the small, human dimensions of the bay lent a sadness to the setting. The grave was marked by a simple stone slab stuck upright among the stones near the beach, and the brief inscription was still quite legible:

AUGUST SONNTAG
died
December 1860
aged 28 years

Off Qilavik, the ice foot we had traveled along on April 2 had broken up. We advanced into the snow-covered valley of Taserartalik and climbed up onto the plateau, doubling and then tripling the teams. Since my experience in living alone, Kutsikitsoq had been unusually amenable. Perhaps he considered that I had passed some kind of a test? On the steepest slopes, he pushed his enormous load with such zest that he strained a nerve in his left leg—dear Kutsikitsoq, excess in everything! We stopped. Out in the open, I pulled his boot off, massaged his leg with a counterirritant, and bandaged it. He submitted to this like a child. I had him lie down on his sledge, and there he stayed immobilized, under the ironic glances of his wife ("Why not tie me down?" he said jokingly), while we pulled him to our depot at Cairn Point. We did not reach it until April 18, for our progress was slow, very slow. I kept stopping to work on my maps, record observations, collect samples of rocks, shingle,

301

and gravel, take sightings, and compute altitudes. We pitched camp at either the mouth or the upper end of the main valleys, staying as long as necessary for the work.[32]

To celebrate our arrival at Cairn Point, we opened our few cans of vegetables. We spent the evening drinking tea together and I talked on and on about nuna, "the earth," the homeland, my homeland: its light, its landscape, what its mountains look like, how its waters always run freely, about its birds, its people, and their way of life and language. Hesitantly, but with expectant delight, the Eskimos one by one asked me to speak in French. "To us it sounds like music," they said. Our good humor expanded, and they asked me to sing. They knew only two kinds of sounds: their traditional *ajaja* (usually consisting of a pentatonic tessitura over melodic base lines that were pretty much the same throughout the entire Polar Eskimo group) and Lutheran hymns. "La Madelon" enchanted them; "La Claire Fontaine" moved them; the "Marseillaise," "Le Chant du Départ," and the "International" impressed them. Tino Rossi left them cold. I whistled passages from the overture to *Don Giovanni* for them, and to that they listened attentively. The Eskimos themselves never whistled. Several weeks later, they asked me to whistle the most intense passage in the overture again. The past winter, they had been indifferent to all classical music broadcast over the radio. Now, *Don Giovanni* made them uneasy. Was it because I had given them some idea of what the drama was about by describing how the Commendatore reappears as a statue seeking justice? Then they asked for "La Madelon" again. The only musical instruments brought into the country until then had been the accordion and the harmonium. No violin, no piano. I am sure that the flute would have moved them profoundly, in particular the Andean flute.

That evening, for the first time, the sun did not set. One after another, we glued our eyes to the small window in the tent: a cold red ball hung low on the misty western horizon.

The next day, I suggested to Qaaqqutsiaq that he take the best dogs from our three teams and move our depot from Cairn Point north to Uunartoq—a distance of about twenty-two miles—in as many trips as necessary. As things turned out, however, he could not take this job on until we reached Force Bay. All the way up to Anoritoq the jumble of ice was to prove particularly bad, and we needed all three sledges to transport our supplies over that short but arduous stretch. We proceeded more slowly than usual and kept close together so that we could help each other.

Before leaving Cairn Point, I used it as a base for topographical treks together with Kutsikitsoq. Our system was this: Natuk stayed behind in the tent to see to the food, while Kutsikitsoq and I set off along the coast in the morning. In the case of each major ravine, I would climb two miles inland to the plateau by myself and walk along it, roughly parallel to the coast, while Kutsikitsoq, who had stayed behind on the ice bank with his sledge, proceeded up the coast.

He would turn into the first snowy valley he came to and drive the dogs up to where I was. If it was a big valley, we would follow it together to a depth of three or four miles. There were two advantages to this: I could orient the surface cartography along a natural axis, the valley; and I could record the dimension of the rise because we almost always covered the altimetric distance —the height above sea level—within a given day.

Polar Eskimos cannot be overpraised as partners on expeditions such as mine. Trained in the methods of men like Peary and Lauge Koch, some of them —notably Qaaqqutsiaq—functioned as genuine assistants. On this expedition, we were quick to synchronize our movements at each stopping place, and my two companions became indispensable to me. For example: we would arrive at the observation point we had chosen; while I unharnessed the dogs, the Eskimo would lay out my surveyor's table, binoculars, compass, graph paper, clips, and eraser, and sharpen colored pencils as needed. Once the dogs were unharnessed, I would warm up my fingers in my pockets.

"Naammappoq! Everything's ready!"

I would start work, sometimes using the Eskimo's body to shield me from the wind. Presently, he would prepare a cup of scalding-hot tea while I took a few measurements and jotted down my notes. Once the survey was finished, I would hold the cup of tea in both hands to bring the blood back into my fingers. Qaaqqutsiaq or Kutsikitsoq would pack my equipment carefully, harness the dogs, and, while waiting for me, take a look at the map so that we could discuss it on the way, if necessary. He would answer my questions at length, telling me about the fauna and flora; the location of sea-peat deposits; the dates of the melting of the snow, of the torrents, of the ice field, the ice ledge for each of the stretches we covered. When we got back to camp, he would often want to consult our three companions to be sure that he had answered all my questions correctly.

On the afternoon of April 21 we arrived in Anoritoq, where we were joined again by Qaaqqutsiaq, who had completed his transportation job. The name Anoritoq means the place where the wind blows incessantly. So much for etymology, for this cape is known as one of the least windy places in the country, and in the summer the water here is wonderfully smooth and calm. We had no sooner arrived in the area, which had been uninhabited for decades, than Kutsikitsoq became very excited and told us about yet another of his family's great exploits. We were walking back and forth along the shore, looking for the site of the old camp. I saw what remained of the hut of the famous Dr. Cook—Tatsekuuk. He had set out from here on February 19, 1908, bound for Cape Svartevoeg (now Stallworthy) on Ellesmere Island, with eleven sledges, a hundred and five dogs, and nine Eskimos (including Pualuna), carrying four thousand pounds of provisions and other necessities for the trip across the Polar ocean, as well as two thousand pounds of walrus meat and fat, making three tons in all.

Suddenly Kutsikitsoq pointed to a triangular stone embedded in the frozen ground.

"You see this stone, which is shaped like a head," he said to me. "The

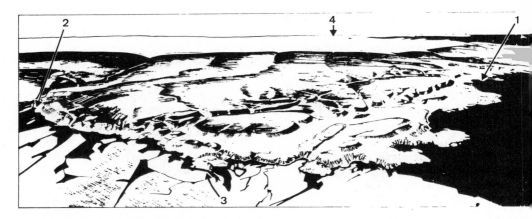

Inglefield Land: Qeqertaraq and Force bays. The glacier, or ice cap, is in the background; in the foreground is the fissured ice field of July. My camps at Qeqertassuit and Qeqertaraq (1) and Force Bay (2) were set up in these bays. The others were at Cape Inglefield, or Anoritoq (3), and Etah (4). (*From Malaurie*, Thèmes de recherche géomorphologique)

eyes? They're these two tiny slits; the mouth is lower down; then this little round hole, slippery like an utsuuq—a vagina—with hair even. Well, it's a woman, arnaq. Yes, it's a woman—and there's a long story about her."

The Legend of Anoritoq

"A long, long time ago, a very old woman lived here. Her name was Anoritoq. She had only one son, Angulligammak. Maybe he was too sensitive, maybe just clumsy—in any case, he became the scapegoat of the camp. Since he had never been hunting, one day the Inuit said they would take him. Off they went. Evening came. The hunters stopped for the night. But Angulligammak did not know how to go about sleeping outdoors. He asked the others. Making fun of him, one man said: 'All you do is take one leg out of your pants. Pissortut! You'll be asleep in no time.'

"Angulligammak followed this advice. But no sooner had he uncovered his leg than one of the hunters took up a harpoon and buried it in his rear end. The wretched boy leaped around a bit and then, without a sound, fell down dead. The next day, his companions returned to the camp, went bawling to his mother, and told her: 'Some Inuit came, and they killed your poor son. Aii! Aii! It's too bad, too bad. . . .'

" 'Aii! Aii! Aii!' Anoritoq wept. Between sobs, she suddenly shouted: 'At least bring me back a bear with a fetus if you find one! Aii! Aii! A very pregnant, very pregnant female! That fetus can be my son!'

" 'Angutit pissortut? Aren't we men?' the hunters answered, and they went off at once.

"After a while, they were lucky enough to find a pregnant female. They took out her fetus and carried it back alive to the camp to give to Anoritoq:

" 'Here, here's a little fetus that will make you a very nice son!'

"Anoritoq took it in her arms and rocked it and sang softly to it, as if it were a real baby.

"Soon her neighbors' children and the neighbors themselves named him Angulligammak, like Anoritoq's real son. They said to him: 'Come on, Angulligammak, we want to play with you!'

"And they amused themselves by playing at bear hunting and sticking him in the back with their little harpoons. But Angulligammak, like the true son of a bear, knew very well how to defend himself.

"As he grew older he began to go out hunting. If he killed an animal, he would bring it back to his 'mother.' But then it happened that for several days he caught nothing, nothing at all. He and Anoritoq began to die of hunger.

" 'If I get nothing again today,' he said to her one morning, 'I'll go to a settlement I know of and if I make no noise I will manage to steal a little meat.'

" 'Oh, dear, oh, dear! Be careful,' Anoritoq said to him. 'They would be quite capable of killing you and eating you. . . . And above all, be careful of your cousins.' (That was what she called dogs.)

"But each day he kept insisting until at last she let him go. With tears in her eyes, she gave him endless advice. As she was thinking things over, she hit upon a wonderful trick to protect him from danger. She colored one whole half of his body with lampblack and spread the word about in the area not to kill a bear of two colors because it was her son, her very dear son. . . .

"Alas! Alas! Angulligammak did not come back and one morning Anoritoq was told that 'over there, near a large rock, someone had killed a poor young bear of two colors. The hunters were very intrigued by it. . . . Some people were saying that it could very well be Anoritoq's son. Of course, the hunter had seen him only from one side!'

"When Anoritoq heard this she turned very, very pale. Mad with grief, she climbed onto the roof and began to sing loudly: 'No more bear, no more child, I must wait once more and call for a bear, a bear, a bear.'

"Since she refused to come down and kept on singing for a new bear she might adopt, in the end she turned to stone."

As he spoke these last words, Kutsikitsoq bowed before the stone with mock seriousness; he took one of my dry biscuits and some margarine and seal fat out of his pocket; he offered them to the stone, saying in a shrill voice: "Accept these presents, Anoritoq, and favor us in our bear hunting!"

He smeared the grease not only on her mouth, as was customary, but also over her whole body, not forgetting her utsuuq. Kutsikitsoq liked to show his independent turn of mind by continuing to offer the old ritual sacrifices. The rest of us approached the stone in turn, half serious, and each clumsily offered it his present—marmalade, a cigarette. . . .

Yes, Anoritoq, may you favor us!

The Sunday Service

April 22 was a Sunday. "The Sabbath!" Qaaqqutsiaq said to me jovially. This would be our first "day of rest" since setting out on the expedition. And what do you do for fun on a Sunday? The opposite of what you do every other day: we stayed in bed.

Come ten o'clock, I was tired of lying around. I rolled over and looked at Kutsikitsoq.

"Back in Qinnissut, aren't you something of an ajoqi, catechist? . . . Well, why don't you conduct a service for us this morning?"

First Kutsikitsoq had to be urged, then he left it up to the others: "The Inuit would have to want me to. I wouldn't say no."

Everyone was in favor, which obviously flattered him. While we were getting dressed, he went to a corner of the tent and prepared himself. He rummaged around in his suitcase and pulled out a thick book bound in thick black cloth and interleaved with dried flowers: a Bible in Eskimo, including prayers and songs, published by the Lutheran church. From a cardboard box he took out a white cap with a black band and visor.

"Kommunere!"* he said to me, as he put it on.

He had no white anorak, but he would make do without. We gathered around him. The seal meat and the chamber pot—here serving all purposes except the one for which it was designed—were pushed into a corner; the Primus was turned down. Then Kutsikitsoq began, in a beautifully grave, meditative voice:

"Sapaammi poorskip king. Sisamaanni . . . Qinuniarta tamatta! The fourth Sunday after Easter. . . . Let us all pray! Naalagaq, Gutip ataata! . . . Lord God, our Father!

"Maannali aallartitsisinnut aallalerpunga, arlassinnilla ima aperineqann-gilanga. In those days . . ."

After reading the New Testament scripture about the Holy Ghost, Kutsikitsoq offered a quick commentary. The meaning is indeed difficult, and he did not dwell on it overlong. When we asked him to go on, he took up his Bible again and leafed through it:

---

*The Danish title given a native of standing to whom the government assigns public functions that carry with them a measure of authority.

"Here's the Gospel I understand best. I can explain it to you if you like."
Very much at ease, he took up his book and read slowly:
" 'In those days, Jesus said to his disciples: Do not worry about what you will drink and what you will eat, nor about the clothes to cover your body. . . .' "
I looked at him a little uneasily.
" 'Is life not more than food, and the body more than clothing?' . . . You understand, Natuk? Life, eternal life, as the palasi[33] puts it so well. Of course, I can't talk the way he does," he remarked in passing, "but the idea is the same.
" 'Consider the birds of the sky,' " he continued, and he gestured broadly. " 'They do not sow, they do not reap, they do not gather anything in their store rooms. Your Heavenly Father feeds them! . . .'
"Now, that's true. That's the way it is for our birds, the appaliarsuit, the guillemots."
"Ieh, ieh," his audience assented, impressed. During the homily they sat with lowered heads, the better to concentrate on their devotions.
" 'Who is the one among you, yes, who is the one among you who, no matter how hard he tries, can add to his height by one cubit?' "
Everyone straightened up. Evidently that question had hit home. They looked at me. Those small men, the tallest of whom hardly reached as high as my chest, glanced at me and bowed their heads again.
"It's easy to grasp, I think," Kutsikitsoq remarked casually.
" 'And consider how the lilies of the field grow. . . .' "
"What are 'lilies of the field'?" Padloq asked timidly.
The ajoqi gave an adequate answer: "It's a flower, a pretty flower—just a flower. . . . 'I say to you that Solomon'—even Solomon," he said, stressing the syllables, "who was, as you know, a kungissuaq from the land of the Tuluit*—'in all his glory was never dressed like one of them.' "
Then Kutsikitsoq ended the parable. Calmly, like a real palasi, he said: "Don't get worried and don't say: Where will we find something to eat, something to drink, something to cover ourselves with? . . . That kind of worry is for the heathen."
The atmosphere was becoming a little heavy. Kutsikitsoq knew better than anyone else how low our provisions were. He cleared his throat.
"I know my brain is small, very small," Qaaqqutsiaq ventured shrewdly,

---

*Great king from the land of the English. *Tuluit* is a phonetic alteration of "Do you?" Possibly the Eskimos identified the English with the locution they heard constantly during expeditions (Do you, Tou you, Tulu. . . .) and formed the Eskimo-English word. The singular is *Tuluk;* the plural *Tuluit.* Long ago, Tuluit were known as *upernaagiit,* the men of the springtime (the whalers); the Norwegians were the *umiitormiut* (the great beards); the Americans were the *piulikormiut* (Peary's men); and the Danes were the *kunukormiut* (Knud Rasmussen's men). There was no name for the French, since I was the first Frenchman they had seen. Two whaling captains well known to the Eskimos of Thule in 1850 were called Alamisi (Adam Smith) and Ittupaluk (Nice Old Man).

"but I must be a heathen, as Christ says. When we arrived in Etah in April, if we hadn't hunted—well, the dogs would all be dead by now and maybe a few others as well."

"Ieh," Kutsikitsoq said, "but hunting isn't work, after all. Picking up a gun or harpoon and going after seal or bear isn't really work for an Inuk. . . . And anyway, it's Gutip, God, who puts them there, the puisi, ussuk, nanoq, aaveq, timmiat—the seals, great seals, bears, walruses, birds—all of them. They've got to be there in the first place or else you couldn't hunt them—right? Work is doing something for money, doing something for someone else, for a white man. Now, don't ask me any more questions. Like in our old legends, look at what lies beneath, look at the meaning. Don't go by the words, by every little detail."

Kutsikitsoq wiped his forehead. Everyone was silent, visibly impressed by the effort he had made and confounded by such wise arguments.

Spring Bay

We started out again that afternoon. The ice bank was beautifully smooth. Two days were spent studying Force Bay, our first long step since leaving Etah. There was little snow on the shore. During the night of the twenty-third, the weather, until then beautiful and calm, turned colder. The temperature fell from a daytime −10°C (14°F) to −17°C (1.4°F). In the morning our camp, which was on the beach, was smothered in fog. There were signs indicating seals—active allut that had recently been visited. But this was not the best area for them. "Uunartoq! Uunartoq!" I was told again and again. "That's really the only place where there are seals!" I had already sent Qaaqqutsiaq and Padloq on ahead to hunt in Uunartoq while we waited in Force Bay.

By pushing myself hard, I finished my work at Force Bay in the late afternoon of the twenty-fourth. I had a good collection of fossils[34]; I had made the usual surveys of stranded beaches and taken altimetric readings, from which a graph could be plotted of the speed at which the continent, once relieved of its burden of ice, has risen in the eight-thousand-year-long postglacial period.

After pausing to eat, Kutsikitsoq and I built a cairn on the right bank of the stream above our tent site. A message was placed beneath it. At five in the afternoon, we broke camp. Even though Qaaqqutsiaq had cleared a way through the piles of ice (in some passes he had had to use an ax), all night long we had terrible trouble making any progress. We kept running into extraordinary tangles of hummocks. Here, skill counted for more than brute strength. It was a miracle that the heavily loaded sledges did not break when, having been arduously hoisted to the top of six- or nine-foot-high walls of ice, they then plunged down the other side. (A sledge's pine thwarts and two oak stanchions are attached by sealskin thongs tied fairly loosely so that the framework is very flexible; no nails are used to hold it together.) At one point, as we came out of a narrow passage where the dogs had got all tangled up and were jostling one another as they pulled, the waving plumes of their upraised tails blocked our view, and all of a sudden a crack and a wide water hole appeared before us. The stronger dogs managed to cross it; the others splashed around in the freezing water. Three balanced blocks of ice, one of them pointed, made it possible for my sledge, which I hadn't been able to bring to an instant halt, to pass over. A combination of dogs' pluck and driver's skill propelled the heavy sledge forward, although the back end was in the water and the front was raised at a 60 degree angle. I was standing on the transverse bar at the base of the back stanchion, leaning forward. With straining haunches the dogs, at a signal from Paapa, gave one hard pull and the nose of the heavy sledge crashed down on firm ice.

Twelve or fifteen hundred feet to our right lay two massive capes, Grinnell and Ingersoll, with their parallel red, yellow, and ocher strata. At about two in the morning, as we were entering the wide Uunartoq Bay—Bay of Early Spring—I glimpsed a strange sight through the frosty fog; way out here on the ice field a woman was silently, steadily driving a team of dogs in circles around a seated man. It was Padloq and Qaaqqutsiaq! They had been hunting for seal since the day before.

Puisi! This animal plays a vital role in the Eskimos' life. In the Thule district in 1950, the local civilization could still be called a seal civilization. The ringed seal is the most common species here. What betrays the presence of this marine animal—and leads it to its doom—is the fact that every five or ten minutes it must surface to breathe. During the summer, well and good; it takes its time breathing and lingers, floating, on the water. But with the arrival of cold weather, matters become more complicated. Starting in the autumn, in fact, when the sea is freezing, the seal must open from ten to twenty holes for himself within a given area, which apparently he does not leave. With his black claws, he carefully keeps these holes open as the ice thickens—to a depth of three to six feet in March. Riddling the ice bank until it looks like an enormous sieve, these peepholes or allut can be spotted on the surface by excrescences that resemble molehills. Beneath the shell of ice, they are bell-shaped, and are variously slanting, straight, narrow, fat, or bulging. With a special stick, the Eskimo takes soundings to determine where to aim his weapon. Usually, the allu is fairly large. The seal has plenty of room as he breathes on, and melts, the thin film of ice that has formed and blocked the air passage since he was last there, and so the allut grow. During the months of darkness, this animal, who is a good geographer, gifted with an astonishing memory for topography, moves fearlessly from hole to hole. Fearlessly—and yet up on the ice, man also fights hard to survive, and preparations are under way that spell death for the seal. A hunter, encased in furs, approaches slowly; guided by his dogs, he has spotted an allu. He moves noiselessly, for he carefully places his feet on a piece of caribou skin to prevent the snow's crunching. He kneels; his bearskin-clad

Seal hunting. Drawing by Qavisanguaq (twenty-three years old). Neqi, March 1951. (*Private collection*)

buttocks rear up in the air like a gargoyle's as he thrusts his nose into the little hole.

He smells the water slowly, methodically, in a series of short sniffs almost imperceptibly punctuated by his exhalations. With his gloves, he delicately brushes away chunks of ice from the lead-colored water. He grimaces, straightens up, then bends down again. Once more he thrusts his head into the allu. Minutes pass, a long time. Not a sound is audible except for the creaking of the ice. At last the man grunts softly and stands up. The question is settled: this allu was recently visited by an animal. The hunter stations himself by the allu; the seal does not have long to live.

What does it matter to the man that he must wait? Is he not able to make the animal do what he wants? Look at Padloq, proudly playing the man. She kept driving the dogs in smaller and smaller circles, systematically blocking all the peepholes except one. The suffocating, terrified animal was being driven toward the allu chosen for his death.[35] Qaaqqutsiaq sat by it, motionless, impassive. His "indicator" was in place—a float of three or four fox hairs tied at the outer edges by a supple thread made of sealskin. When the thread moved, it would mean that the tapered body of the seal was rising for air—and that would be the moment to run it through.

Usually seated on an antiquated stool, grasping a harpoon in his right hand, holding in his left a supple rope moored to the ice, the hunter waits: one hour passes, two, often more. . . . "Psttt!" The cord gradually slackens. The man hurls the harpoon with the speed of lightning; in response there is a tragic splashing of water. Red-stained ripples slap against the snow. Even before he could get his ration of air, the seal has been struck on the shoulder, and the blood spills from him. He struggles, thrashes about, and pulls against the tip

Seal hunting on the ice field. To the right, the hunter's companion restrains the excited dogs with his whip. To the left, the Eskimo, protected by a canvas screen, draws as close

of the harpoon which has bitten into him; but the rope holds fast, tightens, twists, and smacks the snow. With his remaining strength, the exhausted, panting animal pulls one last time. Too late. Already his convulsive jerks are growing weaker; in a few minutes, the man will take his broad-bladed knife, widen the hole, and with a satisfied smile put an end to this unequal battle, this small daily drama.

When we reached Qaaqqutsiaq, he was at his fifth hole and still had caught nothing. In the old days, the Eskimos used to say that in such a case the hunter should be beaten black and blue so that his body would be freed of the evil spirits that frighten off puisi.

"Come on, now you can hunt," they would say to the unfortunate man. "Now the seals will come to you."

Qaaqqutsiaq no longer believed in these practices and went empty-handed from one allu to another.

"Unni! What's the use!"

But then old songs for bewitching the seals rose irresistibly to his lips:

Nunallu sermillu
Akorngagut tammarnaanga
Aia ia ia. . . .

Between earth and glaciers
I hid myself, falling. . . .

This murmured song, solemn and reverent, faded away in the fog as the dogs pulled with all their might and we made our way to the shore.

as possible to the seal, which is sleeping on the ice. He is about to kill it. Drawing by Bertsie. Siorapaluk, December 1950. *(Private collection)*

Hunting seal at the breathing hole. Drawing by Imina. December 1950. *(Private collection)*

There were piles of boxes and cartons on the ice, plus a few jerrycans: this was where our main depot of foodstuffs would be established. Qaaqqutsiaq had left the final decision to me as to where it would be, and had simply unloaded the bags onto the ice. We would choose a suitable place later; for the moment, we were so utterly worn out that we could do no more than put up the tent and go to sleep.

Early on the morning of April 25, I was awakened by jubilant shouts. My eyes squinted from fatigue as I looked out to see a sledge gliding over the ice toward us with some sort of jinn waving from it.

He was seated on the far side and to the fore of the sledge. Then he leaped off and with short steps ran ahead of his dogs and to their right, to guide them toward the best passage through the hummocks on the ice foot, or coastal ice belt.

"A . . . Assut! Faster!"

He swept down upon us in a cloud of white dust. It was the indefatigable Qaaqqutsiaq coming to tell us that he had killed a seal at last and that Padloq had seen many—*amerlaqaat*—hare prints.[36] She had killed twelve hares. We ate together in high good humor. The morning mist, caused by a sea wind from the south, had cleared. There was now not the slightest breath of air. The sun was warming and thawing one side of the tent and now stood so high above the horizon that we took off our heavy qulitsaqs. A few days more and it would be spring. With axes, we cut a wider passage through the hummocks and, using all three sledges, hauled our freight to shore. At high tide, we threw bridges of wood and ice over the crevasses so that we could cross them. We built the depot—a cube about three feet by three at the base—in a secure position on the right bank of a small deltaic cone. Located a short distance from the head of Uunartoq Bay, it would have the enormous advantage of being accessible to us via the ice foot in June, when we would be returning from Washington Land, ready to go on to Canada.

As soon as we had finished the depot, we went up to the very head of Uunartoq Bay, to where Padloq had already set up her tent. The good woman was very excited and bustled about when she saw us. Smoke was drifting from her tent, where six pink-fleshed hares—insipid fare for anyone used to seal and walrus—were cooking at a fast boil. We pitched camp on the edge of the crescent-shaped beach, in the shelter of a small island of muddy, dingy-yellow ice. We were camping on the very spot where, ninety-eight years before, the second Grinnell expedition—sent to look for Sir John Franklin and led by the American physician and naval officer Elisha Kent Kane—had spent two winters in 1853–55.

In his short life Elisha Kane carried out remarkable explorations throughout the world. Intimately bound to the celebrated nineteen-year-old medium Margaret Fox, Kane was an engaging and strong-willed man. He and his crew wintered farther north than anyone ever had before. He gave one of his family names, Rensselaer, to the bay where he spent his two harsh winters: the bay known to the Eskimos as Uunartoq or Spring Bay. His personality dominated this famous expedition, during which he faced grave problems: his ship, the *Advance,* was icebound for two winters; scurvy, rheumatism, snow blindness, and several cases of madness struck the members of his expedition; there was a mutiny among his crew. He had to cope with not only continual tension and insubordination but also severe cold (at the end of the "little ice age," around 1840, this region experienced a brief return of intensely cold weather), and problems with the Eskimos, with whom he had to negotiate agreements.

Kane was not helped—to put it as charitably as possible—by the two Danes who accompanied the expedition. "Pedersen was always a cold-blooded sneak. Ohlsen, double-faced, fawning and insincere. They have left the expedition. . . . They carry not the respect of good men," Kane wrote in his private journal. The attitude of the doctor, Isaac Hayes, who was later to lead his own Arctic expeditions through this region, was equivocal. During preparations for the first departure for the south, he persuaded part of the team to attempt to run away, leaving the main body of the expedition to its fate. The flight, begun August 28, 1854, came to a pitiful end on a day in December 1854, when Hayes and his fellow mutineers engineered a shabby betrayal of three Eskimos who had tried to help them out. The Eskimos were put to sleep with opiate drinks and stripped of all their clothes, including their boots; their dogs were stolen. When they woke up, they managed to reach the Americans after dressing in ponchos fashioned of blankets and boots made of strips of cloth. The Americans threatened them with guns and made the Eskimos take them back north. On December 17, 1854, Hayes reached Uunartoq and was welcomed back by Kane. They endured another winter together, and on March 20, 1855, the expedition abandoned ship and headed south for Upernavik, pulling their long boats on sledges. After eighty-four days of risky navigation on land and by sea, they arrived at their destination.

I remember Kane especially for the extraordinary agreements he worked out with the Eskimos: he assured them that he, the white sorcerer, would not use the power he possessed to torment them, on condition that they give him some dogs and fresh food. After 130 years, the favorable memory that Kane has left among my Eskimo friends is vague, certainly, but tenacious. He pushed farthest north at the time, despite his obvious inexperience in traveling by dogsledge over ice. During the winter he used to read passages from *David Copperfield* to his companions, and he wrote a book—*Arctic Explorations*—which was a best seller that set all Americans to dreaming. He inscribed in their consciousness the first indelible images of what was an Eskimo.

A few bits of debris bore witness to Kane's expedition of nearly a century before: a pile of stones, some scraps of iron. After looking about for three hours on the rocks, Kutsikitsoq found an arrow pierced by a hole. (Later, on my return to Copenhagen, I learned that the explorer D. B. MacMillan had also seen this arrow.) Undoubtedly a message or the copy of a message had been deposited in a fractured rock to which the arrow pointed; we searched for it but could not find it. Nor did we find the grave of Kane's companions, Baker and the cook Pierre—the tumble-down pyramid Hayes spoke of in his report.

In this vast landscape of rock and ice, then, nothing remained but one arrow and a scrap of iron to recall the twenty-four months of daily struggle, the striving, the last adventures of that courageous and fruitful American expedition—no local trace of it other than in the confused memories of the Eskimos and, far to the south, in libraries where the travel diaries and works of scientific observation are preserved.

Uunartoq—the Bay of Early Spring—is aptly named. The weather we encountered was good, the heat stultifying. As I sat at the door of my tent shortly before dawn, everything was gray and shadowy until the sun appeared by the headland. It lingered indolently on the tops of the great bare plateaus. Its rays caressed the brows of the slopes, paused for a moment, and then an orange stain spread across the horizon. Beams of sunlight swept over the gray-tinged ice. The frozen sea was still contained in darkness, but the massive icebergs looming above it sparkled with myriad reflections that ranged from pink to lilac, from sea green to royal blue, all seemingly enameled. The light enveloped me as I watched, and warmed my face.

As the nighttime pallor of this immense space yields to spangled, sparkling brightness, the landscape assumes color and form in the dim light. Reflections are so strong that even shadows are tinged with color. The tall sandstone cliffs, only moments before swathed in colorless scree, redden and emerge elegant and proud. The deep, dark ravines, the faults, the ribboned strata that darken where they join, the superimposition of these heavy masses one upon another, without lacunae lend the powerful ensemble an indescribable lightness. From Uunartoq or Rensselaer Bay to Cape Scott, this imposing skyline extends over a distance of some sixty miles, broken only at the midpoint. A scree slope stands out with youthful distinctness, straight as a sheath, facing the frozen sea as if it were the fold of an ample, pleated gown of stone. Along a shore once battered by pre-Cambrian waves, unceasing erosion has carved out ledges and spurs. Frost, glaciers, and water have pushed nine-cubic-foot blocks before them, as well as rock masses encased in more than six-foot-thick reddish moraine, a whitened fluvial marl, its angles blunted, and here and there grayish yellow wilt. The rounded gneissic hummocks at the back of the bay stand in dull contrast to all this: they rise out of the snow one after another, as if on parade, marching eastward in continuous undulations of pebbly plateaus and meandering valleys.

Fed by the immense dome of the sparkling ice cap to the east, in July tumultuous torrents of water and mud will rush down, push the snow aside, hollowing and scouring out a bed for themselves; and thus they will restore to this ancient, beaten, worn land, exposed since the dawn of time, its miserable pre-Cambrian, crevasse-wrinkled face.

Every day I went either up onto the plateau to work on the map or out onto the taluses to survey scree slopes and make section drawings. On the morning of April 27, as I was crossing the bay from south to north I discovered the back reaches of the fjord, more than a mile long and a good half mile wide. This area had never been mapped before. I cannot believe, however, that when Kane's ship lay within shooting distance of it for two years in a row, the American explorers had never noticed it.

"As I sailed along the coast," Hayes wrote in 1868, "I passed a succession of places which were already engraved in my memory. Those high sandstone rocks were as familiar to me as the rows of warehouses and stores on Broadway. I had explored the area surrounding Port Rensselaer so often that I recognized every gorge, every headland, every ravine, as if I had seen them the day before."

Well, this is what he says, yet there is no trace of the fjord, at least not on the map published in 1867. I say this without irony. Speaking for myself, I admit that now I would be incapable of drawing an exact map of the fjord at Siorapaluk (Robertson Fjord), although every twist and turn of it is vivid in my memory, for the simple reason that I never sketched it. The same was true, I believe, of Donald B. MacMillan at Etah and Cairn Point and of the Dane, James Van Hauen, at Neqi. The first attempts to make an exact map of Thule date from the time of Lauge Koch (1930) and the English geologist Wright (1939), despite the fact that from 1903 on, dozens of experts had passed through that famous station, beginning with Knud Rasmussen, who occasionally lived there. It often happens that far-ranging expeditions neglect the area around their point of departure.

Most of the time I went out alone and found myself carrying on a conversation with an imaginary companion. When the two Eskimos were not hunting, they idled away their time sitting on some hilltop looking through my binoculars. They wanted to get some idea of the countryside too, they said.

For several weeks now, I believe, we had hit our stride—a slower, freer pace. Now that the sun was higher in the sky, more seals were coming to the allut. Soon our familiar table companions would be pulling themselves up onto the ice to sleep more comfortably in the warmth and fresh air. The specter of hunger faded. At mealtimes, Kutsikitsoq grew agreeably lyrical. "Maloringuaq, eh? It's nice here. Pinnerpoq! . . . You'll tell them, won't you? You'll explain everything to them—about the colors, the dogs, the silence, the immense spaces. . . ."

That evening while Natuk was cutting my hair, Kutsikitsoq proposed: "Why don't we set ourselves up here at Uunartoq for good—Natuk, you, and me? You know, we would live here like brothers. Nuannigijuk! Oh, it would be a good life. . . ." (I was Qaaqqutsiaq's barber; I cut his hair Eskimo style, bowl-shaped, or à la Joan of Arc, whichever he preferred.)[37]

We were finishing dinner when Padloq and Natuk suddenly straightened up and pointed to a spot out on the ice field.

"Qamutit! . . . Qamutit!" they cried.

Four sledges were moving out from Cape Leiper, to the north of us, and fanning out on the horizon. Padloq ran back and forth in great excitement:

"Inuit, takkuut! Eskimos, look!"

She seized our ocher-colored tent, clambered up on the rocks, and waved it back and forth. To make the tent more conspicuous, she moved up to the crest of the first foothills above the bay. Her silhouette must have been visible against the snow. We stood in a group and shouted in unison. Had they seen us, heard us? The file of sledges slowly altered course. Padloq and Natuk kept hopping about, laughing nervously. The Primus stove was pumped up, and two pans of coffee were prepared. In this desert, miles from any inhabited place, one's first reaction to an imminent encounter is great tension: Who is it? What is it? What will we find out? What's going to happen?

The men combed their hair. Skins were shaken out, and the interior of the large tent was made tidy. I noticed the women in one corner hastily freshening up, mirrors in hand. As the sledges drew near, we went outside and sat down on our jerrycans, facing the ice field, and like chieftains we watched the strangers approach.

The leader of the group was far ahead of the others. His dogs were not much to look at; they were thin, the fur along their backs was worn and flat, and long clumps of sticky hair hung from their bellies. The man was visibly excited. He was pushing his sledge awkwardly, got caught in the hummocks, and had trouble getting over a ridge. We heard him laugh as he yelled "Qaa! qaa! qaa!" at his dogs. Then he simply went on laughing heartily. He was incapable of saying a word as he appeared before us, a bent figure in an old qulitsaq, which was worn at the elbows and in front; his face was blackened by the sun and powdered with frost. Whip in hand, he strode vigorously toward us. We three stood; each took off one glove and shook his hand silently, in true Inuit style. Then the women came waddling up in turn; with eyes lowered, they waited for the man to condescend to put out his hand. Meek and gentle, they leaned over, touched his palm lightly, and then, rather gracefully, stepped to one side and stood slightly apart. No one had yet said a word. But there was a genial sparkle in everyone's eyes. After a few banal remarks about the weather and the joy of having met, this man—his name was Sorqaq, and he was the naalagaq from Qeqertarssuaq—left us to see to his team. His movements were precise. We did not stir; according to Eskimo protocol, it is not proper to take care of someone else's dogs. Only after several minutes could we go over to his sledge and discover what treasures he had brought.

There were four bearskins, three of them large; they elicited little cries of admiration from the women. Feeling very much at ease, Sorqaq praised the skins and invited us to feel them.

"Qamutit!"

Uisaakavsaq, from Qeqertaq, the second member of the group, arrived; leaving Sorqaq to show off his goods to the women, we went to meet him. We went through the same ceremony again, then broke up into small groups. For fear of not seeming enthusiastic enough, everyone forced himself to be exuberant. One had to talk loud, even shout, to be heard. Suddenly Uisaakavsaq rushed to the front of his sledge. His dogs—many of them were young, between six months and a year old—had lunged at Kutsikitsoq's dogs. A free-for-all ensued, with more shouting, punctuated by shrieks from the women. Uisaakavsaq thrashed his animals with his whip handle, striking them left and right on their backs. Their howls were earsplitting, and they took off, limping, in all directions. No one turned around to look; Uisaakavsaq was a clumsy fellow, and everyone immediately deserted his sledge.

When news of the hunt is good, the Eskimo likes it to be doled out so that it percolates slowly into his listeners' minds; and so, in due course we learned that, in all, seven bears had been killed sixty miles from where we were, near Humboldt Glacier: three by Sorqaq, two by Uisaakavsaq; and one each by the hunters who had not yet joined us: Mattak, one of Pualuna's sons, and Aleqasina.

The hunters stood before their sledges, whips stuck tips up in the snow, and kept an eye on their teams. Sorqaq was leaning casually against his napariaq, his stomach pressed against it; then he propped his elbows on it. Occasionally, he vouchsafed some detail in his cavernous voice. We had our first cup of tea beside his sledge, on the side of which the women were perched. An hour went by. The hunters talked on, managing to appear both nonchalant and important. I invited the whole noisy group to coffee in my tent. We squeezed inside; every square inch was occupied. The tent filled with the friendly smell of tobacco smoke.

"Cigarette?"

"Lift your leg. . . . Move your arm forward. . . . Pass me your knife. . . ."

There is nothing Eskimos enjoy so much as being together like this, especially when they have come back from a big bear hunt. After hours of cherished solitude, they have a chance to satisfy their old gregarious instinct. We passed the first piece of meat around and everyone had a bite. We had hardly settled down when the last two members of the team, Mattak and Aleqasina, arrived with great commotion. They were late, and for them etiquette was almost ignored. No one got up. The emotion had passed.

Nine o'clock came and went, eleven o'clock, midnight, two in the morning:

they sat there still telling stories, elaborating, arguing, beaming with pleasure; after all, they were alive!

Nanoq this, nanoq that. . . . Every ten seconds, the word *bear* was on their lips. Each hunter was eager to explain in the minutest detail the tactics he personally used to approach the bear and take him by surprise.

". . . But the bear shuffled off," Uisaakavsaq said, "and then the sledge rammed into the edge of an iceberg and then I was late taking out my rifle, and then a thong got tangled around the barrel. . . . I took aim, but my foot slipped a little. . . . I fired again. It was very dark, as if it were going to snow. Peerujoq ajoq! Fog! What bad luck! The bear was getting farther and farther away. I took my knife and cut the traces of two of my dogs very close to the harness so that they could join the other three. This took some time. The ice was bad and the last four dogs in my team—they were pulling hard, but they were all pulling in different directions because they were so keyed up.

"At last the bear slowed down," Uisaakavsaq continued. "He bit himself, stanched his wound with snow, and then came to a complete stop. He leaned back against an iceberg and looked slowly to the left and to the right. He crapped again and again. My five loose dogs had stopped in front of him, pointing, but the damned animals were no good—too young! Only one of them had the courage to get near enough to the bear to bite his paws. . . . Then," Uisaakavsaq said, in conclusion, "I arrived. Toquvoq, nanoq—death, bear!"

There was a long silence. Then the men twitted Qaaqqutsiaq and especially Kutsikitsoq, "the great hunter," because so far they had not caught anything. Their glum faces grew even glummer. A good five minutes went by before they unclenched their teeth. (I once knew two normally very arrogant Eskimos who for days on end had behaved with the greatest humility toward everyone because they felt so mortified at having returned empty-handed from a bear hunt.) But these hunters did not taunt Kutsikitsoq long. He had given proof of his worth, and also they were afraid of his irony. Teasing must be light and brief; at times like this, it must never wound. The Eskimo is thin-skinned, but he accepts a measure of sarcasm with a smile; raillery forces him to outdo himself—it is a form of self-criticism via humor. This sarcasm constitutes a weapon against the forces of inertia that threaten: it is important to encourage the best members of the group to lead the others, who are always more or less lazy.

Now the laughter turned on the youngest member in the group, Aleqasina.

". . . He was lost for hours—he's got to be really clumsy! Ha, ha, ha! . . . And Mattak's dogs are no good!" Ducking his head and hunching his shoulders, Mattak smiled and capped the taunt: "Yes! No good at all. Absolutely, totally no good."

Sorqaq's hoarse voice was heard again. With false modesty and the greatest precision, he described how he had killed his third bear: in what weather, with whom, what he saw, what the sky looked like, what he felt, what he should have felt, and also what others might have thought . . . and what he would do and could do about that. . . . It was by now three in the morning. The pots of coffee and tea—Eskimo tea, black as ink and speckled with brown leaves—were emptied and refilled tirelessly. After drinking, we proceeded to the bear. The meat is tough and stringy: we ate it boiled and spread with bear fat. The bear's tongue is much coveted, and this was scrupulously divided among us all. Then more tea, some hare, then back to the bear meat, then on to some seal liver, which we ate raw. After cigarettes, we had some chocolate; then once again back to the bear. The Eskimos crushed each bone either with their teeth or between two rocks, and sucked out the marrow. They ate and ate—they filled their bellies with enough to last them a month. *Ukaleq,* or hare, is a pale, soft meat with a sweetish taste: fit for women or in periods of scarcity. But today it was spice to the good meats, part and parcel of the varied banquet. Today we were rich. . . . The feast continued. Once more, the Eskimos addressed themselves to the bear.

They ended up eating every last bit of its organs. Would they ever stop?

When they reverted to raw, frozen seal, with its pinkish white, gelatinous fat, I seized on that as an excuse to go off to bed. Kutsikitsoq and Qaaqqutsiaq did not join me until early next morning, dead tired, hiccupping and belching like beasts.

*This Country Was
Born Cruel: The
Law of the North*

On the afternoon of April 28, we started out again. I left first; by now it was a habit—I would go ahead and leave my friends to break camp. An hour later, they caught up with me on the ice field. That night we arrived at Cape Taney, where for two days I worked by myself while the Eskimos hunted food for the dogs.

The new month began with a dark, snowy day. A north wind had driven the temperature down. We felt much more tired than we had in March, and

Seal's head. (*From Kane,* Arctic Explorations)

more than once caught one another dozing on the sledges. We took advantage of the fact that the surface froze during the "night," and traveled then, when the sun was low on the horizon. Our skin had to become accustomed to the cold again—it tightened, our nostrils stung, and our ears burned. I was reminded of the dim wintry hours I had spent near Savigssivik.

We did not slide down into Inuarfissuaq Bay until May 2. Inuarfissuaq—the Bay of the Great Massacre.

Great Massacre? Qaaqqutsiaq described it to me briefly. Although it is an old story it is worth telling, for it is still very much alive in everyone's memory here. It has been told so many times, however, that no one is very sure anymore what is legend and what fact.

Two boys were fighting on the shore of the island we had just reached. They were fighting pretty roughly, the way many children do. One boy was thrown down by the other. He cried out, and to make him be quiet, the other kicked and punched him. By chance, the grandfather of the boy on the ground saw what was happening. He ran over to them and intervened, as was right. There was a fight. The man was very angry, and struck the other child so hard that he fell down on the rocks, quite dead. The other grandfather was furious, and he intervened in turn, and then the fathers, the shrieking mothers, the mothers-in-law, uncles, aunts, cousins, nephews, and nieces. The whole camp was embroiled. There were insults and curses—horrifying scenes. Everyone was in a state of indescribable violence. People hurled rocks and bones at one another's heads, flung themselves on one another savagely. One man chased a woman, grasping a bloody harpoon. In the end, they all efficiently finished each other off. Not a living person was left.

The story does not say how the last person died, or who witnessed the event and told about it afterward.

When I awoke in Inuarfissuaq, I had the strange feeling of having traveled backward in time. The change in latitude from Etah was permitting me to witness the coming of spring for a third and last time. A snow bunting had perched on the tent pole. Puffing out his small silvery breast, he began to sing. The air was cool and light. On the snowy ice, pools of opaline-green water sparkled in the sun. When Natuk glanced at me, her smile was tremulously expectant. The new season was taking triumphant possession of Great Massacre Bay.

Who could still doubt it? After six winter months spent as prisoners of the sea, the seals made no mistake about it. They saw their dark caverns begin to take on an emerald tone from the upper layer of water, they recognized a new smell in the air, and they hoisted themselves up through their tunnels of ice into the sun. Three or four of them emerged from a single allu. Along the steaming crevasses, there were even whole colonies—ten, fifteen, sometimes thirty or forty. Sprawled out on the shining surface, the creatures would forget to eat for weeks. "Uuttoq!—seal sleeping on the snow, June seal, no good seal," Kutsikitsoq said to me.

This country was born cruel. Is there any pleasure greater than to hunt an animal when it is resting? The polar bear, with his strength and cunning, is even better at this than we are. Gliding over the snow, he adroitly takes up his position downwind and facing the sun. His calm gaze narrows in on his prey —a corpulent seal. He is 300 feet away from it. With catlike stealth, the sinuous bear creeps forward slowly and heavily. He is now 250 feet from the goal, then 200, then 100. He blends into the ice field almost perfectly. I say almost because although the approaching bear has a chance, the seal, sunk in his indolence, has a chance too, slight though it may be. Nanoq's snout is black. He is so aware of this that he wrinkles it nervously; he has even been seen to thrust his big nose into the fleecy snow, trying to whiten it. Now he is 75 feet away, now 50, now 30. The seal is all languor; he glances to the left and right, but his black eyes are near-sighted, and dimmed by a melancholy rheum, and by sleepiness. The bear attacks! One tremendous leap forward, one blow of his paw—wham!—crushes the animal's head where it lies.

Is the bear a glutton? Watch the wet-lipped animal dragging his victim over to an iceberg. He sits down, leans back against it, and sets about tearing his prey apart with his powerful claws. The white blubber he lays aside for himself. The blood-red meat and the formless, stinking entrails are fit for the terianniaq, the fox flunkeys that follow him.

The human hunter identifies so successfully with seals that, especially when low-lying clouds deaden all sounds, he is able to come very close as they lie sleeping on the ice. He uses various kinds of mimicry: he raises and lowers his head at the right moments, he imitates the seals' cries, and thus manages to slip up to the allut where the colony is resting. He quiets their apprehension by making little seallike barks and bobbing his head up and down. Then suddenly he straightens up, runs to the allu, and sits down on it, blocking the seals' escape. Like an all-conquering god, he kills two or three helpless seals around him.

Some fifteen hundred feet from our island, a seal was sleeping near a hole. I masked my rifle behind a white canvas screen mounted on two skates—a Danish *skydesejl.* Six hundred feet away from the seal, I prepared my silent attack. Hidden by the screen, I began to crawl toward him. With my legs dragging behind me, I inched forward on my elbows. Whenever I could, I made a twenty- or thirty-yard dash but always crouching behind the screen. Vaguely uneasy, the seal lifted its head, stirred, and changed its position. Now I could hear it breathe. I flattened myself against the snow and lay still. I was planning to move again when the seal drew a breath, since it is unable to hear then. Suddenly it lifted its small, round, bald head and turned a bewildered, mustachioed face in my direction. It peered around with its dim, wrinkled eyes. If it grew suspicious, it had only to drag itself over to the allu with one supple movement and disappear.

I advanced twenty-five yards more, then five. It was a plump female, a swollen bottle shape molded inside her varitoned skin. Her body undulated and a tremor rippled over her flesh.

We had no meat for the dogs. I delayed no longer, reluctantly took up my rifle, and aimed between her eyes. The shot, reverberating from the cliffs, made a tremendous noise. The animal was fatally wounded; her body quivered; in her bulging eyes, which suddenly seemed to me enormous, I could see her oily gaze slowly dying; then, very quickly, it was all over. The seal was hauled back to the camp, leaving a trail of blood behind it. This was the first *puisi* we had killed on the ice this year. The Eskimos were delighted and gave me an enthusiastic welcome. I knelt, thrust my knife into the seal's flesh, and pulled the liver from among the steaming entrails. Carefully I laid it on the snow. The five of us squatted down in a semicircle. Somewhat bemused, we watched the still-warm liver sink into the blood-spattered snow. I cut off a piece and threw it out toward the ice field; the Eskimos glanced at me fleetingly, the expression on their faces both complicitous and aloof as they saw me participate in one of their ancestral rituals. Then Qaaqqutsiaq carved the remaining liver into equal shares; like communicants, we ate in silence.

The afternoon was given over to routine work—mapping the fjord, plotting the levels of the stranded beaches, taking samples of weathered rocks. Around Inuarfissuaq Bay and on the small island of Avoortungiaq opposite it, I looked for skeletons near some tumbledown igloos. I confirmed that among the many traces of animals there were no human remains. The Inuit told me that here the practice had been to throw bodies into the sea. The people on Avoortungiaq had been descendants of an Alaskan migration, so it was not out of the question that burial customs peculiar to that culture should have prevailed here.

We traveled over excellent ice and arrived at Dallas Bay on May 6. Our departure had been delayed by an inexplicable illness which kept me in the tent.[38] Kutsikitsoq and I stayed in the bay two days while the other three hunted near Cape Scott. A long-hoofed caribou—*Rangifer pearya*, a smaller, more delicate species than the Canadian caribou—had leaped up at their approach but had quickly vanished from sight. It had been agreed that as soon as my work was finished we would pick up Qaaqqutsiaq and the women on our way north. We reached Qaaqqaitsut on May 8, and until the twelfth traveled along a stretch of very heavily indented coast. It was a maze of fjords and islands where a geographer would have the greatest trouble in orienting himself. Many of the innumerable islets were so tiny that one could easily cross them in a few steps. I stood on a hilltop trying to record this profusion on paper, with Kutsikitsoq watching beside me. When he saw the point of my pencil snap as I was dotting in yet one more minute island, he asked me: "Why don't you just put them in everywhere—here, and here. . . . It's just so many dog droppings out there!"

Inland, the details of the relief were no less complex; the Eskimos are right to call this region Qaaqqaitsut, or "the country of many small mountains," with no true mountain. Seen from above and through a halo of fog, the panorama of hills and valleys looked like a boundless expanse of whitecaps. With Qaaqqutsiaq I had the good fortune to explore a hitherto unknown fjord and to go by sledge up a river which led through a series of lakes to the ice cap itself.

At the edge of it we built a small cairn. I forgot to leave a message, as Polar explorers traditionally do here and there along their routes, so that if they do not return, a search expedition will have some clue to their itinerary. For a long time we stood on the edge of the glacier. We were surely in the same surroundings where, in 1917, a Danish expedition had lived through one of the most poignant dramas in the history of Polar exploration. If we had not reached the exact spot, we were certainly very close, no more than three to five miles away. Since Lauge Koch, I was the only white man to have ventured into the area of the tragedy, so I looked for a monument or a cross. There was nothing. It was as though the event had been effaced from the memory of man. Qaaqqutsiaq, whose brother Aajuku had been a partner on this mission, known as the Second Thule Expedition, told me what he knew about it.

14

THE SECOND
THULE
EXPEDITION

Knud Rasmussen, the founder of Eskimology, was in every respect a first-rate man. Thirty-eight years old at the time of the Second Thule Expedition, he had already established the store at Uummannaq. Rasmussen had a rare warmth and an incomparable ability to organize and inspire other men; additionally, he was an experienced explorer and possessed extraordinary endurance. He was of mixed Danish and Eskimo blood and spoke the language of Thule perfectly; he had spent the year 1903–4 there, made another extended visit there in 1907–8, and continued to visit fairly regularly after 1910, the year he started the store at Uummannaq.

The second so-called Thule expedition, unlike his first (1912), included men who were real scientists. Perhaps Rasmussen relied too much on his legendary Eskimo intuition, which leads one to challenge fate, and over-estimated this gift in others. In any case, his confidence was to prove fatal in this expedition that included scientists as well as hunters. Rasmussen hoped he would be able to cope because of his Eskimo teammates. He knew he could count on their selfless support, especially in times of danger. This rare and complex man was a passionate adventurer—an Eskimo, and therefore unpredictable, strong, capable, a self-taught scientist with only "primitive" training, since he had learned his ethnology on the spot with the Eskimos, by living among them. Now he was eager to accomplish, together with more formally trained colleagues, a great work. He always had the gift of making people outdo themselves.

Thorild Wulff, the second member of the expedition, was a well-known Swedish naturalist; he had several expeditions to his credit, notably in China; then forty years old, he was in mediocre health but was, Rasmussen said, a "quick and enduring walker." Although Wulff lacked the spirit of adventure and a willingness to cooperate with the Eskimos—they did not like him, according to Peter Freuchen—Rasmussen appreciated his skill as a scientist and was personally resolved to work with him. Wulff brought prestige to Rasmussen's early expeditions.

The youngest white member of the expedition, the Dane Lauge Koch, twenty-five years old, was willful, ambitious, and reserved, concerned that scientific research be perfectly organized and nothing be left to chance; he proved to be a remarkable geological and geographical explorer. He had been staying at Disko, and the Second Thule Expedition was his first big exploring venture. His physical resistance and his energy were exceptional.

In addition to these three qallunaat, there were three Thule Eskimos and one Greenlander of mixed blood, Hendrik Olsen. The Eskimos were Aajuku, Inukitsupaluk (called Harrigan by Rasmussen), and Nasaitsorluarsuk, more commonly known by his Christian name Borseman (and called Bosun by Rasmussen). Aajuku was Qaaqqutsiaq's brother, now deceased. Inukitsupaluk and Borseman I knew very well from my stay in Thule, and they talked to me at length about the tragic expedition. One of them eventually gave me a written account of the expedition which showed how psychological relations among the expedition members became more complicated as their situation worsened. Also, in May 1952, Lauge Koch had dinner with me during one of his visits to Paris, and he described to me very simply the fearsome hours he had lived through. He gave me some specific, terribly violent details that accounted for the tragedy. To avoid any ambiguity, before I try to recapture the events of those long past days I want to express my respect and deep admiration for Knud Rasmussen and for the irreproachable decisions he made during this essentially inner drama of six—and in particular three—starving men.[39]

The Second Thule Expedition had set out to explore the unknown coast of northern Greenland between St. George Fjord and de Long Fjord. On August 24, 1917, after covering 1,000 miles, the group stopped at Qaaqqaitsut, on Cape Agassiz, Peabody Bay, on its way home. The men had experienced days of great hardship as they crossed Greenland's immense ice cap. Food had run out, the last dog was eaten on August 24, and they were still 155 miles from Etah, the nearest inhabited native camp where they could hope to get help.

"We all agree," Rasmussen wrote in *Greenland by the Polar Sea*, "that our arrival on land means salvation." Although the situation was dangerous, it offered some favorable aspects. On the plateau, hares and reindeer are relatively abundant. One of the Eskimos had just killed five hares which provided two meals on the twenty-fifth. With the number of cartridges they had left, the explorers could reasonably count on quite a few days of food. The expedition, planned according to Eskimo practices, had deliberately traveled light. It therefore depended mainly on the luck of the hunt. But as Rasmussen said, "all travelers in the Arctic know the risks they run when they leave their homes for unknown shores." What's more, the partners, to whom the plans were submitted at the time of departure, had endorsed them all enthusiastically.

Now that they were headed south, "everyone understands," Rasmussen wrote on August 24, "that our dangers and difficulties are over." This comment is significant: it shows the mood they were in.

At that point, the group included six men—three whites and three Eskimos. The Greenlander partner, Olsen, had mysteriously got lost a month
earlier and, despite hours spent searching for him, had never been found. He
was the first to die.

After deliberating among themselves at length, the six men—they were
exhausted from crossing the northwestern section of the ice cap and their
equipment was in miserable condition, especially their very worn clothes—
agreed that, for the time being, they would leave their geological specimens
and their notes at Cape Agassiz and would split into two groups. Knud Rasmussen would leave the team and, accompanied by Aajuku, would go to seek
help in Etah; the two men would cut across the Inglefield Land plateau. There
was no question in Rasmussen's mind that his strong empathy and his powers
of persuasion would enable him to convince the Etah Eskimos to act promptly.
"We will advance by forced marches with no regard whatever for the hunting
conditions," wrote Rasmussen. "So we agree that Aajuku and I must go to Etah
for relief; we are both of the opinion that we are able to set out for the long
walk without a preceding rest. Harrigan and Bosun remain in order to hunt for
Wulff and Koch, who have no longer strength to pursue the game." Such were
the arrangements unanimously agreed to by the group. Help would then be
brought as far north as Iceberg Lake, which was relatively close to Cape
Agassiz, thirty-seven miles away as the crow flies, sixty by the land routes.

The second team, consisting of four men and led by Wulff, would make
its way to the lake as slowly as hunting en route required. This, then, was how
the group was divided up. The decision was important: necessary perhaps, but
dangerous, considering Wulff's depressive personality. On the ice cap, again
and again, he had refused to go farther, and Rasmussen well knew that he
himself was the only one who could fight successfully against the botanist's
terrible crises of discouragement and force him to go on.

The Wulff-Koch group kept two rifles, eighty cartridges of small shot, and
forty rifle cartridges. On August 25, "in the best of spirits after a feast of newly
shot hares" (K.R.), Rasmussen and Aajuku set off. They took one rifle and
thirty cartridges with them. Rasmussen felt very confident. In a little over two
days, killing only one hare, he and Aajuku covered the distance of sixty miles
to Iceberg Lake, which is astounding when one remembers that all six men had
been exhausted by weeks of living on the scantest rations while they crossed
the great glacier. Rasmussen and Aajuku did not stop; they had to press on to
Etah for food and help. It eventually took the survivors of the second team
twelve days to cover the same sixty miles to Iceberg Lake by a different and
slightly longer route, killing twenty-four hares, six ducks, and two reindeer
along the way (K.R.). On his first day, Rasmussen had allowed himself only four
hours of sleep after traveling for thirteen hours; the second team spent its first
day resting and walked only eight hours the second day.

This extremely slow pace was to become even slower, until it seemed likely
that the group would be forced to split up again. The men were, in effect,
handicapped by the weakness and demoralization of their leader. Wulff had

Knud Rasmussen scaling a barrier of hummocks. (*From Mylius-Erichsen and Moltke,* Gronland)

headaches and complained about his stomach; his eyes were dull and his knees weak; he had the greatest difficulty getting to his feet.

Many times during the previous month on the glacier, when the expedition had finally been obliged to eat its dogs, Wulff, who made no secret of how repugnant he found the meat, had declared that without food he could go no farther. On two occasions, according to Freuchen, Rasmussen had to cross a frozen torrent to persuade his miserable teammate, who was lying on the bank, to get up and go on. After Rasmussen left them at Cape Agassiz, Wulff became terribly gloomy and, over their meal of hare, he told Lauge Koch for the first time that he felt he was "dying" (L.K.). On August 25 and 26, he told his three companions that he could not go on eating hare, the only game the area afforded. Only reindeer meat would give him back his strength and save him. But reindeer was very rare there; they had seen no trace of any. He spoke of his extreme fatigue and referred to their crossing the ice cap as if it had been a nightmare (L.K.). After considering various plans, the four men decided they would leave together in the direction of the preestablished rendezvous site at Iceberg Lake. As had already been decided, Wulff resolved to leave his scientific journal and his botanical collections at the depot. Lauge Koch left only his geological specimens; his geological and cartographical notes he kept with him. Wulff was still very reluctant as they broke camp; in fact, twenty minutes after they left he wanted to turn back. But the others made him go on. They killed a hare half an hour after this difficult departure.

Every time a hare was killed and eaten—sometimes raw—Koch, Inukitsupaluk, and Bosun ate only the entrails, giving Wulff the fleshy meat over his vehement protests. Apparently Wulff, who was clearly at the end of his tether, tolerated only meat broth and raw meat: cooked hare revolted him and made him vomit.

The terrain they were covering, Qaaqqaitsut, I have already described: it is rough and cut up by ravines, a true roller-coaster kind of landscape which is not only exhausting but disheartening to travel over because distances seem to double.

The autumn mist on August 26 completely defeated the Swede's morale. He could no longer eat anything but soup. On the twenty-seventh, after thirteen hours of rest, the exhausted group managed to resume its slow advance. It took them three hours to go two and a half miles. Wulff complained to Koch about his heart, about his increasing anemia. He spoke of Danish hospitals, dishes of oatmeal, eggs, malt extract (L.K.). Yet, despite his fatigue, he continued to make botanical observations, the work he had been engaged to do. He was too weak to take notes and had to dictate them to Koch. Over two days, August 25–26, the four men ate nine hares—a bit more than one hare per man per day, which was very little in relation to their hunger and great need, but was still a fairly substantial amount. During the night of the twenty-seventh, quantities of wet snow fell, lowering the temperature and slowing their progress even more. The damp, cold air, the low sky, and the poor visibility were all discouraging for men who were very weak and far from any help. Another serious drawback of fresh snow is that it hides hare tracks. Nothing was brought back from the hunt this time except a young hare, which was quickly devoured. The two Eskimos, who had been scouring the countryside for game—and now with no success—were beginning to grow very weak too. After walking southwest for four hours on the twenty-eighth, the four men decided to head northwest so as to reach Cape Scott, where the hunting might be better.

Wulff was becoming more and more irritable, however, and he kept stopping again and again. The other three had to wait for him. According to Freuchen's account, several times Wulff begged them to go on without him; then, when they had disappeared over a hill, he would shout to them to wait for him. He was extremely nervous and at times seemed delirious (L.K.). That day, the twenty-eighth, in twelve hours they covered five miles. Then they rested for twelve hours. Wulff remained awake most of the night; it was one of those disagreeable autumn nights—cold and damp. He was chewing tobacco and seemed thoughtful. Koch and the two Eskimos watched him from their sleeping bags. The next day, after three hours of walking, for the first time, Wulff very calmly expressed his desire to give up and wait for help or for his own death, which would not be long in coming now. Koch was afraid that he himself would not be able to hold out one more day. Yet he persuaded his companion to go on, showing him a lake a good mile away. He also pointed out that the difficulties which lay ahead were nothing compared to what they had been through already. "Maybe," Wulff said, "but for all that, this is like being accompanied to one's own funeral" (L.K.).

At last, one of the Eskimos spotted some reindeer excrement, which he immediately ate. If there was a reindeer close by, might they not be saved? They followed the animal's trail, but soon lost it. Wulff was deeply cast down by this. The men chewed on willow roots.

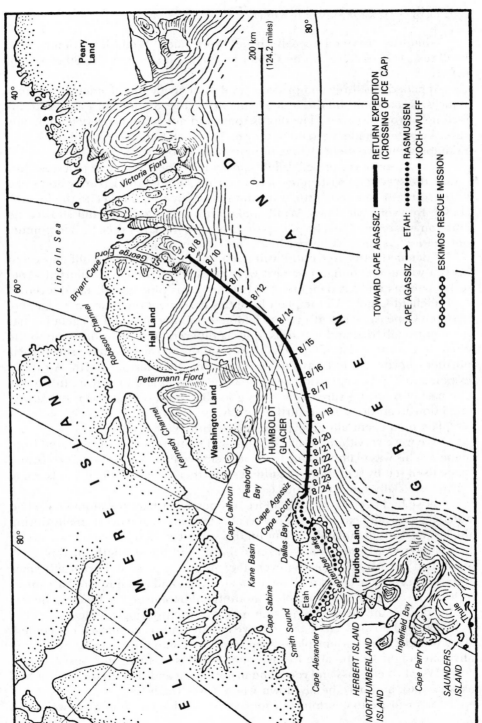

MAP 9. Itinerary of the Second Thule Expedition

When they reached a small ravine, Wulff said, "Well, dear friends, here I will rest; I think there will be shelter by the great stone on the other side of the river" (L.K.).

Appalled, his three companions tried to dissuade him. Under the circumstances, what would be the best argument to use? Should they appeal to his feelings or to his reason? The discussion could not go on for very long, in any case. To enter reindeer territory, they had to reach Cape Scott at all costs. The Eskimos grew impatient. It was urgent to move on.

"No, I cannot continue," Wulff said again. "There is an end to it now. Just do me the service to write a few letters for me, and let the Eskimos boil some water so that I can get a little warmth in my body whilst I dictate the letters" (L.K.). Everyone sat down. Wulff spoke with a strange calm and showed no emotion whatever. Then he got up to go over to the large rock he had pointed out before. As soon as he reached it he lay down at its foot.

A detailed letter to Knud Rasmussen was dictated. In it, Wulff expressed his last wishes, as though his spirit were already elsewhere. He himself wrote to his parents and his daughter.[40] Then he lit his pipe and dictated a report on Inglefield Land: "All the plant localities here mentioned lie on N. Lat. 79° between Cape Agassiz and 15 to 20 kilometers to the west of it. Vegetation has been unusually rich and vigorous, quite a different and luxurious type to the one of the north coast of Greenland. Several of the varieties have surely their northern border here. I have not seen sign of them farther north. A careful examination of the vegetation between Cape Agassiz and Etah from July to the first part of August is sure to give very good botanical results. In my exhausted condition I can do nothing further" (L.K.).

The men spent altogether two hours with Wulff.

"We were very thin," Inukitsupaluk said in his report, "and suffered from anemia. This was plainly visible from our veins, which almost disappeared, and made itself felt by sensations of giddiness; further, we had difficulty in keeping warm, especially our hands and feet.

"If we had been on the inland ice or open ice, where we should have had a sledge, we would have tried to pull Wulff along, as we did occasionally during the last days on the inland ice. But on this snow-bare land of cloughs it would be a matter of carrying him—and none of us had the strength for this. . . ." Wulff had been slowly starving ever since August 4 or 5, and especially since the seventeenth; he could no longer eat anything, and certainly not hare meat. "Of our last bag he tasted merely a mouthful of hare liver. . . . I believe he was ill, for during the last few nights he moaned often during his sleep.

"We had no alternative but to leave him behind, as he himself demanded. If we found a reindeer in a place from which we could return whilst he was yet alive, we might still be able to save him. But this was the only possibility.

"We plucked grass and roots and made as soft and sheltered a bed for him as we could, and here he lay down when it was ready.

"As we arose to continue our journey, he nodded a smiling farewell. And this smile from the poor man who had lain down to die was my last impression of Wulff."

Worried about their own safety, the Eskimos were impatient to pursue their hunting, Koch tells us. The Swede's resolve to stop only spurred his companions on to leave; otherwise the expedition would be headed for disaster. It was agreed that they would come back if they killed a reindeer. Wulff explicitly asked them to go on if they killed only hares. When they parted company on the twenty-ninth, the weather was foggy. Koch adds that as they left, he himself had "a feeling of walking to meet my own death." In fact, the next day he felt the first symptoms of exhaustion—dizzy spells and frequent blackness before his eyes. Then, on the thirtieth, the three men had some good luck; after eating boiled moss, they were able to kill six ducks on the lake. At last they reached the approach to Cape Scott, where again luck smiled on them. They killed six hares. They weighed the possibility of returning to Wulff, who lay dying twelve miles away. This would have meant a twenty-four-hour trek at least, considering the three men's state of exhaustion (L.K.). Every day they were now killing enough hares for themselves, but not enough to provision a journey to Wulff and back, assuming that he was still alive (L.K.).

It was three days after their arrival at Cape Scott—five days after they had left Wulff—that late in the afternoon of September 2 they at last killed two reindeer. "But at the same time a thick fog settled on the land. We then definitely abandoned any thought of returning to Wulff, for not until ten days after his last meal could we be with him again, and it was not probable that in his exhausted condition he would have been able to resist the night frost and hunger for so long" (L.K.). So the three men ate the two reindeer and rested for two days.

"There was now no other alternative but to go down to Etah, and as quickly as possible report to the leader of the expedition Wulff's death" (L.K.).

But on the morning of September 4, there was a new development, Koch tells us. Near where the reindeer had been killed, Koch and his companions were joined by one and then two Eskimos sent by Rasmussen, who, they deduced, had undoubtedly arrived in Etah. One of the Eskimos had just killed a caribou. It meant salvation for everyone. Lauge Koch learned that Knud Rasmussen had arrived in Etah on August 30 at two in the afternoon, after an exceptionally fast journey of five days, and had remained there.

He also learned that on the fourth day of the trip, some ninety miles south of Cape Agassiz, the expedition leader had met three sledges of reindeer hunters in good health but with no extra provisions to share. After carefully weighing the various possibilities, he had decided to take a sledge and continue very quickly by way of the ice cap to Etah, sixty miles to the south, to seek more help, rather than act immediately with the forces at hand. (Rasmussen had calculated that on foot it would take them nine or ten days to find the second group, given their exhaustion after the forced march.)

There was much discussion at this point among the survivors. Impressed

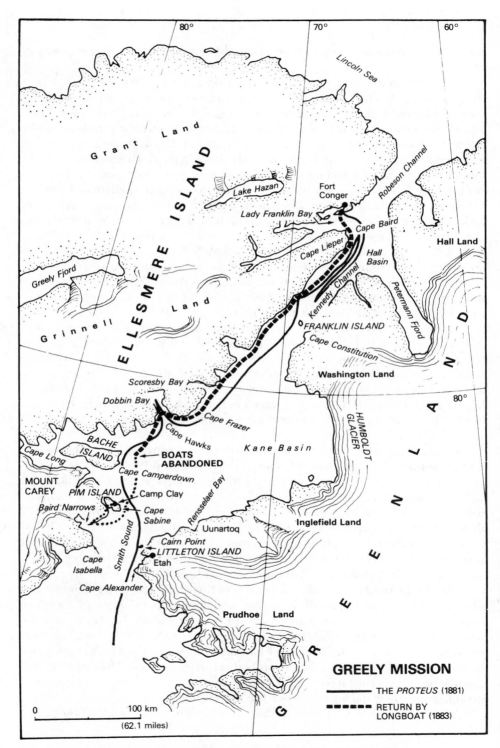

MAP 10. Itinerary of the Return of the Greely Expedition

by Rasmussen's decision, Lauge Koch thoughtfully made his way toward Iceberg Lake—in commemoration later named September Lake—the rendezvous agreed upon earlier. He and the two Eskimos arrived there September 7. Five new sledges from faraway Etah were waiting for them with coffee, tea, sugar, oatmeal, biscuits, canned food . . . and sleeping bags, a precious addition for exhausted men at this time of year, when the weather had already turned cold. There had been no time to make them new clothes. The six experienced hunters sent by Rasmussen had been orally instructed to set up a depot on the shore of the lake and to leave two Eskimos there.

The other four, supplied with provisions, were to search the countryside north of the depot for Wulff's team. Two of them, as we know, had met Koch at Cape Scott.

Thus there were six fresh men now on hand. A crucial decision had to be made: to return to Etah, or immediately to get help to the unfortunate Swede if, against all expectations (can one ever know?), they would still be in time. In any event, to look for his body.

It was finally decided to return to Etah; who made the decision the reports do not say. The entire group headed south, abandoning the unfortunate Wulff a second time. As in a Shakespearean tragedy, it was as though the protagonists were fleeing the place where the drama had occurred. By returning immediately to Etah, Koch no doubt felt he would be restoring responsibility to the leader of the expedition, but Rasmussen, exhausted himself, was deeply affected by the terrible news and did not go back then or ever afterward.

The nine men reached the Etah fjord at ten o'clock at night.

When he was told they were coming, Rasmussen, who had hardly begun to recover from the fatigue of the expedition and from the famine, hurried to meet them. He saw Koch first.

". . . As I came up with them Koch sat down on a stone, pale and without a word, and the tears which rolled down his cheeks told me everything I needed to know.

"A catastrophe had overtaken the expedition. . . ."

It was only a month and a half later that Koch and Aajuku undertook to look for Wulff's body and bury it. It was already the end of October. The sun was low in the sky; everything was covered with snow. The chances of finding Wulff were very slight. Rasmussen had asked Freuchen to go to the area, which he did; he went first to Cape Agassiz to look for the cases of samples, and then, from the Eskimos' description, he recognized the place where Wulff had been left. But neither his body nor any other trace of him (bones, watch, or papers) was ever found.

It was after this great drama that Rasmussen and Koch went separate ways. From then on, Rasmussen led expeditions to the Canadian Arctic, Alaska, and the southeast of Greenland, while Lauge Koch organized large-scale geological expeditions to the north and east of Greenland.

To arrive in this distant desert and find no monument or cross in memory of the Swedish botanist was disconcerting. A stream running along this sector and a Land at 82° were named after the brave scientist, to perpetuate his memory. No cairn or special monument was ever built by Rasmussen or by Lauge Koch when the latter visited the spot in 1922. From what I know about the drama and from my own experience in leading expeditions, I feel very strongly that had Rasmussen stayed with the second group at Cape Agassiz, it would surely have been doomed. Only fresh men bringing help from Etah could have saved the expedition, and only Rasmussen, with his drive and his authority, could have secured that help. All things considered, Rasmussen's was really the only possible solution, and to some extent it worked.

Since, for all my looking, I had not found the exact spot where the drama had taken place, and since no one before me had found any remains either, I did not feel authorized to choose a place arbitrarily and construct a monument there without anyone else's consent.

"I am sure," Freuchen wrote, "that [our friend] regretted his decision to stay behind and tried to follow his companions, and that he lost his way— otherwise we would have found his body. . . . As the Eskimos said to me, the very fact that Wulff did not shoot himself led them to believe that he still hoped he would be saved."

The only indications we have about Wulff's state of mind as his companions left him is the last page of the journal he gave Koch:

"August 29th. I am half dead, but found Woodria ilv.

"Lay down at 7 P.M. for I will not hamper the movements of my comrades on which hangs their salvation."

THE SECOND THULE EXPEDITION

Lauge Koch. Northern Greenland, 1920 or 1921. (*Nygaard, Arktisk Institut, Copenhagen*)

Departure from Etah, on April 13, 1917, of the Second Thule Expedition. In the back row, left to right, are Knud Rasmussen, Aajuku (Qaaqqutsiaq's brother), Thorild Wulff,

Hendrik Olsen, Lauge Koch. In the front row, left to right, are Borseman
(Nasaitsordluarson) and Inukitsupaluk. (*American Museum of Natural History*)

Thorild Wulff. Disko Island, July 1916. *(Arktisk Institut, Copenhagen)*

15

NUANNAARPOQ: GROUP LIFE DURING AN EXPEDITION

I knew my own powers of endurance: I was sustained by my work, and that was only temporary. But what about the great stamina that Eskimos exhibit during ordeals?

"That isn't muscle," one of them told me one day, making me feel his arms and then his body. "That's bone! Take my hand—it's like a pair of pincers. And my mouth is my third hand. I could hold back a dog with it if I had to."

I used to talk to Qaaqqutsiaq sometimes about what had happened to Wulff. I asked him how many days he could go without food in the autumn if he were forced to.

"If I started out in good condition—if my body was 'fat' enough—from two to four weeks. But only if I had water to drink every day, of course. From Cape Scott to Etah you would have to count on a four-day journey, cutting across the top of Qaaqqaitsut. If everything went well . . . I would have walked without stopping—until I died in my tracks like a true Inuk. . . . I would have managed to get back eventually to Etah the way Koch and the two Eskimos did. No Eskimo has ever died of hunger in a hunting area, even when game is scarce, especially if there's hare about. We eat everything, even hare and reindeer droppings, if necessary! We fight to the end!"[41]

It seems—this was the opinion of Peary and Nansen—that the optimum age for Polar expeditions is twenty-five to thirty-five, which is not to say that an older man would be unfit. Peary was fifty-three when he ostensibly reached the North Pole, and Cook was forty-three in the same period. Nansen was thirty-four when he undertook his daring, remarkable expedition to the Pole after quitting his wooden ship, the *Fram;* Amundsen and Scott were, respectively, thirty-nine and forty-two when they conquered the South Pole; Rasmussen was forty-three at the beginning of the Fifth Thule Expedition, to Canada and Alaska.

Physical endurance must be sustained and controlled. The question frequently asked—Does it matter that a man is married or not?—is secondary. What is important is will, a disinterested involvement, and the inner joy one has in pursuing a clearly defined work project.

When you talk about an expedition, you are talking about a team. A leader's primary qualification is the ability to recruit his partners. To make a sound choice calls for breadth of vision, an understanding of psychology, and tact; it is difficult, and you must be extremely careful. The team's homogeneity depends on the leader's choice. Conflicts are inevitable. These conflicts are unimportant if, like the Eskimo, everyone is infinitely patient, and if the bond that unites partners is interest in the joint undertaking, a feeling of admiration or friendship for the expedition's leader, respect for what he is attempting to do. In times of trouble it is up to him to use his competence, his persuasiveness, his empathy, his inner strength, his qualities as a man—generosity, intelligence, modesty, and courage—to make up for whatever this or that member may lack. In the end, the value of the team depends much less on the value of its individual members than on the bonds which unite them to the person who initiated the project, assuming that the methods have been clearly agreed upon at the outset. Empty talk and pretense break down very quickly: a man of no character—a "little" man, a "shallow" man—is very quickly shown up when he faces the challenge of the cold. Nothing is so odious to an Eskimo as egotism and incompetence: "That show-off is no good. Seqajuk! Good-for-nothing! See his head—he looks like an actor! In a big cold there'd be nothing left of him," the Eskimos said to me about a Polar explorer to whom the magazines were then giving a lot of publicity.

A leader is defined by the group he chooses. The mediocre leader attracts and keeps only mediocrities.

Obviously, certain precautions must be taken in dealing with the Eskimo. However well paid, a native who agrees to go on an expedition never thinks of himself as an employee: he knows that his freedom lies in his own hands. He scorns money. What mattered to Kutsikitsoq and Qaaqqutsiaq was, above all, to join me in an adventure that seemed to them different and worthwhile; to participate in a "scientific" *(ilisimasassarsiorneq)* trip that would enhance their status in the eyes of their people and in their own view; to be indispensable to this white man at whose disposal they were happy to put their technical competence in their hunting grounds; and also to accumulate stories to tell during the winters to come. Yet they would only have gone on the express condition that the day-to-day atmosphere seemed to them sufficiently "pleasant." "Nuannaarpoq!" as the Eskimos say.

Blasted *Nuannaarpoq!* How much arguments, how much despair that word has caused! It is hard to define *nuannaarpoq* or its variant, *nuanni.*

It is both a need and a state of being. For example, it is tobacco after you have been without it for a cruelly long time; or bear meat, lots of bear meat; or cold that is intense enough to shatter an oilcan and that people will talk about for years; or being together again after a long, arduous hunting trip; or a beautiful religious service with harmonium music; or an exuberant, sensitive *asasaq*—friend, lover; it is an appetite for living—living intensely, immediately —and for the unexpected; it is a mixture of joy and violence; it is "having fun."

I know a qallunaaq from a sprawling town in southern Greenland who told me how surprised he was that his Greenland maids kept leaving him, one after another. "The little idiots," he said, "they don't even wait to be paid. Psst! One evening the door will shut softly. I'll never lay eyes on them again." How could it have been otherwise? This qallunaaq was the personification of anti-nuanni!

The intuitive sensitivity of the Inuit is apparent in their judgments of men. Their mental pantheon includes a *Piulissuaq,* the great but authoritarian Peary; a *Naalagapaluk,* * the amiable leader (MacMillan); a *Kunuunnguaq*—"Our Knud"—or *Kunuupaluk*—"very dear or nice little Knud"—or later simply *Kunuuki*—"our dear Knud" (Rasmussen). There is also a *Kuukkok* (Lauge Koch), and a *Tatsekuuk* (Dr. Cook), "Tatse" being an alteration of "Doctor." For various reasons, neither of these two earned the privilege of a true surname. Then there is *Amaroq,* wolf, the translation of the name Wulff, whom apparently the Eskimos did not like very much, and *Daigtipaluk,* Dr. Vincent, Peary's doctor, who argued with Peary over his severe treatment of the Eskimos. His Eskimo surname means "the nice unhappy doctor who makes you feel a little sorry for him." Each of these names expresses a nuance in their opinion, which changes according to the circumstances.

I have been called, successively, Malaurie, Malorinnguaq, Maloripaluk, and finally Malorissuaq. Plain "Malaurie" denoted the stranger, the unknown person, and I remained that for four months while they observed me. Then I was Malorinnguaq—the Malaurie who is beginning to be one of us, who is integrating himself into our group. Then Maloripaluk, graduated into the group and occupying a certain place determined by him and the group and changing according to the circumstances to a person we have come to know well, with his good and his bad qualities, someone to like but also to criticize —someone "intimate." I quickly discovered that *paluk* was nothing but nuances. It was an extremely disconcerting surname, since the slightest change in intonation—which my untrained ear could more or less detect—conveyed affection in varying degrees but also criticism and, depending on circumstances, mood, or some feeling of resentment; it could even express distance and lack of compassion. Perhaps the use of it was also a kind of defense against an authority or some sort of "power" on my part which they always distrusted.

I was not to earn the right to the most honorable *suaq*—Malorissuaq—until much later, after I had showed my mettle with some success and also—unfortunately—grown somewhat older! I should add that actually a person is very

---

*The suffixes vary in meaning according to the intonation: *suaq* means "the great," but also, in certain cases, "the ugly," as in *meerarssuaq,* "the bad boy." In the Thule dialect, *paluk* has emotional overtones which are sometimes protective—"dear," "nice." As Schultz-Lorentzen points out in his Greenlandic dictionary, *Kunuupaluk* means "dear Knud," *Suvfiapaluk,* "dear Sofia," and *Palasipaluk,* "the good pastor."

rarely addressed by his surname or name, and never by a first name, which is unknown here. The Eskimo is still afraid that he will paralyze the forces of nature with the spoken word.

The Eskimos have a very fair sense of values. For example, they understand that a scientist is not a businessman, that he is not rich, and for him they will spontaneously lower their fees; in fact, nothing honors or flatters them more than to contribute to the success of an important project, to hold a theodolite or an altimeter. They are aware of how far behind they are technically, and like to learn things that can be useful to their society. They are keenly observant; my Eskimo companions used to take mental note of each of my geomorphological operations, and were anxious not to make a mistake or appear ridiculous when they reported to the group on my activities and accomplishments.

They have a very harsh opinion of the tourist who misjudges the country, the Sunday explorer who is loaded down with equipment but lacks personality or purpose in life—even if he is lavish in his fees. Here everything is gauged and appraised by intuition and tact. This is why it is so hard to give specific advice to people traveling in Eskimo country. The rules cannot be taught; you have to sense them. While on a long journey, you must have a humble attitude toward the Eskimos' daily tasks—care of the dogs, loading the sledge, hunting, predicting the weather, deciding on the itinerary and schedule, building the igloo. Nothing irritates the Eskimo as much as the "Boy Scout" who thinks he knows it all. After his guide has loaded the sledge, he goes around shifting things and tying queer knots; the jerrycan should go in back, not in front; the pan should be on the right, not on the left; the chamber pot won't look good in a photograph and is modestly covered with a cloth. This is all wasted effort. The Eskimo is sure of himself and slowly moves in, overturns the load, and reties it the way he wants it. Don't meddle in what does not concern you! Here you are a mere "transient." "They" have centuries of experience behind them. Even if they were wrong about something, it would be a waste of time to try to convince them of it. They expect almost no help from you in what they are doing. One example from among many: two men are on the trail; the cold is penetrating; time seems endless. Ten, fifteen hours go by without a break, as the sledge glides forward. The white traveler is hunched down on the low floor of the sledge behind the hunter, who sits up straight and for hours does not condescend even to turn around. The white man, a newcomer, begins to moan and complain: "When are we going to get there? Is it far?" Silence. "Oh, what a country! Is it much farther? Tell me, is it far?" Nothing exasperates an Eskimo more, because these questions betray the traveler's lack of interest in his surroundings. He will answer, in a monotone, that today the weather is clear and beautiful, that the snow is *manngertaq*—crackling under the dogs' feet; he will be thinking that this qallunaaq does not talk enough, is not nuanni, that his dogs are suffering because the sledge is heavily loaded, etc. He will point out that behind that little island there are lots of seals and it's a great pity he can't go there this minute, that this trip is causing him a lot of trouble. . . .

Because of the white man his children will certainly suffer from hunger this winter. . . . He will not have had time to do enough hunting. Then the white man will protest that he has paid him quite a lot of money and they must go faster. . . . This is just what the Eskimo has been waiting for: he whips his dogs, pretends to be speeding on, but actually prolongs this stage of the trip. The run will be finished in glacial silence and the white man will have been put in his place.

To maintain his authority, the leader of an expedition must know how to be uncompromising about certain specific things, such as the choice of itinerary and the schedule to be followed, how provisions and chores will be divided. If the expedition leader has decided how long one lap of the trip will be (after consulting with his Eskimo guide, of course), and the guide then wants to shorten it for no apparent good reason, the leader must insist, no matter what, that the original plan be followed.

"Ajornara," Kutsikitsoq would sometimes say to me. "It's impossible to go any farther. I know the country better than you do."

It is up to you to know, to sense whether or not he is lying. If you think it is possible to go on, then risk it. But whatever you do, make no mistakes— it would be the last time the Eskimo went with you.

What if the wretched Inuk won't listen, what if he turns stubborn? Then compromise; give in with a smile! But when you get the upper hand again, be sure to make him feel it. In this harsh country, where a high price is paid for everything, life is a silent daily struggle. Like an accountant, the hunter keeps track of your credits and debits; sooner or later accounts are settled.

At all costs you must avoid outbursts of anger and threats. There are numerous causes for disagreement, but anger erupts only for serious, rare reasons. Most of the time criticism and backbiting give way quickly to harmony and reconciliation. To quarrel with one Eskimo is almost sure to alienate the whole group. Prolonged misunderstandings are intolerable.

The little white man is getting angry, they will think. *Kamappoq!* An atmosphere of mutual defiance will develop between you and the Eskimo. "That qallunaaq? Not at all nuanni." And at the first chance your companion will say that his eyes are bothering him, or he has a headache, or he has sprained something; he will leave you where you are and return home.

The Eskimo will be all the more stubborn if he feels that his honor has been attacked. When the Marvin group was on its way back from Peary's last expedition, in the spring of 1909, a tragic incident took place. Professor Ross Marvin was the only genuine scientist on the expedition and was perhaps critical of Peary; returning from the 86°, he was following instructions to make his way toward the ship with two Eskimos, one of whom was Inukitsupaluk. Like the white men, the Eskimos had been frightened by the dangers they had faced and were worn down by the daily struggle. Evidently their freedom of spirit was undiminished, though, for Bartlett spoke of "constant slacking off" and MacMillan, Peary's companion, went so far as to say that the famous Uutaaq was a "quitter" and an "agitator." Peary never reported this tension. The cold was severe. Suddenly the three men found themselves in trouble: it seemed that Inukitsupaluk could not go any farther. At this point Marvin may have given orders that, for the sake of the team, Inukitsupaluk be abandoned, although no one knows for certain—the facts are unclear. However it may be, Inukitsupaluk's cousin, Kulluttu (actually, all Eskimos are in some sense cousins), chose to kill Marvin rather than abandon his fellow Eskimo, who was in danger. A few days later, the two Eskimos arrived safely at the ship. According to the official version of the incident, Professor Marvin had "accidentally" fallen into a crevasse.

"The Eskimos' staying power has been greatly exaggerated," noted Adolphus Greely, head of the American expedition during the Second International Polar Year. "These people are absolutely incapable of appreciating the goal of a trip like this; how can they help becoming gloomy and losing all their moral resiliency?"

Given the experiences of Peary, Cook, Vilhjalmur Stefansson, Rasmussen, Koch, and myself, these criticisms seem to me wide of the mark. Is it not possible that Lieutenant Greely, who was certainly a remarkable explorer, might have avoided the disaster that struck him if he had set out with a different opinion of the value of the assistance the local natives could have given him?

Trust the Eskimos judiciously, and you will be surprised to find that they will work extremely hard and even risk their lives for you.

One last remark—the Eskimo does not like to be swindled. He is aware that he plays an important part in many expeditions. He senses that these big voyages of exploration are more often than not profitable for the men who organize them. He knows that they go back to America or Europe and write books and sell their photographs, as well as the pelts and souvenirs they have bought on the spot for very little. Peary set up a real business in furs and ivory that he obtained by bartering with these poor men. The Eskimo leaves detailed arrangements up to the white man, but as a principal actor in the drama he still expects a fair share of the benefits. If in addition to providing information, collecting salable objects and furs, and acting as guide, the Eskimo often saves the lives of the men who put themselves in his care, the reasons for his bitterness are not hard to sympathize with.

16

A
BEAR
HUNT

We were at Qaaqqaitsut, on the edge of Humboldt Glacier. As we moved north, we saw more and more tracks. One night, Kutsikitsoq plunged his harpoon into the snow in front of the igloo, point upturned. He covered the point with his qulitsaq.

I looked at him, startled. Apparently this used to be a kind of signal. A man who was being chased by a bear had thought up this trick to save himself. In a rage, the nanoq had thrown himself at the disguised harpoon and impaled himself on it.

Near Cape Agassiz, we became so excited that when the Eskimos saw a very recent track, they got the sledges unloaded in seconds, throwing things every which way. The first trail we followed was deep and distinct. No doubt about it: it had been made the day before and the bear was large.[42] The dogs were all keyed up and kept a good pace, following one another at regular intervals; the sledges crossed a cape, rounded an iceberg, and passed near the same allu three times. Countless fox prints cut across the trail. For more than two hours the Eskimos doubled back and forth. It did not seem that the animal could have left the fjord, in which there were no icebergs; I had already set up camp there and had decided to name it Martonne, after a great French geographer who was encouraging me in my Polar studies. At four in the morning, a white fog gathered around the base of the slopes and slowly crept out over the ice field. The dogs' red tongues were hanging out, and they were dragging their feet. The snow was not hard and frozen, as on previous days. Under the sun it had become thick and soft—melting sugar crystals.

To warm up and to give the teams a rest, the Inuit stopped for a bit and made some tea. We were at the mouth of the fjord, near the more easterly of the two large islands that close it off to the north. We started to talk, and everyone sounded skeptical and disillusioned.

"I will never dare face the other Inuit again," Qaaqqutsiaq groaned.

Bear hunting. According to the Eskimo, this is how we should understand the scene: to the left, the dogs have surrounded the bear, who cannot escape; however, earlier he bit the hunter, who is sitting off to one side. The two sledges on the right are coming

"Not even one tiny little bear, ajor!

"This nanoq-tupilak, this bear-spirit keeps going back and forth; it's enough to make you lose your way!" But then Qaaqqutsiaq explained that in April and May the bears are seeking mates, and that is why they wander around, seemingly aimlessly.

"If it were winter, all we would have to do would be to follow a trail as straight as this whip handle. Nothing stops the bears then! No matter what's in their way—lakes, plateaus, mountains—they go straight ahead. Unless there's a precipice, of course, an ippik. But look at them now. And I'm sure, absolutely sure," he added, "that he is here in the fjord. He's roaming around here somewhere. As long as he hasn't smelled us, he might come by here— but it isn't possible that he hasn't smelled us! So where will he go by? When is this nanorsuaq, this big bear, going to show himself?"

It was then that Padloq, who had gone off, pipe clenched between her teeth, to satisfy her needs, suddenly found herself face-to-face with him: the joker, paws curled inward, was watching her curiously, his small triangular ears cocked toward her.

A leap, a shout, and the dogs lunged forward in a cloud of snow. The men had thrown themselves on their sledges. They yelled to their teams: "Sjorfaa! . . . Sjorfaa!"

The dogs quickened their pace. The bear, his belly close to the ground,

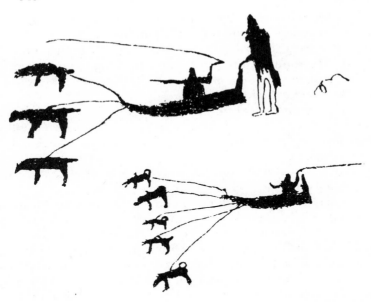

to his aid; the person standing behind one of the sledges has been drawn so tall because he is a qallunaaq. Drawing by Mitsoq. (*From Steensby,* Contributions)

was running at a prodigious speed. It was wonderful to see the normally lumpish animal now so streamlined and agile.

There was no open water nearby where he knew he could not be harmed. He was heading northeast, toward Humboldt Glacier, approaching an area covered with hummocks where it would be hard to catch up with him. He bounded along, his neck outstretched; then he changed tactics and kept turning his head to look back. We were gaining on him, and he swerved toward the glacier wall: he was doomed.

Each man took out his knife, pulled his dogs to him, and cut their traces as close as possible. If the bear caught hold of the harness he would swing the poor animals around in the air like missiles. Fifteen raging dogs raced after the animal, surrounded him, and brought him to a standstill. They attacked him only from one side, for every good dog knows that bears are left-handed. Clearly nanoq himself felt that this was the end. He raised up on his hind legs and faced them. He turned his elegant head right, left; his haggard, sharp, dark-brown eyes stared into space. Now the sledges drew up. The bear turned suddenly, took a gigantic leap along the wall, and managed to disengage himself. Desperately he dug his claws into the ice and inch by inch pulled himself up a fault. The dogs howled and leaped to snap at his dangling paw. Was nanoq going to make his escape? The men intervened. With military precision, they fired.[43] The bear paused, clambered higher, and clung to the cliff. The snow turned red. Large drops of blood fell one by one. The animal was still only wounded, and he dropped turd upon turd; at last a bullet bore into his skull near his ear; he fell into a small crevasse. He made one last attempt to get up. His snout looked moth-eaten, his blue tongue protruded between his teeth, and he collapsed on the ice. Silently, the men looked at his outstretched body—silently and even sadly.

"After all, he's the one closest to us!" Kutsikitsoq said. (The bear is so closely identified with man that, according to Inuterssuaq, when one killed a bear one was to observe a period of mourning as for humans—three days for a male, five for a female.)

Regret quickly vanished, however; the pleasure of hunting and the need to eat were more powerful.

It took more than two hours to pull him out of the crevasse. Meanwhile there was a rattling of iron, loud laughter, and much calling back and forth. Once he was out, we stripped off his fur with broad strokes of the knife. Then the men gutted the animal, taking care to remove the gall and bury it in the ice, otherwise it would poison the meat and make our hair fall out. All the meat except the intestines and lungs was divided into seven parts. We found grass and shreds of Arctic willow branches in the bear's stomach; the animal must have been cruelly hungry. "Here, take these!" Natuk gave me the teeth and claws, for my wife if I ever married: "They will make her remain faithful to you!" I was assured. With irony, a piece of meat was thrown to Nerrivik, goddess of the waters; then came the dogs' turn; then, at last, ours. As the men ate the raw marrow and fat and the cooked tongue, which was considered most delectable, they told hunting stories.

Bear hunting. (*From Mylius-Erichsen and Moltke,* Gronland)

An ancestor goes out into the ice field: he sees an extraordinary bear coming toward him, a sort of jointed bear skeleton. Is that not surprising? But the hunter, who is something of an angakkoq, does not panic and quickly manages to remove himself partially from his own material envelope. And behold he, too, becomes a skeleton! As he is doing this, he takes care to put his son to sleep by magic. He walks up to the bear, who is dumbfounded to encounter another skeleton. The angakkoq takes advantage of the bear's amazement and kills him. He puts his own self back together with no difficulty, and awakens his son, who marvels at such a fine hunt. . . .

Such things may happen to an old angakkoq, but sometimes the struggle is harder. Three men are out hunting, one of whom has only recently become a sorcerer. They come across an enormous bear, which straightaway leaps upon the angakkoq. Before he can protect himself, the bear rips his stomach open so wide that the poor man sees his intestines spill out and form a little heap on the snow. Though he is only a beginner, he is an angakkoq nonetheless, and the moment the animal draws back to attack again, the man gathers up his intestines with one sweep of his arms, puts them back in his belly, and, walking bravely forward, fells him with one blow.

The Bear in Love

A young male bear loved a young Eskimo woman very much.

He used to go to see her in her igloo every day.

Her husband would be out hunting—bear, to be exact.

And while he was gone, the little woman and nanoq embraced each other in the warm igloo.

The bear said: "Listen, little woman, I live up there, you go that way, keep going that way, then you turn right, you walk for two hours: and you are there. I would love to have a little wife like you. . . ." Then, in a loud voice, he said: "But don't ever tell your Inuk where I live. . . . Remember that even from very far away, I will hear you."

"Ieh . . . ieh," the little woman answered, hiding in her lover's warm, tufted armpit.

The days went by. The Inuk had still not killed a bear.

This put him in a bad humor every night. Sometimes he sniffed the air and said:

"Tipi! that's strange, it smells very bad in here, like . . . you'd almost say like bear."

"No, no, of course not," his wife would answer. "It must be your kamiks, which I'm mending."

Soon the Inuk became so peevish that he no longer cared about anything.

Yet his qulitsaq was well sewn, his house was clean, a supply of snow for water was always within reach, and the floor was regularly swept and covered with fresh snow every morning.

"Oh, I don't care about all that," he grumbled. "All I know is, I haven't killed a bear! Hmm!"

Then one night, when once again he had pushed his little wife away to the other end of the bed on the illeq, she put her mouth close, close to his ear and whispered into it as softly as she could: "Nanoq!"

The man started up, and leaped for his harpoon.

"Nanoq! Naa! Where is it? Where?"

"Laaaa, laaaa . . . ," she said to calm him, and again she whispered in his ear: "Up there, high up in the mountain . . . you go this way, that way, keep going that way, then you turn right, you walk for two hours, and there it is. In a hollow full of snow—yes, that one."

The man ran from the igloo. Quickly, quickly, he flew up into the mountain with his harpoons and his dogs.

But up there the bear's igloo was already empty. Nanoq had heard.

Back home, the woman had crawled beneath the illeq, trembling so hard that her fingernails dug into the snow.

A kind of thunder poured down the mountain.

It was he—can you hear him? Panting, he ran down, and he went straight to the igloo. He was about to crush it; he raised his enormous paw . . .

No.

Betrayed and grieving, the bear limped away on his long solitary journey.

In Washington Land

Early on the morning of May 12, I broke camp at Cape Agassiz and we continued on our way along Humboldt Glacier. This glacier, the largest in the Northern Hemisphere, has been lyrically described by Kane, who discovered it, and his account can hardly be matched. We were gliding along beside an awesome wall of ice, 150 to 300 feet high and some sixty miles long, a labyrinth paved with hummocks and icebergs. There were innumerable bear tracks, and at each more or less zigzagging trail the four Eskimos' euphoria grew.

From time to time they scaled icebergs and inspected the immense desert with an old pair of field glasses. "Many bear tracks, but no bears!" they muttered. Suddenly the dogs broke into a gallop. In our three sledges, we arrived, breathless, near a large iceberg that was facing south. A bear had been sleeping at the foot of it: at one spot, the snow was still pressed down. A trail of blood led from an allu, and it was easy to reconstruct the scene: two or three days earlier the bear had caught a seal, which he had dragged to the iceberg; he had eaten half of it. Our dogs, milling around but silent, devoured the frozen remains with a few laps of the tongue. It looked as if the bear had headed north. In an effort to take the animal by surprise, we laid aside our whips. The dogs were excited again after their meal; with tails straight up, they trotted on, still refraining from making the slightest noise; they were all bunched together. We spoke in undertones. The sledges were wrapped in silence as they sliced through the thick snow like sailboats.

Behind us, the tragic land of Qaaqqaitsut widened in an extraordinary way. From where I sat I kept watching it. Not until afternoon did that bluish horizon blur and then vanish in a cottony fog. The bear's trail, unhappily, was lost. We continued to push ahead. On the thirteenth—the morning of Pentecost—we saw, high on the horizon against a gray sky, the first dull-brown signs of a new country: the foothills of Washington Land. But the weather was turning bad. As we passed over the northern spur of the glacier, a strong northeasterly wind and gusts of snow struck us obliquely. After four hours of very difficult travel, we reached the desolate shores of Benton Bay. The valley corridor was like the outlet of a powerful bellows. We tried to set up our tent on the delta, but were forced to make camp at the foot of the cliff on the left bank of the valley. We secured the tent with stones. The instant the shelter was set up, we crawled into our sleeping bags, completely done in. We had been on the move for twenty-three hours almost without a break.

We stayed in Washington Land only until May 20. We skirted the coast from the little island of Pullassuaq to Cape Jackson, stopping over in Benton Bay, Cass Fjord, and the bays of Nygaard and Wright. On Pullassuaq I found a cairn Koch had built twenty-nine years before; there was no message in it. There were many traces of prehistoric sites—circles of stones, etc. Koch had arrived here, almost starving, and with no dogs, having just crossed the glacier on his way back from Peary Land. It was from here that he sent two of his three companions, Inuteq and Nukapianguaq (Sakaeunnguaq's father), on foot across a broken ice field to alert an Eskimo named Qisuk, who had stayed at Nunataq on Wright Bay all winter—which was unusual—and who was spending the summer there as well. It was this hunter, Qisuk, who saved the four men, with the help of Talilenguaq.

I went up the clay-covered plain to the northeast of the glacial outflow and arrived at the first lake. But the thaw was already well under way and my dogs floundered around in the mud. On the Benton coast, near the stream, I found the remains of the prehistoric Eskimo camp Rasmussen had reported.

Exploring the northern sector of Cass Fjord, I reached the northernmost point on my itinerary (80° 15′). I was working under a cloudy, gray sky on what was the fourth day of high winds in a month. Excellent ice enabled Qaaqqutsiaq and me to reach all the places we were aiming for on the ice field off the western coastal platform, to make important rectifications in the topographical map, and to continue my geomorphological mapping project. The coast near our base was covered with gravel and pebbles, and here Padloq discovered vestiges of human habitation (carved flint, etc.). When I came back from a day spent measuring scree slopes on the plateau, I found her squatting on the ground burrowing for still more fossil harpoons to add to the pile she had kindly placed in front of my tent. Clearly, during an earlier and warmer period, this whole coast had been inhabited. No study of it had yet been done. I built a cairn on the spot, in which I placed a third message, the last but one that could be found by a rescue team if we had not returned to our point of departure by the time winter came. The Eskimos added a crudely written letter, and I put the papers in a hermetically sealed Nescafé packet. We stayed on the Nunataq beach for several fine days, during which time I worked very intensely on an in-depth study of the processes of formation of the thin scree on the slopes. At last, on the nineteenth, we reached Cape Jackson, the farthest point on our expedition. A large water hole washed against the shore here; ducks were paddling around in this free water, and a seal showed its clownish face. This small polynya is well known: bear hunters come here in March for the walruses and seals they will need on their expeditions along the Humboldt Glacier in April and May.

From Cape Calhoun, I saw the first birds of the year pass by, borne along by the south wind: gulls, geese, ducks, even some guillemots or sea kings, who seemed to have got lost in the previous week's heavy fog; they were crying. They had come too far: they were 140 miles north of where they should have

Block diagram of Washington Land. In July: the ice field is broken up. Nunataq Bay is in the foreground, center. Our second camp (X) in Washington Land was set up at the foot of the second combe of the southernmost cliff. In the right background the entrance to Cass Fjord can be seen. I set up a small supply depot there. In the left foreground is Wright Bay. (*From Malaurie,* Thèmes de recherche geomorphologique)

been, the last rookeries being in Etah. The gulls hovered on their white wings in the sunshine.

These were a bad sign! They meant the season was well under way. The ice field was going to break up, and I had completed only part of my program: I had still to get to Ellesmere Island in Canada for the balance of the isostatic and geomorphological measurements. I had to hurry.

Even if I had wanted to, it would have been impossible for me to go any farther north along Kennedy Channel via the Greenland ice field. Everywhere the ice was beginning to fragment. The ice foot I had walked on along the vertical cliff of Troedsson to reach Cape Calhoun was now only twenty to thirty inches wide. We lingered for a moment at the bottom of one of those massive and very interesting scree slopes. The coast of Canada was not far, less than eighteen miles across Kennedy Channel. I was 10° from the Pole, or some 690 miles away. Thule was about 310 miles to the south by sledge, and Savigssivik 370 miles.

On the evening of the twenty-first, I decided to head back to Uunartoq, where we would find our depot of provisions. As soon as we had loaded up with cartridges and oil, we would go west; in other words, toward uninhabited Ellesmere Island. Our pace was slowed by the fact that my bitch was about to whelp. Brave Pikuli was too proud to let herself be carried on the sledge like a vulgar package. Swollen belly notwithstanding, she courageously ran her twelve to forty miles per day; it was pitiful to see her look at us with her dim, gentle eyes every time we stopped. Qaaqqutsiaq kept diligently searching for bear tracks. Those we found were all tangled up, as though the bears were loafing about. We wandered to the right and left along our route, first going straight south, then veering toward the east. We were following a still-fresh track when we were enveloped in snow and intermittent fog rising from the open waters to the south. The search for bears was causing us to describe figure eights over a mosaic of icebergs, and we gave up.

17

FROM GREENLAND TO CANADA BY DOGSLEDGE

We reached Inuarfissuaq on May 23. There our group was to split up. Kutsikit-soq and I, each on his own sledge, would go inland to September Lake, on to Hiawatha Glacier, and explore the back of the plateau, working our way southwest to Uunartoq. Qaaqqutsiaq and the women would travel by short stages southward along the coast to the depot at Uunartoq, with our equipment. They would have ample time to hunt seal while waiting for us, and thus our food reserves would be largely assured. We separated on May 26. A few moments before I gave the signal to take off, Pikuli gave birth to the first of her five puppies. We hurried over to the rock where she had taken shelter; with my fingernail I tore open one fibrous membrane and turned the still wet animal over:

"Angut! It's a male!"

Honor was safe. Holding them by their back paws, so that their heads hung down, we examined them one by one to see which had strong bodies. When a pup is strong, it will raise its head. As was the custom, those not strong enough were thrown to the other dogs, who devoured them. The angut that passed the test I distributed as gifts, and gave the signal to leave.

Our route along the fjord presented no problems. The ice was smooth and flat. As we went up the stream bed leading to September Lake, we entered an endless valley.

This country had never been mapped. I took sighting after sighting, although I was soon plagued by the number of things to be done: I had not only to sketch the topography and make cross sections of the terrain but I also had to guide my dogs, shout encouragingly to them, and push my sledge, which did not move easily through the clumps of melting snow that covered the gravel in the riverbed. When runners got jammed between big rocks jutting up out of the snow, the sledge jolted to a stop. In the most difficult places, we ran ahead of the dogs, pulling them forward. We noticed many signs of caribou, but we were shouting so loud that the reindeer probably fled as we approached. A qupannaaq (snow bunting) followed us for a while. To thank him for his little aria, I threw him some symbolic biscuits, as is the Eskimo custom.

On the afternoon of the twenty-sixth, we arrived at the lake that was renamed September Lake, in memory of the Second Thule Expedition. Also variously called Hiawatha and Iceberg Lake, it lies at an altitude of 900 feet. As we stood on the shore, we were surprised to see that a bear had been there a few days before; he had come from the east side of the glacier and, according to Kutsikitsoq, he was one thin, listless flatfoot. We bivouacked on a large rock of spangled gray gneiss which looked comfortable. We did not put up a tent, but lay on our sledges under the open sky. My friend, tired from our climb the day before, slept heavily for nine hours. The only way I could rouse him was to take him his tea.

"Tii massakkut! The tea is ready!"

Like a big, disheveled, half-conscious monkey, he hesitantly stretched out his arm toward his cup; as it filled, his arm drew back. Then crafty Kutsikitsoq woke up. He was in a bad humor, displeased with his dreams. All morning long he was worried, uneasy. Whenever our sledges were side by side, he told me about his troubles: Kutsikitsoq was sad and weary. He was far away from his people, far away from Qaaqqutsiaq and the two women. Every evening he imagined being inside gay, noisy igloos filled with seal meat and friends. "Admit it, I'm not as good as Qaaqqutsiaq. He's alert, he's lively, agreeable. For me, it's all over. I see it very clearly; you two get along well. The way we did last winter in Savigssivik. I don't know how to explain it to you, but nightmares depress me completely. For several days now, qivittoqs have been pursuing me in my dreams. And then I see things more clearly. Yes! I must be too old. Black thoughts thin your blood. Kutsikitsoq—taama, finished."

And he spat into the air.

"Look at my head—look at it! There's no hair left on top; you see what I'm saying—it's too dry. . . . How unlucky I am! Dead children . . . puak . . . tuberculosis, the doctor said. . . . They're at Qaanaaq, lying beneath stones; I go there with Natuk every summer . . . just to 'see' them. . . . You don't have any children—oh, that's right, you're not married.

"My son Masaannaa is about to get married, and I won't be at the religious ceremony. . . . Oh, dear . . . I have nothing left—just Natuk, some dogs, and these. . . ." He showed me his harpoon and his gun. "That's all I have. My house? I have no house. I live in a hole in Qinnissut . . . fit only for animals. Natuk's brother, Inuterssuaq, is rich, and he knows it. Have you noticed how he acts when he has guests? He's told me he would take me in when I get too old. Huh! He also told me I don't know how to save money. I don't understand those . . . those kroner. I can't hold on to them. But he acts like a white man; he keeps accounts and reports. A real qallunaaq. He picked that up when he was working at Thule as a kiffaq in Kununnguaq's [Knud Rasmussen's] store with Pitersuaq [Peter Freuchen], those sanctimonious manners and that sugary tone of voice. Well, you've heard it, you know what I mean—when he's talking to white men. There he is in front of them, with his hands folded on his knees, and he speaks slowly, and he bows and wags his head, and he listens with such attention and patience, using the same words they do in their 'pidgin' Eskimo. He knows very well that white men like those meek manners. But that's not the Eskimo way—that pious tone of voice, those expressions. . . . Yet he is a real Eskimo. His father, Ulloriaq, was a great hunter. His sister, Navarana, married Pitersuaq. She was extremely beautiful and sweet. Why are you making me talk about him so much? You know Inuterssuaq as well as I do. He is good at organizing and acts the leader in Kangerluarsuaq. 'Nunaga! my land, my country,' he says. Soorlu kongi! As if he were a king! What kind of talk is that? The land belongs to everyone. He even set up a small shark-oil factory. That blasted Inuterssuaq! But he is no hunter anymore; he doesn't go adventuring on impulse the way we do, just for the pleasure of hunting and being together, men among men. What's more, he doesn't go bear hunting anymore and he has kiffaqs like the white men. With him everything is planned, organized so he can pile up possessions. He's a clerk. Those aren't Inuit ways of thinking. The way he condescends, the way he acts like a rich man, like someone accepted by white men—that goes against my grain. And during the winter it hurts him to give me meat when I have no more for my dogs. A real shopkeeper. Yes, that's the word. When you ask him for help, he puts on that tired voice of his or he acts superior. I don't want to be a beggar. Kutsikitsoq living in Inuterssuaq's house? Never! Naamivik!" He went on and on, intoning his never-ending hymn about the golden age when Eskimos truly loved one another like brothers.

"In the time of my father, Uutaaq—oh, how different everything was. . . ."

Like a dethroned prince, he wearily snapped his whip across the dark backs of his dogs.

It was late in the morning when we reached the high cliff of the ice cap. The thaw had already done its work. The glacier looked bad, and obviously Kutsikitsoq had no idea where the pass was. He made a great effort and walked all over the place, grumbling.

"Ajornara!" he said to me. "There's no way."

It was clear he had understood none of Qaaqqutsiaq's patient, detailed explanations. As we floundered through the rushing torrents, I measured the position of the glacier so that I could calculate how far it had advanced or retreated since my predecessor, Lauge Koch, had been here in 1922. Finally, I tackled the glacier myself, going up a steep ravine on its left side. We climbed from one level to the next, and by the end of the afternoon, according to my altimeter, we had reached an altitude of four thousand feet. We discussed which route to follow going southwest. We were thinking that we could stay above the thaw area, when to the north the sky clouded over. Big clouds, which meant snow and fog coming from Kennedy Channel the next day. So we decided to go as far as we could that night, dropping slightly lower on the ice cap but proceeding very cautiously, for this area, which was on the edge of Hiawatha Glacier, was bound to be riddled with crevasses. Our forecast was not mistaken. A few hours later, we were wrapped in a milky fog. We laughed when we glimpsed each other's frost-battered faces. The barometer continued to fall throughout the twenty-eighth. We felt as though we were drowning in a watery fluid. The occasional holes in the thickening fog began to seem like harbors. Kutsikitsoq was not enjoying this experience. He was the one, however, who had insisted on going with me. But unlike Qaaqqutsiaq, he did not know how to find his way over a glacier by guesswork in such fog. Now that the plateaus were hidden from sight and the weather was threatening, he started complaining again; he followed me so slowly that I kept having to stop and wait for him. We did move forward cautiously, our sledges tilted at a 20 degree angle on the side of the glacier. To be sure of staying on my route I watched my altimeter carefully, although I could not rely on it completely because the pressure kept changing; indeed, that was evident just from observing the weather. I walked at right angles to the rivulets of water formed by the melting iceberg. If we were to veer too far to the west-southwest, inevitably we would end up at the edge of the ice cap, and that was a sheer vertical cliff more than 300 feet high. . . . Peerujoq! Peerujoq! Fog and more fog. At times I could hardly see the tails of my own dogs.

After walking thirteen hours in zigzags, we pitched camp for the second time. What was left of our two seals we divided among the dogs and ourselves, and we made ourselves snug in our shelter. After we had eaten, I tried to determine our position. Figuring our progress at one to two miles an hour, I could tell our position within several miles. The point was not to go beyond the longitude of Uunartoq—70° 30'—or we would risk wandering endlessly over the glacier. Kutsikitsoq had calmed down, and he was watching me as I made these calculations; he picked up my compass carelessly and held it in this and that position, to show me that it was worthless.

"Oh, I know about that. That doesn't impress me. Uutaaq had one, but they're of no use to us. No use at all. Like qallunaat books. Our books are in our heads. This is the Eskimo compass"—he pointed to his eyes and his nose. "But now that I'm old, you're right, a pujorsiut* might be useful to me. . . . That must be it. . . . But look at the needle. It's going to the right; then if I tilt the pujorsiut to the left, look what happens. It's going in all directions.

"Ajorpoq! No good," he concluded, putting the compass away less carefully than usual.

After this streak of sarcasm, Kutsikitsoq suddenly became servile and began speaking to me in a sugary tone of voice. He kept going to get me more snow for tea; without my asking, he repaired the tip of my whip. He tidied up

---

*Siut: ear; pujoq: fog. By extension, "something that helps you find your way in the fog"; that is, a compass.

the tent again; he handed me the pile of rough notes he had seen me throw down. This was a bit too much! The clown was hiding something from me. I marked our position on my map and wrote down the main events of the day in my journal. I acted as if I had noticed nothing out of the ordinary. Kutsikitsoq, who knew me very well, grew even more irritated. He was afraid, I realized —afraid of this part of the country, which he was not familiar with, afraid of himself, afraid of my silence. And when an Eskimo, who by nature is such a pragmatist, feels the reality of things eluding him, he is seized by a genuine inner panic. He puts himself in the hands of the shaman (or what today has taken the shaman's place) or of the white man, although he has very little confidence in the white man where the life of his country is concerned. If both appear to let him down, he does the impossible to go back home immediately —and I mean *immediately*—whatever the risks, as if, once he is on his home ground, new strength will well up through his feet, through the air he breathes, through communication with his immediate family.

It was true that our situation was difficult, though not really perilous. The fog might very well continue, and we were already short of provisions. The more distant features of the landscape were hidden by the mist and if we did not make a sharp change in direction at a certain latitude—but how would we know, in this fog?—we would, at a point beyond a large north-south depression, penetrate farther into the ice cap which ended at Cape Alexander. At that moment, our situation in this crevassed desert of lifeless ice would no longer be merely delicate; it would become dangerous.

I would have to be careful in my navigation and hardly rely on the Eskimo, who was disinclined now to cooperate with me since he did not know the area at all. Kutsikitsoq's tousled head was bowed as he sat holding his bowl of steaming tea in both hands, Eskimo fashion. In a low, sheepish voice which seemed to emerge from his qulitsaq, he said: "I'm going back where we started from. To join the Inuit again. I'm going alone," he added, in a whisper. "It's no good here. I have to go back. Pissortut!" The "pissortut," blurted out softly, showed how unsure he was. I said something brief and ironical to the effect that that was a very bad attitude! It was just as dangerous to go back as to go forward. The fog was the same behind us as in front of us. "There's no tupilak on the glacier! Besides, Qaaqqutsiaq has talked to me about these phony theatrical fits of panic you've been subjecting me to ever since Etah. What has happened to our happy trip through the Polar night over the fjords and glaciers from Siorapaluk to Savigssivik? Tell me what has become of those days? Sometimes I feel that was so long ago a year might have passed since then."

Kutsikitsoq was furious; he stood up, his mouth slightly tensed. He said nothing. Calmly, slowly, he gathered his things together. His strong fingers, their nicked nails looking as though they had been hacked away, some of them broken, were a few inches from my hands. He was looking for the needle we used to clean the tube of the Primus; it belonged to him. But the Primus belonged to me. He took the needle anyway. I did not say a word. With his back to me, having got all his things together, he ripped open the flap of the tent and closed it behind him slowly, very slowly, taking great care over the last few inches. I had not moved a muscle. I had not turned a hair. I heard him outside gather his dogs together and harness them, more and more slowly. Five minutes later, I heard "Qaa! Qaa! . . . assut!" He was gone.

And there I was, alone—alone and abandoned. Like an Eskimo, I reacted to my problem by having something to eat. I had one-fifth of a seal left. I could think best while chewing: by recovering the natural rhythm of the body, it was possible to regain serenity and strength. I looked over my notes again. Three hours went by, at the end of which I had decided on my plan: first, I would sleep; then, early in the morning, I would leave with my dogs, following the route I had chosen.

It would not be the first time; in November, alone with my dogs, I had had to negotiate rotten sections of the ice field, foot by foot. But a glacier is treacherous. Since I could not calculate my position as long as the sun was hidden, I decided to proceed this way: for a certain number of hours I would go southwest. Then I would go north toward the plateau. I would have to descend the side of the glacier very cautiously. . . . But, what the devil, it would not be the first time I had had to travel through the fog by guesswork. The time passed and my thoughts wandered. I was about to go to bed when I heard the muffled footsteps of dogs near my tent. Kutsikitsoq?

I did not move. It was best to act as if time had stood still. I could sense him hesitating to pull aside the flap of the tent, as if it were stuck. Then it opened normally, slowly. Kutsikitsoq stuck his head inside and looked at me uncertainly. His face was covered with frost and set in a forced smile. Then he quickly stepped inside. He handed me a chunk of seal, his last, and immediately checked the pressure in the Primus. I went on with our conversation as if nothing had happened.

Kutsikitsoq spoke of his father and his youth. We ate together in a friendly spirit and slept side by side, like two difficult brothers.

Visibility was no less poor the next day. The observations of the high area of Inglefield Land which I had planned to take during this trip were out of the question. We were caught in whirlwinds of snow, and as we crossed the ravines where the melting ice ran down, our sledges swayed back and forth on the hard, bare ice like old carts. To orient ourselves, we descended the glacier almost perpendicularly; we reached the firm ground of Inglefield Land again at the edge of a small lake. I did a geomorphological study of this sector, which had been uncovered—perhaps 100 years before?—by the receding glacier. The wind was turning into a storm, however, and hastily we put up the tent and rested for three hours. We could not delay here any longer; unfortunately, the last of the dogs' provisions had been eaten the day before. So we started off again in the blizzard, and on the thirtieth, after a forced march, we finally reached the frozen stream of Uunartoq.

So I had not made any mistakes; I had navigated well. And one more bond had been woven into my Eskimo life on the trail with proud, choleric Kutsikitsoq. I left our surplus oil beneath a cairn. We descended the snowy valley rapidly. The next morning at about nine o'clock we arrived at Uunartoq Bay, a landscape now almost familiar to me. The rising sun was dissipating the fog; the crevasses in the ice bank smoked in bays of light. Colonies of seals were asleep on the ice. At last I saw the expedition's big yellow tent in the lee of a talus already bare of snow. But there was not the slightest sign of life.

"Takkuut! Look!"

The canvas rippled; the pole trembled. Helter skelter, adjusting their qulitsaqs and their pants, our three friends, who had been asleep, came running out. After several days apart, we greeted one another as gravely as if we had not seen one another for years. In Eskimo fashion, Kutsikitsoq and I strove to appear lordly and indifferent to everything around us; we were entirely taken up with unharnessing our dogs. But when our hands touched, feelings overcame all ceremony. Kutsikitsoq began talking. In his precise way, Qaaqqutsiaq kept interrupting and questioning him. Every detail of our adventure was described and discussed.

"Tii," Natuk chirped, busy as always. Inside the tent, Kutsikitsoq sat with bowed head as, holding his bowl of tea in both hands, he ate and told about the trip: the bear tracks, the caribou, the fog, his depression. Came noon, and we were still talking. He was grateful to me for saying nothing about our disagreement and his dubious behavior. But the Inuit had not failed to notice his hangdog air, and would soon understand everything.

That night, my bitch Pikuli—she was happy to see me back—slipped under the canvas of the tent three times, carrying her three puppies, one by one, between her jaws, and gently laying them down near my face. Pikuli wanted to sleep beside me like a pet. She did not like being alone. Unhappily, she gave off such a strong smell that, despite my affection for her, all night long I had to keep rejecting her friendly overtures. In the days that followed Pikuli, her belly swinging back and forth, painfully trotted after the convoy as we moved from place to place. The three puppies rode atop the sledge in a half-open fur sack. If we were moving fast, Pikuli was outdistanced and became a mere dot on the horizon. When we stopped, she hurried to catch up. I would lay the puppies on a caribou skin on the ice field. While I was having something to eat with my companions, Pikuli would finally arrive, lie down on her side, and offer her teats to the puppies.

We restocked the sledges at my main depot at Uunartoq: oil, tobacco, margarine, and the balance of the ammunition. We would hunt for meat en route. On June 1, I decided we would leave for the west.

We set out at night to take advantage of the frost, definitely resolved to sleep by day. To the west, the high summits of Ellesmere Island stood out against the snowy blue. The weather was favorable. If the ice was good too, we would need a scant twenty hours to pass the "liquid frontier" and complete the crossing.

In fact, off Cape Grinnell we had the benefit of smooth, bare ice. We made rapid progress westward; we might even shorten the time we had estimated.

On the trail once again: the three sledges, one behind the other; the trotting dogs with their flatulence, their complicitous eyes; the smell that rose from our skin clothes; the tired glances we exchanged; sweaty faces; a routine carried out while half asleep. But then abruptly we ran into the most formidable tangle of pressure ice I had ever confronted. It was so dense and so increasingly high that it seemed it might force us to backtrack. We had all leaped from the sledges, and as if propelled by a new force, we scattered to look for a better route. For miles, piles of six- to twelve-foot-high blocks of ice marched on—a succession of veritably crenellated walls that had pushed up from the depths. This ice was old, dirty, and sharp. Our group reassembled. For seven hours we fought our way along the foot of the cape by carving a passage through this barrier. Working with stakes and axes, we opened trenches and passes; we smoothed sharp angles; we filled in crevasses with chunks of ice.

At about two in the morning, we rested briefly, lying on our sledges, and then went back to work. As we were making our way through the labyrinth of rubble, Qaaqqutsiaq discovered a pass which allowed us to travel southwest over a relatively flat surface for five hours. We took heart again; but in the late morning, twelve miles from our destination, our difficulties increased. At the mouth of Bache Fjord, on Ellesmere Island, we were confronted by a field of gigantic hummocks encircled by a thick continuous belt nine to twelve feet high —winding walls of ice that had been compressed, packed together, and thrust up from the depths. Unless we were to make a very wide detour to the north, which I had no time for, our attempt seemed sure to fail.

With our three sledges nose to nose in a circle, we stopped for a half hour to catch our breath and then started off again. The sledges filed through the ice.

We were groping our way through a maze of gorges and passes. On one side there would be a wall, on another an open space of sorts. We had no clear idea where we were going. One of us would go ahead and, with his ax, chop a path for the others. Twice already we had had to cut steps for the dogs. They would pull themselves up the walls, whimpering, their tails low. We would unload the sledges and push them up with our shoulders until they fell down heavily on the other side. Then we had to lug the baggage and equipment on our backs and stash it on the sledges again. The slightest accident could hold us up, so we had to be as quick and adroit as possible. Yet danger always threatened: we could so easily step into a hidden crevasse, or catch and fracture a leg while putting all our strength into pushing the heavy sledge up the old compact ice. A few dogs were showing signs of exhaustion. Several were limping; their paws had got abraded and the salt in the ice was eating into them painfully. We had to make time: there would soon be no meat either for the dogs or for us if we did not speedily manage to find a passage through to a hunting area. Under such old, hummocky ice there are no seals—the ice is too thick for their claws to open allut.

The ice field sometimes shook violently under our feet, reminding my companions that at this time of the year there is the danger of the ice breaking up, which would cut them off both from their homeland and from our provisions. Although at this latitude the ice field does not normally break up until mid-July, it has been known to do so three or four weeks earlier than that and in a single night to be swept off by the southward drift toward the mouths of Lancaster Strait. If we were to be isolated on Ellesmere Island—that desert of northern Canada, which has been uninhabited for years—we might be in for a hard early winter before new ice formed.

I thought our situation over, studying the figures again and again: our ammunition was ample for the moment and, if we rationed it strictly, would last us another eight months. In September, we would build an igloo of stone and peat, reinforced by a second wall of peat—if we found any peat—and covered with snow, like my hut at Siorapaluk. For food, we would be entirely dependent on hunting. We still had enough ammunition, 2,200 cartridges, from my initial supply of 2,700 cartridges, so that was no cause for serious concern. To run through the figures again: four shots per day per hunter (two men) during our enforced stay over the summer on the deserted Canadian coast. That meant we would have used 720 cartridges by September, when we would still have to reckon on four more months of hunting—October to January—using six cartridges per day per Eskimo hunter, because then the hunting would be more difficult. This would leave a reserve of nearly 100 cartridges in January in case of an emergency.

There was another source of food once the ice field formed again: a number of seals could be killed at their allut with a harpoon, rather than with a rifle. So we would have to find out which area had allut. Judging by the number of seal colonies on the Uunartoq ice field in June, we could predict that Alexandra Fjord, on Ellesmere Island, would be a good place to hunt seal in the winter. But why, then, had Greely during his disastrous expedition in 1882–84 hunted so little in the winter during his forced stay? True, the seal was a migrant animal. . . . Yet the situation in June 1884 should have been the same as the situation in June 1951, since both years fell during periods in which the climate had warmed up.

Not until January or February would we be able to travel on the newly formed ice field to our depot of provisions at Uunartoq, in Greenland, and cross the ice cap, whose crevassed edges would then be filled in with snow, to my hut in Siorapaluk. These were close calculations; there would be risks—but then there always are risks. The Eskimos had been duly warned before we started that our provisions might run low and that we might be isolated in uninhabited Canadian territory, and they had accepted these possibilities with smiling equanimity. Nevertheless, now they expressed their doubts and fears in quick, silent exchanges. When five people are forced to spend seven winter months alone together, anything can happen; the margin of supplies, large as it may be, cannot cover unforeseen emergencies—absence of seal (the ice being too thick if the winter is abnormally cold), illness, accidents, quarrels. In our case, I must emphasize how isolated we would be: I had chosen not to bring a radio with me, and Ellesmere and Inglefield lands were totally deserted. So, we simply had to get through. . . . This resolve took clear and definite shape within me, despite a great and mounting fatigue which warned me that we could not maintain such effort much longer.

After hours of struggle and countless detours, we had managed to advance only about 300 feet to the west. Kutsikitsoq, alas, became demoralized and began to complain again:

"I can't go on any longer. . . . Ajornara, it's too high; we'll never make it. Look, the dogs are about to collapse. You're a qallunaaq, you can't see that. There's no seal left for them. Ajoq! Ajoq!"

And he sat down on the snow. After a second and final reconnaissance, I set out with the ever ready and willing Qaaqqutsiaq. We floundered through the soft snow back and forth, back and forth, along the wall with its translucid opal scallops, in search of a new opening. Whenever I could, I climbed up on an iceberg to scan our surroundings through my binoculars. We surveyed the area with meticulous care. Qaaqqutsiaq, unlike Kutsikitsoq, seemed to have more energy and enthusiasm the more difficult things became; we talked over our situation, agreed on a route, and traced it out roughly. The next few miles proved to be exceptionally difficult. Every time we painfully perched the three sledges on top of a rise and let them fall down the other side, it seemed that the wide wooden thwarts with their flexible fastenings must surely come apart from being banged around that way.

The dogs were dazed by our blows, and they kept flopping down. They, too, were terribly tired; the sun and the glare reflected by the snow bothered them, and they squinted and thrust their noses into the snow where they lay. Light kicks to their bellies brought them to their feet. In spite of their fatigue, before they started pulling they managed to look at us understandingly. Our destination was right ahead of us now, within reach. Kutsikitsoq had recovered and was doing his share. There was not a sound to be heard but our shouts and curses. We were caught up in a sort of fever. Whether we went forward or backward, we had to get out of this "trap" fast. The two women made themselves as inconspicuous as possible, silently freeing the traces when they got stuck in the ridges of ice. Whenever the two men and I talked something over, they stayed out of the discussion; their faces were expressionless and one could not tell whether they approved or not. I kept steadily encouraging everybody. Whenever a large obstacle loomed in front of us, Qaaqqutsiaq and I would move ahead to reconnoiter. We negotiated that enormous wall of ice literally yard by yard.

Until at last a long, smooth surface lay before us. One more leap and we were there. On June 3, I reached Ellesmere Island, the first Frenchman to have made the crossing from Greenland to Canada. After three grueling days we were dirty, sunburned, and heavy-eyed. I must admit that before we even set foot on land, our thought was not to unfurl some flag or other but simply to pull our sleeping bags off the sledges and go to sleep in full daylight.

When we woke up and looked around in the morning, the Canadian panorama did not look any different from our familiar Greenland. On the horizon to the north, there were large scree slopes at the foot of the imposing brown cliffs that mark the coast of the Bache Peninsula. Mountains that had been rounded and polished by the glaciers stood to the southeast. Between two of them lay the bluish ice of Buchanan Bay, with its dendritic network of fjords. Along Alexandra Fjord, which we had entered, I could see stranded beaches of rounded pebbles and white shingle. My contentment was all the greater when I saw that the hunting prospects were promising. On the perfectly smooth ice field—it was the young annual ice—a great number of black dots signaled scattered colonies of sleeping seals, as I had hoped. At least we were assured of being able to replenish our own stores of meat and to feed our teams.

The crackling snow was thick and hard enough for the sledges to move quickly where I wanted, and I immediately set to work in the area. I took cross sections of the scree, measured the slopes, and made systematic studies of fragmentary erosion in comparable sections of terrain. Things were looking up.

By returning along the path we had opened up en route to Canada—by way of Smith Sound—we seemed assured of getting back. Hunting looked good and could readily provide us with the reserve we anticipated we would need for the first three months—but after that would come autumn, and then winter. How could one not remember the people who had been here before us? We were on the very spot where, nearly seventy years before, on Cape Sabine, eighteen American explorers, blocked by the ice, had died of hunger, one by one, after long months of agonized waiting. Cape Sabine had been a camp of hunger and lost hope. Admiral Peary called it "that black moment in the history of America in the Arctic." What seemed possible for us in 1951 had not proved possible for them in 1884. Why not?

The Starving Men
at Cape Sabine

In 1881, First Lieutenant Adolphus Washington Greely was assigned by his government to direct the American Polar station at Fort Conger, near Hazen Lake on Ellesmere Island. This station was part of the program of the First International Polar Year. At the time, it was the northernmost station in the world. Because of inadequate government support, it was also one of the most poorly equipped. Assisted by Lieutenant James Lockwood, a first-rate explorer who had beaten the Englishman Markham's record by reaching latitude 83° 24′, Lieutenant Greely, of the Fifth Cavalry Regiment, carried out his mission with remarkable energy for two years. In voluminous notes—magnetical, meteorological, oceanographical, zoological, and botanical—he recorded the most important scientific observations any Polar team had gathered to that point. As spring 1882 came to an end, the explorers cheerfully prepared to return home. According to plan, that summer a ship was supposed to make its way to Fort Conger, on the southwestern coast of Robeson Channel, and transport the expedition members back to the States. It had been agreed that if the ship did not manage to reach them, it would leave provisions on Littleton Island, near Etah, and on Pim Island, by the headland of Cape Sabine, immediately east of the entrance to Alexandra Fjord, near which I was now bivouacking. The men were expecting the ship any day, but nothing appeared on the horizon. The relief ship had failed to advance beyond Smith Sound that year.

In 1883 the alarmed United States govenment hastily outfitted a second relief ship, the *Proteus,* a 467-ton sealer. Unfortunately, before the *Proteus* reached Fort Conger it was wrecked on Smith Sound, more than 200 miles south of the station.

Greely was a very authoritarian man, and increasingly he found himself challenged by his companions. Indeed, from the day his ship sailed, he had refused to speak to his second in command, Second Lieutenant Frederick Kilingsbury, communicating with him only through written notes! The problem was further aggravated by the fact that, thanks to a special disposition, the members of the exposition had the unusual right to go on strike or to break their contracts. Everything conspired, therefore, to set the stage for a drama. As the weeks and months went by, a drama did unfold, and the atmosphere at the Greely base transformed it into a camp of hatred and slow death.

By the time the summer of 1883 came, Greely and the twenty-four other men, including two Greenlanders from Upernavik who proved later to be excellent hunters, were terribly worried to see no sign of their relief ship. By then they had been expecting it for two years. They left their base on Lady Franklin Bay and headed south, using what means they had—two canoes and one small dinghy. Adhering to written orders "to be followed in case of difficulties," Greely kept to the west side of Kennedy Channel and Kane Basin—in other words, to the east coast of Ellesmere Island, which was uninhabited and heavily frozen over. This was a major error, and one that is hard to understand after the experiences of the Americans Kane and Hayes, whose familiarity with the Polar Eskimo of northern Greenland had helped if not saved them during their expeditions in 1853–55 and 1860–61. Greely's strange route along a coast of desolate, lifeless ice could not lead to any contact with the Eskimos of Etah and could not, therefore, result in the expedition's gaining any help from them.

Near Cape Sabine, on a small knoll, Greely came upon the crates of provisions left by the *Proteus;* they contained 500 rations of bread, some tea, and canned food. Simultaneously, Greely learned that the *Proteus* had been wrecked north of Cape Sabine on July 23, 1883. In a message found among the crates on October 1, 1883, the ship's captain, E. A. Garlington, had written that the American government had not given up hope of saving the expedition;

what he said in substance was that Greely and his companions should keep up their courage. Accordingly, Greely postponed his retreat southward. Besides, winter was coming on and there was only time enough to build a shelter that would better enable them to confront the cold weather. He set up camp on the northern shore of Pim Island, west of Cape Sabine, and called it Camp Clay. My camp on Alexandra Fjord was only a few miles from that site.

Camp Clay was at latitude 78° 3' west. The expedition's third winter was spent in a hut covered by their whaleboat, which had had to be abandoned and then was miraculously restored to them by drifting ice floes. The men had only forty days' worth of provisions, but still felt confident they would be picked up soon.

They were to wait more than 250 days. That year there was a great deal of ice, and the ships that had been dispatched to find them were unable to get through to them. What's more, Greely felt that the drifting ice would prevent him from reaching the coast of Greenland. I am not convinced by this: even if the sound can often not be crossed by boat in the summer because of bad weather or ice, in the winter, starting in December, it can be crossed by sledge or on foot: my own voyage of exploration testifies to that. But it seems that Greely, who was exhausted, clung to his instructions and to this last little depot at Cape Sabine. He remained anchored to the uninhabited Ellesmere coast and did not attempt to make his way to the west coast of Greenland, to the Eskimo villages of Anoritoq and Etah, which were well known ever since the expeditions of Kane and Hayes. He did not send a mission to ask for help, but instead, from time to time, set off exploring the west coast of Ellesmere Island with his starving men.[44]

Hunting yielded little, despite the presence of the two Greenlanders. The explorers, whose clothes were in tatters, were soon reduced to eating lichens they found on the rocks. At first they caught a few shrimp at the edge of the ice field, and even caught and ate several foxes. But soon they faced starvation.

In time, the fishermen would use rotted human flesh for bait. After unspeakable suffering, eighteen men were to die, one by one, of cold and hunger. One died on February 18, just before the sun returned; six died in April, four in May, and seven in June (the last died in Godhavn on July 8, after the rescue). Among them were Lockwood, the Greenlander Christiansen, Jens, who drowned while out hunting seal, the second-in-command Kilingsbury, to whom Greely refused to speak up until the moment he died, and Octave Pavy, the French explorer-doctor whom everyone liked and who, sensing that he was doomed, committed suicide on June 6 by swallowing what was left of their medical supplies. He threw himself into the water so as not to be eaten. But let us turn to Greely's distressing account:[45]

"February 25 . . . Lieutenant Lockwood's condition worse," he notes in his detailed and implacable journal. "There are no signs of scurvy about him, only a general break of his physical and mental powers. . . ."

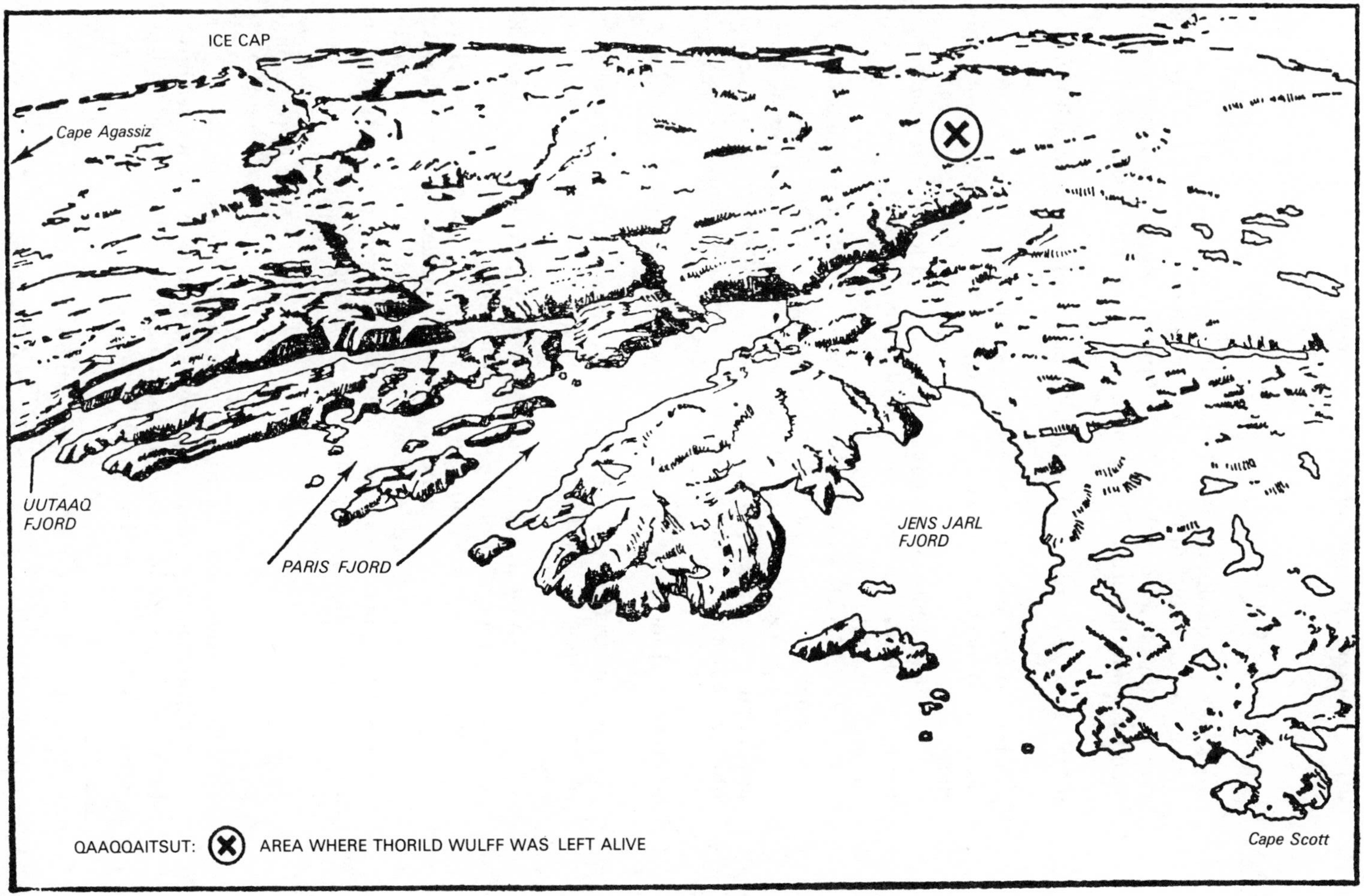

ICE CAP

Cape Agassiz

UUTAAQ
FJORD

PARIS FJORD

JENS JARL
FJORD

Cape Scott

QAAQQAITSUT: ⊗ AREA WHERE THORILD WULFF WAS LEFT ALIVE

MAP 11. Qaaqqaitsut

In early April, he noted:

> Lockwood's condition after Christiansen's death alarmed me very
> much, and on April 6th I commenced issuing him extra food—four
> ounces daily of raw dovekie. . . . On April 8th, he fainted, and his mind
> wandered much during the evening but never unpleasantly so. . . .

On May 20, Greely recorded, Israel, the astronomer, was much weaker.

> In order to give Israel the last chance, and on Dr. Pavy's recommenda-
> tion, four ounces of the raven was given him today, that being our only
> meat. . . .
>   May 23rd. Ralston died about 1 A.M. Israel left the [sleeping] bag
> before his death, but I remained until driven out about 5 A.M., chilled
> through by contact with the dead. . . .
>   May 26th. —How we live I do not know, unless it is because we are
> determined to. We all passed an exceedingly wretched night. . . .
>   Summer opened wretchedly, with a howling gale and driving snow,
> and a temperature near the freezing point. . . . We were yet fourteen in
> number, but it was evident that all must soon pass away. . . .

The entry for June 4:

> We had not strength enough to bury Salor, so he was put out of sight
> in the ice-foot. . . . Our condition grows more horrible every
> day. . . .
>   June 5. —A clear, calm, and fine warm day. I crawled on the rocks
> today and got a canful of tripe de Roche—half a pint. . . .
>   June 6th. —Henry [long suspected by his companions of stealing]
> admitted he had taken . . . contrary to positive orders, seal-skin thongs*;
> and further, that he had in a bundle, concealed somewhere, seal-skin.
> He was bold in his admissions, and showed neither fear nor contrition.
> I ordered him shot, giving the order in writing:

Near Cape Sabine,
June 6, 1884

SERGEANTS BRAINARD, LONG, AND FREDERICK:
    Notwithstanding promises given by Private C. B. Henry yesterday,
he has since, as acknowledged to me, tampered with seal-thongs if not
other food. . . . Private Henry will be shot to-day, all care being taken

---

*In their dire extremity, the explorers made soup out of pieces of sealskin.

to prevent his injuring anyone. . . . Decide the matter of death by two ball and one blank cartridge. This order is *imperative* and *absolutely necessary* for *any chance* of life.

[Signed] A. W. Greely
First Lieutenant Fifth Cavalry, U.S.A.,
and Assistant, Commanding L.F.B. Expedition

About two o'clock shots were heard. . . . Everyone, without exception, acknowledged that Henry's fate was merited. . . .

June 8th. —Clear and calm all day . . . managed in five hours' time to pick about two quarts of tripe de Roche. . . . Obliged to eat the last seal-skin thongs in stew this afternoon, with which we mixed the tripe de Roche and reindeer-moss. . . .

June 9th. —. . . Schneider . . . signs of scurvy . . . in his swollen, stiff knees . . . this evening appeared to wander a little. Had nothing but tripe de Roche, tea, and seal-skin gloves for dinner. Without fresh bait we can do little in shrimping, and so live on lichens and moss alone. Elison expressed a desire that his arms and legs should go to the Army Medical Museum in the interests of science. His case is most singular. . . . Biederbick is engaged in writing up the medical case. . . .

[no month] 20th, . . . Six years ago to-day I was married and three years ago I left my wife for this Expedition, what contrast! When will this life in death end? . . . 21st, 11 A.M., it commenced snowing. . . .

By the morning of the 22nd . . . it was only through the energy and devotion of Frederick or Brainard, I do not remember which, that we obtained, about noon, some water. . . .

Near midnight of the 22nd I heard the sound of the whistle noise of the Thetis.

I feebly asked Brainard and Long if they had strength to get out, to which they answered, as always, that they would do their best. . . . [But] nothing was to be seen. . . . Long . . . set up the distress flag . . . which had blown down. . . . A fruitless discussion sprang up as to the noise. . . . Suddenly strange voices were heard calling me. . . .

In fact, some sailors were hurrying ashore from an American ship, the *Thetis.* They were horrified at the sight of the two men dragging themselves across the beach. Presently, on a small rise, they saw a wind-battered tent from which groans could be heard. One of the sailors burst into tears. They could not find the door of the tent fast enough, and slashed it open with a knife.

What we saw before us was a horrible spectacle. On one side, near the door, his head facing outside, a man was lying, apparently already dead. His jaw hung down and he looked at us with his eyes open, fixed and glassy, his lips lifeless. On the other side was another man, alive but with no hands or feet, with a spoon attached to the stump of his right arm. . . . Opposite us, walking on his hands and knees, was a black man with a long tangled beard wearing a dirty, torn robe and a little red skull-cap, his eyes fixed and shining. When Lieutenant Colwell appeared [adjutant to the commander of the *Thetis,* Captain W. S. Schley], he got up and put on his glasses. "Who are you?" Colwell asked him.

The man did not answer and looked at him with a vacant expression.

"Who are you?" he asked again.

One of the men looked up.

"That's Greely, Major Greely."

Then Colwell crawled toward him and taking him by the hand, said to him:

"Greely . . . could it really be you?"

It is very likely that the dead men had become the last resource of the starving survivors, who waited impatiently for them to die so that they could cut up their flesh. No doubt it was Pavy, the doctor, who, skillfully using his scalpel, cut out the useful flesh from between the ribs, and thus enabled the group to survive. Thighs, arms, and legs were also cut up. As final marks of respect, the hands, feet, and faces were left intact. Pavy was so skillful that only careful examination of the bodies made it possible to detect his subcutaneous surgery. After Pavy died, the bodies of four others were picked clean by the starving men and so dismembered that the scattered remains could not be reassembled. These four men, as well as Pavy, were considered to have been lost at sea. To make the coffins of the others heavier, the rescuers put stones in them in lieu of the corpses.

Snow Blindness
and Return Home

I went up Alexandra Fjord with Qaaqqutsiaq a number of times. We used only one sledge—Qaaqqutsiaq's, since it was the smaller—with both his and my team, along with some of Kutsikitsoq's dogs. In this way, we were able to make very good time.

The geomorphological work which I methodically carried out along different alluvial levels was interesting, but there was not enough time to pursue it as far as I would have wished. I did some useful snow cartography of slopes and took measurements of scree slopes. But however reassuring the brilliant sun might be, the moving ice and flowing rivulets kept reminding us of the danger of being cut off from our base in Greenland if the sea should suddenly become an expanse of free water. Not one day could be lost, so morning and night we made trips right and left. We saw the star-shaped footprints of the qupannaaq, some gulls, many polar hares, but not the slightest trace of musk ox or reindeer. Qaaqqutsiaq's health prevented my keeping up the pace I would have liked. At each geomorphological station, he would lie, face down, on the floor of his sledge, his head in his arms. On the morning of June 4, after fourteen hours of uninterrupted work along the southeastern coast, he took me aside and complained of a headache and pain in his eyes. All he could see in front of him was a sort of halo. Although he had been wearing sunglasses, he was the first of us to suffer from the painful affliction of snow blindness. He begged me not to let that stop me: "Just let me sleep," he said, leaning against the napariaq, "and let's not go back to the camp until the work is finished." Before we rejoined the group, his wife suggested the powerful but painful remedy commonly used by the Canadian Eskimos and sometimes by those of Thule—a few drops of oil in the eyes[46]—but he refused vehemently. I also was beginning to notice a heaviness in my head, and my eyes were inflamed and teary. So whenever we could while I worked, we took shelter near icebergs, staying in their shadow. Thanks to my Polaroid sunglasses (unfortunately I had only one pair), my condition did not get worse, and Qaaqqutsiaq, nursing himself in his own fashion—he lay on the sledge with a band over his eyes—gradually recovered. Then it was Natuk's turn to be affected, and her case seemed fairly serious. All day long, she sat sideways on the back of the sledge and kept her head down. She became almost exhausted, for she slept hardly at all for ten days.

The season was moving forward; summer seemed to be coming very early that year. The snowdrifts on Alexandra Fjord dripped water, and the glaciers gleamed wetly in the sunlight. At their feet, the bits of mica in the gray and black rocks along the coast glittered. There was not the slightest breeze over the ice field, where an irregular upward movement of reflected particles formed a cloud as high as a man. Under an aggressively blue sky, nature seemed festive. The icebergs were fringed with little trenches of water. At the mouth of the fjord, the ice pack was breaking up at the edges of the coast. The zigzagging fissures had widened since our arrival. Accordingly, I postponed to another year the geomorphological exploration of the Knud, Bache, Cook, and Darling peninsulas.

The reverse, or inside, of Kutsikitsoq's bone *(ixxaun)* sunglasses. Qinnissut, 1950. *(Private collection)*

On the fifth I very regretfully gave the signal to return to Greenland. To my partners' credit, they had not once asked that we advance the date of our return, despite the dangers we faced.

We built one last cairn with a final message on the south coast of Alexandra Fjord. A few hours later, we were crossing Cape Sabine again, this time heading east. The expedition was nearing its end.

The trip from Canada to Greenland was as quick and easy as the crossing from Greenland to Canada had been difficult; the path had, after all, been cleared. We found the traces of our earlier passage: the corridors hacked out of the ice by ax, dog turds, constellations of our own yellow urine on various walls of ice, here and there bits of straw we had removed from the soles of our skin boots, bits of laces and whips. We had left Buchanan Bay, on Ellesmere Island, on the morning of June 5, and we reached our depot at Uunartoq, in Greenland, on the evening of the sixth! We were greeted by gloomy weather and fog. Extremely tired as we all were, my companions were bursting with exuberant joy to be back in their nuna, their homeland. Like a child, Kutsikitsoq jumped up and down in front of his dogs and tossed his whip into the air. The women giggled at everything anyone said.

I looked over the work I had done. In the larger sense, the expedition had fulfilled its basic objectives. The map testified to that. Thanks to the work we had done, plus some valuable aerial photographs, five morphological sheets would later be drawn up of Inglefield and Washington lands, extending from Etah to Cape Agassiz in Inglefield Land and from Pullassuaq to Cape Jackson on Washington Land. The maps covered the inland area to a distance of up to two miles depending on the itineraries.[47] On the basis of these five sheets at 1:100,000, two large sheets at 1:200,000 would be drawn up and published in Paris by the Imprimerie Nationale.[48] The Danish government granted me permission to give eleven French names to identified capes, bays, rivers, and fjords. And so in these northern latitudes there would be henceforth a Paris Fjord, which has a large mouth and is broad and deep as it extends inland; a Martonne Fjord, named after the great geographer to whom I referred earlier; and a Cape Joset, named after the French geophysicist who lost his life in a crevasse in central Greenland in 1951 and to whom I was very close. I wanted to honor the Eskimos too, since they are always forgotten when maps are made, so I baptized one fjord Uutaaq; one river Aqajak, after an Eskimo who died with Krueger in 1930–31; another river Aajaku, after Qaaqqutsiaq's relative who accompanied Rasmussen back to Etah during the Second Thule Expedition. The Aajaku River is not far from the area where Wulff died of hunger. Now there is also Depot River, so named because it ran by my second small depot of provisions in Washington Land, and Polaris River, in honor of Charles Francis Hall.

We had collected six crates of geological samples, fossils, samples of sand and clay, and bags of pebbles from riverbeds. I had filled five notebooks with notes, sketches, and observations about the geomorphology of the terrain we had covered[49]; these notebooks provided material for in-depth analyses and also laboratory studies of frost action at the French CNRS's Cold Station which I later carried out using various simulated conditions as close as possible to the natural conditions so carefully identified. We had also brought back collections of samples of altered rocks and coastal fossils, and substantial photographic documentation of the trip.

It seemed that our hardest days lay behind us.

I owe the success of my expedition to Kutsikitsoq and my three other companions because they did not hesitate to risk the danger of possibly spending the winter in Canada under the very precarious conditions I made clear to them.

The practical intelligence of the men, who were able to solve every problem that arose—and God knows there were many—and their generosity of mind and heart were invaluable to me. As for the women—they functioned as temporizers; in a subtly ambivalent way, acting now as witnesses, now as arbiters, they exerted a really beneficial influence.

I want to offer special tribute to Padloq, who was perhaps more adventurous than Natuk. In difficult moments, Padloq was able to inspire her with the spirit of our group, which had gradually knit together and was caught up in a shared mission I had infused with such meaning that it became larger than we were.[50]

18

RETURN
TO
SIORAPALUK

Qaaqqutsiaq had been lucky enough to kill two seals. This enabled us to celebrate our crossings in the usual fashion, by consuming a large meal on the desolate beach. We cooked the meat; the liver we ate raw. We talked about the days ahead, and about the farewell party we would have when we reached Siorapaluk.

From then on, we were so rich in food that we kept only the seals' meat and left the fat on the ice.

On Thursday, June 7, we struck camp and loaded up the 150 pounds of my geological samples. I took one backward look at the broad expanse of Uunartoq Bay and at the depot of provisions and equipment which had been on my mind so constantly. I felt a tug of regret, but then was caught up again in the life of the convoy.

We went up the valley, heading for the great ice cap, tacking back and forth among the rocks and marl that were already cropping up on the valley floor. Except in the hollows, the plateau had been almost completely cleared of snow by wind, evaporation, and then by the thaw. Our actual ascent of the glacier began only on the ninth. There were no moraines—or very few—to cross; this was true all along the ice cap in Inglefield Land, at least in the areas where I was able to observe the point where glacier and plateau met. We did not encounter any serious problems. At that time of year, the crevasses were still filled in. After climbing a succession of broad platforms, we stopped on Hill 900. According to the terms of our agreement, Qaaqqutsiaq and Padloq were supposed to leave us at this point. They would return to their people in the Etah camp, traveling along the edge of the ice cap. It was the most direct route; also at this time of year, the ice foot from Uunartoq to the Etah fjord was not dependable, especially around the larger capes. It had been agreed that as soon as we transported my samples up onto the glacier en route to Siorapaluk, the couple would be free to go. Padloq had been too tired to climb the glacier with us, and was waiting below for her husband. We aligned our three sledges in a triangle. One of us got some firm snow from a hollow, and the traditional cup of tea was slowly prepared. Pipes and cigarettes were brought out; there were long silences. Kutsikitsoq and Qaaqqutsiaq looked at each other through puffs of smoke. They lived hundreds of miles apart; they would not see each other again for years, perhaps never: here accidents happen often. The circles under our swollen eyes, which were inflamed by the glare and weariness, our thin, sunburned faces, our torn clothes—these things bespoke the group's weeks-long effort better than anything we could say. I wrote out a payment order on a leaf of notebook paper. Qaaqqutsiaq took it, inclining his head slightly. He did not know how to read English, and it would be five or six months before he was paid the crowns which I instructed the Danish store at Thule, nearly two hundred miles to the south, to give him, but he trusted me and without saying a word or examining the paper, he put it into his cartridge pouch. We shook hands, each of us equally moved and upset. Patient, precise, unassuming, extraordinarily supportive, the reticent little man said to me simply: "I won't forget you." I may be wrong, but that kind of statement I believe.

Like a gentleman, he made his departure a quick one; he leaped on his sledge, rapidly descended the slope, and disappeared in the west, waving his arm and shouting "Aroo! Aroo! . . . To the left! To the left!" so that his dogs would cross the streams of melting water carefully on a slant. Our farewells were prolonged by salvos of gunfire that died away in the distance. We started up the glacier again. Kutsikitsoq, as if overwhelmed by the separation, had lost all his buoyancy. Natuk sat, expressionless, at the back of her husband's sledge. Every time it jolted, the pain in her eyes made her groan. It took hours for our team to recover its usual verve. We all felt the emptiness created by the departure of our two comrades.

We had long since lost sight of Inglefield Land, to the north and behind us. Before us we could see nothing but our shadows, the pale sky, and a ridge that seemed to float between sky and ice. We were walking in front of the dogs in order to open a way for them through the snow. When we happened to glance up at that elusive horizon, we half expected to see some fantastic apparition rise up from behind it.

I kept the needle of my compass pointing due south, as I had while we were climbing earlier, and then I shifted to south-southwest. It was important that we keep strictly to our route, but I had with me only a compass table for 1950. Our only possible pass was the Neqi pass, and Qaaqqutsiaq had told me it was not easy to find. And once again, Kutsikitsoq—blast him!—was not very familiar with the area.

On the tenth, we stopped climbing. We were at an altitude of 4,300 feet. I had no sextant and made rough calculations (the number of miles per hour, the route we were following) to determine our approximate position. The terrain continued to be flat for several miles and then by slow degrees began to descend. I changed our direction so that we were heading south-southeast.

At about two o'clock I noticed dark spots in the sky. It was a phenomenon common in the Arctic and involves reflection: the sea appears to float in the clouds. We were seeing a water sky. Only late in the afternoon did we see the sea itself, at the foot of the glacier. The water was black and marvelously open. Far in the distance we could see the shining, snowy summits of Northumberland and Herbert islands. At this point fresh troubles arose.

The silence surrounding us was broken by tearing, cracking noises. Several short, dry sounds followed, first muffled, then grating; then came a long-drawn-out grinding. We were in the border area of the glacier, and on that sunny surface, the crevasses were warping. Natuk was terrified; she swore she would never set foot in the mountains again. Kutsikitsoq kept better control of himself, but admitted that all he knew about this glacier was that it was very dangerous in June. We stopped to take out our sealskin ropes and slip them under the runners in front of the sledges; our harpoons were within arm's reach. Through my mind passed images of crevasses as deep as the naves of cathedrals; I had visions of chasms, of a crystalline world bristling with spikes. Kutsikitsoq felt absolutely sure he was going to fall straight into a chasm! Meanwhile, zebralike stripes seemed to be forming all around us. Natuk thought she saw one to her right, ahead of the dogs. We sat on our two sledges, which were moving very slowly, braked by the friction of the sealskin thongs; our thought was that even if they tipped over the edge of a crevasse, we would be held back by the sealskin. Later I was to learn that, at the same time I was confronting these obstacles, the geophysicist Joset, after whom I named a cape, and the Dane Jens Jarl completely vanished together with their sledges in such an abyss 930 miles to the south in Greenland.

I went ahead to reconnoiter and mark out a trail. Kutsikitsoq ran to catch up with me, and we positioned ourselves at an agreed distance from each other. We were not roped together; that is not an Eskimo tactic, and no one could have persuaded them to use it. The way they see it, if one man falls the other will not be able to help him. Help each other? . . . If the fall is a bad one, there is nothing to do but get the sledge away as fast as possible. Our sealskin traces, tied end to end, would be long enough to pull up someone caught in a crevasse. My mountain rope was fifteen feet long. If it were attached to the sealskin harness, would it be long enough to lower someone down to look for the body? Whoever fell would undoubtedly have been knocked out by the fall.

With Kutsikitsoq's harpoon and my piolet, we cautiously tested all suspect snow and every doubtful pool of soft slush. When necessary, we sounded the ice in different places. By tacit agreement, we had divided the area to be explored. We moved as lightly as possible by walking on the tips of our toes and leaning as far forward as we could—our bearskin-clad rear ends comically raised as far as balance allowed—while we resolutely poked the snow around us. From the top of a small rise, we saw one possible route, but none that seemed perfect. We agreed not to slip over to the west, where there was a questionable basin. I walked ahead some seventy feet, signaled, and Natuk, who was afraid, started forward. Kutsikitsoq went back to encourage her. I chose my own route slightly to one side. With infinite caution, we inched forward. The path wound from bump to bump, forming a capricious network over the slope. At the most dangerous stages, we called back and forth to each other, rejoined, and crossed the snow bridges at a slow trot. The only way to discover whether the bridges would hold was to try them. Then we observed some dark shadows, indications that a gorge opened out down below. Our descent quickened. The dogs were excited to smell salt and they speeded up. We halted one last time, while I got my bearings. In this area no two glacial valleys could be so big—this had to be the right way.

"Imaq!" Kutsikitsoq shouted. "The sea!"

A gap in the cold, pink-tinted morning light revealed an expanse of ice field and icebergs. At the far end lay Neqi. We were dropping lower and lower into the gorge by the minute. The altimeter read 2,600 feet. But was it correctly adjusted? The pressure must have changed since we left Uunartoq, at the edge of the sea (point zero). We were surely well below 2,600 feet. This far down it was dark; our voices echoed, reflected off the valley walls, and we laughed at the sound like children. After five more minutes of rapid descent, we stopped again, this time to adjust the load on one of the sledges. We paused long enough to light a pipe and then moved on. Natuk felt better and was running in front of the dogs like a little girl. She was soaked in sweat, her cap was askew, and her hair was disheveled. "Assut!" she shouted to the dogs. "Assut! Faster! Faster!"

She was extremely happy to reach solid ground again. We did not look our best: our clothes were greasy and spotted; the laces of our damp kamiks hung loose. The melting snow was so soft that we sank into it up to our calves. No matter; an immense desire gripped us. After weeks of solitude—weeks that, because we were living at such an intense pitch, had seemed like months—we were about to see people again. We were delayed briefly by a snow bridge that had collapsed. If we were not to be trapped in the gorge, we had to negotiate a sheer drop of some nine feet. We unharnessed the dogs. Expecting to break our necks at any moment, we found a way. I maneuvered my sledge down some scree. With consummate skill, Kutsikitsoq slid his sledge, although more heavily loaded than mine, straight down the side.

The valley opened out into a wide delta. We could hardly make ourselves heard! Thousands of guillemots were wheeling above the slopes, crying "piuli! piuli! piuli!" Some were swimming in water holes on the ice field, now and then plunging their heads abruptly beneath the surface. Many gathered on the scree and balanced there. Fluttering from one heap of rocks to another, they chose the stable slopes, never making a mistake about the earth's unpredictable dynamics. The wind carried fresh salty air to us from the coast. On the terraces with the best exposure, the thick grass, fertilized by fat from the camp, was beginning to turn green. Yellow and red flowers and tall grass with white catkins lent the severe landscape a festive note. The creeping dwarf willows with their purplish red roots were reappearing on all the hillsides. Spring was more advanced here than it had been in the north, and it was bursting out in all its diverse splendor.

The moment we caught sight of the first igloos, we halted. We set the teams in order. Blushing, Natuk tried to hide her emotion as she dabbed perfume on her face and under her arms and behind her ears. She was fore-handed. Kutsikitsoq combed his hair. With my feet close together, I leaned forward, and the Eskimo stitched the bottom of my bearskin pants. In return, I brushed him off and lent him a clean anorak. We quieted the dogs so that we would surprise everyone when we arrived. Then walking in front of our teams, we approached the camp. But . . . not a sound, not a shout greeted us. Doors banged on the deserted, stinking igloos. The roof of one had been caved in. The ebony-black peat walls were drying out and turning lighter. Scattered over the ground was the detritus of the winter: bits of tow, oakum, scraps of animal skins, some dirty yellow raw fat. The little station had been abandoned by the Eskimos. Natuk was disappointed and began to whimper. Kutsikitsoq went into an igloo, then walked back and forth along the shore, his head bowed. At last he sat down, with his legs spread wide, and philosophically tossed an occasional pebble into the water. . . .

The three families of Neqi had moved on. Not far, though! A short dis-tance farther along our way, we found them. At the edge of the ice field we came upon tents, root fires, and the smell of juniper. Harpoons and scraps of meat lay on the ground. This was living prehistory. Lying on the shore, men in animal skins basked in the sun, enjoying the arrival of the warm season. Half-naked children played in the spotted snow amid puppies and seal car-casses. As soon as they saw us, they began yelling.

"Inussuaruna? Are you a spirit or a man?"

"Inussuanga. I am a man."

This was the ritual exchange among Inuit after a long separation.

Our animals were excited, and though their feet were dragging, they ran as fast as they could. An Eskimo came to meet us and clear a way for us. As we approached, the women disappeared. A few minutes later they returned, and as if we were patriarchs, they offered us raw guillemots, auk eggs, and fresh salmon.

What a welcome! Caribou skins were thrown on the ground, and lying down, Oriental fashion, we began to exchange news. Questions were asked on all sides. Natuk was moved, and spoke so softly that she seemed to have lost her voice. In the midst of a hubbub of words and laughter, it was impossible for me to take exact notes. What was happening in the south, in Siorapaluk and elsewhere? Apparently no one had any idea. This was the season of rotten ice, and there was no way to move about either by sledge or by kayak. The villages and camps were closed in on themselves.

"Siku?" I asked Qaavianguaq about the sea ice. Siku naammattoq! The ice field was still good. It might still be good the day after tomorrow; it depended on the wind.

If I did not want to miss the annual ship at Thule, 120 miles away, and

Eskimo camp near Neqi. Drawing by Ivalu. Qeqertaq, June 1951. *(Private collection)*

risk spending another winter here, I had no time to lose. The ice could break up any day. So, although we had barely arrived and in spite of our hosts' insistence, we decided to set off again.

Traveling on the ice next to the shore, we managed to get around the difficult Cape Tuluriaq, which was piled high with scree, and then we set our dogs trotting at top speed along the now well-known route. At Illuluarsuit, we saw traces of human beings. There were twisted dog turds and some footprints. At that point we left the ice foot and went onto the ice field, skirting a coast whose every detail was as familiar as an old friend. Nervous and tense, we kept looking for a human face to appear. Nothing, no one. Our tension grew. All of a sudden, up on the cliff, a hunter came into sight. When we shouted, he turned around; then, throwing down his bag, he came on the run, his bird net over his shoulder; in the beautiful spring sunshine, he looked like a happy vacationer on the ice. It was Sakaeunnguaq. We shook hands; Natuk embraced him; everybody laughed.

We quickly exchanged news. No deaths. One birth—at Kangerlussuaq, the summer camp near Kangerluarsuk, on the south bank of Inglefield Fjord. And there was news for a proud father:

"Ulrikka, your daughter-in-law, is as round as a barrel, fat as two seals."

Kutsikitsoq smiled with pleasure.

"Masaanna keeps postponing his wedding to give you time to get back," Sakaeunnguaq told my companion.

Once we had rounded the last little cape, the three official buildings of Siorapaluk—the store, the school, and the catechist's house—rose before us like large red-daubed toys; and there, too, stood the nine brownish, dirty igloos and my empty cabin, whose surrounding wall of snow had melted away.

As soon as I had pitched my tent near the cabin, all of Siorapaluk—washed and dressed as if it were Sunday—came by. They arrived in little clusters, so as not to "overcrowd," as they put it. In ways that were sometimes moving, each one told me how glad he was to see us return safe and sound. The crates of pebbles seemed to impress them. Kutsikitsoq gave a voluble account of our adventures. If only Qaaqqutsiaq and Padloq had been there with us! Kutsikitsoq went from igloo to igloo. The men squatted down, resting their forearms on their thighs, a morsel of seal and fat on the tips of their knives, as they stared at the ground before them and listened attentively. Now and then they asked to have some point explained which did not seem to them completely clear. Ieh, iehs of approval punctuated the story and encouraged Kutsikitsoq to go on. The expedition passed before my eyes again as though on a screen.

I listened to the story with one ear and followed the pictures with one eye. Groups were forming apart from me. Suddenly I felt I had become a stranger, a qallunaaq again. Natuk had left us. She was telling a story, too. There was no question about it: our team was dead.

I tried repeatedly to establish contact with Thule through the radio transmitter I had left in Siorapaluk. It was no use. Not only was I unable to pick up any communication on the usual frequency but on all the other frequency bands I was deafened by an amazing din of pure Brooklynese. The transmitting station seemed close. Were the rumors I had heard from the Eskimos going to turn out to be true? Was there a war going on? It was not out of the question that the Korean War would have spread to the Pole. But Radio Sottens, the clearest station after the German station in Cologne,[51] made no mention of a conflict in the Arctic in its daily news bulletin. After resting for two days and one night, I prepared to leave my base for good. In spite of my attachment to the hamlet, ice conditions did not permit me to stay any longer.

I easily persuaded Sakaeunnguaq and Qaalasoq, Ululik's brother, to go with me, especially Sakaeunnguaq, who did not wish to separate from me. Kutsikitsoq, who was tired and eager to see his son, Masaanna, again, would follow us only as far as Qaanaaq, an Eskimo camp that had been abandoned six years before. Sakaeunnguaq came into the room and bustled around. In a moment I was to go to the farewell party being given for me in the building which served as both school and chapel. I had a few minutes left; I took a last look around the cabin—I had not moved back into it because I was too used to living in a tent at this time of year. Wanting one last time to touch things I was leaving behind in the room I had lived in, I pushed open doors, shifted crates around, opened the little window. For a moment, I walked back and forth alone. I tried to engrave every detail on my memory. Eleven months of life among the Eskimos were coming to an end.

OUR EXPEDITION

Departure of the expedition from Etah, April 15, 1951. Kutsikitsoq and Natuk are standing with their backs to the camera.

Loading of the sledges for the expedition,
in front of the author's hut or igloo.
March 30, 1951.

Etah lies on the upper left beyond
the second large peninsula. In
the foreground is Cape Alexander, the
westernmost point of Greenland. In the
background is the uninhabited Inglefield
Land. (*Geodaetisk Institut, Denmark*)

Campsite on the ice field. Our two tents: that of Qaaqqutsiaq (seated, on the left, repairing his whip), and the author's tent (toward which Padloq is heading). The reindeer skins are drying. Jerrycans of gas and sledges are serving as ballast. May 1951.

Hunting at the allu, or niparneq—the seal's breathing hole. The hunter (Kutsikitsoq here), having found the allu, scents the animal and harpoons it when it comes up for air. The Inglefield Land ice field (Uunartoq), April 25, 1951.

Qaaqqutsiaq in the labyrinth of ice hummocks. Uunartoq Bay, June 7, 1951.

Natuk doing water duty: cutting off slivers of ice on iceberg walls facing south. May 1951.

Kutsikitsoq's team and sledge skirting the cliffs of Inglefield Land. April 1951.

Qaaqqutsiaq (born 1902). April 1951.

(ABOVE) Jean Malaurie and his sledge.
Washington Land, May 1951.

(RIGHT) Padloq, in Peabody Bay,
searching for bear with a telescope.
May 1951.

(RIGHT) Principal leg of the Humboldt
Glacier advancing toward the Kane Basin
ice field in Peabody Bay. In the foreground are the detached icebergs that
will start drifting south. (*Geodaetisk
Institut, Denmark*)

At our base camp, on the stony beach.
Kutsikitsoq feeds his dogs with a seal that
has just been killed. Cass Fjord, May 15,
1951.

Difficult crossing through
the hummock barriers
between Greenland and Canada.
June 2, 1951.

Padloq (born January 2, 1910). Uunartoq, April 27, 1951.

Return of the expedition; at the foot of the great Inglefield Glacier, which will have to be crossed. The runners of the sledge are being polished with a file. June 9, 1951.

Kutsikitsoq (born April 15, 1903). Cass Fjord, Washington Land, May 15, 1951.

After the rough crossing of the Smith Strait hummock barriers. From left to right are Qaaqqutsiaq, Jean Malaurie, and Kutsikitsoq. Ellesmere Island, Alexandra Fjord; June 3, 1951.

FORCED MARCH TO THULE

It was raining. The farewell party took place in the evening in the chapel-school. It was what you could expect after a year of living closely together. Almost everyone was there—Inuk, John, Laura, Sakaeunnguaq, Pualuna, Jaku, Kutsikitsoq, Appalinnguaq, Imina, Bertsie, Ann Sofia, Olipaluk, Ululik, Aqatannguaq, Igapaluk, and Atangana. We drank the traditional "café-mik" together. One of the men present felt moved to make a little speech.

I answered him in the Thule dialect, improvising a little speech which clearly affected them. They seemed touched that I attached any importance to protocol. I tried to express our relationship in a more serious, feeling way, looking at it not from a day-by-day but from a higher perspective. We had more to eat, reminisced a little, and then everyone quietly returned to his hut, igloo, or tent.

The wind storm continued all night. From inside my tent, I could hear the raindrops smacking on the almost bare ice, which made an unpleasant metallic sound. In the morning, around seven, the prospect for my return trip looked bleak. The day was overcast and wet. But there was nothing for it. My luggage, which weighed about sixty-six pounds, not counting the heavy cases of rock samples, was quickly tied together. I was starting to harness my dogs when I saw all the people coming toward my hut in little groups.

"Inuulluaritse assut!* Good-bye, everyone. . . . Good-bye from the bottom of my heart, dear friends!"

After a salvo of gunshots, I gave the signal to leave. The dogs howled; crackling gunfire answered them from the shore. Outlined against the horizon,

---

*Assut has different meanings, depending on the intonation: (1) fast, faster; (2) with all my strength, with all my heart.

old Pualuna, standing a little apart from the group, was still waving his hand hesitantly when we plunged into the fog.

Ten minutes after we left the camp, the first torrential rain of the season poured down on us. We were four—Kutsikitsoq, Sakaeunnguaq, Qaalasoq, and myself, riding on four sledges. Our runners sank into the melting ice. Again and again, we had to get off the sledges and push with our shoulders until the convoy bumped along again. Once we had passed Cape Cleveland, the dogs began to flounder through water that lay a foot deep on the ice. It rose above the openwork bottom of the sledge. We were "navigating" in a lake of fresh water lying upon a frozen salty sea.

I piled my luggage into a pyramid and placed my notes and sketches on top of it. It was a useless precaution. In the midst of that gray water, and beneath a low sky, it was very hard from a distance to detect the crevasses in which accumulated rainwater was flowing.

Near Nunngarutipaluk, I did not notice a large channel until it was only three feet ahead of me. My eleven galloping dogs tried to avoid it. They stopped short at the edge, afraid, but the sledge bumped against them and pushed them all into the sea, a confusion of bellies and paws. I was suspended over the crevasse: in front, the runners had bitten into the edge of the ice, while in back the sledge rested firmly on the surface. The action of the wind could slowly widen the channel. One clumsy move would precipitate a disaster. It was Paapa, my lead dog, who saved me. He paddled over to the sledge, raising swirls of water. We exchanged one understanding glance. I grasped him by his harness and threw him, or pushed him, rather, to the other side of the channel. Every second counted. I had time to grab two more dogs. The three of them looked back, waiting for a sign from me. Cautiously I lay down and crawled over the sledge/bridge to the farther side. Once safely there, I whistled, and with a concerted pull, the three dogs yanked the sledge forward. I had simply to fish out the other eight miserable animals who were still splashing around in the icy water.

On all sides, the ice field was so broken up that for a while we had to travel by way of the mountain. Once again we were obliged to carry the equipment on our backs. When we returned to the ice field, we saw a little white tent in the distance on a deserted shore. It was Majak and his young wife peacefully enjoying their honeymoon. Majak had taken fifteen days' worth of provisions with him. He had nothing to do but abandon himself to his lovemaking. Who would dream of disturbing him? His closest neighbor was on the far side of the hill, thirty miles away.

Our first stop was by the abandoned camp at Qaanaaq. The hamlet was well situated in a place where whales and narwhals passed by. In the old days it had been inhabited by generations of Eskimos. (According to the latest radiocarbon datings I made on the peat, Qaanaaq as an archaeological site is nearly a thousand years old.) Yellow and green grass grew on the low coastal hillside; the earth was rich, the peat having been fertilized by oil from the seals and whales hunters had cut up on the spot. Kutsikitsoq and Natuk would be leaving us here to go to their son's wedding. First, however, they intended to spend several hours because five of their children—dead of tuberculosis—were buried here.

I lingered for a while, standing with Natuk and my friend. Once they were gone, our little team would have completely dissolved, marking the end of several months of living together through happy moments and times of danger. I turned my head one last time. Kutsikitsoq was looking at me with a miserable smile. My last glimpse of him was of a man standing, a little hunched, before five heaps of stone, facing the sea.

After traveling for four hours, Qaalasoq, Sakaeunnguaq, and I crossed the large Inglefield Fjord. We reached Itilleq late in the day. To our astonishment, we found two women living alone in a tent. One of them was old Irolu. We spent a good hour with them and changed our clothing. They showed childlike pleasure at our visit. Shortly afterward, for the fourth and last time, I climbed the Itilleq Glacier, to the east of Politiken Glacier. We had no serious problems with it. Our three sledges traveled over the ice cap without stopping, following a south-southeast route that was new to me; because the weather was unusually calm, we were able to cover the last several miles during the night. On June 15, we stood above Wolstenholme Fjord, fortunately still covered with ice; at last we were within sight of the famous mountain of Uummannaq-Thule.

PART FOUR

THE
IRON
AGE

*What sorceress is about to rise
in the white sunset?*
—ARTHUR RIMBAUD

20

THULE-BLUE JAY: THE EIGHT-HUNDRED-MILLION-DOLLAR BASE

Sakaeunnguaq, Qaalasoq, and I stood discussing which route to follow. We were all three dirty and smelly; I was worn out and leaned on my napariaq. Suddenly one of the Eskimos touched my shoulder.

"Takkuut! Look!"

A thick yellow cloud was rising into the sky.

"Qallunaat!" he added.

I pulled out my field glasses and, squinting, slowly brought them into focus. Beyond the compact ice field, an extraordinary spectacle took shape on the spotted lens; for a moment, I thought I was seeing a mirage.

A city of hangars and tents, of sheet metal and aluminum, glittering in the sun amid smoke and dust, rose up in front of us on a plain that only yesterday had been deserted. The most fantastic of legends was taking shape before my eyes.

"Takkuut! Look at that!"

Like pustules erupting from the depths, rows of storage tanks stood along the mountain. Their being orange made the vision all the more absurd. As we went down the slope of shining snow, surprise changed to stupefaction. As far as the eye could see, there were lines of trucks and cranes, and mountains of crates. Steel skeletons raised thin metallic arms toward the sky. Along the slopes, the enormous jaws of tentacled diggers chewed away amid smoke and steam, lifting tons of mud and stones which, in one uninterrupted movement, they vomited into the sea from buckets. The sound of the breathing, the panting of this "city," reached all the way to where we stood, and from then on it was to stay with us—the muffled grinding of ceaselessly turning motors. Planes by the dozen wheeled about in the gray sky. One, nearer than the rest, flew back and forth like a huge bumblebee, adding its own deep buzz to the hubbub. Seen from the glacier, the spectacle created by this sudden eruption of civilization looked sinister. Our dogs were howling their heads off. Two of the teams attacked each other. We intervened, but not very energetically. This return to the world of men was a letdown.

We continued our descent toward the coast. The glacier was in very bad shape; the season was too far advanced for us to be able to cross without problems. Small holes opened up in the surface at our feet. The rotten snow did not hold. At one point during the last few miles I was almost engulfed when the bridge over an enormous crevasse suddenly collapsed a moment after I stepped off it. I had no sooner escaped this danger than the whole slope seemed to begin to move; the ice was swelling in the heat of the rising sun. Section after section slid down toward the valley. We traveled the last few miles prepared for the worst.

On the shore we found a wet, yellowish rock on which we rested for a while. We left the two Eskimos' sledges and their equipment beside it and crossed a torrent, carrying my material on our heads. We threw my dogs forcibly into the icy water—they were terrified of it—and with a rope hauled them up onto the opposite bank. We did the same with my sledge.

On June 16, after crossing the frozen fjord, we were finally arriving at the Eskimo "capital" of Thule; in the eyes of the qallunaaq I had once more become, this seemed like a very big word to denote a disorderly cluster of twenty or so molehills—igloos whose relative importance could be assessed by the height of the rubbish pile before each door. We were greeted by an unusual silence; even the dogs slept on. The two Eskimos, disappointed, grumbled and thrashed their teams as they passed through the camp. Discarded wrappers from packs of Camel cigarettes and chewing gum littered the snow.

At one window I glimpsed the chocolate-smeared face of a child. A few yards farther on, a door opened slightly and from a cloud of cigarette smoke a young woman in blue jeans and makeup called out to me, "Hello, boy!" Whatever had happened since February, when I was last here?

We set up our tent near Knud Rasmussen's little white house, which was vacant. The south wind smelled of diesel oil. A message of welcome from Krogh, the Danish administrator, was delivered to me. Old Uutaaq paid us a visit; a few minutes later, he was joined by Inukitsupaluk. Little by little, I heard the news.

"Thousands and thousands of Americans," Uutaaq said in his hoarse voice. "Amerlaqaat, you lose track of how many. They come down from the sky every day. There's the atomic bomb, too. . . . We've been here a thousand years, we Inuit. We always thought Thule was an important place on the earth. . . . After all, we were the ones who discovered it. . . . Thule . . . Inukitsupaluk learned from Tatsiannguaq that fifty big ships sank beneath the ice down there. . . . The Inuit also say that they're going to heat the ice field and make it melt; that way there will hardly be any winter anymore. . . . Then they're going to send us to the North Pole. That's why Piulissuaq spent fifteen years trying to go there with the Inuit. . . . Ah! we understand everything now. . . . None of these Amerikamiut have women. That isn't normal. Sofia has heard that they'd like our hundred girls. . . . The poor things! They could never satisfy those thousands and thousands of men. . . ."

He went on for two hours. I was skeptical and listened with only half an ear. A little later, I was to confront the truth.

Qisuk personified it. Wearing a gray-green jacket with the words "United States Navy" in black block letters on the back, he was pushing a sledge piled high with cases of tinned corned beef, ham, marmalade, and bundles of magazines over the rocky ground. The dogs were struggling to pull the load. Qisuk, streaming with sweat, forced them on by belaboring them with cans of vegetables. He was followed by a crowd of kids wearing jockey caps; Lucky Strikes drooped from their mouths. They were coming from the store; the stock had been replenished, the Americans having generously given their surplus to the Eskimos through the Danish administrator. Already the shore was strewn with empty tin cans and scraps of clothing.

"Now we are richer than the danskerne. We don't have to work anymore," the natives announced. "What are we going to do? No more hunting, no more kayaks." Then, immediately contradicting themselves: "That's just a manner of speaking. You can't eat half of what's in these cans; it's too salty." The Eskimos could not tolerate even lightly salted canned food.

In the village, everyone was arguing and haggling and swapping rumors.

People were indeed talking a lot, but it was something else that really preoccupied them. The return of the sun, the heat, the abundance had awakened basic urges in them. This was the season for love. Although by now, the first half of June, the period of seasonal rut was almost over, it was still in full swing. Furtive meetings ended in some well-sheltered place. The few loose women were approached often. Glances were exchanged. People made jokes and erotic remarks in front of the elderly. They laughed loudly. Children were not the last to burst out laughing at the most daring sallies. Kujaakitsoq pointed out a small hut to me, the "young people's house." One hundred thousand qallunaat might land with airplanes and ships, but they could not stop spring from awakening sexual desire. That year—1951—the explosion of sensuality had an unusual and serious result. Because it monopolized the Eskimos' attention during those last weeks of June, it prevented their being clearly aware of the tremendous event that was to upset their entire existence.

I could say, almost without exaggeration, that the Eskimos watched the birth and building of the "city" in June and in July without apparent reactions. The daily spectacle of the constantly expanding base accustomed them gradually to what was happening, and when they awoke from their lovemaking, it was too late. The shock effect had been missed. Men who lived by the harpoon found themselves in the atomic age.

One afternoon, I left the Eskimo village where Qaalasoq was staying to call on the small Danish administrative group and find out what was really happening. The Danish government's representatives in Thule were three: an administrator, a doctor, and a radio operator. Krogh, the excellent young administrator, received me in a very friendly way, but gave me only vague and cautious information.

"We don't know anything," he said, preparing to leave his office. "I'm supposed to have coffee with one of the Americans in charge and then go on to the movies at the base. You aren't going? My wife is overwhelmed by these invitations. Do excuse us and come by tomorrow. Undskyld, undskyld. What can I do about this base?"

Standing near his house and, in a way, detaining him, I made a futile effort to convince the young administrator to enjoin the Americans, at least nominally or temporarily—in the name of the Council of Hunters, of which he was president and which had not been consulted about this operation—from making further landings until a local agreement had been reached on behalf of the Eskimos, who were obviously threatened. I urged on him the tactical advantage of taking a strong position, no matter how artificial, in order to negotiate a local agreement that the Americans would have to sign, since they had already proceeded so far with the operation.

"Look at the Eskimos' long-range interests," I insisted. "This way the immense piece of land on which the Americans are installing their base could be leased them by the Council of Hunters, which is the de facto communal authority; the money would be paid to the council and used in its investment program. . . . To the Americans the sum would mean nothing. For the Eskimos, for the local administration, it would be a gold mine. It would finance a modernization of hunting, and it would be something that has never been attempted anywhere else in the Arctic. Such an agreement," I said, "which could be used by the Danish administration as an argument in its diplomatic discussions, would be to the credit of the local authority in the tradition of Knud Rasmussen and could help ensure a better future for everyone. It's now or never. . . . If nothing is done locally, the diplomats in Copenhagen certainly won't waste their time over details that to an archaic society are all-important."

I talked and talked . . . but to no end. The answer was "Undskyld, undskyld. Excuse me, excuse me. I have an appointment. . . . A cup of coffee with some American officials and I'm several minutes late already. . . . Copenhagen will surely do whatever is necessary in good time. . . ."

I took my sledge and headed for the base, accompanied by an Eskimo who wanted to see everything. In less than fifteen minutes, crossing the ice field on North Star Bay, we reached our destination. A year before, the valley had been peaceful and empty, a flowering, virginal tundra. On a clear day only the summer before I had set up my tent here. Now, as we moved onto the beach we were almost crushed by an enormous truck with twelve six-foot-high wheels. The driver, wearing a red-and-yellow striped shirt, immediately brought his machine to a stop with a volley of gas and air-brake explosions. The dogs were more used to bears than to this strange din, and they leaped into the air in every direction. Paapa looked at me in consternation. From the glassed-in cab where he was perched, the American waved.

THE IRON AGE

The July 9 landing, North Star Bay, Thule. (*USIS*)

American base. The steam pipes are always elevated above the ground to avoid melting the permafrost. Thule-Dundas, 1972.

Typical Eskimo houses. Thule-Qaanaaq, 1972.

Three rows of housing on the left, supplied by water pipes, are for the Danish administration and staff. The long buildings are the infirmary and school. Eskimo houses are to the right and in front of the oil storage tanks. Thule-Qaanaaq, 1972.

Two "modern" Eskimos with the Danish administrator. Thule-Qaanaaq, 1972.

The arrival of goods for the year. Siorapaluk, August 1972.

Tunnel dug by the U.S. Army
beneath the Thule ice cap.
(*USIS*)

Kutsikitsoq. Siorapaluk, 1972.

Bertsie. Siorapaluk, 1972.

"Want a lift?" Then he caught sight of our team; he threw up his arms in surprise.

With a thunderous noise a bulldozer took up its excavation work. The machine lifted pounds of mud, which looked like the mud of a mangrove swamp because of the thaw. We were spattered with earth. Jeeps, half-tracks, caterpillars, and all kinds of other machines went back and forth, jolting from rut to rut. They poured rubble from the mountain into the sea to wall off the bay with a 2,000-foot-high embankment; the port thus formed would have water so deep that the tides would not affect it. Roads ran everywhere. Like insects, we crawled from one muddy hole to the next. The dogs were terrified and hung their heads as they walked. Suddenly a whistle shrilled. I looked up, intrigued. Two minutes later an explosion split the mountainside. Rocks flew through the air. Yellow dust fell back onto the ground. There were two more warnings. We went on.

We headed toward a signpost, and we reached a road, a real road, straight and flat, along which cars with red lights were streaking in both directions. From time to time, their horns blared. I was hesitating to cross the road when we met a man on foot. He must have been surprised to see two primitive men, one tall and one short, both miserably dressed in animal skins and with a dogsledge in tow. He shook his head in disbelief. I asked for some information, which he gave us.

Headquarters was a dusty wooden hut. I tied up the dogs, left the Eskimo outside, and went into a sort of air-conditioned, enameled snack bar. It was empty and smelled of fresh paint and light tobacco. From a radio in one corner came the murmur of a song. Magazines scattered on tables, colored photographs of movie stars on the walls. . . . I was motioned to a rocking chair.

Some high-ranking officers at the base came in. All of a sudden I was introduced to a general, the commander of the United States Air Force here in Thule. He gave me a quick, piercing look; I said a few words about my expedition and the fact that I was a scientist and a native of France. He looked at me again, with cold, inscrutable politeness, and then shut himself in a room with two of his fellow officers. In English, I explained to the people who were still standing around me firing absurd questions at me that I was a "native from Paris."

The men were surprised:

"What have our intelligence people been doing all this time? This base is supposed to be top secret, and a Frenchman has been staying here for a whole year. And now he's about to go back to Europe. . . . It's impossible. . . . French? Maybe he's a Communist. . . ." There was a pause—had it gone on much longer I would have found it unpleasant—and then an officer came out of the conference room and gestured to one of the men standing near me: "You are cleared," he said to me. I was free to go!

Then one of the men told a joke, and the atmosphere, which had been filled with doubt and suspicion, changed suddenly.

"Notre Pariss!" said one of the men. I looked at him, wide-eyed.

"Folies-Bergère! Amie la France!"

Jokes crackled; someone put his hand on my shoulder.

"Drink?" I was handed a glass of tomato juice.

They sympathized with the "poor Frenchman" who had been stuck up here all alone, surrounded by savages. A tall, thin man pushed his way through the group and looked at me out of China-blue eyes.

"How much does your business pay? You must make a pile! I'm interested."

He crushed my fingers in his enormous hand.

By this time, everyone was full of good will and eager to take me around to see everything. At the Signal Corps, while they were fixing my Foca camera, they showed me the plan of the future city, which was tacked up on the wall, and explained it in detail. Who was going to object to the fact that I was paying this visit? For the moment, everyone was content to ignore the question of where I would get the visa I needed. Left in limbo between the rules of the government and the principles of international law, I constituted an embarrassing case no one wanted to take cognizance of. It was my good luck and my protection. Since governments hate unusual cases, they are only too happy to ignore them.

"Hello! Come on, John!"

They led me from street to street; we ended up at the movie house. Tomorrow they would be showing *Kon-Tiki,* but tonight the movie was a thriller in the best American tradition: one long brawl punctuated by a few kiss-me-quick love scenes. Close-ups, chases with blasts from machine guns, free-for-all fights. The Eskimo who had come with me that afternoon was so overwhelmed that he left in the middle of the show. I thought he had gone for a walk, but as it turned out, I did not see him again for a long time. Nor Sakaeunnguaq either, for that matter. I learned from the Eskimos that my dear friend was so stunned by what he had seen during the previous few days that he had simply taken his sledge and returned to Siorapaluk.

Every morning I walked around the city as a tourist, my camera around my neck and a notebook in hand. I had been "cleared," so I went everywhere. Following the arrows at each crossroad, I walked through dirty white dust in step with the heavy tread of power tools and machines. In less than ten weeks, the world's most formidable air base had risen up on this desert.

Imagine a valley three miles wide and nine miles long, at one end terminated by a glacier, and at the other end closed off by the sea, which was frozen nine months out of twelve. Packed into this valley was a group of Americans numbering more than one-quarter of the native population of Greenland. In the space of a few weeks, the Americans had apparently spent as much as, or more than, the Canadian government had invested in its Eskimo colonies in the last hundred years. The monies for the annual work on the base would amount to more than double Denmark's expenditures for the whole of Greenland since 1721. The creation of this base was part of Operation Blue Jay, which was said to be the biggest military enterprise since the Allied landings in Normandy. Apparently Thule would be the Strategic Air Command's most powerful atomic base.

Even the Thule pastor, a native Greenlander who was usually very calm, was overwhelmed by events; in the evening, he would take a piece of chalk and try to analyze the cost of the operation for me on his blackboard. According to him it was astronomical, considering that vehicles, manpower, provisions—everything down to the last nail needed during the initial period of the operation—had to be brought in by air freight. We floundered our way through the figures, adding zeroes as we went. (According to later official figures, in eighteen months the base had officially cost nearly $200 million; in 1951, $1,140,000 in salaries had been paid before any work could begin on the site. The cost of equipping and installing the base was later estimated at nearly $800 million!) The plain was already studded with giant cranes for miles on end. Six heated hangars were planned to house the largest planes, on two of which construction had already begun. As far as the eye could see, prefabricated houses were being put together and roofed. The little Danish meteorological station was surrounded by rows of brand-new huts, barracks under semicylindrical shelters, and warehouses. Operating on fixed schedules, buses serviced all four corners of the city. On one street, I chatted for a moment with a traffic policeman. He held a clipboard and was carefully marking down each vehicle that passed in either direction.

"Good job," he said to me, waving his clipboard.

I agreed: he got five dollars an hour and worked a ten-hour day.

When finished, the runway, which was the whole reason for this gigantic complex, would be more than 9,000 feet long and 200 feet wide.

Some projects either envisaged or already under way were: the movie theater; the electric system and its generating station; the telephone system, providing instant communication with DEW line[1] bases from the Aleutians to Iceland; a baseball diamond; a radio tower higher than the Eiffel Tower; two types of radar, one of them a detection radar with a fixed antenna 435 feet long and 164 feet high monitoring 3,000 miles—into the heart of Eurasia—the other a search radar for enemy missiles with a rotating antenna 82 feet in diameter, 154 feet above the ground; a restaurant; an ultramodern hospital, the largest distillery of sea water in the world (at first water had been taken from a nearby lake, which had soon gone dry); a model laundry, a tunnel beneath the ice cap; pillboxes in the ice, and a library.

Planning for Operation Blue Jay had begun secretly in Washington in January 1950, and the secret had been so well kept that the Eskimos had had no hint of it. The operation had to be carried out quickly. The ships had to be unloaded in July and August, before the ice field froze. The news from Korea seemed likely to hasten things even more. All the men I met were working seven days a week for astronomical salaries—from $1,500 to $2,000 a month—and had a lively sense that they were taking part in a great patriotic enterprise. There was no feeling of romanticism about the North Pole here. I doubt whether these Americans had even heard of Kane, Hayes, Greely,

Peary, Cook, Rasmussen, Wulff, or Lauge Koch, or cared to get to know their Eskimo neighbors. Each had been hired for a specific task with a view to achieving the greatest efficiency and output. They worked, they ate, they slept.

John Hubbard, an architect and the nephew of Charles Hubbard, who had designed the base, walked around with me for a bit. He was intelligent and friendly, and we had a pleasant chat. I visited a house equipped with a refrigerator, bathroom, lavatory, and central heating. Elsewhere I was shown the piling pipes which they planned to sink into the permafrost* to stabilize its temperature. I was taken to the mess hall. For the occasion, the person with me wore the insignia of his profession, a large yellow circle, on his chest.

"Arctic expert," he said to me, laughing.

This was the man's first visit here, where a whole generation of young engineers would get on-the-job training. Thule was the first field of experimentation for the American army as it invented on the site its own methods of Arctic engineering; not until twenty years later, around 1972, would it reach a point where in a few rare fields it was more sophisticated and developed than Soviet science, which was otherwise preeminent in dealing with cold regions.

We strode over piles of excavated earth, a network of wires and pipelines, as we made our way toward a large hut used as a communal mess hall by the whole base. Inside an enormous room with pastel walls a crowd of men stood in line. We took our places. For fifteen minutes I had nothing to do but decipher the hieroglyphics on the cowboy shirts of the men around me. On the walls were slogans like: "Watch out. . . . Don't play with other people's lives. Enemy ears are listening to you: Be quiet." In the background the radio ground out popular songs twenty-four hours a day. At last we reached the food. Giant vats and enormous percolators stood on the oil stoves. I was handed an aluminum plate with the inevitable little divisions, which indifferent cooks in white chef's caps filled as we moved along. We sat down at a long metal table. A group of "scientists" sat on my right. We chatted for a few minutes. They were here only for several days and clearly did not want to be confused with their military hosts. It was a difficult, cautious conversation. Across from me, two engineers were talking. They could not see how Thule could be considered "top secret" any longer.

"But it's an open secret! It isn't serious. Officially, we don't know where we are. We're not allowed to tell our families, even though some evenings we hear Radio Moscow discuss how the work is progressing here. After some planes left Goose Bay [Newfoundland], Moscow even announced the names of the passengers coming to Thule!"

". . . And you can't sew up the lips of the people who go home at the end of September when their contracts expire, or the Danes in the village or the

---

*In Thule, the ground is permanently frozen to a depth of a thousand feet. During the summer, the ground thaws to a depth of three feet at the most.

Danes manning the radio. And what about you? Are you a friend or an enemy? I say it's an open secret. Sooner or later, it will all have to come out."

Then they went on with their meal, discussing road systems and motors.

I wandered from one office to another. A dozen vehicles were lined up in front of the headquarters' service station. I spotted a strapping young man with red hair: Joe was from Michigan and worked in the convoy. He was driving his ten-ton truck to the airport to mail a letter to his girlfriend.

"Okay!" he said.

He took me aboard. We rolled along a sort of highway a hundred feet wide,* using short blasts of a pedal-operated horn to warn lines of cars that we were about to pass. We passed a road roller, which was going over the ground again and again and making an infernal racket. Joe drove at top speed, whistling the latest blues tunes. To our right, we could see an expanse of caterpillars aligned with perfect precision, and a parking lot filled with jeeps. To our left, there was already a graveyard of cars and broken tools dwarfed by mountains of crates of spoiled food.

The noise was growing louder. The dust was so thick that Joe put on his headlights.

"Airport!" he yelled in my ear.

The truck stopped. The American jumped out and waddled off to mail his letter. I got down, too, and was immediately enveloped in a cloud of sand raised by the propellors of planes landing and taking off every ten minutes. Imagine a northern landscape, flat as your hand, without one tree, and a gravelly runway blackened by oil and striped with furrows made by exhaust gas.

"Next September," a pilot yelled in my ear, "we'll have jets and superbig four-engined planes, the biggest in the world."

The air smelled stale and dry—it smelled of gas and of burning. I was jostled by a crowd of busy men going back and forth. Pilots in helmets and flying suits covered with piping were talking together. A loudspeaker bleated order upon order. Now some officers came onto the runway with microphones in one hand, while with the other they kept their caps from being whipped off by the wind. A Superfortress was arriving from Goose Bay. Its propellers had hardly stopped turning before its left side opened and out onto the landing area poured sections of houses, jerrycans, cars, and cranes. An enormous fourteen-ton shovel had been brought to the site this way. Not far away, a Dakota which was on the point of leaving was swallowing up passengers. I was told they were engineers who were going to spend the weekend inspecting a base some 600 miles away. They gave a casual wave of the hand; I responded vaguely as they disappeared into the belly of the plane.

Certainly nothing is stranger than the outskirts of an airport—especially at the North Pole. I had never seen such a cosmopolitan atmosphere within

---

*Eighty-nine miles of similar roads were eventually built around the base, linking the different stations.

such a small area. I met a group of American engineers of German origin; some of them had just come from Florida. Like schoolboys on a picnic, they walked along in orderly fashion, carrying their little flight bags. Tagged and herded together, they headed toward their hut, where bunks had been assigned them. Tomorrow, they would be at their jobs. None of them knew exactly where he was. When two of them learned that they were in Greenland, they protested violently. They were supposed to be going to a meteorological station in Baffin Island, Canada. They had been unloaded by mistake, like spoiled fruit. It did not matter—within two hours they would be reshipped, this time in the right direction. The 7,500 workers at the base all came from Rosemont, Minnesota, where they had been recruited in the spring with great secrecy. Most of them had been flown over to Greenland. About 3,000 would remain for the winter. All in all, from June 1950 to the summer of 1952, 19,000 people would pass through the airport at Thule.

To leave the base, all I had to do was follow a precarious path along the cliff. Near the ice field I would find the Eskimos of Uummannaq-Thule sitting on cans and crates, talking together.

They would ask me all sorts of questions. I gathered that most of them, especially the women and the old people, had confidence in their local administrator and the Danish king. But one could also sense bitterness and fear welling up in them, particularly in the thirty- and forty-year-old men: "We have been abandoned by the danskerne! What is going to happen to us? Ajor! Ajorpoq! What terrible troubles lie in store for us!"

The women were proud of the gossip they overheard at the store; they came and went, gleaning a bit of news here and passing it along there. What worried them was that hunting would become difficult. The seal, uuttoq, who had pulled himself up on the ice field to sleep in the sun, was—even he!— disturbed by the unpleasant noise of motors; it made him uneasy. The old people kept repeating that the waters had been polluted by diesel oil and that the walruses and seals would not return; they would never return.

"All that"—they pointed to the base—"is not for us. Nothing good will come of it. And Pitugfiik, the valley where the Amerikanski have settled, used to be full of foxes and partridges. We won't be able to hunt there anymore, even if they're still alive. . . ."

Uutaaq, who had just moved into a beautiful frame house given to him by the Danish government in recognition of his past as an explorer, took me aside:

"An engine, an airplane, is very lovely, very complicated. But we are not impressed. You white men have equipment, books. But we—without knowing much, look what we've been able to do with nothing, not a piece of wood or iron except for what is in Savigssivik. A sledge, an igloo, is also a very good thing. . . . We have been here for hundreds and hundreds of years. We have some say, some right to speak—after all, this is our home. I'm the oldest of them all. . . . Oh! if Piuli were alive, I would go talk to him. . . . We Inuit helped the Amerikanski a lot, Piulissuaq, Tatsekuuk, Kane. . . . I'll remind them that we have some rights over them."

When I started to leave he said, "Wait, I have a pile of papers here. I can't read very well. Have a look at them."

There were two envelopes postmarked New York City. I tore them open. One contained a large sheet of paper with a letterhead. "Dear Mr. Uutaaq," it read, "We have the honor and pleasure to inform you that our assembly has unanimously elected you a member. . . ." The other letter was unexpected, to say the least: Uutaaq, whom the secretary's office had undoubtedly confused with other members of the club, was invited to attend various demonstrations and a lecture.

The Eskimos were very upset. Torben Krogh, the young administrator, explained to them what had happened and told them to be patient. Steps had to be taken. But what steps? The Eskimos discussed it again and again.

"Go north? Run away? But it isn't possible. Ataaq, ataataq, ataatataq, ataatatataq—our parents, our grandparents, our great-grandparents—are buried here. Then stay? But with all this noise, who can sleep anymore, or hunt! Ajoq! Ajoq!"

And the lamentations continued.

The fifty large boats had not sunk, contrary to what Inukitsupaluk had said. On July 9, preceded by helicopters and ice breakers, a formidable armada, the largest ever sent into the American Arctic, dropped anchor in Thule Harbor. In this convoy alone there were 4,400 passengers and 300,000 tons of cargo.

The Eskimos were overwhelmed! Their springtime lovemaking was forgotten. From the ship, hundreds of pairs of eyes and binoculars were trained on the coast. Sitting on the beach, we watched the spectacle no less fixedly. We imagined those hulls crammed with vehicles, machinery, prefabricated houses, derricks, tents, meat, cigarettes, candy, fuel. After a seventeen-day wait in the ice in Melville Bay, and more than a month of difficult navigation (many propellers were damaged by the ice and had to be replaced en route), the men on board were impatient to land. Since early morning, Eskimo kayaks had been slipping like eels around the tall gray steel hulls. Jostling one another along the rails, the "boys" tossed dollars, watches, knives, and breakfast rolls down to the Eskimos. The noise of engines at the base was drowned out now by jazz from the loudspeakers on each ship.

One evening, the landing ships ran into trouble and drew alongside the Danish-Eskimo beach, which was, theoretically, off limits to them. Open-faced men who seemed no older than eighteen or twenty stepped ashore; they were dirty and unshaven, bundled into shiny black hip boots yet shivering with cold. At first they were shy; then they began to come up to me confidently because I welcomed them politely in their own language. "There aren't any Russians here, are there?" they asked, in their knowing, nasal voices. "These Mongolians"—pointing to the Eskimos, who were standing a short distance away—"are

they Samoyeds or Chukchis?" It was as though this were a commando operation. They had no idea of where they were landing—Greenland, Spitzberg,
Bear Island, perhaps Siberia?

They were friendly. They gave us a crate of oranges and plums. The fruit
was wrapped in mimeographed ship's newspapers. Reading those papers, one
got the impression that a grave conflict was about to break out. We talked of
one thing and another, while we warmed our hands around a brazier stuffed
with boards. After an hour, the boys returned to their ship.

"We'll come back," they said.

And did they! For the next two or three days, the coming and going
through the Eskimo village was incessant. There were young men of all sorts.
College boys from Harvard and Berkeley—already dubbed the Thule bobby-
soxers—had come to "see" the Arctic. They worked mornings at the base to
reimburse the army for their passage; during the afternoons, their ambition
was to discover the Pole. This group was outnumbered, however, by sailors
and working-class fellows who would stand in front of the igloos, loaded down
with merchandise—cartons of cigarettes, axes, ropes, large cans, shoes, and
caps—and barter with the Eskimos. The souvenir hunt was phenomenally
successful from the outset. A small bear crudely sculpted in ivory brought the
sum of twenty dollars; an old whip, ten dollars; a pair of worn-out "primitive"
boots, seven dollars. I witnessed some absurd scenes. One young American
asked me to say something for him to an Eskimo who had carved an ivory
figurine:

"Please tell the Eskimo to carve a lot more like that for me. They must all
be exactly alike. But tell him the price will be lower. I'll pay him five dollars
each, instead of ten."

I translated. The Eskimo was startled.

"Ajorssiva! I can't do it! Tell this silly qallunaaq that the more of them I
make all alike, the more expensive it will be, because it will be more boring to
make them!"

The traffic between the boats and the Eskimos increased. The Americans
began taking still photographs of the Eskimos and filming them. Let a "native"
make a move—a man pick up a harpoon or a woman nurse her baby or a hunter
prepare to eat seal meat—and five cameras would aim and click away.
"Thanks!" Light meters in hand, the visitors would walk off, chewing gum,
discussing "shutter speeds" and "poses."

The villagers were becoming impatient. Something had to be done. One
morning, rumor had it that the general agreement reached between Copenhagen and Washington in April 1951 for the defense of Greenland strictly for-
bade all contact between natives and Americans on the base. Torben Krogh,
who had at last been officially informed of what was going on, was irritated.

"I have stopped the Eskimos from approaching the ships in their kayaks,"
Krogh informed the Americans. "Now it is up to you."

The reaction was immediate and harsh.

One afternoon when I was trying to prevent two Yankees from making

God knows what deal with a native family, some American officers were suddenly silhouetted on top of the plateau. The two sailors moved off quickly.

That evening, I learned in the camp that because they had been caught in the act, the two men had been sentenced to several months in detention; while their ship was in port, they would have to remain in the storerooms belowdecks. The authorities had struck, and this one punishment was enough. From then on, an iron curtain descended between the base and the village. Its tangible form was rifle-bearing soldiers on patrol.

The administrator Krogh, respecting and wishing to protect local customs, could congratulate himself with a clear conscience. Yet these measures could not prevent the brutal collision between two different worlds. All contact was forbidden, true, but who could stop the Eskimos from thinking?

From their igloos, these primitive people had watched a fortress rise. They had heard its muffled throbbing. Even if they managed to forget the days of July 1951, that hammering would be enough to remind them. Everything they had once longed for, had obtained only in small quantities after hard days spent hunting, was now handed to them, even showered on them, by the government. A few weeks later, they saw rollicking festivities succeeded by organization, hole-in-the-corner trafficking replaced by accountancy. Money, that prime agent of corruption, held sway everywhere. The younger hunters were now aware of how mediocre their material way of life was. Who was going to be able to persuade them that this was not true! The second chapter in the history of Thule and of northern Greenland had begun: Inuk, the man with the harpoon, was doomed.

In 1954 the Minister of Greenland announced that the Polar Eskimos had decided to move 125 miles to the north to Qaanaaq, on the edge of the Murchison Strait. The kings of Thule had refused to raise their glasses in salute to the new era.

One could only cheer. Yes, of course legendary Thule was not dead. It had not mistaken one military base for the whole of our civilization.

A fine gesture. . . . But wasn't it futile? The airport and its defense area would grow every year, while the hold of the white man—the technocrats and the engineers—on the entire country would become tighter and tighter.

21

RETURN
TO THULE,
1967, 1969, 1972

July 26, 1967: Kastrup Airport, Copenhagen. SAS Flight 713 Copenhagen–Thule. Gate 12. Departure 11:00. Immediate boarding.

In the big Danish air terminal, a luxurious building of marble and chrome, voices were muffled. Whispery announcements in Scandinavian languages and English filled the air. Hurried travelers dressed in summer clothes were leaving for the south—the Balearic Islands or Rome or New York. In response to the brief summons of a dry, neutral voice, I entered the passageway, a gray antechamber to the white frozen expanses of Greenland. I queued up in a melancholy line of a hundred or so people waiting to embark on the bimonthly jet that joins Denmark to the American military base in Thule.

The passengers were mostly Danish civilians who were employed, under the terms of the NATO treaty, in construction, maintenance, and service jobs at the base. Engineers, foremen, truck drivers, taxi drivers, post-office clerks, cooks, waiters were going back, after vacation, to their jobs.

The Copenhagen–Thule crossings used to be made by boat; in July 1950 it took me several weeks by sea. This day, at an altitude of 30,000 feet, my flight would cross in four hours and fifty minutes.

We took our seats on the plane. I absently observed the comings and goings of the stewardesses, but my mind kept returning to the odyssey of my past seventeen years.

This was not my first return to the Arctic. Between 1960 and 1963, I spent several months on three missions to the eastern and central Canadian Arctic, part of that time in Illulik, Foxe Bay, part around the Boothia Peninsula. Earlier in 1967, I had been to the Bering Sea, to the islands of St. Lawrence. And whenever I had got permission from the U.S.S.R. Academy of Sciences, I had pushed on into eastern Siberia—Oymyakon, to the east of Yakutsk, and Suntar, along the Vilguy River.

Flying in comfort over the Norwegian Sea offered a wry contrast to some

396

of those difficult exploratory missions, which were carried out by umiaq or monoplane in the fog of Bering Strait. In my mind's eye, I could see those villages, which bear traces of Japanese and northeastern Siberian influences: the intense ceremonial life, the whale hunts dominated by the spirit of shamanism. I encountered there the memory of a form of military organization unlike anything I have been able to study elsewhere in the Bering Sea area: warlike armor, small forts, lookout posts, groups of slaves. How radically different those complex powerful societies of the past were in comparison with the simple, stocky, and vital Greenlandic Eskimo group in Thule! Kutsikitsoq, Qaaqqutsiaq—and all my dear Thule friends—were on my mind as we flew over the immense Greenland ice cap at an altitude of 15,000 feet. What had become of them since July 1951? When I left them, they were worried and anguished but also tempted by the unknown future before them.

In those intervening years and later on, I had acquired considerable experience as consultant to government on the difficult problems posed by the integration of the Eskimos into the modern world. Now the Danish government's Minister of Greenland had sent me as consultant on a similar mission to Thule. The question was simple, although the answer was not: "What do you see as the future of Thule? Give us your ideas and proposals, and work out a plan of reform."

The plane was losing altitude. We had to be over Melville Bay, but it was concealed by cottony clouds and pockets of fog.

I left the immense military base and walked to the shore, which was dominated by Knud Rasmussen's little white house; it was empty still, but its presence seemed to bear witness to a nobler hope. Out in the bay, once busily plied by kayaks, a solitary sloop was swaying in the water. In answer to my shout, a man came up on deck and waved to me warmly. I soon learned that three Eskimos had been waiting two days for me.

Two of the young men had been children at the time of my first visit. Kresunguaq was the son of Imina, of Siorapaluk; Avataq was the son of Anaakkaq, the black Eskimo of Savigssivik; the third man I didn't know. We shook hands, nothing more. The emotion was mine; for them, it could only be vicarious. It was their fathers who knew me.

The majesty of the bay was intact, and it gripped me as it always used to. We slipped along silently, though now and again the ice floes were still closely packed, and the boat thrust its way slowly through the cracks, pushing large fragments of ice before its prow. The sloop had to maneuver and countermaneuver; it sundered the larger fragments, recoiled, then moved quickly forward, patiently widening the channel.

The sky was clear. On our left was big, flat-topped Saunders Island; its high rust-colored cliffs, grooved by gullies, stood tall and distinct. Sea birds —agpats, gulls, sea mews—wheeled above our heads. Two Eskimos were in the stern, at the tiller. The third was stationed in the prow, and with gestures indicated our route through the floating ice. I chatted with Kresunguaq— cautiously, for I'm afraid I had forgotten most of the Thule dialect. The young hunters were extremely courteous. Their eyes sparkled encouragingly, and they said, "Of course, everybody knows you speak the way we do. . . . People remember you very well . . . with your dogs!" I ventured some elementary Eskimo, a child's syncopated pidgin. From those long-past days, groups of words from their dialect, then sentences, the intonations in their accents and inflections gradually returned to my lips. We skirted Nullit and Cape Parry. I glanced at the surface with a professional eye: "Well, I never noticed before how very flat that shingly plain is!"

We moved into gray patchy fog; the mingled odors of salt and ice stirred old memories in me. We were advancing very slowly, only a few miles per hour. The putt-putt of the diesel engine and the vibration of the boat gradually lulled me into a pleasant drowsiness. Suddenly, I was aware of hurried steps on our port side. The men had sighted a spot on a distant moving ice floe, barely visible through the cottony fog. I picked up my binoculars, then handed them to Kresunguaq. It was a reddish haired dog marooned on drift ice. As we learned later, he had been looking for scraps of seal that bears would have left and was caught off guard when a section of the ice field suddenly broke loose; the poor dog had been drifting for three weeks and was facing a horrid end when we happened along and saved him. His bristling hair and brown eyes were full of a kind of wild gratitude and told us clearly what suffering and anxiety he had endured. . . .

It was seven in the morning when I recognized the high, grassy beach where on my return to Thule by dogsledge in June 1951, I had changed my wet kamiks in old Ivalu's lonely tent. We drew near, round a cape, and like a blow to the face, a kind of mining town rose before me: Qaanaaq, the new Thule, a checkerboard of brightly painted small square houses; the flat roofs looked as if they had been sliced level or left somehow unfinished.

The houses were tiered on either side of a sloping main street, the ones higher up supported on the horizontal by posts. Two big tanks, like enormous pimples, added a final defacing touch to the landscape. I noticed a section of row upon row of black shanties. Would they be the native "huts"? We dropped anchor a half mile offshore and, as the boat rocked, Kresunguaq watched me with a slight smile.

We waited twenty minutes for a boat to come pick us up and deposit us on the shore of the new Eskimo capital of northern Greenland. The beach was strewn with dirty rags and empty cans. Four men—Danish officials—appeared. Emerging from a big jade-green and white parka, American-made, the senior official walked up to me: "Thank you for coming back! You are awaited by all of them. Undskyld—excuse us, but, last night there was a celebration and they drank a lot. The district administrator is still asleep, too. I am here to welcome you in his name."

An elderly man was walking down the hill with short steps, his kamiks unlaced. They pointed him out to me, but I was not sure I recognized him. He was wearing dungarees; a big shiny white button closed a collarless shirt too tightly around his skinny neck. A few coarse white hairs on the chin and upper lip, the eyebrows still coal-black, short hair, a furrowed pentagonal face, a slightly opened mouth that revealed a few widely spaced teeth, body squat but still solid and erect—Qaaqqutsiaq!

He faced me—stiff, bowlegged, his weight firmly on his heels—and wordlessly shook my hand. His eyes, set in pockets of fat, were laughing with what seemed to be affection. To break the tension of my own feelings, I leaned down and rummaged in the bag at my feet. I handed him a fat copy of my printed thesis, the result of our 1950 expedition to Inglefield Land, and copies of the morphological maps that we worked so hard together to draw up. He accepted them gravely. I knew that he would keep them in his old sailor's chest and, when the igloo was empty, would put on his glasses and examine the material, page by page. I could visualize his thick finger following the drawings as if to make sure that they were accurate, and in my head I could already hear his half-critical, half-approving Ieh! Ieh!

The young government assistant came up to suggest that I lodge for as long as I liked in the new school building. It would make it easier for me to see people, he added, during my stay in Qaanaaq. We set out. To reach the school one had to climb a steep slope. The new Thule was tiered to a height of 180 feet.

As we walked along, I glanced at the large silent houses on my right. "They belong to the danskerne," Qaaqqutsiaq whispered to me. The left side of the wide street was lined by wretched little hovels like so many rabbit hutches. This was the Eskimo slum built by the thrifty Danes in place of the old Thule. Here and there were a few white tents. "For us, for the Inuit—no better than dogs!" Qaaqqutsiaq said under his breath, looking around to make sure that the officials did not hear him. "Just wait. . . . People will tell you. . . . The administrator lives up at the top, he has the finest house, next to the clinic. . . . People will tell you about it. Just wait a bit, just wait a bit. . . . Qaanaaq ajorpoq! Everything's bad in Qaanaaq. . . ."

It was a slow walk. Thule-Qaanaaq was waking up. Yellow smoke was rising from the shacks: the Eskimos had lighted their coal stoves and would be shuffling about to clean their coffeepots. Three children, perhaps ten years old, came out of a hut and walked toward me. They stopped me and, staring me straight in the eye—unthinkable behavior according to traditional civility—asked me straight out my name and age. Twenty years ago such impudence would have made one blanch.

No sooner was I settled into some young boarder's plain, narrow room than there was a knock at the door. It was Kutsikitsoq. He was thinner, but his face was still noble, and less lined than Qaaqqutsiaq's. As he walked forward crabwise, his head sunk deep in his sealskin anorak, he stared fixedly at the floor. His bald spot had grown—it was now like a monk's—but the long locks of hair falling over one eye lent him a scoffing air. His slightly forced smile revealed pink gums. His teeth were all gone but one, in front. He who used to boast of having them all. His eyes were as mocking as ever. "Back again?"

he murmured. We were standing some distance apart, each equally ill at ease. Then, in one movement, we embraced, Eskimo fashion, clasping each other close around the shoulders. "Malaurie!" I was too moved to speak. Presently, we sat down on the bed, feeling awkward once more. I gave him the same fat book as to Qaaqqutsiaq. He accepted it with the same reserved dignity. His gestural language might have been translated thus: "You've done what you thought you had to do. We are happy to have helped you do it, but you are the only judge of it. I hope that it's for the good of everyone, and particularly of yourself, because we like you."

The news fell from his lips in a rapid, scrambled way, as if I had gone away only yesterday. "Natuk and Padloq? You'll be seeing them, they're getting themselves made up a little—just a very little, they're nothing but old women now. . . . Uutaaq, Pualuna, Nukapianguaq, Gideon? Dead, all dead, ajor. . . . Your cabin in Siorapaluk isn't there anymore. The walls, floor, everything down to the last nail—no more. No one, I guess, has wanted to rebuild there. Your dogs? . . ." Dear Kutsikitsoq was answering all the questions I was asking silently inside. "Caporal died last—he was a good dog. After you, Angutil-luarssuk adopted him—you know him, you met him in Qeqertaq, and you thought he had a good head on his shoulders. . . . Aamma? She's fine, you'll see her."

The dentist, who also stayed at the school while he was passing through town, discreetly brought us two bottles of beer so that we could reminisce in festive style.

Later in the morning, I took a short walk. The sun was shining, the fog had lifted, and everybody who was anybody in Qaanaaq was abroad. Boys looking like movie cowboys in their black leather jackets and their embossed and studded leather belts walked up and down, a cigarette or cigarillo in their mouths, cans of beer in their pockets. I saw a few blue jeans, but mostly the gray or black trousers of the qallunaat, and pointed street shoes of cheap leather.

The women wore light, usually floral-print dresses over blue wide-legged pants, and rubber boots in bright colors. Red nail polish. . . . I passed a few fat women with their hair in curlers, but the young ones wore their hair short, pageboy style. A Dane strode by, a rifle slung over his shoulder; he must have been on his way to hunt on the ice. The man looked like a worker, and this would be his day off. An Eskimo woman sporting a superb poncho, which she wore like a cone over her pants, was trotting near the Dane to point out the way he should go. I was busy greeting people and shaking hands. Some old women waved to me hesitantly from their windows. They shouted in hoarse, happy voices. My sortie into the main—the only—street was beginning to resemble simultaneously a mayoral tour of inspection and a distant cousin's visit for some anniversary. I felt a little uncomfortable, and decided to take refuge at Ululik's house; I had been told he was living here. I called to one of the young cowboys, and he came over, snickering. I commissioned him to act as my guide, which he did with authority, his friends crowding on his heels. I arrived at a suburban style of detached house, with a flat roof; the entranceway was tiny, and I could hardly imagine hunters with their furs and their expansive gestures in it. This hall led into a large room about sixty feet square, with sleeping platforms paired like bunk beds along the walls, accommodating eight people. The illeq, the soul of the igloo, had disappeared in the designs of the Danish architects responsible for these prefabricated houses. Colorful coverlets were scattered about; on one I noticed a fat pillow with a red and black floral pattern.

Wearing bearskin pants, Ululik welcomed me with his great laugh: "Nuanninguyu! What a real joy to see you again!" Once he had got me seated, he reminded me, swallowing his words in his contentment, of our first fox hunt in Illulorsuit. His memory for time and geography was still precise. I looked at him: as always, his eyes were sunk in rings of fat, the greater or lesser depending on how he felt. His perpetually sweaty face crinkled in ironic smiles; he kept running thick fingers through his mussed hair, turning his head mechanically as he clucked "What's all this!" and spit now and then into a small tin beneath the table. I noticed him counting on his fingers. Then he stared at the floor in silence, his head bent low. Presently, he looked up abruptly, as if he were scenting something, and told me he was sorry he had nothing but seal to offer me. No sooner said than done: an earthenware dish—new—was placed on the floor, a small Woolworth's-style knife—also new—was laid beside it. I got ready to eat. Then Ululik took his personal knife from his pocket. Ekrariussaq, his wife, picked up her ulu. I tore my meat with my teeth; my own knife was back at the school, and I did not want to cut seal with the white man's knife.

When they heard of my arrival, others joined us: Paulina, Peary's granddaughter, now married to Kresunguaq, the man who came to fetch me; old one-eyed Ivalu, now even older; her husband, Qaalasoq, the brother of Ululik, who, when he was about to speak, opened his mouth, pursed his lips, threw himself back, and shook himself as if he were shaking his ideas out; also Aamma of bygone days; she was now a toothless grandmother, yet for me she still had her discreet charm.

I cut myself adrift among reminiscences. I noticed that with this older generation civility preserved all its virtues. In this modern, dirty house, each visitor made it a point of honor to allow his cigarette to burn long; at the last possible moment, he got up and, cupping his hand, knocked the ash into a can or the wastebasket by the door.

Hours flew by. As we shared the seal, with no apparent change of expression each person evoked the past, his eyes alight with pleasure. Suddenly the young black-shirts pushed open the door. They did not stand back and a little apart, as young people did in the past. With chests thrust forward, hands in pockets, speaking bad Danish among themselves, they cheekily walked to the center of the room to sweep up whatever was on the table. Ululik eyed them with a dry, scornful look that made them retreat and station themselves flanking the door. Deference was short-lived; the boldest of the lot came forward again, though hesitantly. On the table were two packs of cigarettes and some cigars that I had left, as is the custom, for people to take as they please. Eskimo politeness required that one wait until they were actually offered. The boy snatched the two packs of cigarettes, ripped them open, and, with an air of disgust, dropped them; he picked up a cigar, sniffed it, threw it down on the table also, and rejoined his chums, muttering an oath in Danish. Ululik lowered his head; Ekrariussaq had gone back to her washing.

I paid a visit to A——, who was forty years old. Like Maassannguapaluk and all the men of his age, he already looked like an old man. The cold, frost, unsuitable food, and, above all, alcohol had destroyed his vigor. A few steps away from him, a man, unbuttoned, lay sprawled against N——, a woman of thirty. When I came in, both turned their heads, like animals caught in a trap. The man was a hunter whom I know very well. His drunken eyes stared at me fixedly.

In the house, a girl turned on the radio. Reception was limited to one wavelength, which brought in the American base. Blues and rock music, announced in a Yankee twang, were brought twenty-four hours a day into these igloos. A woman imitated Elvis Presley: ". . . loove viumenn nayce. . . ." She slipped her hands over her body, her hips, her thighs. Everybody laughed. "Okay, Amerikanski," the woman said, and sat down again.

"When the Amerikanski come by plane," she went on, "they have tollars, handfuls of tollars. The Danski don't like. They don't like that the Amerikanski who like the Eskimos ever since Piulissuaq give us whatever they have—tollars, chewing gum, cigarettes, knives. . . . People like the Amerikanski better because they're rich. All you have to do is look at the map—Denmark is little, America's big."

Padloq—old Padloq—had just come in. Fixing me with her yellow eyes, she said to the woman: "Tell him, yes, yes, tell him. He is one of us. Tell him everything."

The woman continued: " 'Here, take that!' . . . That's what the American says to the Eskimo. 'Take that . . . and that, and that, and that, too,' while the Danski aren't looking. . . . What's all this? The Danes don't want us to have tollars? Amerlaqaat! Full of tollars. . . . They give us cigarettes, lots of cigarettes. Camel . . . Lookay Straik. . . . Good for the Eskimo, they say, and it is good for the Eskimo because now people have beer so they smoke more. Why do the danskerne want people to buy their cigarettes when the Americans give them to us? Eh? Why? If it weren't for the Amerikanski, what would people be wearing? Eh? Shirts, anoraks, boots, caps, gloves! And all the rest—chewing gum, cigars. . . . Everything is U.S. except the flag, which is Danish. What's the sense of that?"

An Eskimo took me aside. His eyes glittered as he grasped the lapel of my jacket and said: "For years I've been saying that the Danski are not fair with the kalaallit and the Inuit. The qallunaat can drink as much as they want to; we can't. Why not? They have their 'parties,' as they call them. Inuit are never invited. Why not? And the Danish workers who come in the summer to build our houses, sometimes they are very rough with our girls. Why? Why? They're the ones who taught us to drink. . . ."

Later, while I was examining the records of the Fangeraade—the Council of Hunters—I came upon further complaints. Another Eskimo who came from Moriussak, a village some twenty-five miles southwest of Qaanaaq, declared "People can't hunt anymore. All the foxes are attracted by the smell of refuse at the Americans' Dump Dundas, in Thule. They walk around the planes like so many rabbits, it seems. But we haven't got the right even to go to the base; we aren't allowed within twenty miles of the base. . . . They're stealing our foxes away from us. In the mountains around our villages, there are almost none left. So, who is going to get the foxes at the base for free? Some qallunaat —Danish, American—of course! We've learned—because we know everything, we Inuit—that last year there were so many foxes that they killed them with machine guns and the Danish police burned them. What does that mean? Here we work hard to trap and sell foxes in good condition, and down there where the qallunaat are, the foxes are drawn by their refuse dumps and people burn them! That's disgusting, and it'll come to no good end. They treat us as if we were weaklings. And it's the same with the immiaq. Why don't they give us as many bottles as we want, like the Danes in Denmark?

"Ajorput! Ajorput! It's all wrong! I can give you more examples of ajor-puts than you know what to do with. . . ."

A young man in a black jacket whom I didn't know bore down on me threateningly. The fixed look and clenched jaw did not lie: he had to have gone to Denmark for technical training, and belonged to the new generation that had learned to despise the white man there. "Ajorput, qallunaat! You can put that in your little notebook. Write it down now, while I'm watching you"—he laid a finger on the page—"and that way, I'll be sure all the world will hear it. People know you write books about us. In Denmark I saw one with photographs from twenty years ago. Well, you write down that we, the Inuit, do not have the right to stay more than three days in Thule-Uummannaq, where our fathers used to *live*, because the base is nearby. The Americans could corrupt us, it seems. Ah! Ah! Ah! But if the Americans can corrupt us, why couldn't the Danski from Denmark corrupt us too? Why not? Since they send us to their technical schools? And the Danskis who live at the base, they're not delicate? They're not corrupted? . . . And if our parents haven't got the right to go to the base, why do we young people who take the plane to go to Denmark have the right to go there? We're younger, and when you're young aren't you more impressionable? . . . And the hut we are allowed to stay in for three days at most! Ajorput! Thule-Uummannaq used to have twenty-five houses, and our dead were buried there. . . . For centuries and centuries and centuries our old people were there, and now just one hut. You've seen for yourself how misera-ble it is—the broken crates, the abominable filth . . . fit for dogs. That's what they offer us in return for having driven us out of the country—and the right to stay there three days, and not one more. . . .

"You want more ajorput? You've seen the dumpsuaq, the big refuse dump for the base? Now the soldiers are forbidding us to go there to pick up nails, lumber, sacks. . . . 'Order of the Danes' is what they say, and to keep us from taking anything they pour benzine over it all and burn it. That way, we have to buy nails and lumber and sacks at the Danish store! Qallunaat, tamarmik! White men, all white men—good-for-nothings!"

What did the Danes in Thule say?

I went first to call on the doctor in his clinic up above the town; it had some ten beds. The medical service for Eskimos was separate from the island government, and its members were very independent-minded. At least, that was how it had been in earlier years.

My welcome was cordial. The doctor, in his thirties, seemed friendly. But he warned me immediately, in a hurried voice: "I am awfully busy!" And his wife, who was a nurse, added: "We're leaving in two weeks for our vacation in Denmark."

We visited the clinic together. Familiar hands reached out to me, and I shook them. Old—now old indeed—Natuk; Tukuminguaq, the paralyzed young wife of a hunter from Siorapaluk; old Borseman, the onetime member of Rasmussen's Second Thule Expedition. I went from one bed to the next: "Tikerak? Nuanninguyu! You've come back? How good for us!" Heads were raised, eyes shone. . . . Nikikanguaq, who kept house for me twenty years ago in Siorapaluk and whose one hand had been paralyzed, came up to embrace me. She was living in the nearby home for the elderly.

At first the doctor was amused, then visibly annoyed by the noisy friendship these poor and old people felt for a foreign qallunaaq; he went back to his office, where eventually I rejoined him. The conversation took a drier, more official tone, as if it were necessary to reabsorb the flow of affection.

We spoke of this and that. The doctor reminded me that he was the sole medical officer for the entire district, and that this small clinic was a heavy responsibility. When he visited outlying villages, Qaanaaq was without a doctor. With characteristic Danish irony, he mentioned de Gaulle and his concept of grandeur: since France was very weak, how were we supposed to go about achieving grandeur? . . . There was a polite inquiry about my research. . . . I asked after his children. . . . The civilities having been duly observed, I questioned him about local birth and death rates; the group he treated totaled 500 Eskimos and the birth rate was low—1 percent per annum.

"Is it true, Doctor, that the pill and other contraceptive devices have been introduced here?"

"Actually, the coil was given to all Eskimo women who asked for it," he answered, "and in Qaanaaq all the girls who want it now receive it. In the small villages, however, it is less widely used than in Qaanaaq."

I learned that the birth rate had gone down by half. The doctor seemed satisfied. I took my leave at that point, to make my own calculations. The birth rate had dropped by half: abortions were performed for social reasons (for unmarried mothers, etc.). From the point of view of Eskimo mentality, these Western contraceptive methods represented a genuine revolution. But were they particularly appropriate for a traditional society such as this?

The group's natural demographic growth—0.8 percent in 1940–50—was already very slight before the adoption of contraceptive methods. What, then, would become of these people whose young men, in addition, often went off on distant bear hunts, particularly during the three months, April, May, June, when the women's fecundity peaked?

In 1967 in Sweden—a society that practiced contraception widely—it took 1,100 sexual encounters to produce a single birth. Wasn't there every reason to be concerned about this Eskimo group in which sexual activity has always been very specific, and female fertility was formerly seasonal? Having numerous children had constituted, in fact, the surest guaranty of continuity for this old Eskimo people that was now confronting the white man, and it had been their one true happiness as well.

Didn't the government's seemingly philanthropic Malthusianism mask their political concern of reducing the bill Denmark had to pay?

The dentist was a transient. I needed only look at Kutsikitsoq, Sorqaq, and a few others to see why. At the age of forty-five, these two Thule Eskimos were completely toothless. In 1951, they had excellent teeth.

Thule was not alone in this problem: in some Eskimo areas in the eastern Canadian Arctic, children of fourteen had already lost their teeth. "Starting at the age of five, which is to say starting with their second set of teeth, Eskimo children who are fed at air bases no longer have a single dental crown in their mouths. All the crowns have been completely destroyed by caries. Some vestiges of roots may survive in the sockets, and above each socket one finds abscesses, osteitis, and purulent infections. When the child's first big permanent molar appears at the age of six, it is intact, obviously. Three months later, the crown has been completely destroyed and socket abscesses appear."[2] In fact, I saw the Qaanaaq Eskimo children around me chewing gum: from morning to night their teeth were bathed in the sugary juice.

This problem is a genuine threat: without teeth a man can no longer chew meat, which must therefore be swallowed as is. Serious gastric troubles soon ensue. It is to "details" of such a nature, to the candy, molasses, sugar, and other gifts from the missionaries and officers, that the Polynesian Islands, which were visited in the nineteenth century by foreign navigators, owed the eradication of their populations.

When, later on in my visit, I shared Sorqaq's life, I was horrified to see how frugal his meals were: tea with milk, biscuits, margarine, and a lot of cigarettes to dull his hunger. He could eat frozen meat only in very little bites, which he swallowed without chewing. The great hunter of yesterday was no more. Sorqaq and I were about the same age, but while I went out on the trails he, simply for lack of strength, stayed behind in the igloo to grumble. (Eventually he got himself appointed shopkeeper in Qeqertarsuaq.)

Kutsikitsoq was another toothless man, but he had not lost his sense of humor; he told me the story of how long a time it took him to obtain a set of dentures.

"It used to be that the dentist pulled teeth when he was passing through a camp. For the government that was the surest way of getting the trouble at the root. Now we are given false teeth that fit more or less. My set is much too big and I often lose it. While I'm hunting walrus, I have to hold it with my left hand while I am throwing the harpoon with my right . . . and sometimes both fly off together! They've promised me another set, but who knows for when?"

It was not just bad food, and alcohol, that was affecting the Eskimo's health. They also smoked to excess—an adult smoked almost one pack, or twenty cigarettes, every two days. And, for whatever reason, one-tenth of the group wore glasses, whereas in 1950 only four or five wore them, generally because of age. In the sectors we visited, one-quarter of the children between the ages of five and fifteen now needed glasses; in 1950 in Siorapaluk or Neqi, not a single child needed them.

In Thule-Qaanaaq most of the running water was reserved to the Danes. The water was brought to their cisterns by Eskimos in town-owned trucks. To fill their sinks, the Eskimo villagers had to fetch water from the town tap, and to shower they had to go to the clinic.

A knock at my door: I got up and opened it to admit Q——, a hunter from Qeqertaq. He had fine, shining brown-black eyes; his poorly shaved face looked feverish. "Malaurie, uneye! Hello! The Secretary of the Commune isn't here, is he?" I reassured him. The young Danish assistant he was referring to (actually, a very intelligent and nice fellow and because he had just arrived, seemingly eager to act in the best interests of the Eskimo residents) was indeed not with me. So the man sat down. For one month, he had been Thule-Qaanaaq's street cleaner. Early in the morning, he went with his truck to every Danish house to pick up the refuse and collect the contents of the slop pails that awaited him.

As he sat stiffly on the side of my bed, with his arms crossed, his cap held in one hand, Q——began with news: "Kaalipaluk made the trip back and forth to Qeqertarsuaq by boat. . . . You've seen him! Sorqaq came too, but then he couldn't leave—still can't. His rudder's broken. Savigssivik has still got solid ice."

He stopped. There was a long silence. We smoked a cigarette.

Q——, still very stiff, rolled his cap between his fingers. He lit a second cigarette and, brusquely, he attacked:

"You have said, so the Inuit are telling each other, that it is bad that the qallunaat treat us as they do. You have said that the white men are always the naalagaqs, the bosses, and that we Inuit do the dirtiest work. You were telling the truth. You know what I do. . . ." He stood up. "I am anaqarssuaq. I am the Big Shit of the qallunaat of Thule, that's what I am now. A long time ago, when you were in Qeqertaq, I was a hunter. Now I am a big shit.

"Why don't the whites take a white man on to do this job? We Inuit, we don't ask the qallunaat to pick up our shit. We throw it ourselves to our dogs. . . ."

He sat down again.

"Soon all of us will be the white man's kiffaqs. You have written that soon there will be no more hunters and that that is not good. I have come to say to you, thank you. Thank you!" He grasped both my hands. "You say out loud what we think to ourselves, so my friends the Inuit are grateful to you. Thank you, thank you."

From where he was sitting, stiff and upright, arms crossed, he looked at me intensely. "I've been drinking, it's true! Utoqqatserpunga! Excuse! It gives me courage to speak.

"The niivertoq, the district administrator, it's all right, him, the money: he had kiffaqs. When he calls us together, we are all agreed: we are going to say everything, and we get all worked up and then it's pitiful. We talk loud and a lot, a lot, a lot. . . . We get lost in little things, little things—like repairing this man's shack or repairing the communal hut in Neqi. We talk about increasing some old man's pension from three hundred to three hundred and twenty-five kroner a year. And then we say, 'Thank you, thank you.' But we know that some white men here are earning ten thousand kroner a month. And then the officials offer us a coffee-mik with some little cookies and everybody is happy. But when we get back to our wretched igloos, no one is happy anymore. Yes, and it's bad that our children are sent to Europe for 'technical training,' as they say. They'll get married down there to some Danski. We'll never see them again, and if they do come back they'll be stuck up and they'll look down on us. You see the son of So-and-So and the daughter of So-and-So. They've been sent to Denmark, and they come back home two weeks out of a year, dressed in their fine clothes. Ajorput!" Then, immediately contradicting himself: "But it's the most intelligent ones that must study in Denmark. They'll be doctors, engineers, managers. That's good for us. They'll protect us."

"No, you're wrong," I retorted. "If the most intelligent ones leave, only the stupidest ones will remain to be your hunters, and that's not good for the Inuit. Inuit—in Thule that means mainly hunters. To be a hunter calls for a great deal of intelligence. The hunter has to come from among the best Inuit. Look at Siorapaluk, for example. I'm told that now there are eleven hunters there, but actually there are only three, maybe four: Qaarnaaq, Inuterssuaq, Qaaqqutsiaq—the young one—and Imina. Without them there'd be no more village. They are the first, the ones who lead and train the peqatigiit by their ingenuity, their courage. You don't modernize yourselves by setting your sights as low as possible but by pulling yourselves up by the highest."

"You're right, I hadn't thought it through. Taamarpunga—so much for my thinking—but all in all that's what I meant. I just got a little ahead of myself. But we'd need doctors, engineers, too. So it's good that they go to Denmark. But they don't come back!"

We were facing each other, smoking one cigarette after another. He was still seated, still rigid, his arms still crossed on his chest. Now he leaned slightly forward; his eyes were dark, inward-looking. He hadn't finished telling me what had been building up in his head for days.

"But I haven't told you everything." His voice became jerky and muffled. "Some children don't respect their parents anymore, the old people aren't listened to anymore, an ajoqi now takes the place of a father. The Danski want the children from the villages to be boarders in Thule-Qaanaaq from September to May. All right. We gave our consent. But the parents now are very unhappy in the igloos without their children. And now who is going to teach our children to hunt and to sew? It's not in books that you learn that. The kayak, the dogs, sewing—our children know nothing about these things anymore. Just enough to strut about and be kiffaqs. So, when they come back home they do nothing, nothing at all. A lot of seqajuks . . . They don't go hunting anymore because they don't know how to hunt. So, they look down on the hunters, and since they stay behind in the village, they run after the girls and they drink. And some girls—they aren't worth anything anymore. Above all it's the girls who aren't worth anything anymore. They don't want to marry hunters anymore. It's too hard to be the wife of a hunter, they say, and hunters don't make enough money, they say.

"Nothing's right anymore. At the clinic—you've been there—it's a mess, too. The food is qallunaat food, but the old people and the Inuit want seal and walrus, not white people's canned food. That doesn't give us strength. So, the Inuit are unhappy."

The Eskimo was on his feet again, angry and at the same time discouraged. "Ajorpoq! They don't listen to us. It's as if a person didn't exist. . . . But wait a little, just wait a little. Soon we'll have some real leaders. Not this one or that one—they're soft, they kowtow to white men and they're afraid to get angry. But the Inuit are *very* intelligent." He struck his forehead. "Wait a little, wait a little. People want no more of it. You've seen U——. Now he realizes what's got to be done. He knows where the young people are who know. . . . If the officials don't get better, they'll be put out to sea, and all the qallunaat with them. Say this everywhere, write it in your notebook: Nunauut! It is our land! There's iron—you know that, you've seen it in Savigssivik. There may be oil beneath our feet"—he smiled ironically and scraped his boot against the floor —"and then, in any case, we always have seal, walrus, birds. We're not all that poor! Just wait a little, wait a little."

I walked with Q——to my door.

"Sinudluarna! Good evening!"

"Illillo! Thank you!"

I watched this Eskimo prophet walk with a steady step back to his slum. Then I glanced at the leaden sea. For a moment, as if seeking relief, my attention fastened on the shining dark gleams that the south wind scattered over the fjord. Blocks of ice stained by moraine floated in wide circular movements in the channel. A kayak returning from the west slipped through the emptiness of the clear night. In the iron-gray sky, white clouds with orange caverns drifted by. The triangular flight of ducks extended the length of the beach, low over the water. My mind would not be long beguiled; abruptly, the night fog veiled the distant seascape. That night the surface of the sea would freeze again.

P——worked as a domestic in Qaanaaq. She was the widow of a Qeqertaq narwhal hunter, who became entangled in the rope of his harpoon while out in his kayak and drowned. P——lived in a small detached house near the clinic; she had one daughter.

"You mustn't be surprised that some Eskimos are discouraged," she said to me. "They are desperate. They have been robbed of their future. The Eskimo hunter became poor the day money was introduced by you people, you whites. Now we do everything for money. In Siorapaluk, for example—I know that that interests you—out of seven kayaks only one is a sealskin kayak. The others are made of canvas. Eskimos would rather sell the sealskins that are meant for making kayaks in order to pay for their cigarettes and their beer; today Eskimos would sell everything they have. They're not bad, those canvas kayaks, but they're damp and they don't slip through the water as well. In Qaanaaq, things are worse.

"In any case, speaking for myself, I don't think I would marry a hunter again. The only men who are making any money are the ones who work for the Danes at the store. A hunter for a husband? He would live on the wages I earn as a cleaning woman at the hospital. I put all my money in a savings account. . . . I've sent my daughter—look, this is a photograph of her—to Denmark. I don't see her anymore, and I mind that very much, but at least she'll speak Danish. Maybe she'll marry a Dane. . . . Who knows? Only the ones who speak Danish have a future. Five or six Eskimos in Thule, no more, speak Danish. But just wait a bit. In a few years, all the young people who've been sent to Denmark for technical training will speak Danish. . . . The qallunaat. . . . Ah, ah, ah! Before, there never used to be any money when they had to pay for our seal and our fox. We were poor, and they used to answer us: 'What can we do? The market's bad. It's the war! Your sealskins are too small,' and so on and so on. . . . If they're spending a lot of money now, it's because they are afraid of us! Now they find the money to turn our children into little Danes. . . . A lot of Eskimos don't like white people, while some still do, like me, and say that they're nice, but many Eskimos hold this against them.* Twenty years

*A Polar Eskimo woman, an excellent bookkeeper, told me that it was painful for her to live in her country because the Ancestors kept reproaching her for "always favoring the Danski" in her accounts. She preferred to emigrate to the south, and she married there.

more, and there'll be no hunters left. Draw walrus one by one away from the group—and they die. With us, it's about the same thing."

Back to my past: I was returning to Siorapaluk.

It was late in the majesty of evening when I entered Robertson Fjord. The fjord was more dramatic, more impressive than I had remembered it. At the foot of the ice cap, the slopes looked wild and verdant in a Cézanne-like light. The igloos, to which some huts have been added, seemed to huddle together at the mouth of the big torrent whose delta created the twin bays that accounted for this human settlement.

In the peaceful evening, Siorapaluk, the "pretty little sandy beach," presented the same charm as it did seventeen years ago. The boat was heading toward shore. People had caught sight of us, and no doubt we were being examined through binoculars. I adjusted my anorak without taking my eyes from a black spot that, little by little, became a group of men and women.

Inuterssuaq glanced at me quickly; sixty feet offshore, he stopped the motor. In the general silence, he threw the anchor overboard in what he would have liked to be a masterful gesture.

So as to look at no one in particular, I lowered my eyes, as was the custom. I went ashore in the dinghy. The moment I set foot on land, a hoarse but joyous shout—"Sainang sunai!"—welcomed me. It was dear, dear Imina!

"In truth, that's how it is," I said gravely, as I shook hands with the old man, then with Sakaeunnguaq, then with Bertsie, who was half hiding behind her husband.

"And me too?" someone whispered. It was Ann Sofia, now old and toothless but smiling with every wrinkle in her tanned face.

Behind her came all the others—Iggianguaq, Qaarnaaq, Nivikannguaq, and still more. How they had changed! Without further ado, I settled down in Imina's house. On the ill-fitted gray planks of the floor, some salmon caught the evening before awaited us. While we were eating heartily, we exchanged memories. "Nuanni!" punctuated our stories. The Eskimos talked, talked, and I, too, did not stop remembering, recalling. . . . We let ourselves go, interrupting one another, in our pleasure in recapturing and reliving the past.

"We knew for sure you would come back," Sakaeunnguaq whispered to me. "I often saw you in my dreams." I paid a visit to Qaarnaaq, whom I knew only slightly before, but at his house were several of my old close friends. Then I went from one to the next, wanting to shake hands with the nine heads of igloos in the hamlet.

Once the wonderment of returning was past, would I find that Siorapaluk had been spared the fate of Thule-Qaanaaq? The next morning at dawn I discovered the new Siorapaluk.

In the afternoon, I called on Sakaeunnguaq. The "little angakkoq" remained a close friend. Now he lived in a cabin recently built by the government and allocated to him on the basis of a very modest installment-plan contract. For him, however, it would never be more than a qallunaaq's igloo. So he allowed the plywood and plaster to deteriorate. The tar roof leaked; rainwater splashed, drop by drop, into pails and cans. . . . Eight people lived in this perhaps 250-square-foot space. Three of them were quite ingenious, capable in the course of a day of repairing a motor or carving a harpoon head with great skill. But it seemed they were glad to see the wounds in this house widen. A woman's blue leather shoe was lying in front of the door on a ripped bundle of shirts. In place of the illeq, four beds were ranged along the damp walls. Bertsie was stitching a kamik, sitting beside one of the two windows, both with broken panes.

There were only two signs of life: the bloody carcass of a seal that hung from a heavy hook in the middle of the room, and a black avataq—the inflated sealskin used in hunting walrus—that was suspended from a nail. Kaali, now twenty-two years old, was plugging the holes with ivory teeth he had carved perfectly.

Sakaeunnguaq glanced at the weather through the broken pane, which had a rag stuffed in the hole. He slipped on one kamik and looked for the other, not remembering that Bertsie was mending it for him. When he had slipped the second on, he sat down before the radio and twirled the knob to bring in the everlasting rock music broadcast over United States Thule.

Why today should anyone go hunting? The store and Danish welfare payments took the place of the hunting days past. People lived on biscuits, tea, coffee; cigarettes made the boredom pass.

Suddenly, short, sharp cries were heard: "Qilalugaq! Qilalugaq!" Four belugas were swimming some thirty feet offshore. Alerted by the children—still the village outlooks—a few young men who felt like playing at hunting rushed for whatever was within reach: kayaks, repeating rifles. A boat was pushed out into the water. For one hour, they labored to isolate and kill one poor little whale weighing 130 pounds.

Imina was sitting in front of his cabin. He had been watching their puerile antics with scorn. Like all the old men, he refused to have anything to do with these parodies of the past.

We were alone in his house. He was seated on his illeq, his right leg extended before him. His eyes were grave, almost remote, as he asked me to listen to him for a moment. It was the same tragic balance sheet all over again:

"You did well to come back. I am getting old and I should not have wanted to die without seeing you again. I want to talk to you. Nothing is going right, but I have some hope. A young and active generation is standing up—but it's urgent. You see Siorapaluk now. The girls sew badly, they no longer marry, and they have children by different fathers. Those children are real iliarsut. With no father, they go from one igloo to another, to live with anyone who is willing to take them in. Nedjlinara—poor little things. Last winter in Kangek, Inuterssuaq's net had no seals—they'd all been stolen by a hunter who was passing by. A long time ago, when you were there, everybody in the village would have known who it was, and the guilty person would have been reported. But now. . . . It's the same with the fox traps. The man who has a complaint goes from one hut to another. Ajor, ajor. The Inuit don't talk to one another anymore because they don't know what is happening anymore, here or there. Some young men are living like little old men—you know, like the little old men in the Qaanaaq clinic: up at eleven . . . a meal . . . a visit with this one . . . a visit with that one . . . until the end of the afternoon, when they sleep some more, and then wake up a little later to visit some more. . . .

"Do you know how many young men in the whole country go bear hunting? Maybe twenty! Wait a bit longer, and there'll be no more bearskin even for our trousers. And then the Inuit are angry among themselves. Parents no longer understand their children, who speak to them in Danish. Their experiences and hopes are different. The Inuit do not get along with the Greenlanders who come from the south. In Savigssivik and Qaanaaq there are a lot of them and that makes for a lot of trouble, and then there are Danes in Qaanaaq. . . . We like the Danes, we like the Americans—they've done us a lot of good, but here are too many of them, and then there is the beer—I like beer, but only a little bit. A lot isn't good, especially not a lot of whiskey, which makes people very mean. Ah! Where is the time when the Inuit were all as one—ajor! But maybe I am wrong to say that; maybe I am too pessimistic. Surely the younger generation will stand up and change everything for the better. I hope it won't be too late."

The Eskimo, once a free man, was in fact becoming the white man's kiffaq. Colonization had become apparent:

1. Numerically: The Thule base comprised 3,000 men, and the administration of this district of 500 Eskimos plus 100 Danes (civil servants and their families) was increasingly onerous.

2. Politically: The management of public affairs was in white hands. Appropriations came from Denmark. The administrator was Danish, as were the chief of police and the manager of the store.

3. Technologically and racially: The Eskimo was being assimilated into our ways of life and methods of production; the number of mixed marriages was already large.

The Eskimo was humiliated by what had befallen him; he had caved in; he drank, and he wept. But his protests were beginning to make themselves heard; revolt was rumbling; the dying man was returning to life. He was growing tired of the occasional sweetener he was given; his eye was turning to his children, and he saw their fixed smiles and closed faces. He had no doubt that they would be the ones to avenge the lies and pretenses he had been fed.

The economic situation of the Polar Eskimos—whether or not it was desired by the government—accounted for the depth of their social and moral crisis. Let us look at Siorapaluk, which was representative of village life in general. The situation there was appreciably better than in Qaanaaq, where, because of the concentration of whites and their influence, the hunting society was rapidly declining and was on the verge of disappearing. In 1950, Siorapaluk had thirty-four inhabitants and seven dog-teams-with-hunter. In

413

1967, with a population of ninety-eight, the work force had not even doubled: there were thirteen dog teams belonging to adult hunters, plus three teams belonging to adolescents, and three motorboats, belonging to Inuterssuaq, Imina and his son, and Qaarnaaq.

These hunters were grouped in three peqatigiit (as opposed to two peqatigiit in 1950)—Inuterssuaq, that of Imina and his son, and that of Qaarnaaq. Out of sixteen producers, there were in fact only three major ones. With their activity and their intelligence, which was translated into regular gifts of their hunting surpluses, these three maintained the community as a whole. Of the thirteen others, there were regular kiffaqs of one or another of the big producers; ten worked by the day and, depending on need, moved from one peqatigiit to the other. Of these ten daily workers, four, by virtue of their personalities, managed to remain independent.

In 1950, Siorapaluk was producing more than it consumed. Only five individuals received old-age or sick benefits, which were most modest.

In 1967, Siorapaluk was producing only one-quarter of what it consumed, and out of ninety-eight inhabitants, fifty-four were receiving public assistance —salaries (six), family allowances (thirty-one), aid to young mothers (two), old-age pensions to those over fifty (eleven), and payments to the totally or partially disabled (four).

In 1950, the village had one salaried inhabitant—the catechist, John Petrussen, who was also simultaneously shopkeeper and teacher.

In 1967, there were six salaried people: the shopkeeper, shop assistant, teacher-catechist, a cleaning woman for the school, and a midwife.

Productive life for the Eskimo had always meant life itself, yet it was being doubly discouraged. First, there was less need to work because a family could at least subsist without hunting by living on the pensions due its old members, and on allowances provided for children; second, hunting was underpaid, if one compared what it yielded to the hourly wages the government ensured Eskimos working as guides, unloading cargo, etc. One could hardly be astonished that the system was collapsing. A welfare system was replacing a system of production. This society was discouraged from making any effort.

Siorapaluk was not an isolated example. The same conditions prevailed in the two other villages I revisited—Qeqertaq and Savigssivik—and in Qeqertarsuaq.

The abandonment of hunting in northern Greenland was not the result of some ethnic or cultural crisis but rather the result of systematic underpayment.[3] Taking into account his personal investment in materials (lumber for the sledge, rifles, dogs, etc.), during his seasonal work in 1967, the hunter received one-third the salary of an Eskimo street cleaner or storekeeper; one-sixth the salary of a nonspecialized Danish laborer at the American radar base, who, in addition, received lodging and food free; one-ninth the salary of a specialized worker at the same base (such as a taxi driver); one-fourteenth the salary of a carpenter or a foreman at the same base.

The figures speak for themselves. At best, the pelt of a seal or fox brought

100 kroner ($16), the average price being about half, or 50 kroner ($8). In addition it took from two to four hours to dress a fox skin. Despite his strenuous work (about 1,000 hours per year), plus his expensive investment, at best a hunter could count on a monthly income of 600 to 800 kroner ($100–$125). The majority earned about one-half that amount.[4]

On the other hand, the Eskimo employed in the store worked an eight-hour day in a warm shop, was guaranteed a paid vacation, and received a 1,000 to 1,100 kroner per month, which he could supplement by hunting on weekends. Furthermore, the progressive concentration of the population for administrative reasons (education, trading) in five villages (in 1950 there had been ten) obliged the hunters to travel long distances to reach the hunting grounds, so one must adjust the figures given to reflect the ever larger amounts of essential travel time. From September to November, boats setting out from Siorapaluk more often than once a week ensured an eighteen-hour round trip to the walrus-hunting grounds off Pitorarfik, in the northeast. During the winter, the hunters made a thirty- to fifty-mile trip twice monthly by dogsledge in order to hunt walrus. Several times a week, they had to travel twenty to thirty miles to check their trap lines, which lay farther and farther away. Thus, a good half of their working time was lost in moving about. Formerly, hunters used to locate their igloos—by definition not permanent—in the immediate proximity of the hunting terrain chosen for that year. A lively system of exchange enabled them to enjoy mutually the various hunting possibilities afforded by all the sites inhabited by the group. Considering the accumulated burdens the hunters now had to cope with, it should be no surprise that production was declining at the very time when new dietary, dress, technological, and cultural needs were being awakened.

Public assistance, direct or indirect, was destroying this society. From 1910 to 1936, the Thule store under Knud Rasmussen accounted for the economic activity of the entire territory, and in the main its effect was beneficial: production exceeded both imports and consumption in value. In 1967— and here I refer to Siorapaluk's store only—production covered less than one-third of expenditures in this village where all residents were Eskimos or Greenlanders.[5]

The low remuneration of the hunter seems the more flagrant when one considers that in 1967 his work entailed an initial investment of more than 30,000 kroner ($5,000) carrying an optimum interest rate of 0.5 percent. The underpaid producer was involved in absurd expenses: a $5,000 boat could not be amortized by a three-month-long hunting season (the sea is frozen nine months a year); the rental/purchase of a house that had a fixed location forced him to travel; he had to pay to heat that house with coal (one-half to two tons per year) imported from the United States—and this in a country rich in animal fats and oils. In a word, the hunter was caught up in a market economy that for him was murderous; for how long could he wear himself out in a futile effort to produce?[6]

The 500 Polar Eskimos in the land of Thule—who may stand as symbols for the total Eskimo population of 100,000—are a mere handful compared to the huge numbers of Asian peoples.

In our modern world, the fate of this handful of men may not seem important. Yet what is at stake is crucial: is not each of these Eskimos the custodian of human capital, of a fund of experience, knowledge, and traditions handed down through generations? Every time a so-called minority culture is eradicated mankind's patrimony is undeniably impoverished, for like the greater civilizations, the more limited cultures also participate in the history of man and contribute to a fuller knowledge of his destiny. The future of this primitive population, symbolically situated at more or less the top of the globe, will tell us a great deal about the merits of our civilizing techniques; we should therefore watch it closely.

Following Knud Rasmussen's 1910 initiative, in 1937 the Danish government took charge of this group of Eskimos. Like the outstanding explorer, the Danish government, with disinterested resolution, set out to integrate this isolated group first into the community of Greenland, then into the larger community of Denmark, without altering its essential characteristics.

A delicate and difficult task, if ever there was one.

For forty years, the program benefited the people of Ultima Thule, first by preserving their isolation, thus protecting their culture; then, through a prudent, sometimes severe policy of expanding their natural resources, by raising their standard of living until it was much higher than that of many hunting regions in western and eastern Greenland and in northern Canada. However useful this policy of "enlightened restraint" might have been at a certain stage, the problems posed by the arrival of an ancient society into the modern world remained unsolved.

It is not a matter of denying these traditional societies the chance to be modernized. Every effort should be made to raise their standard of living by improving their technology, but this does not mean the establishment of an absurd system that is costly for the government and that, in addition, could only lead to the ruination of the society that was presumably the object of such solicitude. What was true on the economic level was even more so on the sociological. The introduction of the fox trade (sporadic from 1880, systematic after 1910), of currency (local money starting in 1910, Greenlandic after 1936, Danish since 1960), and of the individualistic, capitalist system of profits and markets ran counter to Eskimo tradition and rules. When the new economic forces came into play, they destroyed social cohesion and group laws. Individual capitalization was utterly contrary to the tradition of this communal group; the sharing of the catch was discouraged by the producer's need to save up in order to amortize his loans on schedule; individual ownership of boats and houses was alien to a tradition that called for joint ownership of possessions other than those directly required for hunting—dogs, guns, etc.

The profit motive and the examples set by the qallunaat incited the Eskimo to become critical of the hierarchies his traditional society had utilized for the common good. He came to see that the more skillful hunter, with a better entrée among whites, would of course be able to equip himself with the most modern tools: repeating rifles, motorboat, etc. He would bring in more game, he would earn more. He would obtain loans from the bank. When in debt, he would try to build up his resources. First, he would sell his surplus game— something that had been unknown, since extra game always used to be shared; then he would use the labor of others.

To put it more generally: a class society was established, in which the rich employ the poor. An egalitarian society became plutocratic; the weakest became the kiffaqs of the well-off. Approximately over the years 1940–56, this happened with the Thule Eskimos: the peqatigiit of free and equal men gave way to a society in which the richest man used the labor of the most defenseless (the orphan) or unlucky. Earlier (1910–50), the peqatigiit had been a temporary partnership of hunters; the partners were equal, in the literal sense of the term, and settlements were made in kind, the hunters simply grouping around a man who was better off, more powerful, and, for example, owned a boat that was used in common. In Thule in 1950, the process of class formation was so little embryonic that indirectly—through various holidays such as births, anniversaries, and Christmas—the richest member of the community was obliged to give back to the group his surplus of the goods he had accumulated at the store by selling fox skins. But very soon (1950–60), under the pressure of new needs sparked by the store and of the monetary system gradually put into effect that included old-age and disability penions, family allocations, wages for working for the government, the erstwhile partners became more demanding and insisted on becoming salaried employees.

The small Eskimo experience I was witnessing here exemplified in microcosm a moment of great importance in economic history. The notion of exchange value was gradually introduced to people who previously had not the slightest idea that any such thing existed. The Eskimo had never looked on the surplus game he caught as merchandise. To have extra walrus or seal was, for him, an auspicious event that reminded him how fundamental was the alliance between nature and the group. His obligation to share his surplus was all the more compelling inasmuch as he was a mere agent in the alliance; the division was made without the least idea of individual investment. The concept of value as our industrial societies know it was utterly foreign to the Eskimo's mentality. After 1920, he became familiar with a store that supplied some of his basic needs (lumber, rifle, knife, etc.), but it required the progressive opening up of this isolated region, which began in 1950, for the idea of exchange, with value added, to develop in the minds of these people. Then the Eskimo began to perceive surplus differently: game ceased being, in a social sense, a part of the group; gradually a hunting system came to be invested with an exchange value. And I repeat, the introduction of the notion of individual profit, of capitalization, and of capital interest destroyed the socioeconomic foundations of the communitarian group.

The decline of this plurimillennial hunting society has derived more from an economic system and from the civil law that sustains it than from any so-called cultural shock. It was not Danish culture or Christianity that initially undermined it but rather the capitalist mercantile system of exchange, which was insidiously introduced to coexist with the traditional system of joint possession.

In a game-rich country, a "capitalistic" colonialist system, obviously originating elsewhere, could only impoverish the Eskimo and reduce him, in terms of development, to zero. Two societies were juxtaposed, and the one could only absorb the other: the Danish-Greenlandic—rich; the Eskimo—poor. Two systems opposed in spirit: an individualistic capitalism eager for immediate profit, and a communitarianism eager for solidarity and ecological equilibrium with its natural milieu.

What we are witnessing, then, is the historical process of dispossession and impoverishment of a marginal people. Up until about 1955, this society relied on mutual aid and collectivism; it abided by moral and religio-ecological rules, the underlying principles being to live in harmony with nature and to possess its gifts in common, and to preserve a historical and cultural heritage. This has been replaced by a "legal code" that seems to have been devised for an "ideal" citizen who is born an orphan and dies celibate; a code that makes everything one-generational, under which the family is an inconvenience, all collective and all long-term work is forbidden, moral unities are dissolved with each death, the clever man is the egoist who so arranges his life as to have the fewest responsibilities, and property is conceived not as a moral entity but as a possession always convertible into cash.

In 1967, after my long absence, I rubbed my eyes in disbelief when I counted nineteen motorboats for the entire district. Before, inadequate equipment had been evident; now, an excess of equipment burdened individual budgets and destroyed any communitarian policy. Furthermore, the noisy, intrusive traffic of these boats with their outboard motors made the indispensable use of the kayak impossible.

In the difficult yet necessary period of adaptation, the Eskimo society of Thule was a civilization that needed to develop from within, according to its own nature, and following its own rhythm, moving at its own speed. This was not happening. In order to modernize it from within, to not become a cultural zoo, the authorities should have concentrated first on technical problems. The school should have been a technical school, and should have introduced the Eskimos to the most modern methods of hunting and a rational exploitation of the tundra. These methods have long been taught in Sweden and in the U.S.S.R. In areas already familiar to him—hunting, stock breeding, biology, tools and hunting equipment—the Eskimo would have quickly acquired the sense of being on an equal footing with the white man.

Were the hunting grounds considered too small, then surely it would have been easy to obtain from the Americans the free annual transportation of five

to ten brigades of hunters to the northern game-rich coasts far from Thule—
this would have compensated the Eskimos for their loss in earnings caused by
the transfer of a part of their hunting terrain to the American base. The hunters
could have returned south by their own means, by dogsledge, while hunting
seals en route. In this way, their innate sense of adventure would have been
reconciled with the objective need to expand their overcongested hunting
grounds. Given the Eskimos' wish to be located in the vicinity of the white
man's stores and schools, it would also have been necessary to make a biological study of the country's game potential in order to plan the hunting program
and to devise a policy of genetic improvement of wild species—fox, seal. In the
villages, the husbandry of furred animals, with the stock fed by the hunting
surpluses of walrus and shark, would have opened up useful new horizons for
the Eskimos.

The "modern" Eskimo of 1967 displayed a rather passive spirit, and he had
been unable, at least in this first generation, to form elites and formulate
long-range views. What he wanted above all was to benefit from the advantages
of the consumer society—to enjoy it and get his fill. Only afterward did he want
to face the difficult problems posed by the integration of a hunting society into
the modern world. Natural pride had convinced the Eskimo that he would be
able to surmount these problems as successfully as he had been able to dominate the problems of cold, solitude, and famine throughout his history.

While awaiting a national mystique that would end up being formulated in a
political program, the Polar Eskimo was in danger of being progressively
corrupted into a welfare dependent. And though he felt grateful for the aid he
received, the Eskimo presented another side as well. The white man had killed
off hunting by allowing the market for fox and seal to collapse, he said. From
then on, it would be the white man who would be the game. And through his
lobbies, the Thule Eskimo pursued subventions and grants both in Godthaab
and in Copenhagen.

   On my trips to Greenland in 1967, 1969, and 1972, I could observe how
the Eskimo was playing an extortionist game with the transient white man.
Politics was a kind of revenge. People felt they had claims on the white man,
and the instant he arrived his true value was assessed with consummate skill.
Always an excellent actor, the Eskimo would mime before his unknowing
victim. He would wander, tattered and dejected, from hovel to hovel, but
always within his prey's sight, playing the ailing Eskimo. Either the white man
paid up or he was judged stingy. He would be thanked barely, with a condescending expression: after all, by paying he showed he was guilty. The North
Pole was to become a sort of purgatory for the transient Westerner. He would
never pay enough for what the Eskimo unconsciously felt he had been robbed
of—his joy in living.

   The Godthaab radio—Grønland Radio—was widely listened to, and it fed
this bitterness. In 1965 Knud Hertling, the first president of the Independent

Party of the Inuit, was declaring that "the investments of the Danish govern-ment must be considered in the perspective of reparations for wrongs inflicted during the colonial period." Since that period extended from 1721 to 1955, even the substantial monies already granted—for the industrialization of fishing in southern Greenland, for example—would never be enough.

Embittered by the decline in his purchasing power, the Thule hunter learned from Grønland Radio that he was no longer alone in pushing his demands. From uncertainty to bitterness and from bitterness to violence: the escalation was worldwide.

Anguiasset: money. *Anguiasset . . . anguiasset. . . .* The word was forever on the Eskimos' tongue. People who had settled into a kind of apathy roused themselves only to claim higher salaries, more opportunities, more time off.

Pay, pay. . . . The Eskimo seemed to take pleasure in infecting his wounds in order to humiliate and pressure the white man. To the Eskimo's way of thinking, the important thing was not that he receive the grants; what mattered was that the principle of the grant represented revenge; for him, it was in the nature of restitution.

A number of Eskimos questioned me about Denmark's—ergo Greenland's —joining the Common Market. (This did then happen in 1973.) I explained the pros and cons. The pluses: the Common Market would open Greenland to the world and could facilitate increasing business activity. In an insular, provincial, and colonial context, the exchange of goods and ideas would be like an infusion of much-needed oxygen. The minuses: they were not well enough organized and protected to stand up to aggressive capitalism. This is what I told them: "Get a price policy. Get from the Americans, who are occupying a part of your communal territory, a substantial rental fee, to be paid into a communal fund that would guarantee the hunters high price ceilings. Get yourselves organized: unless traditional societies protect themselves, they will be absorbed by a profit-oriented economy that is more concentrated and in a position to take advantage of dumping prices. Stop thinking of the hunter's life as something left over from the past. In Greenlandic society of today, belong-ing to hunters' groups must be seen as a privilege that is sought after. Only those who belong to these groups should be authorized to hunt. Danish public opinion is not informed about what is going on here, but the Danes in Copen-hagen would support you if you asserted yourselves as independent hunters. Danes have a great admiration for you; Danish people love Greenland. Be yourselves. Master the most modern techniques. A lot of people in the West will become your allies. What a surprise, if people were to learn that up at the Pole there was a society of free men resolved to live apart from the industrial world, live by its own rules and customs, while borrowing from Western society its weapons and its tools." The Communal Council of Thule, consisting en-tirely of Eskimos, met unofficially in August 1969 to hear the report I had prepared. It gave me its views. The report was approved with, however, this comment: "You must stay here with us to help us carry it out. Stay, stay here. You must not be very happy in your own country, since you keep coming back to us. Anyway, this is all too new for us, and you can talk to the white man as an equal."

Winter was already approaching. It was October 1972, my third visit to Siorapaluk since my return in 1967. The guillemots had left us. The gulls were still here, still screaming in the cloudy autumnal sky. I had come in July. Once again it was time for me to return to France.

I had already alerted the village of my return south. Knowing that, for reasons of dignity and feeling, Imina would prefer we be alone when we bid each other farewell, I had sent to say that I would visit him that evening.

I stood in front of the pretty lettuce-green Danish house and coughed before I pushed the door open. Like an Oriental sage, Imina was seated on his illeq, his right leg stretched out before him. His smiling eyes and a gesture invited me to come sit beside him. We exchanged a few casual remarks; then he stood up and pointed to the calendar: December 22. "Inuvok, your birthday. I will not forget it."

After a moment's hesitation, we threw ourselves in each other's arms, holding close. I wanted to keep this old man against my chest, this friend of my youth and silent brother of my older years. I felt myself being gently pushed away. Imina seized my shoulder and looked straight and deep into my eyes. In a grave, sad voice he said: "You will not come back! I feel it. . . . I see it. . . . Tnudluara! Good-bye, Malaurie. And know that you are thanked: you have brought light to my life."

The next day, a small group gathered on the sandy beach. Kresunguaq, deputy to the Greenland Council, was there. He was Imina's son, and the one who had escorted me to Qaanaaq on my first return trip, in 1967. I had known him when he was twelve, running among the scree slopes hunting guillemots with a net and searching under the rocks for their eggs. His being chosen deputy was in keeping with the habitual humor of these men: he was not an authoritarian, but a diplomat.

My three bags lay on the beach; the canoe that would take me south was waiting. Two men would accompany me; Kaali, the son of Sakaeunnguaq, and Kutsikitsoq, who was passing through and was taking advantage of this opportunity to get back to Thule-Qaanaaq.

The silence was uncomfortable. Men and women were standing in a group some thirty feet away. I walked over and silently shook everyone's hand. Upright on his bowed legs, Qaarnaaq said casually: "Tomorrow, with Nivikannguaq, I'll be leaving to hunt reindeer in Inuarfissuaq. I like reindeer meat. . . ." I hastened my leave-taking, waved one last time, and in a few moments my family of the fog and ice was a dot on the horizon.

My family! How did it happen that these few men, so far away, were so dear to me? Was it that I recognized them, that in them I found the nucleus of my own nature: a respect for strength and for the energy of despair?

It was true that although I was apart from them for dozens of reasons and by thousands of miles, not only did they remain in the center of my thoughts but I also felt, at a certain level, "responsible" toward them. And no doubt that was the reason that mobilized me afresh once I was back in France, and drove me on to look, with them and on their behalf, for new lines of defense adapted to the new times.

22

TOWARD
A
CONCLUSION

On May 2, 1973, in Le Havre, I chaired an international conference on Arctic oil. The meeting was significant in that it was the first to be held on this subject in the history of the oil industry. The Arctic was entering into world economic competition, and events were moving fast. Representatives from the major international oil companies attended. This meeting of 200 experts naturally aroused immense interest in oil circles throughout the world, the more so since it brought together for the first time not only directors of the big international oil companies, engineers, geologists, and bankers but also ecologists and large native—Indian and Eskimo—delegations.

Why such a conference? The situation in Thule and in other regions of the Alaskan and Canadian Arctic where I had led numerous expeditions had convinced me that before the remaining virgin areas of the Northern Hemisphere were exploited it was of primary urgency that a balance sheet be drawn up of past errors and future prospects and that, on an international scale, each interested party confront its own responsibilities.

People are more and more concerned about the numerous conflicts between science and politics. It is through international meetings of this sort that one can try to find answers to one of the basic questions of our period: how to put science at the service of man.

The 1973 meeting aroused greater advance interest because it was held in the wake of a congress, held also in Le Havre, in November 1969, on the theme "Economic Development of the Arctic and the Future of Eskimo Societies." That congress, which I had organized and directed with my friend, the Nobel Prize winner René Cassin, had caused considerable repercussions in the Arctic, from Alaska to Greenland. Actually, it had been the first time in the long history of the North that Alaskan, Canadian, and Danish delegates (and one Soviet expert, who came a day late)—natives, civil servants, and scientists—met to discuss together the present and future of the 100,000 Eskimos who occupy a 900-mile front, or almost one-half of the boreal ice cap.

The problems that confronted the Eskimo people, who had been divided for three or four centuries by political frontiers that were extraneous to them, were now felt the more passionately by virtue of their being tardily pointed out. In concretizing the situation, the petroleum industry was dramatizing it. By the early seventies, everyone was aware that the Arctic—because it depends directly or indirectly on the three big world blocs, including Japan—was destined within ten years to be industrially exploited on a large scale. The energy shortage and rising costs accelerated programs for the prospecting of oil and the exploitation of Arctic franchises in North America as well as in Siberia. Oil and gas were known to exist in such abundance on the northern coast of Alaska, in northwestern Canada, and in eastern Siberia that by even a prudent estimate these reserves constituted almost one-quarter of all hydrocarbons on the planet. The exploitation of these vast mining sectors means that by the year 2000, 20 percent of the globe's surface will have come under the control of the big nations and the industrial multinationals. Here, surely, is an epochal change of still-unforeseeable geopolitical consequences.

All of us realize that this historic step will not be taken without great damage to the still-unviolated natural world of ice. Ecologists and clear-thinking defenders of the environment multiply their warnings, and everyone agrees that in no way should the desertification and pollution of the tundras and Polar seas be the price of the tremendous battle already engaged. There is nothing, however, that the most modern technology cannot undertake to solve. And the debates at the oil conference proved as much.

The essential point lies elsewhere. It so happens that the regions involved are not uninhabited. That a company spending $20,000 a day in the Arctic prospecting and drilling for oil would deny any royalty to the people who have lived in these regions for thousands of years is inadmissible; all the laws on the books cannot gainsay that this land is theirs. Their rights must be the point of departure in any discussions.

The purpose of the conference was to specify the respective rights of the parties concerned, but of course, to revert to Edouard Drumont's terrible dictum: "Everybody has some rights; the point is knowing how to make use of them." How in this ridiculously, tragically unequal struggle between the poor hunters of the Great North and the kings of banking and oil was one to find any possibility of equity? In the immense conference hall, each speaker, with condescending courtesy, acknowledged the presence of the large Indian and Eskimo delegations. The long hair, the motley clothing, the provocative badges ("Indian Power," "Eskimo Power") caused smiles. The wives—Danish, Canadian, American—were reassuring tokens. Then the tone changed: the natives' behavior—very attentive—was at first surprising, then disturbing. People were struck by the care with which these "primitives" noted and recorded everything; they were constantly sending sealed messages from table to table.

Now and then, this or that person got up and joined that person or this person in a private room where they conferred at length. Occasionally one caught their eyes flashing with anger. Their youth was no longer misleading. This was no group of innocents; they knew that for them time was measured, that there are historic moments when days count for centuries.

The meeting given to "The Rights of Minorities" was approaching. As president of the conference, I found placed before me various protests from certain delegations. They were evidently disturbed by "subversive" statements made in an international gathering to which the press, radio, and television might give a circulation felt to be inopportune. The authorities on which I was dependent financially gave me to understand "Don't overdo! We know your generous ideas as a scientist. . . . However, the foreign delegations are the guests of France and under no circumstances do we wish to receive diplomatic protests over unwarrantable interference in the domestic affairs of other nations." In other words, calm down your protégés.

I answered that the very meaning of this colloquy was to have the oil companies be publicly challenged by the native delegations. There was no reason to fear, I added, that Indians and Eskimos would precipitate an incident. I was persuaded by their level-headed statements that they at least would have the virtue of being clear. I was more apprehensive about extreme statements from some clearly reactionary oil and banking groups. To make sure that the ten native delegates would make an exemplary impression, I called them together on the evening before the meeting. We hoped to stay clear of the French and foreign radio and television reporters, but we had the greatest difficulty finding a quiet, isolated café open in this city of Le Havre. Either we were told, "We're closing" (do Indian braids and coppery Eskimo faces frighten Normans?), or else a delegate whispered, "Not there, not there!"—having caught sight of someone representing more or less officially the Canadian (or the American or the Danish) government—"he'll spy on us!" Finally, we found a bar on the second floor of a building that usually served wedding banquets. The oval table posed some protocol problems among Lapp, Finnish, Canadian, and Alaskan Eskimos, Greenlandic and Indian delegates, but the latent rivalries were quickly resolved, even though several wives of Indian delegates were present. Anglo-Saxon in the main, they were the more heated for feeling that they were at issue. But their husbands packed them off to a corner, and they did not share in the discussions.

The three Greenlanders asked me to preside over the meeting, which was conducted mostly in English. First problem: What should we drink? To my surprise, only fruit juices and mineral water were ordered. "Tonight we work!" The Lord be praised, for very soon a lively discussion set the Yukon Indians and the Canadian Eskimos at loggerheads.

It emerged that the Yukon Indians were disputing the title to thousands of acres on the borders between them and the Mackenzie Eskimos—lands that were likely to be the object of requests for oil licenses. Historic rights. . . .

Imprescriptibilities. The Greenlanders and I watched in dismayed silence as the fight, worthy of a Western film, raged. The only element lacking was the phony middleman to divide them and steal from both.

Finally the arguments began to meander, and I managed to observe that it would be truly regrettable if such discussions were to take place tomorrow in front of the assembled delegates: "People believe you are strong because you are united for a cause. . . . Raise the tone of the discussion. Be inflexible in matters of principle, but show that you are bigger than other speakers who will talk about dollars and profit margins. This is the price you must pay if your political strength is to be recognized. Appoint one spokesman!"

I did not have to insist. A rapid exchange of glances, and with one voice the mouthpiece was named: the Mackenzie Eskimo James Wah-Shie. The Greenlanders—shrewder politicians—and the Alaskans opted to bide their time and speak up during the discussion. Moses Olsen, the deputy from the north of Greenland (therefore, from Thule), and Angmalortok Olsen, born in Qaanaaq and president of the Society of Greenlanders in Denmark, would voice their autonomist views at the opportune moment. It was agreed that the botanist Yrjo Vasari, representing the North Lapp Council, would close the natives' participation in the discussion by presenting the problem as it existed in Finland. And thus, in two hours, without further problems, the order of the day was established.

One might well have feared that, come the moment, these men would be verbose and their language violent, but these young Indians and Eskimos, while they did not forget the depredations they had endured, realized that their fellow delegates were indulging in double-talk. The native delegates were precise, confining themselves to facts and to affirming their resolve to live by their customs and their own wishes. Like genuine politicians, they had decided to say as little as possible regarding subjects about which they felt they were still inadequately informed. And they were to learn that their silence and dignity would make a greater impression than long speeches.

"Do not presume to ignore our rights," James Wah-Shie said straightaway, and his voice broke slightly. "Any exploitation would then be out of the question. We will avail ourselves of our rights and we do not doubt that from now on the government itself will support us. I address you as spokesman for all the natives of the Arctic who are represented here, but also as president of the Federation of Canadian Natives North of the Sixtieth Parallel.* We have come to this conference, as have you, in order to learn. For three days, we have listened to you express your ideas about lands that once were ours, and we have heard how you intend to exploit them. Now the moment has come to tell you what our wishes and our plans are. . . . We think that, as indigenous peoples, we indeed have certain rights both from a moral and from a legal point of view. These rights are part of a juridical concept that has been recog-

---

*More than half of the total area of Canada.

nized for centuries in the Western world. They are territorial rights, hunting rights, fishing and other rights that are based on our traditions and on the fact that we have dwelt in these territories from time immemorial. These rights rest also on certain more recent legal decisions.

"Those among you who have been in the North have some firsthand knowledge of the frightful conditions, social and other, that our people are now enduring. We have not chosen to live in this way; it has been imposed upon us by the immigration of white men to our land. We are therefore concerned for our future. You will understand that we cannot accept the exploitation of the North unless we are sure that it will profit us in the years to come. If we are sure that we will have our share in the wealth, and that the resulting prosperity will permit us to compete with other countries on a footing of equality, then we will accept development. We must be equally sure that we will be able to participate directly in the planning and in the decisions relative to any development. That will allow us and our children to play not a passive but an active role.

"The monies from a settlement of our territorial claims should permit us to establish an economy that is better adapted to our value systems and our culture. If our territorial claims were met, we would again be able to be our own masters. But if our territorial claims were not to be recognized, the oil companies would find themselves in the courts."

A long silence followed this statement. To prevent the tension's slackening, Robert Petersen, a Greenlander born in Sukkertoppen, intervened immediately. He was president of the Greenlandic delegation.

"We are deeply concerned about pollution, most especially of the seas. If pollution were to become a reality, it would threaten to put an end to the productivity of hunting and fishing, which are essential to fifty thousand Greenlanders. Customs and traditions would be in danger of disappearing. And one could challenge the ownership of the land. At the moment, in principle it lies with the state of Denmark. Actually, at the beginning and according to tradition, there was no private property in Greenland. There are arguments for, there are arguments against. However it may be, to this point there is no official position with regard to the ownership of territories in Greenland. Many people are trying to defer any discussion of this in order to avoid complications. But if one delays too long, conflicts will surely arise and they will be all the more serious. For the first time in the long history of Danish-Greenlandic relations, it is now perceived in Greenland that the interests of Greenlanders are not necessarily the same as those of Denmark."

Moses Olsen, born in 1938 in Holsteinsborg, the son of a hunter and elected member of the Danish Parliament (in Copenhagen) since 1971, spoke next in his capacity as secretary general of the Organization of Greenlandic Hunters and Fishermen:

"In the course of the last few years, the search for oil has made it possible to envisage a new source of revenue. We are skeptical. We do not think that the major benefits will be for the indigenous people, no doubt because of a lack of education and training. Until the present, there has been no technical program to educate and train them. It is essential that the means be found to train the natives so that they, too, can work at all levels in the oil industry. It will be impossible to avoid pollution if these industries are established in the country. These are the major reasons for which we wish to delay the exploitation of our resources in oil and gas particularly."

Angmalortok Olsen spoke last. Born in Thule-Qaanaaq, son of one of the first missionaries in Thule, he was an electrical engineer, living and working in Copenhagen, and married to a Danish woman. He was representative of the Greenlandic intelligentsia that in Denmark included some 10 percent of the Greenlanders resident there—the youngest and technically best-trained element. He was president of the Society of Greenlanders in Denmark (Peratigi Kalaallit).

"We have come to listen and to learn in order to collect the information that will permit us to deal with these problems in an effective way. We are not specialists. We can receive information only by being content to look through the small end of the opera glasses. We have realized that the sudden interest the world shows in Arctic oil represented initially a response to the world's overall energy needs. Then we asked ourselves whether that was the best way of solving the problem. In Greenland, we are in an altogether special situation in relation to Denmark. There are constitutional and juridical questions that must be clarified. It is necessary and vital for Greenlanders to know clearly who owns the natural wealth of Greenland. It must be said that royalties or taxes will not suffice to resolve the problem. We must be able to exploit our resources. This must be an activity of the government of Greenland. We will reply, therefore, that we are not interested in the development of an oil industry in Greenland if we cannot be responsible for it. For us to participate, we need time to train our people. Let us wait, then. If you look at the map on the wall here, you will see that this Polar region can be humanity's great refrigerator. You, your children, the children of your children, will need these raw materials even more than we need them ourselves, and perhaps they will be able to use them more productively. So perhaps one should leave such resources in the Frigidaire for the moment."

And so the oil companies and their national governments were for the first time challenged on the international scene. Mr. Tagak Curley, of Coral Harbour, on the Arctic island of Southampton, president of the Eskimo Federation of Canada (Inuit Tapirisat) went even further, insisting that Eskimo governments quickly become a reality: "We want our countries to be truly in our own hands," he declared. (Delegates were encountering the same violent protests that had been voiced by the Quebec Eskimos at the Federal Provincial Conference on a New Quebec, in 1972.) "The Eskimos have to manage their own affairs on their own land; this is not the land of the whites. You white men have your own bosses in your own land; we wish also to have ours in our land. . . . Every province in Canada has its own government. Eskimos have eyes and ears like white men, and they can manage their own territories without being guided by other governments."

The protests and claims put forward in these terms by Eskimo and Indian delegates were answered by a Canadian, in these words: "The last time I came to Le Havre was twenty-seven years ago. I came here to fight. Today, such is not my intention. And it is on this note that I will conclude my statement."

It is not with such threatening words that one makes history; at most one risks infuriating the dispossessed hunter—like the radical leader from Point Barrow, Alaska, Etok (formerly Charles Edwardson, Jr.), who in the style of a revolutionary nationalist proposed that a commando group should seize an American radar station. (The United States Department of Defense had a chain of stations stretching from the Bering Sea to Greenland.) The radar stations were manned by twenty to fifty men and were vulnerable, he said, to an Eskimo raid. "During the Arctic night it would be easy for young Eskimo activists to surround some stations," Etok claimed. "The men on duty would become hostages and once the operation was over, the attackers would launch an appeal by radio to the whole world—to the United Nations, claiming independence for a free nation and for a confederation extending from Siberia to Greenland, constituting a circumpolar Eskimo action." Never, according to Etok, would the American government, thus disarmed, dare bomb and destroy the stations, for such reprisals would kill the hostages also. In this way, the whole world would learn of the Eskimos' tragic fate, he added, in effect. "When a situation has deteriorated so far, activists have only limited alternatives, and sometimes such acts are necessary to get things moving."[7]

These desperate words cannot be taken seriously, of course, but it would be a mistake not to listen to them. It is impossible to defeat a people whose courage mounts in step with the injustices it endures and its indoctrination. At the Le Havre conference, one could entertain doubts about the youthful native representatives; they were of mixed blood and perhaps of mixed commitments; accompanied by white wives, for the most part they were young politicians who had broken all professional ties with the country they were supposed to be representing. And one might well guess that they would be easy to manipulate. Neither their style, dress, eating habits, financial ambitions, nor tourist interests set them apart from the European, Japanese, or North American delegates —not even the language of their fathers, which most of them could not speak.

Some were attracted by promises of technical cooperation even to the point of entering into unofficial negotiations with the oil-company people. Cooperation, promotion, cooptation—the process is familiar. Dubious representatives? Maybe. But who is not? Generally, the masses of the Third World are betrayed by their first-generation elites, but they come very quickly to recognize their true spokesmen. At the conference, ideas were advanced and of necessity were heard, for ideas cannot be gunned down. It was clear that a dialogue was possible, because both oil companies and governments were eager—I can vouch for that—to have a clean conscience. They did not want to be held responsible—once again—for ethnocide. Nonetheless, the economic and financial system is ever present, and its inertia is such that neither governmental nor industrial management—sluggish, blind, and deaf—will be able to control events unless dramatic reforms are adopted. In the light of what we know, of what other colonial histories and other unhappy experiences of the Third World have taught us, could we not, in this one remaining unviolated area on our planet, avoid a process that we now know is not inevitable? It was in no one's interest that the situation be allowed to deteriorate.

1982: Time passes. . . . Things have come a long way since that summer day in July 1950 when, on the cliffs of Siorapaluk, I came upon men dressed in bearskin trousers using nets to catch birds that they then ate raw.

As in Africa, as in Asia, as in the Caribbean, a wave of chauvinism has swept over Greenland. An Inuit nationalism that, reflected in the blurred mirror-image of an Eskimo hunter out of an already legendary past, seeks to meet the challenge of occidentalization and an industrialized economy.

In July 1976, I had the rare privilege of being one of the guests invited to attend the first Pan-Inuit Congress at Point Barrow that culturally unified the Eskimos of Alaska, Canada, and Greenland. Only the Siberian Eskimos did not participate in this meeting.

This Pan-Inuit League held its second reunion, this time at Nuuk (the Inuit name for Godthaab), in July 1980. Its affirmation of Inuit strength was all the more striking because Greenland had only just then acquired, on May 1, 1980, its regional internal autonomy within the context of the kingdom of Denmark.

At this historic congress, I had the opportunity to speak with Greenlanders from every region of the great island, and particularly from Thule. They were proud, and still wore bearskin pants.

Were the pessimistic impressions I formed during my preceding sojourns in Thule in 1967, 1969, and 1972 to be permanent? Apparently not. At the Nuuk congress the Greenlandic delegates succeeded in convincing me that the last empty decade spent by the Polar Eskimos, and in fact experienced by all of Greenland, was the very momentary consequence of an economic and mental colonization. The laws and resolutions passed by Greenland's rising young elite prove they are anxious to grapple with the problems common to all new nations. I particularly noted:

- a new system of quotas aimed against alcohol—the cancer of Greenland;
- Danish-Greenlandic bilingualism in the schools;
- local taxation and increasing economic autonomy;
- establishment of a commission to study the future of hunting communities in northern Greenland.

The Inuit power prophesied by Anaakkarsuaq at Thule-Qaanaaq is at last becoming a reality.

Perhaps the most important sign of progress is the growing sense of

Greenlandic nationalism, which has already produced a February 1982 referendum calling for the withdrawal of the country from the Common Market. A large proportion of Greenlandic people apparently feel that as a Danish province they have been constrained to join the Common Market when their first priority is to regain cultural and economic autonomy. The nation has to be put back on its feet before it can be integrated into the uncontrollable European infrastructure. Besides, the geography of Greenland links it to the American continent, not Europe.

Although most Greenlanders favor continuing the historic ties with Europe, certain Greenlanders have told me that they are ready to give up their present artificial standard of living if this would enable them to "Greenlandize," on the essential levels, their political and economic power. The Inuit Atakratigit party, though minor among the three political parties in the new Greenland, is indicative of the depth of this developing revolution. Within the confines of Greenland's conservative society, this party, with its extreme-left tendencies, is spreading more and more widely among the nation's youth.

A new Greenland is searching for itself. Its mineral riches, notably uranium, are essential to the West and will play a role of major importance in coming years. Beyond the limits of the old traditions, Greenlanders seek to build a new Inuit society balanced between a liberal capitalism all too eager to devour them, and a bureaucratic and totalitarian socialist state that most of them completely reject.

Thirty years have gone by and the geographer-explorer that I was back in Inglefield Land is discovering today that in the Arctic the social sciences are subject to radical modifications.

The past belongs to the ethnographer who came first and who, with obstinate patience, carefully described what was then called a "primitive society" from the exterior. Then came the time of the ethnologist who knew how to discover the cultural wealth of ancestral customs and imbue them with a philosophical structure. The time has now come for the "scientist of synthesis," and for the ethnohistorian who is able to integrate the archaeological past with the present so as to situate a civilization in terms of its destiny.

My geomorphological studies of scree were for me not only a science, but an Ariadne's thread leading to the realization that all natural systems are governed by an order: rocks, in their fragmentation, have, for each petrography, a dimensional limit. Reduced through weathering, they crumble to a certain dimension in equilibrium with humidity, temperature, and mechanical resistance, and it is this process we call a physical geosystem. It was as a geographer that I first observed the social "physiology" of a small group of hunters, which oscillated between minimum and maximum—but which can only hold its own by following similar well-learned principles of equilibrium.

During all the Inuit congresses I have attended, I have never ceased interpreting the decisions of the representatives as a demonstration of their search for an equilibrium among the past, the present, and the future; between the traditional economy and an industrial eventuality.

Will the alcoholic despair of that last decade at Thule prove to have been a sign of a salutary violence, the expression of the search for identity?

The Eskimos of Thule are an extraordinary symbol, not just for Greenland, but for all of the West as well: they recall the Arctic legends, the primordial humanity of Genesis, in which the sons of God gave birth to a race of northern giants, and the Greek myths in which the Hyperboreans were consecrated to Apollo, god of the sun.

In 1910, when Knud Rasmussen baptized the capital of the Polar Eskimos with the legendary name "Thule," he gave a concrete form to the fabulous destiny of this people. The Eskimos of Thule constitute, by the very name of their capital as well as by their geographic location, a reference, a place of hyperborean perpetuity, and an aristocracy for all Greenland.

Let no one be surprised to see the wish for an Eskimo Gaullism expressed by the pen of a Frenchman. The reader will be less inclined to smile if he is willing to view Eskimo Gaullism together with all its consequences: it means sustaining one's historical dignity, becoming the ethnologist of one's own past, appealing for group effort, producing only what one consumes, denying oneself the degrading regime of welfare, returning to vital sources in defense of an economy that is adapted to the philosophy of life of these youthful boreal nations. In a word: autonomy. For the sake of such aims, who would not be a Gaullist! Not to wish for such an awakening would be to will an ethnocide, the first manifestations of which are already evident among some in hoboism, alcoholism, and drug addiction.

I am confident about the future of Greenland if it masters money, which threatens to serve, there also, as an end in itself, and to transform the nation's fragile groups into ghosts manipulated by outside forces. It is an article of faith, an internal voice of the heart and of memory that whispers to me: Have confidence in the perenniality of the Eskimos of Thule, of the entire Eskimo people.

Sujumut—forward, people of Thule. It is for you to give a new reality to the Hyperborea of our most ambitious myths.

NOTES

1. *Le Monde,* September 10, 1952.
2. Greenland, an integral part of the kingdom of Denmark, has an area of 837,780 square miles, six-sevenths of which is covered by ice. In 1979, the population was 49,338. The high annual growth rate of the population, which was 4 percent in 1961, has dropped dramatically due to the policy of contraception. It is now (1978–79) only 0.4%. A population of 66,000 is predicted for 1985. In 1979, 17.3 percent of the population had emigrated from Denmark, whereas in 1967, the proportion was 14.7, and in 1950 was only 4.5 percent. Two-thirds of the largely interbred population lives in the towns on the southwest coast. Less than 12 percent of the population has remained in traditional hunting villages. The island income depends mainly on cod and shrimp fishing. *Hunting and trapping account for no more than 10 percent of revenues.* The general standard of living is much lower than that in Denmark. A broad program of Danish investments was begun in 1955, when the so-called colonial regime was abolished. Considerable sums are involved: 1,496 million kroner in 1979 alone, or approximately 100 million dollars, or nearly 2 million per person. The welfare program and economic colonization have had predictable results: Greenland produces less than one-fifth of what is spent on the island each year. The Danization of the country and the falling off of native production of cod, shrimp, seal, etc., and hunting and agricultural products have been the visible results of this very generous and, for Denmark, costly program. In giving a new dimension to Danish-Greenland relations, it has worked against the goal desired by everyone—the affirmation of the Greenlanders' ethnic and political identity—a goal which was first articulated by the great administrator and scientist H. J. Rink.

1. Knud Rasmussen, the celebrated Eskimo-Danish explorer, was born in Jacobshavn, Greenland, in 1879, and died in Copenhagen in 1933. In 1909 he founded the first Eskimo "store" in Uummannaq, which he poetically baptized "Thule." Beginning in 1910, Captain York was the pilot of Knud Rasmussen's ship, the *Sokongen;* it was used both for the needs of the Eskimo store and for scientific expeditions. It was Captain York who led the famous Thule Expedition—1921-25—from Copenhagen

to Thule and on to Danish Island, south of Southampton Island, in Hudson Bay, where it arrived on September 18, 1921. Captain York's real name was Peter M. Pedersen.

2. Julianehaab is a town in southwestern Greenland. John Petrussen later became a Greenlander pastor. In 1972 he was assigned to the capital, Godthaab.

3. Was this, perhaps, a response born of a group memory of fear caused by the nineteenth-century whalers, who were often unpredictably violent? Whale hunting began in 1819 and ended in 1910. Roughly 150 ships per year came from Dundee, Aberdeen, and the Shetland and Orkney islands, in Scotland; after several hours at anchor offshore from an Eskimo settlement, particularly off Cape York, near Savigssivik (200 miles south of Siorapaluk), the whalers would invite entire families aboard to trade. The epidemics of flu and other diseases caused by these visits of the white men have not been forgotten. In 1902 many Cape York Eskimos died from widespread flu: the few survivors lost all their hair. The terror created by these qallunaats, or whites, who were considered curiously short-legged, has been remembered. I was told that they arrived in boats with high poops. Disembarking unexpectedly, the crews would visit the villages in force. The Eskimos' ancestral fear was such that, Rasmussen wrote, after a century—in 1907—when a child saw an iceberg that looked like a ship without a mast he would cry "Qaqqaatsorssuak-kut! We have to flee to the mountains!" and everyone would take to the hills. However, some good memories remain, too. Ivalu, an old woman, told me that once, when she was a girl, she decided to go out to two big ships near Appat. Her parents told her, "You stay home!" But she went anyway. Another time, she climbed aboard a whaling ship and traded little auks, a bearskin, leather straps, and sealskins for a rifle, a knife, tobacco, and matches. It made her happy for a whole year.

4. In 1950–51, the population of the Thule district was still untouched by venereal disease. Considering the people's isolation and their sexual promiscuity, it is surprising that they had not been affected during the years 1818–1910 when whaling ships were often in the area. I know of several cases of the disease—gonorrhea having hit the Eskimos in Etah during this period, particularly in 1907–8—because the victims described their symptoms to me. Since no doctor was working among them, I can only conclude that there was some sort of spontaneous resorption.

5. One family caught annually about fifty fish, weighing around eleven pounds each, which was very little, and this figure applied only to the most active families. In the village, sharing was the rule.

6. The narwhal—*Monodon monoceros;* in Eskimo, *qilalugaq*—is, like the white whale, helpful in preventing scurvy thanks to special properties of its skin (*mattak*). Its fat is used as a lighting fuel; its meat makes it an essential food animal. Formerly its horn, or tusk, was used as a spear or, since the Eskimos had no wood, as a main beam for igloos. The narwhal's body is fifteen feet long and eight feet in girth; divided into eleven parts, it can feed a team of dogs for one month during the winter. Its tusk, usually found only among males, can grow to five and more feet in length; it fetches a high price on the market—at least $1,000—but the ends are often broken. This cetacean comes and goes, depending on the winds, the currents, and its mood. It has a predilection for the water near old and bad ice. During the summer, it stays exclusively in the waters of the Inglefield Fjord, especially in the area around the glacier. The mating season is April–May, and copulation is practiced vertically in the water, belly to belly. Births occur only every other year, and

take place in June and July in deep water. The future mother is surrounded by numerous females who take turns massaging her stomach with their heads. At birth, the baby is immediately placed on the mother's back.

The male spends the summers in deeper waters than the female. The narwhal fears both the walrus and the orc. In the 1950–51 period, thirty male narwhals and a hundred females were caught each year by the district's seventy hunters.

7. The fox, or *Canis lagopus;* in Eskimo, *terianniaq.* The foxes in this mountainous region, which is cut by fjords and has little snow because of the dryness of the upper latitudes and the wind from the ice cap, are (by mimicry?) mostly dark—brown or bluish. (In the "flat" tundra of northern Canada and northern Siberia, their fur is almost always white, like the snow around them.) Foxes have their own territories. The blue foxes of the Thule region, for example, never cross the borders of their area to mix with the white foxes in the flat tundra of the barren grounds—the northeast Canadian Arctic—even though this biological border (Kane Basin) is crossed by the bear, the reindeer, the musk ox, and the white Polar wolf.

8. The angakkoq is called *tungralik* by Alaskan Eskimos.

9. This is the worst insult possible. The Eskimo cannot stand a shopkeeper who cheats or someone who gives false information. His inner peace, indeed his whole life, depends on exact information concerning the ice, the wind, wild game, etc.

10. Some small help was given the old by relatives and friends. In 1950, a very modest pension provided them with just enough to get by on: 200 kroner a year for a single man over fifty, and 300 kroner for a couple. Very rarely, a hunters' council would give a supplementary but extremely modest sum.

11. Few Eskimos in Siorapaluk fished for seal with nets. It did not belong to their tradition, whereas in the southern part of Melville Bay, in Upernavik, it was common. "The net is not for hunting; it's good for women," I was told. As if in response to some biological force, the society resisted any innovation that did not spring directly from it.

12. Hunting for walrus, or *Odobenus rosmarus*—in Eskimo, *aaveq*—is the only form of big hunting regularly practiced which gave Eskimo society some power before trading in fox furs began with the Europeans. A walrus that measures ten feet in length and nine in girth weighs a ton and a half. Enveloped in a tough skin and a layer of fat one foot thick, the animal can be divided into twenty-two pieces. One walrus provides a team of ten dogs with food for two months in the winter. Bad walrus hunting means hardship, if not famine. The walrus looks for its food (mussels, crustaceans) in shoals and stays close by the coast, near a polynya, or expanse of free water, during the winter; it is hunted all year round. Probably the most ancient form of walrus hunting is to harpoon the animal at its breathing holes and beneath thin ice. To this end, the Eskimos have perfected a particularly ingenious hoisting technique using ropes. Before the kayak was reintroduced, in 1863, the Polar Eskimos had the advantage of being able to hunt unsuspecting walruses who used to sleep on rocks that had been polished smooth by the continual friction of their bodies; today the hunted walruses have deserted these little islands in the sun and it is no longer possible to pursue them on foot.

While walruses have been known to go south of Melville Bay, the greater part of the herd spends the winter in the waters of this region: in the strait of the Neqi Fjord, and west of North Star Bay, between Wolstenholme Island and Saunders Island. When they are unable to make breathing holes in the thick ice (unlike the seal, they must break through in one stroke, which can be done only when the ice is no thicker than three feet), they gather in the holes of free water by capes and straits. If the walrus is trapped in a fjord by ice, like the white whale it will make its way to free water by creeping over the ice bridge for a distance of as much as six or eight miles—a feat that can require several days. The walrus's reproductive cycle is two years, the gestation period is ten months, and the young are born in July and August. A baby walrus travels on its mother's back. When danger threatens, she carries it between her fins. The young reach maturity at three years, and the average life span exceeds sixteen years. One herd includes a single male, several females, and their young. To avoid the extinction of the species, the Eskimos in this exemplary tribe had developed a strict habit—custom having the weight of law—in hunting walrus: despite the dangers, they harpooned the animal *before* finishing it off with a rifle when, every ten minutes or so, it came to the surface to breathe. The animal has few vulnerable spots: the neck, the temple, and the eye. It reacts violently when wounded and is helped by the other walruses.

Two hundred walruses were caught annually by the seventy hunters in the 1950–51 period; or about three walruses per hunter. The statistic merely suggests a norm, for walruses are hunted in *peqatigiit*—groups of four or five hunters. Before 1860, the walrus was not fearful, as we have seen; it would sleep on rocks along the coast and could be hunted from the shore. Between 1860 and 1951, the hunter used also to attack the animal from his kayak and harpoon it before shooting. Since about 1960, the animal is harpooned only after it has been wounded by bullets. This method would make for considerable losses if the animal had not got used to the noises of the motor and did not swim off as soon as it heard the vibration of the propeller in the water. The walrus has begun to adapt to the new hunting techniques and to defend itself against them. The walrus is becoming acculturated.

Note that the word in Eskimo for walrus is *aaveq*, and that for the bowhead or Greenland right whale, *arfeq*. In Eskimo, the two belong to the same linguistic family.

13. Numerous instances have been reported of shamans being "resurrected" after lying three or four days in a cataleptic state. Perhaps this is the principal reason behind the prohibition against burying men until four days after their death (for women, five days) and the strict taboos connected with the burial: for example, the sealskin enclosing the dead person had to be left unlaced at the mouth, or a hole had to be made at that point; the corpse had to be carried from the igloo by an exit other than the door, and the igloo was then abandoned; certain animals might not be hunted for a month, certain words not pronounced; women were not to sew, etc.

It is curious to note as an example of the unity among religions that before the birth of Jesus it was a widespread practice for rabbis to teach that for the first two days after a person died the soul wandered around the body, from which it had trouble separating. Only on the third day did the soul depart, and the body become inert.

14. The language of the shamans is secret. Several words from the shaman language of Thule as reported by Rasmussen are: *pungo* (*qimmeq* in ordinary language), meaning dog; *sittalik* (normally *aaveq*), walrus; *ajappattoq* (normally *nanoq*), bear; *nuvelik* (normally *illu*), house.

15. The white whale, or beluga (*Delphinapterus leucas*)—in Eskimo, *qilalugaq qaqortaq*—is fifteen feet long and can easily be hunted with harpoons. Few risks are involved. Dreading the orca, the white whale looks for water that is not very deep. In an

emergency, it will head for the shore, where the Eskimos wait for it. The white whale is sought for its meat, its blubber, and especially its skin (mattak), which, like normal skin, helps to prevent scurvy.

It migrates in August and September along the coast in groups of four to six. In 1950–51, about a hundred belugas were being caught annually by the seventy hunters among the Polar Eskimos.

16. On both the southwest and east coasts of Greenland, these boats were once made of seal or walrus skin and used exclusively by women. Today they are made of wood. The Thule Eskimos began using the kayak again about 1863, but they never had the skin umiaq. Polar Eskimos are not sailors but men of the ice. Since the ice floe was their first raft, from which they hunted seal and walrus in open water, they did not need to venture farther out into the open water itself. The ice pack was wide enough in summer—from Savigssivik to Cape York—for them to hunt seal and seabirds from it.

17. The seal, *Phoca phoetida* or *Phoca hispida* (in Eskimo, *puisi, natserq*), is very common in all the bays of the region, but is rarely found in the areas favored by walruses, since the seal is afraid of them. It was an essential animal in 1950, constituting a source of heat and light (its fat is superior to that of the walrus) as well as of food and clothing (boots, gloves, anoraks), and used in building tents (twenty to thirty skins were needed for a large family tent). Today it is still used for equipment— kayaks, harnesses, whips, buoys, kiviaq, and sacks for birds—though less so. It is the only seal whose skin is sold commercially. The seal winters in the Thule district. The young are born in March and April. An adult measures from three to four and a half feet in length, three and a half to four feet in girth, and on the average weighs a hundred pounds. In the winter it is hunted by the *niparneq* method (through a breathing hole or *allu*) and by net (rarely); in summer, by the *uutoq* method (the seal lies on the ice in May and June) and in kayaks. In the spring, the seal is thin and has no fat. It is nearsighted and protects itself by its hearing and its exceptional sense of smell. It swims in a zigzag pattern, guided by its back flippers, and it is hard to catch up with. The seal is special in that it eats only while in the water. It can remain underwater for seven minutes without breathing, and in the event of danger, for more than fifteen minutes. When it surfaces to breathe, it stays up for only thirty seconds to a minute if it is uneasy. In 1950–51, three thousand seals were killed annually by the seventy hunters in the area.

The great seal, *Phoca barbata* or *Erignatus barbatus* (in Eskimo, *ussuk*), is much sought after because of its tough hide, but its skin is not sold commercially. Six feet long and five feet in girth, it also spends the winter in the Thule district. The great seal is not afraid of the walrus, and can be found in all medium-depth waters. During the winter when, like the *Phoca hispida*, it is relatively immobile, it looks for cracks in the ice. It has no breathing hole. It is not easy to catch, since it is not myopic and is most vigilant. Because it dives very fast, it must always be harpooned first. Fatter, stronger, and bolder than the common seal, this animal defends itself with great energy. Today the Eskimos prefer to attack it only in groups. In 1950–51, one hundred seals of this species were killed annually off certain beaches and in shallow waters of the Thule district. The carcass would be divided into seven parts. Today (1980) the hide of the great seal is still indispensable for sledge straps, whips, harnesses, and especially boot soles. The gut, although hardly translucent, was once used for windows.

The Greenland seal, or *Phoca groenlandica*, and the hooded seal, or *Cystophora cristata,* do not winter in the Thule area. About a hundred and ten were caught between July and October by the seventy hunters (1950–51). The skin of both is still valued as leather, but only on the local market.

In 1950 it was advisable to have available one *Phoca hispida* every two days in winter to feed ten dogs, one seal every three days in the fall and spring, and one seal every seven days in summer. All in all—taking into account the other animals hunted: walrus, white (or beluga) whale—about fifty seals were needed for each sledge and family per year.

18. The orca or great killer whale, *Orcinus orca*—in Eskimo, *aarluk*—is the undisputed king of the sea. It lives only in deep water and in the large fjords. It is feared by all, men and animals alike.

The orca rarely attacks a walrus. The two animals have distinct territories, each excluding the other, each dreading the other; an encounter, however, is not impossible. As soon as a man sees the crest of the orca's caudal fin slicing through the water, the fjord empties: the kayaker hurries to an iceberg or to the shore as fast as possible. Prodigiously intelligent and organized, the orca, with its fearsome jaws, attacks the bowhead whale according to an unchanging strategy. The largest member of the pod stations himself at the entrance to the fjord while two scouts place themselves in front of the whale who, at top speed, tries to reach the shore, where —so great is his panic—he will run aground. But the two orca scouts block his way. One of them approaches the bowhead and bites the edge of its lip to force it to open its mouth. At that precise moment, the second orca thrusts itself into the vast mouth and tears out the tongue. Smothered in its own blood, the disabled whale floats helplessly. Alerted—by ultrasonic messages?—the big orca swims up and finishes the animal off.

In Thule, there is no particular ritual connected with the orca. In Alaska (St. Lawrence Island and Bering Strait), it is considered to be a friend of the Eskimo. One might say that it hunts for them, and the tide and currents do the rest by washing onto the shore what the orca has not eaten. Propitiatory rituals have always been held in its honor so as to win its good graces. I have been told that during these rituals in Savoonga (St. Lawrence Island), the orca, which stays at a distance, waves its fin contentedly.

19. I chose this dream from among others that were told to me. As one might suppose, the most common dream themes deal with hunting, food, love, and with evil spirits and ghosts who, armed with knives, chase you. The spirits (every Eskimo believes that he has a particular spirit who protects him, while the evil spirits—qivittoqs, tupilat—try to harm those who do not know how to protect themselves) haunt everyone's dreams. Not a week went by without someone's relating to me hellish nightmares that had paralyzed him. Sakaeunnguaq once took advantage of my being alone to confide in a pathetic, detached voice that from time to time he dreamed of a qivittoq with the body of a man and the feet of a reindeer which Inukitsupaluk had encountered with Lauge Koch in 1923 in Polaris Land five hundred miles to the north of Thule. "When I am half asleep, these horrible monsters sometimes come close to me to grab hold of me. They frighten me out of my wits." Dreams can have a premonitory value. Oneiromancy, long practiced here, was still held in high esteem in 1950, and even somewhat today.

20. It is rather curious that in 1950 the Thule Eskimos had no sense of the signs of the zodiac. On the other hand, it should be noted that for obvious reasons they took great interest in the moon—its movements and its haloes. The hunter knew at least

ten stars very well, which he used to guide him during his winter expeditions. The angakkoqs sometimes took off on "information journeys" to the moon.

21. The days of the week were counted numerically except for Sunday—*sapaat*—which derived from a concept foreign to the Eskimo. *Ataasinngorneq*, or the number one, was Monday; *marlunngorneq*, or two, was Tuesday, etc. It seems that this system had been used since 1920.

  Before the white calendar was adopted, the calculation was lunar, and therefore monthly. It appears that the Polar Eskimos of "prehistory" (theoretically, prehistory means prior to 1818, the date of their discovery but, practically, 1910, the date of the first store) did not divide the months into days and weeks. In the first place, they did not think it useful, their notion of time being completely different from ours. They calculated the duration of their journeys in *siniks*—the number of times they slept en route. They still counted this way; the Western calendar was used only for administrative purposes. The Eskimos referred to the movements of the sun and moon and to the position of the stars, with which everyone was entirely familiar. Because daylight is continuous during the summer and four of the winter months are dark, it is often easy to mistake the "days" of the calendar, whereas, naturally, the movements of the sun and moon can be followed with relative accuracy, if one pays attention.

22. Long fallen into disuse after 1600 because of the englaciation of the water, the kayak was reintroduced (1863) in the Thule area by an emigration from Baffin Land. The kayak is still used only in a limited way, as its form testifies. It is least developed in Greeland. When the Polar Eskimos were discovered by John Ross (1818), they did not even know the word *kayak*, although their ancestors had used it in the same area, as archaeological digs illustrate, before 1600, the year in which the two-century cooling period began. In this instance, the Eskimos display selective memory, deliberately forgetting or obliterating whatever does not have immediate practical meaning for them.

  Once the kayak was introduced, it came into use only slowly, because the Eskimo feared the walrus and its furious attacks in the open sea. Its practicality was also limited, since the water was free of ice for only eight to ten weeks a year, and the walrus, which was unafraid of people until the rifle began to be widely used, could be hunted from the shore or from the ice field, the harpoon being anchored to stones and hurled at the walrus as it lay on its rock "islands." Since 1904, the construction of the kayak has been little improved: it measures about eighteen feet in length, the width at the midpoint is a scant two feet, and the depth of the hole for the rider a scant eight inches. The overall length of the double paddle is about eight feet; it is divided into three approximately equal parts—two blades and the handle in the middle—each about two and a half feet long. The Thule Eskimo is less skillful with the kayak than the southern Greenlander. The tradition of the kayak, although a revival—the pre-eighteenth-century Inussak and Thule cultures were sea and seal cultures—is recent.

23. If summer is the season of isolated camps and family life, winter is the season of social life, from the northern to the southern boundaries of the tribe. Winter is the time for exchanging news, for friendships to be formed and marriages to take place. It is also the time for changing igloos: the Polar Eskimos move every three years in order to make use of the resources peculiar to each area—bears in Melville Bay; walruses in Neqi-Etah; seals in Savigssivik; walruses and foxes in Thule; stones for oil lamps north of Neqi; birds and seals in Siorapaluk; sharks in Kangerluarsuk;

narwhals in Qeqertaq and Nunatarssuaq; birds in Etah and on Saunders and Herbert-Northumberland islands, whose surrounding waters are rich in walruses; reindeer in Inuarfissuaq; and bears on Humboldt Glacier. The exchange practice has been maintained in a moderate degree so that the complementary arrangement continues to make sense. The Eskimo is always eager for change, of course—he wearies of living for years on end in the same surroundings. As for the group as a whole, it tries to maintain general unity by forbidding families to appropriate this or that portion of its territory and instead encourages long-term residence. This is the price of political unity.

24. Twelve inches thick in early November; twenty-eight in early December; forty in early January and February; forty-four in early March, forty-eight in early April; the maximum reached at the end of April, fifty-two inches (Qaanaaq, 1963).

25. Around 1890, reindeer were hunted in the Thule district with bows and arrows. For lack of wood, the bow—two and a half feet long—was made of three pieces of reindeer ribs lashed together by narwhal tendons. According to Imina, this bow was weak and could not shoot far; its effective range was from fifteen to thirty feet. The bow string was a length of narwhal tendon. The bow was held vertically.

The arrow, about a foot and a half long, was tipped with a small piece of meteorite iron (from Savigssivik) or flint. This arrow often could not kill the animal, which then had to be finished off with a lance.

The reindeer had usually to be followed until it was exhausted, but the Eskimo was trained from childhood to run long and swiftly. The hunter wore boots soled with bearskin so that they made no sound on the snow.

The deer was best shot when cornered or worn out. But it was protected by its hairy hide, and a wounded deer would often get away.

There is no question that the fathers of today's Polar Eskimos were heirs to a maritime culture—the so-called Thule culture—based on seal and walrus hunting. Because of hunting and dietary taboos, during the 1600–1860 cold period it had been forbidden to hunt reindeer. When the thaw came, the taboos were lifted, but the animals were soon decimated by a food shortage.

In a thirty-year period (1860–90), it was enough during a mild winter that the ice set, and the snow then melt and refreeze, to create a barrier so solid that the hooves of animals looking for lichens and grass could only scratch the surface of the ice. By the 1890s, the reindeer in the Thule region, which had—both males and females—very developed antlers, were almost totally wiped out and their carcasses lay strewn about the glaciers and ravines.

Accordingly, it was for only one generation (1920–50) that this ancient form of hunting of the Canadian Eskimos (the Eskimos of Illulik, the source of the last migration) could be practiced in the Thule district. Reindeer were hunted more for pleasure than out of necessity; they were never an important food resource for the population, according to Imina. Today there are no reindeer on the slopes and plateaus of the vast area between Savigssivik and Etah. The only surviving deer now graze in Inglefield Land. They are the small-bodied *Rangifer pearya*. (As for the musk ox, it has survived only on Ellesmere Island.)

Reindeer meat is eaten by the Eskimo only after it has been boiled or in winter after having been frozen for three days. The viscera and the lining of the stomach are eaten in their entirety. The bone marrow and the stomach lining are particularly appreciated.

26. The biggest lamps were about a foot high, seven inches wide, and one inch deep;

made of soapstone from three "quarries," these cup-shaped lamps were fueled with seal, whale, or walrus blubber. The wick was made of flax down. The lamp produced a yellow flame about a quarter of an inch high. The wife had to tend the wick with a root or small stone tool to prevent its smoking or burning up. She also diced the lumps of blubber that form the top layer of fat, and chewed them so that they melted more easily.

27. Bearskin pants, with the fur on the outside, still worn in 1980. The pants reach slightly below the knee and are laced around the calf; they fit very snugly around the thighs and have a flap opening in front; the belt is made of sealskin, a clothing innovation due to Greenlandic influence since 1910.

The nanu used to be held up at midhip by a strap (until 1910). When he leaned over, the man exposed his naked back between his jacket and the top of his nanu, thus providing enough ventilation for the jacket. In 1964, this was still the case among the Utkukikjalingmiut (Back River, Canada). In Thule, during periods of severe cold, a fox skin used to be tied below the pants, at knee level. In 1950, a wide sealskin belt served the same purpose among the majority of young hunters. In rare cases, the fox tail was wrapped around the top of the knee—if the man was wearing short pants.

All the men sported their bearskin pants, a sign of their dignity, both summer and winter. They seldom owned a second pair. (Only the poorest hunters wore the less warm pants made of dog skin.) A large bear provided skin for two pairs of pants. A new pair of pants was acquired every five years. As Birket-Smith helpfully reminds us—and I myself observed it constantly—the Eskimos take great care of their clothing, whether while hunting, or during the cutting-up operation, or when at home in their igloos. Thule, too, had its fashions, even if they varied little from decade to decade—i.e., the length of pants or of caribou jackets; jackets without fringe, as among the Canadian Eskimos (Kutsikitsoq wore his jacket in this style to underscore his Canadian Eskimo origins); bearskin chin straps; the shape and length of the tongue at the back of the qulitsaq; etc. Fashion apart, the Eskimo has always insisted on a generous cut so that he can move easily.

At the turn of the century, men and women lived almost naked in their igloos. Two oil lamps and animal heat—five to seven people crowded into some eighteen square feet with very little air, a high-caloric meat-based diet, and a then higher metabolism—would raise the temperature halfway up the igloo to 15° or 20°C (59° to 68°F). The women wore only a fox-skin loincloth or even just a narrow strip of fabric secured by a belt over the pubic area. In order to be more comfortable than in their fur garments, the men were also half-naked, sometimes wearing their nanus, sometimes not. The Eskimo has always liked to be warm, even to sweat.

28. The legend of the pigtail and narwhal tusk is very popular. The Eskimos remember it by the title "The Blind Child and His Sister." There are variants. I heard one related by Pualuna, as I indicated above, but here I have preferred to give the version found in Holtved (see Bibliography), for a portion of Pualuna's tale seemed incomprehensible and ambiguous to me.

For the other legends recounted in this book, my informants were Amannalik, Kutsikitsoq, Bertsie, Imina, and, of course, Pualuna. Thirteen years earlier, Amannalik had been the source for my friend and colleague Erik Holtved. When there are two versions of the same legend, I have followed Holtved, the linguistic authority—but adapting freely.

Since 1967 I have used a tape recorder to collect stories and unpublished songs. In 1950 carrying a recorder was impracticable, given my geographic purposes.

29. Actually, in recent years there has been a tendency to assume that in the pre-Christian era the Indians might have been one of the elements that made up the Eskimo people of Canada, beginning with the Dorset culture.

30. The Greenland right whale—*Balaena mysticetus*, commonly known as the bowhead whale, in Eskimo, *arfeq*—is some fifty-five feet long. It can yield twenty tons of oil. Swimming at a speed of eight miles an hour, it can be seen only off Cape York and Natsilivik (Cape Parry). Heading up the coast of Melville Bay toward Cape Parry, it turns westward at this latitude to Pond Inlet and winters in the vast polynya known as the North Water, which does not freeze. In July, it enters the so-called whale strait in the direction of the Inglefield Fjord and Qeqertaq. The whale mates in these waters, as close as possible to the glacier; no doubt the waters in this area have special physical and chemical properties. In August, the whale swims up toward Qaanaaq and Siorapaluk and the Etah region, which is the most northerly part of its northern Greenland circuit.

Unlike most mammals, the baby whale is born tail first. The birth takes place in the water. The mother rises slowly, Harris tells us in his fine book *The Whale* (Stock, 1973), because the newborn calf must draw its first breath on the surface. "The mother helps him, carrying him gently to the surface so that he will not drown. The other females in the group take a keen interest in the birth and help the mother to keep the baby on the surface" (p. 63).

The Polar Eskimos have never hunted the whale (as opposed to the beluga or white whale, which they *do* hunt). Their traditions make no mention of it, nor have they either the appropriate harpoons or umiaqs, unlike the Bering Strait Eskimos, who were their direct ancestors. The great whale bones used in building their igloos could have been taken from whales that now and then were grounded on the beach.

31. The figures above relate to 1950–51. In 1910–25, according to Inuterssuaq in Knud Rasmussen's store, that trading post operated with the following tight price list: one blue fox brought the Eskimo ten kroner ($1.60); one white fox five kroner (80¢); one walrus rifle, 1889 model, cost him seven to ten blue foxes or twenty white foxes; one Mauser rifle ten blue foxes; one seal rifle two blue foxes; ten walrus gun bullets one blue fox or five kroner; one large knife one blue fox; one steel trap two kroner; a hundred grams of tea, one kilo of sugar, and five kilos of oats cost ten white foxes or fifty kroner ($8.00). Around 1930, prices, both sale and purchase, became slightly less tight for the Eskimos.

32. Each singer has his own rhythm and tone *(pisia)*. Melodic themes are handed down, it seems, but vary according to the singer. There are songs with words and songs without words, either handed down or original. If original, they are the property of the composer, and during his lifetime are never sung by another. Many archaic terms are used, which the Eskimos do not always understand. The Thule Eskimos are not familiar with the pentatonic scale, and the halftone is rarely used. The drum song is called *ingmerneq*.

33. Despite the ice's screening action, phytoplankton is very abundant. Once the ice-field surface is clear of snow, in the upper layers of water solar action is not impeded. Furthermore, during the six weeks when the sea is free of ice, the confluence of cold and warm waters encourages the proliferation of phytoplankton, especially the *Limacina heliciana* (with shell) and the clionids (boring sponges). This

plant plankton is the basic component of krill that the whale, who sojourns in these fjords and sounds, consumes by the ton. The seal's essential foods are decapods, amphipods, and cod.

34. Although over the whole of the territory no portion of it belongs to any one individual, the "living space" immediately surrounding a village is the specific property of that village's inhabitants. Another village, for example, could not regularly install fox traps in this area without prior negotiations with the first village. The Neqi sector (Pitorarfik-Sorfalik) constitutes a special area in the district. It is the only hunting ground for walruses—they abound here for hydrographic reasons too complex to enumerate in this book—and is, accordingly, a communal hunting territory. It serves as a kind of domanial land, *res nullius,* but also as a marketplace, a fairgrounds, and a social meeting place. In February and March, two-thirds of the tribe foregathers here, is briefly reunited, and then scatters once the hunting is over. This socialization of space at the tribal level had begun to change as of 1967. I noted, for example, some attempts by villages to appropriate neighboring fjords. But all the critical areas, such as Neqi, Inglefield Fjord (the only place narwhals go in August), Saunders Island (for walrus hunting), the guillemots cliffs, and the distant ice fields used for bear hunting (Kane Bay, Melville Bay, and the eastern coast of Ellesmere Island) are still (in 1980) owned by everyone.

35. She married Ulloriaq after Peary left, and in 1917 had one son by him, Talilenguaq. She died in Qaanaaq in 1921.

36. Boots—kamiks—are made of depilated and blanched sealskin. In winter, bearskin boots are worn. The inner boots are made of rabbit fur turned inside out. The feet are bare inside the boots. In severe cold, a kind of slipper made of reindeer skin or bearskin is worn over the boot, laced above the foot; it is called a *kamikpang.*

37. Skins are basics of a hunter's life. One double boot is made of one sealskin and lasts one or two years. A hunter has two or three pairs of boots. A sealskin jacket requires three skins and lasts three years. A pair of bearskin pants, which calls for one whole bearskin, is worn out after five years. A qulitsaq, or hooded reindeer jacket, is made of two deerskins and lasts four years. A kayak requires five sealskins and is usable for five to ten years. A family tent takes fifteen skins, which are turned back at the peak of the tent to let some light in.

38. *Arctic Adventure,* by Peter Freuchen, p. 12. It is not impossible that this is the same Atitak who later married old Pualuna.

39. The house for young people is small here, and differs from the Alaskan assembly house for men and women. In the central Canadian Arctic (Pelly Bay) during the winter, this communal building can reach (according to a missionary) twenty-four feet in diameter for big gatherings. It is then a huge bright snow igloo constructed of connecting units, with a single roof.

Among the Polar Eskimos, each village has a house for young people. It is usually the house occupied by an unmarried man or woman. Adolescents, beginning at the age of eleven or twelve, discover one another here, especially during the winter. In 1950–51, their caresses were rather audacious, but hardly anything more. Married adults were usually not allowed in. In Siorapaluk, the house for young people was the one lived in by Jaco, a thirty-year-old bachelor.

Since 1961, it has been the practice for some Eskimos to live there for four or five months with a partner before marrying; the relationship is not considered an engagement. But this liberal practice is possible only with parental consent, and is still followed by only a small number of the young people. I was a guest several times, but no matter how close I was to them, it was not before the end of the winter that they began to forget I was white. Joining in with the young with their rules and tacit understandings was more difficult. It was a subtly permanent situation. Only while hunting or on an expedition did I join with them most completely—although it was never total.

40. D. B. MacMillan, *Four Years in the White North* (New York, 1918), p. 275.

41. J. Malaurie, L. Tabah, and J. Sutter, *Population* (Paris), No. 7, November–December 1952.

42. J. Sutter and L. Tabah, *Population* (Paris), No. 3, 1956.

43. It is curious to note, Sutter remarks, that this is the same interdiction theoretically imposed by the Catholic Church.

44. Let us consider sexual taboos on the assumption that they were established to promote fecundation of the woman. One is always surprised to learn of the profound empirical knowledge of female biology in ancient and primitive societies. These populations adopted concrete and precise policies centuries before theoretical and experimental scientific knowledge confirmed their usefulness. The Babylonian Talmud, which was completed in the fifth century A.D., is significant in this respect. Conjugal relations were very strictly defined in it. The woman was considered pure for only sixteen days each month and could not be approached by her husband except during that period. Later studies have shown that the first three or four days of this sixteen-day period corresponded exactly to the period of maximum fecundity (ovulation) in the woman. What about the Eskimos? Unfortunately, we do not yet have enough information to say.

But are these various sexual interdictions and exchanges of women sufficient in themselves to account for the mechanisms by which the group increases or decreases in size?

When it is a question of relatively small differences, it is undoubtedly possible to answer affirmatively. But how can the population increase of 1860–95 be explained? Let us briefly recall the facts: in 1855–60, life for the group was difficult. After a long period of bitter cold, it had endured a terrible famine. Led by the shamans, the Eskimos managed to survive by limiting their diet to birds, abandoning the kayak, and hunting seals only occasionally from ice floes which functioned as rafts, or at breathing holes or in areas of water opened in the ice by storms. Some families were able to survive only by eating their dead when the opportunity offered itself. By Eskimo calculations, there were only thirty-two women able to procreate. The biological characteristics of the group, as observed in 1950, would have been the following, at the very minimum: a thirty-two-month period between babies without recourse to contraception or abortion, such practices being unknown among the Eskimos (coitus interruptus and other contraceptive methods were unheard of in 1950–51); a rate of at least 140 males for every 100 females (the figure for 1950); most likely a high rate of sterility among women of child-bearing age (it was 16 percent in 1950); an average life expectancy of twenty-two for women and twenty-eight for men (1950); a higher mortality rate among women (as in 1950); and an infant mortality rate considerably higher than 60 percent of all births (mostly perinatal deaths). We can arrive at the following figures on the basis of the stable 1950 information: the thirty-two fertile women in 1855–60—assuming there were no cases of infanticide—could not have given birth to more than sixteen surviving female babies up to 1872, of which 16 percent were sterile (by 1950 figures); only fourteen subjects would therefore have been fit for reproduction. But what are we to make of a collectivity whose fate rests on fourteen people? In fact, supposing that for the period under consideration there was a complete ban on infanticide and that marriage and genetic rules and interdictions were not a factor, the figures for fertility, sterility, the interval between births, and mortality that we arrived at above would necessarily limit the annual growth rate of the population to a maximum of 0.8 percent.

And yet, even though general conditions in the past were incomparably more difficult than they are today, the growth rate increased almost 300 percent, if Peary's census is to be believed.

(Readers interested in this problem should consult the various demographic studies I have published with Tabah on this subject. They are based on the precise information gathered by Kane [1852], Peary [1895], and Rasmussen [1918], which were all simple numerical counts of the population, as well as my own genealogical census in 1950–51. Because the parameters are so numerous and do not all work in the same way, it is difficult to do a statistical analysis, especially since we are dealing with such small numbers and simple variations on minor points can throw all calculations off.)

What can we conclude except that the various controls on genetic freedom or regulation, the practice or banning of infanticide—which was used with great wisdom by the Eskimos as a way of planning their demographic renewal—are not enough to explain the history of the group?

We are forced to assume that this small, very specific human group, which in its isolation has been subject to considerable physical constraints for a hundred generations, undergoes fundamental changes during certain periods. It is impossible to pin down the nature and scope of these changes, but we can conclude that they affected fertility, life expectancy, the interval between births, characteristics of masculinity, and infant mortality.

Consider these possibilities. The age of puberty for women (thirteen to fourteen in 1950) and for men (sixteen to eighteen in 1950) could have been earlier or later depending on the needs of the group. The time between the first menstrual period and the first possible conception, which was between four and six years in 1950–51, could have varied depending on climatic and historical conditions.

Is this a unique biological case? Various examples—particularly in the area of immunology and animal demography—even if they are no more easily explained, suggest that a kind of organic intelligence exists. I could cite the case of the rat in our temperate latitudes. In high latitudes, I will cite the case of female seals which reduce their gestation period to adjust to the cold season; the more or less cyclical changes in the numbers of lemmings might be an indication that some system of correction exists, either to increase or decrease the size of the group. There is no question that animals live within a biological order; in certain cases, when their survival is at stake, they can sometimes modify terms of biological regulation which one might have considered to be unchangeable.

45. Anthropology has not inquired closely enough into when it was that man became aware of his paternal function, which is to say, when he first understood that he engendered his own children. All man's connections with woman (consanguinity, promiscuity) and with society were altered thereby. We do know that Lascaux males were aware of their propagative function, and recognized the cause-and-effect

relationship of intercourse and conception. In the case of the Eskimos, within the memory of man semen has always been associated with cynegetics (the science of hunting); i.e., ejaculation was favorable to hunting. If one takes the wintertime amenorrhea and the seasonal pattern of sexual desire, especially the male's, into account, it is more understandable that the men of the North did not readily associate coitus and pregnancy. Nonetheless, Thule's mythic accounts establish the fact that, like the Lascaux man, the Eskimo early on grasped his generative role. That understanding led to family planning with regard to blood ties. To study the question in depth, studies should be based on sculptural and graphic images that would permit us, perhaps, to learn more about a subject that will always remain obscure.

There is general agreement that man's comprehension of his biological capacity was a fundamental discovery in human social history.

46. Inugarssuk's song, according to Erik Holtved, *The Polar Eskimos.*

47. Slightly adapted from the version in W. Thalbitzer, *Légendes et chantes esquimaux du Groenland* (Paris, 1929), pp. 55–56.

48. The qulitsaq is a long-sleeved jacket of reindeer to which a hood bordered by a blue foxtail is attached, with bearskin cuffs and chin strap. The jacket is made of separate skins, cut to order by the women and sewn along the side. A man's qulitsaq has a little rounded point in the back suggesting a bear's tail. All the clothing of the Polar Eskimos is of one color. In the Canadian and Alaskan Arctic, the different colors of different articles of clothing are determined by deep-seated beliefs and strict rules.

Beneath the qulitsaq the Eskimo used to wear (1920) a sealskin *natsiluaq*, a kind of shirt. Next to his skin he wore a woollen shirt. Prior to 1910, he wore a single *atisaq*, a jacket, which was very warm but extremely fragile, made of squares of bird skins stitched together with thread made from tendons. (It took about 100 birds to make one atisaq.) Before 1920–30, he wore the warm, elegant *kapatak*, the hooded jacket made of fox skins (ten fox skins for each qulitsaq), in the winter, which is now only worn by women. At the top of the hood, and at the shoulders and wrists, it was white; in front and back, dark blue. In recent years, I have seen this kind of qulitsaq worn only by the best young hunters with somewhat dandyish tastes.

49. Although as yet there is no general agreement, the most recent studies trace the roots of Eskimo back to the Proto-Indo-European languages and its structures to the Turco-Altaic language groups.

50. The information was provided by P. Fournier.

51. H.B.C.: The Hudson's Bay Company, which was founded in 1670, proudly called itself H.B.C.: Here Before Christ. It had a legal monopoly over trading with the Eskimos in the Northwest Territories until 1867, and an effective monopoly until 1964, when the first government trading posts were established. In spite of the fact that the H.B.C. was a powerful financial association, it naturally felt no moral responsibility for the material condition of these people: the Eskimos suffered periodically from famine until 1963.

52. Subjects that should have been regularly taught, beginning in the lowest grades, include: Arctic history and geography, glaciology, natural sciences (biology, elementary physics, and chemistry), modern techniques in hunting and the raising of furbearing animals, animal biology, ecology, oceanography, meteorology, mechan-

447

ics, airplane flying, and map reading. Then young Eskimo students would grasp the
true meaning of "school," which could become a form of general education
through the study of techniques.

53. According to a local law drawn up by Rasmussen on June 7, 1929, based on local
custom, both men and women could vote for deputies to this Fangaraade, or
Council of Hunters. This ordinance marked the beginning of a political society with
written statutes.

54. In 1867 there was a second and final migration.

55. In music and myth themes, there are clear signs that the Eskimos of northeastern
Canada (Illulik, Pond Inlet) acculturated this small isolated Polar group. In technical areas it is also evident. This was my principal reason for making two expeditions
(1960, 1961) into the Illulik region.

56. Before the fourteenth century, the fully clothed body was apparently left lying on
the ground on its back, surrounded by a circle of symbolic stones. In the rituals of
Alaskan Eskimos who migrated as far as Inuarfissuaq, the body was thrown into the
sea.

57. The important moments of daily Eskimo life are still governed by old beliefs.
Consider, for example, these scenes which took place in Illulik (Hudson Bay)—the
place from which the immigrants to Thule came in 1863.

All activity in the Awadjat settlement had stopped. Ataguttaaluk's second husband, Ikjugaarjuk, was the leader of the Illuliqois group (Hudson Bay). All his sons
had gathered around him. In a low voice, he told them his last wishes concerning
the division of his goods, the fate of his wife and daughters, his burial, the marriages
of this one and that one.

After his death, a vigil was held around the body, which was not put in a coffin;
after being dressed in his most beautiful winter garments, gloved, and booted,
Ikjugaarjuk's body was wrapped in a stitched reindeer skin that was left open at the
level of his mouth. His kin them carried him not to the "cemetery of the missionaries" but up onto a tall hill that he himself had chosen and where he would lie alone.
The things he had used every day were laid nearby. His body was covered with
stones—care being taken that none should weigh on his chest. His telescope, which
was especially coveted by everyone, was placed within his reach. One morning, on
the advice of the missionary, Ataguttaaluk, in spite of her violent repugnance,
removed the telescope from the grave. The next day, everyone noticed that it had
been slipped back in its place among the stones.

Also, relatives and neighbors were forbidden to live in the camp for two years
after the death. The date of these incidents is difficult to determine. Ataguttaaluk
had been born sometime in the 1870s.

Awadjat has been uninhabited ever since. In the graves of men, one finds
kayaks, strangled dogs, hammers, knives, harpoons, and whips. In the tombs of
women—pearl necklaces, boxes of bone needles, and ulus, or curved knives.

58. K. Birket-Smith, *Moeurs et coutumes des Esquimaux* (Paris, 1937).

59. The Eskimos of northwestern Greenland are Lutherans, as are the south Greenlanders. Not until 1960 was there a Catholic missionary in Godthaab, in the south
—a prominent Greenlander, Father Finn Lynge.

60. It is interesting to note that in 1967 the only souvenir shop in the Thule region
that sold for a good profit the various sculptures carved by the Eskimos was set up
right next to the church and was run by the catechist.

61. Hugh Eames, *Winner Loses All* (Boston, 1973), p. 108.
62. W. Herbert, *Par-délà le sommet du Monde;* preface by Jean Malaurie (Paris, 1974).
63. From Theon Wright, *The Big Nail* (New York, 1970), pp. 253, 265, 304; and Eames, *Winner Loses All,* p. 255.
64. I may add that according to what Floyd Bennet said confidentially, Admiral Richard Byrd was lying when he claimed to have flown over the Pole on May 9, 1926. The first people, then, to have verifiedly done so are Amundsen-Nobile on May 12, 1926, aboard the dirigible *Norge*; the Russian Ivan Papinin, who landed with a group by plane on May 21, 1937; the crew of the American submarine *Nautilus* on August 3, 1958; the American Ralph Plaisted by snowmobile on April 19, 1968; the Englishman Wally Herbert on April 5, 1969; the Italian Guido Monzino on May 19, 1971. Herbert and Monzino traveled by dogsledge, and they as well as Plaisted had aerial and radio control. More recently, on August 17, 1977, the Soviet nuclear-powered icebreaker *Arktika* reached the Pole, as did the Japanese Naomi Uemura on April 29, 1978; Uemura traveled by dogsledge and alone, but had air support and control.

   Cook perhaps believed that he had reached the North Pole, although the means he had at his disposal leaves room for doubt; might Peary have led others on to believe that he had?

   What concerns me as an Eskimologist has to do with quite another matter. The more I think about the debate that has continued for some seventy years, the more I am struck by the great indifference shown with regard to the Eskimos. In the United States, where the Cook–Peary controversy became a nationwide debate, all sorts of investigations have been carried out. Yet never was any decision taken to appoint an official commission of inquiry with the staff support of qualified interpreters in order to question the Eskimo companions of Peary and Cook—and they would seem to be indispensable witnesses. I must conclude that both public opinion and the responsible authorities judged the Eskimos to be, in effect, nonexistent; they were just blind, deaf, and dumb participants. Apart from Knud Rasmussen, I am, I fear, the only independent scientist who has systematically—albeit very tardily—questioned some of those men.

   I will permit myself one further comment: considerable sums, on the order of hundreds of thousands of dollars, were variously raised and earned by each of the two leaders as a result of explorations that could not have been carried out without the cooperation of the Polar Eskimos. If one may judge by the documents published by Cook and Peary, neither man troubled to do what would have redounded to his credit—first and foremost, to sponsor a public fund-raising campaign out of gratitude to this tiny group, which was in severely straitened circumstances at the time. The best among them had risked their lives for the glory of America or for what, in American public opinion, then epitomized it: the Stars and Stripes' priority in being planted at the Pole.
65. The four principal winds are: *nigeq,* the south wind, which blows in off the sea and brings with it fog, rain, snow, and gusts of wind; *avannaq,* the dry but violent wind; *kannaq,* the east wind; and *assaeneq,* the west wind.
66. The Eskimos put oil-soaked moss or, even better, dry peat soaked in oil on the tips of their harpoons, and this provided them with light as they went from one igloo to another on moonless days during the Polar night.
67. A story told to Kutsikitsoq by Qvaviarssuk, who went with Rasmussen on the Fifth Thule Expedition, to Hudson Bay. The story takes place near Illulik.

Part III
One Thousand
Miles of Exploring

1. Hunting of musk ox on uninhabited Ellesmere Island is forbidden by Canadian law.
2. In planning the equipment for this French geographical expedition to Thule, I was guided by the report that the Danish geologist Lauge Koch wrote following the Jubileaum Expedition (1920–22). On my return to France, Lauge Koch and I often discussed the problems involved, for in the intervening thirty-odd years, transportation techniques had changed very little for the scientific geologist intent on sticking close to the terrain.

   Because the basic purpose of the expedition was scientific, it was essential that it not be allowed to turn into what Koch called "a hunting party," with the Eskimo determining the itinerary in relation to a search for game.

   One option for me would have been to assume the burden of a three-month secure supply of food for men and dogs. However, the program I had set for myself in Paris made it imperative that the expedition be able to travel as rapidly as possible over long distances.

   For the operation to be carried out properly, on arrival at a given camp our main group of five people had to be divided into two detachments. The function of one was scientific: using his sledge and the best dogs available, one Eskimo would transport me as a passenger to the sites and locations required for my mapping and morphological surveys. The second group, of three people, was concerned with hunting. Working out of our campsite, they would keep our teams supplied with seal. Each of the two women would take care of her husband's clothing and repair his team's harness; they would take turns in attending to my personal effects and equipment. Such was the plan. It worked out well except for provisioning the dogs from Etah to Inuarfissuaq. The number of seals we were able to catch on old hummocky ice from March 26 to April 15 could be counted on the fingers of one's hands. Those were hard, not to say anxiety-provoking days. As a last resort, we could have fed flaked oats to the dogs, but they were very weak and several seemed unlikely to survive long on such a diet in such cold. At that point, my two Eskimos very "sportingly" agreed to risk losing some of their own animals and if things became truly desperate give them to the others to eat—so anxious were both men not to compromise the success of my undertaking. But every morning, we used to assure one another that better days were coming, and meanwhile we ourselves lived on our reserves of meat.

   By the time we reached Inuarfissuaq, our meat supply was finished, but here the area was rich in game. It took Qaaqqutsiaq no more than one alert week to largely replace our stock. And except for the crossing to Ellesmere Land, for the balance of the mission hunting, whether with harpoon by the allu or with a rifle, sufficed to assure a good diet for the dogs.

   For ourselves, we had an adequate supply of foodstuffs at hand. A part of these supplies I had purchased on my return to Paris from Africa.

3. We had brought with us three Danish Army rifles, with a seven-cartridge magazine, which were excellent but heavy. Also, one 16-millimeter rifle for ptarmigan. The ammunition supply was generous: ten cartridges per day per person, for a period of three months. This might seem a lot but was not excessive, since one had to

consider a possible forced wintering over in either Greenland or Canada. The entire supply was carried with us to Ellesmere Land.

4. Oil for heating and cooking was our biggest load. We transported 150 liters in five jerrycans and one large drum. (One-third was left at our depot.) A jerrycan is such an encumbrance that, on my orders, as each one was emptied it was left behind, to the despair of my companions. Our consumption of oil was high in March–April because the cold was severe ($-30°C$ or $-22°F$), but it dropped greatly in May–June ($-10°$ to $+5°C$ or $14°$ to $41°F$).

5. In the end, I had decided against taking my little transmitter with me. Its weight would have been an extra burden, and I would have had to take great precautions to protect it during difficult stages of our trip. And lastly, it would have been useful only on deserted Ellesmere in the event of our having to winter there; even assuming that the set would still be functioning, I was sure that any SOS it would have permitted me to send would have been futile. In the autumn, no large motorized boat was available at the Danish Thule station, and in winter, no dogsledge mission would have risked crossing such long distances during the full Polar night in an attempt to reach us. The fact that we would have failed to return to my Siorapaluk base in August 1951, five months after our departure, would have been as meaningful as a radio appeal and at least as effective. No help could be expected to reach us before January 1952, nine months after our leaving Siorapaluk, or at the latest by April–May 1952, almost a full year after our setting out. The messages that I had purposely and regularly left under cairns at essential stages along our route would surely, to my way of thinking, suffice to orient any mission that might eventually come looking for us. One further consideration: at such a latitude and on light expeditions by dogsledge, a radio's efficacy is an illusion, and a dangerous one in that it gives the explorer a false sense of security. In any event, for all that I was on an official mission, I was not counting on the authorities in Copenhagen to act in case of need. No matter how well disposed a government may be, I have always been skeptical about its being helpful in circumstances of this sort, which call not only for the practical means and for imagination but also for the speediest of responses.

6. In intense cold and on icy snow, the Eskimos in northeastern Canada use runners of frozen mud. At temperatures around $-10°C$ ($14°F$), when snow exposed to the sun is beginning to become soft and sticky, whalebone runners are better. When snow is melting, steel runners are just as efficient.

Here we had only steel runners; we would splash them with water, which froze instantly. On good ice, the sledge would slide much faster. But we had to avoid rough places or the coating of ice would crack and the runners would have to be iced all over again. That meant unloading and turning the sledge over, filing the runners, melting snow over a burner, splashing the water on the runners, and reloading.

7. According to Moltke's measurements, before Peary's time, sledges were 8 feet long, 1.8 feet wide, and 6 inches high. The stanchion in back—the napariaq—which is a characteristic feature of Thule sledges, was 2.75 feet high. The runners then were made of 8- to 12-inch lengths of walrus bone. Because materials were scarce, sledges were never alike. In 1875, George S. Nares saw a sledge made of walrus bone with crosspieces of narwhal teeth. Sledges were wider on the bottom than above.

As I have said, Qaaqqutsiaq, Kutsikitsoq, and I each had our own sledge, and all were built to the native design. Kutsikitsoq's was a large model, 13.1 feet long, by 2.1 feet wide, and 9 inches high. Qaaqqutsiaq's sledge and mine were slightly smaller—about 11.5 feet long, all the other dimensions being slightly smaller. The crosspieces and the stanchions were pine, the two supports oak. All runners were single lengths of steel screwed onto the framework. Each hunter had built his own sledge. No doubt a small sledge would have been practicable for travel on the plateau, but it could not have long withstood a hard passage over bad ice without suffering damage. We had stowed two long pine planks against possible repairs; they proved to be unneeded, and we left them in Washington Land.

One big ax with a five-foot-long handle was packed and proved to be a precious tool among the hummocks of Smith Sound when we had to cut steps in the ice to help the dogs over the worst walls of ice. As Lauge Koch recommends in his report, I had asked Qaaqqutsiaq and Kutsikitsoq to bring complete hunting gear with them: harpoon, lance, sealskin buoys, and so forth, in the event of our having to winter over. We had no kayak or inflatable dory. In the future, it would be useful, *even indispensable*, to provide both.

8. A word about the dogs, on whom the success of the mission depended. We had at our disposal three full teams, forty-three dogs in all. A good third of Qaaqqutsiaq's animals were barely adult because an epidemic of perlerorneq had struck his team the year before. My own team was homogeneous and full-grown except for Caporal, who, at not quite eight months, was just beginning to pull well. Clearly, Kutsikitsoq had the best and most impressive team—of his sixteen dogs, only three or four were less than a year old.

Despite unfavorable circumstances at times, we did not lose a single one of our valiant animals. On the contrary, en route we had two litters of five and ten pups, respectively, whom the women cared for tenderly. (I had kept some of them, for they could prove useful as support, indeed as food, for the adult dogs were that to become necessary during a forced stay in Canada.) Our supply of traces, made of bearded seal's skin, was sufficient. At no point were boots for the dogs' paws of any help in protecting them against cuts from the rough surface of floes or against the bite of salt from melting sea ice.

9. We used two tents. One belonged to Qaaqqutsiaq; it was made of a poor quality of canvas in the shape of a helmet, and we kept it for short excursions. The other was mine, made of stronger canvas but not double thickness, which was unnecessary in a calm season with little snow; it was quite spacious, having been enlarged in the course of the winter to accommodate six or seven people; at its highest point the roof was better than four and a half feet from the ground.

Even when the entire group was assembled, the tent served admirably. Harpoons doubled as poles. The nylon guy ropes quickly frayed against the stones and sharp edges of the sledge which were used in place of pegs, and we gradually replaced them with sealskin thongs.

10. Our cooking equipment was most rudimentary but adequate. We had two new Primuses (one of which we left at the depot), plus numerous spare mantles, supplies of Sterno, and two aluminum casseroles. Each of us had, or I supplied, a bowl and an aluminum plate, fork, and spoon. The forks were never used, for we all ate with our fingers, nor were the spoons, for we drank both soup and coffee from our bowls. We ate from a common casserole, and if we were eating in the tent we used the aluminum plate to chill meat by simply setting it on the snow.

11. In 1950 the stone mounds protected meat against the rapacity of dogs, bears, and

foxes (they are scarcely in use today). They must not be too far from the igloos, so that the hunters can get to them easily and also shout to keep the guillemots from feasting on the cache. The mounds are made of stones because the Thule district has no wood, not even driftwood. Only since the 1930s has wood been imported, enabling the larger villages to build individual drying racks for meat.

12. I was unable to persuade my partners to buy or make *qipiks*—sleeping bags—of caribou. In the past, this type of bag was in wide use, but of all the Polar Eskimos I knew, the only person who owned one was Minik, from Savigssivik. During the very cold nights in March and April, my comrades, who were wrapped in nothing but cotton blankets of indifferent quality, felt the cold acutely. To stay warm, they huddled closer together.

13. Dr. H. K. E. Krüger's geological expedition, the only one in this region that came to a totally tragic end. After spending the winter of 1929 in Neqi, Krüger set out in the early spring of 1930 with a single sledge; he was accompanied by a young Dane and a very experienced Eskimo. They left Etah in the direction of Ellesmere Island and never returned. Men and equipment vanished without a trace.

14. One can measure how great a disaster it was when one realizes that an Eskimo must wait nearly a year before he can put a young dog into harness, and that since the district is totally isolated, dogs can be obtained only from the interior of Polar Eskimo country. Negotiations are started with relatives in the nearer villages and extend to the most distant parts of the territory (that is, Savigssivik in the south), with cousins acting as go-betweens. The dogs are either gifts or loans, depending on relations between the parties. Aside from negotiations through cousins, there are also exchanges: one adult dog, say, for a secondhand rifle, one bitch for a telescope, a litter of pups for three planks.

15. Rations of packaged tea, coffee, sugar, and powdered milk sufficient for two men for 10 days out on the trail were supplemented by large purchases I made during the winter of 1950, chiefly at the Danish store. Thus, we totaled enough food for five people for 100 days on full rations, or 170 days on reduced rations. (This figure is very approximate and also minimal. Actually, I had a 290-day supply of tea and coffee. I had upped the quantity of both items, for their consumption here is heavy especially if the basic food is seal, which it would have had to be in the event of our wintering over.)

On hand I had 120 cans of meat; 40 kilos (88 pounds) of dried cod; 30 kilos. (66 pounds) of biscuits (90 days for five people); 10 cans of vegetables; 48 jars of Nescafé (20-cm. size); 44 cans of ovomaltine (enough coffee and ovomaltine for 150 days); 44 cans of a chocolate drink (for 50 days); 9 kilos (20 pounds) of tea (for three months); 50 1-kilo (2.2-pound) cans of jam; 10 1-kilo (2.2-pound) bags of rice; 30 kilos (66 pounds) of sugar (for three months); 7 kilos (15 pounds) of butter and fat; 80 20-cm. cans of vitamin-enriched lemon juice; and a dozen 1-kilo (2.2-pound) cans of condensed milk.

Two-thirds of our supplies were held in reserve at the Uunartoq depot, against the possibility of our having to winter over in Inglefield Land or Ellesmere Land. In this way, during December or, at the latest, in early January 1952, we would have been able to take off from Alexandra Fjord (Bache Peninsula) and be sure of making a connection to reprovision ourselves with foodstuffs and oil. Biscuits, powdered milk, coffee, and tea were packaged either in tin containers or in a heavy oiled paper. This precaution protected them against humidity, and it worked well. Our consumption of coffee, tea, and sugar was considerable, and the jam, butter, and biscuits were no less appreciated, but except for the latter they were not essential. The dried cod was to be a great boon in March and early April. On the other hand, we made little use of the canned meat and vegetables. Our essential meat needs in March were met by the reserves of seal intended for our dogs; in early April, by Polar hare, which abounds at Force Bay and at Uunartoq; in the second half of April, by seal (at Inuarfissuaq, Qaaqqaitsut), and occasionally by bear (Cape Agassiz). Because we moved about rapidly in Washington Land and on Smith Sound, we lived on our reserves but made no great inroads into them. In this "warm"— −10° to +5°C (14° to 41°F)—season of the year, your hunger is easily satisfied by several cups of tea or coffee provided you have been well nourished during the preceding months. Many days we were content with that and no more. Tobacco was in good supply—a must when you are on an expedition with native partners. Every other Sunday morning, I would distribute the tobacco ration. Each man got one package of twenty cigarettes to last him two days, and as much pipe tobacco as he wished. In cold periods, the Caporal cigarette is much desired, but generally Eskimos prefer the mild Danish or American leaf. They could never bring themselves to smoke shag tobacco. Kutsikitsoq wanted to give it a try once, and it made him retch. I had purposely brought no wine or hard liquor. As do many other people, I consider it harmful to drink spirits in the Arctic; furthermore, it would have been practically and psychologically impossible for me to drink behind the Eskimos' backs, and in 1950–51, alcohol was fortunately forbidden and unknown to the Polar Eskimo.

16. An inventory of our resources may be of interest. When our spring expedition left Siorapaluk, on March 29, 1951, its equipment represented the very modest investment of some 7,900 francs or 2,250 dollars.

Dogs, with harness: 600 francs—or 171 dollars—(a dog older than a year and a half cost 12 to 15 francs); food, rifles, ammunition: 3,000 francs or 850 dollars; photographic equipment: 2,000 francs or 570 dollars; camp equipment, sledges, clothing: 1,000 francs or 285 dollars; scientific equipment, some of which had been lent me by scientific organizations: 1,000 francs or 285 dollars (this item not included in the 7,900-franc total); compensation to native partners, in kind and in cash: 400 francs or 115 dollars (by way of bonus, they also received the quite sizable stocks I had laid on against our possible wintering over but which we had not used, together with some of my own equipment, such as two rifles, binoculars, tools, etc.); reserve funds earmarked for the representative of the Danish government: 500 francs or 143 dollars.

17. Walrus is an excellent food, but 65 to 70 percent of its weight is water; each dog needs two to four pounds of meat every other day in the spring, and the same amount daily in the winter.

18. One of the Eskimo terms for cigarette (in Illulik) is "that which banishes weariness."

19. We all wore native-style clothing. I had insisted that the five of us have new qulitsaqs and that our nanus be at least in good condition. Following local custom, our qulitsaqs had the precious chin strap of bear fur. For each partner I was keeping some cotton underwear in reserve; for myself, I had two sweaters in natural wool.

By late May, the sun was so hot that we wore only canvas anoraks. Each of us had three pairs of smooth white sealskin boots; Kutsikitsoq and I each had, in addition, a pair of bearskin boots, with the fur to the outside. Supplementary caribou slippers worn inside the boot were much cherished during the deep cold spells, and rendered true service in particular to the hunters during their long vigils by the allut. The Eskimos also wore socks made of hare pelts, but I could never get used to them. Practical as they are, the skins are very fragile and a white man finds them hard to wear, for apparently his feet perspire more than do an Eskimo's.

Each of us had his winter gloves (sealskin), with one or two spare pairs. The women made us outer gloves of caribou. Natuk had brought along a large supply of unshorn sealskins for making repairs (gloves, boots, harnesses). It is well known that in the spring, ophthalmia is greatly to be feared. I had excellent Polaroid glasses; the Eskimos had supplied themselves with dark glasses. Kutsikitsoq broke his, and when he came to need them, he had to make do with some primitive glasses in bone frames, but he quickly got used to them. My wristwatch, which was a then current model, worked well.

20. This is the definitive version of the legend, as given by Erik Holtved.

21. Actually, the transport was carried out in relays because the ice was so bad. First, part of the depot was carried to Cairn Point by us three men. Then, after my stopover alone in Qeqertaraq, the five of us took it from Cairn Point to Uunartoq, or Rensselaer Bay.

22. In lean times, the dogs are tied up with chains rather than their sealskin leashes, which they would devour out of hunger.

23. To prevent the natives from becoming used to taking drugs in large quantities, in 1950 the administration was carefully rationing the number of pills given out to each small, isolated station. In cases of benign illness, the naturally depressive Eskimo quickly became disheartened—even at the very first signs of a sickness: strong, persistent headache, pustules, etc. He showed a childlike fear and groaned constantly. When he was in true pain, facing an agonizing illness, the Eskimo showed stoic courage and total indifference to death. Turning toward the wall of the igloo, he waited in silence for fate to do its work.

24. The ice foot still exists as a floating platform even after the ice field has melted. On the major capes, it may be no more than three feet wide, and even narrower.

25. Gontran de Poncins, *Kablouna* (Paris, 1948), p. 234.

26. The geomorphological studies of the coasts (glacio-eustatic movement, the duration and force of erosion over a period of 8,000 years) were made possible by an aneroid barometer. The Institut de Géographie of the Sorbonne lent me one of the three in its possession, and it proved to be a very sturdy and precise instrument. Zero is established by the average level of the frozen sea. When one changes altitude, the difference in the prevailing atmospheric pressure should not hinder the reading. Therefore, one must pick a calm day and return quickly to one's starting place to check whether or not the needle has returned to zero.

The equipment of the topographer-geologist is surely among the simplest. Mine included map board, slide caliper, binoculars (B. B. T. Krauss, with an excellent lens), two aneroid barometers, a 36-foot measuring tape, drawing materials (pencils, erasers, graph paper, ruler), a mica map case, photostats of earlier maps, and plastic envelopes for all documents requiring protection against humidity. In order to familiarize myself with the territory I would be traveling through, during the winter I made enlargements to scale of my predecessors' maps. Unfortunately, not until I returned to Europe at the end of my mission was I able to make use of the magnificent Danish collection of negatives from oblique aerial surveys of the region in question. My geology equipment comprised a hammer, piolet (ice ax), sample bags, and two micrometer calipers. There was no point, I had decided, in my taking an odometer with me. I did have four thermometers, two of which were broken en route, and complete photographic equipment protected by waterproof cases. I had slope measurers as well.

27. The tern is a small seabird with a slender beak. It attacks by dive-bombing, screaming like a Stuka. For the tern, the year offers two summers, since it flies as far as South Africa between its two mating seasons. In one year, the tern covers nearly 25,000 miles.

28. The suspicious and very brutal death of Charles Francis Hall, the great leader of the expedition, at 83° 05′ north on November 8, 1871, has always seemed surprisingly sudden. Recent studies of his remains have established that he was poisoned by one or more members of his expedition, who might have been worried by, or tired of, his enterprising spirit.

29. Life Bay Cove is called Qravdlunalik by the Eskimos, meaning: "that place to which the white men came."

30. By "stranded beaches," a geologist means the edges of ancient beaches that rise in tiers above the coastline; they indicate former levels of the sea, which lowers as the land more or less uniformly rises. The highest beaches in Inglefield Land were 500 feet higher than they had been 8,000 years ago. These measurements make it possible to estimate the original volume of the inland ice.

31. This was the only mail carried by sledge from Upernavik to Thule during the winter. Every year, two sledges made the trip across Melville Bay. Because the bay is big, it took two weeks to go and come back. In order to maintain the physical isolation of the legendary group of Polar Eskimos and avoid all infection—for both men and dogs—the mail bags bound for Thule were put under a rock about a mile north of the Upernavik huts. Once the inhabitants of Upernavik had left, the dogs were halted some distance away while the Eskimos went and exchanged inbound for outbound mail.

The air was so pure here and these Eskimos so free of viruses that any infection caused by the arrival of a stranger from the south of Greenland or elsewhere immediately turned into a *nuak,* or bout of flu, lasting four to eight days. No one ever died from it during the time I was there.

32. Jean Malaurie, *Thèmes de recherche géomorphologique dans le Nord-Ouest du Groenland* (Paris, 1968), p. 260.

33. The pastor. The minister then was a Greenlander from Julianehaab who lived in Thule. The office changed hands every five years or so. No Polar Eskimo had ever been considered worthy to be invited to assume the functions of palasi; this was still true in 1980.

34. Lamellibranch and foraminifera fossils—coastal fossils gathered in the sand of streambanks and of stranded beaches.

35. This method of hunting seal is called *aqqaasoq* in Thule. If the man is alone, hunting by the side of an allu is called *niparneq.*

36. *Lepus variabilis.* The hare is valued more for its fur, which the Eskimos use for socks inside their boots, than for its meat. The hare winters over and seems to have no trouble finding food. It is hunted and eaten by owls and foxes. Thus, an abundance of hares often indicates few foxes in the area. In 1950–51 the seventy hunters in the tribe killed between 1,000 and 1,500 hares a year.

37. The bowl cut was adopted after the arrival of missionaries, in 1909. Before that, Eskimos did not trim their hair. The men's heavy locks reached to their shoulders. By letting their hair fall forward they could hide their faces whenever they wished,

but usually an Indian-style leather band held it off their foreheads. The women wore their beautiful blue-black hair in a chignon high on the back of their heads. All sorts of beliefs have been associated with hair. The style of cut varies widely from group to group between Bering Strait and Greenland.

38. During my return to Savigssivik in February with Kutsikitsoq, out on the ice field in the middle of the Polar night and in temperatures of −40°C (−40°F), I was suddenly overcome by weakness—an abrupt loss of tension, accompanied by a violent migraine which weakened my resistance to the cold. It did not last very long, but was no doubt serious enough, for once I was stretched out in our tent Kutsikitsoq, whom I had known for only about two weeks, came over to me, a candle and sheet of paper in hand, and asked me urgently to write that if I died it was because of illness.

Excepting these two incidents, in February and May, I did not suffer from any illnesses during my stay.

Cephalalgia—severe headache—which hinders the body's mobilization against cold, is not unknown among Eskimos. They use the same remedy as everyone else: they stay in bed in the dark, with a band tied tightly around the head.

In November, in Nunatarssuaq, on the Inglefield Fjord, as I was leaving Sauninnguaq's igloo—which was isolated—I fell up to my waist in the freezing water of a hidden crevasse. Supporting myself by the elbows, I managed to hoist myself out and because I got back to Sauninnguaq's igloo on the double quick I was able to avoid getting "frozen" in the air—barely. The temperature was very low at the time: −20°C (−4°F). Luckily, my tightly laced skin boots and my bearskin pants tied around my knees prevented the water from soaking my body.

Falls into crevasses and other accidents of that type occur regularly among the Eskimos. Every two or three years, a Polar Eskimo dies in this way.

Before the arrival of the white man, the only diseases the Eskimos suffered from were pulmonary congestion, diseases of the throat and stomach, and rheumatism. There was no cardiovascular disease and no cancer.

39. The account presented here is drawn from written accounts only, which are indicated in the text by author's initials. My sources are as follows: Knud Rasmussen, "Report of the II Thulé-Expedition for the Exploration of Greenland from Melville Bay to Long Fjord, 1916–1918," *Med. om Gronl.*, Bd. LXV, No. 14, pp. 1–180; maps and charts (Copenhagen, 1927). Thorild Wulff, *Grönlandska Dagböcker*, Introduction by Axel Elvin (Stockholm: Albert Bonnier, 1934). Reports by Lauge Koch and by Inukitsupaluk, published in the Rasmussen cited above. Peter Freuchen, *Arctic Adventure* (London, 1936).

40. The following three letters of farewell dictated or written by Wulff on August 29, 1917, before being abandoned are taken from Thorild Wulff, *Gronländska Dagböcker* (Stockholm, 1934), pp. 404–5.

The letter of farewell to Rasmussen gives a very detailed account of Wulff's last wishes. This is the opening:

My dear Knud,

Continual hunger, the efforts of the summer, and the almost total absence of food these past few days have weakened my physical force to such a point that even in mustering all my will I find myself unable to follow Koch and the Eskimos. As their salvation depends on moving as quickly as possible toward the best hunting grounds, I will only be a burden to the group if I continue to drag behind. With perfect serenity, I bid you adieu and thank you for the good camaraderie during the expedition and hope that you will be able to save yourself and my work.

This letter, dictated to Lauge Koch, was written in Danish.
Only the last line is in Wulff's hand, and is written in Swedish: "Good-bye, old friend. Thorild Wulff."

North Greenland
29/8 1917

Dear Papa and Mama,
    With my stiff and frozen fingers, a last greeting before taking my final rest, exhausted by the hardships of the journey. I await death with perfect serenity, and my heart is at peace. Up to the last moment I have honestly tried to honor our name and I hope that the results of my work will be saved.
    Thank you for all the goodness you have given me as a gift on the path of life since my earliest childhood. Through all the vicissitudes of life you have always been the ones closest to my heart, you and Gun. Thank you and fare-well.

Thorild

This letter, written in Swedish, is in Wulff's hand, as is the following letter, to his daughter.

North Greenland, 79 Lat. N.
29/8 1917

Dear Guvner!
    I think the sands are running out for your Papa. My last thoughts go out to you and the old parents in Göteborg. I had been so happy at the thought of having you with me in Sweden for the whole of next summer!
    May life be favorable to you and your trials not too bitter. Remember that a man's most precious good is his pride. Live well and enjoy everything lumi-nous and good that life holds out to you. A kiss on the cheek!

Papa!

41. In the Eskimo tradition, suicide is allowable only in instances of illness or grave problems of adaptation. In all other situations, a man fights, he confronts his fate with courage. Suicide makes sense to the Eskimo only as social euthanasia (the old people) or in the event of a very serious loss of face.
    It is remarkable—and this observation has a religious value—that the Eskimo does not like to kill except when necessary and, naturally, during conflicts. The spirit of the dead person pursues you: therefore, it is preferable to be killed than to kill. The Eskimo would rather see the person in question do away with himself: that he let himself freeze to death in the water of a crevasse; hang himself from a knotted rope suspended from the ridge pole of an igloo (the wretched man holding himself up with ferocious energy until death comes), between two tent poles, or

between two meat caches (like Orfik, Sauninnguaq's lover in Neqi); shoot himself
with a rifle, which is a common method among women; or walk out into the tundra
until he drops from exhaustion.

A man may commit suicide out of despair over being cut off from the group,
from being alone. In Qeqertaq, Usukitat told me that this had happened with his
brother. The twelve-year-old boy, an orphan, had hanged himself with a rope from
a cliff in Natsilivik.

42. The white bear, or *Ursus maritimus, nanoq* in Eskimo, plays an essential role in
Eskimo life. In 1855, while the Greenlander Hans Hendrick was hunting with the
Thule Eskimos during the Kane expedition, for which he worked as interpreter, he
saw two *black* bears, which the local Eskimos called "A." Hunting black bears was
considered extremely dangerous, according to Hendrick (*Memoirs of Hans Hendrick*
[London, 1878], p. 26). Were they survivors from a warmer period, when the
Canadian forest extended a hundred miles farther north than at present? I hardly
think so. From 1600 to 1800, the North American Arctic had experienced a "little
ice age." In 1950, all bears in the area were white.

In bear hunting the "social test of masculinity" is always in play. The bear's
way of life has taught the Eskimo a great deal. The bear constructs a kind of igloo
for giving birth and for the cub's first year of life. It is an ice shelter covered with
snow (or a snowy rock-filled cave), which has an entrance corridor about 10 feet
long and 2½ feet high, sheltered from the prevailing wind. The female, who has
gathered straw (grasses and moss) and meat, lives with her young. The male
hibernates alone. During hibernation, when its heart beats ten times more slowly
than ours, the bear lives off its own fat. If a male becomes very hungry, he sometimes attacks the females in order to eat the cubs; he will even eat his own offspring
in the event of severe famine.

The white bear of North Greenland measures about six feet in length and
weighs between 300 and 400 pounds. In the Arctic it is indispensable for its fur,
which is made into pants for men. It is hunted each spring in Melville Bay (five days
by sledge from the Greenland coast) or in Kane Basin (near Humboldt Glacier; four
days from Siorapaluk when conditions are good), or on the east coast of Ellesmere
Island (Pim Island, Jones Strait), which is three days from Etah. The skin of the
female is less desirable than that of the male because the fur is shorter. The fur of
the young does not adhere.

The bear carcass is divided into seven parts; in addition, there are the intestines and lungs. When boiled, bear meat is oily and quite tasteless. Eaten raw and
frozen, it is excellent. In 1950–51, at most twenty to thirty bears were killed in the
district annually by the Polar Eskimos. Still today the bear is almost always hunted
on the ice field with the help of unharnessed dogs who run it down and bring it
to a halt. The bear is very vulnerable in the water, for it has no means of self-
defense, but it is difficult to hoist it up onto the ice because it sinks quickly. The
hunter "directs" the bear with his kayak to the point where he wants to kill it. "The
bear swims in front of the bow of the boat, and if it tries to veer to portside or
starboard, a little whack with the paddle is enough to keep it going straight ahead"
(Pedersen, *Animaux polaires,* p. 77–97). As soon as the animal approaches the chosen
spot and lifts himself out of the water, he is harpooned or shot.

The white bear is an unsociable, emotional, cunning animal of remarkable
intelligence. Generally it lives out on the ice field, but in February and March, it
comes in near shore for several weeks to catch baby seals, which are born under

the snow. Then the bear returns to the pack, coming in to the coast again in the fall. Bears mate in mid-April; the unions are brief and each partner returns to its territory, which it stakes out with urine. Birth (often of twins) takes place in mid-January. The interval between births is about three years. The same interval has been noted for the musk ox, the walrus, and even for Eskimo women.

Ruthlessly hunted by tourists in Alaska—from planes and with machine guns —the white bear is on the way to disappearing. In 1950, there were estimated to be no more than ten thousand in the whole Arctic Basin, though the situation is better nowadays. Nearly 15 percent of this number is hunted each year. The bears gather and reproduce in northeast Canada, northwest Greenland (particularly Melville Bay and the Humboldt Glacier region), and in northern Siberia. Fortunately, bear hunting is forbidden in the U.S.S.R. This is one reason why bears are fairly numerous near Svalbard.

43. In the past, before the Polar Eskimos had the rifle—about a hundred years ago, around the time Pualuna was born—bears were hunted in hand-to-hand combat. (Dogs were much fewer then, two or three per team, and often hunters had no dogs at all.) The bear had to be surprised where it had stopped en route—at the foot of an iceberg—and when it had fallen asleep after a meal, a spear was plunged into its heart. But even when wounded to the quick, the bear could often break the spear and violently attack its assailant. Many Eskimos bore the scars of such battles on their bodies. (I saw no such scars in 1950: no one of those who had been old enough to hunt for bears in that fashion in the 1880s was still living.) Then the hunter would dig into the animal's heart with a small knife.

The Thule Eskimos habitually hunt bears in pairs. One man will distract the bear on the left while the other attacks on the right, its weak side. In the past they used a trap inside a ball of meat—a sharp-toothed instrument—expanding in the stomach as the meat was digested and causing the animal to hemorrhage internally; this weakened it, slowed it down, and made the kill easier.

44. Between February 2 and 6, 1884, an attempt at liaison with the coast of Greenland (Inglefield Land) was made by two men on foot, but by that time the ice on Smith Sound had broken up. The men did not apparently persevere hard enough in their attempt because no one believed that the Eskimos of Etah would really be able to save them. First of all, they should have kept the boat intact instead of using it as fuel. Then, if the ice in the strait was broken, they should have gone farther north and crossed the strait near Uunartoq. The success of my expedition in June from Uunartoq to Ellesmere Island is proof of this. Contact would have been made and help obtained in a matter of days, or weeks at most. Naturally the same would have been true in April or May too, when the cold was less severe and the expedition was still in good shape.

45. A. W. Greely, *Three Years of Arctic Service: An Account of the Lady Franklin Bay Expedition of 1881–84 and the Attainment of the Fartherest North*, 2 vols. (London: Richard Bentley and Son, 1886).

46. The Eskimo pharmacopoeia was relatively extensive in 1950, if not always effective. For a boil or purulent sore, the skin of a lemming or hare was applied, fur side out. This was said to drain off the pus. Rotten fish and meat were used as laxatives. (Very fresh meat causes constipation.) For a headache, the sufferer's head was wrapped in a wide sealskin band. The thin membranes adhering to the untanned skin of the reindeer served as bandages. Burns and rheumatism were treated with seal oil and with fat.

Everyone in Thule knew that if one ate too much fat, one's eyesight was impaired and one risked going blind.

47. Jean Malaurie, "Présentation d'une carte de la région littorale de la Terre d' Inglefield (N. W. Greenland) au 1/100,000ᵉ et d'une carte de l'état des glaces de mer au large dudit littoral," *Compte rendu de l'Académie des Sciences* (Paris), June 22, 1953.

48. Jean Malaurie, "Terre de Washington (Côte sud) et Terre d'Inglefield: Groenland N. W. Feuille Nord et Feuille Sud. 1:200,0003ᵉ" (Paris: Imprimerie Nationale [CNRS], 1958, 1968).

49. Jean Malaurie, "Thèmes de recherche géomorphologique: Terre d'Inglefield et Terre de Washington. Baie de Disko," *Mémoires et documents de l'Institut de géographie de Paris, numéro hors serie* (Paris: CNRS, 1968).

50. Here I want to pay particular tribute to Kutsikitsoq, who died during the summer of 1981. In the letter below, I attempt to analyze the complex nature of my special ties to him, which were woven into relations with the group as a whole. As evidence of the very deep friendship I felt, through Kutsikitsoq, for the Polar Eskimos, and the ties I had formed with these people, I gave my only son—who was born in Paris in November 1952, after the expedition—the name of Kutsikitsoq, with the permission of his namesake, naturally.

Dear Kutsikitsoq:

I am writing these words especially for you. I must tell you how grateful I am to you for your constant loyalty during that difficult expedition and how much I owe you for the calculated risks you generously took together with the other people of our team. As I have said, this crossing was the more dangerous because, in order to travel light, I had had to leave food at the Inglefield Land depot which, had the ice broken and we been unable to recover it, would have made our enforced winter stay in Canada very hard, if not catastrophic, since we had taken with us only ammunition and minimal supplies.

To you I owe the final makeup of our team. I had, in fact, at first thought of having Maassannguapaluk join us. This twenty-four-year-old métis grandson of Peary had seemed ideal to me for the role of assistant and intermediary between the Eskimos of the backup group, and you and Natuk and me, the main group. His defection at the last moment created serious problems for me, as you know. In an "emergency," it is not easy to find in a village an Eskimo who has good dogs and an adventurous character; in this case, one who was willing to put up with an expedition based on a white man's calendar and schedule as well as with the demands of your and my personalities; and finally, an Eskimo who had no qualms about the plan that only one woman, your wife, would be sharing our life. Imina and Ululik were too independent; Iggianguaq's personality was not compatible with ours; Olipaluk and Sakaeunnguaq did not have good teams and their clothing was in poor condition.

Time was to prove your choice of Qaaqqutsiaq, a hunter from Etah, the best possible. I will not dwell here on the admirable qualities of our faultless forty-eight-year-old companion—so many pages in this book testify to them—but rather, I would like to think more deeply about our personal relations during our long journey together.

Of course, the great shadow of your father, Uuttaq, forced you to outdo yourself in bringing our mission to a good end. For during our visit to Uummannaq-Thule, in February, he had solemnly said to you: "You will accompany Malaurie since he picked you, and just as I did with Piuli [Peary], you will be with him when he is in trouble."

But, as you know, we first had to take each other's measure, you and I, and learn to put up with each other's often difficult personality. In the beginning, indeed, it was not at all clear that we would "make it."

You, forty-seven years old, with your mocking smile, your celebrated charm, your panache, your sixteen splendid dogs, your thirteen-foot-long sledge, had a prestigious background that was at once your strength and your weakness—the strength that comes from example and the weakness that comes from the fear of a son who hopes to measure up to the greatness of his father.

I, twenty-eight years old, young and strong-willed, aware of my capacities as the leader in authority, but obviously worried about my lack of Arctic experience in comparison to yours. However, I was not lacking in the famous *nuannarpoq* either, without which my other qualities would have been useless. I was fortified by my scientific activity and my ongoing research for which—never appearing to fear that you might be humiliated by it—you felt the liveliest respect. Every day during the winter, you will remember, I wrote down the smallest genealogical detail and ethnological observation, tightening the links during a vast socioeconomic study pursued in common which basically tried to establish through maps and calendars the cost of the hunter's labor and the real value of his earnings. This work interested you. Finally, during the spring, I carried out my geomorphological program in Inglefield, Washington, and Ellesmere lands, covering some hundred and ninety miles of coast and penetrating inland to a depth of nineteen miles. It involved not only traveling six miles on foot per day, but also digging up the earth with you in special areas, describing the findings in detail, measuring the slopes of characteristic screes (which meant that I had to climb to the top, take samples, and determine the altimetric reading), and in the end, systematically establishing a continuous topographical and geomorphological map on the map board. It was difficult work, both physically and intellectually. In addition, I imposed on myself the further task of driving my dogs and feeding my team, which I did not out of any sportsman's impulse but because I felt it was absolutely necessary in order to impress on the Eskimos in the group—and especially on you—that my efforts were at least the equal of yours.

Under the eyes of Qaaqqutsiaq and the two women (Padloq and Natuk, both in their forties)—an uncertain group, at once attentive and guarded, whose judgment of me would be decisive as we traveled and shared life under the big tent—you and I were inevitably going to confront each other, and I was aware that the success of the expedition would depend on this confrontation.

For me especially the test was serious. The bonds among you four Eskimos seemed to have been strengthened by the fact that an exchange of wives had apparently taken place—at least you boasted personally about it. One mistake on my part, and I would risk being abandoned, cast out somewhere and left to my fate—and my expedition would be a failure. The stakes were high.

Terrible Kutsikitsoq! Our winter excursions had been easy, as it turned out, since we were going from village to village. When we were to leave on the hazardous expedition to desert territory, you had to be the one hesitatingly to provoke the battle, to attack first. I have told about your arriving late for the expedition's departure, about your impudent explanations, and how then you harassed me with your sarcasm and criticism on the technical level, how you turned yourself inside out to catch me at fault.

Your whole "act" consisted of getting the audience, our companions, on your side in order to make Kutsikitsoq bigger by humbling and making fun of the white novice—and it's true that in hunting and managing my dogs, I was a novice. Of course my whip did not crack as sharply as yours, but I soon found out that I could expect no help from you on that score. I had to take care of myself. How many times did I brace myself, remembering the terrible moments in the central Canadian Arctic that were described in *Kabloona* with such modest greatness of spirit by my old friend, the lamented Gontran de Poncins!

But what I did not immediately understand was that your way of behaving with me, your acting as a free man and not as a docile guide, in the end was going to be beneficial to me in every way. Did this come to you as a happy—or an unhappy—surprise? The disguised generosity of your behavior and our complicity, on the one hand, and your impenetrable smile, on the other, have left me with no answer even now to that question.

Your critical attitude toward me hastened the changes I had to work in myself. I had very quickly to do violence to my white man's psychology, to learn how to "take it" with a smile, Eskimo fashion, and on my own to assume my triple task as scientist, driver of my sledge, and expedition leader; I had to speed up my apprenticeship in order to integrate myself into the group and to assert my authority by deserving it. In a word, in this foreign "university" with its unspoken rules, I had to stand before a deliberately impenetrable jury and win my Eskimo "degree."

The results of my "examination" were not really given to me until we arrived in Canada, on June 6, after crossing the double barrier of hummocks under the extremely difficult conditions I have described. Of course, I was never explicitly told that I had passed, but I felt it so clearly that I "celebrated" immediately by insisting on the protocol to which you were all most sensitive.

Do you remember? I called the group to a halt. The sledges were drawn up in a star shape and before the keen eyes of my four-member "jury" I walked slowly, very slowly, toward Qaaqqutsiaq and offered him my blue nylon jacket —which each of you hankered after so—right in front of you, as you stood by in silence.

By ostentatiously showing this "preference," I finally asserted myself, in my own way, as the acknowledged leader of the expedition.

It was high time: the second wintering-over that now threatened me could force us to take on very serious responsibilities.

For several weeks, I had been graduated into the group—that is, promoted, as an equal, in all respects, of my Eskimo companions and so bound to them for better or worse that many of the decisions made from May on—notably the long trip to Canada—had been taken wordlessly among us, on the strength of just a glance, Eskimo-style.

And during our return trip to Siorapaluk, in our talks, however brief, one phrase was constantly repeated—*soorlu ataaseq,* everyone as one!—which was blessedly reassuring to me. This I owe to you and to our complex relationship. I wanted to tell you this again, here and publicly, and in that context it is normal that your photograph, which I took at Uunartoq, should appear on the jacket of this book.

51. French broadcasts were inaudible; twenty years later, they were still inaudible, on both short and long wave. "Nuki? Hmm! Hmm! French radio has no strength," the Eskimo would say to me, my attempts to explain away this deficiency notwithstanding.

Part IV
The Iron Age

1. DEW line: Distant early warning line—radar stations spaced every thirty miles from Alaska to Iceland at about latitude 63°.
2. "Dental decay is extremely rare not to say nonexistent among the Eskimos, so long as they preserve their traditional way of life and diet." L. Hartweg, *Le Peuple esquimau aujourd'hui et demain* (Paris: Mouton, 1973), p. 230.
3. Although there was plenty of culture shock as well. One example among others from my 1967 trip: A young Eskimo woman came to me in tears. She told me that she had been painfully shocked by a pornographic picture magazine that a Danish worker who employed her as a house servant had showed her: "It's too ugly! Ajorpoq, the qallunaat!"
    The day was not far off when drugs would be available. In the south of Greenland, drug traffic was already widespread. Several hunters who were more or less aware of what was going on told me how they resented being humiliated in such a way: "We are not a dumping ground for white men!"
4. In 1967 the figures were: 600–800 kroner ($100–$130) per month per hunter, or 7,200 – 9,600 kroner ($1,150–$1,500) per year for a production that can be broken down approximately as follows: 50 seals, 20 to 50 foxes (hunted more or less intensively, depending on the market price), 2 walruses, 1 white (beluga) whale, 2 kiviaqs of birds, 100 to 200 salmon, 8 days' supply of eider-duck eggs, 8 of birds, and 9 to 15 days of work for the whites as docker or guide. Since the methods of reporting economic figures have grown more complicated, they have also grown more obscure, and it is impossible to obtain meaningful figures for more recent years without doing an on-the-spot survey.
5. Siorapaluk, 1950: 80 percent of the disbursements at the store were in the form of payment for the production of skins, ivories, and shark oil; 20 percent went for salaries and subventions. Siorapaluk, 1966: 30 percent of disbursements at the store (43,666 kroner out of a total of 140,214 kroner) was for productive labor; nearly 70 percent went for salaries and subventions. The subsidized welfare state had arrived.
6. A hunter's equipment involved substantial financial commitments both in the cost of materials and in labor. A complete hunting outfit (jacket, reindeer or bear pants, boots) cost from 600–1,000 kroner ($100–$160), and had to be replaced every two to five years. A sledge cost 400 kroner ($64); one dog cost 40 kroner ($6), and one complete team and sledge, 800 kroner ($128). A kayak cost 500 kroner ($80), a

motorboat 30,000 kroner (nearly $5,000). Loans were available at 2 percent over a thirty-three-year period, but low as the interest rate appears, it was very high even in 1967 if one considers that a boat is usable only for the three ice-free months per year. The price of one seal fillet was 25 kroner ($4), or 125 kroner ($20) for five fillets. Other costs: twenty traps at 5 kroner ($.80) each, or 100 kroner ($16); two rifles for 200 kroner ($30); a yearly supply of 500 cartridges for walrus; 1,000 (.22) for seal, fox, and hare; and 200 buckshot. Total expenditures amounted to approximately 33,000 kroner ($5,300).

7. H. G. Gallagher, *Etok: A Story of Eskimo Power* (New York: Putnam, 1974) pp. 157–58.

ACKNOWLEDGMENTS

I wish to thank the Commission de Géographie du Centre National de la Recherche Scientifique as well as the director of this organization for having provided funds, which supplemented monies of my own, for the French Geographic Expedition to Thule, 1950–51. It is scarcely necessary to say that this book is not a report on my geomorphological and anthropological findings. The publications which give an account of those findings are listed in the Bibliography. I also thank my cousin M. Guy Girard de Charbonnières, the French ambassador to Denmark, who greatly facilitated my obtaining Danish permission for this expedition to an area then strictly closed to Europeans and Americans, with rare exceptions, in order to protect the purity of this brave population against an intrusion deemed biologically and culturally harmful. I also thank Professor Emmanuel Martonne and Dean André Cholley (Institut de Géographie); Professors Febvre and Braudel (Collège de France); M. Eske Brun, Minister of Greenland, and the Greenland Department of Transportation; my comrades from the two French Polar expeditions led by Paul-Émile Victor in 1948 and 1949, with whom I had the pleasure of working at that time in Disko Bay as geographer of the French Polar expeditions; Professor Norlund and Colonel J. V. Helk, of the Danish Geodaetisk Institut; the Dansk Pearyland Ekspedition (Eigil Knuth) and particularly Jette Hjelle and the engineer Paul Winther; and, last but not least, the authorities of the United States Weather Bureau.

In addition, I express my cordial thanks to N. O. Christensen, Governor of northern Greenland, and his wife for their hospitality and friendship in Godhavn. I also record my faithful recollection of all my French, Danish, American, and Greenlandic comrades who offered me unstinted help during this enterprise, with special thanks to the Danish authorities who showed considerable regard for a foreign scientist.

In addition to the Polar Eskimos, most notably Kutsikitsoq and Qaaqqut-siaq, Natuk and Padloq, Sakaeunnguaq and Bertsie, and Imina, I cannot fail to mention my Greenlandic friends Peter and Martha Geisler (Skansen), Char-lotte Chemnitz (Godthaab), John and Laura Petrussen (Siorapaluk), and my Danish friends in Copenhagen or Greenland—Professor Erik Holtved; Claus Bornemann; Erling Karup; Tage G. Olsen; Torben Krogh; the pastor of Thule, J. Knudsen; Dr. Busch; the dear radio operator, Leo Christianssen, of Thule; and radio operator John H. Huges (OX3 BC); and lastly, in Paris, my brother, Philippe Malaurie.

GLOSSARY

aak: forward!

aallarpunga, aullarpunga: I'm off

aallarnerpoq: a long time ago

aammalo: again

aaqqatit: sealskin gloves

aarnquaq, aarnuaq: amulet

aavannaamioq: men of the North; the Polar Eskimos

aaveq, auveq: walrus

aaversuaq, auversuaq: great walrus

ajaja: song (traditional)

ajaraarutit: string game

ajoq, ajor, ajornara: it's useless; it's hopeless; what bad luck

ajoqi: catechist

ajornara: it's useless

ajorpoq, ajorput: what a mess; nothing to be done

allerneq: taboo

allernersuit: strict taboo; things that are taboo

allerpoq: in respect to a taboo

allu, *pl.* **allut:** seal breathing hole

amaaq: papoose; hood

amerlaqaat: many

anga: maternal uncle; "he who has precedence"

angajok: elder

angakkoq: sorcerer

angalasoq, angalassoq: partner on expedition

anguiasset: money

angut: male; man

angutit pissortut: aren't we men!

aningaaq: moon (used in legends)

annigaa, aniga: my elder brother (of a woman)

annigsarpok, anissarpoq: it comes out; ejaculation

anu: breast strap for dog

appaliarsuit: sea kings (a type of Arctic guillemot)

aqi: back! (direction)

arfeq: bowhead or Greenland right whale

arnaq: woman; female

asasaq, asasara: friend; dear one; lover (of a woman)

assut: fast; faster; with all my heart

asukiaq, asuk: I don't know

ataa: hey; hey you!

ataaq: parents

ataaseq: one

ataata, ataatak: father

ataataq: grandparents

ataatataq great-grandparents

atisaq: jacket; piece of clothing

avani: north

avataq: seal buoy
danskerne: Danish
eqalugaq: small coastal fish (Polar cod)
eqaluit: salmon trout
equut: window
go da: greetings!
Gutip, Guuti: God
igalaaq, igallaq: igloo window
igunaq: tainted meat
ikkii: isn't it cold!
iliarsuq: orphan
ilisiitsoq: evil spirit
ilisimasassarsiorneq: scientific
illeq: platform, bed
illeraq: a species of small fish eaten by whales
illerioq: chosen relative; ally
illillo: thank you; you're welcome
illora, *pl.* **illoriit:** godparent(s)
illuliaq, illuluaq: temporary house
imaq: sea
immaqa: maybe
immaqa naamik: perhaps not
immiaq: melted snow or ice; beer
ingmerneq: drum song
innaq: cliff
inudluara: good-bye
Inuk, *pl.* **Inuit:** human being; Eskimo
inussut: structures resembling men in silhouette, designed to frighten reindeer
iperaataq, ipirautaq: whip
ippik: steep incline; precipice
issoq: slab peat
isumataq: leader
ittoq: old
kakiorneq: tattooing
kalaaleq, *pl.* **kalaallit:** Greenlander
kamappoq, kamajavoq: in bad humor
kamik: bearskin boot
kapatak: hooded jacket
katak: forward part of entrance passageway
kiffaq: servant; worker
kinaana, kinauna: who is it? who are you?
kiviaq: rotted guillemots

kongi: king
kujappoq: copulate
kungissuaq: great king
kunik: to kiss
kuuk: torrent
malemuk: bird
mammaraai, mamaq: it tastes good!
marlluk: two
massakkut: right away
mattak: whale skin
matu: door
mikivoq: to be little
mitit: eider ducks
naaga, nagga: no; impossible
naajat, naujait: gulls
naalagaq: leader
naalaqarssuaq: great white leader
naamivik: never
naammappa, naammappoq: that's okay; it's good
nakorsaq: doctor
nallinaaq: poor fellow
nanoq: bear
nanorsuaq: great bear
nanu: bearskin pants
napariaq: stanchions at rear of sledge
natserq, natseq: seal; reversed sealskin jacket
niivertoq, navirtoq, nuivertoq: director; district administrator, store manager
neqe: meat; food
nerivoq: eat!
niparneq: hunting at seal's breathing hole
niviarsiaq: girl
nuak: saliva; respiratory virus
nuannarpoq, nuanerpoq: how pleasant
nuanni: how agreeable
nukaga, nukara: my sister; my younger sibling (of same sex)
nuliarpoq: to take a woman
nuna: the earth; homeland
nunaga: my land
oruneq: dish of snow partridge intestines
paaralugo: watch out

palasi: pastor

pania: daughter

peerujoq, persupoq: see also **pujuq:** "like a storm of snow," fog

peqatigiit: group of hunters; any group

perlerorneq: hysteria

perlussuaq: evil spirit

pingasut: three

pisiksi: bow

pisiniarfik: a Danish store in an Eskimo village

pissortut: of course; obviously

puisi: seal

pujorsiut: compass

pujuq: fog

pujut: pipe

pulaar: visit

pulaarpunga: I pay you a visit

qaa, qa: here; to me; come

qaaniarit, qainiarit: come in

qaggi: meeting house

qajoq: broth

qallunaaq: white man

qamutit: sledge

qanoq illit: as you like

qanormi illit: whenever you wish

qanortoq: I want to very much

qarsaaq: a species of Arctic duck

qeersoq, qeersooq: baby seal

qilaat, qilaut: drum

qilalugaq: beluga

qilavik: sea

qilavoq: the process by which Eskimo shamans interpret omens

qingaq: ventilation hole

qivittoq, qivituq: "he who hides in the mountains," legendary evil spirit

qorfa: faster

qujanaq: so much the better; thank you

qulitsaq: caribou jacket

qupannaaq: snow bunting

qvanga, qanga: when?

sainang sunai: greetings

sallutooq: liar

sapinngilaq: it can be done

savik: iron; knife

seqajuk, seqijak: good-for-nothing

seqineq: sun

seratit: spoken charms

sermek, sermeq: glacier

siku: ice bank

sila: air; consciousness; universe

sinik: sleep

sinudluarna, sinidluarna: "have a good sleep"; good evening

siut: ear

soo: yes; why; thank you

soqutaanngilaq, soqutaunngilaq: it doesn't matter

sujumut: forward

sunaana, sunauna: what?

sunalikiaq: what is this now?

taama, taima: finished; stop

taamarmik: good-for-nothing

taatseraaq, taateraaq: gull

taava, tauva: then

taku, takkuut: look!

tangeq: power; force; firmness

terianniaq: fox

ti, tii: tea

tigssarpok, tigsarpoq: have an erection

tiguaq, tiliarnuk: adopted child

tiluttut, tilutuut: wooden snow stick

timmiaq: bird, birdskin jacket

tipi: strange

tnudluara: good-bye

toornaq, *pl.* **toornat:** spirit or shamanic spirit

toquvoq, toqu: death; to die

torssuq, torssooq: entranceway

torssusaq, torssuussaq: passage; entryway; kitchen

tuavi: hurry up

tulugaq: crow

Tuneq, *pl.* **Tornit, Tunit:** imaginary people

tupilak: spirits; ghosts

tupinara: that's hard to swallow

ukaleq: Arctic hare

ukioq: winter; year

ulloriat: stars

ulu: woman's knife

umiaq: large boat

umimmak, umingmak: musk ox
umippigik, umippigit: shut it
una: that one; him
uneye: hello
unni, unnit: it doesn't matter
upernaagiit, upernagiit: whalers
ussuk, ugssuk: bearded seal

usuk: penis
utoqqatserpunga, utoqqatsiuunga: it's bad, impossible; excuse me
utsuuq, utsuk: vagina
uunarpoq: it's warm
uuttoq: seal resting on ice

BIBLIOGRAPHY

The following is a selective bibliography, covering works having to do largely with the Polar Eskimos and not including many specialized or academic works.

BESSELS, EMIL. *Einige Worte über die Innuit.* Braunsweig, 1875.

———. *Die amerikanische Nordpol-expedition.* Leipzig: W. Engelmann, 1879.

BIRKET-SMITH, KAJ. *Anthropological Observations on the Central Eskimos.* Copenhagen: Gyldendalske boghandel, Nordisk forlag, 1940.

———. *The Caribou Eskimos: Material and Social Life and Their Cultural Position.* Copenhagen: Gyldendalske boghandel, Nordisk forlag, 1940.

———. *The Eskimos.* New York: Crown Publishers, Inc., 1971.

COOK, FREDERICK ALBERT. *My Attainment of the Pole.* New York: Polar Publishing Company, 1911.

———. *Return from the Pole.* New York: Pellegrine and Cerdahy, 1951.

EAMES, HUGH. *Winner Loses All.* Boston: Little, Brown, 1973.

EGEDE, HANS. *Description et histoire naturelle du Groenland.* Copenhagen, 1763.

FREUCHEN, PETER. *Adventure in the Arctic.* New York: J. Messner, 1960.

———. *Book of the Eskimos.* Cleveland: World Publishing Company, 1961.

GALLAGHER, H. G. *Etok: A Story of Eskimo Power.* New York: Putnam, 1974.

GESSAIN, R. *Les Esquimaux du Groenland à l'Alaska.*

GREELY, ADOLPHUS WASHINGTON. *Three Years of Arctic Service.* New York: Scribner's, 1886.

HAYES, J. J. *An Arctic Boat Journey.* Boston, 1867.

———. *The Open Polar Sea.* New York, 1886.

HENDRICK, HANS. *Memoirs of Hans Hendrick.* London, 1878.

———. *Contributions to Polar Eskimo Ethnography.* Copenhagen: Med. om Gronl., 1967.

HERBERT, WALLY. *Across the Top of the World: The British Trans-Arctic Expedition.* London: Harlow, Longmans, 1969.

———. *Polar Deserts.* International Library, 1971. Watts.

———. *Eskimos.* London: Collins, 1976.

———. *The Polar Eskimos.* Washington, D.C.: Time-Life Books, 1981.

HERBERT, MARIE. *The Reindeer People.* London: Hodder and Stoughton, 1976.

————. *The Snow People.* London: Barrie and Jenkins, 1973.

HOLTVED, ERIK. *The Polar Eskimos: Language and Folklore.* Copenhagen: Med. om Gronl., 1951.

————. *Contributions to Polar Eskimo Ethnography.* Copenhagen: Med. on Gronl., 1967.

IGLAUER, EDITH. *Inuit Journey.* Seattle: University of Washington Press, 1979.

KANE, ELISHA KENT. *Arctic Explorations.* Hartford, Conn.: R.W. Bliss and Co., 1869.

KOCH, LAUGE. *Au nord du Groenland.* Paris, 1928.

KROEBER, ALFRED LOUIS. *The Eskimo of Smith Sound.* New York: Knickerbocker Press, 1900.

MALAURIE, JEAN. *Themes de recherche géomorphologique sur la côte nord-ouest du Groenland.* Mémoires et documents de l'Institut de géographie de l'Université de Paris, hors série. Paris: C.N.R.S., 1968.

————. *Les Civilisations esquimaudes.* In *Encyclopédie de la Pléiade,* Ethnolgie II, Paris: Gallimard, 1979.

———— (chairman): "Le Peuple esquimau aujourd'hui et demain: The Eskimo People Today and Tomorrow." In Quatrième congrès international de la Fondation française d'Etudes nordiques. Paris: Mouton, 1973.

Narrative at the North Pole Expedition Polaris. Washington, D.C., 1876.

MACMILLAN, DONALD BAXTER. *Etah and Beyond.* Boston: Houghton Mifflin Co., 1927.

————. *Four Years in the White North.* Boston: Medici Society of America, 1925.

MYLIUS-ERICHSEN, L., and MOLTKE, HARALD. *Gronland.* Copenhagen: Gyldendalske boghandel, 1906.

PEARY, JOSEPHINE. *My Arctic Journal.* New York and Philadelphia: Contemporary Publishing Co., 1893.

PEARY, ROBERT EDWIN. *Nearest the Pole.* New York: Doubleday, Page and Co., 1907.

————. *The North Pole, Its Discovery in 1909.* 1910. Reprint. New York: Greenwood Press, 1968.

PEDERSEN, ALWIN. *Animaux polaires.* Paris, 1958.

DE PONCINS, GONTRAN. *Kabloona.* New York: Reynal and Hitchcock, Inc., 1941.

RASMUSSEN, KNUD. *Nye Mennesker.* Copenhagen: Gyldendal, 1906.

————. *The People of the Polar North.* London: Kegan, Paul, Trench, Trübner and Co., Ltd., 1908.

————. *Greenland by the Polar Sea.* London: W. Heineman, 1921.

RAWLINS, DENNIS. *Peary at the Pole. Fact or Fiction?* Washington: R. B. Luce, 1973.

ROSS, JOHN. *Voyages of Discovery.* London: Longman, Hurst, Rees, Orme and Brown, 1819.

SALOMONSEN, F., and GITZ-JOHANSEN. *Gronland Fugle* [*The Birds of Greenland*]. 3 vols. Copenhagen, 1950–51.

STEENSBY, HANS PEDER. *Contributions to the Ethnology and Anthropogeography of the Polar Eskimos.* Copenhagen, 1910.

VAN STONE, JAMES W. *The First Peary Collection of Polar Eskimos' Material Culture.* In *Fieldiana Anthropology,* vol. 64, no. 2, 1972.

WEEMS, JOHN EDWARD. *Peary: The Explorer and the Man.* Boston: Houghton Mifflin, 1967.

WRIGHT, THEON. *The Big Nail.* New York: John Day, 1970.

INDEX

NOTE

Italic numbers refer to maps